InfoTrac Readings

Readings from the InfoTrac College Edition database, specifically chosen for their relevance to the material presented in each chapter. Formerly identified as Online Readings.

Related Web Sites

An annotated list of the most valuable online resources related to political science and American government.

Participation Exercises

Exercises that ask students to gather information, analyze data, or apply theory to practice. The exercises are designed to (1) promote active participation in the political process, (2) allow students to develop the knowledge and skills necessary to become effective citizens, (3) encourage continued involvement in the political process after completing the course, and (4) develop some basic research skills.

MicroCase Data Exercises

Case studies that encourage students to analyze actual data from the most recently available National Election Study and how those findings are likely to impact political outcomes.

Constitutional Convention

A structured discussion in an interactive online forum that allows students to debate the merits of a number of provocative constitutional reform proposals including electoral college reform, school prayer, term limits, flag burning, the line-item veto, and campaign finance reform. Instructors must post each Constitutional Convention discussion topic within the TNOW platform to activate this feature for student use.*

Primary Sources

Important historical documents related to American government including the Constitution of the United States and the Declaration of Independence and classic readings such as *The Federalist Papers*.

*Instructors: see the Multimedia Manager Instructors Resources CD-ROM (MMM-IRCD) for information on how to implement this feature.

THE Web OF Democracy

THE Web OF Democracy

An Introduction to American Politics

Second Edition

Michael C. Gizzi
MESA STATE COLLEGE

Tracey Gladstone-Sovell
UNIVERSITY OF WISCONSIN–RIVER FALLS

William R. Wilkerson
COLLEGE AT ONEONTA, SUNY

THOMSON

WADSWORTH

Australia • Brazil • Canada • Mexico • Singapore • Spain • United Kingdom • United States

THOMSON

WADSWORTH

The Web of Democracy: An Introduction to American Politics, **Second Edition**
Michael C. Gizzi, Tracey Gladstone-Sovell, and William R. Wilkerson

Acquisitions Editor: Carolyn Merrill
Development Editor: Stacey Sims
Assistant Editor: Rebecca Green
Editorial Assistant: Patrick Rheume
Technology Project Manager: Inna Fedoseyeva
Marketing Manager: Janise Fry
Marketing Assistant: Kathleen Tosiello
Marketing Communications Manager: Tami Strang
Project Manager, Editorial Production: Paul Wells
Creative Director: Rob Hugel
Art Director: Maria Epes

Print Buyer: Doreen Suruki
Permissions Editor: Bob Kauser
Production Service: Newgen–Austin
Text Designer: Lisa Delgado
Photo Researcher: Rebecca Seggel
Copy Editor: Donald Pharr
Cover Designer: Garry Harman
Cover Image: © CORBIS
Compositor: International Typesetting and Composition
Printer: Webcom

Printed in Canada
1   2   3   4   5   6   7   11   10   09   08   07   06

Thomson Higher Education
10 Davis Drive
Belmont, CA 94002-3098
USA

Library of Congress Control Number: 2005938051

ISBN-13: 978-0-495-00738-8
ISBN-10: 0-495-00738-2

For more information about our products,
contact us at:
Thomson Learning Academic Resource Center
1-800-423-0563
For permission to use material from this text
or product, submit a request online at
http://www.thomsonrights.com.
Any additional questions about permissions
can be submitted by e-mail to
thomsonrights@thomson.com.

TO
Julie and Nicholas

TO
Jim and
to my mother, Shari,
and mother-in-law, Barbara,
both of whom I lost
during the writing
of this book

TO
Jennifer, Emily, Noah, and
to my late father, Charles

Brief Contents

Preface   xv
About the Authors   xxix

CHAPTER 1	Democratic Citizenship and the Web of Democracy	1
CHAPTER 2	The Constitution and the Origins of American Political Ideals	26
CHAPTER 3	Federalism	56
CHAPTER 4	Civil Liberties and Civil Rights	85
CHAPTER 5	Public Opinion and Ideology	122
CHAPTER 6	The Media and American Politics	153
CHAPTER 7	Parties and Interest Groups	184
CHAPTER 8	Elections and Political Participation	226
CHAPTER 9	Congress	273
CHAPTER 10	The Presidency and the Executive Branch	302
CHAPTER 11	The Federal Courts and Judicial Power	336
CHAPTER 12	Politics, Economics, and Public Policy	370
CHAPTER 13	American Foreign Policy	399

Notes   433
Glossary   446
Index   461

Contents

Preface   xv
About the Authors   xxix

CHAPTER 1

Democratic Citizenship and the Web of Democracy   1

Mary Fetchet: Political Change in the Aftermath of 9/11   2

Democracy and American Politics   4
The Meaning and History of Democracy   5
The Transformation of Democracy   9
Democratic Political Practices   12
Core American Beliefs   15
Individualism and Personal Freedoms   16
Private Property and Capitalism   18
Equality   18
American Nationalism and Exceptionalism   19
The Current State of American Democracy   20
Conclusion: Democracy and the Internet   24

CHAPTER 2

The Constitution and the Origins of American Political Ideals   26

From the Boston Tea Party to Shays' Rebellion   27

Introduction: Constitutionalism and American Politics   30
The Political Principles of the American Founding   31
Enlightenment Political Ideas   31
The Framers' Understanding of Democracy   36
Colonial Political Practices   37
Events Leading to the Revolution   38
The First Contracts: The Articles of Confederation and the State Constitutions   40
The Constitutional Convention   42
The Ratification Debates   44
General Provisions of the Constitution   48
Legislative Power   49
Executive Power   50
Judicial Power   51
Other Key Provisions   52
Changing the Constitution   52
Conclusion: The U.S. Constitution—Continuity and Change   53

CHAPTER 3　　　**Federalism　56**

Medical Marijuana: National or State Concern?　57

　　American Federalism: A Definition　60
　　Federalism in the Constitution　64
　　　　The National Government in the Constitution　65
　　　　The States in the Constitution　66
　　　　Concurrent Powers　67
　　　　Interstate Relations　67
　　Two Centuries of American Federalism　69
　　　　Dual Federalism　69
　　　　The Long, Slow Rise of Nation-Centered Federalism　70
　　　　The Great Depression, the New Deal, and a New Era in Federalism　74
　　　　Johnson's Great Society: More Money and More Direction　75
　　　　The New Federalisms: From Better Management to Less Money　77
　　Recent Developments in Federalism　78
　　　　The Growth of Coercive Federalism　78
　　　　Congress and the Devolution Revolution　80
　　　　The Supreme Court Reins in National Power　81
　　Conclusion: How Much Control Should the Nation Have over the States?　83

CHAPTER 4　　　**Civil Liberties and Civil Rights　85**

R.A.V. v. St. Paul　86

　　Introduction　88
　　Civil Liberties　90
　　　　Freedom of Expression　92
　　　　Freedom of Speech　94
　　　　Freedom of the Press　96
　　　　Unprotected Expression　97
　　　　Freedom of Religion　99
　　　　The Right to Privacy　102
　　　　The Rights of the Accused　104
　　Civil Rights　108
　　　　Understandings of Equality　109
　　　　Equality and the Constitution　110
　　Equality for Other Disadvantaged Groups　116
　　Current Issues　118
　　Conclusion: Freedom and Equality—The Ongoing Debate　119

CHAPTER 5　　　**Public Opinion and Ideology　122**

Sex, Lies, and Public Opinion　123

　　Citizen Participation in the Web of American Democracy　125
　　Political Socialization: How Americans Learn about Politics　127
　　　　Family　128
　　　　School　129

Generational Effects   *130*

The Media   *131*

Community Groups and Peers   *132*

Political Ideology: Are Opinions Connected?   132

An Alternative View of Ideology   *133*

How Much Do Americans Know about Politics?   137

Measuring Public Opinion   141

Who Conducts Public Opinion Polls and Why?   *142*

A Citizen's Guide to Public Opinion Polling   *144*

Conclusion: Public Opinion and Public Policy   150

CHAPTER 6

The Media and American Politics   153

Bloggers Take Down Dan Rather: The Ascendancy
of the "New Media"   154

Introduction: Defining the Mass Media   156

Media Formats   *156*

Media Audiences   *159*

Programming Objectives   *160*

The New Media   160

The Changing Role of the Media in the Political Process   163

A History of News in America   *164*

From the Press to the Media   *165*

Media Ownership Trends   167

The Question of Bias   168

Sources of Structural Bias   *171*

The Mediated Electoral Process   173

Free Media   *173*

Paid Media   *174*

Televised Debates   *176*

The Media and Agenda Setting   178

The Media and Political Socialization   179

Conclusion: Participation and the Media   180

CHAPTER 7

Parties and Interest Groups   184

The Rise of the 527s   185

Political Parties and Interest Groups: Similarities and Differences   187

Political Parties   188

What Political Parties Do   *188*

A Brief History of Political Parties in the United States   *190*

Why Two Parties?   *196*

The Role of Minor Parties   *197*

Three Viewpoints on Political Parties Today   *198*

Reassessing Parties in American Politics   *205*

Interest Groups   206

What Interests Are Represented by Groups?   *207*

Group Membership   212
How Interest Groups Seek to Influence Politics   214
The Madisonian Dilemma of Interest Groups   222
Conclusion: Parties and Interests in American Politics   223

CHAPTER 8

Elections and Political Participation   226

Red and Blue America: How Real Is the Divide?   227
Why Elections Matter   232
The Structure of American Elections   234
Primary Elections and General Elections   234
The Rules of the Election Game   238
Financing Federal Election Campaigns   239
Candidate-Centered Elections   242
The Race for the White House: The Long Road   243
Selecting Presidential Nominees   244
Competing in the Primaries and Caucuses   244
The National Conventions   247
The General Election   247
Running for Congress: The Power of Incumbency   250
Voting   252
The Decline of Voter Turnout   253
Who Votes?   257
How Voters Choose a Candidate   261
The 2004 Election Results   265
The Presidency   265
The Congress   266
The 2006 Election Results   266
Political Participation Beyond Voting   267
Conclusion: Does It Matter If We Participate?   271

CHAPTER 9

Congress   273

Partisanship vs. Tradition: The Case of the Filibuster–Nuclear
Option Confrontation   274
Congressional Organization   277
House and Senate   277
Parties and Party Leadership   279
Committees in Congress   282
The Legislative Process—How a Bill Becomes a Law   287
The President in the Legislative Process   290
Divided Government   291
Explaining Congressional Action   293
The Dominant Goal of Reelection   293
The Incumbency Advantage   295
Who Are Our Representatives?   298
Conclusion: Lawmaking and Representation   300

CHAPTER 10   **The Presidency and the Executive Branch   302**

George W. Bush and Social Security Reform:
Can the President Lead?   303
  Public Expectations of the Presidency   305
    Creating the Presidency   306
    Constitutional Powers of the Presidency   310
    Can the President Meet Expectations?   315
  Presidential Leadership: The Power of Persuasion   317
    Leadership as Persuasion   317
    Term Cycles and Presidential Leadership   321
  The President and the Executive Branch   323
    The Executive Office of the President   323
    The Cabinet   326
  The Federal Bureaucracy   328
    Functions of the Bureaucracy   328
    Controlling the Bureaucracy   331
  Conclusion: Can the President Lead?   333

CHAPTER 11   **The Federal Courts and Judicial Power   336**

Lawrence v. Texas and the Right to Privacy   337
  Courts: Three Institutions in One   339
    Courts as Institutions of Dispute Resolution   339
    Courts as Legal Institutions   340
    Courts as Political Institutions   342
  Court Organization and Structure   343
    The Modern Federal Judiciary   343
  The Modern Supreme Court   348
    Access to the Court   348
    Who Are the Litigants?   350
    Oral Argument and Decision Making   351
  The Politics of Judicial Selection   352
    Selecting Supreme Court Justices   352
    Selecting Lower Court Judges   358
  The Supreme Court and American Politics   360
    The Development of Judicial Power   360
    Debates over the Appropriate Role for the Court   366
    The Court and Public Policy   367
  Conclusion: The Least Dangerous Branch?   368

CHAPTER 12   **Politics, Economics, and Public Policy   370**

There and Back Again: Deficits to Surpluses to Deficits   371
  Politics and Policy   374
    The Public Policy Process   374

The Context for Economic Policy Making   379
    Public Expectations for Economic Prosperity and Their Consequences
    for Economic Policy   381
Fiscal Policy   383
    The Budget Process   385
    Monetary Policy   387
The Politics of Rich and Poor   390
    Income Distribution   390
    Wealth and the Widening Gap Between Rich and Poor   391
    Wealth and Income: Why They Matter   393
Conclusion: Policy, Participation, and the Web of Democracy   396

CHAPTER 13

American Foreign Policy   399

Wal-Mart, China, and the Impact of Globalization on American Foreign Policy   400
American Foreign Policy   403
Constitutional Powers in Foreign Policy   403
    Struggle over the War Power   403
    Treaties and Executive Agreements   405
    Diplomatic Powers   405
The Players in American Foreign Policy   406
    Foreign Policy in the Executive Branch   406
    Foreign Policy and Congress   410
A Brief History of American Foreign Policy   411
    The Beginning of Interventionism   411
    The Two World Wars   412
    The Creation of the United Nations   413
    The Cold War   414
    Deterrence and the Arms Race   415
    The End of the Cold War   416
Current Problems in American Foreign Policy   418
    The War on Terrorism   418
    Al-Qaeda and Osama bin Laden   418
    The Afghanistan War and the Escape of bin Laden   420
    Strategies in the War on Terror   420
The War in Iraq and Its Consequences   421
    Buildup to War   422
    "Mission Accomplished" and the Rise of the Insurgency   423
Global Warming and Foreign Policy   427
    What Is Global Warming?   427
    International Efforts to Curb Greenhouse Emissions   429
Conclusion: Foreign Policy and the Web of Democracy   430

Notes   433

Glossary   446

Index   461

Preface

The American Government course can have direct relevance to the lives of students. Politics is a part of life, and learning about how politics and government work can be a life skill students apply for years to come. However, in order to put those ideas into practice, students must learn to interact with their government and in the political process, and that learning process begins with their American government textbook.

Today, almost every American government textbook published comes with a companion website that includes study questions, web links, and perhaps some brief content to accompany the text. But in almost every instance, the book's website is an afterthought to the printed text. Because we wanted to engage the student in true interaction, we designed *The Web of Democracy* to be different. It is a truly hybrid project—part textbook, part online course—that covers the "nuts and bolts" of the introduction to American government course in a streamlined, thirteen-chapter presentation specifically designed to minimize photos and extraneous boxed features and, as a result, the cost to the student. More importantly, the streamlined presentation allows instructors and students to devote their time and attention to the resources and activities provided online. In our view, *The Web of Democracy* is the first truly interactive introduction to American politics. Each chapter was written in conjunction with its accompanying online content. The online resources that accompany this book are not an afterthought; they are fully integrated component of the text.

The three authors of this text share a commitment to integrating technology into our teaching. We also share a commitment to college teaching. We teach at state universities that have as their first priority undergraduate education. The introductory American politics course is the mainstay of our teaching load. We teach it at least once a year, and usually, we teach it every semester. We also teach without TAs and have class sizes similar to many colleagues who teach in similar institutions.

About the Textbook

Theme

Most students who are enrolled in an introductory American politics course do not intend to be political science majors. They often take the course to fulfill some aspect of their university's general education curriculum, which requires students to take political science in the expectation that the course will instill in them a better sense of their role as citizens. However, improving citizenship skills is not usually the primary goal of the standard American politics textbook. Consequently, although students enrolled in introductory courses may gain an understanding of political science, they often do not leave such courses any better prepared to be active citizens than prior to their enrollment.

The Web of Democracy emphasizes the concept of citizenship and approaches the study of political institutions, actors, processes, and principles from that point of view. This theme is especially relevant at a time when concerns about the declining rate of political participation, growing levels of cynicism toward public officials, and a general lack of involvement in public matters on the part of the average person are particularly high. Another benefit of this theme is that it demonstrates the relevance and importance of politics and the study of politics to students' everyday lives. Providing students with the knowledge and skills needed for active citizenship will not ensure that they will become active citizens, but it will better prepare them for that role should they choose to adopt it as part of their personal behavior.

A Truly Interactive Textbook

The Web of Democracy is similar to other American government texts in its organization, but significantly different in the wide variety of tools it provides students for active learning. We include the standard content desired by instructors for the introductory course on American government, but do so in a compact 504 pages. *The Web of Democracy* is a brief text, but it is thorough in its coverage of important concepts and issues. The text is heavily supplemented by resources placed on *The Web of Democracy*'s online course, which we view as an essential companion to the text.

The World Wide Web offers numerous opportunities to help students become more engaged citizens. The web can be used to provide students with the tools they need as citizens. We believe that a brief text along with interactive pedagogy provides an excellent opportunity to develop future citizens. We have created *The Web of Democracy*'s online course materials with that goal idea in mind.

These tools are flexible. Each of us uses a different mix of the features described below. Instructors may use as few or as many as they choose. Some may wish to start slowly, whereas others may wish to use many features from the website. The *Instructor's Manual* accompanying the text provides valuable tools to help instructors integrate the material within the course.

New to This Edition

Instructors who have used the first edition of *The Web of Democracy* will notice a number of changes in the new edition. Since the book was originally published, there have been further leaps in technology for the classroom that we hope will facilitate the use of this textbook and its online resources.

Accessing the Course Materials

A sign-in card accompanying each new textbook provides an access code and instructions for creating an account for accessing all the materials available with the textbook, including *The Web of Democracy* online course now available via the new ThomsonNOW! platform and the InfoTrac College Edition database, which both come automatically with each new textbook purchase.

Ebook. Perhaps the biggest change in the new edition is that the online resources now include a fully hyperlinked ebook. The ebook provides the same written text and marginal icons that appear in the printed book. However, in the new ThomsonNOW! platform, all URLs and marginal icons are fully functional hyperlinks that take students directly to the materials indicated, making it easier than ever before for students to move between the printed text and the related online course technology. Once students access the ebook, they are able to locate the materials through multiple navigational options: by table of contents, by marginal icons, and by hyperlinks.

All New Features

For the first time, we have added a number of new audio-visual online technology features and a complete tool kit of online student test preparation resources.

New! Political Theatre. The Political Theatre icon links students to archival audio and video clips drawn from key political events from the last seventy-five years: presidential speeches, campaign ads, debates, news reports, national convention coverage, demonstrations, speeches by civil rights leaders, and more, all specifically selected for their relevance to the chapter material. Examples include an audio clip from Franklin Roosevelt's first fireside chat, footage of the infamous Daisy presidential campaign ad, Nixon's resignation speech, Vice President Al Gore's concession speech at the end of the 2000 presidential election, and George W. Bush's address at the site of the World Trade Center bombing in September 2001.

New! In the News. The In the News icon links students to ABC videos related to the chapter material. These videos feature short, high-interest clips from current news events as well as historic raw footage going back forty years. Clips are drawn from such programs as *World News Tonight, Good Morning America, This Week, PrimeTime Live, 20/20,* and *Nightline,* as well as numerous ABC News specials and material from the Associated Press Television News and British Movietone News collections.

New! Video Case Studies. The Video Case Studies are 8- to 10-minute video segments that explore important political controversies and issues directly related to the chapter material. Each case study concludes with critical thinking questions for classroom discussion.

New! Study Tools. A Study Tool link at the end of each chapter takes students to a chapter quiz that evaluates student mastery of the chapter in preparation for the actual classroom exam. Additional hyperlinks direct students to even more study tools, including flashcards, a crossword, puzzle, critical thinking exercises, and an interactive timeline.

Revised Features

Some key features of the previous edition have been revised in the new edition of the textbook.

Simulations. The icon for Simulations now groups together a variety of interactive online modules that step students through a series of critical thinking questions or decision points in order to give them a better understanding of their own political beliefs or how the political process works in practice. Those modules include:

Political Awareness Questionnaire. The political awareness questionnaire enables students to explore their own political views and see how they fit into the ideological spectrum of American politics that is used in the textbook. Students answer a series of questions; based on their answers, the questionnaire then generates a report that describes where their responses place them within the political spectrum and explains how their positions compare with the other ideological categories presented. The categories in the spectrum are the following: moralist liberal, New Deal liberal, pragmatic liberal, traditional conservative, individualist conservative, and moralist conservative.

Presidential Leadership Simulation. In this simulation, students take on the role of President George W. Bush as he is faced with choosing a new justice. The simulation walks students through the initial selection of a candidate to the final Senate vote to confirm or reject the nominee, highlighting the political consequences of each decision made along the way. In this way, the simulation helps students better understand the complexities of presidential power. Although the American president may be the most powerful political official in the world, that power is nonetheless subject to limitations and constraints.

Other simulations focus on current debates such as abortion, the First Amendment, and states' rights; public opinion and the death penalty; balancing the federal budget; and confirming supreme court nominations among others.

Chapter Updates. One of the problems in writing an American government textbook is that at some point the book has to go to print, even though American politics keeps moving forward. For example, as the final page proofs for the first edition of this book were being reviewed, terrorists attacked the World Trade Center in New York City and the Pentagon in Washington, D.C. At the time, we tried to indicate in the book how this event was likely impact the political process, but we were able to do this much more effectively online by adding specific readings and chapter updates as events gradually unfolded. One of the virtues of the World Wide Web is that it is always subject to revision; with this new edition, we plan to make relevant material available on the website and to update it as needed. The Chapter Updates, then, will be posted in response to notable political events that occur after the publication of the printed textbook. The Chapter Updates serve the same essential function as the Additional Content feature did in the previous edition.

Additional Content. These links take the student to supplementary content related to the chapter material. In contrast to the chapter updates, these links typically provide additional clarification or background rather than recent developments in current political events.

InfoTrac Readings. The InfoTrac Readings are readings from the InfoTrac College Edition database, specifically chosen for their relevance to the material presented in each chapter. In the previous edition, these were identified as Online Readings. The first time students try to access these through the ebook, they will be directed to the InfoTrac Login page and asked for their access code. However, once they have officially created an account for themselves, they will be prompted for their user name and password and then directed to the exact article in question.

Updated Features

The following key features from the previous edition have been fully updated and expanded to reflect the changes in the new edition.

Participation Exercises. Each chapter includes participation exercises that provide students with important tools they can use as citizens. These exercises can be viewed as preparation to participate in the political process; however, they can also be seen as examples of class participation. The exercises are designed to (1) promote active participation in the political process; (2) allow students to develop the knowledge and skills necessary to become effective citizens; (3) encourage students to continue to be involved in the political process after the course has ended; and (4) provide students with the opportunity to develop some basic research skills.

Many of the exercises will involve having students gather the information they need to form political judgments. For example, students are asked to identify their representatives at all levels of government and to learn where these individuals stand on issues of concern to the student. Other exercises ask students to analyze data, and still others have them apply theory to practice. Taken individually, these exercises do not involve major "research" on the part of the student, but they do develop research skills that could then be utilized in other projects and in other courses.

Constitutional Convention. Several chapters in the book are also linked to a virtual "Constitutional Convention," an online forum that enables students to interact with one another through a structured discussion format. The Constitutional Convention presents several provocative proposals on the subjects of electoral college reform, school prayer, term limits, flag burning, the line-item veto, and campaign finance reform and provides students with an opportunity to debate the merits of proposed reforms to the U.S. Constitution amongst themselves. In the new ThomsonNOW! platform, instructors must upload each of these features as indicated below in order for students to access them. This setup procedure ensures that only students enrolled in the specific class will have access to the discussion thread, and instructions for this can be found on the Multimedia Manager Instructor Resources CD-ROM available with the adoption of this textbook. Once the instructor has activated the feature, students can post their comments, other students can read them, and students can respond back and forth. As faculty teaching the introductory course, we have used the Constitutional Convention in our own classes for several years and have found it to be an extremely effective learning tool. Students enjoy the opportunity to interact with their peers in a nontraditional format, away from many of the pressures of face-to-face classroom interaction. Often, students who rarely speak in class discussions are among the most active participants in online forums.

MicroCase Data Exercises. *The Web of Democracy* provides students with the ability to "do" political science research using real quantitative data in web-based MicroCase exercises. Using the powerful MicroCase analysis system, students are able to engage in simple empirical data analysis. Students can grapple with the relationships that exist between various demographic factors that are used to categorize individuals and the ways in which these individuals are likely to act in the political process. Unlike the stand-alone version of MicroCase, the data exercises included in *The Web of Democracy* require no additional software. Students can complete data analysis exercises from within the website and easily submit their answers to questions to their instructors. Data exercises include questions from the most recently available National Election Study and from other sources as well.

Primary Sources. In addition to selected scholarly readings from the Info-Trac database, the website includes copies of the Constitution of the United States, the Declaration of Independence, and classic readings such as *The Federalist Papers*.

Changes to the Textbook Proper

In addition to the changes to the online resources listed above, we have made the following changes to the textbook itself.

- Our primary goal with this new edition has been to add key new features designed to help students and instructors navigate between the printed text and the online resources more easily. The new sign-on process, the new online platform, and the new fully hyperlinked ebook have all been implemented with that goal in mind. We have also worked to provide better navigational guides within the textbook itself: a key to the marginal icons that identify the types of online features available in each chapter now appears on the inside front cover of the book for easy reference. We have also added a specialized table of contents for each of the online resources available for each chapter so that students and instructors can more easily assess the full complement of activities and resources available. We have also included an all-new glossary at the end of the book.

- Perhaps most notably, we have added an all-new chapter on foreign policy, which is more relevant than ever now that we are a nation at war. This chapter allows for a focus on important issues of the Iraq War, nuclear proliferation, and the impact of globalization on American politics.

- Content revisions include more in-depth discussions of democracy, social capital, and civic engagement in Chapter 1; the growth of coercive federalism in Chapter 3; a comparative ideology discussion in Chapter 5; new media outlets and their effects on the political process in Chapter 6; and, in Chapter 12, a discussion of the most recent efforts to address the impact of money on the policy-making process.

- Updates include California's most recent ballot initiatives on the use of the Internet by political parties and interest groups in Chapter 7; and, in Chapter 10, the most recent developments in the Bush Administration, including recess appointments, coverage of the Iraq War, use of veto power, public relations issues, and public opinion.

- New features include new boxed features on Trust in Government Post 9/11 and Civil Liberties Post 9/11; text boxes examining the convergence of print, television, and Internet news gathering by single organizations; and new public opinion data and illustrations in several chapters.

- New chapter-opening vignettes include the issues of medical marijuana, federalism, and the scope of the commerce power in Chapter 3; the role of bloggers in Chapter 6; the rise of Section 527 groups in Chapter 7; attempts to reform Social Security in Chapter 10; and budget issues and Hurricane Katrina in Chapter 12.

- New end-of-chapter pedagogy includes key terms with page references a set of annotated web resources, and a Study Tools link that directs students to the online study resources.

Additional Resources

There are numerous additional resources that Wadsworth can make available to both instructors and students. Selections from some of these resources have been fully integrated and linked into *The Web of Democracy* where there was a direct correlation to the specific content, but instructors may choose to supplement those predetermined options with additional content available in the resources below. *Some of them are for college and university adopters only. Contact your local Thomson representative to learn more.*

Instructor Resources

Multimedia Manager Instructor Resources CD-ROM
ISBN: 0495127779
This one-stop lecture and class preparation tool makes it easy for you to assemble, edit, publish, and present custom lectures for your course using Microsoft Power-Point. The Multimedia Manager lets you bring together text-specific lecture outlines and art from Wadsworth texts, along with ABC News video clips and images formerly on transparencies. In addition, you can add your own materials to create a powerful, personalized, media-enhanced presentation. The CD-ROM also contains a full Instructor's Manual with chapter outlines, summaries, and suggestions on integrating the various website components and other resources. You'll also find multiple choice fill-in-the-blank test questions, a completely revised Test Bank in Word format and ExamView, the Video Case Studies Instructor's Manual, and electronic transparencies including tables, charts, and graphs.

JoinIn™ on TurningPoint®: Web of Democracy
ISBN: 0495170208
JoinIn™ content for Response Systems on CD-ROM has been tailored specifically to the text, including content directly related to *The Web of Democracy*, as well as a folder of generic questions related to politics, public opinion, voting behavior, and policy. These ready-made "clicker" questions allow you to transform your classroom, assess your students' progress, and examine concepts in political science with instant in-class quizzes and polls. Our exclusive agreement to offer TurningPoint® software lets you pose book-specific questions related to American politics, or you can use your own custom questions and display students' answers within the Microsoft PowerPoint® slides of your own lecture, in conjunction with the "clicker" hardware of your choice. Enhance how your students interact with you, your lecture, and each other.

Political Theatre DVD
ISBN-10: 0495007218; ISBN-13: 9780495007210
This DVD includes the full set of Political Theatre clips integrated into *The Web of Democracy*. Bring politics "home" to students in a real, visceral way, illustrating

how American political thought is acted out within and for the public sector. Choose clips from dozens of "watershed" moments in politics, including political ads, speeches, and documentary footage. This free instructor ancillary can be shown in class to launch lectures, to prompt class discussion, or to provide a platform for homework assignments and research.

JoinIn™ *on TurningPoint*® *(with Installation CD-ROM)*
ISBN-10: 0495095508; ISBN-13: 9780495095507
Transform your classroom by combining the power of Political Theatre with the innovative teaching tool of a classroom response system through JoinIn™. Instantly poll your students with questions we've created for you! We've done the work by providing more than 100 questions from which to choose. Additionally, you can create your own custom questions. The tool displays students' answers seamlessly within the Microsoft PowerPoint slides of your own lecture, in conjunction with the "clicker" hardware of your choice. *Contact your Thomson representative for more information about JoinIn on TurningPoint and our exclusive infrared or radio frequency hardware solutions.*

ABC DVD: American Government, 2007 Edition
ISBN-10: 0534257380; ISBN-13: 9780534257385

ABC VHS Video: American Government, 2007 Edition
ISBN-10: 0495096784; ISBN-13: 9780495096788
Nineteen two- to five-minute high-interest news stories available on either DVD or VHS will spark classroom discussion and tie current national events to your American government courses. Stories are categorized within seven contemporary issues, including Hurricane Katrina, changes in the Supreme Court, the war on terror and occupation of Iraq, the line between social interests and individual freedoms within our constitutional system, and more. Discussion questions are included to complete the interactive experience.

Video (DVD) Case Studies for American Government
ISBN-10: 0534643140; ISBN-13: 9780534643140

Video (VHS) Case Studies for American Government
ISBN-10: 0155041606; ISBN-13: 9780155041608
A set of twelve case studies, free to instructors and available on either video or DVD, serves as lecture launchers of contemporary policy issues for classroom use. Examples include "Affirmative Action," which reviews recent developments in the debate over affirmative action policy, and "Show Me the Money: Money and the 2000 Presidential Campaign." Each case study concludes with questions for classroom discussion.

Student Resources

Thomson NOW!
What do you need to learn NOW? ThomsonNow! for American government is a powerful, personalized online study companion designed to help you gauge your own study needs and identify the concepts on which you most need to focus your study time. Access to this program is free with your purchase of a new text. How does it work? After you read the chapter, take the diagnostic Pre-Test for a quick assessment of how well you already understand the material. Your

Personalized Study Plan outlines the interactive animations, tutorials, and exercises you need to review and directs you to the convenient ebook with page references you may need to reread. Next, take the Post-Test, which helps you measure how well you have mastered the core concepts from the chapter. Study smarter—and make every minute count! If you didn't buy a new book, but need access to ThomsonNow, visit our website at www.thomsonedu.com for information on getting access. Look for the Single Sign-On card in each new book for instructions on how to access this important ebook resource, which is the first ever fully hyperlinked ebook for *The Web of Democracy.* The ebook provides access to all the activities indicated in the icons found in the margins of the printed text.

InfoTrac® College Edition with InfoMarks™
(NOT SOLD SEPARATELY)

Because specific articles from the database have been selected and tied directly to sections of *The Web of Democracy,* access to this resource is automatically included for each new copy of the text. However, students are not limited to the articles specifically related to the textbook material and can use this resource to do additional research for in-class reports, projects, and other assignments. When you adopt this text, you and your students will gain anytime, anywhere access to reliable resources with InfoTrac College Edition, the online library. This fully searchable database offers more than twenty years' worth of full-text articles (not abstracts) from almost 5,000 diverse sources, such as top academic journals, newsletters, and up-to-the-minute periodicals, including *Time, Newsweek, Science, Forbes,* and *USA Today.*

Your free subscription now includes instant access to virtual readers drawing from the vast InfoTrac College Edition library, hand-selected to work with your book. Check the Instructor and Student Companion Websites that accompany your text for availability of InfoTrac College Edition virtual readers. In addition, students have instant access to InfoWrite, which includes guides to writing research papers, grammar, "critical thinking" guidelines, and much more. Adopters and their students receive free unlimited access to InfoTrac College Edition with InfoMarks for four months. To take a quick tour of InfoTrac, visit http://www.infotrac-college.com/ and select the "User Demo." *(Journals subject to change. Certain restrictions may apply. For additional information, please consult your local Thomson representative.)*

American Government: Readings and Responses (with InfoTrac)
ISBN-10: 053452804X; ISBN-13: 9780534528041

Monica Bauer, Metropolitan State College of Denver, has assembled an impressive selection of up-to-date, universally themed readings to illustrate the main debates of key issues in American government. The readings cover both pro and con positions on various issues, and major writers from right, left, and center are represented. In a feature unique to this text, the author includes an edited dialogue between students of varying political orientations to make the readings more accessible to those struggling with the material. This anthology also includes website selections, press releases, congressional testimony, and student-led interviews with major political figures to give readers a real-world political orientation.

Current Perspectives American Government InfoTrac Reader (with InfoTrac)
ISBN-10: 0495007986; ISBN-13: 9780495007982

Current Perspectives includes sixteen articles on issues in American politics, covering a range of topics from political theory to political socialization—giving students a comprehensive introduction to American government. After each reading, critical thinking questions are provided to give students a better understanding of the readings. Along with the reader, students are given access to InfoTrac® College Edition; they can even create their own online reader in InfoTrac® using InfoMarks.

Election 2006: An American Government Supplement
ISBN-10: 049518747X; ISBN-13: 9780495187479
Written by John A. Clark and Brian F. Schaffner, *Election 2006,* which offers analysis that includes maps, charts, and graphs, is an instructionally interesting and unique supplemental booklet. Factors discussed by the authors include the unpredictable national political climate with our nation at war in an uneven economy. The use of real examples in this election booklet makes the concepts covered come alive for students.

The Quest for the 2004 Nomination and Beyond
ISBN-10: 0534614272; ISBN-13: 9780534614270
This booklet, written by Stephen Wayne, focuses on the issues of the 2004 presidential campaign, the strategies of the candidates, and the outcomes of the party nominations.

Regime Change: Origins, Execution, and Aftermath of the Iraq War, Second Edition
ISBN-10: 0495188832; ISBN-13: 9780495188834
This supplement, available free when ordered together with any Wadsworth text, is written by David Kinsella. The book provides an overview of the recent war with Iraq, including its origins in the failed policy of containment following the Gulf War, the political and legal debate over regime change, the conduct of Operation Iraqi Freedom, and the challenges of postwar stabilization and reconstruction. Includes a short bibliographic essay for further reference.

9-11: Aftershocks of the Attack
ISBN-10: 0495130990; ISBN-13: 9780495130994
This short text (sixty-eight pages) puts the tragic events of 9/11 into political context. It focuses on how the American political system will respond to the challenges posed by the 9/11 terrorist attacks. The author is interested in how the major institutions—such as the presidency, the Congress, and our system of civil liberties and rights—are changing to respond to this challenge. The book is well grounded in historical context as well, as it delves into how other major crises have been handled. Other areas typically covered in an American government course, such as the media, religion, and public opinion, are emphasized as well.

Battle Supreme: The Confirmation of Chief Justice John Roberts and the Future of the Supreme Court
ISBN-10: 0495171077; ISBN-13: 9780495171072
Battle Supreme offers an inside look at the Supreme Court nomination process, examining the confrontation over the replacements of Sandra Day O'Connor and William Rehnquist. The text follows three substantive issues—the right to privacy, religion in American life, and who should die— to give students an opportunity to understand the intersection of law, courts, and politics in the United States. The book is great for bundling or custom binding with Intro to American Government, Judicial Process/Law & Courts, Supreme Court, Presidency, or Congress.

The Handbook of Selected Court Cases, Third Edition
ISBN-10: 0495003522; ISBN-13: 9780495003526
Includes over thirty Supreme Court cases.

The Handbook of Selected Legislation and Other Documents, Third Edition
ISBN-10: 0495003530; ISBN-13: 9780495003533
Updated in late 2004, this supplement includes excerpts from twelve laws passed
by the U.S. Congress that have had a significant impact on American politics.

Thinking Globally, Acting Locally
ISBN-10: 053455329X; ISBN-13: 9780534553296
Authored by John Soares. Designed to help students get involved and become
active citizens. Topics include tips for writing letters to the editor, volunteering,
how to change laws, and registering to vote.

Special Note to Students

We have written this book as a tool to enable you to best learn about
American politics. You will benefit most from all that *The Web of Democracy*
has to offer you by combining the use of the book with the online resources.
We don't expect you to use everything available online, and indeed, we
realize that each instructor will pick different features to require. But we
encourage you to take the time to participate in the Constitutional Convention, should your instructor assign one, and complete the various simulations and exercises that you find in the online course materials.

It is our vision that *The Web of Democracy* can serve as a toolbox for you
to use as active citizens. We want to provide you with the resources you
need to critically evaluate office holders, candidates, and the issues that interest you the most.

The Interactive Study Guide on the online course materials will help you
learn important topics in each chapter. Quizzes offer practice before taking
a test. The Interactive Study Guide is free with the purchase of the text.

Acknowledgments

In writing this book and developing the online course materials, we have ac-
cumulated a considerable debt to several individuals for whom we can only
offer our sincere thanks. Reviewers who provided feedback on the first edition of the book include: John L. Anderson, University of Nebraska, Kearney;
Keith Knutson, Viterbo University; William J. Lipkin, Farleigh Dickinson
University; Leah A. Murray, Weber University; and David L. Nixon, Oklahoma State University. The following academic reviewers offered numerous
constructive criticisms, comments, and suggestions during preparation of
the original manuscript: Akiba J. Covitz, University of Richmond; Larry
Elowitz, Georgia College and State University; Glenn David Garrison, Collin
County Community College; Jesse C. Horton, San Antonio College; Timothy
Hoye, Texas Woman's University; John C. Hughes, Saint Michael's College;
Matthew R. Kerbel, Villanova University; Quentin Kidd, Christopher New-
port University; Tom Oberlink, Kalamazoo Valley Community College;

Stephen Sandweiss, Tacoma Community College; Joseph L. Smith, Grand Valley State University; Bruce M. Wilson, University of Central Florida.

We are particularly grateful to have the excellent editorial support and trust of two editors at Wadsworth Publishing. First and foremost, this book would never have come about had it not been for the vision of Clark Baxter, publisher for political science at Wadsworth. Clark was willing to provide ongoing support and direction for the project since day one, even when he did not understand some of the technical aspects of what we wanted to accomplish with the interactive features of *The Web of Democracy*. He put his trust in us, and for that we are particularly thankful. Sharon Adams Poore, our original development editor, also deserves a great deal of thanks. Not only did she coordinate the reviews of each chapter, but Sharon guided us through our first venture in textbook publishing. She pushed us along when it seemed that the manuscript would never be finished. We also want to especially thank Stacey Sims, our current editor, who helped us through a sometimes difficult revision process.

We also want to thank Michelle Varderman and Inna Fedoseyeva for their technical expertise in producing the online material and the ebook. Sheila Collins at William Patterson University was instrumental in writing the narrative for the presidential leadership simulation. Carrie Schneider at the University at Albany, SUNY, provided considerable assistance updating the simulation for the second edition.

We are grateful to Paul Wells, production manager, and to Gretchen Otto at Newgen–Austin, who handled the day-to-day responsibilities throughout production.

We would also like to thank Julie Aguilar, who was very helpful in guiding us through MicroCase details.

Michael Gizzi thanks several current and former colleagues at Mesa State College for their support and encouragement while writing, including Boyce Baker, Susan Becker, Tim Casey, Sam Gingerich, Bob Mayer, John Redifer, Steve Schulte, Gene Starbuck, Harry Tiemann, and Richard Vail. Cathy Rickley deserves thanks for the numerous requests made of her as department secretary while writing the book. Theresia Holman did the same for the first edition. Six former students provided research assistance: Elizabeth Burin, Judy Craddock, Joseph Haynes, J.D. Lauritzen, Kristen Settle, and Jared Wright. J.D. and Jared were instrumental in providing research assistance for the second edition, drafting introductory case studies for chapters 10–13. Elizabeth Burin wrote the draft of the glossary. Finally, the students in his POLS101 Introduction to American Government course helped make this text what it is by supplying feedback to various participation exercises and serving as willing guinea pigs for the online Constitutional Convention. Michael Gizzi also wants to thank Bill Ball, Chip Hauss, Gary Klass, and Bruce Miroff. Chip shares our vision of using technology to enhance learning, and his input into the development of the book has been particularly helpful. Bill and Gary provided important feedback during the earliest days of this project. Finally, Bruce Miroff deserves thanks for providing encouragement in writing this book, even though it competes against his own fine text.

Tracey Gladstone-Sovell thanks her River Falls colleagues and students. Particular mention goes to fellow department members Davida Alperin, Wes Chapin, and Neil Kraus, who provided much needed intellectual and moral support along the way. She would like to offer special thanks to Joan Kratt, without whose assistance she would have never been able to write a textbook and run the department at the same time. Kurt Leichtle provided a historian's insight, David Schultz was always willing to bounce around ideas, Alan Tuchtenhagen could be counted upon for a good discussion about politics, and Mary-Alice Muraski provided friendship and technical advice. She would also like to thank the university's IT staff, who have supported her various efforts to incorporate technology into teaching. Finally, she would like to thank her students, who provide inspiration and feedback and are the reason she still enjoys teaching after twenty years. Special thanks go to Dannette Neuman and Amber Bowman, who provided research assistance on the first edition, and Jamie Krueger, who did the same for the second.

Bill Wilkerson thanks his current and former colleagues at Oneonta, Richard Barberio, Rob Compton, Paul Conway, Janet Day, Gina Keel, Michael Lynch, Carl Meachum, and Paul Scheele, for conversations about teaching and American politics. Alana Jeydel (Oregon State University) read early chapter drafts and provided encouragement throughout. Thanks to Amanda Lamica and the reference staff of Milne Library, who helped run down citations and data for the first edition—often on short notice. Wisconsin River Falls student Jamie Krueger provided the same support for the second edition. Special thanks to my U.S. government students over the years, who have helped me hone many of the ideas in the text and tools on the website. This project is better because of you.

We also owe considerable thanks to our families, who have endured what has seemed like constant, never-ending work on the book over the last few years. Any errors in the text remain our own. We welcome feedback from instructors and students using *The Web of Democracy*.

About the Authors

Michael C. Gizzi is an associate professor of political science at Mesa State College in Grand Junction, Colorado. After receiving his bachelor's degree at Saint Michael's College in Vermont, he obtained a Ph.D. from the University at Albany, SUNY, in public law and American politics.

Dr. Gizzi teaches courses on constitutional law, judicial politics, criminal procedure, criminal law, and American politics. He teaches an online distance education American government course and is a strong advocate for instructional technology in the classroom. He has written on instructional technology, federal judicial administration, and his current scholarly interests are on trial courts, focused on plea bargaining. Dr. Gizzi is past president of the American Political Science Association's Organized Section on Information Technology and Politics, and a current member of the Section's Council. He is also Associate Editor for Teaching Innovation for the *Journal of Information Technology and Politics*.

Dr. Gizzi is an avid road biker, hiker, runner, and martial artist. He and his son will both test for their black belts in Troy Miller's blend of Jun Fan Jeet Kune Do in 2007. He enjoys spending time with his family, watching movies and satellite television, and playing with all of the technology gadgets he can get his hands on.

Tracey Gladstone-Sovell is professor of political science and chair of the department at the University of Wisconsin–River Falls. Her bachelor's degree is from Penn State University. Her master's and Ph.D. are from Purdue University. Previously, she taught at Northern State University in Aberdeen, South Dakota.

Dr. Gladstone-Sovell teaches courses in political philosophy, media, and constitutional law and has taught the introductory American politics course for 25 years. She has written in the area of popular television and politics and has a continued scholarly interest in the history of American political thought. She has long been an advocate of the use of technology in teaching at her university and serves on its Faculty and Academic Staff Development Board.

She knits and does needlework to stay sane and spends her free time with her husband and walking her dog. She listens to music and watches way too much television for her own good.

William R. Wilkerson is an associate professor of political science and chair of the department at the College at Oneonta, State University of

New York. His bachelor's degree and Ph.D. are from the University at Albany, SUNY, in public law and American politics.

Dr. Wilkerson teaches public law, American politics, and research methods. He was a coprincipal investigator of a National Science Foundation Instrumentation and Laboratory Improvement Program grant and served as the coordinator of Oneonta's Social Science Computing Laboratory. He has served as a faculty fellow in Oneonta's Teaching Learning and Technology Center. He has been a member of the council of the American Political Science Association's organized section on Information Technology and Politics. His current scholarly work examines the use of the Internet in judicial citations and the decline of upstate New York.

In his free time, he enjoys spending time with his family, running, biking, and reading.

Democratic Citizenship and the Web of Democracy

■ Mary Fetchet: Political Change in the
  Aftermath of 9/11   2

■ Democracy and American Politics   4

■ The Meaning and History of Democracy   5

■ The Transformation of Democracy   9

■ Democratic Political Practices   12

■ Core American Beliefs   15
  Individualism and Personal Freedoms   16
  Private Property and Capitalism   18
  Equality   18
  American Nationalism and Exceptionalism   19

■ The Current State of American Democracy   20

■ Conclusion: Democracy and the Internet   24

Mary Fetchet: Political Change in the Aftermath of 9/11

Mary Fetchet testifying before the Senate Committee on Governmental Affairs 17 August 2004.

Brendan Smialowski/AFP/Getty Images

For families and friends of those who worked in the World Trade Center, the events of September 11, 2001, were an unimaginable horror. As Americans watched in shock and disbelief while terrorists flew planes into the World Trade Center, ultimately leading to the collapse of the buildings, these families and friends hoped that their loved ones had survived. Eventually, the death toll rose to over 3,000. For most of the world, September 11, 2001, was a devastating event, but for family members and friends of those killed and injured, the immensity of the attack was compounded by intense personal loss and grief.

In the aftermath of the attacks, many questions were asked: How could this happen? What can we do to make sure that this never happens again? Who should be held accountable for the security and intelligence mistakes that, if corrected, might have prevented the attack from occurring in the first place? How can we take steps to ensure a greater level of safety and security for all Americans?

Among those asking the most telling questions, and continuing to press for answers, was Mary Fetchet, a resident of New Canaan, Connecticut, whose twenty-four-year-old son, Brad, was killed in the attack. He worked on the eighty-ninth floor of the second tower and had been told to remain in his office by Port Authority officials after the first tower had been hit. Had he left the building after the first plane hit, he, along with many others, most likely would have survived. Ms. Fetchet decided that she had to do something to get answers to questions about why the attack happened and how other attacks could be prevented so that she could help protect her remaining family and the families of other people who died that day. Ms. Fetchet founded **Voices of September 11,** a nonprofit advocacy group.

The group's mission is "to provide resources, support and information to all those affected by the 9/11 terrorist attacks."[1] The group has been involved in a wide range of activities in support of its mission, including assisting families by providing support groups, workshops, public lectures, and a wide range of 9/11 information. The group has also helped families who, four years after the attacks, were still being notified that remains of their loved ones had recently been found and identified.

In addition to providing much-needed personal support for the families of the victims of the 9/11 attacks, Ms. Fetchet, along with others similarly affected by 9/11, became involved in the political process to get important questions answered. Professionally, Ms. Fetchet is a social worker who, before 9/11, was not involved in politics other than through voting. Yet, in a relatively short amount of time, she became a tireless and extraordinarily effective political actor. She appeared on a number of television programs, testified in Congress, and testified before the 9/11 Commission. She pushed government officials, including the president, members of Congress, and various local officials, in order to get answers to the questions that remained in the wake of 9/11 and to change the system so that such an event would not happen again.

Despite resistance from the Bush administration, as well as from some members of Congress, Ms. Fetchet and a relatively small group of others brought political pressure sufficient to force Congress to create the bipartisan National Commission on Terrorist Attacks Upon the United States (commonly known as the 9/11 Commission). The commission was charged with investigating the events leading up to 9/11 as well as any possible intelligence failures and mistakes that could have been prevented. The family members put pressure on the Bush administration to ensure that key leaders, from the president on down, testified before the commission and provided it with all the information it needed in order to conduct its investigation. During the commission's hearings a reporter for National Public Radio asked Ms. Fetchet about her reasons for continuing to press government officials for answers. As she responded, "I have two other children, I have a husband and friends. You know, the only thing that I can say is that I would never be able to live with myself if I didn't push for getting to the answers, didn't push for changes being made, didn't push our government officials to set aside their political agendas and to come forward and lay the facts on the table so we don't have another September 11th."[2]

When the 9/11 Commission completed its work, it made a number of policy recommendations that it believed would go a long way toward preventing another 9/11 from occurring.[3] The commission recommended a major overhaul of the federal intelligence bureaucracy. There was resistance, however, on the part of various agencies to adopting the commission's proposals. Again, Ms. Fetchet and others, working with members of the 9/11 Commission and sympathetic senators and representatives, brought the necessary political pressure so that legislation was passed enacting the commission's recommendations. As noted in the *Washington Post*, the visible and active efforts of the families resulted in the president dropping his opposition to the 9/11 Commission and allowing members of his administration to testify before it: "Loud criticism from the family members also moved opponents on the Hill to retreat from efforts to curb the commission's budget and deadline." And finally, "the family members scolded holdouts until the legislation passed."[4]

Fetchet's efforts have not gone unnoticed. She has been the recipient of a number of awards, including the National Justice Award in 2003 and the "Connecticut Hero" award in September 2004. She was also named one of ABC's 2004 People of the Year. Her work illustrates a truism about American politics, but one that is often minimized or dismissed: It *is* possible for a small group of dedicated individuals who have a commitment to a cause or issue to make a difference. It *is* possible to change the system, and one does not need to have huge financial resources or extensive political experience to make change happen. What it does take is time, energy, and lots of hard work.

ABC Person of the Year for 2004.

Democracy and American Politics

As Mary Fetchet's story illustrates, all American citizens—regardless of age and political experience—can have an impact on American politics. Young people can and do hold real power. In the upstate village of Valatie, New York, Jason Nastke was elected mayor at age nineteen. When he was twenty-four years old, George P. Bush played a major role in his uncle's presidential campaign. Jesse Jackson, Jr., was elected to Congress when he was thirty years old. At age twenty-six, Adam Putnam (R-Fl.) was elected to Congress. What they all have in common is that they chose to become involved in their nation's political process. Serving as an elected official is a form of political participation that requires a significant personal commitment. One need not go as far as running for office to be a participant in American politics, yet increasingly it appears that participation in politics is becoming the exception rather than the norm. The lack of participation raises serious questions about the health of a political system that Americans usually point to with pride.

If you were to ask average citizens of the United States what type of government they live under, their answer would most likely be "a democracy." If asked to explain what that means, a typical response might be to quote Lincoln and say "government of, by and for the people."[5] If you pushed further and asked if such a system of government is desirable, the answer would probably be an emphatic "yes." However, if you took the next step and asked why democracy is desirable, you might very likely be faced with a blank stare. If you asked what the responsibilities of democratic citizenship involve, the response would be to "vote and obey the laws," with any additional involvement in public affairs being above and beyond the normal responsibilities of the average citizen. Yet, if you asked the same people to truthfully state when they last voted, only about half would say they participated in the last presidential election. A smaller percentage participated in state and local elections, and an even smaller number were involved in any kind of community organization, much less running for office. (Voter participation is discussed in detail in Chapter 8.)

Citizens of the United States often express great pride at living in a democracy, but at the same time, they are often ignorant of the rationale for such a system of government and are not able to defend democracy in a rational discussion of the subject. The assumption tends to be that democracy is, to borrow from Thomas Jefferson, "self-evident." Because the United States is, arguably, the only remaining superpower in the world, the case for democracy is made both in the United States and for the rest of the world. Americans also tend to assume that the government of the United States has always been a democracy and that the self-evident superiority of democracy as a form of government has been a constant in American political history. Although this assumption is quite common, it is historically inaccurate. Although democratic political systems can be traced back to the ancient Greeks, throughout most of Western history democracy as a form of government was seen as dangerous and undesirable. Democracy was something to be avoided rather than something to be proud of. Most of the founding generation of American politics shared this view, and many were profoundly antidemocratic. Yet those citizens who identified the U.S. government as a democracy were not wrong. The reality is that democracy has come to be seen as a positive form of government. However, the transformation from a government to be avoided to one that the nation aspires to has been the result of a process of historical change precipitated by public discussion, political action, and changing understandings of the nature of democracy.

The Meaning and History of Democracy

To appreciate the transformation of democracy, it helps to start with a deeper understanding of its meaning than can be gained from quoting Lincoln. The word *democracy* comes from the Greek words *demos*, which means "people," and *kratew* (kra-te-oh), which means "to rule." Therefore, the literal translation of democracy is "rule by the people." This may be an accurate definition, but it is not a sufficient one because it leaves open important questions. It does not answer the question why rule by the people is a good thing, nor does it give any guidance as to how such rule can be accomplished.

The first of these questions—why is democracy good?—is known as a **normative question.** Normative questions involve values, principles, and the rationales used to justify why certain actions are desirable. In examining the normative questions surrounding democracy, it is important to realize that from the period immediately following the height of Athenian democracy during the fifth century B.C.E. until the nineteenth century, the predominant understanding of democracy in the West was that it was not a good form of government. The question then becomes why? To answer that, we can look back to one of the earliest analysts of democracy, the Greek philosopher **Aristotle.** Aristotle undertook an examination of all forms of government known to him at the time he was writing. He concluded that it was possible to characterize governments by looking at two questions: (1) Who governs? and (2) Whose interest is served by the decisions made by those in power?

With respect to the first question, Aristotle's observations led him to conclude that there were three possible scenarios: One person could govern, a few (a select minority of the citizenry) could make the political decisions, or the many (a majority of the citizens)[6] could govern. In Aristotle's analysis of existing governments, he noted that there was usually an economic dimension to the question of who governed. The few tended to be the economically privileged, and the many tended to be the less well off. In terms of the second criterion, political decisions could be made to benefit the **self-interest** of the governors, or they could be made to benefit the public at large. Governments that made decisions based on the **public interest** were clearly preferable to those where decisions were designed to benefit the self-interest of the governors. Based on these criteria, Aristotle concluded that there were six possible forms of government, with democracy located in the undesirable category of a self-interested form of governing (see Table 1.1).

Aristotle placed democracy in the undesirable category because his study of existing political regimes led him to conclude that when the majority of people were given political power, they exercised it in a manner that was self-interested rather than based on what was for the public good. To provide a contemporary example of what Aristotle was concerned

Goal?	Who Governs?		
	One	Few	Many
Public Interest	**Monarchy**	**Aristocracy**	**Polity**
Self-Interest	**Tyranny**	**Oligarchy**	**Democracy**

Table 1.1 Aristotle's Classification of Governments. According to Aristotle, governments that rule in the public interest are preferable to those in which decisions are made in the self-interest of the rulers. Democracy is placed into the undesirable category because Aristotle thought that the majority of people would most likely make self-interested decisions that were contrary to the public good.

Source: The Politics of Aristotle, edited and translated by Ernest Barker (New York: Oxford University Press, 1962), pp. 110–153.

about, a majority of people might be likely to favor an action such as abolishing taxes because it would be in their immediate economic self-interest. However, such an action would not be in the public interest because there would be no revenues for legitimate public purposes such as defense and education. Aristotle, as well as others who have been skeptical of the value of democracy, also worried about the dangers of **mob rule** that exist when the majority has political power. Mob rule exists when a majority of people engage in rash, irrational behavior, usually brought about by the influence of a few individuals, and take direct action against the minority, with whom they might disagree. Such action often involves violence and usually does not conform to the rule of law.

Despite his skepticism regarding popular participation in government, Aristotle did think that there was a form of government, which he termed a *polity,* where the majority governed for the public good. In order to have a successful polity, the majority of the population had to be neither rich nor poor. In a polity, most citizens needed to have enough material wealth in order to be independent. The poor were too dependent on others for their well-being, making them susceptible to manipulation. The wealthy had too much power over those who relied on them for their livelihood. Consequently, the rich could exert a disproportionate influence on public affairs. During Aristotle's era, it was extremely rare for a society to have a majority of its population that was neither rich nor poor. Because the economic conditions necessary for a polity were not usually found, Aristotle also concluded that such governments were extremely rare and unstable. In most existing circumstances the majority of citizens were incapable of making disinterested decisions.

The idea that government should serve the public good was a key value that contributed to the ancient Romans' revisions of Aristotle. They wanted a government committed to the public good, and they also wanted a government that was stable and would last. They developed the idea of a **republic.** The Latin term is *res publica,* which means "public thing." Rather than having a system where either the one, the few, or the many held the ultimate political decision-making authority directly, the Romans developed the idea of a "mixed" constitution, with the one, the few, and the many all included in the political process. Such inclusion was possible through use of the principle and the practice of **representation.** In a representative system, individuals would be chosen by the citizenry to make political decisions on their behalf instead of the citizenry making those decisions directly. Republican government was considered "popular" government because the political decision makers were chosen by the citizens to represent them in making decisions. The representatives were supposed to make decisions by considering the public good rather than what was in their own individual or class self-interest. However, republican government was not necessarily "democratic" because most of the population were still not citizens and could not participate in the political process.

Become an informed citizen by completing the Know Your Representatives participation activity.

After the Roman experience with popular government, the West experienced centuries of governments that can best be understood as variations of monarchy, tyranny, or despotism, depending on the character of the individual ruler. During the Renaissance, the idea and practice of popular government were revived, particularly the interest in republics. However, it was not until the Anglo-American world of the late eighteenth century that republics would come to be seen as the best possible governing structure that could exist.[7]

Republics were highly valued because they were seen as the form of government that was least likely to exercise arbitrary power and become tyrannical. However, republics were also seen as particularly fragile because of the demands they placed on the citizenry. Republics required a specific character trait among those who exercise political power, something called **civic virtue.** Civic virtue is a concept that had been associated with republics since the time of the Romans. It means that people making political decisions—whether that decision was whom to choose as a representative or about the wisdom of a proposed piece of legislation—had to put aside their own self-interest and make the decision based on what was best for the public good. This was required despite the fact that, all too often, what was best for the public was bad for a person individually or as a member of a group or class. Even so, a political actor in a republic was supposed to exercise civic virtue and make disinterested rather than self-interested decisions.

A contemporary example of individuals who exercise civic virtue might be the people who do not support a tax cut, even though they might benefit from such a decision, because they think that the nation needs the additional revenue to respond to collective needs such as education or defense deficiencies. Acting in a civically virtuous manner was seen as possible for people, but from ancient Rome through the eighteenth-century Anglo-American world, the dominant opinion was that most people were not capable of civic virtue and that only those who were should be given all the privileges and rights of citizenship. (See Chapter 2 for an extended discussion of the importance of the idea of civic virtue in American constitutional history.)

The traditional Western negative assessment of democracy, as well as the limited understanding of citizenship that was part of the classical republican tradition, was based on an **empirical judgment** about the nature of the people. Empirical judgments are determinations of what actually is the case. In looking at the behavior of average people, most political leaders concluded that average citizens were not competent enough to make good political decisions. To use the terms of classical republicanism, the average citizen lacked the capacity for civic virtue. Given that for most of Western history the vast majority of people lacked much significant education, as well as the opportunity to participate in political decision making, the judgment about their incapacity to make disinterested political decisions seems to have had some empirical validity.

The Transformation of Democracy

The statement "all men are created equal" has come to symbolize democracy. However, when Thomas Jefferson inserted it into the Declaration of Independence in 1776, he most likely did not anticipate how this phrase would come to be interpreted in American politics, especially in terms of who would be allowed to participate in the political process of the new country. When independence was declared, most of the new thirteen states restricted citizenship to white male property holders who had reached the age of twenty-one. Women, slaves, men without enough wealth to be considered "independent," as well as the native people of the nation were not seen as capable of participating in the political processes of the new states and the new nation. A few states did allow free black males to vote, and a few allowed some women to vote for a short period of time, but for most of the early history of the republic, voting was restricted to those who were seen as sufficiently rational and responsible to exercise civic virtue: white male property holders. Although it may be difficult today for us to understand the basis for this restricted understanding of citizenship, it is important to keep in mind that the political leaders at the time viewed their new governments as *republics*, not as *democracies*. They were careful to limit undue democratic influences on the political process by, among other things, restricting who could participate in elections.

"Downloading Democracy," Robert Conquest.

The negative assessment about the character of the "majority" points to one of the often unstated assumptions held by those who think democracy is desirable. To make the argument that democracy is a form of government that should be desired, one must assume that "the people" are worth responding to. In other words, one must assume that the citizens—those empowered to make political decisions—are knowledgeable, rational, and responsible political actors. If this assumption does not exist in practice, democracy does not make much sense. Would a suggestion that public decisions should be made by ignorant, irrational, irresponsible people be likely to convince many people of its validity? Consequently, it was the *empirical* judgment about the fundamental character of the people that had to change before democracy could be transformed from a government to be avoided into one that is seen as the most desirable.

This change started in the United States during the nineteenth century and continues into the present. It came about partially as a result of the changing character of the population, particularly in terms of education and economics. But it also came about as a result of *concerted political activity* on the part of those who were not considered competent enough to be included in the political process. The excluded groups of people formed political movements that challenged the status quo and demanded the right to be included in the political process. They were engaged in a process of trying to convince those in positions of power to open up the political system. They eventually were successful by demonstrating that they, too, were sufficiently rational, knowledgeable, and responsible to be citizens.

The transformation of democracy into a positive goal can be seen by looking at the process of the expansion of the **franchise.** The term *franchise* means the right to vote, and the most pressing and concrete goal for those left out of the political process was acquiring this right. Voting in a representative political system can be considered the most fundamental right of citizenship because it is "preservative of all rights."[8] As the population became more economically independent and with the beginning of westward expansion, a political movement known as **Jacksonian democracy** developed in the 1820s. This movement sought to expand the right to vote to all males. Under the banner of "universal manhood suffrage," the movement argued that economic status should not be a prerequisite to voting rights. The movement was successful over time as, on a state-by-state basis, the property requirement for voting was gradually eliminated. It is important to note that the push for suffrage during the 1820s and 1830s was largely confined to white males. However, by the middle of the nineteenth century, nearly all white males had the right to vote in all but a handful of states.[9]

Other expansions of the franchise came in the form of constitutional amendments beginning with the ratification of the Thirteenth, Fourteenth, and Fifteenth Amendments in the aftermath of the Civil War. The Thirteenth Amendment abolished slavery. The **Fourteenth Amendment** sought to ensure that the former slaves would now have citizenship rights and prohibited the states from interfering with those rights. However, it also officially excluded women and "Indians not taxed" from voting. The **Fifteenth Amendment** formally stated that voting rights were not to be denied to an individual due to race or "previous condition of servitude." This apparent expansion was short-lived, however, because the states of the former confederacy began to restrict the voting rights of the former male slaves and their descendants with procedures such as grandfather clauses, poll taxes, white-only primaries, and literacy tests. These practices generally remained in place until the 1940s, when the Supreme Court began to invalidate them.[10] Other congressional and Supreme Court actions limited the voting and citizenship rights of Asian Americans and Native Americans. Despite the apparent gains made via constitutional amendment, the political reality at the end of the nineteenth century was not very different from the beginning of the century. The only individuals who could fully participate in the political process—by voting in elections—and who had not able to at the start of the century were white males without property.

The turn of the twentieth century also saw actions taken by the national government that restricted citizenship rights for select groups of residents. In 1882 the Chinese Exclusion Act was passed to bar laborers from migrating to the United States and to prohibit Asian immigrants from achieving citizenship status. This act was renewed in 1902. It was not until 1922 that Asian-American immigrants received full citizenship rights when the act was repealed. The native peoples of the country were also denied full rights. In *Elk v. Wilkens* (1884), the Supreme Court ruled that Native Americans were ineligible to vote and were not considered citizens under the Fourteenth Amendment.[11] In 1887 Congress passed the Dawes Act, which permitted Native Americans to become full citizens with voting rights, but only if they agreed to participate in a program designed to break up the reservations. Participation also required that the individual renounce tribal affiliation to become a citizen. Very few Native Americans chose to participate in this program. In was not until 1924 that Congress, in the Indian Citizenship Act, allowed the original inhabitants of the country to participate in its political processes, although local restrictions continued to exist.[12]

It was not until the twentieth century that real gains were made in expanding the franchise. During the early twentieth century, renewed interest in expanding the franchise resulted in *organized political movements* that had explicit goals of attaining voting and other citizenship rights for those still excluded from the political process. The goal of gaining the right to vote for women was attained in 1920 with the passage of the Nineteenth Amendment to the Constitution. The black civil rights movement, through the leadership of the NAACP, began to challenge the second-class citizenship status of African Americans. ***Brown v. Board of Education*** (1954) represented the culmination of a long and hard-fought process to convince the Supreme Court to change its interpretation of the Fourteenth Amendment, thereby requiring that the states treat all their citizens the same regardless of race. During the 1960s and 1970s, Congress expanded on the decisions reached by the Supreme Court and passed the Civil Rights Act in 1964 and the **Voting Rights Act of 1965.** (See Chapter 4, "Civil Liberties and Civil Rights," for additional details about this effort.)

Read *Brown v. Board of Education.*

Women engaged in a long political movement to gain suffrage. In 1920 the Nineteenth Amendment to the Constitution was ratified, giving women the right to vote.

The Voting Rights Act instituted specific measures that provided for genuine enforcement of the Fifteenth Amendment and resulted in African Americans being able to register and vote without fear. Once the act was implemented, it resulted in dramatic increases in voter participation on the part of African Americans. The Twenty-Third Amendment was ratified in 1961. It gave those Americans who lived in the nation's capital, Washington, D.C., the right to participate in presidential elections by allocating three electoral votes to the District of Columbia. One of the means by which African Americans were prohibited from voting was through the use of a poll tax, a requirement that individuals pay for the privilege of voting. In 1964 the Twenty-Fourth Amendment was ratified, eliminating poll taxes in federal elections. The Supreme Court later expanded this prohibition to state and local elections as well.

The final constitutional expansion of the franchise came in 1971, during the Vietnam War, when the **Twenty-Sixth Amendment** lowered the voting age from twenty-one to eighteen. At that time, the argument was successfully made that if individuals could be drafted into the military against their wishes, they should be able to have a say in electing those officials who were making the decisions that were directing the war effort. Ratification of the Twenty-Sixth Amendment, along with that of earlier amendments that broadened the franchise, illustrates the fact that these changes came about only through active participation in the political process. As the twenty-first century begins, it is difficult to imagine a broader franchise than currently exists in the United States. If a person has been born in the country—or has become a citizen through the naturalization process—is eighteen years old, and—in most states—is not a convicted felon, he or she is entitled to participate in the political processes of the United States by voting in elections. It can also be fairly stated that there are no longer any substantial legal or practical barriers to voting, which had previously restricted the ability of members of racial minority groups to participate in American elections. The difficulty confronting the nation regarding voting at this point is that most Americans choose not to participate.

Democratic Political Practices

During the course of the last two centuries, the nation has collectively decided that the vast majority of its residents are in fact competent and capable enough to be included in the political process. Although there is certainly reason to question the overall knowledge, rationality, and reasonableness of the population in terms of its collective political behavior, we no longer question the inclusion of all components of American society under the category of citizen. Now that it has been established that all the "people" are qualified to be included in "government by the people," the next question is to determine the most appropriate procedures for implementing democratic decision making.

In the Greek understanding of democracy, government by the people was understood literally—all the people were directly involved in the decision-making processes of government. Today, this practice is commonly referred to as **direct** or **participatory democracy,** with all citizens directly involved in making decisions that affect the community. This form of democracy was practiced in Greece, where the population was small, citizenship was restricted, and life was comparatively simple. However, as more complex, larger, and more diverse communities developed, direct democracy came to be seen as highly impractical. Citizens generally have neither the time nor the inclination to be directly involved in determining the outcome of all the collective decisions that must be made in highly complex, interdependent, and technologically sophisticated societies.

Go to the Direct Democracy Center for arguments in favor of direct democracy.

To provide for citizen input into political decisions, and also to allow citizens to spend most of their time in other pursuits, the procedures of **indirect** or **representative democracy** were developed. Through the processes of representative democracy, the population periodically chooses individuals from among the citizenry and empowers the representatives to make the collective decisions. Political decision-making power is given to the representatives for limited periods of time and for specifically designated purposes. The practice of representation allows the average citizen to spend most of his or her time and attention on other pursuits. At the same time, by having the time and resources to focus on public affairs, the elected officials are in better positions to make thoughtful political decisions.

The advent of new communications technologies has reopened the possibility of more citizen participation in the political process. Some have suggested using technology such as interactive television and/or the Internet to give citizens the opportunity to exercise more direct political decision-making power. We now have the technological capacity for individuals throughout the country to indicate their personal preferences instantaneously. This could, theoretically, eliminate the need for representatives. But others have argued that representative government is preferable to direct democracy, not just because it is more practical but because it offers what James Madison referred to as a filtering function. Representation refines and enlarges "the public views, by passing them through the medium of a chosen body of citizens, whose wisdom may best discern the true interest of their country, and whose patriotism and love of justice will be least likely to sacrifice it to temporary or partial considerations."[13] Thus, representation provides the opportunity for more reflection, debate, and discussion and, consequently, a more deliberative decision-making process.

Although representative democracy is the norm in the United States, there are procedures at the state and local levels of government known as the **referendum** and **ballot initiative** through which citizens directly decide the outcome of a policy issue. Such procedures are often used at the local level to determine educational issues involved in school funding and property taxation for educational purposes. In recent years, decisions regarding public funding of sports stadiums have also been determined by a direct vote of the citizens being asked to pay for the facilities. Such procedures are also used at the state level, sometimes to determine changes in the state's constitution and other times to determine direct policy outcomes. In the 2004 election a number of states used this procedure to enact state constitutional amendments prohibiting gay marriage. California is a state that relies a great deal on the initiative. In 1996 California presented sixteen different issues for which the voters were to decide the outcome of a policy; in 1998 there were twelve such issues on the ballot. In the 2004 election, California voters were again asked to decide sixteen issues, including ones about Indian gambling, stem cell research, and one designed to alter the state's primary system.[14] At this point, there is no national initiative; however, the procedure has been introduced into Congress as a possible constitutional amendment.

Regardless of whether we use direct or indirect means to make political decisions, in a democracy those decisions are premised on the assumption of **majority rule.** In determining the outcome of a question, the ultimate decision-making practice is to choose the option preferred by the majority: a majority of citizens in a direct democracy or a majority of representatives in an indirect one. In the process of registering preferences, another basic premise of democratic decision making emerges: All votes are counted *equally,* and every vote counts. In an election to choose representatives, each citizen's vote counts the same as every other citizen who has chosen to participate in the election. When voting on proposed legislation, each representative has an equal say—no one can legally vote twice, and no person's vote is weighted more than other people's. Much of the controversy surrounding the Florida vote in the 2000 presidential election involved determining exactly how to make sure that every vote did count and that no one was excluded from having his or her vote included in the total.

Democratic decision strategy is also supposed to be a **deliberative** process. Decisions that are reached should occur after a full examination of the issue in which a variety of perspectives are discussed and debated before making a final determination of what, if anything, should be done. This process should occur at all levels of political decision making—everywhere from the individual citizen's choice of whom to vote for to elected officials' decisions regarding such weighty issues as war and peace and the allocation of public funds to various projects and programs.

A vital democracy also makes demands on its citizens. Obeying the law and paying taxes are necessary, but they are not sufficient to ensure the success of democratic government. Citizens living under a dictator are expected to obey the law and pay taxes, but democracy requires more to be healthy and successful. Democracy demands that its citizens pay attention to public affairs. **Political participation** is essential for a successful democracy. In the United States today, there may be limited opportunities for

Participate in the Constitution Convention's direct democracy forum.

citizens to participate directly in the decisions made at the national level; however, there are multiple opportunities to have an indirect impact on decisions. Voting is certainly the most basic vehicle for participating in the political process, but for a democracy to remain healthy and vital, more is necessary. Democracy requires that citizens stay informed and that they seriously consider various proposals regarding collective problems and collective resolutions. It asks its citizens to think about these questions not solely in terms of their individual interests but also in terms of the common good. Democracy requires collective discussion; it involves communicating one's views to those in positions of power. Participation in the political process may involve coming together with people who have similar perspectives to better promote their position. Individual actions, interest groups, and political parties all provide such opportunities for citizens, yet most people do not actively seek vehicles for political participation.

In recent years, scholars, most notably Robert Putnam, have suggested that in addition to formal mechanisms, democracy also requires a sufficient amount of **social capital** in order to function successfully. Social capital is defined as "connections among individuals" as experienced in social networks and voluntary organizations.[15] Putnam has found that Americans increasingly are not joining the kinds of social, civic, and religious organizations that in the past provided important opportunities for individuals to learn the skills needed to become what J. S. Mill once termed "active citizens." Putnam notes that Americans have moved from direct involvement in organizations to "checkbook" involvement. We join a group by paying dues, but we do not becoming actively involved in the group's overall activities. Putnam notes that Americans today are as knowledgeable about public affairs as in the past, but not as involved: "We remain . . . reasonably well-informed spectators of public affairs, but few of us actually partake in the game."[16] He, and others, have suggested that the decline in social capital and civic engagement has had a detrimental effect on the nation's political system. In short, democracy cannot be successful in living up to its promise if its citizens fail to become involved in the political process.

Read the selection from John Stuart Mill's *Considerations on Representative Government* for a defense of democracy and a discussion of citizenship.

Core American Beliefs

Americans strongly believe in the idea that the people should rule. In the United States, this has come to mean that we should elect leaders to govern through regular elections decided by majority vote. This belief has been remarkably resilient over time. It has been true even in times of conflict when the solution has often been greater participation in democracy, as when eighteen- to twenty-year-olds were given the right to vote in 1971. Americans also see it as an obligation of Americans to vote. In a 1996 survey, 82 percent of the respondents said that voting in elections is either an "essential obligation" or a "very important obligation." Only 9 percent of those surveyed thought voting was a matter of personal preference.[17]

"Tuning In, Tuning Out: The Strange Disappearance of Social Capital in America," Robert Putnam.

Democracy is one of a set of core beliefs shared by most Americans. These beliefs are at the center of **American political culture,** the set of shared beliefs, values, and traditions on which the vast majority of the nation's people agree. American political culture helps define the nation's politics and government and is distinct from the political culture of other nations. Our beliefs shape our politics by helping determine individual and collective opinion on specific issues and by setting the boundaries of solutions to societal problems.

To a large degree, the core American beliefs predate the formation of the United States and were enmeshed in important documents such as the Declaration of Independence and the Constitution. Alexis de Tocqueville found these beliefs among Americans in his travels through the nation in the 1830s. These values have been continuously handed down to new generations of Americans. We are taught about these documents and the ideals that they embody in school, in our homes, and in the media. Although the same basic beliefs have been important throughout American history, the definitions of these ideals have changed. As discussed earlier in the chapter, during most of our nation's history, the values of democracy, equality, and individual liberty applied only to white males. Results from the 1996 Survey of American Political Culture (see Table 1.2) show that Americans want their children taught these core beliefs. The survey also shows that Americans realize that as a nation we have not always fully upheld our high ideals. As you will see, each of these beliefs stands alone, but they also support one another as well. In particular, the remaining core beliefs support American democracy.

Individualism and Personal Freedoms

Although the people of many nations support the idea of democracy, no nation so reveres the individual as the United States. Americans agree that individuals should have the power to control their own destinies, define their own lives, and have the responsibility to take care of themselves. In contrast, many other nations focus on the collective, or national, good and believe that the government should take care of the people.

This strong belief in the individual has also meant that Americans wish to be free from government. Government should be limited in its capacity to control their lives. Liberty and freedom are inherent rights of humans and are possessed by all people. We see an important list of liberties in the Bill of Rights: Free speech and press, the freedom to practice religion as one chooses, and the right to a fair trial are important examples. These rights are central to any effective democracy. Citizens must be guaranteed the right to freely and fully participate in public debates. They must be assured that they have the opportunity to express their views openly and without fear of reprisal. They must be guaranteed that they can converse with others and share their concerns. They must be allowed to freely criticize those currently in political power. They must have the ability to publicize their

	Extremely or very important	Somewhat important	Somewhat unimportant/ very unimportant/leave it out of the story
With hard work and perseverance, anyone can succeed in America.	83%	14%	4%
American democracy is only as strong as the virtue of its citizens.	83	14	4
Our founders limited the power of government so government would not intrude too much into the lives of its citizens.	74	19	8
America is the world's greatest melting pot, in which people from different countries are united into one nation.	73	21	5
America's contribution is one of expanding freedom for more and more people.	71	22	6
From its start, America had a destiny to set an example for other nations.	65	22	13
Our nation betrayed its founding principles by cruel mistreatment of blacks and American Indians.	59	24	17
Our nation was founded upon Biblical principles.	58	26	15
Ours has been a history of war and aggression—our expansion occurred at the cost of much suffering.	58	26	16
America has a special place in God's plan for history.	50	22	29
Our founders were part of a male-dominated culture that gave important roles to men while keeping women in the background.	38	28	35

Table 1.2 How Should Core American Beliefs Be Taught to the Nation's Children? Each question was introduced in the following way: "In teaching the American story to children, how important is the following theme . . . ?"

Source: The Public Perspective (February/March 1997), p. 9 (from the 1996 Survey of American Political Culture, James D. Hunter and Carol Bowman).

perspectives, and they must have access to the necessary information so that their opinions are in fact informed. In a system premised on majority rule, it is especially important to protect minority rights to political expression. An environment with a full range of ideas, no matter how controversial and/or unpopular, is essential to maintaining a vital democracy. (Civil liberties are discussed at length in Chapter 4.)

Private Property and Capitalism

Closely linked to a belief in individual autonomy and individual liberty is the strong support among American people for private property ownership and a market economy. Influential English political thinker John Locke wrote of the fundamental rights of "life, liberty and property" (see Chapter 2). Private property, no less than intellectual freedom, is a fundamental right. Although there is no absolute constitutional right to private property, the Fifth Amendment reads in part that "nor shall private property be taken for public use without just compensation." This clause states a long-held American skepticism over government efforts to limit the use of land and other property.

Private property ownership is fundamental to the capitalist free market system, and the free market is the economic system of choice for Americans. Over the last seventy years, Americans have accepted—even demanded—increasing limits on the market through government regulation, but the belief in a market economy has remained strong. This support is closely tied to our belief in individual autonomy and the American Dream of economic success. Throughout our history, we have consistently idolized the great people of American industry, from John D. Rockefeller and Thomas Edison to more recent investor Warren Buffett and Microsoft cofounder Bill Gates.

Equality

Equality is both closely linked to democracy and individual liberty and in conflict with beliefs in individualism and ownership of private property. Clearly, Americans have a strong belief in political equality; everyone has a right to vote, serve on juries, and participate in the civic life of the nation. The idea of equality extends beyond basic citizenship rights. Americans strongly believe that each citizen is equal under the law and that the rules apply equally to all persons regardless of their wealth, race, gender, and/or status in the community. **Political and legal equality** is important to the American people. Ninety percent of respondents to the 1996 Survey of American Political Culture believe that it is an essential obligation or a very important obligation to "treat all people equally regardless or race or ethnic background."

Similarly, Americans support the idea of **equality of opportunity.** Each person should have the ability to succeed or fail on his or her own merit.

No individual should be excluded from a job because of an immutable characteristic. Every child should have access to a good education. Equal educational opportunities are important in a democracy. If democracy makes sense only when one assumes a knowledgeable, rational, reasonable population, it is essential that the average person have the opportunity to live up to this standard. Adequate education has long been considered a prerequisite to a healthy, functioning, representative government. In the eighteenth century, both Thomas Jefferson and John Adams argued forcefully, though unsuccessfully, for universal public education to guarantee a vital republic. Although their specific plans, which restricted the recipients of such an education in terms of race, class, and gender, have been altered, public education continues to be seen as vitally important for the success of the political process.

Americans value equality, but there are clear limits to the American definition of the term. Equality of opportunity is important, but there is no similar level of support for **equality of results.** Again, people should succeed or fail based on their own ability and work. Americans further believe that the nation has only a limited obligation to help those unable or unwilling to succeed on their own. Although social welfare programs exist, they are smaller than those of other Western democracies, and people on public assistance are often looked on as deficient, even un-American.

American Nationalism and Exceptionalism

Finally, Americans believe strongly in the United States as a nation. In a July 2005 Gallup poll, Americans overwhelmingly indicated they thought of themselves as patriotic: "94.5% of Americans think of themselves as at least somewhat patriotic, and 72.2% say they are either very or extremely patriotic. . . . Only 5% of those polled said they were 'not especially patriotic.'"[18] The vast majority of Americans are patriotic and believe that the United States is a great nation, maybe even the greatest nation on Earth. Americans believe in, and our leaders profess, the superiority of the American people. Some of this belief derives from our wealth and military strength, but it goes further. Americans claim their nation to be morally superior to others and find our version of democracy superior as well. Americans are often averse to looking to other nations for solutions to policy problems.

Americans also hold nationalistic political symbols close to their collective heart. The American flag is flown much more widely than the national flags in other nations. Other symbols such as the Statue of Liberty, the White House, the Washington Monument, the Jefferson Memorial, and the Lincoln Memorial are extremely popular tourist attractions. Major national holidays such as Independence Day and Thanksgiving serve as occasions to celebrate the greatness of the American republic. Many other holidays serve nationalist purposes as well.

The Current State of American Democracy

Although democracy has acquired a positive connotation over the course of the nation's history, politics has increasingly come to be seen in a negative light. If you asked someone today to identify the first thought that comes to mind when they hear the word *politics,* the person is likely to respond with a cynical or unflattering comment that politics is "dirty" or "corrupt." We have certainly experienced a number of events in the last two decades that could lead us to draw such a conclusion, but politics does not have to invoke such a negative reaction. Politics can be understood differently.

Early political scientist Harold Lasswell said in a classic definition that politics is "who gets what and how."[19] David Easton describes it as the "authoritative allocation of values."[20] Whether one chooses either of these definitions, or a variety of others that people have suggested, it is clear that politics involves collective or public choices. Questions about how we choose to distribute the things we value within and among the population, who we decide should make the distributive decisions, and the reasons why such decisions are made are all at the heart of politics. When decisions are made regarding environmental issues, taxes, or the price and accessibility of prescription drugs, we are distributing resources and we are indicating what we see as important in public life. When we enter into debates about the level of government best suited to making political decisions, we are concerned with who makes decisions. When we seek to justify the decisions that are made and demonstrate the basis of those decisions, we are showing why such actions were needed. Political decisions can certainly be made in a manner that harms people and causes the public to lose confidence in the political process, but they can also be made in a manner that enriches the lives of citizens. This is especially true for democratic politics, which holds out the promise and potential of collective decision making for a collective good.

In the United States at the start of the twenty-first century, the prerequisites for democratic politics are all in place. We have political freedoms, we have the ability to communicate with one another, and we have a free press and public education. But by many measures, we do not have a healthy democracy. As mentioned at the start of this chapter, most Americans do not vote, most do not participate in political debates and discussions, and only a small percentage of the population involves itself in community activities. Mary Fetchet, whom you met at the beginning of the chapter, is clearly the exception rather than the rule. Numerous studies show that we say we are extremely dissatisfied with, and even cynical about, politics. As Figure 1.1 illustrates, people have significantly less trust in their public officials than they did before 1970.

Previous generations dissatisfied with their situation sought to change it, often with great success. One can look at the civil rights movement of

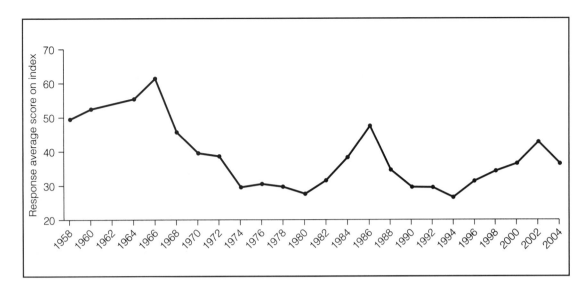

Figure 1.1 Trust in Government over Time. Americans' trust in government has declined significantly since the 1960s.

Source: 1958–2004 National Election Studies, conducted by the Center for Political Studies, University of Michigan.

the 1950s and 1960s, the antiwar movement during the Vietnam era, and the women's and environmental movements that became politically active in the 1970s to see examples of concerted political activity that made a difference. Today, however, the general response to public affairs is to withdraw into private life. In the words of Robert Putnam, a contemporary analyst worried about the state of American political culture, Americans "bowl alone."[21] We do not engage in the variety of political and community activities that are the foundation of a healthy democratic political system. We do not have an active civic culture, which is necessary for democratic practices to thrive. We are more comfortable watching television than we are attending precinct caucuses. Others have taken issue with Putnam's analysis, but it has been convincing enough to generate a great deal of scholarly as well as popular political debate and discussion.

"Politics after the Internet," Yuval Levin.

Although there have certainly been reasons for a great many people to feel that their government has not been living up to its own ideal, there are consequences to our retreat from public life. If citizens collectively fail to participate in the political process, decisions will still be made; however, the likelihood that they will be made taking all perspectives into account and/or for the overall public good is drastically reduced. If democratic politics fails, we have no one to blame but ourselves.

TRUST IN GOVERNMENT POST 9/11

In the immediate aftermath of the 9/11 terrorist attacks on the World Trade Center in New York City and the Pentagon in Washington, D.C., there were outpourings of support for the direct victims of the attack, for the people of New York and Washington, and for the public servants—the police officers, firefighters, and emergency medical personnel—who risked, and lost, their lives doing their jobs. Rudolph Giuliani, the mayor of New York, became a national hero because of the leadership he demonstrated at the time. The confident and competent way he responded to the crisis was an inspiration to many Americans who were sorting through their own reactions to the attacks. The public and other elected officials also rallied around President George W. Bush with a unified and bipartisan show of support.

Americans attended memorial services, burned candles in their windows, and flew the flag in overt displays of patriotism. But did the events of September 11, and the aftermath, alter Americans' fundamental attitudes toward government? The initial evidence suggested that they did. Since 1958, the National Elections Study has been measuring trust in government by asking the following question: "How much of the time do you think you can trust the government in Washington to do what is right—just about always, most of the time, or only some of the time?" When NES asked the question in 2000, 4 percent of the population indicated that they trusted the government "just about always," 40 percent said "most of the time," and 55 percent indicated that they trusted the government "some of the time." In 2002 the responses were 5 percent "just about always," 51 percent "most of the time," and 44 percent "some of the time."[1]

In the aftermath of September 11, other organizations asked the same—or very similar—questions of the American public, and the response was fairly dramatic. In late September 2001, a *New York Times*/CBS News poll found that 55 percent of the respondents said they trusted the government "most of the time." A Gallup poll taken in early October 2001 showed an even higher rate of 60 percent responding in the same manner.[2] Robert Putman and his colleagues also found evidence of increased trust in government, as well as indications of an increased attention to, and interest in, politics. They found that 51 percent of the respondents had increased their level of confidence in the federal government between 2000 and

(continued)

late October 2001. They also found that interest in politics grew by 27 percent among younger people, a much larger increase than displayed by the overall population. Putnam interpreted these results to signal the possible renewal of civil engagement among Americans.[3]

Others are not so sure. The Brookings Institution commissioned a poll in early May 2002 and found a significant decline in the measure of trust in government from the post-9/11 high point. In October 2001, the pollsters found that 57 percent of the public trusted the federal government to do what is right "just about always" or "most of the time." By May 2002, eight months after the attacks, that number had decreased to 40 percent. A 17-percentage-point decrease in public trust would certainly seem to indicate that the initial upsurge in public support for the federal government has faded, but it is also worth noting that the 40-percent level is significantly higher than the 29 percent who had responded in the same way in July 2001.[4]

The early studies of the impact of 9/11 on attitudes toward the federal government suggested that some of the initial increased public support was short-lived. In 2004, this was confirmed in the National Election Study. In 2004, 4 percent of those asked indicated that they trusted the government to do what was right "just about always," 43 percent said "most of the time," 52 percent said "some of the time," and 1 percent said "never." In addition, the NES index of trust in government went from 43 in 2002 to 37 in 2004—a decrease, although it is still at a higher level than during much of the 1990s. Time will only tell what, if any, long-term effect 9/11 will have on the level of trust that Americans have in their governing institutions.

[1] National Election Studies, http://www.umich.edu/~nes/nesguide/toptable/tab5a_1.htm.

[2] Pamela Paul, "Faith in Institutions," *American Demographics,* January 2002, pp. 20–21.

[3] Robert D. Putnam, "Bowling Together," *American Prospect,* 13.3, February 2002, http://www.prospect.org/print/V13/3/putnam-r.html.

[4] G. Calvin Mackenzie and Judith M. Labiner, "Opportunity Lost: The Rise and Fall of Trust and Confidence in Government After September 11," Center for Public Service, The Brookings Institution, May 30, 2002, http://www.brook.edu/dybdocroot/gs/cps/opportunityfinal.pdf.

Conclusion: Democracy and the Internet

Check here for possible post-publication updates to the chapter material.

Visit the websites of organizations seeking to tap the democratic potential of the Internet.

Many individual citizens today are dissatisfied with the political process. Many analysts of the political system are also concerned about its vitality and its future. At the same time, others see in the Internet an opportunity for increased political awareness and a new avenue for political participation. One can argue that the Internet is inherently democratic to the extent that it is open to all citizens. There are legitimate concerns about the ability of people in less advantaged economic situations to gain access, but this problem is being addressed through the increased "wiring" of public schools and libraries. Because of its interactive character, the Internet can provide a forum for public discussion of issues, and it does provide a new means of communication between citizens and elected officials. It has been used as a tool for mobilizing citizens to come together in response to shared political concerns, and it can be an invaluable source of information for anyone seeking to become knowledgeable about particular issues.

We have titled this work *The Web of Democracy* for a number of reasons. A web is an interwoven fabric with individual strands of fiber coming together to create a whole. Democracy is supposed to be like that: People come together as citizens and interact to create something bigger than themselves as individuals. At times, American democracy can also resemble a spider web, something that one can get caught in and "trapped" by without necessarily understanding what has happened. We are convinced that the Internet has a democratic potential. We have used this title because we think the Internet can be a tool through which citizens can be empowered to become more involved in politics and through which they can make a difference. We do not think, however, that such a use is automatic. No tool can improve political participation unless citizens want the system to change.

Finally, we also are convinced that the Internet is an important pedagogical tool. Used effectively and carefully, it provides a means of gaining a better understanding of the operations of American politics—which is, of course, the primary reason for enrolling in an Introduction to American Politics course.

Key Terms

Voices of September 11   2
normative question   5
Aristotle   6
self-interest   6
public interest   6
monarchy   6
aristocracy   6
polity   6
tyranny   6

oligarchy   6
democracy   6
mob rule   7
republic   7
representation   7
civic virtue   8
empirical judgment   8
franchise   10
Jacksonian democracy   10

Fourteenth Amendment   10
Fifteenth Amendment   10
Brown v. Board of Education   11
Voting Rights Act of 1965   11
Twenty-Sixth Amendment   12
direct democracy/participatory
    democracy   13
indirect democracy/
    representative democracy   13

referendum   13
ballot initiative   13
majority rule   14
deliberative   14

political participation   14
social capital   15
American political
   culture   16

political and legal
   equality   18
equality of opportunity   18
equality of results   19

Suggested Web Resources

The following are websites related to democracy.

The Direct Democracy Center promotes the idea that representative democracy has failed and that we should have a direct democracy. Its position is that "It's time for real democracy instead of grossly incompetent government, social aggression, political terrorism, legal anarchy, selfish extremes and media-driven chaos." The site contains an extensive reading list and access to a list of proposed amendments to the U.S. and California constitutions (**http://realdemocracy. com**).

The Initiative and Referendum Institute states that its mission is "to research and develop clear analysis of the initiative process and its use; to inform and educate the public about the process and its effects on the political, fiscal and social fabric of our society; and to provide effective leadership in litigation—defending the initiative process and the right of citizens to reform their government from career legislators who want to take it away." In addition to providing historical data, the site also hosts a companion site, BallotWatch.org, which tracks the status of current ballot measures throughout the country (**http://www.iandrinstitute.org**).

E-The People describes itself as "a public forum for democratic and deliberative discussion. The conversations on E-The People explore the political issues we see in the news, **rejecting the traditional spin and conventional wisdom** that tend to fill the airwaves." E-The People is run by the nonprofit Democracy Project (**http://www.e-thepeople.org/about**).

Project Vote Smart has won numerous "best website" awards since it was established. It provides basic "factual information on over 13,000 elected offices and candidates for public office—President, Governors, Congress and State Legislatures." Through this site citizens can get information about their elected officials, including who they are, where they stand on issues, their voting and campaign finance records, as well as evaluations of the representatives that have been done by more than "100 conservative to liberal special interests" (**http://www.vote-smart.org/index.htm**).

Voices of September 11 is the organization founded by Mary Fetchet to provide support for the families of the 9/11 victims (**http://www.voicesofsept11 .org/**). You can read Ms. Fetchet's testimony before the Senate Governmental Affairs committee (**http://www.911independentcommission.org/ mary81704.html**). You can also watch the ABC News "Person of the Year, 2004" story (**http:// abcnews.go.com/WNT/PersonOfWeek /story?id =363206&page=1**).

A complete study tool kit is available for this chapter and includes the following:
Flashcards
Crossword Puzzle
Critical Thinking Exercises
Interactive Timelines
Chapter Quiz

2 The Constitution and the Origins of American Political Ideals

■ **From the Boston Tea Party to Shays' Rebellion**   **27**

■ **Introduction: Constitutionalism and American Politics**   **30**

■ **The Political Principles of the American Founding**   **31**
Enlightenment Political Ideas   31
The Framers' Understanding of Democracy   36

■ **Colonial Political Practices**   **37**
Events Leading to the Revolution   38
The First Contracts: The Articles of
    Confederation and the State Constitutions   40

■ **The Constitutional Convention**   **42**
The Ratification Debates   44

■ **General Provisions of the Constitution**   **48**
Legislative Power   49
Executive Power   50
Judicial Power   51
Other Key Provisions   52

■ **Changing the Constitution**   **52**

■ **Conclusion: The U.S. Constitution—Continuity and Change**   **53**

From the Boston Tea Party to Shays' Rebellion

© North Wind Picture Archives

The colonies of British America experienced increasing popular dissatisfaction with official government policy during in the 1760s and 1770s. A series of decisions by the British government over these years—the Stamp Act, the Tea Act, and the Intolerable Acts, for example—generated various forms of opposition. The colonists published their concerns in local newspapers. Individuals throughout the colonies formed "committees of correspondence" to ensure that events in one colony were known to residents of the others. Pamphlets that explained the complaints of the colonists were written and distributed. These writings were used to build widespread support for the opposition. Petitions were circulated, collected, and sent to those in power stating the specific complaints and rationale for the concerns. Colonial legislatures passed resolutions attempting to encourage the government in London to alter its positions. From the colonists' perspective, none of these activities yielded the desired results. The British continued to ignore their concerns, and over time, more complaints were added to the already long list. Eventually, the colonists resorted to other tactics—methods that involved more than stating their concerns in writing and actions that involved open defiance of the law and the existing authorities.

In 1773, residents of Boston disguised themselves as "Indians" and dumped tea into the harbor as a means of protest against what they saw as unjust British policies.

Throughout the colonies, one of the largest complaints had to do with tea, a favorite beverage of the day, and the price colonists paid for this imported commodity. The British government had passed the Tea Act in 1773 to ensure that the colonists would have to purchase their tea from the British East India Company. Resistance to the Tea Act was particularly strong in the Massachusetts city of Boston, where the people refused to allow ships carrying tea to unload their cargo. At the same time, the royal governor refused to allow the ships to leave until the tea had been unloaded. On December 16, 1773, average people took matters into their own hands. After the governor again refused to respond to their requests to let the ships leave Boston with their cargo, a group of individuals met at the Old South Meeting House. Samuel Adams sent a signal that meant that those gathered were now to implement a plan they had previously agreed to follow if the governor once again refused to respond satisfactorily to their concerns. At his direction, Adams's followers disguised themselves as Indians and proceeded to the wharf where the ships were located. In an orderly process, without damaging the ships themselves, the "Indians" proceeded to destroy the tea by dumping it into Boston Harbor. It is estimated that the tea was worth 10,000 pounds sterling, a considerable sum at the time.[1]

Read a firsthand account of the Boston Tea Party.

The **Boston Tea Party** was an act of civil disobedience undertaken by Americans involving the destruction of private property and open defiance of a duly enacted law. Yet when it took place, there was widespread support for the action. The Tea Party was seen by many in 1773, and continues to be seen today, as a valiant effort on the part of patriots to exercise their political rights. These actions were deemed necessary and justified to make a distant government more responsive to the needs and concerns of the people.

In the years following the Tea Party, opposition to British policy grew stronger, eventually resulting in the colonies declaring their formal independence from British rule in 1776 and the Revolutionary War. The war was justified based on the idea that governmental authority resided in "the people." Popular support and the commitment of average people to the cause of independence were essential for the long and difficult war effort. During the war, colonies became states, and the states united under a national government: the Articles of Confederation.

When the war concluded, politics in the new nation underwent significant changes. In many of the states, the democratic rhetoric of the revolution was taken quite seriously. There was much more popular involvement in politics than had existed during the colonial era. There was also considerably less deference toward the privileged classes. Within a decade of independence, the democratic impulses let loose by the Revolution were seen by many to be dangerous and in need of being curtailed. In 1786 and 1787, new instances of civil disobedience occurred, also in Massachusetts, but this time in the western region of the state. Rather than being praised, these actions were seen as evidence that a major political crisis existed and that substantial changes were needed to respond to the crisis.

Western Massachusetts in 1786 was populated mainly by small farmers who were having a hard time coping with the economic depression occurring at the time. Many had mortgages on their land and were indebted to Boston bankers and merchants. In the language of the day, the farmers were debtors and they were a majority of the states' citizens. The most pressing issue facing them was economic: They were having a hard time repaying their loans because there was limited hard currency—money backed by gold and silver—in circulation. Unable to repay their debts, farmers were forced to turn over their land to lenders through foreclosure proceedings. The farmers wanted the state to pass legislation that would make paper money legal tender. This would have enabled the farmers to repay their debts.

The state legislature was dominated by Boston economic interests tied to the bankers—creditors who had lent the funds that the farmers were obligated to repay. The creditors were a distinct minority of the population, but they were a privileged minority. The creditor-dominated state government refused to print paper money and vigorously enforced foreclosure actions that were happening with increasing frequency. In their view, to do as the farmers wanted would have added to the already existing inflationary pressures, thereby creating an economic crisis that would erode the fundamental right to private property.

Opposition to the distant government in Boston was widespread among the western farmers. Meeting in their respective counties, the farmers used accepted political practices and petitioned the legislature in Boston to address their concerns. When the legislature did not respond, the farmers took more direct action. Groups of them stormed courthouses in a number of counties, thereby preventing the foreclosure actions. One of the farmers, Daniel Shays, became a leader of the group. Shays had been a soldier in the Revolutionary War and, by all accounts, had fought hard for independence. Under his direction, the farmers armed themselves, forced the state court to adjourn, and took several other actions against the government.

The governor sent the militia into the area to put an end to the lawlessness that came to be known as **Shays' Rebellion.** He also requested assistance from the national government to help the state restore order. But without financial resources, the national government was unable to respond. Eventually, there were a few skirmishes between the farmers and the state militia, and the Shaysites were easily defeated. Their leaders were arrested, convicted, and sentenced to death for treason, although they were later pardoned.

In many ways, the Boston Tea Party and Shays' Rebellion were quite similar; however, the response to them by the leaders at the time was quite different. The "Indians" of the Tea Party were considered righteous citizens attacking an unresponsive, distant, and tyrannical government. Their actions were considered virtuous. Fifteen years later, the farmers of western Massachusetts were viewed as dangerous and out of control. The "rabble," as they were called, were too self-interested to see the necessity of sacrificing their own desires for the public good. The "average citizen" now presented a threat to public order and the future of the new country. Reports of Shays' Rebellion helped convince many that the national government needed additional powers to respond to such rebellious acts on the part of the "people" more effectively. The incident was a clear-cut illustration of what would happen if the people became too involved in politics. Consequently, the people needed to be distanced from government.[2]

These two events, occurring a little more than a decade apart, illustrate the changing political climate that existed in late-eighteenth-century America. The impulse toward democracy and popular participation in politics and government, which inspired the Declaration of Independence and the Revolution, quickly came to be seen as a trend that needed to be stopped. In the eyes of many of the political leaders of the day, the people needed to be contained and their influence on government significantly limited if the experiment in republican government was to survive. The U.S. Constitution was intended to limit the democratic tendencies of the Revolution as well as solve a number of other political problems that existed at the time. The events and ideas that led to the creation of the new nation and to the writing of the Constitution—along with the Constitution's importance in contemporary American politics—are the subjects of this chapter.

Introduction: Constitutionalism and American Politics

One of the most remarkable characteristics of the U.S. Constitution is its longevity. The Constitution has been in place, with very few alterations, for more than 215 years. No other country with a written constitution has had its essential governmental structure last for as long a period of time with so few basic changes. Although changes have been made, our general structure of government and rationale for politics remain essentially the same today as they were in 1789, the date of final ratification of the Constitution. When the Constitution was written and ratified, few people imagined that the government being instituted would last so long. Nor could they envision the complex, diverse, technologically sophisticated nation that would develop over time. Despite the dramatic differences between the eighteenth and twenty-first centuries, we need to spend some time in the eighteenth century to gain a clear understanding of contemporary American politics. In other words, we need to know where we have been to understand where we are today.

Part of the reason it is important to learn about the background and history of the Constitution is because of the role it plays in the overall context of American politics. The Constitution is more than a plan of government and a set of decision-making processes and procedures. It is also a symbol of legitimacy and the embodiment of a specific understanding of the nature of government. It helps define us as a people and a culture. Americans do more than follow the rules that the Constitution establishes; they believe in the authority of actions taken pursuant to its authority and in the illegitimacy of any actions or decisions deemed "unconstitutional." In the words of one author, the Constitution is "the myth that binds us."[3]

"Thinking About Constitutionalism at the Start of the Twenty-First Century," Donald S. Lutz.

Constitutionalism, a term used to describe this belief, is central to Americans' notions of who and what we are. To believe in the Constitution is to believe in limited government. It is to hold that there are, and should be, limits to democracy and majority rule.[4] It means that our politics is premised on the belief that there is a fundamental law, the Constitution, and that all other laws, to be valid, must conform to the Constitution. The constitutional myth includes belief in what, theoretically, can be contradictory ideas. It means to believe in "democracy and liberty; legal equality of individuals and a balance of power among the branches of government; a nation of laws, not of men; majority rule and minority rights; one man, one vote; a free marketplace and the rights to free speech and privacy."[5]

CHAPTER 2: The Constitution and the Origins of American Political Ideals

A good many of our contemporary beliefs about the Constitution were not held by those who created the document, and we tend to forget that the Constitution of 1789 is not the Constitution of 2007. As Eric Black notes, "This creates quite a strain between the facts of 1787 and our need to believe that the framers had their eyes on democracy, freedom and equality."[6] Given this, as you study American politics, you will be well served if you keep in mind the changes that the Constitution and nation have undergone since 1787 as you also remember the original principles upon which it is based.

The Political Principles of the American Founding

When the American colonists expressed their opposition to British policy and eventually asserted their right to separate themselves from the British government, they did not do so to seize power for its own sake. Their understanding of what did and what did not constitute legitimate political actions on the part of governmental authorities inspired their actions. Being very aware of the enormity of what they were doing, they publicly justified their cause through a series of proclamations and pronouncements. The colonists took pains to explain why they were doing what they knew was rebellious and illegal. In fact, their actions make little sense without knowing the political principles and ideals that served as both their justification and their inspiration.

Read the Declaration of Independence.

The clearest expression of the colonists' sentiments was the **Declaration of Independence.** This document set forth the principles that its signers saw as the only legitimate foundation for governmental authority, principles of government, and political ideals that would later be incorporated into the state constitutions, the U.S. Constitution, and the Bill of Rights. Each of these founding statements can be understood as embodying the then current understanding of what constituted the best that people could aspire to in terms of a political system. It would be helpful for you to take some time to read both the Declaration of Independence and the U.S. Constitution, both of which are available in the appendix, before reading the next section of this chapter.

Read the U.S. Constitution.

Enlightenment Political Ideas

The Framers and their ideas were products of their times: the period of intellectual history known as the **Enlightenment,** which covers the seventeenth and eighteenth centuries. During this period, ideas about politics and government changed markedly from previous eras. Although there were differences regarding key political principles among Enlightenment political writers, a set of core ideas distinguishes Enlightenment political thought. To understand these ideas, it is important to keep in mind that people contemplating major political change need to have answers to some fundamental questions: What is the nature and purpose of politics?

What political principles and values are central? And what is the best governmental structure through which to achieve these goals?

Unlike previous eras, Enlightenment thinking about politics started with the individual. Enlightenment thinkers developed the idea that social and political life is rooted in the notion that certain **individual rights** are part of the nature of things and are inherent in every person. Such assumptions about individual rights may seem like truisms today, but they were revolutionary during the Enlightenment. The focus on individual rights was written into the language of the Declaration of Independence, which states, among other things, that all men are entitled to certain "unalienable rights." The Declaration goes on to state that governments are "instituted among men" to preserve those rights.

The Nature of Politics: Human Nature

Facing the prospect of creating new governments forces one to ask fundamental questions: What is it about human beings that forces us to create governments to live together? Why is government needed in the first place? The answer to these questions came from an understanding of the characteristics that defined **human nature.** A range of perspectives on human nature existed at the time, but most colonists shared the idea that human beings were not perfect. Because humans had fundamental flaws, they needed to be limited in their actions by governmental authority. As James Madison put it in *Federalist* No. 51, "if men were angels no governments would be necessary," but since men were not angels, governments were needed. Thus, the real question becomes what form of government is preferred and what constitutes the legitimate foundation of political authority.[7]

Read *Federalist* No. 51.

Individuals, who are the basic units of society and government, may be characterized by fundamental flaws, but they are **rational.** The capacity of human beings for rational thought means that, as imperfect as we might be, it is within our power to compensate for our flaws and weaknesses. We can use reason, rather than fear and/or coercion, to improve the situations in which we find ourselves, including our political situation.

Enlightenment political thinkers viewed government as a human creation that arose in response to the problems encountered in the natural situations that people found themselves in. The "natural" condition was one where there was no government; writers of that era referred to this as the **state of nature.** In that state, human nature would be expressed without restraint. Descriptions of the state of nature varied. **Thomas Hobbes,** who had a very harsh view of human nature, called it a state of "war of all against all," where life was "solitary, poor, nasty, brutish and short." **John Locke** had a more generous view of what life would be like without government. But even he concluded the state of nature became "inconvenient" due to conflicts that developed among the individuals living there. Regardless of one's description, the state of nature was ultimately not the most desirable situation for human life because people could not seem to live together without conflict. However, because humans did have reason, there was a way out. Using their reason, individuals soon reached the conclusion that the state of nature had to be replaced with the artificial creation that was government.

The move from the state of nature to civil society and government came through the creation of a **social contract.** Individuals in the state of nature exercised their reason and recognized that their collective lives would be better if they agreed to a set of common rules and a method of enforcing those rules. Consequently, they entered into a voluntary arrangement whereby they would live under a government of their own creation to provide for their mutual benefit and protection.

The American Revolution put what had been theory into practice. The Declaration of Independence announced the failure and end of the contract between the colonists and the British government. After independence, the former colonists took the social contract idea very seriously. Having accepted the validity of the social contract as the basis for government, it became very important to the colonists to have **written constitutions** that spelled out the details of the governing system that all had agreed to. These written constitutions were seen to represent the **fundamental law** to which all others had to conform. The state constitutions, the Articles of Confederation, and the U.S. Constitution were seen as explicit confirmations of the social contract as the foundation of all legitimate government. These plans were adopted only after a rational process of debate, deliberation, and voluntary assent.

The Purpose of Government: Protecting Individual Rights

General Enlightenment understandings of human nature provided answers to questions about why politics was necessary, but that still leaves open the question of the **purpose of government:** What should government be trying to achieve? Some, like Thomas Hobbes, thought the primary purpose was to provide security and safety for individual citizens. In the aftermath of 9/11, the responsibility of government to provide basic security has become an increasing matter of concern. Others, like Jean Jacques Rousseau, saw government as responsible for enhancing the lives of citizens. But the principles of government that were written into the Declaration of Independence and the plan of government adopted in the Constitution were most directly influenced by two European political philosophers: John Locke and the Baron de Montesquieu.

Locke had been very specific about the rights of individuals in the state of nature. According to him, the natural rights of individuals were **life,** the **liberty,** or freedom, to preserve that life, and the right to have the **property** that one worked for. These principles were incorporated into the assertion in the Declaration of Independence that an individual's "unalienable rights" include "life, liberty and the pursuit of happiness." **Thomas Jefferson** may have meant more than the right to private property when he used the phrase "pursuit of happiness" in the Declaration, but it was clear that happiness could not be found unless one's possessions and the fruits of one's hard work were secure.

Although property was a natural right, it led to a major problem in the state of nature because it produced conflict. In the state of nature, disagreements arose regarding property rights, but there was no agreed-upon way of settling the disputes. Recognizing that this was not a desirable situation, individuals decided that they would be better off if they voluntarily agreed to give up some of their natural freedom to ensure more security and more material wealth. The purpose of the social contract was to protect individual rights, specifically those of life, liberty, and property. Locke was concerned with preserving natural liberty, so he argued that government should be limited, with individuals retaining as much freedom as possible.

Locke also provided the colonists with a justification for rebellion. Locke said that people voluntarily entered into an agreement to form a government to protect their life, liberty, and property. If the government set up to offer such protection was no longer doing so, it was legitimate for the people to declare that the social contract was no longer working. Then they could start over and create a new government better suited to fulfill the purpose for which all governments were initially created. The colonists used this line of logic when they sought to justify their break with Britain. The Tea Party was one of a series of events that culminated in the Declaration of Independence, a document that justified the break with Britain by providing evidence that the government was no longer serving the ends of protecting individual rights.

The Plan of Government: Republicanism

Once independence was declared, Americans, having no desire to revert to the state of nature, had to replace the rejected social contract. They needed to establish new governments. When each of the former colonies adopted its own state government, it focused its attention on what kind of governmental structure would best achieve the goal of protecting individual rights. Looking for guidance, the constitution writers turned to the French thinker the **Baron de Montesquieu.**[8] Montesquieu embodied the conventional wisdom on the correct construction of a **republic,** the only form of government, in the words of **James Madison,** "reconcilable with the genius of the American people."[9] Republics were so highly prized because their authority came from the people, and history had shown that republics were best suited to preserving liberty.

A decade later, when James Madison was preparing for his role at the federal Constitutional Convention, he too spent a good deal of time reading about republics. One of the writers he found most useful was Montesquieu, who had analyzed what defined republics as well as what made them succeed. In a republic, the final political authority rests with the public at large. As noted in Chapter 1, in a government based on representation, individual representatives are elected by those designated as citizens. The representatives are then empowered to make the political decisions that affect the country for set periods of time and through established decision-making procedures. In an **aristocratic republic,** only a minority of the citizenry is given the power to choose representatives; in a **democratic republic,** the entire citizenry has that power. In the late 1780s, Americans created a republic that had both democratic and aristocratic elements but that was not yet a "democracy."

In analyzing what made a republic successful, Montesquieu pointed to a principle that had long been associated with republics—**civic virtue.** As noted in Chapter 1, civic virtue is the idea that the ruling element of society, whether it be composed of a minority or the majority, must put the good of the whole, or the **public interest,** above individual or class interest when making public decisions. Citizens acting in a civically virtuous manner would be willing to make an individual sacrifice if it meant that the public good would be served by so doing. The difficulty, then, for any republic would be to prevent virtue from degenerating into its opposites: greed, self-interest, and ambition.

Montesquieu argued that to maintain virtue and a republic, it was important to pay particular attention to the governmental structure. It was vital to maintain a strict **separation of powers.** The basic powers of government are the legislative (the power to make the laws), the executive (the power to enforce the laws), and the judicial (the power to interpret the laws). To maintain a successful republic, it was necessary to separate those powers so that no individuals were able to exercise more than one of the powers at any given time. By separating the powers of government, the likelihood of political power corrupting officials would be lessened and the chances for civic virtue would be improved. Montesquieu's ideas about the importance of representation and the proper governmental arrangements were taken very seriously by the revolutionary generation, especially James Madison, and these views were incorporated into both the state and national constitutions.

The political principles and ideals that inspired the founding generation of American politics have come to be termed **republicanism.** As Gordon Wood has noted, "Americans did not have to invent republicanism in 1776; they only had to bring it to the surface."[10] By the end of the eighteenth century in the Anglo-American world, republics were seen as the only form of government where individual liberty could be protected against the abuses of arbitrary governmental power, better known at the time as *tyranny.* The problem was that "because republics required civic virtue and disinterestedness among their citizens, they were very fragile polities, extremely liable to corruption."[11] Finding ways to avoid such corruption was the goal of those Americans who designed the new governments. Civic virtue was

"Republicanism and the Founding of America," Marcus Cunliff.

central to republicanism and had to be encouraged and cultivated: "The sacrifice of individual interests to the greater good of the whole formed the essence of republicanism and comprehended for Americans the idealistic goal of their Revolution."[12] Advocates of republicanism argued that education, the proper lifestyle, and relatively small governments were all necessary to promote civic virtue.

The Framers' Understanding of Democracy

The political leaders in late eighteenth-century America may have adhered to a republican political philosophy, but they were not democrats. They shared the general view of democracy that dominated Western political thought until the nineteenth century (see Chapter 1). In particular, they did not have confidence in the ability of the majority of residents in the colonies to exercise civic virtue and be good citizens. Jefferson may have inspired generations with his assertion in the Declaration that "all men are created equal"; however, he and most others of his generation did not have the same understanding of the phrase as we do today. The call to equality may have been inspirational, but the extent of its reach was limited at the time it was written.

To be a citizen, a person needed to be rational and independent. Women, Native Americans, slaves, people of color generally, and those without sufficient property were not thought to have the ability to participate in the political process. They were not included in the "men" of the Declaration. Gordon Wood has characterized the situation as follows:

> The republican revolution was the greatest utopian movement in American history. . . . But the ink on the Declaration of Independence was scarcely dry before many of the revolutionary leaders began expressing doubts about the possibility of realizing these high hopes. The American people seemed incapable of the degree of virtue needed for republicanism.[13]

By the mid-1780s, many of the leading political figures of the new nation worried about the extent to which the common people, or "the rabble" as they were often called, were involving themselves in the business of politics. Shays' Rebellion provided concrete evidence of the dangers that would occur if the common folk took too seriously the principles used to justify the Revolution. Shays' Rebellion also demonstrated that many of those common folk were in fact taking the words of the Declaration to heart. They began to make political assertions that the value of equality expressed in the Declaration should be taken seriously. This was most likely an unintended consequence of appealing to the principles embodied in the document: "Jefferson and others who invoked this egalitarian moral sense, of course, had little inkling of the democratic lengths to which it would be carried."[14] As we shall see throughout this book, the democratic implications of the Declaration are still being contested in twenty-first-century American politics.

Colonial Political Practices

Most of the men responsible for leading the Revolution and writing the Constitution were members of the elite class of colonial society.[15] Thus, they shared a common economic, educational, and ideological background, including the political ideals described in the previous section. Yet they were not primarily political philosophers. They were active participants in colonial politics whose actions can only be understood as reflections of their principles. The political practices of the British government that developed during the seventeenth and eighteenth centuries, when viewed through the political principles of the colonists, did not measure up. This led to the conflicts that arose between the colonies and the British government after the 1760s. Conflicts over the legitimacy of specific political practices and policies made the theoretical principles concrete. The combination of principles and practice led the colonists to war, independence, and the creation of new states and a new nation.

When the colonies were established under British authority, each had its own individual governmental structure. Although the structures were similar, none of the colonies had the exact same governmental organization—a pattern that has continued to the present day. Despite this, certain political practices were firmly established by the 1760s. All of the colonies had governors appointed by the king, and those governors had considerable powers. All of the colonies had some type of popularly elected legislative body. The colonial assemblies were **bicameral**—that is, they had two houses—and were established on the British model, with the upper house seen to represent the aristocracy, or "better sort," in the society and the lower house seen to speak for "the democracy," or the average citizens.[16] There were regular elections to determine who would serve in the colonial assemblies, and there was active debate regarding public issues that took place via pamphlets, newspapers, and "committees of correspondence."

Furthermore, the consequence of these practices was that the colonists were accustomed to representative government, to representatives that they chose directly, and to representatives who lived in the communities they represented. Different understandings of the nature of legitimate representation developed on either side of the Atlantic. The colonists believed in **actual representation,** which is the idea that the only person who can legitimately speak for a group of citizens is someone they actually choose. Representatives needed to be clearly tied to a specific geographic location to fully understand the needs and concerns of its citizens. Virginians should be represented by people from Virginia. In contrast, the British operated on a model of **virtual representation.** They did not believe that representatives had to be directly chosen by the citizens being represented, nor did they have to live in the area represented. If the representative acted in the name and best interest of the nation, all the people were being represented. Therefore, members of Parliament, even though they had never set foot, much less lived, in the colonies, could determine what was in the best interest of the nation as a whole. The Americans strongly disagreed with this understanding.

The **electorate,** those empowered to vote, was generally composed of white male property holders. This was also the case in England. The difference, and it was a significant one, was that it was far easier to own property in the colonies. Consequently, much more of the population was a part of the body politic than was the case in England. It is estimated that those eligible to vote in the colonies constituted somewhere between 50 and 75 percent of the white adult male population.[17]

Events Leading to the Revolution

Although the colonies were formally under British rule, Parliament and the Crown largely let them run their own affairs with little interference.[18] The situation changed in the aftermath of the French and Indian War. As a result of that war, which took place in North America, the British government incurred a significant war debt and needed to raise revenues to repay it. Consequently, the British government enacted a series of laws designed to exact more revenue from the colonies, and these laws met with increasing opposition in the years before independence.

One of the actions taken by the British government was a more rigorous enforcement of existing customs and navigation (trade) laws. Before the 1760s, the colonists regularly neglected to pay the fees required on imported goods and goods transported from one colony to another. The new laws enacted after 1760 not only sought to end the "illegal" activities, but they also established a new court with the authority to try all cases involving violations of the Navigation Acts. Finally, customs officials were given increased authority, and they exercised it. All of these actions were resented in the colonies. They were seen as major interferences with the colonists' internal affairs and as improper interference in their governmental structures.

Find a chronology of the American Revolution.

It quickly became clear that customs revenues were insufficient to raise the amount of money the British government now required, so it decided to impose additional taxes on the colonists. Parliament passed the **Stamp Act** in 1765. It was a tax on all printed material, everything from newspapers to legal documents. As such, it was the first direct tax imposed on the colonies. Because the colonists had not elected any of the members of the Parliament that had instituted this tax, they vigorously objected to what they saw as "taxation without representation."

The Stamp Act generated the first widespread opposition to British policy in the colonies. There were mass meetings, violence, and public protests in response to the act. The revenue agents who were supposed to collect the taxes were harassed and threatened by groups of average people taking the law into their own hands, which resulted in the eventual resignation of many tax collectors. The colonial assemblies sent representatives to the **Stamp Act Congress** in 1765, and they brought a formal petition to the king protesting the law. This was the first time that a number of colonies (nine attended) gathered together formally to complain about British rule. It was a significant step in the eventual uniting of the colonies. Amid all the opposition, the Stamp Act was repealed by Parliament; however, this was not the end to the British effort to exert more control over the colonies and to extract more revenue from them.[19] Parliament passed a series of additional direct taxes on the colonists and greatly enhanced the British ability to collect the revenue by increasing the number of customs officials and by giving them increased authority.[20]

In 1773 Parliament passed the Tea Act, which allowed the East India Company to ship its product directly to the colonies without first landing in Britain, as required for all other tea companies. This seemingly insignificant law became the trigger for increased popular opposition to British policy. The Americans saw this law as limiting their economic freedom by creating a monopoly and granting special privileges to a favored company. The reality was that, by this time, all British policy was immediately suspect as an exercise of tyrannical power. Opposition to the Tea Act appeared throughout the colonies. In Boston the opposition resulted in the now famous Boston Tea Party described in the opening section of this chapter. Although it was hailed as an act of patriotism by the colonists, the British government saw this as an act of rebellion and retaliated by imposing extreme measures known as the **Coercive** or **Intolerable Acts** on the colony. One of the provisions altered the nature of the Massachusetts legislature by appointing, rather than electing, the members of its upper house. Another provision suspended regular judicial proceedings, and still others imposed economic sanctions until the destroyed tea had been paid for. Boston refused to do so and was placed under the control of military authorities.

Although most of Britain's actions were directed toward Massachusetts, opposition to British policy was widespread throughout the colonies. In 1774 the **First Continental Congress** met in Philadelphia. At this meeting, representatives from the colonies expressed their opposition to the Coercive Acts and their support for Massachusetts. The Congress adopted a resolution calling for disobedience to the Coercive Acts and a boycott of British goods. While not yet arguing for independence, the Congress did put forth a **Declaration of Rights** which asserted that the colonists' political rights and freedoms as British citizens were being violated by the British government. It warned that armed resistance might be called for if the Congress's concerns were not addressed. This declaration was a concrete reflection of the colonists' ideal that government existed to protect individual rights, not to violate them.

In the months after the Declaration of Rights, armed conflicts occurred at Lexington and Concord in Massachusetts and later spread to other areas. King George declared that the colonies were in rebellion and sent more troops to attempt to quell the rebellion. Support for independence was growing among the colonies, aided by the publication of Thomas Paine's *Common Sense*, which openly called for the colonies to break their connection to Britain. The **Second Continental Congress** adopted this position in

Read more about Thomas Paine.

Common Sense

June 1776 and directed a committee to write a resolution justifying the action. Thomas Jefferson took the lead in drafting the document, which became the Declaration of Independence. It was agreed to on July 4, 1776, and remains one of the most inspirational documents in American political history. The Declaration was an extraordinary achievement. It meshed together theory and practice and has served as an inspiration for oppressed people both in this country and abroad ever since it was written.

The First Contracts: The Articles of Confederation and the State Constitutions

Once independence was declared, the former colonists had to develop new governments. Consistent with the dominant political philosophy of the time, they drafted written constitutions (social contracts) that were then ratified, or agreed to, by the citizens of each state. When these first constitutions were written, both the theoretical and practical concerns that had been expressed during the revolutionary era were taken into account. Political freedoms such as those of speech, the press, and religion were protected. There were efforts to ensure that adequate representation existed in all the governments. To prevent the government from abusing its power and becoming tyrannical, executive power was limited because this was seen as the branch of government that was most susceptible to corruption. As the states were writing their own constitutions, members of the Continental Congress sought to create an agreement that would govern the relations among the newly independent states.

Read the Articles of Confederation.

Shortly after independence was declared, the Continental Congress directed that a new national government be proposed. The **Articles of Confederation,** America's first national constitution, were adopted by the Continental Congress in 1777 and eventually ratified by all the states in 1781. Because of the fears that existed at the time about too much power being exercised by a distant central government, the Articles were a loose association between the states: a confederation, with each state retaining its own sovereign power and authority (see Chapter 3).

The concerns about excessive executive power resulted in a national, or central, government that had little authority and no executive branch. The primary institution of the government was the Congress. In it, each state had from two to seven delegates, but only a single vote per state. Although the Congress could conduct war and foreign policy, most important actions required approval by two-thirds of the states. Such agreement was extraordinarily difficult to achieve. Under the Articles, there was no means of enforcing national policy on the states. In addition, the central government did not have the authority to tax citizens directly. To raise revenue, Congress assessed the states for their share of funds needed. However, it had no method of collecting if a state failed to contribute its share. Finally, the Articles required unanimous consent from all the states to amend the agreement.

The new nation conducted the military effort under the Articles and eventually was able to establish peace with Britain. But in the postwar period, the weakness of the government created by the Articles started to become apparent. As described in the opening section of the chapter, there was a widespread economic depression, which contributed to economic conflicts among the states. State governments took actions that protected the economic interests of their own citizens, often at the expense of citizens from neighboring states. Some states began to print paper money as a means of responding to economic problems that they were experiencing. However, money printed in one state was not recognized as legal currency in other states. To protect the economic interests of state citizens, some states imposed tariffs (import taxes) on goods that came, not from other countries, but from other states. The result of all these conflicting economic policies was that it was difficult for an individual to conduct business across state boundaries. There were also border disputes between a number of the states because the western boundaries of the nation had not been definitively established.

Additional weaknesses of the Articles of Confederation began to appear. Without an effective means of raising sufficient revenue, the national government was unable to repay the funds it had borrowed from foreign governments to finance the war. The unpaid debt made it impossible for the country to obtain credit. This in turn made it difficult for the bankers and merchants to operate their businesses. The country also had a difficult time getting other nations to take the United States seriously in terms of international relations. Without sufficient revenues, the Congress had not been able to maintain much of a military presence after the war. American merchants were subjected to raids by the Barbary pirates, and they had no navy to call upon to protect their interests. The British were still maintaining forts in the western territories, and there was no U.S. Army to compel them to leave. Finally, it seemed that the national government could not maintain law and order within its own boundaries. The inability of Congress to respond to Massachusetts' request for help in quelling Shays' Rebellion also highlighted the ineffective executive authority of the national government.

There was also evidence that the democratic implications of the Revolution were being put into practice by the less-well-off elements in the society. During the colonial era, the assemblies were dominated by men of property, but after the Revolution, this situation changed. In some states, average citizens now controlled the legislatures. These states were taking actions such as printing paper money and declaring it legal tender with which to pay debts. Although such laws pleased the debtors (who were the majority of the population), they angered the creditors (who were the wealthy minority). In Rhode Island, the legislature declared that its paper money had to be accepted for the repayment of debts. This angered those who had loaned the funds because it was clear that the paper money did not have the same value as the gold that had been borrowed.

Finally, there was Shays' Rebellion, described in the opening section. This was the trigger incident that convinced many of the established leaders of the country to fear that there was too much democracy and that the rabble needed to be removed from the political process. Although there is still debate over how difficult the situation really was at the time, many of the best-known leaders of the nation thought that the Articles of Confederation were not working and that a new government was needed.

The Constitutional Convention

Consistent with their views about the nature of government and the ability of human reason to solve problems, the colonists did not attempt to correct the problems that existed under the Articles through armed conflict. It was a *rational* process of gathering representatives from each of the states together and having them exercise their reason to create a new government better designed to fulfill the needs of the new nation. The process started in 1785, when a group of colonial leaders met at Mt. Vernon, Virginia, the home of George Washington, to discuss the difficulties they perceived to exist at the time. The meeting resulted in a call for the states to send delegates to another meeting at Annapolis, Maryland, to discuss the increasing problems related to trade and other economic issues. All of the states did not send delegates to Annapolis in 1786, but the result of that meeting was a call to all the states to send representatives to Philadelphia in the summer of 1787 for the purpose of revising the Articles of Confederation.

A **constitutional convention** would be held for the purpose of reconstructing the national government so that it better fulfilled the desire of Americans to live under a viable *republic*. The idea of such a convention, with the goal of producing a written constitution, represents the fulfillment of the political principles of the Americans. When the convention first met, nine states were represented; eventually, delegates from three more states were present at one time or another, but Rhode Island, arguably the most democratic state at the time, never sent delegates to the meeting.

The convention's authority was enhanced when George Washington agreed to attend. He was unanimously elected the presiding officer, and his stature lent prestige and legitimacy to the meeting. At the outset of the convention, the delegates decided that the proceedings would be undertaken in private. The doors were locked, the curtains were drawn, the public was not invited, and there were no reporters.[21] This was done to ensure that the debate would be free and vigorous and that delegates would be able to express views that they knew might be controversial without fear of recrimination. The secrecy, however, did raise concerns among those who were not in favor of altering the Articles. Although the secrecy of the convention may have allowed its members to speak more freely, it is unimaginable that such a momentous undertaking could be held behind closed doors today.

In the summer of 1787, George Washington presided over the Constitutional Convention. His personal prestige helped give legitimacy to the convention's work and its final product.

The stated purpose of the convention was to "revise" the Articles, but it soon became clear that revision meant starting over. The Virginia delegation proposed a plan for a new government that has become known as the **Virginia Plan.** It was largely the work of James Madison (see the text box, "James Madison: Father of the Constitution"). The plan called for a strong national government with the ability to veto actions taken by the state legislatures. It also called for representation based on population, which would have given the balance of power to the large states. The plan included a bicameral legislature that would elect the president. Although this plan became the basis for debate at the convention, many of its provisions were modified and compromises were made to accommodate the concerns of the small states.

The small states, led by New Jersey, offered their own plan, known as the **New Jersey Plan.** It adhered to the provision in the Articles of Confederation that gave each state an equal vote in Congress. The New Jersey Plan would have kept the balance of power between the states as it was under the Articles: The small states would have more influence because there were more small states. Although this seemed like it might be an insurmountable barrier, a middle ground emerged.

The **Great Compromise** was reached on the issue of representation: Representation in the House of Representatives would be based on population, which would give more votes to the larger states, but states would be represented equally in the Senate, which resulted in the smaller states having more influence there. In addition, delegates from the smaller states tended to be more suspicious about the national government becoming too powerful and wanted to ensure that the sovereignty of the state governments would be preserved. As a consequence, the provision in the Virginia Plan that would have given Congress the power to veto state laws was dropped.

Read the records of the Constitutional Convention debates.

Another issue that threatened to derail the convention was slavery. Some of the northern states wanted to stop the importation of slaves immediately. The southern states refused to accept the Constitution with that provision. The compromise that was reached was that the importation of slaves could be halted, but not until 1808. How to count the slave population for the purposes of determining the number of representatives each state would have was also an issue. The southern states wanted to count all the slaves as part of their population; the northern states did not think this was appropriate because the slaves were not part of the citizenry. The **Three-Fifths Compromise** resulted, with each slave being counted as three-fifths of a free person for purposes of representation and taxation. The outright abolition of slavery was never seriously considered at the convention.

The Ratification Debates

Contrary to much popular perception today, ratification of the Constitution was not a "done deal." In fact, not all of the delegates in Philadelphia signed the document produced by the convention. The Constitution had provisions establishing the procedures by which it would be accepted as the new national government. Each state had to hold a ratifying convention, where it would decide whether or not to ratify the plan. For the Constitution to go into effect, nine of the thirteen states had to agree to it. It was clear that if any of the large states chose not to ratify, the plan would not be workable, even if nine states did approve. In New York and Virginia, two of the largest states, there was intense opposition to the plan. Such well-known figures as Patrick Henry argued vigorously against ratification. Eventual ratification came about only after a rather heated political debate. It also came about as the result of compromise and an agreement to alter the plan as soon as it was adopted.

To build support for ratification, one of the Constitution's staunchest supporters, **Alexander Hamilton,** conceived of a method to convince people that the Constitution was a better plan of government than the Articles and that it ought to be adopted. Hamilton, James Madison, and John Jay wrote a series of arguments that were initially printed in the New York newspapers and then reprinted in other states. These essays were intended to provide an explanation of how the new government would work once it was implemented. They also sought to counter the criticisms that were raised by those opposing ratification. The arguments

JAMES MADISON: FATHER OF THE CONSTITUTION

James Madison has come to be known as the Father of the Constitution because of his role in the Constitutional Convention and the subsequent ratification debates. Prior to the convention, he had spent a great deal of time studying the history of republics and reading the works of leading political writers, including Montesquieu, on the topic. His plan was not adopted in its entirety, but it was the foundation upon which the Constitution was based. Madison was also one of the most influential delegates at the convention and participated heavily in the debates and eventual compromises that were adopted. His writings were also a significant factor in the ratification debates. His contributions to *The Federalist Papers* helped gather the support needed for ratification in the important states of Virginia and New York.

© North Wind Picture Archives

James Madison was instrumental in the drafting and eventual adoption of the U.S. Constitution. He was a key participant at the Constitutional Convention and wrote many of the *Federalist Papers*.

Read Madison's *Federalist* No. 10.

Read Madison's *Federalist* No. 51.

Madison thought that the key to the future of the republic was in its institutional structure. Based on his studies, he concluded that the single biggest threat to the future of the republic was the existence of *factions*. Factions were composed of people acting on the basis of self-interest. Factions were inevitable, and their existence undermined the disinterested civic virtue that was necessary for the republic to succeed.

Considering the options available, Madison concluded that factions could not be eliminated without undermining the political freedoms that had been secured in the Revolution. Taking his cue from Montesquieu, Madison argued forcefully that adhering to the doctrine of separation of

(continued)

JAMES MADISON: FATHER OF THE CONSTITUTION (Contd.)

powers was essential in curbing the influence of factions. But he went further. In addition to separating the three branches of government, it was also necessary to have what he called "auxiliary precautions" to "control the effects of faction." These precautions are the decision-making procedures written into the Constitution that are better known today as "checks and balances." Madison also argued that having frequent elections and the existence of multiple levels of government (federalism) also served to curb the effect of factions.

Access all of *The Federalist Papers.*

soon came to be known as *The Federalist Papers,* and they are often referred to when there is a question concerning the meaning of the Constitution. They are the first "interpretation" of the Constitution, and because individuals who were actively involved in drafting the document wrote them, the views expressed in these essays are still widely read today and seen as authoritative statements when attempting to determine the "intent of the Framers."

The people against ratification of the Constitution as it was written have come to be known as the **Anti-Federalists** because they wrote in opposition to the Federalists. The Anti-Federalists' efforts to oppose ratification were not as organized as those of supporters of the Constitution. However, their criticisms of the Constitution were sufficiently persuasive to convince people that, once adopted, the Constitution had to be amended to respond to the objections.

Objections to the Constitution centered on four themes.[22] First, the Anti-Federalists charged that the proposed Constitution was too aristocratic. They thought that the plan would ensure that the privileged members of the society would be in the most important decision-making positions and that the average person would be left out of the political process. The second concern had to do with the nature of republics. The Anti-Federalists did not think it was possible to sustain a republic over such a large geographic area. The conventional wisdom was that republics could be successful only if they encompassed a relatively small region. The third concern was their fear that the creation of a new, strong, national government located a great distance from most of the states would bring about a return of the tyrannical political practices that had existed during the late colonial era. The Anti-Federalists were staunch

CHAPTER 2: The Constitution and the Origins of American Political Ideals supporters of their own state governments, where they felt that they had the most influence and which they felt were the most responsive to their concerns. They were afraid that the states would lose their autonomy under the Constitution.

The fourth, and by far the most significant, concern raised by the Anti-Federalists was the absence of a **Bill of Rights.** Many of the state constitutions included a set of fundamental protections guaranteed to the individual citizens of the state. Including limitations on the powers of government in any written constitution was considered by many essential to ensure that the principle of limited government existed in practice as well as in theory. Among the most important of the rights that the Anti-Federalists felt needed to be protected were those of speech, the press, and religion, and guarantees of judicial due process such as the right to a jury trial. These were all examples of what were seen as fundamental freedoms that had been fought for during the Revolution. The Anti-Federalists were worried that these recently secured rights were in jeopardy again with the proposed new Constitution.

Read writings of the Anti-Federalists.

The Federalist Papers responded to the concerns by making a number of arguments regarding the new government that contributed to its eventual ratification. First, the Federalists made the case that the Articles simply were not working. They contended that a stronger, more powerful government than existed under the Articles was necessary to respond to the economic situation described earlier in the chapter. They also claimed that a large republic was better than small ones because it was, as Madison argued in *Federalist* No. 10, better suited to control the effects of factions. **Factions** were groups of people who shared an interest that was contrary to the public good. The existence of factions meant that civic virtue was lacking, but factions were an inevitable aspect of the political process. Madison argued that factions would have an easier time controlling a small republic than one that covered a geographically large and culturally diverse nation. Contrary to the conventional wisdom, a large republic was better than a small one.

Read *Federalist* No. 10.

There was a need to convince people that the new government was not likely to abuse its powers and encroach on the rights of states and individuals. This is where Madison's emphasis on the separation of powers and checks and balances came in. The Federalists argued that the institutional arrangements of the Constitution would ensure that power would be held in check because no one person, or faction, could control the entire political decision-making process.

The Federalists were not as successful in responding to the critique about the absence of a Bill of Rights. They argued that a Bill of Rights wasn't necessary because the new government had never been given the authority to interfere with fundamental individual freedoms; thus, there was no need for concern. Although successful in responding to the other concerns, this argument did not satisfy the opponents. To garner enough votes to ensure ratification in New York and Virginia, the supporters of the Constitution agreed that one of the first acts of the new government would be to offer a set of amendments that would be referred to as the Bill of Rights.

The Constitution was ratified in 1788, and the new government became effective in 1789.[23] The first ten amendments to the Constitution—the Bill of Rights—were among the first items of business and were ratified by the states in 1791. Even James Madison, the Father of the Constitution, became convinced that such amendments were a good idea and introduced a number of them himself during the first session of Congress.

General Provisions of the Constitution

Review the United States Constitution.

The governmental structure established in 1787 has undergone remarkably few formal alterations in 215 years. It established a set of institutional arrangements that has proven adaptable to changes in the societal, economic, and technological foundations of the American people. Although the basics may be familiar, it is worthwhile to review the general provisions of the Constitution in preparation for gaining a deeper understanding of how the system works today.

The Constitution sets up a political system that has a strict separation of powers among the three fundamental branches of government. Members of the legislature may not serve in the executive branch, nor may they be judges. The same holds true for officials in the other branches. A judge may not, at the same time, be a member of the president's cabinet or an elected member of Congress. The three branches are also given distinct sets of powers, the details of which are covered in subsequent chapters in the text.

The three branches are separate, but they are also interdependent. Presidents and judges do not adopt legislation, but presidents may suggest proposals and may veto laws passed by Congress. Judges don't write legislation, but they may rule that a law is unconstitutional. Neither, however, has a formal role in determining the specific content of legislation. Presidents negotiate treaties and conduct foreign policy, but the Senate has to approve treaties before they go into effect. The president may be the commander in chief, but Congress has the authority to "raise an army and navy" and to "declare war." Judges interpret the laws, but the executive branch must enforce those interpretations for them to be effective.

According to James Madison, a formal separation of powers was insufficient to ensure the future of the republic. He argued for the need for what he termed "auxiliary precautions," better known as the system of **checks and balances.** The checks and balances limit the ability of each branch of government to act independently if there is opposition to its actions on the part of the other branches (see Figure 2.1). A prime example of an auxiliary precaution is the president's power to veto acts of Congress that he thinks

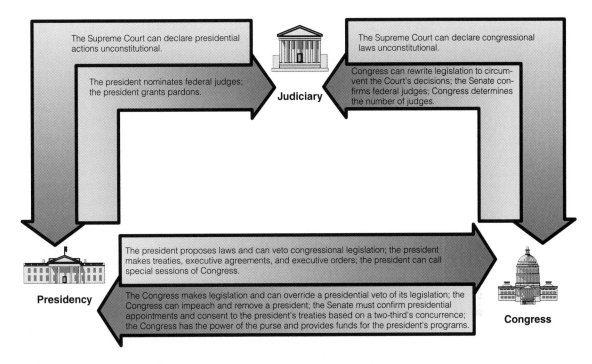

Figure 2.1 Checks and Balances. Most of the major checks and balances among the three branches are explicit in the Constitution, though some are not. For example, the courts' power to declare congressional laws or presidential actions unconstitutional— their power of "judicial review"—is not mentioned.

make for bad law; this is a check on the legislature. However, since it is conceivable that presidents could abuse this power, there is a provision to override a veto if a supermajority of two thirds of each house of Congress still thinks the bill should become law. Another check on the legislative power is built into its bicameral structure. In passing laws, each house of Congress must pass the exact same bill before it can become law, thus separating the legislative power itself.

Review *Federalist* No. 51.

Legislative Power

Article I of the Constitution assigns the legislative, or lawmaking, power to the U.S. Congress, a *bicameral* body. A bicameral legislature has what is usually referred to as an upper and lower house. In the United States, those chambers are the Senate and the House of Representatives, respectively. This means that it has two houses, or chambers, and very few actions can be undertaken without the express approval of both houses. Members of Congress are chosen by and represent the people of their states. House members serve two-year terms, and all of them are up for reelection every two years. Senators serve six-year terms. One third of the Senate is up for reelection every two years. Except in states with very small populations, House members represent a portion of their state known as a district. Senators represent the entire state, and there are two senators for each state.

Congress is one of the institutions that have undergone an important structural change. One of the "antidemocratic" provisions of the original Constitution was to have senators elected by members of the state legislatures. It was thought that this provision would limit the amount of popular influence in the national government. It was also thought that the requirement that the popular branch be reelected every two years was a built-in check on the people. If voters were improperly influenced and made unwise decisions, a new election in two years could correct the mistake. In 1913 the Seventeenth Amendment to the Constitution was ratified, mandating the direct election of senators. So, currently, the House of Representatives and the Senate are both directly elected by the people they represent.

In Article I, Congress is given the explicit authority to pass legislation that, among other things, allows it to raise an army and navy, regulate interstate commerce, establish a post office, raise revenue through taxes, coin money, and, in general, "provide for the common defense and general welfare of the United States." These are known as the **enumerated powers** of Congress because they are specifically listed or enumerated. The last of the listed powers of Congress is the power "To make all laws which shall be necessary and proper for carrying into execution the foregoing powers, and all other powers vested by this Constitution in the government of the United States, or in any department or officer thereof." This is known as the **necessary and proper** or **elastic clause** of the Constitution because it gives the legislature the discretion to pass a wide range of laws about topics that may not be specifically listed in the Constitution but that are consistent with the broad principles and powers that are specified.

Executive Power

Article II of the Constitution established the executive branch by giving a single executive, the **president,** the authority to administer the federal government. It also gave the president considerable power, which has increased during the course of the nation's history. Presidents serve four-year terms. George Washington, the nation's first president, established the precedent of serving two terms in the office. No president served more than two terms until Franklin Delano Roosevelt was elected to four terms beginning in 1932. Although he was one of the most popular presidents in the nation's history, his decision to run for office four times led to an effort to prevent future presidents from having that same option. The Twenty-Second Amendment made formal what had previously been tradition by limiting a president to two terms in office. Although similar limitations have been suggested for members of Congress, at present there are no restrictions on the number of terms that representatives and senators may serve.

Article II assigns a number of specific powers to the president. These include being the commander in chief of the armed services, recognizing other countries, receiving ambassadors, negotiating treaties, and making nominations to the federal courts.

The Framers' attempts to limit the influence of the average citizen in the operations of the federal government were manifest in the method that they adopted to elect the president. To ensure separation of powers, they rejected the idea that the Congress should choose the president. This makes the U.S. government different from most other democracies, in which the executive is selected by the legislature. When the legislature chooses the executive, a parliamentary system of government exists. Although rejected as a practice in the United States, it is the standard in many Western democracies, including the United Kingdom, France, and Germany.

The dilemma the Framers faced was how to balance their commitment to popularly elected representative government against their fear of the potential dangers inherent in the practice of majority rule. To resolve the dilemma, they created an institution unique to American politics: the **electoral college.** The system as it currently operates is described in detail in Chapter 8. Over the course of time, changes have been made that have democratized the system so that currently voters do choose their president, albeit in an indirect manner. However, as it was originally conceived and as it operated into the nineteenth century, the people were largely excluded from the process of electing their president.

Judicial Power

It was very important to the Framers that there be an **independent judicial branch.** The courts were seen as having the least amount of inherent power. As Alexander Hamilton wrote in *Federalist* No. 78, the courts have "no influence over either the sword or the purse," but only the power of judgment. Knowing how fragile this power was, the Framers put provisions into the Constitution designed to ensure that judicial decisions could not be subject to political pressure by either the executive or legislative branches. Most important, the Constitution provides federal judges with life terms contingent on "good behavior." The only way to remove a federal judge is through impeachment, and this has happened only a handful of times in the nation's history. The life-term provision was included so judges could make unpopular decisions without fearing that their jobs would be in jeopardy. The Constitution also states that the salary of judges cannot be reduced, which is another potential means of retaliation against judges who make unpopular decisions. In terms of its method of appointment, the courts are the least democratic branch of government. There are no elections to the federal bench. As described in more detail in Chapter 11, the president nominates, and the Senate confirms the nomination. The Supreme Court also has the power of **judicial review,** which is the ability to declare acts of the Congress and the president to be void because they violate the Constitution. This

Read *Federalist* No. 78.

power is not explicitly listed in the Constitution; rather, it was asserted by the Supreme Court in 1803 in the case of *Marbury v. Madison.* A more complete discussion of this power appears in Chapter 11.

Other Key Provisions

Perhaps the single most innovative aspect of the Constitution is the existence of the national or federal government at the same time that state governments exist with their own constitutions and authority. This arrangement is known as **federalism.** Before the Constitution, it was not thought that such a system would be possible. Sovereignty, or the ultimate governing authority, needed to be located in one place and could not be divided. As we shall see in Chapter 3, federalism is a central feature of the American political system. Because it was understood that the existence of both a national and state governments could easily result in conflicts, the constitution includes what is known as the **supremacy clause:** "This Constitution, and the laws of the United States which shall be made in pursuance thereof . . . shall be the supreme law of the land; . . . anything in the Constitution or laws of any State to the contrary notwithstanding." The purpose of this clause was to make it clear that the national government would prevail if and when there were conflicts between federal and state laws.

Compare the U.S. Constitution with your state's constitution.

There are also other provisions in the Constitution that are tied to the idea that government should be limited in its powers. The first ten amendments to the Constitution are known collectively as the Bill of Rights. Discussed more thoroughly in Chapter 4, the Bill of Rights protects individual citizens against the possible abuse of governmental power by guaranteeing political rights such as freedom of speech, religion, the press, and assembly. It also protects citizens in dealing with the judicial system by establishing a number of procedural guarantees such as the prohibition on unlawful search and seizures and on cruel and unusual punishment, as well as establishing the right to a speedy trial. Even without the Bill of Rights, restrictions on governmental authority are written into the Constitution. Many of them seem archaic today, such as the prohibition on granting titles of nobility, but this is largely because few ever attempted to engage in such an activity once the Constitution had clearly made it "out of bounds." Other provisions, such as the prohibition on **bills of attainder** (laws that punish a person without a judicial proceeding) and **ex post facto laws** (laws that make an action illegal that was legal at the time it happened), remain important limitations on that the powers of the federal government today.

Changing the Constitution

The Constitution incorporated provisions for changing or amending the document. The Framers of the Constitution did not think they were infallible and thought it likely that there would need to be changes made in the future. There was a desire to make the amendment process easier than the unanimous agreement needed to make changes under the Articles, yet not so easy that changes could be made without careful deliberation and an agreement by more than a simple majority that any particular change was needed and desirable.

There are two methods through which constitutional amendments can be proposed. The first is initiated in Congress. If two-thirds of the members of both the House of Representatives and the Senate agree to a change in the Constitution, the proposed amendment is then sent to the states. The other procedure is initiated by the states. If two-thirds of the state legislatures ask for an amendment, Congress will have to establish a constitutional convention. Once sent to the states, there are two ratification methods. An amendment must either be approved by three-quarters of the state legislatures or supported by three-quarters of state conventions held for the purpose of considering the amendment.

All but one of the formal changes to the constitution have come about through the first method: They have been initiated in Congress and approved by three-quarters of the state legislatures. Only the Twenty-First Amendment (repealing Prohibition) was ratified by state conventions rather than by state legislatures. The Constitution has never been amended via a constitutional convention. Although occasional calls for another constitutional convention arise with reference to particular issues, there would be no way of knowing what the consequence of such a meeting would be. Potentially, it could mirror the convention of 1787, which "revised" by starting over. Such a prospect makes some observers nervous.

The procedures are such that the Constitution has been amended rather infrequently over time. When one discounts the first ten amendments— the Bill of Rights, which was added right away as a result of the objections raised during the ratification process—and takes into account that two amendments cancel each other out (the Eighteenth Amendment, establishing Prohibition, and the Twenty-First Amendment, repealing it), there have only been fifteen changes in the basic structure of government since it was adopted. However, many would argue that the Constitution has been amended more frequently than this through the process of judicial interpretation. This issue will be covered in depth in Chapter 11.

Should the Constitution Be Amended by National Initiative?

"Failed Amendments to the Constitution," Morton Keller.

Conclusion: The U.S. Constitution—Continuity and Change

The U.S. Constitution is the foundation for all that happens in American politics. Those who participated in its creation and in the events surrounding the American war for independence were people who believed that political legitimacy ultimately rested with the people, and this had the potential of instituting a radically democratic political system. The ideals and principles that inspired them to put their lives on the line to gain independence still serve as powerful motivations for political action. The events of the period may have set the groundwork for the future democratization

Check here for possible post-publication updates to the chapter material.

of the nation, but the Constitution itself was a step away from the democratic impulses set forth by the Revolution. The Framers of the Constitution were more interested in instituting economic and social stability than in creating a political system that was open to participation by all the residents of the nation. As we move on to examine contemporary political practices in the United States, it is worthwhile to think of the founding period as the beginning, but certainly not the end, of the debate over what type of a political system we want, whom we want to make collective decisions, and how much we are willing to commit to making self-government work in practice as well as in theory.

Key Terms

Boston Tea Party   28
Shays' Rebellion   29
constitutionalism   30
Declaration of
   Independence   31
Enlightenment   31
individual rights   32
human nature   32
rational   32
state of nature   32
Thomas Hobbes   32
John Locke   32
social contract   33
written constitutions   33
fundamental law   33
purpose of government   33
life, liberty, property   33
Thomas Jefferson   33
Baron de Montesquieu   34
republic   34
James Madison   34

aristocratic republic   35
democratic republic   35
civic virtue   35
public interest   35
separation of powers   35
republicanism   35
bicameral   37
actual representation   37
virtual representation   37
electorate   38
Stamp Act   38
Stamp Act Congress   38
Coercive or Intolerable
   Acts   39
First Continental Congress   39
Declaration of Rights   39
Second Continental
   Congress   39
Articles of Confederation   40
constitutional convention   42
Virginia Plan   43

New Jersey Plan   43
Great Compromise   43
Three-Fifths Compromise   44
Alexander Hamilton   44
The Federalist Papers   46
Anti-Federalists   46
Bill of Rights   47
factions   47
checks and balances   48
enumerated powers   50
necessary and proper
   (or elastic) clause   50
president   50
electoral college   51
independent judicial
   branch   51
judicial review   51
federalism   52
supremacy clause   52
bills of attainder   52
ex post facto laws   52

Suggested Web Resources

The following websites provide additional resources related to the U.S. Constitution and its adoption.

There are any number of locations where one can access all of *The Federalist Papers.* Congress' website Thomas (named after Thomas Jefferson) offers complete access (**http://memory.loc.gov/ammem/help/constRedir.html**), as does the

University of Oklahoma Law School (**http://www.law.ou.edu/ hist/federalist**).

Anti-Federalist documents are not as easily accessed. One location is at the Wepin Store (**http://www.wepin.com/articles/afp/index.htm**), which is a site dedicated to the libertarian philosophy of individual sovereignty. Another location is through the Constitution Society (http://www. constitution.org/afp/afp.htm) (see below).

The record of the Constitutional Convention debates (http://memory.loc.gov/ammem/amlaw/lwfr.html) can be found through the Library of Congress's American Memory collection, which also provides access to a wide range of other resources related to the Constitution specifically and American history in general.

A firsthand account of the Boston Tea Party (http://www.historyplace.com/unitedstates/revolution/teaparty.htm) can be found at the History Place.com (http://www.historyplace.com), which is also a good resource for other material related to American and world history.

We have provided a copy of the Constitution on *The Web of Democracy* website and in the appendix; however, some of you may want a more detailed analysis. The annotated U.S. Constitution (http://www.findlaw.com/casecode/constitution) is available via FindLaw and provides links to Supreme Court decisions that are related to the various provisions of the document. Similar material is also provided by Cornell University Law School (http://www.law.cornell.edu/constitution/constitution.overview.html) and by Emory

University Law School (http://www.law.emory.edu/FEDERAL/usconst.html).

The Constitution Society (http://www.constitution.org) adopts the position that the Constitution is often ignored and that it should be adhered to more strictly. There are those who would argue with the view of the constitutional interpretation that the society follows, but the site provides easy access to all of the founding documents as well as other primary and secondary source material.

The National Constitution Center (http://www.constitutioncenter.org) is a nonpartisan and not-for-profit organization established by Congress. The purpose of the center is "to increase awareness and understanding of the US Constitution, the Constitution's history, and the Constitution's relevance to our daily lives so that all of us—'We the People'—will better understand and exercise our rights and our responsibilities."

The National Center for Constitution Studies (http://www.nccs.net/index.html) is another nonpartisan source of information on the Constitution. This website contains a "quiz" on the Constitution that can be taken to test your knowledge of the various provisions of the document.

A complete study tool kit is available for this chapter and includes the following:
Flashcards
Crossword Puzzle
Critical Thinking Exercises
Interactive Timelines
Chapter Quiz

Federalism

■ **Medical Marijuana: National or State Concern?**   57

■ **American Federalism: A Definition**   60

■ **Federalism in the Constitution**   64
   The National Government in the Constitution   65
   The States in the Constitution   66
   Concurrent Powers   67
   Interstate Relations   67

■ **Two Centuries of American Federalism**   69
   Dual Federalism   69
   The Long, Slow Rise of Nation-Centered
      Federalism   70
   The Great Depression, the New Deal, and
      a New Era in Federalism   74
   Johnson's Great Society: More Money and More
      Direction   75
   The New Federalisms: From Better Management
      to Less Money   77

■ **Recent Developments in Federalism**   78
   The Growth of Coercive Federalism   78
   Congress and the Devolution Revolution   80
   The Supreme Court Reins in National Power   81

■ **Conclusion: How Much Control Should
the Nation Have over the States?**   83

Medical Marijuana: National or State Concern?

A medical marijuana patient protests at a Sacramento, California, rally against federal arrests of state authorized medical marijuana users.

Over the last decade eleven states—Alaska, California, Colorado, Hawaii, Maine, Maryland, Montana, Nevada, Oregon, Vermont, and Washington—legalized the use of marijuana as a medication. In early 2005, legislation was pending in seven more states to legalize its use. In most states, the **medical marijuana** laws were passed by initiative or referendum; the general public passed these laws. (Direct democracy is discussed in Chapter 1.) Opinion polls have consistently shown widespread national public support for the medical use of marijuana under the supervision of a physician.[1] Each of the eleven states that have legalized marijuana therapy has established its own rules governing medical marijuana use. Typically, patients must enroll in a confidential registry. Enrollment, estimated to be approximately 113,000 in 2005,[2] is allowed only for people who can confirm they are suffering from a state-established list of conditions. Furthermore, patients and their caregivers are also limited to possession of small amounts of the drug—in most states one to three ounces—and in the number of marijuana plants they may cultivate.

Marijuana is said to provide relief from nausea, vomiting, seizures, chronic pain, and the lack of appetite caused by a number of diseases and their treatment, including various cancers, Crohn's disease, epilepsy, glaucoma, HIV/AIDS, multiple sclerosis, and wasting syndrome. The use of medical marijuana remains controversial.[3] Patients and other advocates are confident that using marijuana works, and some doctors have prescribed it. However, the few systematic studies that have been completed show modest if any medical benefits of marijuana use. Dr. Joseph Sirven, an associate professor at Mayo Clinic College of Medicine, summed up the current state of knowledge on the subject in a March 2005 *New York Times* article: "People subjectively report benefits. There's a whole Internet literature suggesting what a wonderful thing it is. But the reality is, we don't know."

The efficacy of medical marijuana is controversial, but events in California during the fall of 2002 created a second controversy of a very different kind. On August 15, 2002, Butte County, California, sheriff's deputies and federal Drug Enforcement Agency (DEA) officials arrived at Diane Monson's home.[4] Monson suffers from chronic back pain and muscle spasms and was a registered medical marijuana user since 1999 under California's Compassionate Use Act of 1996, passed by the voters as Proposition 215. She cultivated her own marijuana plants. The deputies found that Ms. Monson's cultivation and use of marijuana were lawful under the Compassionate Use Act. The DEA officials found Ms. Monson had violated federal law, the Controlled Substance Act of 1970 (CSA). The CSA defines marijuana as a Schedule 1 controlled substance whose possession, manufacture, and distribution are illegal. After a three-hour standoff, Ms. Monson's half-dozen marijuana plants were seized and destroyed by DEA agents.

Two months later, Ms. Monson and a second woman, Angel McClary Raich, sued. Raich suffers from numerous ailments, including a brain tumor, and uses marijuana for pain relief and nausea relief. Raich is not well enough to grow her own marijuana; she receives it free of charge from two unnamed people. The two sued then Attorney General John Ashcroft, arguing that the Controlled Substance Act is unconstitutional as it was applied to them; the federal government could not lawfully prosecute them under the CSA. They sought to stop future raids by federal officials.

The dispute between Ms. Monson and Ms. Raich and the federal government was over which level of government—the states or the national government—has the power to regulate in this area, the use of medical marijuana. Should states be able to decide if marijuana can be used for medical purposes, or is regulation of marijuana within the power of the national government? We often think of the national government in the United States as all-powerful in its ability to enact laws on the issues it pleases, but it is not. The Constitution limits the national government by providing it with specific, enumerated powers. What are the limits of these powers? It is hard to say with precision, but those challenging the seizures of medical marijuana argue that the Department of Justice went beyond its power when it applied the Controlled Substance Act to noncommercial medical marijuana use. Congress justified the law upon passage as an exercise of its power to regulate "commerce . . . among the several states" as defined in Article I, Section 8, of the U.S. Constitution. Those in favor of state regulation of medical marijuana argue that Congress's interstate commerce power has limits and that the application of the CSA in this dispute is not concerned with commerce at all; no commercial activity—buying and selling—took place because Ms. Monson grew her own marijuana and Ms. Raich received hers at no cost. Therefore, the decision should be left to the states. Supporters of the federal government's position argue that any manufacture, distribution, or possession of a controlled substance such as marijuana regardless of use is interstate commerce and within the power of Congress to regulate and the Department of Justice to enforce. In this view, the problem of illegal drugs is a national problem and requires a national solution.

A federal district court ruled in favor of the federal government. A federal appeals court reversed the decision and ruled in favor of the two women plaintiffs. In a 6–3 decision handed down on June 6, 2005, the U.S. Supreme Court reversed again and sided with the federal government.

View a news story on the Supreme Court's medical marijuana decision.

The decision came as something of a surprise because the Court has handed down a series of federalism decisions in the last decade that have limited federal government power, as discussed later in this chapter. Justices Scalia and Kennedy each sided with the federal government in the medical marijuana case, in contrast to their usual opposition to the expansion of federal government. In a majority opinion written by Justice John Paul Stevens, the Court found that "the regulation is squarely within Congress's commerce power." Congress can regulate "purely local activities that are part of an economic 'class of activities' that have substantial effect on interstate commerce." Stevens also expressed sympathy for the plaintiffs and "the troubling facts of the case," and he encouraged other institutions to find a way for medical marijuana use to continue. He noted that "the voices of the voters . . . may one day be heard in the halls of Congress." Interestingly, in Justice O'Connor's dissent she noted that she opposed the program but believed that there were limits to Congress's power to regulate commerce; if noneconomic activity such as this can be regulated, "it threatens to sweep all of productive human activity into federal regulatory reach." Similarly, Justice Thomas noted in a separate dissent that "Our federalist system, properly understood, allows California and a growing number of other states to decide for themselves how to safeguard the health and welfare of its citizens." The Court's decision did not end the debate, however. Distribution of medical marijuana has continued in several states, even as the federal Drug Enforcement Administration has begun to pursue violators. Proponents of medical marijuana have continued to push Congress to pass legislation that will stop federal enforcement of the ban. Lobbying efforts encouraging Congress to pass legislation that will legalize medical marijuana nationally or at least allow the states to decide for themselves are also being pursued.[5]

Read the opinions in *Gonzales v. Raich.*

Under the Constitution, state governments retain many of the powers they held before the ratification of the Constitution. Among the important areas of state control has been criminal law. Because each state writes its own criminal law, states can vary significantly in how they punish the same crime. The national government has broad powers as well. As is evident in the medical marijuana dispute, the powers of the state and national governments can often come in conflict.

The debate over the scope and nature of national government powers and over which level of government—the nation or the states—should be able to act in a particular area began even before the Constitution was ratified and has continued for more than two centuries. Recently, the debate has been rekindled as the national government has moved into areas that have traditionally been the exclusive concern of the states, such as the collection of child support, combating gender-motivated violence, and combating the drug trade. The federal courts have struck down laws as being beyond the scope of federal government power. These debates have extended beyond federal courthouses into the halls of Congress, to state capitols, and to the American public.

Watch a 1957 news story on the Little Rock crisis.

Listen to President Eisenhower's explanation of his response to the crisis.

The controversy over medical marijuana is only one recent example of federalism and the fight over the scope of the commerce power at work.

Governor Wallace
Resisting Integration at
University of Alabama:
1963.

Federalism means that we all do not live under the same laws. The commerce clause gives the national government the power to regulate throughout the United States. Sometimes we see advantages in giving the states autonomy; the laws of the fifty states can vary to reflect the beliefs of each state's citizens. Furthermore, states experiment with different solutions to social and economic concerns, allowing the states to borrow ideas from one another. But at other times, we see problems in this arrangement and are happy with the national government's power. For example, before the national government stepped in and passed the Civil Rights Act of 1964, many states refused to extend even the most basic civil rights to black citizens. More recently, federal environmental law, the state-established right to die, and federal worker safety laws have all been the subject of federalism debates. In a federal system, who makes policy can have a big impact on what policy is.

American Federalism: A Definition

Federalism is a system of government that divides power and sovereignty over a territory between two levels of government, typically a national government and regional governments. As Figure 3.1 shows, each government in a federal system has its own elected officials and its own ability to pass laws that will affect the rights and responsibilities of the people living in the territory. In the United States, these two levels of government are the national government and the fifty state governments. Federalism does more than divide government; it also divides the authority to govern.

Most nations, however, are governed by a **unitary system,** in which one national government has the authority to make decisions for the entire territory. France, Sweden, Israel, and Ghana are examples of nations with unitary governments. Local or regional governments in these nations can be altered or abolished by the national government. Furthermore, **local governments** do not have the final say on policy matters; this takes place at the national level.

Read Tocqueville on
federalism.

The United States is not unique in having adopted a federal system. Canada, Germany, India, and more recently South Africa and post-Soviet Russia have done so as well. The Founders believed that federalism would protect liberty. As discussed in Chapter 2, the constitutional system created in 1787 was complicated. It created a separation of powers within the national government, and it divided power between the nation and the states. A federal system limits the power of each level of government by allowing each one to check the other. James Madison referred to this as the "double security" of federalism.[6] The Founders also believed that the risk of tyranny would be reduced by this arrangement. Federalism ensures that leaders at many levels of government—national, state, and local—will each have some power and that no leader will be all-powerful. By limiting the power that any government or person holds, liberty will be preserved. Federalism has other benefits as well.

Review *Federalist* No. 51.

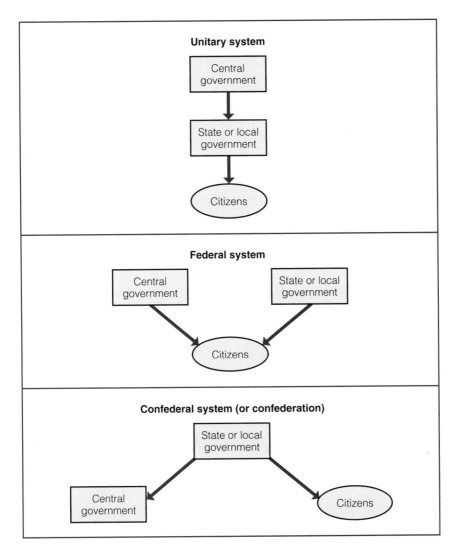

Figure 3.1 Federal, Unitary, and Confederal Government Systems. In a unitary system, power is held by the central government. Regional governments carry out central government decisions. In a federal system, both central and regional governments have independent authority to act. In a confederal system, regional governments hold power, and the central government is dependent on those governments.

It promotes political participation by allowing for many points of access to government. There are more than 87,000 separate governments in the United States (see Table 3.1), and the variety of governments encourages policy innovation. Subnational governments—states and localities—can create varying policies, thereby accommodating and promoting diversity. Finally, federalism allows diverse peoples to live under one governmental roof.

Visit a local government meeting.

U.S. Government	1
States	50
Local Governments	87,525
County	3,034
Municipal	19,429
Township and Town	16,504
School District	13,506
Special District	35,052
Total	87,576

Table 3.1 Governments in the United States, 2002

Source: *2006 Statistical Abstract of the United States,* table 415.

LOCAL GOVERNMENTS IN THE WEB OF DEMOCRACY

Of the nation's 87,576 governments, virtually all (96.5 percent) are local governments. Interestingly, local governments have no status under the U.S. Constitution. Based on individual state constitutions, state legislatures create local governments as they wish—giving localities the powers that they desire. For example, the state legislature can alter the boundaries and powers of localities and other governmental units within their borders. Many of these governments, known as special districts, govern such individual services as airports, seaports, and water treatment facilities. These districts are usually controlled at the state level. Still, there are nearly 50,000 genuine local governments—cities, towns, villages, and school districts—in the United States. These local governments vary incredibly, from mammoth cities such as Chicago and Los Angeles to small towns such as Alplaus, New York, and Chandler, Oklahoma. These local governments generally do their work outside the spotlight of the news media and with little of the public scrutiny that typifies the work of our national and state governments.

Unlike the national and state governments, local governments in the United States offer individual citizens remarkable potential for access and influence. And this access and influence can matter: These governments make important decisions that have an impact on our lives. Local governments decide how land is developed, provide police and fire

(continued)

protection, maintain roads and bridges, and provide for parks in your town. School boards hire teachers for the local schools, build and maintain school buildings, and set policy for schools in the district.

How can you make a difference at the local level? If you have a specific concern, attend a local government meeting and express your opinion. Almost all local government meetings allow for new business from the floor (as those in the audience are called). Better yet, organize a few friends and neighbors and go together. Town boards and city councils can be responsive. Do you want to make a more long-term commitment to your local community? Many towns depend on volunteer firefighters and emergency medical technicians. School districts and municipal governments often seek volunteers to serve on advisory boards. You can even run for office. Unlike running for president of the United States, there is no age requirement—beyond being of voting age—to run for most local offices. Young people serve as local officials throughout the United States.

New Orleans firefighters attempt to extinguish a fire in a looted building after Hurricane Katrina. Local governments provide many essential services in the United States. Firefighting is one example.

Federalism in the Constitution

The notion of a "federal" government was well established in 1787, when the U.S. Constitution was drafted, but the Founders gave the idea new meaning. The traditional idea of a federal government was embodied in the Articles of Confederation. Under the Articles (discussed in more detail in Chapter 2), the thirteen independent states gave the central government, the Congress, the specific power to operate the Revolutionary War effort and negotiate the peace. But even this narrow power was constrained. The central government had no power to levy taxes; it depended on the states to provide financial support. Furthermore, representatives to the central government were appointed by the states—they could be recalled at any time—greatly limiting the government's ability to engage in independent action. This made for a weak government. Today, we would call this form of government a **confederation.** A confederal system is characterized generally as independent governments that have given a limited amount of power to a central authority to pursue a common interest. The European Union is a current example of a confederation.

The United States was the first modern federal government; it included a national government and state governments, each with distinct power. It is important to remember that the Constitution was the result of political compromise. Some ardent Federalists—Alexander Hamilton, for example—wanted to limit the role of the states,[7] whereas Anti-Federalists such as George Mason urged keeping the Articles of Confederation with only minor changes. As described by James Madison in *Federalist* No. 39, the system of government designed under the new Constitution was "in strictness, neither a national nor a federal government, but a composition of both." The government created in Philadelphia was neither unitary nor traditionally federal—confederal—in nature. The Framers redefined the term *federal* to describe their new creation, which was a system that balanced power between the nation and the states. The Framers designed a new, vigorous national government but retained the thirteen states, allowing them substantial independent power as well. Yet they also stripped the states of critical aspects of sovereignty, such as the power to make treaties, to declare war, and to coin money.

Read *Federalist* No. 39.

As you read the Constitution, you may have been impressed by the remarkable detail of many of its provisions. Although the Constitution does concern itself with many detailed issues, it is equally important to notice what is left out. The Constitution both defines and limits the powers of the national government. It provides some guidance on the power of the states and sets forth many limitations on state government power. It also details some aspects of interstate relations. However, the document leaves much to be worked out through the political process. There is no article of the Constitution that definitively fixes the line between national and state power, but there are several provisions that are concerned with the relationship between the nation and the states.

The National Government in the Constitution

The national government possesses enumerated powers, implied powers, and inherent powers. **Enumerated powers** are those expressly given to the national government by the words of the Constitution. Most of these powers are spelled out in Article I, Section 8. Among them are the powers to create a military force, to declare war, to borrow money, to coin money, to establish a post office, to protect intellectual property, and to regulate bankruptcy. Arguably, the most important of these powers in relation to federalism is the power to regulate interstate and foreign commerce. The **commerce clause** has been used by the federal government since the 1930s as a justification for its expanded role in civil rights and social welfare policy. For example, the passage of the Civil Rights Act of 1964 as well as most environmental laws was justified by Congress under the commerce clause.

Americans often speak of the national government as one of enumerated powers, but this paints an incomplete picture. The national government also possesses **implied powers** that derive from the final clause of Article I, Section 8, of the Constitution, the **necessary and proper clause:**

> *The Congress shall have the Power . . . To make all Laws which shall be necessary and proper for carrying into Execution the foregoing Powers, and all other Powers vested by this Constitution in the Government of the United States, or in any Department or Officer thereof.*

This clause is also known as the **elastic clause** because it allows the national government to expand its power. Like the commerce clause, the elastic clause has been used to justify the growth of the national government. Congress has asserted its implied powers in assuming control over the nation's financial system and instituting a military draft.

A third source of national government power, the **inherent power** to conduct foreign affairs, derives from the United States' status as a sovereign nation rather than from any specific written words of the Constitution. The Supreme Court has established that such powers as the ability to make treaties, to acquire new territory, to recognize governments, and to enter into and wage war are the unique province of our national government.[8] It is argued that this would still be true, by virtue of international law, even if the Constitution had nothing to say about conducting foreign relations.[9]

Underlying these powers is the **supremacy clause** found in Article VI, Clause 2, of the Constitution:

> *This Constitution, and the Laws of the United States which shall be made in Pursuance thereof; and all Treaties made, or which shall be made, under the Authority of the United States, shall be the supreme Law of the Land; and the Judges in every State shall be bound thereby, any Thing in the Constitution or Laws of any State to the Contrary notwithstanding.*

Within its scope of influence, the national government is preeminent. Any action of a state that contradicts this is unconstitutional. The supremacy clause also allows Congress to preempt—or take control of—areas of law where federal action is allowed even if state laws already exist in an area. It also requires state judges to uphold the U.S. Constitution, even when the state's constitution runs contrary to it.

The States in the Constitution

The supporters of the Constitution claimed that it was intended to be a government of limited and defined powers. But the Anti-Federalists feared that this new government would excessively infringe on the powers of the states, possibly even totally subsuming state governments and destroying liberty in the process. The opponents of ratification pressed for a constitutional guarantee of the states' role in the system. Their demands were met with the ratification of the Tenth Amendment in 1791. The Tenth Amendment states a basic principle of our federal system: "The powers not delegated to the United States by the Constitution, nor prohibited by it to the States, are reserved to the States respectively, or to the people." The exact meaning of the Tenth Amendment has been hotly debated throughout our nation's history. At times it has been interpreted as but a truism, a statement of the existing relationship between the nation and the states. More recently, though, it has been interpreted to place real limits on the power of the national government and to allow the states more authority. Regardless of precise interpretation, all agree that the Tenth Amendment recognizes a set of **reserved powers** exclusively for the states.

Chief among the states' powers reserved by the Tenth Amendment is what are called **police powers:** the ability of the states to regulate the health, safety, morals, and general welfare of its citizens. This is a broad grant of authority that goes far beyond creation and enforcement of the criminal code. Under police powers, the states establish public health laws, create and run public education systems, define moral standards, and license professions from hair stylists to doctors and lawyers. States define family life by establishing laws governing marriage and divorce, and they play an important role in our nation's economy through the power to define contract law, corporate law, insurance law, property law, and environmental law, among others. The notion of police powers is a flexible one; over the last two centuries, the states have greatly expanded their roles, and the limits of this power have been the frequent subject of court challenges.

Although the extent of state powers is implied, the Constitution—Article I, Section 10, in particular—is much more explicit about limitations on state power. The states are forbidden to engage in foreign policy. They cannot sign treaties with foreign nations, enter into war, or maintain their own military forces without permission of the national government. The state role in interstate and foreign commerce is limited. States cannot coin money, define legal tender, impair contracts, or tax imports or exports. States, like the national government, cannot pass bills of attainder or *ex post facto* laws. The states remain free to act in many areas, but the Constitution makes it clear that there are limits to their power as well.

Concurrent Powers

In our federal system, there are clearly zones where only the nation may act and others where the states alone can create policy. There are other areas, however, where each level of government—nation and state—can exercise power. The most prominent **concurrent power** is the power to tax. There are limits on the power to tax—no state government can tax imports or exports, and no government can tax another government—but both the national and state governments tax widely. For example, both the national government and more than forty states raise revenue through an income tax. Other examples of concurrent powers are the power to borrow money and to create court systems. These concurrent powers are not directly spelled out in the Constitution; they are implied by the existence of a federal system with two independent levels of government. More examples of national powers, state powers, and concurrent powers are found in Figure 3.2.

Interstate Relations

The Framers recognized that for the Union to work, the states must be required to respect one another's legal acts and treat the citizens of other states fairly. So in addition to ordering the relationship between the national government and the states, the Constitution also creates basic rules of conduct between the states. In general, these provisions are intended to promote national unity.

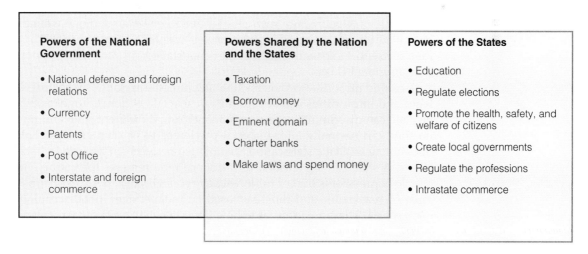

Powers of the National Government	Powers Shared by the Nation and the States	Powers of the States
• National defense and foreign relations	• Taxation	• Education
• Currency	• Borrow money	• Regulate elections
• Patents	• Eminent domain	• Promote the health, safety, and welfare of citizens
• Post Office	• Charter banks	• Create local governments
• Interstate and foreign commerce	• Make laws and spend money	• Regulate the professions
		• Intrastate commerce

Figure 3.2 Current Examples of National, State, and Concurrent Powers Under the Constitution. The U.S. Constitution established a system whereby some powers are given to either the national government or the states. Some powers, however, are shared by the nation and the states.

One way that interstate relations are governed is through the **full faith and credit clause,** Article IV, Section 1, of the Constitution: "Full Faith and Credit shall be given in each State to the public Acts, Records, and Judicial Proceedings of every other State." This means that such documents as mortgages, marriages, wills, and deeds recorded in one state generally must be accepted by the other states as valid.[10] How far does this requirement go? This has been an important policy question in recent years with the controversy over gay and lesbian marriage. Two states now allow some form of same-sex unions. Since 1999, Vermont has allowed same-sex unions, and in 2003 the Massachusetts Supreme Judicial Court ruled that gays and lesbians have a right to marry as heterosexual couples do. Even before the actions of these two states, Congress passed the Defense of Marriage Act (DOMA) in 1996, which declared that no state must recognize same-sex unions even if legal in another state. DOMA also refuses same-sex couples recognition under federal law; same-sex partners will not be eligible for Social Security and other benefits available to heterosexual couples. Thirty-eight states have officially opposed same-sex unions as well and have passed their own laws stating that they will refuse to recognize same-sex unions legalized in other states.[11] The federal courts have allowed policy exceptions to the full faith and credit clause in the past—not requiring states to accept marriages of the very young and between close relatives, for example. Will the states be required to accept same-sex unions and marriages established by couples in other states? If most states have their way, the answer is no. Twenty states have passed state constitutional amendments barring same-sex marriage and 25 others have passed state laws intended to have the same effect. But this issue will certainly be decided sooner or later by the Supreme Court of the United States or by an amendment to the U.S. Constitution. The proposed federal Marriage Protection Amendment (MPA), which would restrict marriage to one man and one woman, has failed to get through Congress since it was first proposed in 2002. A June 2006 effort to pass the MPA in the Senate failed despite public support from President Bush.

A second important provision affecting interstate relations is the **privileges and immunities clause** found in Article IV, Section 2. It means that no state can discriminate against someone from a different state and that no state can normally afford special privileges to its own citizens. This does not mean that a state cannot distinguish between citizens and noncitizens. A state can set reasonable residence requirements for voting and charge nonresidents higher tuition at state colleges, but these distinctions must be reasonable and must be based on independent, nondiscriminatory criteria. There are limits as to how far a state may go in distinguishing between residents and nonresidents. One recent example concerned a 1992 California law that limited the welfare benefits of new residents during their first year in California to the amount of money that would have been awarded in the person's prior state of residence. Because California's welfare benefits were relatively high, this meant that most new residents

We the People

Go to the debate on same-sex marriage.

received reduced benefits. In 1999 the U.S. Supreme Court ruled that this law unfairly discriminated against new state residents.[12]

Finally, Article IV, Section 2, of the Constitution requires that a person who is a fugitive of justice be returned to the state where he or she has been accused.

Two Centuries of American Federalism

One of the enduring questions throughout American political history has been the balance of power between the national government and the states. The basic lines were drawn during the ratification debates from 1787 to 1788. On one side, there are advocates of **nation-centered federalism.** They desire a stronger, more dominant national government. In the early republic, the goal of these supporters was promotion of the nation's economy. They believed that by giving power to Congress instead of to state legislatures, they could best ensure that the United States could compete economically with the great powers of Europe. More recently, the focus of advocates of nation-centered federalism has been on establishing civil rights and equal services to all, regardless of the state in which they live. On the other side are supporters of **state-centered federalism,** who believe that the national government should be held to the enumerated powers listed in the Constitution and that the national government is limited by the Tenth Amendment. Those favoring state-centered federalism believe that freedom is best protected when the governments closest to the people make most of the decisions affecting their lives; to the extent possible, social and economic policy should be made at the state level and not by the national government.

Debates over federalism in American history have been argued through the driving issues of the day. Although at times waged in grand, theoretical terms, at its heart, the debate has often been at the center of American politics. The Civil War was in part about the relative power of the national and state governments. Conflicts over many social issues such as civil rights and the expansion of social welfare programs have often been couched in term of state versus national powers. Controversies over federalism have been decisive in determining the direction of the nation.

All national government institutions have been important in this debate, but the U.S. Supreme Court plays a central role as arbiter of the Constitution. The advocates of nation-centered federalism have largely prevailed since the 1930s, with state-centered federalism predominating before that time. The story is a complex one, but this section will provide a basic outline of central events that emerged in the last 200 years.

Dual Federalism

Until the emergence of the New Deal, the powers of the national government and the states were largely distinct from one another. As James Madison

Read *Federalist* No. 45.

noted in *Federalist* No. 45, the powers of the national government would be "few and defined," whereas the powers of the states would be "numerous and indefinite." The national government was responsible for national security—foreign relations and the military—and the growth of the nation's economy. The scope of economic promotion programs grew over time; early examples included the creation of a postal system and a patent registration office to protect intellectual property, but the powers of the nation were limited.

States, on the other hand, had the broad powers that we described earlier as police powers. As Madison put it, "The powers reserved to the several States will extend to all the objects which, in the ordinary course of affairs, concern the lives, liberties, and properties of the people, and the internal order, improvement, and prosperity of the State." The powers described here define separate spheres of influence for the two levels of government: the nation to preserve and promote the union through the use of its enumerated powers and the states to regulate everyday life by employing their powers protected by the Tenth Amendment. Each level of government was supreme in its own sphere. The view of federalism that James Madison described in *Federalist* No. 45 is known as **dual federalism**, a term used by political scientists to describe the relationship of the nation and the states between 1789 and 1933.

The Long, Slow Rise of Nation-Centered Federalism

Proponents of **state-centered federalism** saw the potential for national government growth and sought to limit this possibility. Those advocating **nation-centered federalism** attempted to use the ideas of implied powers and broad definitions of the enumerated powers to meet their goals. Each attempted to shift the balance to their side through legislation and litigation during the early period of our nation's history.

Chief Justice Marshall Interprets National Powers Broadly

Constitutional powers with a focus on *McCulloch v. Maryland*.

Throughout the first third of the nineteenth century, the Supreme Court consistently interpreted Article I, Section 8, of the Constitution in favor of national government power. Two decisions are particularly important. The first is ***McCulloch v. Maryland***, decided in 1819. The dispute was over the constitutionality of the Bank of the United States, which was for states' rights advocates a particularly odious example of national government expansionism. To destroy the bank's Baltimore branch, the Maryland legislature attempted to tax it. Once in court, opponents of the nationally chartered bank argued that there was no explicit provision for such an institution in the Constitution, and because only enumerated powers were granted to the national government, the creation of the bank by Congress was unconstitutional. Chief Justice **John Marshall,** the nation's greatest Supreme Court Justice, in what is arguably his most important decision, concluded that the power to create a bank could reasonably be *implied* from the specific "powers to lay and collect taxes; to borrow money; to regulate commerce; and to declare and conduct a war"; and, more generally, from the necessary and proper clause. As Marshall put it,

> *Let the end be legitimate, let it be within the scope of the Constitution, and all means which are appropriate, which are plainly adapted to that end, which are not prohibited, but consist with the letter and spirit of the Constitution, are Constitutional.*

Read *McCulloch v. Maryland.*

This alone made the case an important victory for advocates of nation-centered federalism, but Marshall went further. He also stated that since the bank was a valid constitutional act, the supremacy clause meant that the state tax on the bank was unconstitutional. He wrote that the "great principle is that the Constitution and the laws made in pursuance thereof are supreme; that they control the Constitution and laws of the respective States, and cannot be controlled by them."[13]

In the second case, decided five years later, the Court limited the states' role in regulating "commerce among the several states" by interpreting the commerce clause for the first time in *Gibbons v. Ogden.*[14] New York State had granted an exclusive license to run a steamboat between New York and New Jersey. Whether the Constitution allowed a state to pass such a law was at issue in this case. Marshall, again advocating nation-centered federalism, decided that commerce as defined in the Constitution was a broad concept that covered more than simply buying and selling. The Chief Justice also found that the state of New York had overstepped its bounds; interstate commerce was the exclusive purview of the national government. Over the next several decades, the Supreme Court would debate the definition of interstate commerce, but the victory here created a clear limitation on the states' use of their police power. A state could regulate only intrastate commerce—economic activity taking place entirely within its borders.

Read *Gibbons v. Ogden.*

These two decisions planted the seeds for the expansion of the national government and for additional limitations on the states. It became clear that Congress would have broad flexibility in choosing the means for addressing problems of national scope. Furthermore, Congress had the power to regulate interstate commerce—transportation is a prime example. But until the 1930s, the Supreme Court struck down congressional action that affected state and local commerce as well.

The Advocates of State-Centered Federalism Respond

Opponents challenged *McCulloch* and *Gibbons.* Supporters of state-centered federalism argued that the states were sovereign and could choose to ignore national laws with which they disagreed. Particularly at issue were protective tariffs, intended to protect emerging northern manufacturers, and restrictions on slavery. In 1835 Justice John Marshall left the Supreme Court and was replaced by **Roger Taney,** a strong advocate of state-centered federalism and a close associate of President Andrew Jackson. In a series of opinions, the Taney-led Supreme Court moderated, but did not totally undo, the work of the Marshall Court.

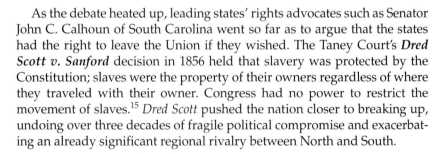

Shown in the foreground is Robert Fulton's boat, *Clermont*. The dispute in *Gibbons v. Ogden* concerned an exclusive license to run a ferry service between New York and New Jersey using a similar Fulton boat. The Supreme Court ruled against New York's power to award the license.

Read *Dred Scott v. Sanford.*

As the debate heated up, leading states' rights advocates such as Senator John C. Calhoun of South Carolina went so far as to argue that the states had the right to leave the Union if they wished. The Taney Court's **Dred Scott v. Sanford** decision in 1856 held that slavery was protected by the Constitution; slaves were the property of their owners regardless of where they traveled with their owner. Congress had no power to restrict the movement of slaves.[15] *Dred Scott* pushed the nation closer to breaking up, undoing over three decades of fragile political compromise and exacerbating an already significant regional rivalry between North and South.

The Impact of the Civil War

Of course, in 1861 eleven states did leave the Union to form the Confederate States of America. The Union's victory in the Civil War ended a fundamental question of federalism. The states retained significant power, but they could no longer argue that they could undo congressional acts or that they could leave the nation. Dual federalism survived for another seven decades, but the supremacy of the national government was now clear. The national government slowly expanded its power until the 1930s, with the essential division of powers between the nation and the states remaining the same. In the aftermath of the Civil War, the states ratified the Thirteenth, Fourteenth, and Fifteenth Amendments. These amendments would eventually be interpreted to give the national government power to enforce limits on state discrimination. (See Chapter 4 for a discussion.)

Federalism and American Industrialization

The end of the Civil War opened a new era for American industrial development. Among the major trends were the rise of the large corporation, the development of national markets for goods, the creation of a national railroad system, and the growth of urbanization as people moved to the growing cities to work in factories. This remarkable economic and social upheaval created political demands. Governments at all levels began to expand their roles. Political reformers—known at populists and progressives—called for new regulations by both state and national governments to deal with the problems of unsafe working conditions, child labor, impure food, the cost of railroad transportation, and monopolistic corporations. Numerous efforts were made by Congress and especially state legislatures to address these problems. Despite popular support, the Supreme Court struck down many of these laws as unconstitutional.

The Supreme Court used the concept of dual federalism to stop these initiatives, arguing that only states had police powers: the ability to regulate the health, safety, welfare, and morals of the public. The Court claimed that efforts by Congress to pass social legislation went beyond its ability to regulate interstate commerce. This limitation made it difficult, if not impossible, for Congress to regulate many areas of American life. In striking down many similar state laws, the Supreme Court took another tack by relying on the right to private property. For example, in a 1905 case in which New York had limited bakers to working no more than ten hours per day, six days per week—a sixty-hour workweek—the Supreme Court struck down the law, arguing that it was the right of every worker to negotiate his own conditions of employment. According to the Supreme Court, the state had no business interfering in this transaction between worker and employer.[16]

Despite the U.S. Supreme Court striking down numerous federal laws, the national government slowly grew during this period. Congress began to create institutions that regulated in much the same ways that states did. The most important nineteenth-century example, the **Interstate Commerce Act of 1888,** is instructive. The Interstate Commerce Commission (ICC) regulated the rates charged for moving railroad freight across state lines. The ICC was created because of demands from small farmers, consumers, and especially business leaders. These groups believed that they were being charged excessive rates. In the early twentieth century, the growth of the national government accelerated. Congress began establishing national police powers. One example was the passage of the **Food and Drug Act of 1906.** It prohibited interstate commerce of mislabeled and impure food, drink, and drugs. The creation of the **Federal Trade Commission** (FTC) in 1914 is another example. The FTC was charged with enforcing antitrust laws and other unfair business practices.

The Great Depression, the New Deal, and a New Era in Federalism

"The New Deal: A New Look," Morton Keller.

The **Great Depression,** a seminal event in American history, began with the stock market crash of 1929. It quickly spread beyond the markets to create deep economic distress: Unemployment was as high as 40 percent; thousands of banks failed; millions lost their homes and had no place to turn. The national government, led by the Republican president Herbert Hoover, reacted slowly and did relatively little to relieve the distress. Historically, under state-centered federalism the national government had no role in looking out for the social welfare of the American people. This had been left to state and local governments as well as to private charity. These institutions were quickly overwhelmed by the magnitude of the problem, and many calls for help were left unanswered. Demands for a larger response by the national government began to grow.

As the Depression continued and deepened, the nation elected a new leader, the Democratic governor of New York, **Franklin Delano Roosevelt.** President Roosevelt and the new Democrat-controlled Congress quickly passed a series of measures intended to stabilize financial institutions, stimulate the economy, and put the nation's unemployed back to work. The program, **"the New Deal,"** expanded the scope of federal power by creating federal jobs and establishing new controls on the nation's economy. The Supreme Court struck down many important parts of the New Deal from 1934 through 1936, asserting that the new legislation passed by Congress had gone beyond the scope of national government power into areas where only the states could act. The Court clung to the idea of dual federalism despite clear popular support for the New Deal. The Democratic majority in both the House and Senate grew after the 1934 and 1936 elections, and President Roosevelt's margin of victory was much greater in his second run than it had been in his first. In frustration with the Supreme Court, President Roosevelt responded with a plan to expand the size of the Supreme Court so that he could create a majority to support the New Deal. The so-called "court packing" plan failed, but early in 1937, the Court relented and upheld the legislation that it previously had struck down. After 1937 the Supreme Court allowed Congress to decide for itself the scope of national government power. This trend continued for the next four decades.

President Franklin Roosevelt's first Fireside Chat, 1933.

Cooperative Federalism

The federal government's response to the Great Depression began a new era in the relationship between the nation and the states known as **cooperative federalism,** the intermingling of government functions that made it increasingly difficult to distinguish any distinct roles for the national government or state and local governments. Political scientist Morton Grodzins developed an easy way to think about the change from dual federalism to cooperative federalism. Prior to the New Deal, most political scientists likened the federal system to a **layer cake:** Each layer or level of government—national, state, local—had clearly defined powers and responsibilities. After the New Deal, these relationships changed, and a more apt description was a **marble cake** (see Figure 3.3). In the words of Grodzins,

> When you slice through it you reveal an inseparable mixture of differently colored ingredients. Vertical and diagonal lines almost obliterate the horizontal ones, and in some places there are unexpected whirls and an imperceptible merging of colors, so that it is difficult to tell where one ends and the other begins. So it is with the federal, state, and local responsibilities in the chaotic marble cake of American government.[17]

The New Deal and its aftermath greatly expanded the role of the national government; nation-centered federalism was to dominate for the next half century. These changes left the national government with more control over the nation's economy through regulation of business and a much greater role in social welfare policy. These new programs gave the national government a more direct relationship with American people and more control over state and local governments. The New Deal was a victory for supporters of nation-centered federalism.

One important development of the Roosevelt era was the expanded use of federal **grants-in-aid,** money given by the national government to state and local governments. Federal grants to the states had been around since early in the republic's history but were traditionally used for only a narrow set of purposes, such as agricultural education. Roosevelt doubled the number of these programs from fifteen to thirty during his first two terms in office.[18] More important, the scope of the grants grew to include funds for programs such as unemployment insurance and Aid to Families with Dependent Children (welfare). In total, the amount of federal funding to state and local governments was small by recent standards, amounting to only $872 million in 1940, but significantly more than in previous eras.[19]

Federal monetary grants to the states.

Johnson's Great Society: More Money and More Direction

The growth in federal grants-in-aid to the states continued throughout the 1940s and 1950s, when new programs in highway construction and in support of higher education began. As one can see from Figure 3.3, the

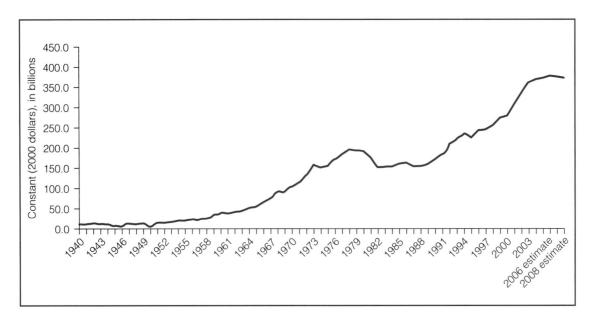

Figure 3.3 The Growth of Federal Outlays to State and Local Governments, 1940–2008. Federal funding for state and local governments has grown immensely since 1940. In recent years, however, the growth has stopped.

Source: Historical Tables, Budget of the United States Government, Fiscal Year 2007 (Washington, DC: U.S. Government Printing Office, 2006), table 12.1, pp. 230–231. The years 2006 and 2008 are projections.

dollar value of these grants grew as well. Most of the money given to state and local governments during this time was in the form of **categorical grants**, money awarded for a specific purpose defined by the national government. In addition, the increase in categorical funds was accompanied by a growing set of **conditions of aid** that told state and local governments how to run programs.

During the 1960s, there was phenomenal growth in federal government programs, led by Lyndon Johnson's **Great Society** and **War on Poverty.** As political scientist Timothy Conlan stated, by the end of the 1960s "[t]he federal government became more involved in virtually all existing fields of government activity—including many that had been highly local in character (for example, elementary and secondary education, local law enforcement, libraries, and fire protection). In addition new public functions were established, such as adult employment training, air pollution control, health planning, and community antipoverty programs."[20] Figure 3.3 shows that there was three times more funding for federal grants to state and local governments in 1970 than there had been in 1960. Most of these programs were run through categorical grant programs; during Johnson's five years as president, more than 200 new categorical grant programs were introduced. In 1960 there were 132 such programs, and by 1968 there were 379, nearly three times as many.[21]

President Johnson called this approach "creative" federalism. In 1964 his administration launched its War on Poverty programs as a national attempt to combat poverty and discrimination. The Johnson administration began to create federal categorical grants that went not only to the states but also to local governments and citizen action groups directly. By funneling money directly to the local level, the federal government could have a greater impact in the fight to alleviate social problems in American cities.

Critics described these changes as **coercive federalism.** As the size and scope of the programs increased, so too did the rules attached to them. The federal government increasingly managed programs in great detail, and the rules were remarkably complex. If state and local governments did not follow these rules, they would lose funding. Leaders of these governments could not afford to lose the money. They had expanded the services they provided to their constituents, and federal dollars were essential to these new programs. By 1970, federal dollars made up 23 percent of state and local government spending, up from 17 percent in 1960. State and local governments had become dependent on the national government money. Once this was true, the national government could establish priorities that state and local governments were bound to follow even though many of the programs were strictly voluntary.

The New Federalisms: From Better Management to Less Money

State and local governments clearly liked the money that the federal government sent them. But at the same time, state and local officials, as well as opponents of federal government expansion generally, were critical of how much the federal government now controlled what state and local governments did. Over the next twenty years, two Republican presidents, Richard Nixon and Ronald Reagan, responded to this criticism. Each proposed a **new federalism,** a plan to return government control back to the states. These programs were motivated by divergent goals and produced different results. But each had in common a belief in a more state-centered federalism.

President Richard Nixon's new federalism (1968–1974) was motivated by a desire to improve management efficiency and to strengthen state and local governments. The primary tools for his initiative were block grants and general revenue sharing. **Block grants** gave state and local governments increased flexibility in deciding how to spend federal money in broad areas—such as urban renewal or public transportation—in contrast to categorical grants. The grants still came with many rules, but states had substantially more control over how to spend the money. President Nixon's most far-reaching proposals for block grants were never approved, but during his term in office, myriad categorical grants were rolled into two major block grants covering community development and employment training. Nixon was also successful in establishing **general revenue sharing** that gave state and local governments at least $6.2 billion per year beginning in 1972. Under this program, state and local governments had the freedom to spend this federal money as they wished with minor strings attached.[22] During the Nixon years, the national government not only gave states new flexibility in how they could spend federal dollars, but it also provided more federal dollars (see Figure 3.3). Not surprisingly, these programs were extremely popular with state and local officials.

President Ronald Reagan's new federalism program (1981–1989) was inspired by a different objective than Nixon's: Returning control of government programs to the states remained important, but the primary aim was to shrink government at all levels. This meant continued use of block grants, giving the states flexibility, but at lower funding levels. Federal aid to state governments measured as a percentage of state budgets shrank from 26.3 percent in 1980 to 20.0 percent in 1990. The impact on large cities was especially dramatic. Many large cities lost more than three-quarters of their federal aid during the 1980s.[23] Furthermore, general revenue sharing was completely eliminated. The decline in funding for state and local governments during this period brought to a halt over three decades of dramatic growth. The problem was compounded by the creation of huge federal budget deficits, which made it difficult to justify ever larger grants the states.

Recent Developments in Federalism

Abortion, the First Amendment, and States' Rights.

Rather than quelling discontent, the new federalisms of Nixon and Reagan stirred up even more demands for change among state and local officials. Despite these demands, the national government continued to make new and more intrusive demands on state and local governments.

The Growth of Coercive Federalism

By the end of the 1980s, advocates of state-centered federalism had a growing list of concerns about their relationship with the federal government. The cuts in funding were one problem, but equally serious in the eyes of governors and other state leaders was increased federal government control over the programs that state and local governments ran. These controls took several forms and had increased throughout the 1970s and 1980s, even as presidents Nixon and Reagan criticized federal government regulation of the states. Under presidents George H. W. Bush and Clinton, the use of these tools continued.[24] More recently, under George W. Bush, coercion has accelerated further. *Coercive federalism* may be the best way to describe the current relationship between the national and state governments. Among the coercive tools used by the federal government are preemption, crosscutting requirements, crossover sanctions, and mandates.

Preemption defines a policy area as the national government's responsibility, precluding state action. A recent example is the Class Action Fairness Act of 2005, which precludes state courts from hearing class action lawsuits

President Bush signing the Class Action Fairness Act of 2005. The law is a recent example of federal preemption.

with more than 100 plaintiffs and $5 million in potential damages.[25] Sometimes, rather than totally push state and local governments out of a policy area, the federal government creates a minimum requirement, allowing state and local governments to exceed this requirement if they wish. This is called a **partial preemption.** An example is the federal minimum wage, currently set at $5.15 per hour. Chicago, Baltimore, Tucson, and Durham, North Carolina, are among the total of forty cities and counties in seventeen states that have increased their minimum wage since 1994.[26]

Crosscutting requirements allow the national government to impose federal rules on the states as a condition of accepting federal money. All governments receiving funds must follow Title VI of the Civil Rights Act of 1964, which bars discrimination in the distribution of federal funds on the basis of race, color, gender, national origin, or disability. A second method of national government control is the use of **crossover sanctions** that require a state or local government to meet specific guidelines to receive the federal dollars. The No Child Left Behind Act of 2002 is an important recent example. To receive federal aid for public schools, state and local governments must conduct expensive testing and meet performance standards. Although many support the idea of improving our nation's schools, state and local officials have been frustrated by the high costs of the program, which have exceeded the new funding provided by the national government. A second example goes back much further. Since the 1960s, Congress has made portions—usually 5 to 10 percent—of highway funding to states contingent on creating a highway beautification program, lowering speed limits to 55 miles per hour,[27] and setting the legal drinking age at twenty-one. Although none of these programs individually seems unreasonable or onerous, collectively Congress has limited the states' ability to set their own priorities. Most recently, Congress has demanded laws with lower blood alcohol levels for driving while intoxicated if states want to receive full highway funding.

But the most significant complaints have come regarding mandates, especially unfunded mandates. A **mandate** is a requirement, an order, that a state or local government implement a national government program. The REAL ID Act of 2005 is a recent example. The REAL ID Act places several requirements on the states, including requiring states to verify that a person applying for a driver's license is a legal resident and to establish security standards for state offices where driver's licenses are distributed. It prohibits financial assistance for the costs involved unless a state joins an interstate compact.

An **unfunded mandate** is a requirement that comes without the money to pay for it. Often, crosscutting requirements and crossover sanctions act as unfunded mandates. Recent unfunded mandate laws as diverse as the Motor Voter Act,[28] amendments to the Clean Water Act, and toxic waste cleanup regulations have a major financial impact on states and localities. One study estimated that state and local governments in the United States were required to spend approximately $10 billion from 1983 to 1990 to pay for unfunded mandates,[29] and political scientist Paul Light concluded in 1999 that approximately 25 percent of state and local government employees work to meet unfunded mandates.[30] A recent report by the National Council of State Legislatures estimates that new laws passed by Congress during the 2004 and 2005 fiscal years cost the states more than $51 billion. Two major education programs alone, No Child Left Behind and Education for the Disabled Acts, are underfunded by $20 billion per year.[31] Mandates create hardships for state and local officials, who must often raise taxes to pay for the programs. But the mandates are appealing to Congress because they allow members to take credit for solving problems without having to face the wrath of taxpaying voters by raising federal taxes to do so.

"An 'Incomplete' for the New Brand of Federalism," Anne C. Lewis.

Congress and the Devolution Revolution

By the early 1990s, public officials' frustration with national government control over states and localities was getting an increasingly sympathetic reception from the general public. By the mid-1990s, there was substantial public support for a change in the relationship between the nation and the states. After the election of 1994, Republicans took control of the House of Representatives for the first time since 1954. The new Republican majority in the House—led by Speaker Newt Gingrich of Georgia—along with the new Republican majority in the Senate vowed to reorder the relationship between the nation and the states by cutting federal government spending and ceding control of more dollars and programs to the states as well as sharply curtailing unfunded mandates. They coined the phrase **devolution revolution** to describe this new effort to shift power and control of programs to state and local governments.

Has Congress been successful in changing the relationship between the nation and the states? Has devolution occurred? Political scientists Ronald Weber and Paul Brace put it this way: "To date, . . . devolution has turned out to be a piecemeal, gradual process rather than a revolutionary or radical transformation."[32] There were two significant successes during the 104th Congress (1995–1996). The first, the Unfunded Mandate Reform Act of 1995, requires Congress to consider the cost of new laws on states and localities. Although mandates are not banned by the 1995 law—and they remain a temptation for Congress—there is some early evidence that unfunded mandates have been curtailed.[33]

One major policy change, giving more control to the states, was a complete overhaul of the nation's welfare system passed in 1996.[34] Described by President Clinton as the "end of welfare as we know it," the new law replaced numerous categorical grants with a major block grant to states, the Temporary Assistance for Needy Families grant. The plan gave flexibility to the states to run welfare programs as they saw fit. Decisions about who would be eligible, the size of benefit payments, and the composition of work and training programs would now be made in state capitals, not in Washington, D.C. There were, however, two major restrictions placed on states. No person could get federal welfare assistance for more than five years, and after two years of welfare, the recipient must work at least twenty hours per week to continue receiving benefits.

Since the election of 1996, the effort to shift power back to the states has lost momentum in Congress and in the White House. The social agenda of the Bush administration and the 9/11 terrorist attacks have brought new efforts by the federal government to limit the activities of state and local governments. The successful efforts by the federal government to stop the medical use of marijuana (noted in the introduction) is one example of the efforts motivated by the conservative social agenda. A move by the Food and Drug Administration to ban the use of drugs for physician-assisted suicide is another. The REAL ID program noted above and stepped-up enforcement of federal immigration laws are examples of the increased costs created by post-9/11 terrorism concerns.

The Supreme Court Reins in National Power

Congress is not the only institution of the national government that has been concerned with federalism of late. In the 1990s, the Supreme Court of the United States struck down more than a half-dozen federal laws

"American Federalism: Half-Full or Half-Empty?" Martha Derthick.

where the Court found that Congress encroached on state power or regulated states directly. Despite the Court's ruling in the medical marijuana case, *Gonzalez v. Raich*, there has been a consistent trend of slowing, if not stopping, the expansion of the national government at the expense of the states.

In the most widely publicized of the federalism cases, the Supreme Court struck down provisions of the Brady Handgun Violence Prevention Act of 1993.[35] Named after President Reagan's former press secretary James Brady, who was shot in the head in the attempted assassination of Reagan in 1981, the law required state and local law enforcement officials to run background checks on those wanting to purchase handguns. Two county sheriffs challenged the law, arguing that it violated the Tenth Amendment by making state and local officials act as agents for the national government. The Supreme Court agreed, ruling that our system of dual sovereignty places limits on the national government. The states are independent except where the Constitution clearly makes them subservient. As stated by Justice Antonin Scalia for the majority, "Congress cannot compel the states to enact or enforce a federal regulatory program." This decision reinforced an earlier decision in which the Court ruled that states could not be compelled to take ownership of low-level hazardous waste produced in their state.[36] Other decisions have overturned congressional efforts to prohibit the possession of firearms within a school zone,[37] stopped federal government efforts to create a new private right to sue in federal court in cases of gender-motivated violence,[38] struck down federal laws empowering suits against states,[39] and found that Congress has exceeded the power given to it to enforce the Fourteenth Amendment's due process and equal protection guarantees against the states.[40] No single decision strikes at any major provision of federal law, but the overall trend is an important one. The Supreme Court has clearly and consistently protected the sovereignty of the states at a level that would have been unforeseen before 1990. It is unlikely that the Court will notably alter its stance on federalism in the near future even with a new chief justice—John Roberts replaced the deceased William Rehnquist in October 2005—and a new associate justice, Samuel Alito, replaced the retiring Associate Justice Sandra Day O'Connor. Roberts and Alito both have established records as states' rights defenders similar to Rehnquist and O'Connor.

In sum, nation-centered federalism is still dominant. Over the last three decades, advocates of state-centered federalism have chipped away at the growth and dominance of the national government. But these strides have been small in comparison to the continued expansion of the national government. Will advocates of state-centered federalism have more success in the coming decades? Only time will tell. But we can be assured that arguments about the proper role of the state and national governments will continue over existing issues and over new issues that will be certain to occur in the future.

Conclusion: How Much Control Should the Nation Have over the States?

In our federal system, political power is divided between the nation and the states. The Founders believed that this system would best protect liberty. The actual division of power was not fixed in the Constitution; rather, it has been decided through politics. The Constitution clearly limited the states, in part by establishing enumerated and implied powers for the national government. Power was reserved for the states through the Tenth Amendment. Until 1937, the national government remained quite small, while the states used their police powers to regulate daily life. With the New Deal, a new era emerged in the relationship between the nation and the states. The national government moved into new areas of public policy, such as economic regulation and the protection of civil rights. Ever larger grants-in-aid flowed from Washington to state and local governments beginning in the 1940s. However, these billions did not come free of obligation. The federal money came with restrictions on its use and required states and localities to carry out national priorities. During the last fifteen years, the power relationship between the nation and states shifted yet again, with Congress and the Supreme Court pushing authority downward to the states. Throughout more than two centuries of history, Americans continue to debate which level of government—the nation or the states—should dominate American politics. As we have seen, how we answer this question has a significant impact on the policies that our government creates.

Check here for possible post-publication updates to the chapter material.

Key Terms

medical marijuana   57
federalism   60
unitary system   60
local governments   60
confederation   64
enumerated powers   65
commerce clause   65
implied powers   65
necessary and proper
   clause   65
elastic clause   65
inherent power   65
supremacy clause   65
reserved powers   66
police powers   66
concurrent powers   67
full faith and credit clause   68
privileges and immunities
   clause   68

state-centered federalism   69
nation-centered federalism   69
dual federalism   70
McCulloch v. Maryland   70
John Marshall   70
Gibbons v. Ogden   71
Roger Taney   71
Dred Scott v. Sanford   72
Interstate Commerce Act
   of 1888   73
Food and Drug Act of 1906   74
Federal Trade Commission   74
Great Depression   74
Franklin Delano Roosevelt   74
the New Deal   74
cooperative federalism   75
layer cake federalism   75
marble cake federalism   75
grants-in-aid   75

categorical grants   76
conditions of aid   76
Great Society   76
War on Poverty   76
coercive federalism   77
new federalism   77
block grants   77
general revenue sharing   77
preemption   78
partial preemption   79
crosscutting requirements   79
crossover sanctions   79
mandate   80
unfunded mandate   80
devolution revolution   81

Suggested Web Resources

The following are websites about federalism from a state and local perspective.

The National Governors' Association (**http://www.nga.org/portal/site/nga**) is concerned with state and federal government issues. The Council of State Governments (**http://www.statenews.org**) represents state executive and legislative leaders. The National Conference of State Legislatures (**http://www.ncsl.org**) is concerned with coordinating the work of state legislatures. It advocates for the states before the national government.

The National League of Cities (**http://www.nlc.org/home**) represents more than 1,500 cities. The U.S. Conference of Mayors (**http://www.usmayors.org**) is also concerned about cities. This organization represents mayors of cities with populations over 30,000 people.

Interested in finding an official state website? The Library of Congress maintains an excellent list of state websites (**http://www.loc.gov/rr/news/stategov/stategov.html**) as well as other information. The National Association of State Information Resource Executives also maintains a wide range of state government links (**http://www.nasire.org**).

The following are links to organizations concerned with the study of federalism.

The Urban Institute is a nonpartisan think tank whose "goals are to sharpen thinking about society's problems and efforts to solve them, improve government decisions and their implementation, and increase citizens' awareness about important public choices." It has a section devoted to the new federalism (**http://www.urban.org/Content/Research/NewFederalism/AboutANF/AboutANF.htm**).

The State University of New York's Nelson A. Rockefeller Institute of Government conducts research on state and local government, federalism, and public policy issues (**http://rockinst.org**).

Many other think tanks, including the Brookings Institution (**http://www.brook.edu**), the Cato Institute (**http://www.cato.org**), and the American Enterprise Institute (**http://www.aei.org**), are all interested in federalism.

Publius is an academic journal that specializes in the study of federalism (**http://ww2.lafayette.edu/~publius**).

Project Vote Smart maintains a page with a number of articles on federalism and states' rights (**http://www.vote-smart.org/index.htm**).
To find federal government agencies begin at (http://firstgov.gov/).

 A complete study tool kit is available for this chapter and includes the following:
Flashcards
Crossword Puzzle
Critical Thinking Exercises
Interactive Timelines
Chapter Quiz

Civil Liberties and Civil Rights

■ *R.A.V. v. St. Paul*   86

■ **Introduction**   88

■ **Civil Liberties**   90
  Freedom of Expression   92
  Freedom of Speech   94
  Freedom of the Press   96
  Unprotected Expression   97
  Freedom of Religion   99
  The Right to Privacy   102
  The Rights of the Accused   104

■ **Civil Rights**   108
  Understandings of Equality   109
  Equality and the Constitution   110

■ **Equality for Other Disadvantaged Groups**   116

■ **Current Issues**   118

■ **Conclusion: Freedom and
   Equality—The Ongoing Debate**   119

R. A.V. v. St. Paul

In April 1990, the Jones family moved into the Dayton's Bluff neighborhood of St. Paul, Minnesota. Dayton's Bluff overlooks the St. Paul skyline and was once a premier area of the city, containing a number of elegant mansions built at the end of the nineteenth century. Over time, the neighborhood lost its appeal. In recent years, middle-class professionals have restored many of the mansions, but for the most part, Dayton's Bluff is dominated by modest single-family homes and duplexes, and populated primarily by white, working-class families. (For those of you who like political trivia, former U.S. Supreme Court Chief Justice Warren Burger's boyhood home was in Dayton's Bluff.)

The Joneses were the first African American family to move onto their street. On June 21, 1990, after several other incidents, including having their tires slashed and their car window broken, the Jones family awoke to a sight that was guaranteed to horrify African Americans, as well as a majority of people living in St. Paul: a burning cross. The fire wasn't large, but the message was clear.

In fairly short order, two young men, both also residents of Dayton's Bluff, were arrested and charged. One was a juvenile who, because of his age, was referred to in court documents as R.A.V. (After he reached his eighteenth birthday, R.A.V. was identified as Robert Anthony Viktora.) The other was eighteen-year-old Arthur Miller III, who lived on the same block as the Jones family. There was never any question that the two had set the fire. There was considerable debate, however, regarding the nature of the crime that had been committed. The two were charged under a St. Paul city ordinance that read as follows:

Whoever places on public or private property a symbol, object, appellation, characterization, or graffiti, including, but not limited to, a burning cross or Nazi swastika, which one knows or has reasonable grounds to know arouses anger, alarm or resentment in others on the basis of race, color, religion, or gender commits disorderly conduct and shall be guilty of a misdemeanor.

The St. Paul ordinance, originally passed in 1982, was amended in 1990 to include bias against gender as well as race, color, and religion as the criteria identifying the kind of expressions to which the law would apply. It was similar to laws that had been enacted in a number of locations during the 1980s generally known as "hate crime" laws. When the law was passed, it had been strongly supported by representatives of major civil rights organizations speaking for groups of people who have been subject to discriminatory practices.

Although the law at issue had been passed in 1982, no one had been charged with violating it until R.A.V. and Arthur Miller in 1990. Miller pleaded guilty to the charge, but R.A.V.—represented by attorney Edward J. Cleary—chose to challenge the constitutionality of the statute. Cleary argued that the ordinance violated the First Amendment's guarantee of the freedom of political expression. He did not challenge the law because he agreed with the actions of Miller and R.A.V.; rather, he made it very clear throughout the entire course of the case that he condemned what they did. But he was very concerned about the nature of the "crime" they had been charged with. He would not have objected if his client had been charged under a number of other laws, including ones prohibiting the issuance of terroristic threats or laws punishing individuals for acts of vandalism and destruction of private property. However, his client was charged under a law that made the expression of particular political ideas—ideas generally rejected by the vast majority of American citizens—illegal.

Cleary chose to challenge the law because he saw it as a direct violation of the First Amendment to the U.S. Constitution. The law as written was designed to punish particular forms of symbolic political expression as opposed to specific acts of criminal conduct. He knew that this would be an extremely unpopular position, particularly among supporters of civil rights in St. Paul and elsewhere. He was correct. He ended up being subject to a good deal of public and personal criticism for the stance he took. However, he felt that an important principle involving freedom of speech and expression was at stake.

In the initial challenge to the law, a Ramsey County district court judge was persuaded by Cleary's argument and ruled that the law was unconstitutional. The county appealed the decision, and the Minnesota Supreme Court eventually ruled that the law did not violate the Constitution. Cleary decided to ask the U.S. Supreme Court to examine the legal issues raised in the case. The Court agreed to hear the case during its 1991–1992 term.

The Supreme Court had decided a series of cases over the years—including *Texas v. Johnson*, the controversial flag burning decision—establishing the precedent that symbolic expression was protected by the First Amendment. The Court had also ruled that neither the federal government nor the states could punish people simply for expressing unpopular political ideas. Nazi swastikas and burning crosses are forms of symbolic political expression that stand for ideas that are unpopular with the vast majority of American citizens.

At the same time, the Court also has a long and well-established history of enforcing and expanding the guarantees available to citizens under the **equal protection clause** of the Fourteenth Amendment. The Court had made it clear that states (and cities) had an obligation to ensure that all of their citizens are afforded equal treatment under the law. The *R.A.V.* case represented a conflict between two bedrock American political values: the idea that all citizens are deserving of respect and should be treated equally and the idea that individuals should be free to voice their opinions, even if those views are unpopular and offensive to others.

The case of *R.A.V. v. St. Paul* presented the Supreme Court with the task of balancing our national commitment to free speech against the desire of St. Paul to guarantee that all of its citizens could live in their homes without suffering threats simply because of their race or religion. In this particular case, the Court unanimously decided that the city had gone too far in attempting to protect its citizens. It was the specific manner in which St. Paul had tried to protect its citizens that proved to be its undoing. By singling out specific areas of expression in the law—racist, sexist, and anti-Semitic speech—the city went too far. As Justice Scalia stated, "The First Amendment does not permit St. Paul to impose special prohibitions on those speakers who express views on disfavored subjects." The Court made it clear that it found the actions that generated the case "reprehensible." But it also noted that St. Paul had means available to "prevent such behavior without adding the First Amendment to the fire." *R.A.V. v. St. Paul* is a particularly illustrative example of the often competing values at stake in questions regarding civil liberties and civil rights. It also demonstrates how many, if not most, civil liberties and civil rights questions ultimately end up being resolved by the Supreme Court.[1]

Introduction

Discussions about civil liberties involve the value of freedom and how it is concretely applied in practice. **Civil liberties** are the individual freedoms that Americans are guaranteed under the Constitution. They are the protections from governmental intrusion into our private lives. Such guarantees are essential to the existence of limited government. We pride ourselves on the amount of individual freedom that we afford citizens. The freedoms that are part of American political culture ensure that minority perspectives, no matter how controversial or out of the mainstream, are protected against any possible efforts by the majority to silence or curtail them.

The ability to express views without official interference is a cherished right of American citizenship, as is the right of the media to publish perspectives that are critical of officials and official policy. The freedoms associated with the rights of political expression are foundational principles of American politics. These freedoms establish the conditions necessary for a participatory political system. Americans are also justly proud of the amount of religious freedom that exists in the country. The government is prohibited from imposing any particular religious perspective on citizens. At the same time, Americans are free to choose for themselves how, and indeed if, they will worship.

At the same time, we also hold to the basic principle written in the Declaration of Independence that "all men are created equal." It is certainly the case that our contemporary understanding of equality and the extent to which it should reach has vastly expanded since Jefferson coined this phrase in 1776. Today, we think of equality as a constitutional right, but the principle that all citizens should be equal under the law has not always been the political reality in the United States. Inequalities associated with the institution of slavery were written into the original Constitution. It has taken constitutional amendments as well as concerted political activity over a long period of time to make the reality of American politics conform to the ideal of political equality. Issues that arise in the area of civil rights are tied to the value of equality and how it should be concretely applied in practice. **Civil rights** are the guarantees that each U.S. citizen has that his or her privileges of citizenship are the same as for all other citizens. Unlike civil liberties, which are protections from government, civil rights are governmental guarantees. They involve the government ensuring that citizens are not discriminated against or treated unfairly.

Freedom and **equality** are the two most important values that underlie American political practices. Although both are essential principles through which we judge a vast array of issues and policies, there are also inherent tensions between the two ideals. Excessive individual freedom can result in a range of inequalities within the society. Imposing equal standards across the nation can result in limits on individual freedom. In debates about civil rights and liberties, freedom and equality are not discussed in the abstract. Debates about the extent of freedom and equality that is desirable in the nation occur within the context of the way in which both ideals have been written into the Constitution. This is why the Supreme Court is often the institution of the federal government that is asked to arbitrate conflicts over civil rights and liberties.

Any number of decisions made by the Supreme Court that have expanded the scope of civil liberties and civil rights have been opposed by segments of the public. As the *R.A.V.* case illustrates, protecting individual rights often involves supporting unpopular causes and less than admirable individuals. The Court's decisions in the areas of symbolic speech—including flag burning—and school prayer have led to efforts to change these decisions by amending the Constitution. The Court's decisions ending racial segregation

"Should All Speech Be Free?" Laura Leets.

Examine civil liberties in a global context.

led to intense and emotional opposition. The opposition included open defiance of the Court's authority as well as attempts to impeach Earl Warren, the Chief Justice who presided over *Brown v. Board of Education.* Large segments of the population do not always support the rights of disfavored individuals and groups within their midst.

What is at stake in civil rights and liberties are conflicts that inevitably arise in a nation premised on majority rule and tempered by an equally strong commitment to individual rights. The tensions between freedom and equality—as well as competing understandings about how each ideal should apply in practice—have been with us since the nation was founded. The questions at stake are ongoing, and we can be fairly certain that new questions will arise in the future. What follows is a brief overview of the state of civil liberties and civil rights in the United States at the start of the twenty-first century.

Civil Liberties

The First Amendment to the Constitution reads as follows:

> *Congress shall make no law respecting an establishment of religion, or prohibiting the free exercise thereof; or abridging the freedom of speech, or of the press; or the right of the people peaceably to assemble, and to petition the Government for a redress of grievances.*

This amendment was attached to the Constitution as the first of the initial ten amendments referred to as the **Bill of Rights.** The amendments were added to answer criticisms that the document as originally written did not sufficiently protect individual freedoms, nor did it establish clear enough limits regarding the types of actions that the national government was prohibited from undertaking. The First Amendment was seen as especially significant because it would guarantee that there would be free and open debate regarding political issues and that citizens would be free to criticize governmental officials without fear of being punished for their opinions. The guarantees provided by the First Amendment help ensure that active participation in the political process by average citizens is possible.

Clearly referring to Congress, the First Amendment was not seen as applying to the states until after the **Fourteenth Amendment** was added to the Constitution. That amendment, ratified in the aftermath of the Civil War (1868), provided for additional limitations on the powers of states. Starting at the end of the nineteenth century, the Supreme Court began to apply the Bill of Rights to the states by relying on the **due process clause** of the Fourteenth Amendment. This process is known as the **incorporation doctrine.**

In 1897 the court began the process by ruling that the Fifth Amendment's protection of private property applied to the states as well as to the federal government.[2] In the realm of civil liberties, the most important instance of incorporation occurred in 1925 in the case of *Gitlow v. New York,* where the court asserted the general principle that the First Amendment applied to the states.[3] Table 4.1 provides a brief history of the application of the Bill of Rights to the states through the incorporation process. It also shows those provisions that have not yet been applied to the states.

Over the course of the twentieth century, the Court has incorporated most of the Bill of Rights, including the various provisions involving criminal

Year	Amendment	Protection/Prohibition	Case
1897	Fifth	Forced states to provide just compensation to citizens when their property is taken for public use	*Chicago, Burlington & Quincy Railway Co. v. Chicago*
1925	First	Asserted the principle that the First Amendment applied to the states by way of the due process clause of the Fourteenth Amendment	*Gitlow v. New York*
1927	First	Freedom of speech	*Fisk v. Kansas*
1931	First	Freedom of the press	*Near v. Minnesota*
1932	Sixth	Right to a fair trial and the right to a lawyer in capital (death penalty) cases	*Powell v. Alabama*
1937	First	Right to assembly and to petition the government for a redress of grievances	*De Jonge v. Oregon*
1940	First	Free exercise of religion	*Cantwell v. Connecticut*
1947	First	Establishment clause (the separation of church and state)	*Everson v. Board of Education*
1948	Sixth	Right to a public trial	*In re Oliver*
1949	Fourth	Protection against unreasonable searches and seizures	*Wolf v. Colorado*
1958	First	Freedom of association	*NAACP v. Alabama*
1961	Fourth	Excludes illegally obtained evidence from criminal trials (the exclusionary rule)	*Mapp v. Ohio*
1962	Eighth	Prohibition against cruel and unusual punishments	*Robinson v. California*
1963	Sixth	Right to a lawyer in all trials	*Gideon v. Wainwright*
1964	Fifth	Protection against self-incrimination	*Malloy v. Hogan*
1965	Sixth	Right to confront witnesses and be informed of the nature of the charges against a person	*Pointer v. Texas*
1966	Sixth	Right to an impartial jury	*Parker v. Gladden*
1967	Sixth	Right to obtain evidence from witnesses	*Washington v. Texas*
1967	Sixth	Right to a speedy trial	*Klopfer v. North Carolina*

(continued)

Year	Amendment	Protection/Prohibition	Case
1968	Sixth	Right to a jury in nonpetty criminal cases	*Duncan v. Louisiana*
1968	Fifth	Protection against double jeopardy (being tried for the same crime twice)	*Benton v. Maryland*
1972	Sixth	Right to an attorney in all criminal cases involving a jail term	*Argersinger v. Hamlin*
Amendments That Are Not Incorporated			
	Second	Guarantee of the right to bear arms	
	Third	Prohibition against the quartering of solider in private homes	
	Fifth	Right to a grand jury in all capital or "otherwise infamous" crimes	
	Seventh	Right to a jury trial in all civil cases involving disputes of more than $20	
	Eighth	Prohibition against excessive fines and excessive bail	

Table 4.1 The Incorporation of the Bill of Rights. The Bill of Rights did not apply to the states until after the passage of the Fourteenth Amendment to the Constitution. The process of "incorporation" has applied most, but not all, of the Bill of Rights to the states over a period of time.

Sources: David M. O'Brien, *Constitutional Law and Politics,* vol. 2: *Civil Rights and Civil Liberties,* 2nd ed. (New York: Norton, 1995), pp. 302–310; Otis H. Stephens, Jr., and John M. Scheb, II, *American Constitutional Law,* 2nd ed. (Belmont, CA: West/Wadsworth, 1999), pp. 348–351.

defendant rights. Although a few of the provisions of the Bill of Rights have still not been applied to the states, it is clearly the case that the First Amendment applies to the states as fully as it does to the national government.[4]

Although the First Amendment may read like a series of hard-and-fast prohibitions, the Supreme Court has never interpreted it in an absolute manner. This is because most questions arising under the First Amendment do not lend themselves to easy answers. There are often competing values at stake, and the Court usually takes a balancing approach to accommodate the tensions involved in protecting individual freedoms while at the same time upholding other societal interests.

Freedom of Expression

Among the rights that the First Amendment protects are free speech, a free press, and freedom of assembly. Taken together, these rights are often understood through the concept of **freedom of expression.** Freedom of

CHAPTER 4: Civil Liberties and Civil Rights

expression is the ability of a person, or group of people, to publicize their views and creative undertakings through a range of communicative technologies and methods. In other words, "speech" is not confined to the spoken word, and the "press" does not mean only the news media. **Symbolic expressions** such as slogans and insignias—everything from the Democratic Party's donkey to the Nazi swastika—are means through which a person can indicate to others his or her political position.

There are different forms of expression depending on the purpose of the ideas. The lines of distinction between them often become blurry, but it is worthwhile to attempt to categorize different forms of expression to better understand the issues that are involved and the amount of protection afforded to each category. If one is putting forth views about public issues, it is known as **political expression.** Since the primary purpose behind the First Amendment was to protect individuals' rights to participate in the political process by voicing their views, this type of expression tends to receive the broadest amount of protection.

There is also **creative expression:** the various means that people have at their disposal to display their creative impulse in the arts, literature, and music. In general, the First Amendment also protects creative expression, although material deemed obscene is not protected. The definition of **obscenity** has been the subject of much debate, as has the question of whether or not "indecent" materials can be banned without violating the First Amendment. In fact, some of the most intense controversies in recent years have involved instances of creative expression.

Finally, there is expression designed to further a business or economic enterprise. Such expression is called **commercial speech,** and although it is protected by the First Amendment, it is subject to governmental regulation. For example, advertisers can be restricted in the claims they make for their products; they are required to tell the truth. Advertisers can also be required to include certain messages if the government has determined it necessary to do so to protect the public. An example of this is the surgeon general's warning about the dangers of smoking that appears on all cigarette packaging.

It is possible for the state to restrict expression in one of two ways. First, a specific form of expression can be prohibited from the outset. This is what is meant by government **censorship.** The formal term is **prior restraint,** which means prohibiting the presentation or publication of certain kinds of material. The second way that government can restrict expression is to punish individuals after the fact. In other words, after a person or group has said or published material that the government finds objectionable, it can charge the person with breaking a particular law.

Prior restraints are unusual in the United States. Most lawsuits concerning freedom of expression take place after the fact. The First Amendment has always been understood to protect against prior restraint; it has not always protected the press after publication.

Freedom of Speech

Freedom of speech does not give individuals the right to say anything they want, in any location, or at any time that they choose. In the classic words of Justice Holmes, "The most stringent protection of free speech would not protect a man in falsely shouting fire in a theater, and causing a panic."[5] In general, the First Amendment does not protect speech that puts people in imminent danger. It is also the case that a community can restrict the time, place, and manner of speech as long as it does not do so on the basis of the content of that speech. For example, it is perfectly legitimate for a city to enact a noise ordinance to prevent loud parties from disrupting a neighborhood. The city could not, however, direct that law only to parties held by college students. A city could also ban loudspeakers from trucks in residential neighborhoods as long as it did not single out specific messages from being announced. In general, these types of restrictions are valid because they are **content neutral.** This means that the purpose of the regulation is something other than the restriction of speech and that there is not a particular message that is being singled out.

In thinking about freedom of speech, it is important to recognize the type of speech that is usually singled out for punishment, and that raises the most serious First Amendment questions. Mainstream views such as those of the Republican and Democratic parties are rarely singled out for punishment, nor are statements of support for the fundamental principles of American politics. It is the critics, particularly those who hold the most extreme views, who are singled out for prosecution. Consequently, First Amendment principles are often established, as in the *R.A.V.* case, by people who are at the margins of American politics and society.

During the first half of the twentieth century, many of the most significant free speech decisions involved members of the Communist Party as well as others who were offering severe and fundamental critiques of the American political system. Most states, as well as the federal government, had enacted **criminal syndicalism laws,** which made it a crime to advocate the violent overthrow of the American government. Such laws were seen as legitimate attempts on the part of the government to protect national security and to prevent violence.

Others, however, saw these laws as violations of the First Amendment because they were punishing individuals on the basis of their political opinions. As people were charged and convicted under the anticommunist and criminal syndicalism laws, the U.S. Supreme Court was called upon to find the balance between free speech and the government's interest in maintaining its own integrity. From the 1920s through the 1960s, the Court developed a set of evolving standards that were applied in First Amendment cases.

The first and perhaps best known was the "clear and present danger" test. Developed in the 1919 decision *Schenck v. United States,* an individual could be punished if his or her speech presented a clear and present danger resulting in a situation that the government had a right to prevent. The Court first applied this test to uphold the conviction of a member of the Socialist Party who had advocated resistance to the draft during World War I.[6] From that time through the 1950s, the court tended to uphold similar convictions. There were, however, significant dissenting opinions during this time authored by Justices Holmes and Brandeis, who argued that no matter how critical or provocative the words of Communists or Socialists might be, they should be afforded First Amendment protection.

The clear and present danger test was modified over time, and the Court began to take into account the probability that the speech would actually result in prohibited conduct. A line was beginning to be drawn between advocacy of ideas and actual conduct. In 1969 a member of the Ku Klux Klan was convicted under a criminal syndicalism law for suggesting at a rally that at some point in the future the group might have to exact revenge against those who did not support its views. The Court ruled that this conviction was invalid. Justice Black wrote that "the constitutional guarantees of free speech and free press do not permit a State to forbid or proscribe advocacy of the use of force or of law violation except where such advocacy is directed to inciting or producing imminent lawless actions and is likely to incite or produce such action."[7] So a person can advocate violent revolution and be protected by the First Amendment up until he or she leads followers to the location of the guns.

As noted earlier, the Court does not confine the scope of the First Amendment to the spoken word. Symbolic expression is also protected, including, or perhaps especially, symbolic expression that the majority may find objectionable or hateful. Perhaps the best-known example is the Court's ruling in the case of *Texas v. Johnson,* better known as the "flag burning case." Gregory Johnson had burned an American flag in protest during the 1984 Republican National Convention held in Dallas. Johnson was charged and convicted under a Texas law that prohibited the desecration of the American flag. The Court ruled that in burning the flag, Johnson was engaging in an act of symbolic political protest designed to convey the message that he was extremely dissatisfied with the policies of the Reagan administration. As a clear form of political expression, the act had First Amendment protection. The only question was whether or not the state's interest in protecting a prized national symbol was more compelling than Johnson's right of political expression. A closely divided Court ruled that flag burning was a form of protected free speech. Recognizing that this was not a popular decision, Justice Brennan wrote: "If there is a bedrock principle underlying the First Amendment, it is that Government may not prohibit the expression of an idea simply because society finds the idea itself offensive or disagreeable."[8]

Find a link to the Supreme Court's opinion in *Texas v. Johnson.*

Public opposition to the decision was strong. Congress responded by passing a national law protecting the flag, but it was promptly rejected by the Supreme Court. Various organizations and individuals continued to protest the Court's decision and tried to find a way to reverse it. Because

According to the Supreme Court, burning a U.S. flag in protest is a protected form of symbolic expression.

the Court has given no indication that it is going to alter its position, efforts have been directed toward a constitutional amendment. Proposed amendments protecting the flag have been introduced in Congress regularly since 1989, but none have garnered the votes necessary to send the amendment to the states for ratification.

Debate this issue at the Flag Burning Forum.

Freedom of the Press

The press has a special place in the U.S. Constitution. It is the only private enterprise afforded special protection in the Bill of Rights. To ensure a participatory political process, it is necessary to have means of mass communications available to the public at large. The press provides citizens with access to essential information regarding the day-to-day operations of the government as well as a vehicle through which the government can be criticized. Because public officials are not always willing to be subjected to such criticism, there have occasionally been attempts to curtail the press. As a rule, the Supreme Court does not accept governmental restrictions on the press.

In 1934 the Court decided *Near v. Minnesota,* which was a challenge to a state law that allowed officials to shut down any "malicious, scandalous and defamatory newspaper, magazine or other periodical."[9] The law was used to close a Minneapolis newspaper that had printed a number of stories maligning local officials using, among other things, anti-Semitic language. This was a clear instance of governmental censorship, or prior restraint. The Court ruled that such an action clearly violated the First Amendment. However, it also stated that government censorship was permissible under certain very narrow and specific circumstances. Seeking to find a balance between a free press and national security, the Court said that, for example, the government could prevent publication of troop movements during wartime.

Find links to the Supreme Court's opinions in *Near v. Minnesota* and the Pentagon Papers case.

The Court reaffirmed this view of press freedom in 1971 in the Pentagon Papers case. During the Vietnam War, the Nixon administration sought a court order to prevent the *New York Times* and the *Washington Post* from publishing a report the newspapers had received that documented the origins of U.S. involvement in Vietnam. The material was controversial and embarrassing to the government, but it did not concern the current military effort. The administration claimed that it should be able to prevent the publication based on "national security" interests. The Court agreed that genuine national security threats would justify such an action. However, the circumstances presented in the case did not indicate that a clear-cut, immediate threat to national security existed. In so ruling, the Court reaffirmed that the grounds for governmental censorship of the news media were very narrow.

Unprotected Expression

In *Near* and other cases, where the Court established that the First Amendment allowed space for government censorship only in the very narrowest of circumstances, it also ruled that there was room for *after the fact* punishment for the publication of materials that fell outside the scope of the First Amendment. In a 1942 free speech case, the Court ruled that there were "certain well defined and narrowly limited classes of speech, . . . which have never been thought to raise any constitutional problems. These include the lewd and obscene, the profane, the libelous, and the insulting or 'fighting' words—those which by their very utterance inflict injury or tend to incite an immediate breach of the peace."[10]

Libel

Libel and **slander** involve statements one private party makes about another that are false and that defame or injure the reputation of an individual. Libel applies if the statement is written; slander applies if it is spoken. Under the First Amendment, there is no real difference between the two, and neither are forms of protected speech. However, the standards that apply in proving an allegation of libel are different depending on whether or not the person claiming he or she has been defamed is a private or a public individual. Private individuals can win a libel suit if they can show that the material was false and that it hurt their reputation. However, the standard of proof is more difficult if a **public official** or **public figure** is claiming to have been libeled.

A public official is someone who holds either elected or appointed public office. A public figure is someone who, through his or her own actions, has placed himself or herself at the center of public attention. Celebrities and sports figures are public figures; senators and mayors are public officials. If a public official or figure wants to file a libel action, he or she has to prove not only that the material in question was false but also that it was printed or stated with **actual malice.** Actual malice can only be shown if the person making the statement either knew that it was false when it was stated or acted with "reckless disregard of whether it was false or not."[11] The Court acknowledged that this standard might result in false information being spread about public officials, but this was the price that had to be paid to ensure full and rigorous debate on public issues. The actual malice standard is difficult to meet, and public officials rarely file libel charges.

Obscenity

"Pornography versus Democracy," Walter Berns.

Another area of expression that is not protected and that has been the source of a great deal of public controversy is obscene material. The Court has made it clear that obscene material does not have First Amendment protection, but it has been difficult to establish a definition of obscenity that can be evenly and clearly applied in practice. After refining the definition over a number of years, the Court announced the following definition in 1973. Material can be found legally obscene only if the works, "taken as a whole, appeal to the prurient interest in sex, . . . portray sexual conduct in a patently offensive way, and which, taken as a whole, do not have serious literary, artistic, political, or scientific value."[12]

In more recent years there has been considerable controversy about the legitimacy of governmental actions aimed at restricting material that is deemed "indecent" but that does not meet the formal definition of obscenity announced by the U.S. Supreme Court. In 1996 Congress enacted the Communications Decency Act, which sought to prohibit material that many might find objectionable and harmful to children from being available on the Internet. The Court noted that it has "repeatedly recognized the governmental interest in protecting children from harmful materials. . . . But that interest does not justify an unnecessarily broad suppression of speech addressed to adults." Perhaps the most significant problem with the law was its inability to define "indecency" with any precision. Because it would be impossible for a person to know with any certainty what material would be considered indecent, the Court acknowledged that the law would have a "chilling effect" on free speech.[13] More recently, the Child Online

Protection Act (COPA), a federal law that seeks to protect children from pornographic material available on the Internet, has been subject to scrutiny by the Court. Enacted in 1998, the law has never been enforced due to various lower court decisions preventing its enforcement. The Supreme Court has not invalidated the law per se, but it has kept in place the rulings halting its enforcement. The Court has indicated that it might be possible for the law to be drawn narrowly enough to withstand constitutional scrutiny, but it has yet to make a final decision with respect to COPA.[14]

Freedom of Religion

Religious freedom is addressed in two separate First Amendment clauses: the **establishment clause** and the **free exercise clause.** The former is a specific prohibition on government. Neither the federal government nor the states can "establish" a religion. Established religions are state supported and endorsed. They were the norm in most nations at the time the First Amendment was adopted, and established religions did exist in a number of states. The establishment clause is generally taken to, in the words of Thomas Jefferson, erect a "wall of separation" between church and state. The free exercise clause is what allows individuals to believe in the religion of their choice or to choose not to believe in any religion.

Explore sites focusing on questions related to religious freedom.

The Establishment Clause

Because governments at all levels have not directly attempted to establish a state religion for quite some time, most establishment clause issues involve questions about the state impermissibly endorsing or favoring religion. Perhaps the most controversial establishment clause cases involve the public schools. Public schools are arms of the state, so any school involvement with religion raises serious questions.

During the first half of the twentieth century, it was fairly common for public schools to start their day with a prayer. For example, the state of New York had a policy that started each school day with a voluntary prayer. In 1962 the Supreme Court ruled that this practice violated the establishment clause. In the following year, the Court reinforced this principle in a Pennsylvania case where the school had required Bible reading and reciting the Lord's Prayer at the start of the school day. This requirement was challenged by a Pennsylvania family as a violation of the First Amendment. The Supreme Court agreed and ruled that a mandatory prayer in the public schools, even if there were provisions so that a student could exempt himself or herself from the practice, constituted an establishment of religion and violated the First Amendment.[15] In the four decades since that decision, the Court has given no indication that it will step back from it. In fact, in recent years, the Court has expanded the reach of this decision. Justices have expanded the ruling to prayers said at official school events such as graduation ceremonies.[16] And in a 2000 decision, the Court controversially ruled that officially sponsored prayers before the start of high school football games also violated the establishment clause.[17]

It is also important to note that "in no case has the Court held that it is unconstitutional for a student to pray voluntarily in the public school classroom."[18] To rule otherwise would raise serious questions under the free exercise clause. In some states, the Court's ruling in the pre-football-game case resulted in an interesting form of opposition. Without formal school endorsement or encouragement, fans began to break into "spontaneous prayer" before games. Such a practice highlights the often blurry line between the establishment and the free exercise clauses. The practice clearly seems to be a not so subtle attempt to circumvent the Supreme Court's decision. However, as long as the school administrators do not officially endorse the practice, it would seem that the free exercise clause makes spontaneous prayer constitutional.[19]

As the previous example illustrates, the Court's rulings in the area of school prayer have generated a great deal of debate and controversy. There are those, including members of the clergy, who are staunch supporters of the decisions. They point to the difficulty in finding a prayer that would not offend members of some religious denomination. They also point to the coercive character of school prayer, noting that even if given an opportunity to opt out of the practice, students might experience peer pressure if they failed to participate. Finally, they argue that prayer is an activity that should take place in a more appropriate setting than the classroom. Opponents to these rulings have attempted to pass a constitutional amendment that would reinstate prayer in public schools. Supporters of a school prayer amendment argue that prayer in school would help encourage traditional values at a time when those values seem to be in jeopardy. They also argue that we are a religious nation and that this should be acknowledged in our schools. Finally, they argue that as long as an "opt out" provision exists, whatever infringement on the First Amendment school prayer might represent, it is a minor limitation and should be accepted as a means to other, more significant ends. As dedicated as school prayer proponents have been, they have yet to generate the support necessary to pass such an amendment.

In addition to the continued debate over the desirability of a school prayer amendment, other establishment clause issues are subject to considerable contemporary public debate. Questions about the appropriateness of religious displays, such as nativity scenes and menorahs, on public property tend to arise every December. Although the Supreme Court has issued opinions, the decisions have not clearly established the constitutional limitations on such practices.

It is still the case that public education is the arena from which most establishment clause issues tend to arise. One public policy proposal that continues to raise establishment clause questions is legislation establishing school voucher programs. Vouchers are public funds that parents can use to send their children to private schools. They are often suggested as a

Participate in this debate at the School Prayer Forum.

means to ensure that parents have choices regarding the schools their children attend. While running for office during the 2000 presidential campaign, President Bush advocated the use of vouchers if public schools did not meet national accountability standards. Vouchers are controversial in terms of reforming the nation's educational system; they raise serious First Amendment concerns if the funds can be used for tuition at private schools that have a religious affiliation. In 2002 the Supreme Court issued its first ruling in a school voucher case. In a 5–4 decision, the Court upheld the voucher program used in Cleveland, Ohio. Cleveland's program made it possible for parents to use vouchers to attend both religious and secular private schools. Ninety-six percent of those participating chose to attend private religious schools. The Court ruled that as long as the program was "neutral" with respect to religion, the program was valid under the First Amendment. This does not end all questions about school vouchers because many state constitutions prohibit all aid to religious schools. Decisions about school vouchers will now most likely be determined by state courts and state legislatures.[20]

The Free Exercise Clause

The free exercise clause guarantees that individuals can hold the religious beliefs of their choice. Controversies surrounding free exercise rights arise when religious practices come into conflict with what would otherwise be legitimate governmental regulations or when conforming to governmental requirements would force a person to compromise his or her religious convictions. In 1972 the Court relied on the free exercise clause to justify an exemption for the Amish from an otherwise valid Wisconsin requirement that children attend school until they reach the age of sixteen. The Amish successfully argued that any public education beyond the eighth grade would expose their children to ideas and influences contrary to their long-established religious practices and way of life.

In 1986 the Court tended to side with the state, ruling that the free exercise clause did not mean that a Jewish member of the air force could wear a yarmulke in violation of the service's dress code.[21] Four years later, the Court ruled that members of the Native American Church could be removed from their positions as drug counselors by the state of Oregon because they engaged in the ritualistic use of peyote—a long-standing practice for members of that church.[22]

At the same time, the Court has also made it clear that any governmental regulations that interfere with a religious practice must have a legitimate governmental purpose unrelated to religion. The city of Hialeah, Florida, enacted a local ordinance designed to stop the ritualistic slaughter of animals—goats and chickens—which was part of the ceremonies of the Santeria religion practiced by some Americans of Caribbean descent who live in South Florida. The Court invalidated the statute because it singled out the Santeria practices for its regulations. The law did not make it illegal for a person to slaughter a chicken for nonreligious purposes, so it was clear that the law was an attempt to interfere with religious freedom. Consequently, the law violated the First Amendment.[23]

We have just touched the surface of First Amendment issues that are constant concerns in American politics. Questions raised in the realm of civil liberties are never definitively answered because new situations and new technologies result in circumstances that force the nation to adjust and modify its view of individual freedom. Usually, these issues are resolved by the Supreme Court. But it is also true that the cases that eventually come before the Court do so only because individuals believe that the issues in their situation are so significant they are willing to undergo the difficult process of getting the Court to hear their case (see Chapter 11). Although we may sometimes disagree with the particular stance of these individuals—such as R.A.V. from the opening scenario—it is worth remembering that without their willingness to become involved in the political process, the personal freedoms of the rest of the public might not be as secure.

Examine the strategies and arguments of interest groups that support different understandings of civil liberties issues.

The Right to Privacy

Not all the civil liberties we possess are noted in specific provisions of the Bill of Rights. The Ninth Amendment makes this clear by stating that "The enumeration in the Constitution of certain rights shall not be construed to deny or disparage others retained by the people." The most important, and controversial, of these unenumerated rights is the **right to privacy.**

The right to privacy in American law is now well over a century old. The idea emerged in late-nineteenth-century legal scholarship as the right to be let alone.[24] During the late nineteenth century and early twentieth century, state and federal courts began to recognize some form of the right to privacy by finding, for example, that individuals had a right to control the use of their likeness in publications and to seek damages when personal information was revealed.[25] Over time, the right to privacy has come to mean something broader. In the early twentieth century, the U.S. Supreme Court began to recognize that individuals were free to make decisions about how to raise and educate their children, whether to have children or not, and whom to marry.[26] When Americans speak of the right to privacy today, they are generally referring to a broad sense of personal autonomy, the right to make choices about their body and lifestyle free of government intrusion.

Contraception

The constitutional right to privacy was established in *Griswold v. Connecticut,* decided in 1965. In that case, the Court struck down an 1879 Connecticut law that made it illegal to use contraceptives or to distribute information about their use. The decision was both extremely narrow and breathtakingly broad. It was narrow in that the Court ruled that the right to privacy in acquiring information about and using birth control extended only to married couples. It was broad because it established, for the first time, a general right to privacy that was based on no single constitutional provision. Rather, it came from "the zone of privacy created by several fundamental constitutional guarantees," including the First, Third, Fourth, Fifth, and Ninth Amendments.[27] This privacy right was applied to the states by incorporating the Due Process Clause of the Fourteenth Amendment. (See Table 4.1.) The right to privacy was quickly expanded to include the use of contraception by all adults.[28]

Abortion Rights

In 1973 the U.S. Supreme Court extended the right to privacy to include a right to abortion. The decision in *Roe v. Wade* ruled that a Texas law that made abortion illegal except in cases when the life of the mother was endangered by the pregnancy was a violation of privacy rights guaranteed by the Constitution.[29] At the time of the decision, forty-six states had laws that made abortions illegal in most circumstances. The right to an abortion established by the Court was broad, but not absolute. The Court found that the state had an interest in the health of the pregnant woman and, after viability, in the life of the unborn child.

Since the 1973 *Roe* decision, abortion rights have consistently been one of the most controversial issues in American politics. This fight has taken place on both the state and national level and has been fought in both legislatures as well as the courts. State legislatures and Congress have passed a variety of restrictions on abortions over the last three decades. The U.S. Supreme Court has consistently upheld the right to an abortion established in *Roe*. In 1992 the Court made this clear when Justices Sandra Day O'Connor, Anthony Kennedy, and David Souter stated that "the essential holding in *Roe v. Wade* should be retained and once again reaffirmed."[30] However, the Court also found that restrictions that do not create an "undue burden" on that right are acceptable.

Both before and after its 1992 ruling, the U.S. Supreme Court has upheld state and federal government laws that limit access to abortions. For example, the Court upheld state and federal laws that require those seeking abortion to wait 24 hours before the procedure is performed; it has allowed for parental notification requirements with a judicial bypass procedure for minors; and it has allowed rules that require women to be informed about the dangers of abortions and be told about possible alternatives to abortion.[31] At the same time, efforts to restrict particular abortion methods have been struck down. In 2000 the Supreme Court struck down a law that banned so-called partial birth abortions.[32] Despite this ruling, Congress passed and President George W. Bush signed a partial birth abortion law in 2003. The Supreme Court has yet to rule on challenges to this law. The right to abortion remains a deeply controversial issue. Recent Supreme Court nomination hearings have confirmed this yet again. Whether the changes in Court membership alter the constitutional status of abortion rights remains to be seen.

Recent Applications of the Right to Privacy

Since the U.S. Supreme Court established the right to privacy in 1965, individuals and groups have asked the courts and legislatures to expand the right to privacy to new areas. Two areas have been particularly notable: sex between consenting adults and the right to physician-assisted suicide. In 2003 the Supreme Court struck down a Texas law that made it a crime for two people of the same sex to engage in sodomy. More details about this case can be found in the introduction to Chapter 11.[33] This ruling overturned a 1986 decision that upheld a Georgia law that prohibited oral and anal sex, but was applied solely to gays and lesbians.

The Court has recognized neither a general right to die nor a specific right to physician-assisted suicide.[34] States, however, do have the power to create rules by which individuals can refuse medical treatment by making their views known in advance in binding documents, such as living wills. Similarly, states can permit physician-assisted suicide. For example, in 1997 Oregon voters passed the Death with Dignity Act. From 1998 through 2004, 208 Oregonians have taken advantage of this law to end their life. The Bush administration opposed the law and challenged the ability of physicians to prescribe medications for the purpose of suicide.[35] The Supreme Court upheld the Oregon law in 2006.[36]

The Rights of the Accused

The rights of the accused are another important area of civil liberties. The Fourth, Fifth, Sixth, and Eighth Amendments establish a number of **due process** rights for those accused of committing a crime. These rights are critically important in the criminal justice system because they are based on the presumption of legal innocence. The state must prove beyond a reasonable doubt that the accused person is guilty, and it must do so following rules of fair play. In the period from the late 1940s through the early 1970s, most of the rights of the accused were incorporated to apply to limit the states as well as the federal government (see Table 4.1). Many Americans are familiar with the rights of the accused through the many police procedures in such television shows as *Law and Order.* What follows is a brief overview of the current interpretation of several of these procedural rights.

Search and Seizure

The Fourth Amendment prohibits "unreasonable searches and seizures." The goal is to protect individuals from harassment by law enforcement officials. In general, this has come to mean that searches cannot be made without a search warrant that is based on probable cause and is granted by a judge or other judicial officer. The Supreme Court has expanded this concept to keep up with technological innovation. For example, in 2001 the Court ruled that a policy of using a thermal-imaging device that looks for unusual heat sources associated with illegal drug manufacturing is the same as entering a home and is thus unconstitutional unless associated with probable cause. The Supreme Court has allowed for a variety of exceptions to this general rule. For example, police may use DWI roadside checkpoints where drivers are required to stop despite the lack of probable cause.[37] Similarly, once a car is stopped, police can inspect what is in plain view and potential evidence can be seized if there is a legitimate fear that the evidence will be lost if the officer does not act.[38] Individuals can also consent to a search. In an effort to make the prohibition against unreasonable search and seizure meaningful, the Court developed the **exclusionary rule,** which precludes the use of evidence gathered by unconstitutional means. The Supreme Court has created many exceptions to the exclusionary rule, including an exception when the evidence was gathered in "good faith" even if it was gathered improperly.[39] Another exception was created in 2006 when the Court ruled that evidence can be admitted even if the police do not "knock and announce" before entering a building with a search warrant.[40]

Self-Incrimination

A person may not be required to testify against himself or herself. The Fifth Amendment ensures that government must prove guilt and that defendants cannot be coerced to provide evidence in their own prosecution. The Court long ago ruled that physical abuse couldn't be used to coerce a confession. In *Miranda v. Arizona,* the Supreme Court went further and required that law enforcement officials notify those accused of their rights before being questioned.[41] The *Miranda* **rule** was reaffirmed in 2000.[42]

Right to Counsel

More than forty years ago, in *Gideon v. Wainwright,* the Supreme Court ruled that states must provide legal counsel for those accused of a felony if they cannot afford one. In 1972 the Court extended this right to any crime that could be punished with incarceration.[43] This right extends to appeals as well. In some places, a public defender's office is established. Full-time attorneys are hired to handle the defense of the indigent. In other instances, private attorneys are hired on a case-by-case basis to handle indigent criminal defense work. The work of those providing legal services to indigent defendants has come under scrutiny in recent years. Public defenders are often overworked and underpaid, and pay for private attorneys is often very low. The fear is that the indigent are not receiving adequate counsel. Criticism has been especially strong in death penalty cases.

Right to a Jury Trial

Juries in criminal trials are responsible for determining the guilt or innocence of the defendant. The Court has ruled that the accused have a **right to a jury trial** in any case—state or federal—where the accused can be incarcerated for at least six months.[44] The Supreme Court has interpreted the Sixth Amendment requirement of an "impartial jury" to mean that the pool of potential jurors must reflect a "cross-section" of the community. Government cannot exclude groups of people based on race, sex, ethnicity, or gender. A defendant has no right to a cross-section of the community on a petit or trial jury, but the Court has ruled that constitutional prohibitions against discrimination extend to the selection of trial juries as well.[45]

Cruel and Unusual Punishment

The Eighth Amendment prohibits cruel and unusual punishment. This has been interpreted to mean that punishment must be proportionate to the crime and that certain forms of punishment—torture, for example—are prohibited. For most of the nation's history, including the time when the Bill of Rights was written, the death penalty has been constitutional. In 1972 the Supreme Court found that the death penalty as then administered was cruel and unusual punishment.[46] Since then, states have created procedures that have met constitutional muster. Most important among them are the requirements that the decision of guilt or innocence and the decision to impose the death penalty must be made in separate proceedings, that juries impose the death penalty, and that juries hear both aggregating factors (justifying the death penalty) and mitigating factors (justifying a lesser sentence).[47]

Currently, thirty-nine states have death penalty laws. In recent years, questions have arisen again about the use of the death penalty. In 1997 the American Bar Association called for a moratorium on the use of the death penalty, expressing concern about poor representation and racial discrimination. Citing the work of investigative journalists, the governor of Illinois suspended use of the death penalty in his state. The public has lost some of its confidence in the death penalty, and juries are not imposing lethal sentences as often as in the recent past.[48] Furthermore, in recent years the Supreme Court has struck down the imposition of the death penalty on the mentally retarded and on those under the age of eighteen. In 2003 the Court overturned a death penalty conviction because of inadequate counsel, finding that the defendant's lawyer had not looked into the defendant's abusive childhood and had not informed the jury about his background.[49] In 2006 the Court reaffirmed its acceptance of the death penalty when it upheld a Kansas law imposing the death penalty when mitigating and aggravating circumstances are equivalent.[50]

The Rights of the Accused in Practice

The rights discussed above are critical to a fair criminal justice process, but it is important to understand that the rules are applied only in cases where the defendant goes to trial. In most cases, over 95 percent of cases in many jurisdictions, criminal proceedings end in a **plea bargain.** Everyone in the criminal justice process is overworked—judges, prosecutors, and defense attorneys alike. It is often to the benefit of all concerned—including the defendant—to conclude a criminal prosecution through an agreement between the prosecutor and the defendant.

CIVIL LIBERTIES AFTER 9/11

On October 25, 2001, just six weeks after the 9/11 terrorist attacks on the World Trade Center, Congress passed the Uniting and Strengthening America by Providing Appropriate Tools Required to Intercept and Obstruct Terrorism Act, better known as the **USA Patriot Act**. The law was passed in such a rush that most members of Congress had not even seen printed copies of the proposed legislation. The stated purpose of the law was to improve the intelligence-gathering capabilities of the federal government. The law passed by an overwhelming majority. In the Senate, only one senator (Russ Feingold, D-Wis.) voted against it, in part arguing that Congress was moving too quickly. However, criticism of the act began to appear almost as soon as the provisions of the **USA Patriot Act** were known. Most of the concerns had to do with specific provisions of the act that the critics thought presented significant threats to civil liberties. These potential threats to civil liberties were taken seriously by Congress when the law was passed. A time limit, known as a sunset provision, was established for some of the most controversial provisions of the law, with sixteen of them set to expire on December 31, 2005. Among the most controversial provisions that were the set to expire included the following:

Information sharing: It is now easier for domestic (**FBI**) and international (**CIA**) intelligence agencies to share information, a practice that had been severely restricted before the act.

Roving wiretaps: One wiretap warrant can now cover all phones and electronic communication devices used by a suspect. Previously, separate warrants were needed for each device.

Access to records: Federal investigators can now obtain records of books purchased, books borrowed from libraries, and a library patron's Internet searches without the purchaser or user being made aware of the request.

Foreign intelligence wiretaps and searches: It is easier for federal investigators to get permission to search a person's home or wiretap the person's communications if they claim that the reason the searches are needed is for foreign intelligence-gathering purposes.

After extensive debate in Congress, the Patriot Act was renewed in 2006. Congress made fourteen of the sixteen controversial provisions that were set to expire permanent and added some additional safeguards for individual liberties. Civil liberties activists continue to challenge the law.[1]

(continued)

Other civil liberties issues have arisen in the aftermath of 9/11, including the rights afforded those being held in federal custody as "enemy combatants." Large numbers of these individuals have been held at a military base in Guantanamo Bay, Cuba, for more than three years without formal charges being filed against them. A few of those being held are U.S. citizens. Many have argued that this practice is in direct violation of the rights of the accused discussed in this chapter. In 2004 the Supreme Court issued rulings in two cases that concluded that U.S. law applies to those being held in Guantanamo Bay, both to those who are citizens and to those who are not. Consequently, those being held as enemy combatants can challenge the legality of their imprisonment in federal courts. After these decisions, some of the detainees were released and returned to their home countries.[2]

In 2006 the Supreme Court ruled that the military commission the Bush administration had created to try the detainees was invalid because it was not authorized by Congress. They also ruled that the commission, as created, violated both the Uniform Code of Military Justice and the Geneva Conventions.[3]

[1] George H. Pike, "USA Patriot Act: What's Next?" *Information Today* 23 (April 2006), pp. 1–2.

[2] Charles Lane, "Justices Back Detainee Access to U.S. Courts; President's Powers Are Limited," *Washington Post*, June 29, 2004, p. 1 (retrieved via LexisNexis, September 15, 2005).

[3] Hamdan v. Rumsfeld, 126 S. Ct. 2749 (2006).

Check the chapter updates for the current status of both the Patriot Act and the Guantanamo Bay detainees.

Civil Rights

Examine equality in the United States.

Questions concerning civil rights involve the political value of *equality* and the extent to which this ideal exists in practice as well as in theory. Equality is more problematic as a political value than freedom largely because support for political equality was not present at the time the Constitution was adopted. Active endorsement for the ideal represented in the Declaration of Independence's assertion that "all men are created equal" has been built up over the course of the nation's history. Even as we, as a nation, have come to endorse a more expansive understanding of equality, the value itself is still controversial because there is a range of perspectives about exactly what equality should mean and how far it should extend.

Understandings of Equality

There are at least three understandings of equality that find expression in American politics, and each perception brings with it increasing amounts of controversy and debate. The first understanding, which today has the greatest range of support, is equal rights or **legal equality,** the idea that the law should be the same for everyone regardless of one's place or status within the society. Although you would not find too many supporters of legal inequality today, it is important to remember that such a state did exist for a significant portion of the nation's history.

The second understanding is **equality of opportunity,** an application of equality to the economic realm. Equal opportunity is the view that everyone should be able to advance his or her own material circumstances based on his or her own abilities and willingness to work hard. What follows from this principle is the position that individuals should not be disadvantaged in their economic opportunities because they happened to have been born with a certain skin color, are of a certain gender, or are characterized by other traits about which they had no, or very little, choice. Most people might agree with this ideal, but there is a fairly large amount of disagreement over how best to achieve it in practice and what role, if any, the federal government should have in bringing about changes in the realm of economics.

The third understanding of equality is **equality of conditions.** This involves the position that people should be guaranteed a certain level of material circumstances by virtue of being citizens. Few people in the United States call for a complete, or even a substantial, equalizing of conditions across the board. However, federal programs such as Social Security, Medicare, and welfare do guarantee specific material benefits to citizens if they meet certain criteria. Some of these programs, especially Social Security, have broad support among the public, but others are more controversial. Exactly how far such programs should extend and whether or not the government has a role to play in affecting the everyday material circumstances of citizens are questions that continue today. Discussions during the 2000 presidential election regarding health-care policy and prescription drug guarantees illustrate that Americans are still engaged in vigorous debates over the question of just how far equal conditions should extend.

Explore the websites of major organizations dedicated to promoting civil rights.

In popular discussions of civil rights, one often finds the term *minority rights* being used. Although widespread, such terminology is a bit misleading. Not all groups of people who have sought equal treatment have been members of groups constituting less than half the population, and not all "minorities" seek equal treatment. It would be more accurate to think of civil rights in terms of disadvantaged, rather than minority, groups. Women constitute a majority of the population but have been subjected to unequal treatment throughout history. Multimillionaires constitute a district minority of the population, but they are a privileged rather than a disadvantaged group.

Changes in both the attitudes of Americans on civil rights and in the laws guaranteeing these rights did not come easily. The changes have been the result of dedicated, prolonged, and at times life-threatening political activity on the part of those who were initially subject to unequal treatment in American politics. When one thinks about the gains that have been made and the profound changes that have come about, it is all that much more remarkable because those who were the catalysts for change were attempting to influence a political system to which they had little or no access. Trying to achieve equal citizenship status from a disadvantaged position within the society is a daunting and difficult process. The successes of the black civil rights movement, the women's movement, and many other groups to secure their rights have also demonstrated that active political participation and involvement in the political process can result in major change.

Equality and the Constitution

As with the area of civil liberties, discussions about civil rights usually start with seeing how equality is protected by the Constitution. They also generally emphasize the pivotal role of the Supreme Court in the process of extending civil rights to all citizens. But it is essential to understand that the Constitution did not include language about equality until after the Civil War. As originally ratified, the Constitution specifically encoded inequality through a number of provisions that endorsed and perpetuated the institution of slavery. These provisions included counting slaves as three-fifths of a person, the continuation of the slave trade until 1808, and the requirement that fugitive slaves (those who had escaped and fled to free states) had to be returned to their owners. In addition, it is important to remember that although the Supreme Court was essential to the expansion of civil rights during the twentieth century, as an institution it did not always support the goal of equality, especially racial equality. Some of the Court's rulings during earlier eras helped perpetuate inequality. Finally, civil rights policy involves the president and Congress as well as the Supreme Court in the decision-making process. Civil liberties decisions have a much greater tendency to be decided primarily by the Court.

The Nineteenth Century

Slavery existed as part of the nation's political system for more than two centuries, and the consequences of slavery remain today. The result is that racial inequality and the struggle to gain equal rights for African Americans remain the paradigmatic case in understanding civil rights in the United States. There were those who opposed slavery from its inception, but concerted attempts to end the institution did not enter the political arena until the abolition movement of the early nineteenth century. Among the earliest national interest groups, abolitionists argued that slavery was morally wrong and inconsistent with the principle that "all men are created equal."

Although opposition to slavery began to grow in the North, the southern states were committed to the institution, which they pointed out was constitutional. The Supreme Court agreed. In 1857 the Court issued the *Dred Scott* decision, which ruled that Dred Scott—a slave—was not a person under the law, but an article of property. Thus, he could not sue in court. In the same case, the Court also invalidated the Missouri Compromise of 1820, a decision that helped precipitate the Civil War. The war was waged in part over slavery, and the South's military defeat ensured the end of slavery as a legal institution. It did not, however, ensure that the former slaves would be accepted as full citizens.

Dred Scott v. Sanford.

In the aftermath of the Civil War, the Constitution was amended. The Thirteenth Amendment (1865) ended slavery. The states of the former Confederacy could no longer allow the legal institution of slavery, but they did enact laws that relegated the former slaves to a subordinate legal and social position. The **black codes** were constraints on the activities of African Americans. They included, among other things, prohibitions on gun ownership and assembling after dark that applied only to the former slaves.[51] The Fourteenth Amendment (1868) was designed to confer citizenship rights on the former slaves. Section 1 of the Amendment reads as follows:

> All persons born or naturalized in the United States, and subject to the jurisdiction thereof, are citizens of the United States and of the State wherein they reside. No State shall make or enforce any law which shall abridge the privileges or immunities of citizens of the United States; nor shall any State deprive any person of life, liberty, or property, without due process of law; nor deny to any person within its jurisdiction the equal protection of the laws.

This language is quite clear, but it was not until the middle of the twentieth century that African Americans in the United States realistically could begin to attain the legal equality promised by this amendment. During the post–Civil War era, additional statutes, known as **Jim Crow** laws, were enacted in the southern states. They required that separate public facilities be established for whites and blacks for everything from education to drinking fountains. These laws might seem to be a clear violation of the Fourteenth Amendment, but in 1896 the U.S. Supreme Court ruled otherwise.

The case of *Plessy v. Ferguson* concerned a Louisiana law that required railroad companies to provide separate cars for blacks and whites. This law was challenged as a violation of the equal protection clause of the Fourteenth Amendment. Despite the dissent of Justice Harlan, who wrote, "Our constitution is color-blind, and neither knows nor tolerates classes among citizens," the Court rejected the challenge. It developed an interpretation of the amendment that legitimated this, as well as all other Jim Crow laws. The **separate but equal** standard held that a state could require a separation of its citizens based on race as long as the separate facilities and services were "equal."[52]

Plessy v. Ferguson.

Segregated public facilities, such as the public restrooms pictured here, were prevalent throughout the South until after the Civil Rights Act of 1964.

The Twentieth Century

At the start of the twentieth century, slavery may have been abolished, but racism still existed. **Racism** is the belief that there are superior and inferior races of people and that individual members of those races should be treated accordingly. In the United States, racism has generally taken the form that whites are superior to members of others races. Although not technically a racial characteristic, a person's national origin (the country from which his or her ancestors immigrated) has also been used to assign inferior status. Consequently, blacks, Asians, Hispanics, Native Americans, and other ethnic groups have all been considered and treated as inferior. As the *R.A.V.* case demonstrates, in a nation committed to freedom of expression, it is not possible to legislate against the existence of racism directly without violating the First Amendment. We cannot pass laws prohibiting racism, but we can adopt an educational philosophy that presents racism as a belief that is contrary to the fundamental American commitment to the principle of equality.

Although it may be impossible to legislate against racist beliefs, public laws have been used to address particular practices that result from racism, especially practices that have been afforded legal sanction. In civil rights discussions, the term **discrimination** is often used to characterize such practices, but this term needs clarification. To discriminate simply means to make distinctions and to treat people differently based on those distinctions. It means to afford unequal treatment to citizens. Yet government discriminates

Hulton Archive/Getty Images

in this way all the time. Only individuals who have reached a certain age can drive a car. Only people with the appropriate education and training can get a license to practice medicine or law. Tax rates differ depending on our income. The list could go on. Although these laws technically represent discrimination, no one questions their legitimacy because the criteria used to differentiate among people are seen to be reasonable. The real question is what are, and what are not, legitimate criteria for such distinctions.

Race was used as a criterion for discrimination for a major part of U.S. history. The most direct form of racial discrimination is **segregation.** To segregate means to separate, so racial segregation means separate treatment of people based on their race. Segregation can come in two forms: *de jure* and *de facto. De jure* means "by law"; it is legally mandated segregation such as the Jim Crow laws. If such a law requires separate drinking fountains, it would be a crime not to provide such facilities. *De facto* means "in fact." *De facto* segregation exists when separate facilities exist, but there are no laws demanding that they do, nor are there any laws prohibiting such a situation. The Supreme Court's decision in *Plessy* endorsed *de jure* or state-imposed segregation.

As Justice Harlan's dissent indicates, there were people in the United States who thought that *Plessy* was wrong from the start, but it was not until the National Association for the Advancement of Colored People **(NAACP)** was founded in 1910 that a focused political strategy emerged to bring about change. The NAACP was, and is, an interest group committed to the eradication of racial segregation and discrimination. In the early twentieth century, it was speaking for those who were politically disenfranchised as well as economically and socially disadvantaged. Because of this situation, the NAACP lacked most of the traditional means available to interest groups to try to effect political change. Because African Americans could not, for all practical purposes, vote, they did not have elected officials to speak for them, lobbying was ineffective, and the NAACP was forced to seek less traditional means to try to influence the political process.

Under the leadership of Charles Hamilton Houston, a Howard University law professor, the NAACP began the slow process of attempting to address racial segregation. Houston trained and then assembled a group of lawyers committed to establishing legal equality by using the judicial system. Houston's students included Thurgood Marshall, who would later argue and win the ***Brown v. Board of Education*** case and eventually become the first African American justice on the U.S. Supreme Court. The NAACP chose to rely on the courts as a means to bring about change for a number of reasons. First, the justice system was the one point of access in the political process that was open to African Americans. Second, the NAACP knew that the Supreme Court's interpretation of the Fourteenth Amendment would have to change if real progress in the realm of racial equality was to occur. Third, because the goal was to achieve legal equality, the courts, especially the Supreme Court, were the governmental institutions that had the political, legal, and moral authority to confer legitimacy on the change.

Brown v. Board of Education.

Houston and his colleagues knew that the Supreme Court did not change direction quickly, so they could be patient and adopt a legal strategy that would take time. Emphasizing cases involving public education, the NAACP started by accepting the "separate but equal" doctrine but attempting to make the "equal" part of it actually apply in practice. The doctrine was eroded through decisions in a series of cases that forced the states to provide genuinely equal educational facilities by focusing on such issues as teachers' salaries. Then the NAACP began a more direct attack on the principle of separate but equal. It won a case in which Texas had tried to establish an all-black law school so that African American students would not have to be admitted into the University of Texas law school. The NAACP successfully argued that there was no realistic way that the new school could be equal to the long-established, white-only state law school.

The lengthy process of change came to fruition in 1954 in the justly famous case of *Brown v. Board of Education*. In this case, the NAACP attacked the separate but equal doctrine directly as it was applied, not to law or professional schools, but to the elementary and secondary schools of Topeka, Kansas. It argued that legally segregated public schools violated the equal protection clause of the Fourteenth Amendment because they placed a stamp of inferiority on the African American students. A unanimous Supreme Court agreed, stating "Separate educational facilities are inherently unequal."[53] The Court specifically overturned its earlier decision in *Plessy*, which was a clear indication that the Court was on its way to overturning all forms of *de jure* segregation.

Brown met with intense opposition throughout the South. Governors and state legislatures openly defied the Court's rulings, vowing that they would continue their practices of legal segregation. The federal courts continued to follow the newly set precedent and ordered school systems to begin the process of desegregation. Although the Supreme Court continued to stand behind its decision, the Court lacks enforcement authority and could do little in the face of open refusal of its decisions. It was not until President Eisenhower sent federal troops into Little Rock, Arkansas, to enforce a federal court desegregation order that the full impact of the *Brown* decision began to be felt. Eisenhower's actions sent the clear message that the full enforcement power of the federal government was going to stand behind the Supreme Court's decision. Eisenhower's actions highlight the important role that presidents have played in the area of civil rights. As the following section demonstrates, Congress also played a major role in extending the reach of the Court's ruling in *Brown*.

After *Brown*

Using the Fourteenth Amendment, the Supreme Court ended *de jure* segregation, but it did not have the authority on its own to address *de facto* segregation. Although the law could no longer require segregated public facilities and states could no longer provide different services to their citizens based on race, there was nothing preventing private persons from practicing racial

"The Civic Meaning of Brown v. Board of Education at Fifty," Lenneal J. Henderson, Jr.

Watch a 1957 news story on the Little Rock crisis.

Listen to President Eisenhower's explanation of his response to the crisis.

segregation and discrimination. To go further in the fight for racial equality, national legislation was needed. To generate support for such legislation, national awareness had to be raised regarding the extent of racial discrimination in the nation. These were the goals of the **civil rights movement** during the 1950s and 1960s.

The best-known leader of the civil rights movement was Martin Luther King, Jr. Under his direction, members of the movement engaged in a range of nontraditional political practices to get the issue of racial inequality on the national agenda. Although their tactics were innovative, the principle of political action that inspired them was nonviolent civil disobedience. The movement attracted a large number of supporters, both black and white. Many college students were inspired to devote time and energy to help achieve its goals. Among the most significant tactics used by the movement was its refusal to obey laws that were seen as morally unjust. Following King's lead, members of the movement were willing to risk jail to make their points. They engaged in a wide range of protests—peaceful mass marches, economic boycotts, and sit-ins—all in an effort to generate enough public support to ensure congressional action.

As support for the goals of the movement grew within the general population, legislation was introduced into Congress designed to extend the impact of the Supreme Court's decision into the private sector. Supported by President John F. Kennedy, the Civil Rights Act was introduced into Congress in 1963. After Kennedy's death, President Lyndon Baines Johnson continued the strong support for the measure. In Congress, the legislation passed fairly easily in the House of Representatives, but it was held up in the Senate by the longest filibuster in U.S. history. Eventually, the efforts to prevent passage were thwarted, and President Johnson signed the bill in 1964. Without this congressional action, the gains of the civil rights movement would have been much more limited.

The **Civil Rights Act of 1964** (CRA) was designed to address problems of *de facto* racial discrimination, which was practiced by individuals and businesses rather than governmental entities. It prohibited discrimination in **public accommodations**—services provided to the general public by private entities. Public accommodations include restaurants, hotels, movie theaters, and other retail establishments. The act also withheld federal funds from state and local governments that continued to practice racial discrimination. The law addressed employment discrimination by private companies and unions, and created agencies within the federal government with the authority to enforce the CRA.[54] Compliance with the CRA did not occur immediately, but since its passage, it has been an effective law in helping achieve the goal of legal equality for African Americans.

The year after the passage of the Civil Rights Act, Congress passed the **Voting Rights Act of 1965** (VRA), which was directed toward removing the barriers that still prevented most African Americans in the country from voting. The biggest obstacle to voting was registration. Most of the southern states made it extremely difficult for blacks to register to vote. In states where there had been a documented history of voter discrimination,

Watch a tribute to Rosa Parks, a key figure in the civil rights movement

Watch President Kennedy's message on civil rights

Watch President Johnson sign the Civil Rights Act.

Presidential Leadership of Congressional Civil Rights Voting: The Cases of Eisenhower and Johnson," James D. King and James W. Riddlesperger, Jr.

When President Johnson signed the Civil Rights Act of 1964, it represented the culmination of a long struggle on the part of civil rights leaders, including the Rev. Martin Luther King, Jr.

the VRA authorized federal registrars to sign people up to vote. The VRA was very effective. As Figure 4.1 illustrates, the VRA had a significant impact on African American voter registration.

Equality for Other Disadvantaged Groups

The Civil Rights Act of 1964 did not only address the disparate conditions that existed for African Americans. It also prohibited discrimination based on religion and national origin, which historically had also been criteria used to unfairly discriminate against individuals. For example, religion had been used as a basis for preventing individuals from entering certain professions or from being hired at all. In the twentieth century, there were limits on the number of Jews who could be admitted to medical schools and signs indicating "Irish need not apply" for job openings. Gender may never have been widely used to prohibit entrance to public accommodations, but it has been used as a criterion in employment decisions, with women consistently earning less than males in the same jobs. The Equal Pay Act of 1963 outlawed different pay for the same work based on the sex of the employee. The provision of the Civil Rights Act dealing with employment practices—Title VII—includes sex along with race, color, religion, and national origin as

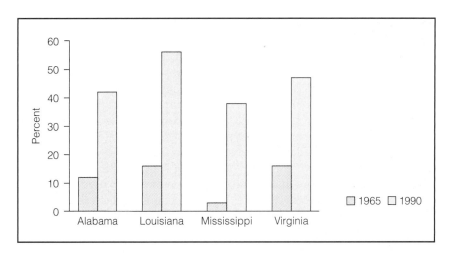

Figure 4.1 Percentage of Black Registered Voters in Selected Southern States. The difference between the number of African Americans living in the South who were registered to vote the year the Voting Rights Act was enacted and in 1990 illustrates the impact that the law had on the ability of African Americans to participate in the political process.

Source: 1990 Statistical Abstract of the United States, p. 264, table 441.

impermissible criteria for making decisions about hiring and promotions. Although sex was initially included in the act as a strategy to prevent its passage—the idea was that senators might vote for racial equality, but never sexual equality—the Civil Rights Act of 1964 has resulted in more equitable treatment for women as well as for racially disadvantaged groups.[55]

The struggle for legal equality for women also has a long history. There was an unsuccessful effort to gain the right to vote for women during the late nineteenth century. After about a decade of concerted political activity, a similar movement during the early twentieth century successfully achieved women's suffrage with the ratification of the **Nineteenth Amendment.** But advocates for women's rights wanted another constitutional amendment as well. In 1923 the **Equal Rights Amendment** was first introduced into Congress. In 1972 enough support had been generated in Congress to send the amendment to the states. The proposed amendment stated: "Equality of Rights under the law shall not be denied or abridged by the United States or by any state on account of sex." The amendment was ratified fairly quickly in a number of states, but it eventually encountered opposition that was strong enough to prevent ratification in the required thirty-eight states. Since then, a number of existing laws have been used to secure more legal equality for women, but some still argue that only a constitutional amendment will truly establish legal equality.

In recent decades, other disadvantaged groups have joined in the effort to achieve legal equality. The passage of the Americans with Disabilities Act requires that government, educational institutions, and businesses

Participate in the debate at the Equal Rights Amendment Forum.

make reasonable accommodations so that people with physical disabilities are not prevented from gaining access to both public services and economic opportunities. Hispanics have been included under the provisions of the Voting Rights Act, with federal registrars sent throughout the American Southwest to guarantee that Hispanics can register and vote. Hispanics continue to be involved in efforts to require bilingual education for Spanish-speaking citizens. The treatment of Native Americans as well as various treaty rights issues remains an area of controversy in states with significant Native-American populations. Advocates for gays, lesbians, and bisexual people have attempted to get legislation and state constitutional amendments enacted to ensure that sexual orientation cannot be used as the basis for denying a person access to rights and protections available to the heterosexual majority. They have also sought legislation recognizing the legitimacy of gay and lesbian marriages or civil unions. This has become an extremely controversial issue in American politics. Hawaii and Vermont passed such legislation, but Hawaii's law was later superseded by a state constitutional amendment and legislation prohibiting gay marriages. In early 2004 the Massachusetts Supreme Court ruled that the state legislature had to rewrite the state's marriage laws so that gay and lesbian couples would be legally entitled to civil marriages. This decision generated a great deal of controversy and resulted in eleven states including anti–gay marriage proposals on their ballots in the 2004 election. All the measures passed.[56] The question of gay marriage is likely to be the source of continued impassioned political debate in the future.

Current Issues

Explore the strategies used by major civil rights organizations to promote their goals.

Most of the current controversies in the area of civil rights center on issues surrounding equal opportunity and equality of conditions. There are still significant disparities in economic status between members of racial and ethnic groups and the majority white population. Women still do not earn salaries comparable to their male counterparts. The existence of sexual harassment continues to raise significant questions about equal treatment of women in the workplace. Women, African Americans, and other ethnic populations still do not have representation in high-level public offices consistent with their numbers in the population. (See Chapter 9 for a breakdown of characteristics of members of Congress.) Nor are they represented in the upper echelon of business and industry consistent with their numbers in the population. Efforts to bring about equality in this area have often centered on the methods that should, and should not, be used to address such continued inequalities.

Affirmative action is the term used to encompass a variety of governmental programs and corporate initiatives that make a concerted, proactive effort to ensure equal opportunity in practice as well as in theory. The U.S. Supreme Court has specifically invalidated some affirmative action procedures, such as the use of quotas in hiring and university admissions. At the same time, the Court has said that it is permissible for government to use other methods in an attempt to make special efforts to reverse the trends associated with long-term discriminatory practices. The Court reiterated this position in 2003, when it validated the use of race as a criterion in the admissions process at the University of Michigan Law School, but at the same time ruled that the undergraduate admissions process, which assigned applicants a specific number of points based on race, was a violation of the Constitution.[57] Critics often claim that such programs constitute reverse discrimination. Supporters point to the continued existence of economic inequalities as justification for more assertive efforts to achieve equal opportunity. These debates are likely to continue because, for all the progress that has been made, we have still not completely fulfilled the promise of equality for all citizens.

Conclusion: Freedom and Equality—The Ongoing Debate

Civil liberties and civil rights present the public with questions that have no final resolution. They are often among the most hotly contested issues in American politics. This is largely because these questions involve the fundamental values of American politics. As events, technology, and our collective experiences change over time, new circumstances will continue to arise that will force us to reexamine what the proper balance between freedom and equality should be. Virtually all of the major political actors in the United States are involved in settling civil liberties and civil rights disputes. The president, Congress, and the Supreme Court play important roles. It is also an arena where citizen participation has often been the most dramatic and effective in bringing about change. Without dedicated individuals and groups, the expansion of individual freedoms and legal equality would not have been possible.

Check here for possible post-publication updates to the chapter material.

Key Terms

equal protection clause   88
civil liberties   88
civil rights   89
freedom   89
equality   89
Bill of Rights   90
Fourteenth Amendment   90
due process clause   90
incorporation doctrine   90
freedom of expression   92

symbolic expressions   93
political expression   93
creative expression   93
obscenity   93
commercial speech   93
censorship   93
prior restraint   93
content neutral   94
criminal syndicalism laws   94
libel   97

slander   97
public official   98
public figure   98
actual malice   98
establishment clause   99
free exercise clause   99
right to privacy   102
due process   104
exclusionary rule   105
Miranda rule   105

right to a jury trial   105
plea bargain   106
legal equality   109
equality of opportunity   109
equality of conditions   109
Dred Scott   *111*
black codes   111
Jim Crow   111

Plessy v. Ferguson   *111*
separate but equal   111
racism   112
discrimination   112
segregation   113
de jure   *113*
de facto   *113*
NAACP   113

Brown v. Board of Education   *113*
civil rights movement   115
Civil Rights Act of 1964   115
public accommodations   115
Voting Rights Act of 1965   115
Nineteenth Amendment   117
Equal Rights Amendment   117
affirmative action   118

Suggested Web Resources

The following websites are provided by groups that are concerned with civil liberties and civil rights. There are numerous organizations in the United States that have these interests. What follows is just a sample of these groups.

Civil Liberties Organizations

The American Civil Liberties Union (ACLU) (http://www.aclu.org) is the most well-known organization dedicated to promoting individual rights in the United States. It is generally considered to have a liberal orientation. The site highlights the specific issues that the ACLU sees as presenting the most threats to civil liberties. Another liberal civil liberties group is People for the American Way (http://www.pfaw.org/pfaw/general). Its stated goal is to organize and mobilize "Americans to fight for fairness, justice, civil rights and the freedoms guaranteed by the Constitution."

The American Center for Law and Justice (http://www.aclj.org) is a conservative organization founded by Pat Robertson. Its goal is to "undo the damage done by almost a century of liberal thinking and activism." It is "dedicated to defending and advancing religious liberty, the sanctity of human life, and the two-parent, marriage-bound family." A similar conservative group is the Rutherford Institute (http://www.rutherford.org). It is "an international legal and educational organization dedicated to preserving human rights and defending civil liberties."

It is worth noting that, in the aftermath of the September 11, 2001, terrorist attack, a variety of groups from the left and the right have expressed concerns that civil liberties might be in danger during this time of national emergency. They created a broad coalition called In Defense of Freedom (http://www.indefenseoffreedom.org) that endorses a ten-point statement of principles. All the organizations supporting this statement are linked from the main site.

Church/State Issues and School Prayer

The ACLU (http://www.aclu.org), People for the American Way (http://www.pfaw.org/pfaw/general), ACJL (http://www.aclj.org), and Eagle Forum (http://www.eagleforum.org) websites all contain extensive resources on a variety of church/state issues, including school prayer. As its name indicates, Americans United for the Separation of Church and State (http://www.au.org/site/PageServer) wants to maintain the separation of church and state. Its site focuses on current issues, court cases, and legislative and public school issue updates and also has an online magazine.

Freedom of Expression and Flag Burning

Flag burning is an intensely emotional issue. It has passionate advocates on both sides of the question. The debate is likely to become even more heated in the aftermath of the terrorist attack on the World Trade Center. People for the American Way (http://www.pfaw.org/pfaw/general/default.aspx?oid=10107) has a special initiative to fight against the proposed constitutional amendment that would make flag burning a federal crime. On the other side, the Citizens Flag Alliance (http://www.cfa-inc.org) is the primary group supporting ratification of the amendment.

Civil Rights Organizations

The National Association for the Advancement of Colored People (NAACP) (**http://www.naacp .org**) was founded in 1909 to combat racial discrimination in the United States. Its site provides links to the organization's past as well as highlights current issues. Its timeline presents a history of the NAACP, which is a good place to begin in order to get an understanding of the U.S. civil rights movement.

The Citizens' Commission on Civil Rights (**http://www.cccr.org**) "is committed to the revitalization of a progressive civil rights agenda at the national level." Its specific goals include fighting "bias and invidious discrimination," promoting "equality of opportunity in education, employment, and housing," promoting "political and economic empowerment," and guaranteeing "equal treatment in the administration of justice."

Sponsored by the Leadership Conference on Civil Rights, Civilrights.org (**http://www .civilrights. org**) identifies itself as a "social justice network." Its mission is to assist the civil rights community in the "fight for equality and social justice in the emerging digital society through the establishment of an online social justice network."

The National Gay and Lesbian Task Force (**http://www.thetaskforce.org**) "is the national progressive organization working for the civil rights of gay, lesbian, bisexual and transgendered people, with the vision and commitment to building a powerful political movement."

The National Council of La Raza (NCLR) (**http:// www.nclr.org**) was organized in 1968 "to reduce poverty and discrimination, and improve life opportunities for Hispanic Americans."

Women's Rights Organizations and the ERA

The National Council of Women's Organizations sponsors a site on the Equal Rights Amendment (**http://equalrightsamendment.org**). It has sections on the history of the proposed amendment, its legislative status, an action update, a strategy for passage, and links to additional information. The National Organization for Women (NOW) (**http://www.now.org**) supports the ERA. It was founded in 1966 in order to promote women's rights. Although there are many other organizations working toward the same goals, NOW remains the preeminent women's rights organization. The Eagle Forum (**http://www.eagleforum .org**) was founded by Phyllis Schlafly to oppose the Equal Rights Amendment and to promote conservative causes. In addition to opposing the ERA, the site also takes stands on a wide range of social issues of importance to conservatives.

A complete study tool kit is available for this chapter and includes the following:
Flashcards
Crossword Puzzle
Critical Thinking Exercises
Interactive Timelines
Chapter Quiz

5 | Public Opinion and Ideology

■ Sex, Lies, and Public Opinion   123

■ Citizen Participation in the Web
  of American Democracy   125

■ Political Socialization: How Americans Learn
  About Politics   127
  Family   128
  School   129
  Generational Effects   130
  The Media   131
  Community Groups and Peers   132

■ Political Ideology: Are Opinions Connected?   132
  An Alternative View of Ideology   133

■ How Much Do Americans Know About Politics?   137

■ Measuring Public Opinion   141
  Who Conducts Public Opinion Polls and Why?   142
  A Citizen's Guide to Public Opinion Polling   144

■ Conclusion: Public Opinion and Public Policy   150

Sex, Lies, and Public Opinion

Upon completing his second term of office on January 20, 2001, William Jefferson Clinton, the forty-second president of the United States, left office with the highest approval ratings of any president leaving office in the last fifty years.[1] Three years earlier, few would have predicted such an occurrence. On January 21,

Monica Lewinsky embraces President Clinton at a White House lawn gathering of interns. Clinton's affair with Lewinsky created a crisis for the president that ultimately led to his impeachment. Throughout most of the crisis, Clinton's public support remained high.

1998, the story broke about a sexual relationship between Clinton and then White House intern Monica Lewinsky. The relationship was sporadic but ongoing, and it lasted from November 1995 through January 1998.[2] There were numerous sexual encounters as well as many other phone calls and meetings between Lewinsky and Clinton during the period. The affair surfaced as part of a civil lawsuit brought against President Clinton by Paula Jones, a former Arkansas civil servant, who claimed that Clinton had made inappropriate sexual advances toward her at an economic development conference while Clinton was governor of Arkansas. When asked about an affair with Lewinsky during a deposition related to the Jones lawsuit, Clinton denied having sexual relations with Lewinsky or ever having been in the same room alone with her. The White House Special Prosecutor, Kenneth Starr, who began his investigation with another Clinton scandal, the Whitewater land deal, began investigating the Clinton-Lewinsky affair as well.

On the morning of January 21, 1998, the *Washington Post,* the *Los Angeles Times,* and ABC News all broke the story, and by the end of the day, every media outlet in the nation could talk or write about nothing else. Analysts began predicting the end of the Clinton presidency. The initial response of the public was negative as well. Clinton's job approval sat at roughly 60 percent before the Lewinsky scandal, but his approval ratings immediately dropped by about 10 points. In addition, polls a few days after widespread coverage of the affair began showed that a majority of the public believed that his alleged perjury in the Lewinsky affair, if proven true, should result in impeachment or resignation.

By the end of January, however, only ten days after the scandal broke, Clinton's job approval rating bounced back to 70 percent in most polls—a

Examine polling data.

remarkable 10 points higher than it was before the scandal and the highest of his presidency. Three events happened during this time. First, President Clinton issued an emotional denial of the sexual affair and of lying about it. "I want you to listen to me," Clinton said, as he glared at cameras. "I'm going to say this again, I did not have sexual relations with that woman, Miss Lewinsky. I never told anybody to lie, not a single time—never. These allegations are false. And I need to go back to work for the American people."[3] Second, First Lady Hillary Rodham Clinton appeared on the *Today Show* and charged that there was a right-wing conspiracy against the president.[4] Finally, the president gave a heavily watched and positively received State of the Union address.

By midsummer, President Clinton admitted the affair both in grand jury testimony and to the American public in an August 17 speech to the nation. A few weeks later, on September 11, Special Prosecutor Kenneth Starr submitted his 463-page report to the House of Representatives. After a week of hearings before the House Judiciary Committee and several days of debate on the House floor, the House of Representatives impeached President Clinton on December 19, 1998. A majority of the House found that Clinton lied to a grand jury and that he had obstructed justice in attempting to cover up his affair with the former intern.[5] The Senate trial began on January 7, 1999, and continued for more than a month. On February 12, 1999, the Senate voted to acquit the president of both articles of impeachment. After more than a year, the attempt to impeach Clinton was over.

Throughout the tumultuous and historic events of fall 1998 and winter 1999, President Clinton's public support remained steady. Even more remarkable was the fact that at each major crossroads in the crisis—his admission of the affair in August 1998, delivery of the Starr report to the House in September 1998, Clinton's impeachment in December 1998, and his acquittal in the Senate in February 1999—President Clinton's job approval rating actually went up. For example, in the week before his impeachment (December 12 and 13, 1998), a Gallup poll found that 63 percent of Americans approved of the job Clinton was doing, and in a poll begun the day he was impeached, his approval had gone up 10 percentage points to 73 percent. Put in a slightly different light, the president's job approval was at 60 percent the week before the Lewinsky scandal broke and stood at 68 percent after his acquittal by the Senate. Although the public's approval of the president's job was clear, it is equally clear that the public thought Clinton's actions were morally wrong.[6]

Two important questions arise about the public's support of President Clinton during this more than year-long crisis: Why did the public continue to support President Clinton? What does this support tell us about public opinion in the United States?

There are several possible explanations for Americans' support of President Clinton.[7] One centers on Clinton's skill as a political operator. There is no doubt that Clinton was a remarkable political survivor and an excellent speaker, but there is little evidence that this was a crucial factor

Learn more about the impeachment of President Clinton.

during this scandal. Most important, Clinton didn't fool the American people. He lost their trust. A majority of Americans, even before his admission of the affair, believed that he lied about it. In January 2001, only 39 percent of Americans surveyed in a Gallup poll agreed that Bill Clinton was honest and trustworthy, and only 41 percent approved of Clinton as a person. Furthermore, no one saw incredible political skills in late 1993 and 1994, as his job approval sunk below 45 percent for much of the time and the Democrats lost control of both the House and the Senate in the 1994 elections. A second explanation focuses on Clinton's adversaries. Congressional Republicans were unpopular during the whole impeachment imbroglio, and Kenneth Starr, the special prosecutor who brought the scandal to light, was seen as mean-spirited rather than as a truth seeker. But again, this disapproval of Clinton's pursuers did not translate into support for Clinton. After his acquittal in the Senate, a *Washington Post* poll found that by a 54 to 42 percent margin, Americans blamed Clinton and not his accusers for the crisis.[8]

The more compelling explanation for Clinton's support is that Americans agreed with his policy positions and credited him with the fine state of the nation's economy. President Clinton's popularity rose as his positions on issues changed.[9] After his early policy fiascoes with health-care reform and support for gays in the military, Clinton staked out a mixture of moderate and conservative positions that resonated with the public. Welfare reform, open trade with Mexico and Canada, a balanced budget, increased crime fighting, and education are only a few examples. Clinton was also the beneficiary of a growing economy. Throughout his term, including during the scandal, real income grew and the stock market soared.

What does this tell us about public opinion? There are two important conclusions. First, the American people *can* understand policy and arrive at conclusions based on this understanding. At each crossroad, analysts predicted that the public would abandon their president, but they never did. While opinion was swayed for a short time by the salacious media coverage of the Clinton-Lewinsky scandal, the decline of support was short-lived. As time went on, Americans become even more convinced of their policy assessment. Second, public opinion *can* matter. It is hard to imagine that Clinton would have survived the Senate trial without strong public support. As the American people continued to stump the Washington pundits, Senate leaders became convinced that the best approach in handling the Senate trial was to make it go away as quickly and quietly as possible. It was time for the nation to move on.[10]

"Monica Lewinsky's Contribution to Political Science," John R. Zaller.

Citizen Participation in the Web of American Democracy

The public's support of President Clinton during the Lewinsky sex scandal and the subsequent impeachment process are examples of how citizen participation can be important in American politics today. Similarly, as discussed in Chapter 1, after much lobbying by victims' families and subsequent public support, the 9/11 Commission was created, despite the president's reluctance to do so. As we will detail in this chapter, the nation's citizens can play a significant role in the complex fabric that is American politics. And their role is larger now than at any time in American history. Chances are you think this is good: "Our nation is a democracy," you might say. "Clearly, the people should play an important role in government." But this has not always been the dominant view. The writers of the U.S. Constitution intentionally limited the role of the people in their government. In Chapter 1, we found that participation by the public was seen as a frightening concept throughout much of world history. The founders of the American republic knew that citizen participation was important to the success—even the continued existence—of the nation. At the same time, they were skeptical about the ability of the people to participate responsibly. As Madison wrote in *Federalist* No. 10,

Review *Federalist* No. 10

> The effect of [elite representation] is, on the one hand, to refine and enlarge the public views, by passing them through the medium of a chosen body of citizens, whose wisdom may best discern the true interest of their country, and whose patriotism and love of justice will be least likely to sacrifice it to temporary or partial considerations. Under such a regulation, it may well happen that the public voice, pronounced by the representatives of the people, will be more consonant to the public good than if pronounced by the people themselves, convened for the purpose.

The creation of the new national government distanced the governed from the governors. The citizenry directly elected only the House of Representatives in the new government. The Senate (selected by state legislatures until the early twentieth century in many states), the president (selected by the electoral college), and federal judges (nominated by the president and confirmed by the Senate) were all chosen, indirectly, by elite bodies. The government was further insulated from the majority faction, as James Madison called dominant public opinion, by the separation of powers in the national government and the division of power between the nation and the states. In short, our government was not designed to act based on mass public opinion; it was established as a government of elites checked by public opinion.

Over time, Americans have come to believe strongly in rule by the people. In a democratic government, we expect that the views of the public should matter in government decision making. This chapter examines the role of public opinion and political ideology in the web of American democracy. **Public opinion** is the collective view of the people on a political issue or idea. **Political ideology** goes further; it is a well-developed set of views that guides an individual's thinking on politics.

A great deal of time and effort is spent trying to understand what the American people think and believe about politics and issues of public concern. The most common way of gauging the views of Americans is through polling. It is now unusual for a day to pass without a headline about some important poll results, telling us what the American people think about a policy or who is leading an electoral race. If the government is going to respond to the people, our leaders must find out what the people know and think about politics and political issues.

These polls can be important in American politics. Public opinion can influence the decisions of our leaders. At times, leaders act because they want to fulfill the desires of their constituents. At other times, public opinion matters because it can be turned into votes; elected leaders fear removal from office. Public opinion can also influence individuals, who often have relatively little knowledge about or interest in politics. But discovering public opinion is hard, and although the techniques for studying it are sophisticated, they are also limited.

More active forms of participation—voting, for example—will be discussed in Chapter 8. Chapter 7 will investigate the role of groups—political parties and organized interests—in American politics. These three chapters, taken together, discuss the various ways that the American people communicate with their leaders and how this communication affects the behavior of government. We will examine what Americans know about politics and how Americans come to learn about our system. We will also look at the ways that Americans individually and collectively participate in politics. In investigating these issues, we want to keep in mind two questions: To what extent do the people participate in and influence politics in the United States? And to what extent should Americans participate in and influence politics?

Political Socialization: How Americans Learn About Politics

We saw in Chapter 1 that most Americans share a set of basic beliefs in democracy, individualism and civil liberties, private property and capitalism, equality, and American exceptionalism. Why is this so? Where does this nearly universal support come from? This raises broader questions: How do Americans learn about politics? How is individual public opinion formed? These questions are central to the study of **political socialization,** the process through which individuals learn about and form beliefs about government and politics. As we shall see, the process is complex and highly individualized. This helps create diversity in how we view candidates and government policy. Yet common sources of information are important for many of us, and Americans share basic values.

No one is born having political views and beliefs; rather, they are acquired through life experience. Childhood and adolescent experiences are particularly important in forming our views of the political world. Early learning is significant because it tends to be what we learn best. It influences how we process new information and ideas that we come in contact with later in life.[11] Early learning remains important in forming our views on the issues of the day as well as our general orientation toward politics.

Young children do not possess the capacity to understand much about abstract concepts such as politics and government. But by age six, children generally identify police officers as government officials, and they know who the president is. They often believe these officials have enormous power, far exceeding their real capacity to act.[12] They also have overall positive images of these officials. As children reach age ten, they often have an understanding of such concepts as elections, voting, and democracy, and they have a sense of nationalism. In a 1998 national survey, not only did 94 percent of fourth graders know that Bill Clinton was the president, but 77 percent knew that one must be eighteen years old and a citizen to vote.[13] By the age of fifteen or sixteen, many adolescents have developed views on issues and political party support similar to those of adults.

As adults, we continue to learn about politics and form views about political issues. Although we are predisposed to keep the political beliefs that we acquire as children and adolescents—especially core beliefs such as party identification, general ideological orientation (conservative or liberal), and racial attitudes—many events can alter our political beliefs throughout our lives.[14] These are especially likely to occur in early adulthood.[15] Examples include moving to a new region of the country, marriage and divorce, changes in social status, and acquiring or losing wealth. Attitudes about complex political issues are less likely to be consistent over time.[16]

Most of what we learn about politics is obtained informally. Although we learn about our political system in school—the course for which you are reading this text is an example—most of the learning takes place without an explicit lesson. Rather, we learn about politics through contact with family, experiences at school, interaction with social groups, and through the media. Key events during formative periods of our lives are also important in defining our political beliefs. These institutions and events are known as **agents of socialization.** As each agent of socialization is discussed in turn, ask yourself how it influenced your positive and negative views on politics as well as your attitudes on political issues. Did your family discuss politics? Do you know what the political attitudes of your parents are?

Family

For most people, parents and family are particularly important to political learning early in life. Children trust their parents and generally form strong bonds with them. Families help to shape personalities and define a child's worldview. This often causes children to parrot the political views of their parents. Typically, parents and other family members are not actively teaching their children about politics, but they do have conversations about politics and important local, national, and world events. Children pick up on their parents' political views and adopt them as their own. Although children might not understand a discussion of a complex issue such as the USA PATRIOT Act, they likely will understand and acquire

	Democrat	Independent	Republican
Both Parents Democrats	**59%**	29%	13%
Both Parents Independents	17%	**67%**	16%
Both Parents Republicans	12%	29%	**59%**

Table 5.1 Party Identification from Parent to Child. Children generally follow in their parents' footsteps when it comes to political party identification.

Source: 1992 National Election Study, Center for Political Studies, University of Michigan.

views on more basic concerns. Examples include more closely identifying with labor or corporations, developing attitudes about social class, and forming a perspective on the value of the natural environment.

Not surprisingly, parental views have the most powerful influence when the political views of the parents are clearly expressed. A relevant example is the way that political party identification is carried from parent to child (see Table 5.1). When both parents identify themselves as Republicans, for example, the child is likely to be a Republican as well. As the table shows, this is not true for everyone. Some children identify themselves as independents even when both parents have the same party affiliation, but only about one in eight children affiliates with the other major political party.

School

Schooling is profoundly important in the political socialization of American children as they grow older. From kindergarten through college, school is central to transmitting the core American beliefs discussed in Chapter 1 from generation to generation. As a nation, we have long acknowledged that a central goal of the U.S. public education system is to prepare citizens. Horace Mann (1796–1859), America's first great advocate of universal public education, put it this way:

> In order that men may be prepared for self-government, their apprenticeship must commence in childhood. The great moral attribute of self-government cannot be born and matured in a day; and if school children are not trained to it, we only prepare ourselves for disappointment.[17]

Schools did then and do now teach citizenship just as they teach reading, mathematics, and science. Schools have long been a major tool for Americanizing immigrants.

In general, the curricula of public schools are examples of a long-existing tension in American politics between encouraging uniformity and tolerating diversity. Currently, we see this tension in debates over school prayer, charter schools, and school vouchers, the teaching of creationism, as well as debates over the inclusion and exclusion of ethnic culture and history in the curriculum.

In school, students learn about politics in two distinct ways: through explicit instruction and through cocurricular activities that promote democratic citizenship and love of country. In **civic education** throughout the elementary and secondary years, students learn about important events and figures in our nation's political history. National holidays are recounted and celebrated; national heroes are praised. Students are taught that citizenship is both an important obligation and a source of rights and privileges. In addition, the Pledge of Allegiance is recited in most American schools at the beginning of each day. Developing a love of country—nationalism—is an important part of education in the United States.

Beyond formal instruction, students are taught about elections, democracy, and citizenship in a number of ways. Student government begins as early as first grade and takes on a growing role in high school. Students are taught to active citizens and taught that representative democracy is good. Selective programs such as Boys State and Girls State help mold future leaders with democratic values. Inside and outside the classroom, students are taught about rules and order. Even more broadly, children are taught about tolerance and differences by exposure to a wider range of people, often for the first time.

Generational Effects

For some people, major social events—the Great Depression of the 1930s and the social upheaval of the 1960s are two twentieth-century examples—can have a notable impact on their political thinking. These events can create important **generational effects** on public opinion. Millions of Americans who lived through the Great Depression became lifelong Democrats and have continued to view government as a positive force in society. The Depression took place when the Republican Party had been dominating national politics since the Civil War. It was the Franklin Roosevelt–led Democratic Party that instituted the New Deal, providing people with hope and with jobs. Previous generations had accepted the very small and inactive national government of the time, but this new generation applauded the new government programs and generally favored continued expansion of the national government for the last half-century. For later generations, the Great Depression was only a historical event that had a limited effect on their political beliefs. Four decades later, the Watergate crisis and the Vietnam War led many people coming of age at the time to become increasingly cynical about government and our elected leaders. It seems likely that 9/11 and the subsequent military actions in Afghanistan and Iraq will have a long-term impact on Americans' views on politics, but it is too early to tell what that impact will be. It is also possible that the Clinton impeachment has had a significant effect on many of the readers of this text.

View President Bush introducing history and civic education initiatives.

The 1968 Democratic convention.

Nixon's resignation speech.
These scenes are examples of the turbulent times of the Vietnam and Watergate eras. These events had an impact on the political views of a generation.

SARA K. SCHWITTEK/Reuters/Landov

Major events, such as the bombing of the twin towers of the World Trade Center in New York, New York, on September 11, 2001, can have a serious impact on political thinking for years to come.

The Media

The mass media—television, radio, newspapers and magazines, the Internet—have an influence on the views of adults and children alike. Television is particularly important because most Americans spend hours per day watching. Since television became widespread in the 1950s, American adults today spend 40 percent more time experiencing the media in general.[18] The world we experience through the media can control our actions. For example, suburbanites are frequently afraid to go downtown. Their knowledge of the city often comes almost exclusively through television news, which has focused heavily on violent crime over the last quarter-century. Although crime rates rose during the 1970s and 1980s, suburbanites' perception of crime grew much faster, but as crime declined in the 1990s, the public perception of America's cities was slow to change. Through the selection and placement of stories, the media can be particularly influential in defining what issues and stories are seen as important. Finally, the routine coverage of news events reemphasizes the socialization we get elsewhere. In general, news programming and the media rarely challenge the legitimacy of our system.[19] (For a more detailed discussion of the influence of news and entertainment programming on politics, see Chapter 6.)

Community Groups and Peers

Peers and the groups that people associate with also have an impact on individual political beliefs. This is especially true in late adolescence and adulthood. For the most part, these associations reinforce existing views. People make friends with, live among, work with, and join organizations with people who have similar beliefs. Among the groups that are likely to influence political views are churches and unions. Churches help develop strong belief systems that guide a person's views on social policies such as abortion as well as a larger worldview. Unions spend a good deal of energy promoting pro-union candidates and issues. In the case of both churches and unions, this influence can be powerful. However, as membership in both churches and unions has declined in recent decades, these institutions influence fewer Americans.[20] Interest groups are politically active; they promote issues of special concern to them and endorse candidates for political office.

Political Ideology: Are Opinions Connected?

When discussing the public opinions of Americans, we refer to a position as liberal or conservative. For example, supporting a woman's right to choose an abortion is the liberal position on that issue. Even if you do not follow politics on television or in newspapers, you have probably heard officeholders or positions described as liberal or conservative. Someone may have asked you if you are a liberal or conservative. You may be wondering what these terms mean and why they matter in the web of American democracy.

When we talk about liberal and conservative, we are attempting to characterize a **political ideology,** which is a well-developed set of views that guides an individual's thinking on politics. A political ideology provides a worldview that, if well developed, enables us to interpret and provide order to the world around us. As we will see in this discussion, Americans have divergent views about politics, but these ideological viewpoints are based on the core American beliefs discussed in Chapter 1. There is a narrower range of ideological positions in the United States when compared to many other democracies. There is no strong socialist tradition in the United States as there is in Europe. Europe also has a much more influential and well-defined environmental or "green" movement than in the United States. Similarly, in Europe a well-organized ultra-conservative movement exists in many nations. These movements are highly nationalistic and xenophobic. Although some Americans hold these views, they are small in number and not well organized.

The standard understanding of **liberals** is that they favor a more expansive role for government in solving society's problems. Liberals support environmental regulation and more government services, oppose the death penalty, and support abortion rights. Liberals also see equality as their primary political value. Conversely, the conventional view of **conservatives** is that they are characterized by a desire to constrain, or limit, the size of government, believing that private solutions are often the best way to work out societal ills. Conservatives favor business over government regulation, see the private sector as responsible for providing jobs, oppose abortion rights, and favor school vouchers. Conservatives value freedom and tradition more than equality. In addition, we often speak of a third category: **moderate,** or middle-of-the-road, Americans. These individuals characterize themselves as neither purely conservative nor purely liberal. Rather, they believe in a mixture of support for a strong government in some areas and a desire for limited government in other areas. The last three decades have seen only modest changes in the self-depiction of Americans' political ideology (see Figure 5.1). Currently, about 32 percent describe themselves as conservative, 23 percent declare themselves as liberal, and 26 percent characterize themselves as moderate.

Who are liberals and conservatives?

An Alternative View of Ideology

Interestingly, 19 percent of those questioned in the 2004 National Election Study—about one in five people—responded that they did not know what their ideology was. Although this seems like a high number, it is the lowest

Look at the results of the National Election Study.

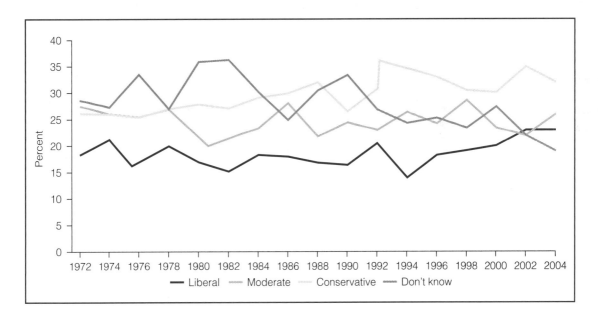

Figure 5.1 Ideological Self-Identification, 1972–2004. Although the self-identified political ideology of Americans has fluctuated in recent decades, there have consistently been more conservatives and moderates than liberals since 1972.

Source: 1972–2004 National Election Studies, Center for Political Studies, University of Michigan.

percentage of "don't knows" ever found in the National Election Study. Only about 55 percent of the respondents to the 2004 National Election Study defined themselves as either conservative or liberal. There is no question that Americans are not focused on the three categories that we have just described. Individuals often take positions that are neither consistently conservative nor liberal. In part, this is because Americans do not usually think in such grand terms. Remember, politics is only a small part of most people's lives. They are much more likely to think about specific issues—especially issues that affect them directly—than about some overarching view of politics. Therefore, the popular ideological terminology—conservative and liberal—is a problem. It is overly simplistic. Because we believe it is important for active citizens to think about where they fit in the American political spectrum, we have set out to create more useful descriptions of political ideologies. The following subsections present six ideological types that can be found in American politics today. As with any typology, it is a simplification of the world; not every possibility is listed. But we believe that these descriptions include the ideological positions of many, if not most, Americans.

Moralist Liberals

Described as idealists, this group is passionately committed to their particular political cause, believing that there is a realm of "right" which is often rooted in deeply held religious or spiritual convictions. **Moralist liberals** see their political role as striving to achieve a more just and equitable society. They often adopt a radical egalitarian perspective, championing the underrepresented and underprivileged elements in society. Willing to reject mainstream politics, they accept no policy as legitimate that does not adhere to their standard of justice. People who fall into this category are typically ardent pacifists and tend to adopt a more global understanding of the political landscape; they have opposed the military actions in Afghanistan and Iraq. They are often willing to disobey laws seen as contrary to their understanding of what is truly just or right. Individuals in this group tend to identify closely with environmental and feminist causes as well as multiculturalism.

New Deal Liberals

New Deal liberals are the traditional base of support for the Democratic Party in the United States. Their highest political values are equality and social progress. This group of people believes that the existing political system works. They generally try to achieve their ends through the use of mainstream strategies such as electoral politics and lobbying efforts. They are often involved in interest group politics. New Deal liberals support an active government that plays a positive role in improving the lives of individual citizens through policies designed to increase the income and security of

Cindy Sheehan, the mother of an Iraqi War casualty, became the face of the antiwar movement in the summer of 2005 when she camped out near President Bush's ranch outside of Crawford, Texas. She is shown here at a candlelight vigil with an Iraq veteran.

those in need. Based on this view, New Deal liberals are committed to organized labor (unions) and the family farmer. They are suspicious, if not antagonistic, toward the interests of corporations and big businesses. Generally, New Deal liberals view material economic benefits—such as health care—as rights that should be available to all.

Pragmatic Liberals

This group has values similar to New Deal and moralistic liberals, but they are tempered by a strong belief in capitalism and a willingness to compromise. More open to business and economic development, **pragmatic liberals** seek to bring about social progress more through economic growth than through redistributive policies. They have a positive view of the government, believing that it can and should be used to improve individual lives, but they are also open to nongovernmental solutions to public problems. More fiscally conservative than New Deal liberals, pragmatic liberals are also more likely to want to "reinvent" government rather than shrink it. Although principles matter to them, pragmatic liberals are willing to compromise with those who have different political orientations if progress toward their goals is made.

Traditional Conservatives

Committed to preserving the values and institutions that they believe are the real source of the nation's greatness and well-being, **traditional conservatives** are concerned with the decline in standards and civility in contemporary culture. They tend to extol the values of classic literature and philosophy and want to preserve the canons of Western culture. Traditional conservatives are suspicious of grand governmental programs designed to improve society. However, they believe that government is necessary to adjust the conflicting interests within society. Traditional conservatives are concerned with the integrity of nongovernmental institutions such as churches and schools. They encourage public service and volunteerism, and look to someone such as former Secretary of State Colin Powell as the embodiment of American values. They are supportive of business interests, although they often criticize the values associated with excessive materialism. Like pragmatic liberals, traditional conservatives can work with frequent opponents to reach common goals.

Individualist Conservatives

Individualist conservatives are committed to the idea of individual freedom and the nineteenth-century ideal of rugged individualism. They believe in limited government. Individualist conservatives believe in a strong national defense, but in domestic politics, they take the view that less is better: Government is more often the cause rather than the solution of social problems. Individualist conservatives are generally critical of government regulations of all types. They support the interests of business, particularly entrepreneurial initiatives, and tend to adhere to a free market economic philosophy. Following their preference for limited government, individualist conservatives are tolerant of various lifestyles, opponents of censorship, and strong advocates of the distinction between church and state. When pushed to an extreme, individualist conservatives become libertarians.

Political Awareness questionnaire. Complete a brief political awareness questionnaire that will place you in one of the six ideological types described in this section. You may be surprised where your ideology lies!

Moralist Conservatives

Rooted in a fundamentalist or evangelical religious perspective, **moralist conservatives** have a passionate commitment to a clear and true set of moral rights and wrongs, which comes from the word of God. Moralist conservatives want to uphold traditional values such as those of the nuclear family. They tend to be highly nationalistic and patriotic, often to the point of being isolationist and protectionist. Moralist conservatives are highly critical of the materialist values of consumer culture and are concerned with the perceived decline in the nation's moral character. They believe that the decline can be remedied through an infusion of church into the government. Moralist conservatives are often more interested in cultural politics (for example, the content of television programs) than in mainstream public policy issues. In contrast with other conservatives, they are willing to use government to help achieve their goals of such policies as mandatory school prayer, government censorship of objectionable and indecent materials, and the institution of covenant marriages. Moralist conservatives are opposed to abortion and to stem-cell research. They are highly antagonistic to alternative lifestyles and are opposed to gay marriage and civil unions. Moralist conservatives are an important part of President George W. Bush's political base.

How Much Do Americans Know About Politics?

We have been discussing the political views of Americans. How much faith should we place in these views? Do Americans express views about politics from a firm base of knowledge? We will address the first question later in the section, but the short answer to the second question is no, Americans do not have a firm base of political knowledge. Since the 1950s, political scientists have consistently found that many Americans have only limited knowledge of the political system. Two National Election Studies confirm this finding. A 1991 study (Figure 5.2) found that Americans have only limited knowledge of the basic rules of government. Although three-quarters of those surveyed knew in 1991 that the president can serve two four-year terms, only one-quarter knew that senators serve six-year terms. In the 1991 survey, only 23.4 percent answered at least five of six questions correctly, and 25.8 percent missed at least five of six questions. A second, more recent study shows limited knowledge, but it is also more promising. The 2004 National Election Study (Figure 5.3) indicates that many Americans do not know the jobs that important national and world leaders hold, nor do they know who is in control of Congress. While 86 percent of those surveyed knew that Dick Cheney was vice president of the United States in 2004, only 11 percent knew that Dennis Hastert (R-Ill.) was Speaker of the U.S. House of Representatives. About one-half of these surveyed knew that the Republicans held a majority of both the House and the Senate. Although these numbers are discouraging, Americans do gain knowledge about government and political leaders over time. For example, the National Election Study asked Americans to identify Tony Blair, the prime minister of Great Britain, in both 2000 and 2004. In 2004 almost twice as many of those surveyed could accurately identify Blair as in 2000.

Why do Americans know relatively little about politics? Three factors are needed for a person to learn about politics: the capacity to learn, the opportunity to learn, and the motivation to learn.[21] Some level of raw intelligence and education is important for political learning. Each of the fifty states requires that children attend school, and nearly all adult Americans

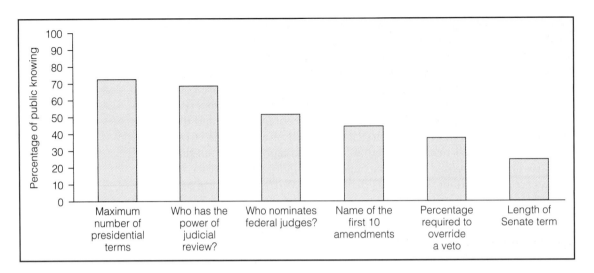

Figure 5.2 Knowledge of the American Political System. Americans have limited knowledge about the American political system.

Source: 1991 National Election Study, Center for Political Studies, University of Michigan.

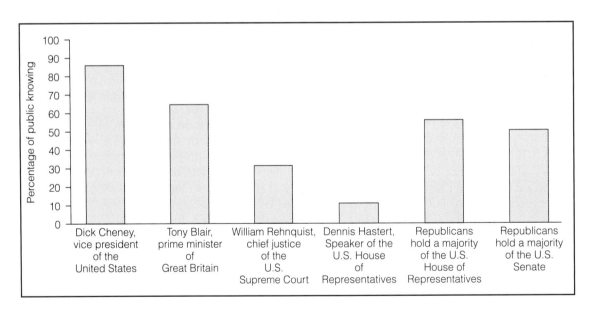

Figure 5.3 Knowledge of Political Leaders and Control of Congress. The percentage of Americans polled who know which leader holds the job listed or which party controls the two houses of Congress.

Source: 2004 National Election Study, Center for Political Studies, University of Michigan.

Do you know who this man is? In a 2004 survey of American adults, only 11 percent knew the name of the Speaker of the U.S. House of Representatives: Dennis Hastert (R-Ill.). Nancy Pelosi (D-Calif.) replaced Hastert as Speaker after the 2006 election.

can read and write. Most adult Americans have sufficient intellectual capacity to learn about politics, but the opportunity to learn and the desire to learn are more complicated.

With time and the proper research skills, one can uncover a remarkable amount of in-depth information about the U.S. government. As the participation exercise in Chapter 1 demonstrates, some information—the name of the vice president or a senator—is easy to find. And in an average local library or with an Internet connection, detailed information about and the text of proposed legislation and the voting records of a member of Congress are readily available. The United States is an open society. Government and

Learn about the U.S. government.

private organizations work hard to gather and disseminate information about government. Clearly, information is out there, but that is only part of what an opportunity to learn about politics means. An equally important aspect of the opportunity to learn is time. American adults are busy. The two wage-earner household and the lengthening workweek have exacerbated the burdens of modern life. Caring for children, maintaining a household, and educational and leisure activities leave little time for anything else. We wish it weren't so, but learning about politics is a chore, and it is work that relatively few people feel compelled to do. For many, after a long day of work and family life, the latest episode of *CSI: Crime Scene Investigation* or *American Idol* looks a good deal more appealing (and requires less mental alertness) than reading about the latest world crisis or policy debate.

In this light, you may be asking yourself other questions: Why does anyone ever learn anything about politics? What motivates Americans to develop and maintain political knowledge? First, for some Americans, learning, discussing, and participating in politics are enjoyable. Some people follow baseball, others watch the latest films, and some care about politics. Just as with baseball and film, there are magazines, newspapers, and websites that cater to a large group of political junkies. Another reason is that some issues are directly relevant to our life and work. For example, farmers often know a great deal about complex agricultural policy, and parents of school-age children are often knowledgeable about the implications of school budget changes. Third, there is a sense of **civic obligation.** Most of us agree that we should educate ourselves about the political world, and some act on that feeling of obligation.

Finally, civic involvement—engagement with the social and political community—is part of what makes us human. In modern American society, we are no longer encouraged to do this; rather, we focus on economic pursuits. As Americans increasingly "bowl alone" (see Chapter 1), as we interact less with the community around us, it is important to remember that political participation can increase our knowledge, broaden us, and create a more fulfilled life. Politics is humanizing.

The capacity, the opportunity, and the motivation to learn are clearly related. With even a small amount of capacity and motivation, one can learn some basic and important information about American politics. One can learn about what government is, but learning about what government does can be more difficult (see the text box, "What Americans Should Know about Politics"). The concepts and ideas are more complex, and details are often more difficult to come by. Thus, knowledge of what government does is likely to be acquired only by those of moderate or higher capacity to learn with high motivation. We should not be surprised that most people do not know or understand the details of complex public policy decisions.

Although it is disappointing that Americans do not know more about politics, the more important questions are whether this is crippling for political participation and democracy as well as who benefits from this lack of knowledge. The answer here is more complex. Political scientists

"Don't Know Much About Politics: The Curse of the Ignorant Voter," Kate O'Beirne.

"How Much Knowledge Does Democracy Require?" Eric R.A.N. Smith.

Michael X. Delli Carpini and Scott Keeter, authors of an important study of political knowledge, argue that although knowledge is lacking, a majority of Americans know enough about politics to function as citizens.[22] Furthermore, Benjamin Page and Robert Shapiro argue in their study of more than 1,000 poll questions, *The Rational Public*, that while individuals are not always well informed and individual polls are subject to the problems of validity discussed later in the chapter, "Americans' policy preferences are real, knowable, differentiated, patterned and coherent."[23]

The collective opinions of the American public do change, but they tend to change in response to significant events and other trends. This change, Page and Shapiro say, is rational. The public's response to the Clinton-Lewinsky scandal and the reaction to subsequent impeachment proceedings are yet another confirmation of this idea. Similarly, the erosion of support for the military action in Iraq has been based on three years of steady bad news and rising U.S. military death tolls.

Is there hope that Americans will be able to realistically know more about politics in the future than they know today? The pattern of political knowledge over the last half-century says no. Despite remarkable changes in communications and the increasing relevance of the rest of the world to Americans' lives, Americans have about the same level of political knowledge as they did in 1950. At the same time, it is remarkable that despite concern over our education system, the increasing superficiality of news coverage, and the widely reported alienation of the American public with politics, Americans are still as knowledgeable as they once were.[24] Although the World Wide Web holds a promise to educate—and the Internet has greatly expanded the amount of political information that is easily accessible—new technology can only help willing and motivated learners.

Only when Americans become more seriously engaged in the civic life of the nation will the political knowledge of the American public grow. The level of civic engagement is important. When the mass public is paying attention and is active in politics, it can have an impact. But when the public is less engaged, it leaves politics to the few.

What should Americans know about politics?

Measuring Public Opinion

Efforts to measure public opinion are at least as old as the United States. People are naturally curious about how others will vote and what they think about current political concerns. News organizations attempt to satisfy that appetite. Early efforts to gauge opinion were rudimentary compared to today's scientific polling. In the nineteenth and early-twentieth centuries, public opinion polls generally took the form of informal surveys. Newspapers and magazines asked readers to send in their views on candidates and issues. Other methods of measurement were estimates of crowd size at political rallies and the use of political party workers to estimate

The history of opinion polls.

candidate support. For the most part, these early surveys were not used to predict the outcome of elections.

By 1936, the magazine *Literary Digest*'s **straw poll** had for two decades fairly accurately predicted the outcome of the presidential election every four years. For the 1936 election, *Literary Digest* sent out more than 20 million surveys to households throughout the United States. Over 2.3 million people responded, and the survey showed a clear victory for the Republican candidate, Kansas governor Alf Landon. Of course, the poll was wrong. The Democratic candidate, incumbent Franklin Roosevelt, won a second term in one of the largest landslides in modern political history. This famous poll blundered by drawing its sample from lists of automobile owners, magazine subscribers, and telephone books, which were all signs of some wealth—and Republican voting—during the Great Depression. This example demonstrates many potential problems with polling, some of which will be discussed later in this section. But this poll is also important because it occurred when modern scientific polling was in its infancy. George Gallup, Elmo Roper, and others were creating a new business—the public opinion and polling business—which has grown immensely since. And by the way, the scientific Gallup poll correctly predicted the outcome of the 1936 presidential election.

Who Conducts Public Opinion Polls and Why?

Examine poll results.

Public opinion polls are widely used today for a variety of purposes. The most obvious as well as the most widespread use is to gather information about the views of a population. News organizations such as the *New York Times*, ABC News, and *Time* magazine regularly conduct polls to understand the political views of the American people. These surveys often ask citizens about the major issues of the day, about potential campaign match-ups, and whether they approve of the job public officials are doing.

Other special kinds of polls are also conducted on a regular basis. Two that are particularly pertinent at election time are tracking polls and exit polls. **Tracking polls** are often conducted in the late stages of a political campaign to gauge last-minute changes in candidate support on a daily basis. Pollsters survey a slightly changing group of voters over several nights, looking for trends in voter attitudes. These polls can help citizens and candidates alike get a feel for shifts in the political winds. **Exit polls** are used by major news organizations to predict the outcome of elections before the polls are closed and the votes are counted. Using sampling techniques, voters are interviewed as they leave the polling place. The use of exit polls became controversial in 1980 as the television networks reported the outcome of state-by-state returns in the presidential election early in the evening on the East Coast, long before the polls closed west of the Mississippi River. When the incumbent, President Jimmy Carter, conceded the election to Ronald Reagan before the polls closed in the western states, many feared that it would reduce voter turnout in these states and have an impact on the outcome of other races. Although the networks are now more careful in their reporting of exit polls, the 1980 scenario could happen again. The 2000 presidential election showed an additional problem with exit polls: In close elections, they can be unreliable. The television networks' problem in declaring a winner in Florida is an example. First they declared Gore the winner, then Bush was given the victory, and finally the networks declared Florida too close to call. Making the problem worse is the growing number of absentee ballots, ballots cast by voters before election day. The larger the number of absentee voters, the less reliable exit polling will be.

Why do news organizations conduct public opinion polls? One reason, mentioned earlier, is to try to provide insight on what Americans think and how they are likely to vote. Polls clearly generate interest with the American public. Just as important, however, is that polling creates exclusive news that a newspaper, magazine, or television network hopes will draw readers or viewers. News organizations seek to make news by polling. The practice of media polling also contributes to the dominant pattern of media coverage of elections: horse race stories. Polling makes it possible for such stories to be written (see Chapter 6).

In addition to news organizations, candidates for elective office, incumbents, and interest groups frequently conduct polls. Decisions about whether to run or not are often based on polling data. Candidates and elected officials alike use polls to find issues that resonate with the American people and to discover how best to present their viewpoints to voters. Modern presidents seek to know what Americans think about a whole range of issues. In addition, the results of polls are often used to raise campaign funds early in a race. Reporting strong early support in the polls, a candidate can often raise money from potential donors who first want to be sure that a candidate is viable before writing a check. Similarly, poll results may prove helpful late in a campaign. "The race is close," the candidate might report to a potential donor. "I need your contribution to ensure victory."

Presidents of the United States are particularly voracious users and commissioners of polls.[25] Beginning with President Kennedy in 1961, presidents have conducted and analyzed public opinion for themselves. They use these poll results in two distinct ways. First, they use them to develop political strategies and agendas. Presidents look at what is popular as one factor in deciding what policy solutions to pursue. Second, polls are used to manage opinion. Presidents cite their polls as indicators of public support and seek to use the results to gauge the effectiveness of their appeals to the public. Bill Clinton was a particularly active user of polling data. More than presidents before him, Clinton looked to the polls to decide on policy options to pursue.

President George W. Bush claimed upon taking office that his policy goals would not be poll driven.[26] Time has proven him at least partially right. Bush's aides make wide use of polling data, but unlike his predecessors, Bush himself does not review polling data.[27] Strong public support of his leadership and his objectives certainly bolstered Bush's decision to go to war in Iraq in 2003. However, as support for the war effort and the Bush presidency declined notably in 2005 and 2006, he continued to insist that the United States would stay in Iraq until the job was done. As he said in August 2005, "Our efforts in Iraq and the broader Middle East will require more time, more sacrifice and continued resolve."[28] At times, President Bush has advocated policy changes despite the polls. He was notably unsuccessful in 2005 when he pushed a major revision to the Social Security system (see Chapter 10). The more he talked to the American people about his proposal, the less Americans supported it.

Other elected officials also use these same strategies. Newt Gingrich and congressional Republicans used public opinion research both to develop their Contract with America, a strategy to take control of the House of Representatives in 1994, and to gauge the success of their efforts during the fall 1994 campaign.

Interest groups sponsor many legitimate, well-done public opinion surveys, but sometimes groups, political parties, candidates, and elected officials conduct polls for less than honorable purposes. One analyst describes these as "pseudo-polls."[29] An example is the mail-in surveys often sent by state legislators to constituents. At times, the questions are slanted to encourage the respondent to agree with the legislator. Although an elected official may have a genuine interest in the views of his or her constituents, for the most part pseudo-polls are simply efforts to curry the favor of voters by showing that their legislator cares about their views.[30] Political parties and interest groups also use polls as part of fund-raising appeals. At the end of a mail-in survey, often containing slanted questions, the respondent is asked for a donation. Similarly, an interest group will sometimes commission polls containing questions carefully written to show support for the group's point of view.

An even more nefarious use of survey research is the **push poll.** These are phone calls, often made just before the election, in which the interviewer seems to want to understand your views, but instead wishes to give you negative information about an opponent. The goal is to "push" the respondent away from voting for a particular candidate.

Most public opinion polls are conducted with an interest in democracy: They seek to understand what the American people think about important issues. But there are many other interests that motivate the growing number of public opinion polls. Making news, persuading voters and campaign donors, and communicating a point of view are all examples.

A Citizen's Guide to Public Opinion Polling

As a citizen, you should be a discerning reader of polls. Since the 1930s, the number of polling organizations and the sheer number of polls reported have grown immensely. These surveys both inform us and at times confuse us. Like the growth of information generally, the mass of public opinion data thrown at us on a regular basis can be overwhelming. As we just discussed, we are right to question the honesty and intent of some polls, but most polls reported in the media are of high quality. This does not mean, of course, that you should accept every fact you read or hear. Public opinion polls can provide useful information, or they may be nothing more than an enjoyable diversion. However, because polls are powerful tools, in the wrong hands they can also create misinformation.

One critical distinction is whether or not a poll is based on the principles of **scientific sampling** (discussed in the next section). One should always be wary about the results of unscientific pseudo-polls. These polls come in many varieties, such as Internet polls, shopping mall polls, person on the street interviews, magazine surveys, and phone-in polls. The results of these surveys may be interesting—it is fun to discover which team that ESPN's Internet site visitors think will win the Super Bowl, the dating habits of fellow readers of a magazine, or which candidate callers think won a debate. However, such polls are not likely to provide an accurate portrait of public opinion. Elected officials and interest groups widely use these polls, but they are not scientific.

The following section presents a series of questions to ask when presented with public opinion polling data. With answers to as many of these questions as possible, you as a citizen will be able to evaluate the validity of the poll and analyze the data for yourself.

How Is a Scientific Poll Conducted?

Many people cannot understand how pollsters can know what Americans think about an issue without having talked to them personally or at least having interviewed someone they know. A survey by the Gallup Organization on the level of trust Americans have for public opinion surveys—yes, it was a poll on polls—found that most Americans did not believe that a poll of 2,000 or fewer people could represent the views of American adults. Yet scientific public opinion polling is based on well-established mathematical and statistical principles known as **probability sampling.** When polls are done well, their results are quite reliable statistically. The particulars are complicated and require the use of mathematical formulas that most of us—the authors included—would not understand. However, the underlying idea of the probability sample is fairly simple: By interviewing a small number of individuals—typically between 1,000 and 1,500 people—one can understand the views of an entire population, be it a nation, a state, or any group whose opinions one cares to know about, provided that each person has an equal chance of being selected for an interview. The goal is to produce a sample that is exactly the same as if the entire population was interviewed.

A random sample does not mean that the names of people to interview are simply picked out of a hat. Rather, a process called **cluster sampling** is used. To create a sample, the members of a polling organization might begin by picking regions of the country. Within each region, they pick a number of counties, and within each county, they select one or more cities or towns. In the city or town, they choose a group of blocks or a series of telephone exchanges. They then choose households or phone numbers in each of the subareas. At each stage, the choices are random, usually with a computer program making the selection. For example, a pollster's computer might begin with the Southwest; then select Dallas County, Texas; and then select the city of Richardson (a suburb of Dallas) within the county. Within Richardson, it might pick a number of residential blocks (the 400 block of Canyon Creek Drive, for example) or a few telephone exchanges (972-248-XXXX) and then select specific households to contact. The poll is random in that it identifies a location of a household, not a specific person to interview.

Most interviews are now done by telephone using computer-assisted telephone interviewing programs. This method helps reduce errors in data entry and makes data analysis faster. To further ensure a random sample, pollsters generally try to contact interviewees multiple times if they do not reach them the first time. Otherwise, the sample would be made up of older married people, who are more likely to be home and who spend less time on the phone.

Who Conducted and Sponsored the Poll?

Many polls discussed in the media are conducted by or for the media organizations themselves. Most major newspapers, television networks, and newsweeklies (*Time, Newsweek,* and *U.S. News & World Report*) conduct polls or contract with others to conduct polls for them on a regular basis. These polls are generally professional, and after considering the questions that follow, you can often learn from them. Professional polling organizations, such as Gallup and Harris, have a vested financial interest in maintaining the integrity of their polling processes.

Interest groups, candidates, elected officials, and others also conduct or contract for polls. They too may be reliable, but take extra care with these polls. Remember, simply bringing the public's views to light is only one potential reason for a survey. If you cannot figure out who paid for the poll or who conducted it, you are best to be wary of the motives and the results.

How Many Persons Were Interviewed?

It is important to know the sample size of the poll. As we saw with the 1936 *Literary Digest* poll, a large sample does not guarantee poll accuracy. However, in scientific surveys, the number of persons in the sample is key because the larger the sample, the more statistically accurate the results are likely to be in general. The reason is that as the sample gets larger, the **sampling error**—the potential difference between the sample gathered and the population from which the sample was drawn—becomes smaller. For a sample of 100 people, the sampling error is 10 percent, but for 1,000 to 1,500 people, the sampling error drops to 3 percent. The benefits of a larger sample diminish quickly, however, as a sample of 5,000 still has a 2-percent **margin of error.** Most polls conducted by major news organizations have

	Poll Result	Range of Error
Candidate A	51%	48%–54%
Candidate B	49%	46%–52%

Table 5.2 An Example of Sampling Error. Question: Who would you vote for if the election were held tomorrow?

$N = 1250$; sampling error $= \pm 3$ percent.

Source: Simulated data.

samples in the 1,000 to 1,500 range because they believe that this size best balances the goal of an accurate poll with the costs of conducting a poll. The sampling error is usually stated as "plus or minus (±) 3 percent." In practice, this means that if a poll, such as the one in Table 5.2, with a sample of 1,250 people found that 51 percent of likely voters support Candidate A, there is a high degree of confidence—about 19 of 20 samples—that between 48 percent (51 − 3) and 54 percent (51 + 3) of the electorate support the candidate. For most purposes, this is sufficiently detailed. Sometimes in a tight election race, however, 3 percent does not allow the reader to know clearly who is ahead. In Table 5.2, you see that given the margin of error, the support for the two candidates overlaps, making the race too close to call. On election night and beyond, the 2000 presidential election remained too close to call because the exit polling in many states was too close to call.

How Are the People in the Survey Characterized?

It is important to know from what population the sample was drawn: Who was interviewed for the poll? This can have an impact on the accuracy and interpretation of the results. Was the sample of "American adults," "registered voters," or "likely voters"? These distinctions may seem picky, but they are important. For a survey on presidential performance, a sample of average American adults makes sense, but if your goal is to understand who will win the presidential election, then a sample of likely voters will provide more accurate results. A related issue concerns minority groups. A standard national sample of 1,000 to 1,500 people will contain too few blacks or Hispanics to interpret the views of these groups accurately. Sometimes a process called **oversampling** is used so that there is a more sizable sample of smaller groups. Similarly, pollsters sometimes use **weighted results** of polls so that the results correspond to the demographics of the population being studied.

How Were the Questions Worded?

A major concern in any public opinion poll is the **wording of the questions.** It is fairly easy to ask a question that will elicit the response one wants. Knowing this, news organizations are careful in how they word questions.

Compare poll results.

Being careful does not mean that the job is easy or that the pollster will be successful. For example, people are much more likely to favor "spending on the poor" or "needy" than "welfare spending," although the two questions are asking about the same thing and the wording does not seem biased. Public opinion surveys are highly sensitive instruments. They must be carefully constructed to be successful. This fact also means that polls can be easily manipulated, which is why proponents and opponents of controversial issues such as abortion and gun control can each cite survey results that support their positions.

A similar concern is the ordering of questions. Sequencing can have a substantial impact on survey results. Sometimes, previous questions will help prime a respondent. During an economic recession, for instance, presidential approval ratings will be higher if the approval question is asked before questions about the state of the nation's economy. To guard against this, polling organizations will test the ordering of questions. Some polling organizations publish the questions in order, with their exact wording. Others place them on websites, and most reputable polling organizations will send a copy of a particular survey if asked.

When Was the Poll Conducted?

The **timing of a poll** can be important in interpreting its meaning. The dates on which the survey was conducted are usually reported with the results. So, for example, was the survey of presidential approval taken before or after an international crisis began? If the crisis was handled well, we would expect the president's support score to increase afterward. Was the election poll completed before or after the debate in which one candidate clearly stumbled? Such a performance may divide voter support of the candidate. No clearer example can be found than the change in President Bush's approval ratings before and after the 9/11 attacks. In late August 2001, the *New York Times*/CBS poll found 50 percent of those surveyed approved of the job that George W. Bush was doing as president. By September 14, the *New York Times*/CBS poll found that Bush's approval rating had soared to 84 percent.[31] (For a detailed discussion of President Bush's approval ratings, see Chapter 10.) Although this change is unusual, major events regularly move presidential approval ratings, at least for a short time.

How Was the Poll Conducted?

Most surveys are now done by telephone, but some are conducted by mail or in person. Each method has its own strengths. One of the advantages of computer-assisted telephone polling is that results can be reported quickly—even the same day on television—after the poll is completed. Creating a good sample is relatively easy with telephone polls, and they are less costly than in-person interviews. There is some minimal inherent bias in phone polls. Although 95 percent of Americans have phones, those who do not are

REPORTING A SURVEY: AN EXAMPLE

The text that follows describes a March 9, 2000, poll that appeared in the *Wall Street Journal* under the title "Race, Religion & Politics." (Note: An oversample is an effort to ensure that there are enough interviews with a relatively small group of the population, such as blacks and Hispanics, to allow separate analysis of this group's data.)

How the Poll Was Conducted

The *Wall Street Journal*/NBC News poll was based on nationwide telephone interviews of 1,213 adults, conducted Thursday to Sunday, March 2–5, by the polling organizations of Peter D. Hart and Robert M. Teeter. (In addition to the main sample of 1,213, there were 156 interviews on certain questions among an oversample of blacks, for a total of 266 interviews among blacks, and 155 interviews among an oversample of Hispanics, for a total of 231 interviews among Hispanics.)

The main sample, black oversample, and Hispanic oversample were drawn, respectively, from 505, 105, and 105 randomly selected geographic points in the continental United States. Each region was represented in proportion to its population. Households were selected by a method that gave all telephone numbers, listed and unlisted, an equal chance of being included.

One adult, eighteen years or older, was selected from each household by a procedure to provide the correct number of male and female respondents.

Chances are 19 of 20 that if all adults with telephones in the U.S. had been surveyed, the finding would differ from these poll results by no more than 2.9 percentage points in either direction among all adults, 6.1 percentage points among all blacks (when the oversample is included), and 6.6 percentage points among all Hispanics (when the oversample is included). Sample tolerances for subgroups are larger.

The *Wall Street Journal* does an excellent job of explaining the survey in this description. The sponsor of the poll, its size and makeup, and a discussion of sampling error are all presented. This discussion, which is typical of what is provided by major publications, but not typical on television, is generally of high quality.

poorer than those who do. Because random dialing, not the phone book, is used to contact people, unlisted numbers are not a problem. Mail surveys are inexpensive, and the privacy they provide the respondent can bring in detailed responses. However, they take a long time to conduct, and relatively few people respond. Furthermore, the sponsor never knows for sure who completed the survey. In-person interviews are still used by some groups. They allow for longer questionnaires—people feel more obligated face-to-face than over the phone—and get the highest response rates. People are also more truthful in person. However, in-person surveys are expensive to conduct. Face-to-face surveys are more likely to be conducted by academic researchers than by participants in the political process.

Where Do I Find This Information?

View major news organization poll archives.

When newspapers and newsweeklies report on polls they sponsor, information similar to that just presented will generally appear as a sidebar somewhere near the story. Quick summaries are often given in television reports. This information is less likely to appear if a news organization is simply reporting the results of polls completed by others. With the growth of the World Wide Web, it is likely that if you know who conducted or sponsored the poll, you will be able to find details about the survey on their website. Major news and polling organizations typically keep archives of polls on their websites. These archives generally include all of the key information you need to analyze a survey.

Conclusion: Public Opinion and Public Policy

Check here for possible post-publication updates to the chapter material.

Public opinion creates a voice of the American people that is often heard by our leaders. The Clinton impeachment trial example is important. The creation of the 9/11 Commission and the reorganization of the federal government in the area of homeland security are other examples. Studies by numerous political scientists over the last twenty years show that government institutions—Congress, the president, and even the courts—often support and create policies that agree with public opinion as measured through polls. Congress passes laws that agree with public opinion, presidents push policy that has public support, and a majority of the decisions by the U.S. Supreme Court find majority support by the American people. When public opinion moves, public policy often moves with it.[32]

Public opinion and the death penalty.

Does this mean that government officials are simply following the polls and abrogating their jobs as leaders? No, or at least not most of the time. Our leaders also seek to shape opinion. Presidents, congressional leaders, and others spend a good deal of effort "going public": communicating about what is important to them with the people and trying to convince the people that their position is the correct one. Not surprisingly, policy change often results when leaders are successful in convincing the people that they are correct.

Public opinion, while important, does not run rampant over our government. The influence of public opinion is constrained by the structure of our government; our complex system of elections and overlapping governmental power makes change difficult in American politics. But public opinion is an important asset. It is better to have the American people on your side than against you. Public opinion can help persuade others that your position is the one they should take for their own. Thus, public opinion is not left to go where it may. Elected leaders and others do not only seek to know opinion; they seek to influence and manage it as well.

Key Terms

public opinion   126
political ideology   126
political socialization   127
agents of socialization   128
civic education   130
generational effects   130
political ideology   132
liberals   132
conservatives   133
moderates   133
moralist liberals   134

New Deal liberals   134
pragmatic liberals   135
traditional conservatives   136
individualist
    conservatives   136
moralist conservatives   136
civic obligation   140
1936 *Literary Digest's* straw
    poll   142
tracking polls   142
exit polls   142

push poll   144
scientific sampling   145
probability sampling   145
cluster sampling   145
sampling error   146
margin for error   146
oversampling   147
weighted results   147
wording of the questions   147
timing of a poll   148

Suggested Web Resources

The following websites are related to the study of public opinion.

The *Washington Post* provides an excellent and detailed account of the Clinton impeachment (**http://www.washingtonpost.com/wp-srv/politics/special/clinton/clinton.htm**).

Polling data can be found at a variety of sites, including the Gallup Organization, one of the oldest and most respected polling firms (**http://www.gallup.com**); the Roper Center for Public Opinion Research, which is affiliated with the University of Connecticut (**http://www.ropercenter.uconn.edu**); and the Pew Research Center for the People and the Press, which does regular national surveys that study policy views as well as attentiveness to the media (**http://pew-people.org**).

Among the major news organizations, the *Washington Post* (**http://www.washingtonpost.com/wp-srv/politics/polls/polls.htm**) and the *New York Times* (**http://www.nytimes.com/library/national/index-polls.html**) provide outstanding archives of polls they have run. The *Post* provides

a searchable database of all polls it has conducted in the past year and presents the data in graphs as well as tables. The site also provides an excellent directory of polls on the Web (**http://www.washingtonpost.com/wp-srv/politics/polls/datadir.htm**). An excellent blog by Marc Blumenthal, mysterypollster.com, examines polls on a regular basis (**http://www.mysterypollster.com/main**).

The Polling Report provides polling data from many sources. The polls are well organized by topic and date. Major categories include politics and policy, the economy, and the American scene. Another outstanding source of public opinion data on policy issues is PublicAgenda.com (**http://publicagenda.com**). Public opinion polls and nonpartisan issue guides are provided on a diverse array of issues, including abortion, campaign finance, major social programs, the death penalty, and health care.

Major academic sources of social science data are the National Opinion Research Center (**http://www.norc.uchicago.edu**), which conducts the

General Social Survey, and the National Election Study (NES) (**http://www.umich.edu/~nes**). Both sites describe the major research they do and allow you to download data sets to analyze. Data at both sites go back more than forty years.

For tables and charts on key questions from the 2004 National Election Study, go to the NES Guide (**http://www.umich.edu/~nes/nesguide/ nesguide.htm**). The site also provides a good deal of historical data.

A complete study tool kit is available for this chapter and includes the following:
Flashcards
Crossword Puzzle
Critical Thinking Exercises
Interactive Timelines
Chapter Quiz

The Media and American Politics

■ **Bloggers Take Down Dan Rather:
   The Ascendancy of the "New Media"**   154

■ **Introduction: Defining the Mass Media**   156
   Media Formats   156
   Media Audiences   159
   Programming Objectives   160

■ **The New Media**   160

■ **The Changing Role of the Media in
   the Political Process**   163
   A History of News in America   164
   From the Press to the Media   165

■ **Media Ownership Trends**   167

■ **The Question of Bias**   168
   Sources of Structural Bias   171

■ **The Mediated Electoral Process**   173
   Free Media   173
   Paid Media   174
   Televised Debates   176

■ **The Media and Agenda Setting**   178

■ **The Media and Political Socialization**   179

■ **Conclusion: Participation and the Media**   180

Bloggers Take Down Dan Rather: The Ascendancy of the "New Media"

Dan Rather on his final CBS Evening News Broadcast.

View an interactive timeline: "The Unraveling of Rather's Report," created by the Poynter Center.

On November 23, 2004, Dan Rather announced that he was stepping down from his position as the anchor of *CBS Evening News*. Unlike Tom Brokaw, his counterpart at NBC, who had announced much earlier that he planned to retire after the 2004 presidential election, Rather had given no previous indication that he was considering stepping down from the position he held since taking over from Walter Cronkite in 1981. Rather's position at CBS, as well as his status as one of the nation's most well-known and respected journalists, changed September 8, 2004, after a story reported by Rather aired on the CBS Wednesday *60 Minutes* program. As the CBS News website story about his retirement noted, "Rather has come under fire for his *60 Minutes* report on President Bush's service in the National Guard during the Vietnam War. The report relied on documents that cast Mr. Bush's service in a negative light. Critics charged that the documents were forgeries, and CBS News was unable to vouch for their authenticity."[1] But the CBS story did not describe the process through which these allegations came to light.

Issues and questions about George W. Bush's National Guard service during the Vietnam War were nothing new. They had been raised during the 2000 presidential election as well as during his campaigns for governor in Texas. However, there had never been any evidence that demonstrated unequivocally that Bush had gotten special treatment or had failed to fulfill his military obligations. The *60 Minutes* report purported to have finally unearthed such documentation in the form of memos that were supposed to have been written by Bush's commander during the time of his National Guard service—certainly a journalistic achievement worthy of note during a presidential election. The problem was, as CBS was later to admit, the documentation that the report relied on was a forgery. The fallout from the report was significant, eventually resulting not only in Rather's decision to step down from the anchor chair but also in the firing of four CBS executives and producers.[2]

As significant as the incident was, there was more to the story than might be evident at first glance. CBS accepted responsibility for airing a story based on false evidence. It acknowledged that CBS News failed to properly authenticate its sources before airing the story and, as mentioned earlier, fired a number of employees as a result of its own investigation into the incident.[3] But the CBS version of the incident did not note where the evidence that the documents were forged had come from, nor did it describe the process through which the questions about the memo's authenticity were raised. Looking in more detail at how the forgery story first came to light tells us a great deal about the changed and continually changing contemporary media environment. CBS undertook its internal investigation only after questions about the veracity of the documents were raised by other media.

As *New York Times* columnist William Safire noted in the days following the story, the journalistic community, most specifically the Associated Press, began to examine fairly quickly the evidence that *60 Minutes* used in its story, but only after "a blogger on the Web site Freerepublic.com" raised questions about the typeface used in the memos. It seems that typewriters used at the time the memo was alleged to have been written were not capable of printing the specific "superscripts" that appeared on the document.[4] Before the broadcast was over, bloggers had started to point to the superscripts as evidence that the documents were fake. Within four hours of the airing of the story, more-mainstream media were beginning to look into the issue as well. Although there are still all sorts of open questions about the documents—who forged them, how they got into the hands of the folks at CBS, and who, if anyone, was behind the forgeries (as well as the bloggers unmasking them)—one thing seems clear: The incident highlights the increasing conflicts between the "new media" and the "old media."[5]

Blogs are part of the "new media," a concept that will be covered in more detail later in the chapter. The term "blog" began to appear in the late 1990s. Initial versions of blogs were referred to as "web logs," which rather quickly morphed into the now familiar term "blog." When they started, blogs were generally the online musings of individuals on everything from their own personal struggles to the major events of the day. In 1999 there were a handful of blogs on the Web, but in 2006 there are millions that touch on just about any topic imaginable, as well as some that are hard to imagine. Part of this explosion is attributed to the development of software and websites that made it easy to create blogs as well as to find the writings of other bloggers in cyberspace. Blogger.com, launched in 1999, was the first major step in making it possible for virtually anyone with a computer and online access to have his or her own blog. The growth since then has been astronomical, and as the above incident illustrates, the writings of bloggers have begun to challenge the mainstream media in a variety of ways.[6]

Watch a story on bloggers.

Dan Rather epitomizes the "old" media. CBS News is part of one of the five major media corporations that dominate the mainstream media in the United States. CBS News has a long and gloried journalistic tradition in reporting the news in a manner that most Americans have trusted. When Rather's predecessor, Walter Cronkite, used to end his broadcasts with the saying, "And that's the way it is," Americans believed him without question.

With Rather's resignation in March 2005, the retirement of Tom Brokaw in December 2004, and the death of Peter Jennings from lung cancer in August 2005, the old media television news landscape in the United States changed dramatically in the space of about nine months. One illustration of this is that the American public no longer trusts television news to report fairly and accurately on the events of the day to the extent that they used to. The reports of all mainstream media are now regularly open to criticism by the millions of bloggers who regularly attempt to refute the messages broadcast and written by "old" media sources. In the process, bloggers have become a visible presence in American politics. In addition to the Rather incident, bloggers were also instrumental in forcing Senator Trent Lott (R-Miss.) to step down as the majority leader of the Senate, in forcing the resignation of a CNN producer for comments he made about the military in the Iraq war, and for exposing the somewhat dubious credentials of a White House journalist, as well as a number of other incidents.[7]

Whether this transformation of the American media landscape is ultimately a good or bad trend depends on one's perspective. On the one hand, blogging is inherently democratic: Any citizen can have her or his say about the events of the day without constraint and with minimal resources. On the other hand, the "old media" have canons of professional ethics and standard journalistic practices that, while not always successful, attempt to verify the truthfulness of claims that are made in stories. There are no editors or publishers in the blogosphere to hold individuals accountable for their stories. In fact, bloggers often write under assumed names. A blogger who made the kind of errors involved in the Rather story can't be fired if he or she puts forth a falsehood. All of this can easily leave the individual citizen in a bit of a quandary in terms of navigating the current media landscape.

Introduction: Defining the Mass Media

To understand the role of the mass media in the political process, it is first necessary to learn something about the media themselves. What are the mass media? The **mass media** include any method of communicating the same message to large numbers of people more or less at the same time. Different types of media exist. They can be distinguished based on the technologies they use to convey information, the primary audience receiving the information, and the main objective of the medium under consideration.

Media Formats

The oldest form of media is print. In **print media,** messages are conveyed through the written word on paper. The print media also make use of still photographs. The main forms of print media today are newspapers and magazines. To publish print media, one needs access to paper and some type of reproduction technology. However, to create print media capable of being read by large numbers of people (that is, mass media), printing plants, distribution networks, and people to gather, write, and edit the words and pictures are necessary. To access the print media, a person needs to be able to read and must purchase the newspaper or magazine. Print media require a certain amount of "lead time" to write, print, and distribute before an individual can read them.

More Americans now get their news through broadcast and electronic technologies, such as television and radio, than from the print media. **Broadcast media** can send messages in "real time." Radio is limited to transmitting sound, whereas television carries video images, which include pictures, sound, and movement. To transmit messages via broadcast media, one needs expensive transmission equipment as well as a government license. This presents a barrier that only large corporations with major sources of revenue can overcome. To access the broadcast media, a person must own a radio or television that can translate the silent and invisible airwave signals into sounds and images that human beings can decipher. After the initial purchase, broadcasts are available without direct monetary cost to the listener and/or viewer. The technology of over-the-air broadcast television permits only a limited number of channels to be aired at the same time in the same location. The new delivery technologies of cable and direct satellite enable more channels to be delivered with clearer signals. These technologies involve additional equipment and charges from the service provider. The providers can also demand additional fees for certain "premium" programming.

Over time, the public has altered its media consumption habits as well as its collective perception of which media format is most credible. Starting in 1963, the public increasingly came to rely on television and television news as its primary source of information regarding public affairs. At the same time, the public began to feel that television is a more trustworthy and credible source of information than are the print media. Although there may be reasons to question such a judgment, network television clearly is the venue of choice for most Americans when they want to learn about political and current events.

The newest form of communications technology is also electronic, but its mode of access is the computer. The **Internet** had its origin in the early 1960s as a means for scientists to share data; it was not until the late 1980s that it began to have wider applicability. During the 1990s, its use and pervasiveness spread, so that in 2000 it was estimated that over 64 percent of Americans have access either at home, at school, or at work.[8] In 2000 the percent of American adults having access to the Internet was 56 percent; in 2004 that figure reached 68 percent. With the increasing availability of the Internet, questions about the **"digital divide"** have become less pressing. At the same time, it is still the case that access to the Internet is not spread evenly throughout the population; those who have less income, those who are members of racial minority groups, and those with less education are less likely to own computers and have access to the Net than are middle-class whites. In addition, there is also clearly a "generation gap" with respect to the Internet; 84 percent of those aged 18–29 have access to the Net, but only 26 percent of those over 65 have access (see Table 6.1).

The Ever Decreasing Digital Divide: Demographics of Those Online in 2000 and 2005		
	2000	2005
All Adults	56%	—
Gender		
Men	58%	74%
Women	54%	71%
Race		
Whites	57%	73%
Blacks	43%	61%
Hispanics	47%	76% (English speaking)
Age Cohorts		
18–29	75%	88%
30–49	65%	84%
50–64	51%	71%
65+	15%	32%
Income Brackets		
Under $30,000	38%	53%
$30,000–$50,000	64%	80%
$50,000–$74,000	72%	86%
$75,000+	82%	91%
Educational Attainment		
High school or less	37%	—
Less than high school	—	40%
High school	—	64%
Some college	71%	84%
College degree or more	82%	91%

Table 6.1 The Changing Internet Population. A recent study of Internet use shows a lessening of the "digital divide," yet there are still Americans who do not have access to the Internet.

Source: Pew Internet and American Life Project (2000 data), www.pewinternet.org/reports/reports.asp?Report 30&Section ReportLevel1&Field Level1ID&ID 105 (2006 data) http://www.pewinternet.org/trends/User_Demo_4.26.06.htm.

Internet communication is a hybrid of print and electronic media. It makes extensive use of the written word, although paper is optional. More recently, still images, sound, animation, and full-motion video became transmittable via computer technology. The Internet also offers instant access for the user. In the more traditional media, access is controlled by the media organization; that is, the networks schedule their nightly newscasts at a specific time each day. However, with the Internet, the individual user decides when and where he or she will log on. The ability to publish as well as receive material over the Internet requires specific hardware and software purchases. However, the costs for an individual to reach large numbers of other people via the Internet are significantly less than through the use of other forms of communication. This is clearly evident in the rise in the number of people involved in the kind of blogging described in the introduction. Blogs could not have become as numerous as they are today if it were not for the relative ease and low cost of disseminating information on the Web.

Media Audiences

Media organizations are also distinguished based on the primary audience for the information that is offered. The main distinction is between **national media** and **local media** outlets. The national media are composed of the entities that are available to people throughout the nation. In the print context, these include a handful of genuinely national newspapers, such as *USA Today,* the *Wall Street Journal,* and the *New York Times.* National media also include the weekly newsmagazines *Time* and *Newsweek* as well as magazines that have a more pronounced political perspective, such as the *New Republic* and the *National Review.*

Although the national broadcast media are still dominated by three major commercial television networks (ABC, CBS, and NBC) that broadcast over the airwaves along with the noncommercial Public Broadcasting Service (PBS), they are increasingly being challenged by newer technologies. Television networks are created by linking local broadcast stations to one another through programming that is simultaneously aired on local stations across the country. Examples of such programs include the evening news programs as well as your favorite sitcoms. Local television stations produce some of their own programs, most notably local news shows, but local stations rely on the networks for much of what they broadcast. The primary limitation of local television is that it can only be seen within the reach of the station's particular broadcast signal. As new technologies have emerged in the last decade, the television audience has been shifting away from traditional network programming to the more specialized formats available via cable and satellite.

The advent of cable and satellite technology has blurred the lines between national and local media by making what used to be local programming available nationally. WGN, which is based in Chicago, and TBS, based in Atlanta, are examples of this trend. Satellite technology has also

Find links to the major national news organizations.

expanded the reach of local television stations. People who would never have been able to access the direct signals of local stations can now do so because they have been designated the "local provider" by providers such as DirectTV and the Dish Network. The new technology has led to the rise of the FOX, UPN, and CW networks, which now challenge the over-the-air networks' dominance of the medium. In addition, the advent of the Internet has given the more traditional media a new format through which they can reach their audience. You would be hard-pressed today to find a television station, newspaper, or newsmagazine that does not also have a presence online. In terms of audience, the Internet is a national, even an international, media format. The Internet has provided the platform for a wide range of independent sources of news, such as bloggers, as well as alternative-perspective websites.

Programming Objectives

The final distinction made in broadcasting is based on the type of programming that is offered. The main distinction here is between the "news" media and the rest of the programming that is available. The primary business of broadcasting is **entertainment,** and most of its offerings are designed to entertain the audience through comedies, dramas, talk shows, and sports programming. The **news media** do have the most direct impact on the political process; however, entertainment television also presents a picture of politics to the viewer that influences our collective perceptions of the political world. In any case, the average viewer spends much more time in front of the television being amused rather than being informed. There will be more on the influence of entertainment on politics at the end of this chapter.

The New Media

The term "new media" has been used in recent years to characterize a variety of new information sources that began to emerge during the late 1980s. Although somewhat loosely defined, the term **new media** refers to new ways to communicate with the public about politics and is generally seen to include talk radio, television talk shows, television news magazines, electronic town hall discussions, MTV, print and electronic tabloids, and the Internet. Although a number of these formats have been an important aspect of entertainment programming for a long time, they started to be seen as having a significant influence on the political process during the 1992 presidential election.

During that election, a number of crucial events took place on television, although not on the traditional news and public affairs programs. Ross Perot became a candidate via his appearance on *Larry King Live*; he also sponsored a series of electronic town hall meetings and pioneered the use of the "infomercial" for political purposes. Bill Clinton had to respond to reports of an extramarital affair with Gennifer Flowers that was first reported in the tabloid press. The story was quickly picked up by the mainstream news media, and his response appeared on *60 Minutes,* a newsmagazine that can be seen as a quintessentially "old" media institution. After surviving that incident, Clinton boosted his popularity by, among other things, appearing on MTV and playing his saxophone on the late-night *Arsenio Hall* show. MTV also became involved in the election by sponsoring Rock the Vote—a get-out-the-vote drive focusing on its audience of younger voters. After being elected to office, Clinton held a number of televised town hall meetings enabling him to communicate directly with citizens and without the news media interpreting and analyzing the events.[9]

Visit the MTV Rock the Vote site.

The Internet, the newest of the "new" media, made its first major appearance in the 1996 presidential election. All the major candidates had websites for the first time. In 1998, then Reform Party candidate Jesse Ventura was able to win the Minnesota governor's race by making use of a website to contact and mobilize voters, mostly young people, who did not usually participate in the political process.[10] Ventura is an example of the ways in which entertainment and politics are now interwoven. A researcher has coined a new term, politainer, to describe him.[11] Part politician and part entertainer, Ventura used his celebrity status and former careers as a professional wrestler and talk radio host to connect with people using the new media. More recently, Ventura's friend and sometime movie co-star Arnold Schwarzenegger used his celebrity status as a major movie star to help him become governor of California.

The 2000 election included extensive use of the new media. During the primaries, Republican candidate John McCain raised significant campaign funds via his website. The blurring of the lines between entertainment and politics was widely apparent. First Lady Hillary Clinton, a candidate for the U.S. Senate from New York, appeared on the *David Letterman Show* complete with her own "top 10 list." As a guest on the show, she made herself known to a television audience who may not be regular viewers of the news, but who are often exposed to political jokes and satire during the late-night talk shows. Both presidential candidates made several appearances on *Letterman* as well as the *Tonight Show.* They also showed up on *Regis, Oprah,* and MTV.

The same pattern was evident during the 2004 elections. John Kerry and George Bush appeared on both the traditional and "new" media. Some people may find such appearances demeaning for the candidates, but they chose to appear on these shows to reach audiences that do not watch *Meet the Press* or the nightly news programs on a regular basis. The Pew Research Center has been tracking the increase in the number of people indicating that they get at least some of their information about political candidates from late-night comedians, *Saturday Night Live,* and MTV. The trend was particularly evident among young people. In 2004, 13 percent of those under age thirty said they were regularly informed about the candidates by the late-night talk shows, and 21 percent said they regularly learn something

"The Kids Are All Right—Young People and News: A Conversation" (with Jon Stewart), Robert Love.

During the 2004 elections, an increasing number of people, mostly in the younger age brackets, got their news about the election from watching Jon Stewart's *Daily Show* as well as Jay Leno and David Letterman.

from comedy programs such as Jon Stewart's *Daily Show*.[12] It is no wonder that the candidates decided to risk their dignity and appear with Jay Leno.

The overall impact of the new media on the political process has yet to be determined. These communications formats generally have had nonpolitical foundations, but they have increasingly become part of the political process.[13] Their impact has been seen most dramatically in the election process, but it is not confined to this area. The new media are increasingly influencing public policy debates. For example, in 2000 television talk show host Rosie O'Donnell brought considerable attention to the gun control movement when she publicly endorsed its efforts on her program and when she became involved in promoting the Million Mom March in support of the movement. Oprah Winfrey has used her talk show to bring considerable attention to children's issues, especially those involving child abuse and neglect.

Some components of the new media, especially the Internet, offer the potential for greater citizen involvement in the political process by providing a means for direct communication between the average citizen and public officials, between voters and candidates for office, and between citizens themselves. The interactive dimension of call-in talk shows and electronic town halls offers the possibility of involving more people in the political process. The Internet, in particular, provides a means through which citizens can interact with one another and generate support and opposition for various public policy proposals. During the 2004 primaries, millions of people were mobilized to support Democratic candidate Howard Dean through the use of "meet-ups" that were formed by people using the Internet to connect with one another. However, the new media, including the Internet, have been infused with the entertainment values of the larger industry of which they are components, and their primary purpose is to generate profits. The commercial dimension of the new media may be stronger than their potentially democratizing impact.[14]

The Changing Role of the Media in the Political Process

The idea that the media have an impact on the political process is a view generally shared by members of the public, elected officials, candidates for office, and political scientists. The media have a number of functions in the political process: They inform the public about ongoing events, they influence political elites, they contribute to determining the political agenda, and they provide the context in which contemporary elections occur.[15]

Since the mid-twentieth century, a number of changes have occurred that help explain the current role that the media play in the political process. The media themselves have changed, if for no other reason than there are many more media outlets. Previously, the focus was on the role of the press. Today, the impact of the mass media on the political process is no longer confined to the news media. There are more different types of media available, and they have penetrated deeper into the everyday lives of Americans.

Who watches what?

In the 1950s and 1960s, the media consisted of the traditional print media (newspapers and magazines) and the electronic media (radio and broadcast television). Radio stations were numerous, but over-the-air broadcast television brought at best six to eight channels into the average viewer's home, and that was possible only in major metropolitan areas such as New York City. At the start of the twenty-first century, print media still exist, although with fewer outlets than forty years ago. Television has been dramatically altered by the advent of cable and satellite technology, which provides the average viewer access to more television programming than any one person could possibly watch. In addition, an entirely new form of media, the Internet, expanded rapidly during the 1990s. The influence of the Internet is growing on a daily basis and changing our society and politics in the process. For example, in 2000, 23 percent of the American public went online for their news; in 2004, 29 percent did. In 2000, 30 percent of the population said they regularly watched the national networks' nightly news programs. In 2004, the response was 34 percent. If these trends continue, the Internet may well become the primary source of information within the next few years and may surpass network news audiences in the not too distant future.[16]

Contributing to the new environment are the simultaneous changes that have occurred in the political process, especially in terms of the decline of political parties. As parties have lost their dominance in the electoral process, and as candidate-centered campaigns have replaced party-centered campaigns, the media have become increasingly significant (see Chapter 8). Many analysts now argue that the media currently play a role in the political process once performed by political parties. They also argue that the media are not particularly well equipped to play that role.[17] The media are no longer simply neutral observers and reporters of political events; they now shape events as well.

A History of News in America

To understand the contemporary state of the mass media in the United States, one needs to know the history of the news. When the nation was founded, the Framers took care to provide the press with formal constitutional protection through the First Amendment; however, the term "media" was nonexistent at that time. In addition, the communication technology at the time was extremely limited by today's standards. Political communication was limited to the printed word, the "press." The primary forms of print communication were newspapers and pamphlets. Given the labor-intensive process involved in printing papers, they did not appear with the same frequency as they do today.

The newspapers that existed during the late eighteenth century were offshoots of political parties, which used them to convey and promote specific political agendas. During the American Revolution, the **partisan press** both supported and opposed the break with Britain. The debates over ratification took place in the newspapers, with the Federalists and Anti-Federalists making their cases to the public via their own newspapers and pamphlets (see Chapter 2). When formal political parties developed in the early republic, they had their own newspapers that promoted each party's candidates, perspective, and agenda. Readers of the day were fully aware of this, for the names of the papers often had the party affiliation as part of the title. Because there were competing parties with different points of view, there were competing newspapers that reflected the various political perspectives that existed at the time. It took resources to produce these newspapers, and they were sold to the public, but their primary purpose was political, not commercial.

During the course of the nineteenth century, print technology improved, which allowed for faster and more efficient newspaper production. The telegraph made it possible to gather and convey information in a more timely manner. Newspapers became businesses that generated revenues from both sales and private advertising. To generate more revenue, publishers began to move away from a partisan orientation, which limited potential sales, to a nonpartisan or "objective" format. If a paper was partisan, it ran the risk of alienating readers who had competing party loyalties. If it took an avowedly neutral or objective stance, the paper could appeal to more people, thereby increasing direct sales and advertising revenue. As objectivity became the standard for reporting, editorial pages, rather than the news section, became the place in newspapers where editors and publishers made their political views known and explicit.

Publishers also found that stories about lurid crimes and scandals sold newspapers, and this practice, known as yellow journalism, began to take hold. The term comes from the yellow ink used in the comic illustrations run at the time. To broaden the scope of their readership, papers focused on and sensationalized crime stories. They also increased their revenues by adding an increasing number of nonpolitical topics to their routine coverage—everything from sports to women's sections.[18]

Technological advancements in communications during the twentieth century transformed the press into the mass media. Traditionally, newspapers had a local or regional impact mainly due to distribution limitations. The rise of radio and television networks created a national culture by making the same information and programming available to people throughout the country. This started the process of blurring regional differences by allowing people from across the county to share in the same real-time experiences in a way that had not before been possible while the means of communication was confined to the written word and still photographs.

From the Press to the Media

The technological changes also brought a new role for the media in the political process. The media began to be used by candidates and elected officials to make direct contact with the public without the press serving as an intermediate interpreter of events. The first president to make use of the electronic media was Franklin Roosevelt. His use of radio, through his famous **fireside chats,** enabled him to speak directly to the American people. His words were broadcast directly into Americans' homes, and people did not have to read a newspaper to learn what the president was proposing. They were able to hear him. Listening to a person speak is a different experience than reading the same speech on a piece of paper. To a nation of people suffering through the Depression, FDR's voice was as comforting as his words. Radio was also significant in bringing the immediacy of World War II closer to the average citizen. The voices of journalists became familiar to people who began to trust those they could hear in a different way than they had trusted the printed world.

Listen to one of FDR's Fireside Chats.

Television made its way into many American homes during the Eisenhower administration. The first political commercials occurred during the election of 1952. The cartoonlike, now quaint "I Like Ike" ads began to change the nature of the electoral process as candidates had a new means of conveying their messages directly to the people with both words and pictures. During the 1950s, television's ability to bring the public into the decision-making processes of the national government also became apparent. Congressional hearings were televised, the best known of which were Senator Joseph McCarthy's investigation of communist infiltration into the U.S. State Department. Through television, these hearings were brought into the

President Franklin Delano Roosevelt was able to communicate with the American people directly by using the "new" technology of radio.

Visit "The :30 Second Candidate" site for a history of political advertising.

Watch a political advertisement for Eisenhower.

Watch the infamous "Daisy ad."

Watch a political advertisement featuring "Harry and Louise."

nation's living rooms with an immediacy that the print media could not convey. The McCarthy hearings also contributed to the rise of celebrity journalism. When CBS television's *See It Now,* hosted by Edward R. Murrow, exposed the unfounded nature of many of McCarthy's accusations, it demonstrated the power of television to change the public's perception of an issue and an elected official. McCarthy's political influence was never the same after the broadcast.[19] The journalist, Murrow, was more believable and credible to the viewing public than the senator, McCarthy.

In the 1960s, the first televised presidential debate occurred, between John F. Kennedy and Richard Nixon, demonstrating the impact that the visual dimension of television could have on viewers. Kennedy was America's first television president. Everything from his inaugural address to his press conferences, the first lady's televised tour of the White House, the beautiful pictures of his family, as well as his assassination and funeral, were all brought into America's living rooms. The 1960s also brought Lyndon B. Johnson's Daisy ad, arguably the first instance of genuinely negative political advertising on television. It brought color coverage of Vietnam into our homes and changed our perception of war. It was also during this period that CBS anchor Walter Cronkite was the most trusted man in the country. When he started to question the nation's policy in Vietnam, it had a tremendous impact on the public's view of the war.

The 1970s were characterized by the rise of investigative journalism spurred by the Watergate crisis. It began the trend that continues to the present, of the news media viewing elected officials as adversaries and as scandals ready to happen. Watergate contributed to the rise of celebrity journalism by advancing the careers of journalists such as Dan Rather and Sam Donaldson. Each became famous by challenging the president in front of the cameras. During the 1980s, Ronald Reagan mastered the art of the political image, emphasizing the visual over the substantive and using the power of television to go directly to the public to gain support for his programs. The 1990s moved politics more firmly into the entertainment arena, as described earlier in the chapter. Then 1998 brought Congress's impeachment action against President Clinton, an action that started with the story of Clinton's affair with an intern that appeared, not in print or on television, but on a website—*The Drudge Report*. The Internet now makes information available instantaneously, often without the same editorial filters as exist in other media formats. The early 2000s have seen the expansion of the influence of the Internet as more and more people get their news from online sources and as political organizations increasingly use the Web to mobilize their supporters.

This brief history of the media in the United States illustrates their transformation from avowedly partisan participants in politics to nonpartisan interpreters of events. It also shows how changing communications technology influences the presentation of the news and our political perceptions. The result of all these changes has been to make the mass media major influences in American politics.

Media Ownership Trends

One of the most important contemporary trends in the mass media concerns its economic base. Over the course of the nation's history, America has become a country of increasingly fewer media outlets owned by a small number of extremely large corporations. This is referred to as the **concentration of ownership.** In the early years of broadcasting, most stations, as well as most print media, were independently owned; today, however, almost all of the nation's news sources are part of large conglomerates. The trend has dramatically accelerated during the last twenty-five years. In 1984 fifty companies controlled the nation's media outlets, but in 1987 the number was down to twenty-six. Three years later (1990), the number was twenty-three. In 1993 there were twenty companies, in 1996 there were ten, and in 2001 there were nine.[20] Today, there are five major corporate media enterprises: Time Warner, Disney, Viacom, News Corporation (Fox), and Bertelsmann—the German-based company that is the largest publisher of English-language books.[21] Ben Bagdikian, who has studied this phenomenon for more than twenty years, finds it to be a very disturbing trend:

> At issue is the possession of power to surround almost every man, woman, and child in the country with controlled images and words, to socialize each new generation of Americans, to alter the political agenda of the country. And with that power comes the ability to exert influence that in many ways is greater than that of schools, religion, parents, and even government itself.[22]

All of these corporations are multifaceted and have widespread holdings in seemingly disparate areas, but they are all, broadly speaking, part of the entertainment industry. These are businesses that earn huge profits by convincing Americans that we should spend our leisure time enjoying products created by their company rather than the products offered by their competitors. These are entities that are accountable not to the American public, but to their shareholders. Their primary obligation is to maximize profits, not to provide citizens with the knowledge they need to make informed political decisions. The creation and dissemination of the "news" to the American public are a relatively minor area of concern to the overall operations of such corporations (see Table 6.2).

Detailed information about media ownership is provided by the *Columbia Journalism Review.*

As the concentration of ownership has increased, the competition between sources of information has decreased. Despite the increasing size of the media companies, there are fewer sources of news and information available to the average citizen than before. Newspapers are the best example of this trend. In 2003, there were 1,456 daily newspapers in the United States. In 1970, the number was closer to 1,750. In most cities, only one newspaper is available. Fewer than fifty cities have competing newspapers. In twelve of those cities, the competing papers are owned by the same company.[23] This means that most localities have monopolies in the reporting of local news. In addition, much of the news that appears in local newspapers and on local newscasts comes from one of the major wire services: the *Associated Press* (AP), the *New York Times,* and the *Los Angeles Times–Washington Post* syndicate. The result is that the exact same story can appear on local television, radio, and in the newspapers simultaneously. The wire services also supply much of the news that appears online.

Before the passage of the 1998 Telecommunications Act, companies were prevented from controlling all the print and electronic media outlets within a single market. The new ownership rules that were part of this legislation have relaxed this safeguard and perhaps eliminated it entirely. This allows for a **convergence,** or bringing together, of media sources. In the past, there were different owners for different types of media, but today, it is likely that the same company will own print, electronic, and online sources of information. Furthermore, it will coordinate its efforts across sources, often in ways that the average viewer may not be aware of. The decreased opportunity available to many Americans to have access to multiple perspectives through which they can learn about politics certainly runs counter to the Framers' goal of ensuring that the people would have many sources of news and information to make informed choices about public issues.

The Question of Bias

One of the most persistent questions that arise regarding the media and the political process is that of bias. Claims that the press is "biased" are heard frequently. Liberals argue that the press is conservative, whereas conservatives

Online

ABC.com
ABCNEWS.com
Oscar.com
Mr. Showbiz
Disney.Com
Family.Com
ESPN Internet Group
NBA.com
NASCAR.com

Movie Production/ Distribution

Walt Disney Pictures
Touchstone Pictures
Hollywood Pictures
Caravan Pictures
Miramax Films
Buena Vista Home Video
Buena Vista Home
Entertainment
Buena Vista International

Resorts/Theme Parks

The Disneyland
Resort, Anaheim, CA
Hong Kong Disneyland*
Disneyland Resort Paris
Tokyo Disney Resort*
Walt Disney World,
Orlando, FL (Animal
Kingdom, MGM Studios,
Epcot, Magic Kingdom)
Disney Cruise Line
Disney's Vero Beach
Resort

Television

(Broadcast and Cable)
ABC Television
Network
Ten owned and operated
television stations
throughout the United States
ABC Family
The Disney Channel
Toon Disney
SoapNet
ESPN Inc. (80%—includes
ESPN, ESPN2, ESPN
News, ESPN Now, ESPN
Extreme)
Classic Sports Network
A&E Television (37.5%)
The History Channel
Lifetime Television (50%)
Lifetime Movie Network
(50%)
E! Entertainment (with
Comcast and Liberty Media)

Book Publishing

Hyperion
Miramax Books
ESPN Books
Disney Publishing

Music

Buena Vista Music
Group
Hollywood Records
Lyric Street Records
Mammoth Records
Walt Disney Records

Television

(Production/Distribution)
Buena Vista Television
Touchstone Television
Walt Disney Television
Walt Disney Television Animation
(has three wholly owned production
facilities outside the United States—
Japan, Australia, Canada)

Sports

Anaheim Sports, Inc.
Mighty Ducks of Anaheim
(National Hockey League)

Radio

More than 60 local radio stations
throughout the United States
Radio Disney
ESPN Radio (syndicated
programming)

Retail

The Disney Store

Magazines

Automotive Industries
Biography (with GE and Hearst)
Discover
Disney Adventures
Disney Magazine
ECN News
ESPN Magazine Family Fun
Institutional Investor
JCK
Kodin
US Weekly (50%)

Table 6.2 Disney Holdings (Partial List), August 16, 2005. Disney Corporation includes a wide array of media and entertainment properties. The range of enterprises that make up Disney illustrates both the concentration of ownership and the convergence of disparate media sources.

Source: Columbia Journalism Review, http://www.cjr.org/tools/owners/disney.asp.

*Disneyland Tokyo and Disneyland Hong Kong are partially owned by the Disney Corporation.

CONVERGENCE IN THE HEARTLAND: THE CASE OF LAWRENCE, KANSAS

Lawrence, Kansas (population 85,000), located about halfway between Kansas City and Topeka, may well be one of the least likely locations to find one of the nation's most well-developed examples of the convergence of media formats, as well as a local example of the concentration of ownership. Home to the University of Kansas, Lawrence is a "small market" by corporate media standards. The "news" in Lawrence is dominated by enterprises that are all owned by the World Company, a private corporation. The World Company owns Lawrence's only newspaper, the *Lawrence Journal-World*. News6, the local cable television station that reaches about 80 percent of Lawrence households through the local cable system, is also owned by World. The result is a concentration of media ownership in Lawrence.

In part because World Company does not answer to a large corporate board, it is free to move in whatever direction its chairman, Dolph Simons—who is also the editor and publisher of the newspaper—chooses. In the mid-1990s he decided that he was in the "information" rather than the newspaper business and began the process of converging the various news organizations under his ownership in Lawrence. At the same time, he created one of the first online news sites: LJWorld.com.[1]

Explore the "converged" media world of Lawrence, Kansas.

In 2001, "The World Company became one of the first media groups to combine its print, television and Internet news-gathering into one newsroom."[2] The combined news-gathering entity is called the "converged news center." It includes writers, photographers, video producers, and editors, whose work may appear in one, a few, or all the formats served by the same newsroom. The editors successfully overcame the initial reluctance on the part of the reporters, who, if they were print reporters, were used to seeing the television reporters as "competition," and vice versa.[3] The center of the converged news presence in Lawrence is LJWorld.com, a state-of-the-art website providing access to all things Lawrence, including local and KU sports information, podcasts, and MP3 downloads. Lawrence may be ahead of the nation, but in all likelihood we will see more of this type of convergence in the future.

[1] Timothy L. O'Brien, "The Newspaper of the Future," *New York Times*, June 26, 2005, Sunday Business, p. 1 (retrieved via LexisNexus August 5, 2005).

[2] "News6: About Us," http://www.6newslawrence.com/about (retrieved August 26, 2005).

[3] Dirck Halstead, "Driving with Your Brights On: A 20,000 Circulation Daily Takes Care of Its Community (and Convergence)," digitaljournalist.org, 2003, http://www.digitaljournalist.org/issue0308/ljw_intro.html (retrieved August 27, 2005).

argue that it is liberal. Republicans say it favors Democrats. Democrats argue the opposite. Organizations on the right, such as the Media Research Center, accuse the media of a liberal bias. Fairness and Accuracy in Reporting (FAIR), a liberal group, provides its own evidence of a conservative bias in reporting. Such accusations are called **content** or **political bias.** It is the idea that reporters and news organizations are promoting a specific political perspective or agenda in the content of their stories. The difficulty with this perspective is that most of the scholarly research into this question does not confirm that content bias occurs. The perception that it does is related more to the political orientations of the critics than to the political orientation of the content of media messages. Those with strong views see any competing perspectives as "wrong" and their own views as correct. Consequently, a report that provides an evenhanded analysis of a competing point of view is seen as biased, but someone holding the competing view would see the same report as fair.[24]

"The Liberal Media Myth Revisited: An Examination of Factors Influencing Perceptions of Media Bias," Tien-Tsung Lee.

Claims of political or content bias are tied to the idea that the media are supposed to be unbiased or "objective" in reporting events. As noted earlier, the standard of **objectivity** in the news emerged in the nineteenth century as newspapers began to lose their partisan character and started to appeal to mass audiences. In addition, as journalists became more "professional" in their orientation, they developed a set of accepted standards and practices that culminated in the idea that reporting on politics should be "value free."[25] Nonpartisan critics of the news media have argued that the standard of objectivity is what should be questioned. Reporting the news is a process of selecting and interpreting events that are inherently value laden. Thus, the important questions are what values and practices are contributing to the selection process because most evidence suggests that these values are not ideological or partisan in nature.

The kind of bias that researchers do find in news coverage is referred to as **structural bias.** Structural bias "is that which occurs as a result of the approved routines of news people and news organizations, as the result of their system of selecting some kinds of information as news and rejecting other kinds as 'not news.'"[26] Structural bias results in patterns of coverage that consistently appear in news reporting. These patterns result from limitations, constraints, and demands that are built into the practice of journalism. Structural bias is also the consequence of the medium itself; it has different manifestations in television than it does in print formats. Structural bias is especially important in television news because this is where most people get their news. The existence of structural bias may be more subtle than content bias, but it is also more pervasive.

Find links to groups on the left and on the right who claim the media are biased.

Sources of Structural Bias

Most sources of structural bias are rooted in the corporate foundation of the nation's media companies. As noted earlier, the national media are controlled by a handful of very large corporations that are primarily concerned with generating revenue. They are only tangentially interested in serving the public interest. All of these corporations are also part of the entertainment

Structural Bias: Explore the sources of structural bias by completing this exercise.

industry: They make money by offering people various means to amuse themselves. Television makes money by keeping people tuned in to its programs; newspapers make money based on the number of subscribers they have. The number of people who watch a particular program or read a specific newspaper determines what is charged for advertising time or space in that format, and advertising is the main source of revenue in the for-profit media. Consequently, the primary goal is to keep people watching and/or reading.

The consequence is that **entertainment values** have become increasingly evident in television news. Reporters are chosen as much for their appearance as for their journalistic skills. Nightly news anchors are celebrities who are regularly featured on *Entertainment Tonight*. They are profiled, along with movie stars and television actors, in *People* magazine. The networks have found that they can package public affairs programs in an entertaining format, and the result is the proliferation of shows such as *Primetime, Dateline,* and *60 Minutes*. These shows may appear news oriented, but their definition of news is more likely to emphasize human-interest stories, as well as "true crime" and celebrity interviews, than to focus on traditional hard-news items.[27]

News programs do not generate nearly as much revenue as other forms of programming for the networks. Consequently, a relatively small portion of the daily programming is dedicated to the news. **Time constraints** are a key component of structural bias. The major commercial networks devote a half-hour of programming each evening to their national news show. When commercials are eliminated, the airtime is approximately twenty-two to twenty-four minutes. Individual stories on the news are usually no longer than ninety seconds. This is simply not enough time to cover public policy stories in detail, particularly stories that are about complex issues and proposals. The time constraints have also led to the proliferation of **sound bites.** These are short clips, usually no longer than ten seconds, of statements that people in the news have made. Given the length of time they are allotted, the statements need to be catchy phrases, and the full context of the statement is often not clarified.

The entertainment values of television place major visual demands on its presentation of the news. Since it is a visual medium, pictures are essential. News events without an inherently visual component, such as economic policy concerns, have a difficult time getting television airtime. Conversely, events that are inherently visual, but have limited public significance, often appear on the news because of the pictures that accompany them.

The **definition of news** is another element of structural bias. The five most widely used criteria for choosing news stories are (1) strong impact; (2) violence, conflict, disaster, scandal; (3) familiarity; (4) proximity; (5) timeliness and novelty. The most important of these are conflict, proximity, and timeliness.[28] The criterion of timeliness means that ongoing issues or public policy problems are usually not seen as news because they are routine and not new or novel. The emphasis on conflict also means that compromise and consensus, which occur on a regular basis in political decision making, are not newsworthy. This results in the one-sided impression that politics is always about conflict. In addition, news is generally defined as bad news. Editors are more likely to air and print stories about public policies that are failing than about those that are succeeding. This leaves the viewer with the mistaken impression that nothing ever goes the way it is designed because political success stories do not conform to the prevailing understanding of what constitutes news.

The Mediated Electoral Process

Arguably, the aspect of the political process in which the media have had the most impact is that of campaigns and elections. It is also where one can see the effects of structural bias most clearly. With the decline in political parties, the news media have taken on the role of interpreting the campaign and election for the voters. The mass media, especially television, are the means through which the public is made aware of the electoral choices presented to them. Most people never have the opportunity to hear candidates in person; their contact with those running for office is through their television sets. From the point of view of those running for office, the media, especially television, have become the primary campaign tools. They have eclipsed political parties as the organizational vehicles through which candidates deliver their message to the electorate. The impact of the media on elections can be seen in three specific areas: the news coverage of the campaign, paid political advertising, and televised debates between candidates.

Free Media

News coverage of political campaigns is referred to as the **free media** because those running for office can reach the public through this medium without paying for the airtime. Numerous studies have shown that news media coverage of elections falls into discernible patterns. The dominant pattern that has emerged is to tell the story of elections in terms that emphasize the "horse race" aspect of the campaign. Horse race stories highlight the "game" aspects of an election by focusing on the strategic decisions made by the campaigns and by neglecting the issues and policy stands of the candidates.

Horse race coverage frames an election by emphasizing who is ahead and who is behind in the campaign. It relies on the results of public opinion polls to assess who is winning and losing at any given point. Horse race stories analyze campaigns mainly by focusing on the "game plan," or the strategic choices made by the candidates. These stories place much less attention on the public policy components of the campaign. In the horse race or game story, the reporter becomes more of a handicapper of events than someone describing the events that have occurred. This is what Thomas Patterson has described as the movement away from descriptive to interpretive journalism. Descriptive journalism focuses on the "what" of events, whereas interpretive journalism focuses on the "why." When reporters interpret events, they do not use partisan criteria; their evaluation is tied to the "game," and they tend to focus on who is ahead and behind in the race.[29]

Another pattern of campaign coverage is the **soap opera story.** Such stories focus on "campaign issues" in contrast to public policy issues. The essence of soap opera is gossip—who did or said what and the responses that the initial statements or actions generated. Election coverage that follows this pattern emphasizes scandal, missteps, and personality questions. The question of "character" is seen as the most important campaign issue, and it has become the primary focus of soap opera coverage. One example of an issue that arose during the 1992 presidential campaign concerned then presidential candidate Bill Clinton's college use of marijuana. Whether or not he "inhaled" was not a public policy issue, but it was a campaign issue. In pursuing the soap opera story, the media often engage in "gotcha" journalism, attempting to catch a candidate in a contradiction or misstatement. A prime example occurred during the 2000 presidential primaries when GOP candidate George W. Bush was given a "pop quiz" on foreign policy. Although the stated purpose of the interview was to examine Bush's competence in the area of foreign policy, the underlying intent of the interview seemed to be to catch Bush in a mistake. The Dan Rather report described in the introduction was an attempt by CBS to engage in "gotcha" journalism, albeit one that did not work in the way that the producers of the segment probably anticipated.

Campaign coverage has also become increasingly negative in tone. Thomas Patterson found that campaign coverage became increasingly negative from 1960 until 1992. During the 1960s, most evaluations of candidates made by journalists were positive; in 1980, negative judgments outweighed positive ones. This trend was accentuated during the 1988 and 1992 presidential campaigns.[30] Other analysis has confirmed that this pattern continues. The Center for Media and Public Affairs has been tracking patterns in the news coverage of presidential elections since 1988. Its findings illustrate the trends in the types, tone, and amounts of coverage over the last five presidential elections As Table 6.3 illustrates, in 2004 horse race coverage decreased, but it still constituted almost half of the stories aired by the major networks.

The patterns seen in campaign coverage illustrate the consequences of structural bias. Telling the story of campaigns as either a sporting event or soap opera fits into the constraints imposed on the media through structural bias. These patterns mimic successful entertainment formats, and they also lend themselves to coverage in short segments. The time and visual constraints as well as the definition of news work together to tell the story of political campaigns in a manner that fits the needs of the major media outlet but that tends not to provide citizens with the kind of information they tend to seek about candidates or issues.

Paid Media

The largest expenditure in any campaign for office is the money spent to buy time and space in the media. Political advertising has existed since the early days of the republic; however, with the rise of television, it has become much

	1988	1992	1996	2000	2004
Amount of Coverage					
Number of stories	589	728	483	462	504
Number of minutes	1,116	1,400	788	805	1,007
Average soundbite (seconds)	9.8	8.4	8.2	7.8	7.8
Focus of Coverage					
Horse race	58%	38%	48%	71%	48%
Policy issues	40%	37%	32%	40%	49%

Table 6.3 Patterns of Election Coverage. The Center for Media and Public Affairs has been tracking election coverage on ABC, NBC, and CBS for the last four presidential elections. It has documented the decline in the amount of coverage and the changes in the patterns of coverage.

Source: Media Monitor, 18.6 (November/December 2004), http://www.cmpa.com/mediaMonitor/documents/05.03.02.Election.Final.pdf (retrieved August 9, 2005).

more pervasive and much more central to the campaign process. The first televised political commercials were aired during the 1952 presidential election. By today's standards, they were primitive, featuring black-and-white cartoon elephants along with the catchy "I Like Ike" campaign theme song. Campaign ads are a form of free speech and, unlike product advertising, are not subject to regulation. Campaign ads are created by the candidates' campaigns, but in recent years, some of the most controversial spots have been created and sponsored by groups independent of the campaigns themselves and involve the use of "soft" campaign funds. All political advertising is required to include a statement regarding the group or person who paid for the commercial. However, with ads paid for by political parties, advocacy interest groups, and individuals other than the official campaign committees, it is often difficult to determine, simply from the name of the group alone, what the sponsoring group stands for and who is financially backing the organization. (See the introduction to Chapter 7 for a description of some ads that appeared during the 2004 election.)

Campaign ads can be distinguished by looking at the central focus of the ad and by examining the overall tone of the message. When broken down this way, campaign commercials can be seen as focusing primarily on issues or images, and they can be seen as either positive or negative in tone. The result is that ads generally fall into one of four categories: positive issue, negative issue, positive image, negative image. In **positive issue ads,** a candidate will promote his or her stand on specific public policy issues such as Social Security and gun control. In **negative issue ads,** the candidate will criticize his or her opponent's positions on the same issues. In **positive image ads,** the candidate will try to present a picture of himself or herself that appeals to

Watch a political advertisement for Eisenhower.

Watch the infamous "Daisy ad."

Watch a political advertisement featuring "Harry and Louise."

voters' ideas about what constitutes a good leader. The candidate will be trying to show that he or she has the right character to hold the office in question. In **negative image ads,** the candidate will suggest that his or her opponent does not have the integrity needed to hold the office. Such ads will often rely less on outright claims and more on innuendoes and suggestions.

It is certainly legitimate for one candidate to criticize another based on the issues, but in recent years, increasing attention has been paid to negative advertising. Such ads become controversial if the allegations made about the opponent are distorted and/or if the opponent's record is taken out of context. "Ad watch" articles have become increasingly common as news media organizations try to assist voters in determining the validity of ads. A major difficulty in assessing political advertising, whatever its tone or focus, is the fact that many of the claims are made via the pictures and images depicted in the ads as opposed to the words of a candidate. Often, citizens are not fully aware of the subtle messages that are conveyed via the images presented in the ads. An unflattering picture of an opponent can be as effective as a series of statements critiquing the candidate's positions on the issues.

Historically, the use of political advertising was confined to the electoral process. However, during the 1990s, various interest groups as well as political parties began to use advertising to influence public opinion on public policy matters. During the debate over the Clinton health-care proposal, an interest group aired an ad with a fictitious couple dubbed Harry and Louise. In this ad, they offered a number of criticisms of the Clinton plan as understood by a typical middle-class family. Although the ad was aired in only a limited number of markets, the news media presented numerous stories about it, thereby increasing the number of people exposed to the message. This ad has been given a great deal of credit for turning public opinion against the Clinton plan. Since the success of the Harry and Louise ad campaign, interest groups have aired ads promoting their positions on various public policy issues. In the last few years, we have seen a number of commercials advancing specific positions in the debate over Social Security reform and prescription drug benefits. (This subject is discussed in detail in Chapter 7.) In assessing the significance of this trend, it is important to note that such advertising campaigns are very expensive and not within the financial resources of less well-funded groups and organizations.

Campaign commercials: Categorize political ads based on their content and tone.

Televised Debates

The first televised debate between presidential candidates was in 1960. The **Kennedy-Nixon debates** have come to be seen as one of the key events that heralded the increasing importance of the role of the media in elections. Those who watched the debates on television came away with the conclusion that Kennedy had "won"; those who listened on radio thought otherwise. The primary reason for the difference was because of the image projected by Kennedy and Nixon on the TV screen, not because of the content of either's comments. Kennedy looked much better on the air than did

During the 2004 presidential election, candidates George W. Bush and John Kerry participated in three televised debates, continuing a tradition that began in 1960.

Nixon, who had been ill before the debate and who did not allow the television producers to use makeup to improve his appearance. After his experience in 1960, Nixon refused to participate in another presidential debate.

The next presidential debate was during the 1976 election between Gerald Ford and Jimmy Carter. The format of the debate was similar to 1960; panels of journalists asked the candidates questions about a range of public policy issues. Since that time, there have been debates between the presidential candidates in every general election and increasingly during the primaries as well.

The debates have changed their formats over time in ways that reflect the changing nature of the media. In tune with the time constraints imposed by structural bias, the length of time the candidates are given to respond to particular questions has been shortened. Kennedy and Nixon spoke for as long as five minutes in response to a single question. During the 2000 primaries, the candidates were given forty-five seconds to respond. The influence of the new media was seen during the 1992 election when one of the debates used a town hall format rather than traditional journalistic questioning. During the Richmond town hall debate, average citizens were given the chance to question the candidates. Unlike the journalists, who tended to ask campaign issue and horse race questions, the citizens asked about a range of issues and public policies.

Over time, the interpretive turn in reporting has affected the debates as well, with the focus more on who won or lost the debate rather than on the idea that the debates allow citizens to gain a better understanding of where the candidates stand on issues of concern. This trend was quite obvious

Watch a clip from the Kennedy-Nixon presidential debates.

Watch a clip from the Carter-Ford presidential debates.

Watch a clip from the Reagan-Mondale presidential debates.

during the 2000 presidential debates. As soon as the candidates were finished speaking, the networks were on the air with instant analyses. Instant polls and live focus groups were used in an effort to determine who won and who lost the debates. The networks also used their websites to invite viewers to register their opinions about who won and lost through online polls despite the fact that—as noted in Chapter 5—online public opinion polls are notoriously inaccurate.

The Media and Agenda Setting

"Presidential Debate Questions and the Public Agenda," William L. Benoit and Glenn J. Hansen.

An agenda is a list of items that an organization intends to act on. The term **political agenda** refers to the set of issues and concerns that are seen as legitimate topics for public discussion and public policy decisions. The mass media are an important aspect of the **agenda setting** process in American politics: They raise the issues that are deemed important to the public, and they frame the manner in which we discuss those issues. The most effective way to bring an issue to the attention of the American public is to have the mass media take that issue seriously. Without media coverage, many topics of serious public import have a difficult time gaining the attention of the public as well as the attention of decision makers.

The media affect the political agenda through the issues they choose to focus on as well as through the issues that they choose not to cover. The way in which the media frame, or interpret, events has an impact on how those events are perceived. For example, during the civil rights movement of the 1950s and 1960s, the media played an active role in generating attention and sympathy for the movement through the manner in which they framed the events. By portraying the protestors as the victims of racism rather than as lawbreakers, the media helped generate public and elite support for the movement. During the Watergate scandal, little attention was paid to the story as long as it was reported as a campaign story. However, once the issue was framed as an example of pervasive corruption at the highest levels of government, the story was perceived differently, and its impact on the political process was dramatic.[31]

The media can also affect the political agenda when they engage in direct political activity. For example, during the 1990s, the corporate parents of the major broadcast news outlets had a large stake in the outcome of congressional efforts to revise the nation's telecommunications laws. Lobbying groups representing media interests contributed large sums of money to candidates and political parties to promote their economic interests. As a result of their efforts, they were able to get legislation passed that reduced the amount of control the FCC has on the broadcast industry, and that relaxed the ownership rules in a way that contributes to the continued concentration of media ownership mentioned earlier. It is worth noting that the news media did not devote a great deal of coverage to the efforts of their own lobbying organizations.[32]

It is important to realize that the media alone do not set the public agenda. A variety of other political actors also contribute to this process. Interest groups and political parties engage in a variety of activities, not the least of which involve gaining media attention, designed to place specific public issues on the agenda. Political decision makers are also an integral aspect of this process, as is the public. The media alone cannot place an issue on the public agenda. If stories do not resonate with the public and if they do not cause decision makers to take notice, the issue may not become part of the public policy agenda.

The Media and Political Socialization

As discussed in Chapter 5, **political socialization** is the process through which individuals learn and form beliefs about government and politics. Most of the attention paid to the role of the media in the political socialization process focuses on the news media. The news media certainly affect what and how we learn about politics. The news media, particularly television, are the primary information resources regarding public issues for most Americans. It is through the news that we acquire knowledge about specific political events and public policy issues. These are the reasons that learning how the news media frame issues and questions and how they tend to tell stories about events and people are so crucial. For example, the trend toward a negative bias in all reporting helps perpetuate the idea that politics is corrupt and that public officials are self-interested.

However, most people spend more of their time being entertained by the media than watching the news. The entertainment influences on public opinion and on individuals' perceptions of the political process are a topic that is often neglected. Yet it is hard to conclude that an activity, such as watching television, that constitutes such a large part of people's lives has no impact on public perceptions, including perceptions about politics. Indeed, many people do acknowledge that such an effect does exist.

This view is seen most clearly in the public realm in political debates that regularly arise regarding the content and implications of entertainment television. Such discussions often involve concern about the importance of maintaining family values. Perhaps the best known of such concerns involves questions about the content of programming aimed at children. Children watch little news, but they pick up information about politics in entertainment programming. Children's programming often has strong messages about authority. In the 1950s, authority was positively portrayed on television. Superman was a clean-cut hero who worked with the local authorities. If you sat down today to watch an afternoon of Nickelodeon, you would see authority figures depicted as insensitive tyrants or silly buffoons. Another example of this type of public discussion is the debate that took place after the "wardrobe malfunction" suffered by Janet Jackson during the 2004 Super Bowl halftime show.

Criticism of the amount of violent behavior in children's programming as well as messages about standards of morality that are evident in prime time programming are expressions of concern that people have about the impact of what we watch on our perceptions of the world. Those who question the manner in which women and members of racial minority groups are depicted on television express similar concerns. Television helps perpetuate racial and gender stereotypes through the characters that populate entertainment programming.

An aspect of entertainment programming that has a direct bearing on the political process is the manner in which elected officials are depicted on television. Until the appearance of the NBC drama *The West Wing* during the 1999 television season, the predominant portrayal of elected officials was either as criminals or idiots. This pattern helps contribute to a cynical and negative perception of elected officials.[33] Since *The West Wing* became a critical and commercial success, other dramas have also presented depictions of American presidents. The FOX program *24* featured an African American president, and ABC brought us the first female prime-time president in its short-lived *Commander-in-Chief*. However, both *The West Wing* and *Commander-in-Chief* were canceled in 2006 and no new presidents are currently on the prime-time network schedule. In assessing the manner in which the media affect the political process, it is important to think about the effects of entertainment programming as well as public affairs and news programs.

Conclusion: Participation and the Media

Check here for possible post-publication updates to the chapter material.

Links to alternative news sources.

As this chapter illustrates, the traditional mass media do not provide much room for direct citizen involvement. From the media's perspective, citizens are consumers of news rather than active participants in the process of creating the news. Decisions about programming and the selection of material are made by corporate executives with much more of a concern for the bottom line than for the political process. However, this does not mean that the average citizen should take the position that there is nothing he or she can do to affect the media's impact on the political process. The most important thing that an average citizen can do is to become a critical viewer and consumer of news.

The mainstream media are just that, mainstream. The country's national television networks, major newspapers, and newsmagazines are decidedly middle-of-the-road, and they all have a vested interest in maintaining the status quo because they are an integral component of the nation's existing power structure. Even PBS, which is often pointed to as a good source of public affairs information because it is not subject to corporate pressures, regularly relies on Washington insiders as its sources. Given this, the mainstream media tend to present a picture of political events without any ideological or evaluative assessments of the substance of political decisions. A critical consumer of news might want to form his or her judgments of public affairs by seeking out alternative views of the news. This would provide a means of learning a wide range of perspectives and evaluations about candidates and proposals rather than relying on only the mainstream media. This is relatively easy to accomplish on the Internet, where one can seek organizations with particular points of view. To seek out partisan and ideological interpretations of events would be, in effect, a throwback to the early days of the republic, when news was self-consciously filtered through a partisan lens.

To become a critical consumer of news, one needs to become visually literate. More and more, it is the case that the impact of the media on the political process is tied to a visual component. Therefore, it is incumbent on citizens to develop skills designed to help decipher the impact of images. Pictures often convey much more than words, and the messages that are sent via images are often subtle and not easy to recognize without a conscious effort. Visual literacy skills are especially important to cultivate in terms of assessing political advertising as well as television news. Watching ads and the news more closely to recognize the visual and verbal messages that are conveyed is vital to making truly informed decisions.

Another strategy is to make use of the potential of the new media, especially the Internet. The bloggers profiled in the introduction to the chapter did just that. They used the Internet to challenge assertions made by the mainstream media. Increasingly, there are online forums, discussion groups, and chats devoted to public issues. The traditional media are making many of these available through their own websites. The new media are increasingly being used to prompt conversations among citizens. It is still too early to fully judge the new media's ability to reinvigorate public debate and participation. However, it is certain that the more use average citizens make of these vehicles to engage in political discourse and action, the more likely it is that the participatory potential of the new media, especially the Internet, will be realized.

Key Terms

mass media   156
print media   156
broadcast media   157
Internet   157
digital divide   157
national media   159
local media   159
entertainment   160
news media   160
new media   160
partisan press   164

fireside chats   165
concentration of ownership   167
convergence   168
content bias/political bias   171
objectivity   171
structural bias   171
corporate foundation   171
entertainment values   172
time constraints   172
sound bites   172
definition of news   172

free media   173
horse race coverage   173
soap opera story   174
positive issue ads   175
negative issue ads   175
positive image ads   175
negative image ads   176
Kennedy-Nixon debates   176
political agenda   178
agenda setting   178
political socialization   179

Suggested Web Resources

The following links point to websites related to the study of the media. The following are links to the online versions of the major broadcast news organizations:

ABC News (**http://abcnews.go.com**) and CBS News (**http://www.cbsnews.com/sections/home/main100.shtml**) have their own websites. MSNBC (**http://www.msnbc.msn.com**) is a joint venture of NBC and the Microsoft Corporation. It is the gateway to NBC News as well as the MSNBC cable news service and *Newsweek* magazine.

Noncommercial news is available through the sites of PBS Online NewsHour (**http://www.pbs.org/newshour**) and National Public Radio (**http://www.npr.org**).

CNN (**http://www.cnn.com**) is the oldest of the cable news networks. It has an international presence and often has reporters in places where the rest of the electronic media do not. The FOX News Channel (**http://www.foxnews.com**) is the newest cable news network. It has a significant emphasis on entertainment news along with public affairs reporting.

CSPAN (**http://www.cspan.org**) broadcasts the day-to-day proceedings of the U.S. Senate and House of Representatives. In addition to airing the actions that take place on the floor, it also broadcasts selected congressional hearings and a series of other public affairs oriented programming.

The *Columbia Journalism Review* (**http://www.cjr.org/tools/owners**) is a good source to discover who owns what in the world of corporate media.

The following are links to selected national newspapers and magazines.

The *New York Times* (**http://www.nytimes.com**) is generally recognized as the premier newspaper in the United States. It will require you to register and log in to enter its site, but it does not charge for access to the current week's articles. The *Washington Post* (**http://www.washingtonpost.com**) and the *Washington Times* (**http://www.washingtontimes.com**) are the daily newspapers of the nation's capital. *USA Today* (**http://www.usatoday.com**) is the nation's only genuinely national paper because it

can be purchased throughout the country. The *Wall Street Journal* (**http://online.wsj.com/public/us**) is also a national newspaper, but unlike the others listed, it charges for its online edition.

Newsweek (**http://www.msnbc.msn.com/id/3032542/site/newsweek**), *Time* (**http://www.time.com/time**), and *US News & World Report* (**http://www.usnews.com/usnews/home.htm**) are the nation's major national newsmagazines.

The *National Review* (**http://nationalreview.com**) presents its readers with a conservative analysis of current events. For a more liberal perspective, try the *New Republic* (**http://www.tnr.com**).

The following are links to organizations that study and analyze the media. Some are more scholarly organizations; others have an avowedly ideological perspective.

The Pew Research Center for the People & the Press (**http://people-press.org**) is an organization that "studies public attitudes toward the press, politics and public policy issues. The Center's main purpose is to serve as a forum for ideas on the media and public policy through its research."

The Poynter Institute (**http://www.poynter.org/default.asp**) "is a school dedicated to teaching and inspiring journalists and media leaders. It promotes excellence and integrity in the practice of craft and in the practical leadership of successful businesses." Its website offers tools for journalists as well as a wealth of background information on important news events.

The Center for Media and Public Affairs (**http://www.cmpa.com**) "is a nonpartisan research and educational organization which conducts scientific studies of the news and entertainment media." In addition to studying election coverage, CMPA also analyzes political humor on late-night television.

The Freedom Forum (**http://www.freedomforum.org**) "is a nonpartisan foundation dedicated to free press, free speech and free spirit for all people." The forum sponsors the Newseum, an interactive museum of news, and the First Amendment Center.

Accuracy in Media (**http://www.aim.org**) says that it "is a non-profit, grassroots citizens watchdog of the news media that critiques botched and bungled news stories and sets the record straight on important issues that have received slanted coverage." It, along with the Media Research Center (**http://www.mrc.org**), analyzes the media from a conservative perspective.

A liberal perspective in found in the organization Fairness and Accuracy in Reporting (**http://www .fair.org/index.php**). It is a self-identified "progressive group" that "believes that structural reform is ultimately needed to break up the dominant media conglomerates, establish independent public broadcasting and promote strong nonprofit sources of information."

Blogs have become so numerous that it is impossible to list more than a few sources. Google has a special search engine that allows one to search for blogs on specific topics (**http://blogsearch.google.com**). CyberJournalist .net also has a list of blogs organized by categories and topics (http://www.cyberjournalist .net/cyberjournalists.php).

In order to see and hear illustrations of key events in the media's role in American politics, you can go to the History Channel (http://www .historychannel.com/speeches/speeches.html) to hear FDR's speeches. You can also access a range of political commercials at the :30 Second Candidate (http://www.pbs.org/30secondcandidate/ index.html) and Living Room Candidate (http:// livingroomcandidate.movingimage.us/index.php) sites. Finally, for an example of the new media's role in the political process, go to MTV's Rock the Vote site (http://www.rockthevote.com).

A complete study tool kit is available for this chapter and includes the following:
Flashcards
Crossword Puzzle
Critical Thinking Exercises
Interactive Timelines
Chapter Quiz

Parties and Interest Groups

■ **The Rise of the 527s**   185

■ **Political Parties and Interest Groups:**
Similarities and Differences   187

■ **Political Parties**   188
What Political Parties Do   188
A Brief History of Political Parties
   in the United States   190
Why Two Parties?   196
The Role of Minor Parties   197
Three Viewpoints on Political Parties Today   198
Reassessing Parties in American Politics   205

■ **Interest Groups**   206
What Interests Are Represented by Groups?   207
Group Membership   212
How Interest Groups Seek to Influence Politics   214
The Madisonian Dilemma of Interest Groups   222

■ **Conclusion: Parties and Interests**
in American Politics   223

The Rise of the 527s

Senator John F. Kerry of Massachusetts, the Democratic Party's 2004 presidential candidate, was proud of his service in the U.S. Navy during the Vietnam War. He was awarded a Silver Star for bravery under fire while saving a fellow sailor's life, a Bronze Star, and three Purple Hearts. The Kerry campaign believed that his service helped establish his credentials as a potential commander in chief and set him apart from his rival for the presidency, the incumbent George W. Bush, whose Air National Guard record had been questioned. Kerry's war record was prominently displayed at the Democratic National Convention in late July 2004. The theme was a large part of the biographical film shown before his speech accepting the Democratic nomination. Kerry began his acceptance speech with a dramatic military salute and deadpanned, "I'm John Kerry, and I'm reporting for duty." Later in the speech he noted that "I defended this country as a young man, and I will defend it as president."[1]

Candidate Kerry's version of his war record and qualifications to be commander in chief did not go unchallenged. Less than a week after the close of the Democratic Convention, a group named Swift Boat Veterans for Truth (now known as Swift Veterans and POWs for Truth)—a group of Vietnam veterans who, like Senator Kerry, served on "swift boats," a name used to describe small patrol boats used by the U.S. Navy to patrol the coast of South Vietnam during the late 1960s—began running a series of television advertisements opposing the Kerry candidacy. The advertisements never actually stated this directly (to do so would violate federal law), but to anyone watching the ads the message was clear: John Kerry could not be trusted, and he should not be president. These ads were powerful. The first ad, "Any Questions," ran in early August challenging his war record and claiming that he "betrayed all his shipmates." The second ad, "Sellout," ran approximately two weeks later, showing a photograph of John Kerry testifying before Congress in 1971 about war crimes that he claimed were committed by American forces in Vietnam. Interspersed between audio of Kerry's claims were statements of Vietnam veterans expressing their views of the impact that Kerry's testimony had on them and their fellow veterans. One veteran stated that Kerry "gave the enemy for free" what Americans "took torture to avoid

The 527 group Swift Boat Veterans for Truth ran a number of ads during the 2004 presidential campaign that criticized Democratic-nominee John Kerry's war record. The ads, including this one featuring retired Admiral Roy Hoffman, leader of the Swift Boat Veterans, was broadcast in August 2004.

Examine the honesty of political ads.

saying," while another veteran urged that, "He betrayed us in the past. How can we be loyal to him now?" By Election Day, the Swift Boat Veterans would spend over $22 million to run a total of ten television ads in hotly contested states and nationwide on cable networks. As they were summarized in the *Washington Post*, the ads "accuse [Kerry] of cowardice, hogging the limelight and lying. Far from displaying coolness under fire, they say, Kerry was never fired upon and fled the scene at the moment of maximum danger."[2] The veracity of the advertisements was challenged throughout the campaign—independent researchers at factcheck.org and others argued that the claims were exaggerated—but the ads clearly had an impact on the campaign.

These ads were notably controversial, and they reverberated through the campaign, but the Swift Boat Veterans were not alone in trying to influence the 2004 presidential campaign. The advertisements run by the Swift Boat Veterans were just the most prominent of a not-so-new but fast-growing phenomenon in American politics, issue advertisements developed and paid for by groups independent of the candidates. The Swift Boat Veterans are a 527 group—the name comes from the section of the federal tax code that defines them. These nonprofit organizations must report their contributions and expenditures to the Internal Revenue Service but can accept unlimited funds from any source. They have existed since at least the 2000 campaign, but they exploded during the 2004 election.

Other prominent 527 groups active during the 2004 presidential campaign included MoveOn.org, America Coming Together, and the Media Fund. The groups all worked to defeat President Bush, but they put forth very different public faces. MoveOn.org became well-known as the result of using the Internet to do grass-roots organizing. America Coming Together and the Media Fund, on the other hand, became prominent because they were financed by billionaires George Soros and Peter Lewis, who alone contributed just over $50 million to try to defeat President Bush.[3] Like the Swift Boat Veterans, they ran television advertising that played an important role in the presidential campaign. In the spring of 2004, the Bush campaign spent $40 million on a series of ads criticizing John Kerry as a "flip flopper." The Media Fund and others spent $50 million in counter-advertising.[4] Overall, 527 groups spent over one-half billion dollars during the 2004 election cycle. In contrast, during the 2000 presidential campaign they spent just under $150 million. The Center for Public Integrity found that 53 of these groups focused their efforts on the 2004 presidential campaign and spent $246 million.[5]

Many analysts expected the rise of independent spending by interest groups to hurt political parties. Parties had once been allowed to collect unlimited donations as well, but this practice was eliminated with passage of a new campaign finance reform law in 2001. But as political scientist Michael Malbin put it, "It looks as if early fears that [campaign finance reform] would mean death for the parties were highly exaggerated."[6] The national organizations of the Democratic and Republican parties raised even more than the 527 groups. Although less prominent, they ran their own advertising and "get out the vote" drives. For example, one Democratic Party ad was intended to combat the Swift Boat Veterans' attacks on Kerry. In the ad, which was run in twenty-one battleground states, retired Air Force Chief of Staff General Merrill McPeak endorsed John Kerry, stating that "Nothing is more important to me than protecting America. . . . John Kerry has the strength and common sense we need in a commander in chief." McPeak had endorsed Bush in the 2000 campaign.[7]

The efforts by 527 groups and political parties did not end with Election Day. Groups continue to raise millions to influence the American people on a whole host of policy issues and political controversies. Tens of millions have been spent by issue advocacy groups on both sides of the Social Security reform debate, including prominent groups from the 2004 presidential campaign and new groups. Millions more were raised for a Supreme Court confirmation battle even before Sandra Day O'Connor announced her retirement in late June of 2005.[8] We can expect that these efforts will continue to grow in the future if left unchecked.

The advertising paid for by interest groups and political parties during the 2004 presidential election and beyond illustrates the role of these organizations in our electoral system. Although the candidates put their own commercials on television, interest groups and political parties also made extensive use of the paid media to make their case to the voters. Political parties and interest groups are important political actors in the United States. They try to influence governmental decisions, and they make extensive efforts to influence the voting public's choices about who should hold, and not hold, office. Parties and interest groups are integral to the political process. It is impossible to understand the dynamics of contemporary American politics without them.

Political Parties and Interest Groups: Similarities and Differences

As we shall see, political parties and interest groups have several similarities as well as some clear differences. A **political party** is an organization that seeks to elect candidates to office under its label and, once elected, run the government. In contrast, an **interest group** can be defined as an organization that seeks to promote its interests by trying to influence public policy. Both political parties and interest groups are nongovernmental political actors. They are private associations that seek to influence—and even control—the work of government. Each also supports candidates for elective office with both endorsements and financial backing. Both political parties and interest groups provide average citizens with opportunities to participate in the web of American democracy.

There are significant differences in the way that political parties and interest groups operate and try to influence government. Because the primary goal of political parties is to elect officials and control government, they try to bring diverse groups together. They seek to form and mobilize electoral majorities that can bring them power. In choosing candidates and policy positions, they often try to appeal to the broadest group of voters possible. The power of political parties is measured by their success in winning elections. In contrast, interest groups are not concerned with operating government. Rather, they wish to pursue a narrower goal of ensuring that government policies benefit them. Thus, interest groups can be divisive. An interest group's support of a candidate is based on the candidate's support of its position. Although winning is important to interest groups, they are unlikely to support a candidate who disagrees with them just to be winners.

Political Parties

Political parties can be thought of as coalitions of interests; parties and interest groups can work closely together. Successful parties manage to balance the needs of a variety of interests to form winning electoral coalitions. For example, since the 1930s, labor unions have had a close alliance with the Democratic Party. Unions have supported Democratic candidates by organizing members to do party work. But political parties also compete internally. Although many Republicans seek to downplay opposition to abortion rights, the Christian Right, which is an active and influential part of the Republican Party, pushes hard on this issue and at times threatens to withdraw support if pro-choice candidates are nominated.[9]

Political parties and interest groups are both important political actors with significant roles in American politics. Each will now be considered in turn.

Political parties have been around since the beginning of the Republic, and despite the fact that George Washington warned against the undue influence of parties by stating, "Let me now . . . warn you in the most solemn manner against the baneful effects of the spirit of party," they have always played a central role in the workings of the American political system.[10]

What Political Parties Do

Although political parties have always played an important role in American politics, their role is different now than it was a century ago. The central goal of political parties, to win elections, remains the same as it has always been, but what it takes to achieve this goal has changed considerably. As part of meeting this goal, parties undertake a variety of functions. As we begin to examine political parties and their role in American politics, we should examine these functions. How well do parties perform them? Have other institutions, including interest groups, taken over these functions from the parties? The following sections examine the functions of political parties.

Recruiting Candidates

The central aim of political parties is to win elections and control government. To achieve this, parties must recruit candidates who have the skills to run winning campaigns. Political parties are always on the lookout for talented people who might be interested in running for office. At times, several individuals wish to seek the party nomination for a single office. If this happens, a primary is held (see Chapter 8, on primaries). In other cases, nominations are made when party leaders designate a nominee. Finding a candidate, especially a viable candidate, may be difficult. When a well-entrenched incumbent is running for reelection, attractive candidates can be hard to come by.

Organizing Elections

Running elections is officially a task of state and local governments, but parties are important as well in two ways. First, they generate interest in the election and encourage participation. Political parties register voters and educate the electorate. Second, parties recruit workers to supervise the polls and oversee vote counts to ensure that fraud is minimized.

Raising Money

Although raising money to conduct campaigns is primarily the job of candidates in the United States, political parties also raise funds. They use these monies to run the party organization; generate interest in the party through voter registration drives and party advertising, such as the ads described in the introduction of this chapter; and support candidates in a variety of ways.

Uniting Diverse Interests

The American people are a diverse lot with many interests. Parties seek to bring together a majority coalition of these different peoples to win elections by emphasizing common goals. This is no easy task. Despite the fact that parties seek to appeal to a broad cross-section of the public, there are differences between our two major parties. The Republican Party is more conservative, whereas the Democratic Party is more liberal. Each party has regular followers as well. African Americans are much more likely to support Democrats, and the Christian Right leans toward the Republican Party.

Simplifying Voter Choice

The electoral landscape is complicated, and voters have limited time to organize information about competing candidates. The labels "Democrat" and "Republican" provide valuable information in helping voters make choices in the voting booth. The information is not perfect—not all Republicans hold the same view on any issue, for example—but it is generally reliable.

And although information on presidential nominees is easy to find, in many other races little information is available. For these races, party labels may be the only real guidance a voter has.

Organizing the Government

Congress is organized along party lines. The majority party has the power and responsibility for running Congress on a day-to-day basis. Without parties, mustering a majority to pass legislation would be difficult. When a new president is elected, loyal supporters brought in to carry out the president's vision of government lead the executive branch. In addition, political parties are essential in bridging the separation of powers. Members of the same political party work together across institutional lines. Common party membership can help members of the House and Senate work together and assist relations between Congress and the president. Similarly, party membership helps coordinate relations between state and federal officials.

Developing Policy Solutions

The leaders of political parties, both in and out of office, work to develop a clear agenda to present to the public. By identifying problems and posing solutions, they hope to develop support among the electorate. Successfully transforming ideas into law provides a record of accomplishments that the party can use to run for reelection. Similarly, the opposition party will attempt to use its alternative proposals to gain electoral advantage. This competition serves to educate the public about the important issues of the day. Every four years, in national conventions, the major political parties draft and ratify a **party platform** that includes the guiding philosophy and the issue positions of the party.

Compare political party platforms.

Political parties, when they function well, serve to make our complex democratic system more workable. Without political parties, the tasks of voters, candidates, and government officials would be more difficult. Voters would have to invest much more time in making intelligent electoral choices. Candidates would have to work even more to run for office and connect with voters. Congress would need another way to organize itself, and the separation of powers would be even more difficult to bridge. Elections themselves would be run differently, and new checks against fraud would have to be developed. Thus, political parties are important, even essential, in the American political system. This makes their limitations all the more frustrating.

A Brief History of Political Parties in the United States

Political parties have a long history in the United States. They have been around nearly as long as the nation itself. Furthermore, the nation's two major parties—the Democratic Party and the Republican Party—are among the oldest political parties in the world. The Democratic Party traces its heritage back to the 1790s and the leadership of Thomas Jefferson. It was founded in 1828 as an Andrew Jackson–led splinter group of the Jeffersonian Republicans and formally became known as the Democratic Party in 1840. The Republican Party emerged in 1854. By 1860, the Republicans controlled the White House—with the election of Abraham Lincoln—and both houses of Congress.

For more than 140 years, the United States has had the same two major parties. Americans see this party system as constant, even permanent, but this belief is inaccurate. Beneath this surface of stability have been two centuries of change for political parties in the United States. This history of change can be divided into six distinct party eras. The dates are approximate but do provide a rough outline. The eras of political parties are depicted in Figure 7.1.

One remarkable feature of this history of change has been the regularity with which it occurs. Within a party era, one party consistently dominates politics by winning elections on a regular basis. Historically, party control of American politics has changed every thirty to forty years. Students of parties and elections call the change between one party era and the next a **critical realignment,** and the election in which the change occurs is a **critical** or **realigning election.** As we will see, critical realignments have a variety of causes. They can occur because of major crises, such as the Civil War and the Great Depression, or other still important but less profound events.

1796–1824: The First Political Parties

At the founding, there were no formal political parties in the United States. The Constitution makes no mention of parties, and it is clear from the method of selecting the president that parties were not anticipated. But parties formed quickly as some of the political differences that emerged in the fight over ratification carried over into the politics of the new republic. Thomas Jefferson and James Madison formed the first coalition, known as the Jeffersonian-Republicans or the **Democratic-Republicans.** The early party formed in opposition to Washington administration economic policy, and its support came primarily from agrarian interests in the South and West. In response, supporters of the Constitution, the **Federalist Party,** formed a second loose coalition or political party. Its support came largely from commercial interests, the cities, and generally from the North. These parties differed significantly from parties today. They were made up of the elite in society, for only white male property owners could vote.

In the first contested presidential election in 1796 (George Washington had no opposition in 1788 or 1792), the Federalist John Adams defeated Thomas Jefferson. But in their 1800 rematch, Jefferson was victorious, and the Federalists quickly faded as a national political force. Democratic-Republicans won every presidential election from 1800 until 1824. By 1820,

Preparty period
before 1796
1789   Washington unanimously elected president
1792   Washington unanimously reelected

First party system
1796–1815 (Democratic Republican dominance)

Democratic Republican Jefferson (1800, 1804) Madison (1808, 1812) Monroe (1816)	**Federalist** Adams (1796)

"Era of Good Feelings"
1815–1828 (No party competition)
1820   Monroe
1824   J. Q. Adams

Second party system
1828–1856 (Democratic dominance)

Democratic Jackson (1828, 1832) Van Buren (1836) Polk (1844) Pierce (1852) Buchanan (1856)	**National Republican Whig** Harrison (1840) Taylor (1848)

Third party system
1860–1892 (Divided government)

Democratic Cleveland (1884, 1892)	**Republican** Lincoln (1860, 1864) Grant (1868, 1872) Hayes (1876) Garfield (1880) Harrison (1888)

Fourth party system
1896–1928 (Republican dominance)

Democratic Wilson (1912, 1916)	**Republican** McKinley (1896, 1900) T. Roosevelt (1904) Taft (1908) Harding (1920) Coolidge (1924) Hoover (1928)

Fifth party system
1932–1964 (Democratic dominance)

Democratic F. D. Roosevelt (1932, 1936, 1940, 1944) Truman (1948) Kennedy (1960) Johnson (1964)	**Republican** Eisenhower (1952, 1956)

Sixth party system
1968–(Partisan dealignment)

Democratic Carter (1976) Clinton (1992, 1996)	**Republican** Nixon (1968, 1972) Reagan (1980, 1984) G. H. W. Bush (1988) G. W. Bush (2000, 2004)

Figure 7.1 Major Parties in American History. There have been six distinct party eras in American political history. They are noted above along with the presidents elected during each era by party and date of election.

the Federalists became so weak that they did not even put forward an opposition candidate; James Monroe ran unopposed for the presidency. This period was known as the Era of Good Feeling, and for a time it seemed as if partisan competition was a thing of the past.

1828–1856: The Emergence of the Democratic Party

The Era of Good Feeling ended quickly. By the election of 1824, internal squabbling had torn apart the Democratic-Republican Party. Four candidates ran for the presidency: General Andrew Jackson, Speaker of the House Henry Clay, Secretary of State John Quincy Adams, and William H. Crawford. Each was a member of the now splintered Democratic-Republican Party. Jackson received the most popular votes, but no candidate received a majority of the electoral college. In the House of Representatives, Adams was awarded the presidency. Outraged, Jackson moved beyond the elite in control at the time and appealed directly to the vastly expanded electorate. Jackson, along with his associate Martin Van Buren, formed the **Democratic Party.** The Democrats largely controlled American politics until the 1850s and were the first modern mass political party. They began using national conventions to nominate presidential candidates and awarded government jobs to their supporters. A second new party, the **Whig Party,** emerged out of the Adams-Clay faction of the old Democratic-Republican Party. The Whigs would elect two presidents: William Henry Harrison in 1840 and Zachary Taylor in 1848. They were a diverse, often splintered coalition of northern industrialists and southern planters.

1860–1892: The Emergence of the Republican Party

By the mid-1850s, the party system was again sent into chaos. This time it was the issue of slavery as well as other economic issues that divided the then dominant Democratic Party and split, once and for all, the already fractious Whigs. The central question was the expansion of slavery into the western territories. The Democrats, strong in both the North and the South, unsuccessfully tried to avoid the issue, and by 1860 there were two Democratic candidates for president, a southerner (Vice President John C. Breckinridge of Kentucky) and a northerner (Senator Stephen A. Douglas of Illinois). The Whigs were weak already, and other parties had emerged in the late 1840s, such as the Free Soil Party and the Know-Nothing Party. As these parties were disintegrating, the **Republican Party** emerged in 1854 from former supporters of all these parties, as well as antislavery Democrats, who were all united against the expansion of slavery. Abraham Lincoln won only 40 percent of the popular vote in 1860, but he emerged with a strong electoral college majority of exclusively northern states. The Republicans also took control of the Senate in 1860. After the Civil War, the nation remained sharply divided regionally along party lines. The Republicans dominated the North and

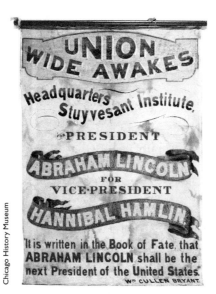

A poster for Abraham Lincoln's 1860 campaign. The election of 1860 led to the emergence of the Republican Party as the dominant party in American politics until 1932.

Chicago History Museum

West, while the Democrats controlled the South (where they would remain dominant until the 1960s). During the 1880s and 1890s, control of the presidency and Congress went back and forth between the Democrats and Republicans. This was a period of divided government. No one party consistently won the presidency and majorities of both the House and the Senate at the same time.

1896–1928: A New Republican Dominance

The election of 1896 put the Republican Party largely in control of the national government until 1932. The election was hotly contested, and turnout hit an all-time high of 80 percent. The Democratic Party, which was controlled by radical farmers, nominated William Jennings Bryan, a populist, for president. He and the Democrats supported reform of the currency system ("free silver") and generally opposed big business. With a platform of high tariffs, a continuation of hard money based on the gold standard, and industrialization, the Republicans and their presidential candidate, William McKinley, won the election of 1896. Although the Republican Party had been in power earlier, 1896 was a critical election. It reaffirmed Republican power with a new expanded electoral base of eastern industrialists, urban blue-collar workers, and many westerners. A victory by Democrat Woodrow Wilson in a three-way presidential race in 1912 broke the Republican stranglehold on the White House. The incumbent, William Howard Taft, ran as a Republican while former president Theodore Roosevelt ran on the Bull Moose Party ticket. The boom economy of the Roaring Twenties, however, swept the Republicans back into power until 1932.

1932–1964: The Great Depression Puts the Democrats in Power

The Great Depression that began in 1929, along with President Hoover's handling of the crisis, led to a new party era. The election of 1932 brought the presidency to Franklin Delano Roosevelt and the Democratic Party, which was to dominate national politics for the next four decades. The **New Deal coalition,** as supporters of the Democrats were known, was a remarkably broad and diverse group: blue-collar workers, southerners, northern liberals, intellectuals, Catholics, Jews, African Americans, and the poor. The election of 1932 is one of the clearest examples of a critical election in American politics.

Aside from the election of World War II hero General Dwight D. Eisenhower as president in 1952 and 1956, the Democrats controlled the White House until 1968. Dominance in Congress was even greater; Republicans won a majority of the House and Senate only in the 1948 and 1952 elections. By 1968, however, the New Deal coalition was breaking up. Conflicts over civil rights and the Vietnam War divided the Democratic Party. The Democrats have controlled the White House, the House of Representatives, and the Senate at the same time for only six years since 1968.

1968–Today: Party Dealignment?

Many analysts saw the election of Richard Nixon in 1968 as the beginning of a new Republican era. For the first time in generations, Republicans made inroads into the once solidly Democratic South. The Watergate scandal stopped Republican expansion for a time, however. In 1980, when Ronald Reagan was elected and Republicans took control of the Senate, analysts looked for electoral realignment. But this did not occur. The Democrats regained control of the Senate in 1986. Republican George H. W. Bush won the White House in 1988, but Congress remained in Democratic hands. With the election of Bill Clinton in 1992, Democrats controlled the presidency, the House, and Senate until the 1994 election. Republicans won control of both houses of Congress after 1994. In the 2000 election, for the first time since 1952, Republicans gained control of all three elected branches of the national government. But this control was weak and short-lived. The 2000 presidential race was the closest in history, the Senate was equally divided at fifty Republicans and fifty Democrats, and the Republican majority in the House was razor thin. With the May 2001 switch of Republican James Jeffords (Vt.) to being an independent, control of the Senate went to the Democrats. In 2002 the Republicans regained control of the Senate. In 2004, for the first time since 1988, a presidential candidate won a majority of the popular vote. Unlike in 2000, George W. Bush won a clear victory in a close election, and Republicans slightly increased their majorities in both the House and the Senate. The 2006 election reversed the control of Congress yet again, with Democrats gaining a sizable majority in the House and a 51 to 49 edge in the Senate.

"The Jeffords Switch and Public Support for Divided Government," Stephen P. Nicholson.

The last three-plus decades are best characterized as a period of **divided government,** a circumstance in which neither of the major parties consistently controls both houses of Congress and the presidency at the same time (see Chapter 9). Divided government goes beyond the national government to the states. The percentage of state governments controlled by one party has steadily declined since 1948.[11]

Why do we have divided government? Some have argued that we are now in a period of party **dealignment** because political parties are too weak to organize the electoral system or command allegiance from the electorate (we will talk more about the weakness of parties later in the chapter).[12] Others discount this idea, noting that parties are weaker, but believing that with the right leaders, one of the major parties can again dominate politics. Some have argued that voters like divided government. Voters use **split ticket voting**—selecting candidates from more than one party on a ballot—to ensure that no one party gains control and political gridlock continues.

Why Two Parties?

Even in our current era of divided government and weak political parties, one fact remains: We have two, and only two, major political parties in the United States. This makes the United States different from most other democracies, where multiparty systems flourish. In other nations, parties are often formed around more distinct ideological orientations or ethnic and religious groups. Yet our two-party system has persisted for more than two centuries.

One key reason that we have two parties is our electoral system. Discussed in more detail in Chapter 8, our winner-take-all plurality system of elections encourages two parties. In this system, candidates for a specific office are running to fill one seat. The winner is the candidate receiving the most votes—a plurality—regardless of whether that person garners an absolute majority or not. This winner-take-all system works in the electoral college as well. Nothing is gained by coming in second or third, as would be the case in a proportional representation system (see Chapter 8).

Other reasons for the perpetuation of the two-party system are tradition and culture as well as state and federal laws that favor two parties. The first two parties, the Federalists and the Democratic-Republicans, derived from supporters and opponents of the Constitution. Whereas many nations are divided by major economic, cultural, and religious schisms,

Is the two-party system still viable?

this has not historically been the case in the United States. For example, the vast majority of Americans accept the basic ideals of capitalism, and the United States has managed to successfully separate religion from politics for most of our history. Now, two centuries later, Americans simply accept and expect two parties. The two major parties further encourage this by being open to change in their ideals to attract new members.

State and federal laws also benefit the two major parties. Republicans and Democrats are often given automatic places on state ballots, but other parties are required to gather signatures on petitions to gain ballot access. The order in which parties are listed on the ballot is often determined by the outcome of the last election. As a result, minor parties generally appear further down on the ballot, making them less visable to voters. Presidential candidates for both the Republican Party and Democratic Party nominations potentially receive matching government funds (see Chapter 8). Minor party candidates are not automatically eligible for these funds. In the general election, the two major party presidential candidates receive automatic government funding. In contrast, minor party candidates qualify only if they win a minimum of 5 percent of the popular vote.

The Role of Minor Parties

Although the odds are stacked against their success, **minor parties,** sometimes known as **third parties,** are continuing features of the American electoral landscape. Take the 2004 presidential election as an example. Seventeen candidates appeared on at least one state ballot. Seven candidates were on the ballot in at least three-quarters of the states. In addition to George W. Bush (Republican) and John F. Kerry (Democrat)—who combined to win 99 percent of the vote—the names of Ralph Nader (Independent Party), Michael Badnarik (Libertarian Party), Michael A. Peroutka (Constitution Party), and David Cobb (Green Party) were found on most state ballots, and each received over 100,000 popular votes.[13] Of these, Nader won the most votes, nearly 464,000 (.38 percent of the popular vote).

It is unusual for minor parties to have an impact on the outcome of an election, but there have been exceptions. In the twentieth century alone, Theodore Roosevelt's Bull Moose Progressive Party split the Republican vote with William Howard Taft, allowing the Democrat Woodrow Wilson to win. Some argue that Ross Perot's independent candidacy in 1992 cost George H. W. Bush a second term and that in the remarkably close 2000 election Ralph Nader gave George W. Bush the presidency.[14] Since 1924, only three minor party candidates have won electoral votes: Strom Thurmond in 1948, Harry Byrd in 1960, and George Wallace in 1968. In all three cases, the candidates were southern Democrats who pulled away from the party over civil rights policy. Minor party candidates do sometimes win significant political office. Two recent governors, Angus King of Maine and Jesse Ventura of Minnesota, won without major party endorsement. Congressman Bernard Sanders of Vermont has served for more than a decade as an independent. But the success of these politicians is unusual.

Vote totals alone do not capture the true relevance of minor parties in American politics.[15] Minor parties serve as a political home to those whose ideologies fall outside the political mainstream. Two long-standing ideological parties are the Socialist Party and the Libertarian Party. The Socialists appeal to the political left and were a significant political force early in the twentieth century. More recently, the Libertarians, supporters of personal freedom as well as a small and narrowly focused government, have been particularly active. Minor parties also serve as a safety valve in American politics. They allow those who are dissatisfied to express their frustration. Finally, minor parties have been a source of policy ideas. Direct election of senators, the graduated income tax, and Social Security are all examples. In 1992 Ross Perot made the budget deficit a major issue. Like many issues brought to American politics by minor parties, the deficit was taken over by the two major parties. Throughout the 1990s, the Green Party—pushing an environmental and governmental reform agenda—captured the interest of many Americans, including young people.

Three Viewpoints on Political Parties Today

One of the major themes in American politics since the 1970s has been the decline of parties. Analysts have argued that political parties in the United States have fallen on hard times. Voters are not attached to them, organizations are weak and ineffective, and leaders of the same party do not work together.[16] More recently, however, some political scientists have seen a resurgence in political parties.[17] To examine these claims and counterclaims, we will look at political parties from three perspectives: **parties in the electorate, parties as organizations,** and **parties in government.**

Parties in the Electorate

Party membership in the United States requires little commitment by the average person. Anyone who thinks he or she is a Democrat is a Democrat. The same holds for Republicans. By way of contrast, in European countries, political party membership indicates that one has formally joined an organization. One pays dues and can participate in selecting leaders. As we will see in the next section, party organizations in the United States are made of relatively small cadres of activists. Party membership for Americans is an emotional or psychological link often carried over from generation to generation in a family (see Chapter 5).

This link between individuals and political parties, known as **party identification,** is important in American politics. Often, this emotional link is converted to a vote. Those who think of themselves as Democrats vote for Democratic candidates. Since 1952, the National Election Study has asked the same question to a sample of Americans: "Generally speaking, do you usually think of yourself as a Republican, a Democrat, or an Independent?" Figure 7.2 presents the results of this question over the last five decades.

In examining partisanship since 1952, several key trends can be identified. First, the percentage of independents steadily rose from 1952 through 1972 and has remained fairly stable since. Second, although support for both the Democratic Party and the Republican Party has declined, Democrats have suffered the larger loss of support. Third, throughout the period, however, Democratic partisans have outnumbered Republican supporters. Table 7.1 presents the characteristics of party identifiers.

Finally, it is important to note that about two-thirds of Americans still identify with either the Republican or Democratic Party. Furthermore, many independents are "leaners," people who lean toward supporting

Examine who supports the two major political parties.

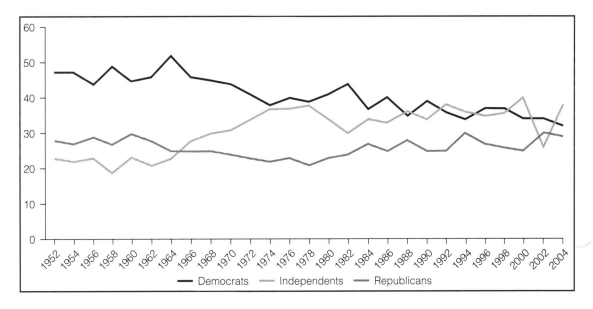

Figure 7.2 Partisan Identification of Americans, 1952–2004. Since 1952, the percentage of independents has increased, largely at the expense of Democratic supporters.

Source: 1952–2004 National Election Studies, Center for Political Studies, University of Michigan.

one party or the other. The rise of independents has largely come from increasing numbers of leaners. The number of true independents—those without leanings toward one of the major parties—has grown little since 1952. As seen in Figure 7.3, about 10 percent of Americans were true independents in 2004.

Republicans are more likely to be:	Democrats are more likely to be:
• male	• female
• college graduates	• high school graduates or less
• people with incomes over $50,000	• people with incomes below $50,000
• born-again Christians	• union members
• conservatives	• liberals
• whites	• African Americans
• Protestants	• Jews

Table 7.1 Who Identifies Themselves as Democrats and Republicans?

Source: Author analysis of the 2004 National Election Study, Center for Political Studies, University of Michigan.

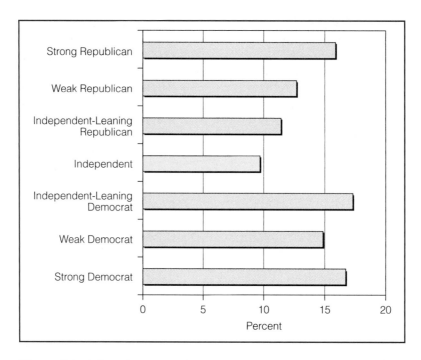

Figure 7.3 A Detailed Look at Partisanship in the American Electorate, 2004. Relatively few people are true independent voters. Most at least lean in the direction of one of the major parties.

Source: 2004 National Election Study, Center for Political Studies, University of Michigan.

These last two points are important. All is not lost for the parties, as some have argued over the last thirty years.[18] There was a decline in support for the two parties in the 1970s. But beginning in the 1980s, Americans have become more attached to political parties again. In examining voting behavior in national elections since 1952, political scientist Larry Bartels found that partisan voting has increased in every election since 1972. American voters are more likely then in the recent past to vote for candidates of only one party. When a voter selects only candidates from one party, it is known as **straight ticket voting.** Split ticket voting—where an individual votes for candidates of both parties for different offices on the ballot—is still an important phenomenon. But if Bartels is correct, it is less important than it once was. All political scientists do not agree with this assessment, but there is considerable evidence that political parties have made a significant comeback in the American electorate.

Parties as Organizations

There is no one Democratic Party or Republican Party in the United States. Rather, there are complex networks of party organizations at the national, state, and local levels. Fragmentation and autonomy best characterize these organizations. In many complex organizations, such as a large corporation or a military unit, orders come down from the top. The leaders, a corporate president or a general, hand down orders to subordinates who carry them out. Political parties in the United States look very different. Independent party organizations exist at the local, state, and national levels for both parties. Although they sometimes coordinate their work, the three levels of each political party most often work separately.

For most of their history, local party organizations were the most active and vibrant level of party organization. Since the 1960s, however, American politics has changed considerably. Most important, for political parties, elections have become money intensive and candidate centered. Extensive party organization is no longer as important to winning elections as it once was. In part, this has led to a decline in local party organizations, but national and state party organizations have grown in expertise and influence. National and state parties have retooled themselves as service providers to candidates. These higher-level party organizations still cannot command either candidates or local parties, but they do play a more significant role in American politics.

National Party Organizations Each of the major parties has a national committee, and that committee sponsors a national convention every four years. The convention meets to nominate presidential and vice presidential candidates, to write a party platform that states the party's philosophy and policy positions, to create rules for the next presidential nomination cycle, and to serve as a place for party activists to meet like-minded individuals and make connections. Between conventions, a national committee made up of representatives from each state supervises the party's operations. A national chairperson runs the day-to-day operations of the party.

Over the last three decades, the national parties have grown and become more prosperous. The parties now have large staffs that support electoral activity. In the early 1970s, both major parties had staffs of approximately two dozen. By the mid-1990s, those staffs had grown to several hundred each.[19] The national organizations serve as support organizations for candidates. They train candidates and campaign staff, conduct and pay for polling, do media consulting, and provide administrative support. This work is supported through aggressive fund-raising. The methods for raising this money have changed in recent year as Congress has passed new laws regulating political fund-raising. Parties may now raise only "hard money," funds subject to federal contribution limits. (The details will be discussed in Chapter 8.) But the parties raise hundreds of millions of dollars during each two-year election cycle. For example, in the last 2003–2004 presidential election cycle, the Democratic National Committee raised over $310 million and the Republican National Committee raised over $392 million. Affiliate organizations raise millions more.[20]

In addition to the national committees, fund-raising committees exist for both the House and the Senate members of each of the two major parties. They are known as the Democratic Congressional Campaign Committee, the National Republican Congressional Committee, the Democratic Senatorial Campaign Committee, and the National Republican Senatorial Campaign Committee. All four committees target their money—each has raised in the tens of millions of dollars in recent campaign cycles—to close races in the hope of winning as many seats for their party as possible.

State Party Organizations State party organizations look much like their national counterparts. They have a state chairperson who runs the organization, and a state committee is selected to oversee the operation. State parties also hold conventions, where they nominate candidates, draft platforms, develop rules, and select delegates to the national convention. Like national parties, many state parties have expanded their operations in recent years, and now they function as service agencies, providing candidates in their state with professional staff expertise and money.[21] State legislative campaign committees have emerged over the last decade to become major players in state legislative elections.[22] In recent years, however, the national parties have been able to exert some power through increasingly large transfers of funds from national parties to the states.[23]

Richard J. Daley, shown here celebrating his first mayoral victory, served as mayor of Chicago from 1955 through 1976. During his time in office, Daley led one of the most powerful political machines in the United States.

Local Party Organizations Early in the twentieth century, local parties were at the center of American politics. Powerful local party organizations, known as **party machines,** controlled government employment and government contracts. Patronage—jobs, contracts, and other benefits controlled by party leaders—was granted to those who supported and worked for the party. Leaders of these machines decided who ran for office. The faithful were rewarded, and those who displeased the leadership were not. To keep the electorate happy, local party bosses provided social services through their vast networks of party workers. The success of party machines came from the combination of controlling city payrolls, access to the ballot, and the dispensing of city services.

Machines were most prevalent in the cities of the Northeast and the Midwest. Chicago was the home of one of the most powerful political machines. Consolidated in the early 1930s, it was led by one of the United States' most powerful and famous mayors, Richard J. Daley, from 1955 until 1976. Only the remnants of the great machines continue today, in such cities as Chicago, Philadelphia, and Albany, New York.

Local parties, now usually centered at the county level, have been hard hit by two important structural changes. First, patronage jobs were eliminated with the advent and expansion of the civil service. Rather than appointing political friends to jobs, most government jobs are now awarded to those who score well on civil service exams. Second, the organizations that were central to electoral success for so long are no longer needed. Rather than go door to door to speak with voters individually, candidates today use the mass media to communicate with thousands, even millions, of voters at once.

Local parties today are largely volunteer organizations, with no staffs and little funding. Local party organizations often gear up for elections. They distribute literature, post lawn signs, encourage loyal supporters to go to the polls, and recruit workers to watch the polls. In a much more limited way than before, local parties communicate with voters on a one-to-one basis. Although not as significant as in the past, local party organizations do provide citizens with the opportunity to become involved in party politics in their own communities.

Parties in Government

The party in government is the group of elected and appointed officials who are affiliated with a party. The parties present alternative policy ideas to the electorate during campaigns. The policy ideas put forward are most often associated with presidential candidates, but as was true with the 1994 "Contract with America," a ten-point Republican agenda developed by then House Speaker Newt Gingrich, policy leadership can come from Congress as well.

The news media tend to focus on policy promises that are not kept. President Bush's "read my lips: no new taxes" pledge in 1988 and President Clinton's failed promise to open the military to gays and lesbians are two examples. This has led many Americans to believe that politicians don't keep their campaign promises.[24] Despite what many Americans believe, party leaders in government work hard to ensure that their campaign promises turn into law. Political scientist Gerald Pomper found that the party that captured the White House *on average* carried through on more than 75 percent of its platform promises with new laws. In most other cases, efforts were made to carry through on promises, but action failed. Few promises were ignored entirely.[25] This means that the party that controls our institutions of government—the presidency, the House, and the Senate—matters.

All presidential initiatives are not equally likely to be successful. Much depends on the party makeup of the presidency and Congress. To examine this, let's look at presidential success rates, a widely used statistic that is the percentage of votes in Congress that the president wins where the president has taken a clear position.[26] The records of presidents Bill Clinton and George W. Bush are instructive. During Clinton's first two years in office, with a Democratic-controlled Congress, measures that he supported were successful a remarkable 86.4 percent of the time. After the 1994 congressional elections, with new Republican majorities in both the House and Senate, President Clinton's success with Congress took a nosedive during his last six years in office. Clinton's success rates then ranged from 35 to 55 percent. George W. Bush, with Republican majorities in both the House and Senate, had an 81-percent success rate during his first term. During periods of unified government, the majority party, led by the president, is likely to be successful in making laws and moving a policy agenda. But during periods of divided government, presidents are likely to be frustrated, unable to effect policy change.

Another way to examine the role of parties in government is to look at Congress. Congress is organized along party lines, with the majority party controlling chairmanships and the lion's share of staff. (This subject is discussed in some detail in Chapter 9.) Partisanship plays an important role in congressional voting as well. Figure 7.4 presents **party unity scores,** the percentage of votes on legislation in which a majority of one party votes against a majority of the other party, in the House and Senate since the 1950s. A higher party unity score indicates that the Republicans and Democrats of the two chambers of Congress are more unified—they are voting together on legislation—and that the two parties are more divided. Figure 7.4 indicates that the parties were less cohesive, and less partisan, in the 1970s than in the 1950s and 1960s. Partisan voting rose significantly during the 1980s and has remained high since. Similarly, in the last few years Republicans and Democrats in both the House and Senate have voted as more unified groups than at any time in the last four decades. For example, an average of 88 percent of Senate Republicans supported the party position on roll call votes during 2005. House Republicans supported their party's position at an 88 percent rate. Both Senate Democrats and House Democrats supported their party's position, on average, 88 percent of the time.[27] House Democrats set a record for the highest level of partisan voting in 2005. The other groups were unified at near record levels.

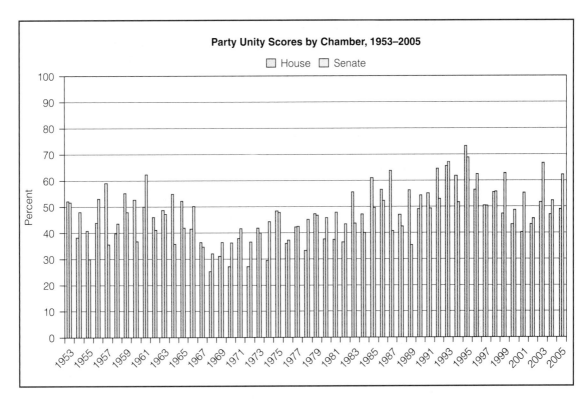

Figure 7.4 Party Unity Scores in the House and Senate, 1957–2005

Source: CQ Weekly, January 9, 2006.

Students of Congress agree that partisanship in Congress has grown in the last two decades and may even be at its highest point since the nineteenth century. Congressional partisanship increased in the 1980s and early 1990s as Republicans regained strength. It surged again after the Republican takeover of Congress in 1994 as the new majority moved aggressively to assert control. As the parties generally have become more ideologically cohesive (see Table 7.1), so too have members of Congress. This combination has led to high levels of partisan rancor in the current closely divided Congress.

Reassessing Parties in American Politics

Our examination of American political parties from three viewpoints shows that the parties have made a significant comeback since they were presumed dead in the early 1970s. Political parties today are more energetic and more effective organizations in the electorate and in government than they were in the 1970s. Americans still look to party labels in deciding which candidate to vote for. Party organizations have regrouped—their roles are different from before—and are currently stronger than at any time since the 1950s. In Congress, too, party unity has resurfaced. These changes go hand in hand. For example, as Congress has grown more partisan, the public has responded with more partisan voting. Although parties do not dominate the political landscape as they once did, they have quietly returned to a place of prominence in American politics. Political parties today still perform most of their traditional functions. They simplify voter choice, organize elections, and organize government. However, parties must now compete for the American electorate's attention with candidates, the media, and interest groups. Candidates run their own campaigns, and parties do not control ballot access as they once did. The public looks to the media for information on politics, and political parties have only a limited ability to shape the information that Americans get about politics.

In short, the role of political parties in American politics has become more limited over the last century. But parties are better able to compete now than in recent decades.

Interest Groups

One of the common themes of American political history has been concern with the role of **factions,** the term James Madison used to describe interest groups in *Federalist* No. 10. Madison argued that humans by their very nature are driven to promote their private interest over the good of the whole. He saw factions as the primary threat to republics. If factions were successful in meeting their private goals, the consequence would be the erosion of liberty. The preservation of liberty was, for Madison, the essential purpose of any government. Yet Madison also saw that the pursuit of self-interest was closely tied to the existence of liberty: "Liberty is to faction what air is to fire." The solution to "the mischiefs of faction" was the republican government created in the U.S. Constitution. As Madison put it, the separation of powers and checks and balances built into the system would serve to "control for the effects" of faction. (For more on Madison, see Chapter 2.)

Read *Federalist* No. 10.

Much has been written about interest-group politics since, but nothing has been more elegant than Madison's *Federalist* No. 10. The concern that Madison identified more than 215 years ago is still with us today. To make matters worse, critics of interest groups argue that the scale of the problem is tremendously larger today than Madison could ever have envisioned. Interest groups are no longer simply small groups of citizens. Groups today can have millions of members or be made up of the corporate elite. They can have professional staffs that number in the hundreds, and their large pools of campaign funds can alter the outcome of elections. Some argue that organized interests have grown so powerful that they have destroyed the very system they seek to use.[28] But as Madison also pointed out, the pursuit of self-interested policy goals is an example of exercising the liberty that an open society affords citizens.

Other modern commentators emphasize that interest groups provide vital roles in a complex nation.[29] The most basic is that interest groups are a form of representation. They provide a link between the American people and their government, giving individual citizens a real chance to participate in the political process. In short, the dilemma that James Madison identified in *Federalist* No. 10 in 1788 is still with us today: How do we balance the public good against the self-interested political claims of groups of like-minded citizens?

What Interests Are Represented by Groups?

There have always been organized interest groups seeking to influence politics in the United States, and Americans have long been known as joiners. Lobbying in Congress began with its first meeting in 1789.[30] Even the term *lobbyist* is 170 years old. The famous French chronicler of American life in the 1830s, Alexis de Tocqueville, noted the proliferation of groups in the United States:

> *Americans of all ages, all stations in life, and all types of disposition are forever forming associations. They are not only commercial and industrial associations in which all take part, but others of a thousand other types—religious, moral, serious, futile, very general and very limited, immensely large and very minute.*[31]

The American political landscape is now characterized by a plethora of interest groups, but all groups are not alike. They vary in a number of ways. Some groups are made up of members, at times millions of them, who join voluntarily. Other interests are not really groups at all. They represent a single member, most commonly a corporation. Many groups have large professional staffs; others are made up primarily of volunteers. Groups may have a broad range of interests in government, or they may focus narrowly on a single interest. Some focus on national and even international issues, others on local issues. Over the last three decades, the range of interests that groups represent has grown as the number of interest groups in the United States has grown. Their interests vary greatly. But what is clear in Figure 7.5 is that the interest-group landscape of Washington, D.C., is still dominated, in number and in spending, by business interests.[32]

Business Associations, Trade Associations, and Corporations

Clearly, the largest single type of organized interest active in American politics is business interests. In the most recent survey of its kind, using data from 1996, almost 60 percent of the groups with representation in our nation's capital seek to further the goals of corporate and business interests. These groups spent over three-fourths of the money spent by all groups to influence policy in Washington, D.C.[33] Recent evidence suggests that business interest groups are more active than ever before.[34] Government activity—taxes and regulations of all kinds—has a major impact on the

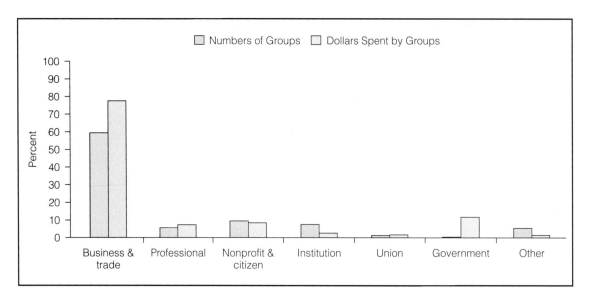

Figure 7.5 Types of Interest Groups in American Politics. Business interests dominate the Washington, D.C., interest-group landscape.

Source: Baumgartner and Leech, 2001.

profits and losses of business. Recently, with a president and Congress receptive to their goals, business interests have become even more aggressive in their lobbying efforts.

One of the most prominent ways that business interests are represented is through peak business and trade associations. **Peak business associations** promote the general interests of corporate America. Examples include the National Association of Manufacturers, the U.S. Chamber of Commerce, and the Business Roundtable. They seek to lower taxes, to limit regulation, and to hold down wage costs. For example, in its 2004 report to members, the National Association of Manufacturers (NAM) reported on a number of policy victories, including tax relief, changes in the way corporate pension plans are funded, and trade agreements with Australia and Chile that the NAM hopes will increase exports. NAM also worked to stop expansion of the Family and Medical Leave Act to apply to more workers and successfully pushed for Labor Department rule changes that allowed employers to pay for overtime work with "comp" time instead of overtime wages.[35] Other peak associations worked on similar issues.

Trade associations bring together competitors in a business area who seek to promote common interests. The 150-plus members of the American Chemistry Council (formerly the Chemical Manufacturers Association) may compete on many fronts, but each member seeks to limit the role of environmental regulations on its business and promotes the idea that chemical producers are responsible corporate citizens. Similar associations exist for hundreds of other industries. Some are large and powerful, including the American Bankers Association, with more than 8,000 institutional members, a staff of over 4,000, and a $62-million budget. Others are less well-known but equally important to their members. For example, the Wine Institute has a $6.5-million budget, more than two dozen headquarter employees, offices in seven other cities, and lobbyists representing it in forty states as well as Washington, D.C.[36] These organizations are not unique, but most of the thousands of trade organizations are smaller and less prominent.

Individual corporations are also active in representing their own interests. The nation's business community has many interests in common, but industry groups and specific corporations may be at odds over specific government policies. Virtually all of the companies on the Fortune 500 and Forbes 400 lists have government relations offices or other representation in Washington, D.C. Many are represented in state capitals as well. Anheuser-Busch, America's largest brewer, has a lobbyist in all fifty state capitals in addition to two full-time representatives, plus a dozen or more outside firms under contract in the nation's capital.[37] Although large corporations often hire full-time lobbyists—even staffs of lobbyists—firms large and small hire consultants as needed, who may represent many businesses to represent their interests in government centers. For example, Hewlett-Packard spent $734,000 in 2004 on lobbyists. This turned out to be money well spent, for the company's representatives convinced Congress to pass legislation that saved it millions of dollars in taxes.[38]

Professional Associations

Professional associations bring together individuals with the same occupation, most commonly occupations requiring some technical training or expertise. These associations are as varied as the work Americans do. Architects, financial planners, piano tuners, and zoologists all have one or more professional associations. Even political scientists are organized, through the American Political Science Association. These groups have a variety of nonpolitical goals, from providing information on new developments in the field to hosting conferences. The level of political involvement for most associations is dependent on the profession's interaction with government and is generally focused on areas of specific interest to its members. The Graphic Artists Guild, an association of 3,000 illustrators and graphic designers, has worked hard in recent years to protect the copyright interests of its members. Health-care professions—the American Medical Association, the American Dental Association, and the American Association of Nurse Anesthetists are just three examples—are especially active in trying to influence government health-care policy. Government heavily regulates who can provide medical services, how and where medical care is delivered, and how much hospitals and providers will be paid for their services. Not surprisingly, business and trade associations are active in the health-care area as well.

Unions

Examine union membership and other data about interest groups.

Many fewer Americans are members of **labor unions** than a half-century ago—only 13 percent of the total work force and eight percent of the private-sector work force are now union members, whereas 33 percent belonged to a union in 1956—but unions remain a significant political force in the United States.[39] Most unions bring together workers who share an occupation or work in the same industry. The United Mine Workers and the National Education Association (the largest teachers union) are examples. Some, such as the Teamsters, have more diverse memberships. Not surprisingly, individual unions work on issues of concern to their membership. For instance, teachers unions are concerned with ensuring that funding for our nation's schools is adequate and work to ensure that teachers have strong professional credentials before entering the classroom.

Unions generally seek to promote better working conditions and improved wages. They have also been active supporters of liberal causes throughout the twentieth century. Labor has supported unemployment insurance, Social Security, Medicaid, Medicare, and civil rights. A major national force for unions has been the American Federation of Labor and Congress of Industrial Organizations (commonly known as the AFL-CIO). It is a union of unions that is one of the most powerful lobbies in Washington, D.C. Its influence rivals that of peak associations.

Citizen Groups

The range of citizen groups active in the United States is staggering. Most of these groups can be referred to as **public interest groups** because the ends they support—a cleaner environment, for example—will benefit the larger community, not just group members. Many of these groups are large national membership organizations, but others are small and concerned with local issues. Some have a broad range of concerns, but others focus on a single issue. Environmental groups include some of the largest membership organizations in the country, such as the National Wildlife Federation (4,400,000), the Nature Conservancy (1,000,000), and the Sierra Club (700,000). Many groups focus on civil liberties and civil rights. Two long-established groups of this kind are the American Civil Liberties Union (ACLU) and the National Association for the Advancement of Colored People (NAACP). The ACLU fights government intrusions into such liberties as free speech and the rights of the accused, and the NAACP promotes equality for African Americans.

Over the last thirty years, new interest groups have emerged to defend the rights of groups of Americans, such as women (for example, the National Organization for Women), gays and lesbians (Gay and Lesbian Alliance Against Defamation), Latinos (National Council of La Raza), and the disabled (American Association of People with Disabilities). Some groups seek to improve and reform the political system. For example, the

League of Women Voters encourages voter participation and advocates campaign finance reform. Common Cause promotes a similar agenda. Other groups promote child welfare (the Children's Defense Fund) and consumer protection, such as the Ralph Nader–led Public Citizen.

Not all groups of this type are liberal. Many conservative groups exist as well. The Pacific Legal Foundation advocates for the power of landowners over environmental regulations. Focus on the Family and the Family Research Council promote evangelical Christian values throughout American society. The American Center for Law and Justice promotes a conservative agenda that includes encouraging school prayer and tolerance for home schooling. The National Taxpayers Union seeks the general downsizing of government, including lower taxes and less government regulation.

The role of interest groups in stem cell research.

Some of the most influential groups in American politics are narrowly focused single-issue groups. Often, there are groups that clearly oppose one another in a single area. One example is gun control, where the 4,000,000-member National Rifle Association is countered by the smaller, but still substantial, 400,000-member Brady Campaign to Prevent Gun Violence (formerly known as Handgun Control, Incorporated). Groups in favor of abortion rights, such as the National Abortion Rights Action League, stand in sharp contrast to groups opposed to abortion; the National Right to Life Committee is an example. Other single-interest groups favor making English the nation's official language (English First), seek tougher drunk driving enforcement (Mothers Against Drunk Driving), and advocate zero population growth (Population Zero).

Government

A relatively new set of influential interests in the United States is the **intergovernmental lobby,** governments seeking to influence government. The growth of government interest groups has been spurred by the post–New Deal growth of government (discussed extensively in Chapter 3). States, counties, cities, towns, and school districts have their own associations to further the interests of their members. Some examples include the National Governors' Association, the Council of State Governments, the National League of Cities, and the U.S. Conference of Mayors. These groups seek favorable treatment in the form of more money and programs as well as more flexibility in how they spend the aid that they receive. Over the last decade, state government organizations have focused on reducing unfunded mandates, which are programs imposed from above without furnishing the money to pay for them (see Chapter 3).

Most of the intergovernmental lobby is bipartisan, with Democratic and Republican officials working together. At times this can create tension, as was the case during the efforts to reform welfare in the mid-1990s. Democratic and Republican governors sharply disagreed, with Democrats opposing reform and Republicans favoring change. The result was that the

National Governors' Association (NGA) became paralyzed and ineffective as an interest group. When interest groups have sharp internal disagreements, its members may act alone or in smaller subgroups. In the case of welfare reform, individual state governors and the Democratic Governors' Association and Republican Governors' Associations acted on their own, replacing the NGA in the welfare reform debate.[40] Similar problems often afflict other types of groups as well.

Other Types of Groups

Many other groups are not easily categorized. Foreign groups, farm groups, veterans' groups, and religious groups are all examples of interest groups not included in other categories. This does not mean they are unimportant. Veterans' groups—such as the Veterans of Foreign Wars and the American Legion—are important supporters of veterans' benefits, a major expenditure of the federal government.

Group Membership

In this section, we examine why individuals join interest groups and who these individuals are.

Why Do Americans Join Interest Groups?

One question that naturally comes up in discussing interest groups that depend on membership is very simple: why? Political scientist Robert Salisbury argues that groups provide three types of benefits to encourage membership: material benefits, purposive benefits, and solidary benefits.[41]

People who become members of interest groups are offered **material benefits** in the form of financial incentives and information. Members of the Graphic Artists Guild (GAG)—who are largely self-employed illustrators and graphic designers—receive access to favorable group health insurance rates and discounts on travel, shipping, and long-distance phone services. They receive a handbook, *Pricing and Ethical Guidelines*, that provides guidance on proper business practices. The Graphic Artists Guild also has local chapters around the country, and it sponsors an annual national conference. For many members of GAG, these benefits provide concrete reasons for joining. The benefits save members money and provide guidance that is hard to find elsewhere.

Individuals also join groups because they care about the goals of the organization. These are known as **purposive benefits.** Environmental groups attract members because people support the goals of clean air and protecting land from development. Groups on both sides of the abortion debate are also good examples. People feel passionately about the issue and want to join others in making sure their beliefs are translated into public policy.

The *Fortune* Washington Power 25.

Finally, members may be motivated to join a group because of **solidary benefits,** which include the sense of community, the friendship, and the connections a group might provide. The Adirondack Mountain Club (ADK) exists to preserve the upstate New York mountain range as wilderness, but its twenty-six local chapters serve an important social function as well. They organize outdoor trips and conservation projects of all types in the Adirondack Park. The ADK brings together people who enjoy the outdoors and want to preserve it. Members of a local chamber of commerce seek solidary benefits of another kind. Regular luncheons and other functions allow small-business owners to connect with other small-business owners for professional and social purposes.

Because people join groups for a variety of reasons, interest groups often provide a vast array of benefits and services, some of which are not closely related to the central mission of the organization and are distant from politics. The AARP (formerly known as the American Association of Retired Persons) provides many services to its members: discount prescription drugs, health insurance, mutual funds, a monthly magazine, and a travel service, along with the advocacy for government programs, such as Social Security and Medicare, that benefit seniors. In an AARP member survey, fewer than one in five members joined it for public policy advocacy. More joined for the publications that came with membership. Still others joined AARP for the prescription drug discounts and the mutual funds it offers.[42]

These significant benefits are necessary because of what is called the **free rider problem,** the fact that members and nonmembers alike will enjoy the fruits of an organization's work.[43] All seniors potentially benefit from the new, prescription drug coverage recently added to Medicare, not only AARP members. The passage of a tax cut for business will benefit all regardless of whether they are a member of a chamber of commerce. Although some people will join groups because they are committed to the mission, others need more. Over recent decades, interest groups have become increasingly sophisticated in providing these additional incentives. Groups are in competition for members and donations. Successful membership groups are those that find the right mix of benefits and advocacy.

Who Joins Interest Groups?

In 1960 political scientist E. E. Schattschneider argued that the interest group "chorus sings with a strong upper class bias."[44] In the almost half a century since Schattschneider wrote the *The Semi-Sovereign People,* this idea still rings true despite the fact that many new groups have emerged and citizen groups in particular have grown in number and influence. We have already learned that the vast majority of interest groups represent business. Many professional associations are also composed of affluent members. Doctors and lawyers are only two examples.

Also important is the fact that all Americans are not equally likely to join interest groups. Similar to what we will learn about those who vote and generally participate in politics in Chapter 8, Americans with high incomes are more likely to be members of interest groups than are those with low incomes. For example, in a survey conducted by three political scientists in 1990, 73 percent of those surveyed with incomes over $75,000 were affiliated with a political organization, but only 29 percent of those with incomes under $15,000 had similar affiliations.[45] The type of group that has historically represented working-class Americans, labor unions, has long been in decline. Still, even the poorest Americans are active in the interest-group system.

There is a clear upper-class bias in American politics. Elite interests are better organized and better funded. They have better access to government decision makers. This does not mean that these groups always agree on what public policy should be, but it does mean that upper-class Americans largely control the policy agenda.

How Interest Groups Seek to Influence Politics

When interest groups decide that they need to become involved in the political process, they choose from among a number of methods to try to influence political decisions. Often, the nature of the group's goals will help it decide from among a number of political strategies. In addition, every method of trying to influence the political process requires that the group has resources (funds and people). The method(s) chosen also depend on the resources available to the group because some methods require more resources than others.

Regardless of the method used, the initial goal of the group will always be to gain entry into the political process. **Access** is key to the success of the group. Without a way in, the group will not be in a position to influence the decisions that are made. Consequently, the group will have to decide where it is going to enter, or have access to, the system as well as what methods it should use to try to achieve its goals.

Lobbying

"The Persuaders," Jeffrey H. Birnbaum.

The essence of lobbying is persuasion; the point of access is through public officials. **Lobbying** involves a variety of methods to convince those already in positions of authority to make the decisions that the group feels are in its best interest. The attempt to convince decision makers to adopt a particular position occurs at all levels of government: national, state, and local. It also occurs with a wide range of elected and appointed officials, but lobbying is used most extensively when a group is attempting to convince legislators to adopt the group's perspective as they craft legislation and decide what should, and what should not, become law.

Lobbying is a growth industry in Washington, D.C., these days. In the period from 2000 to 2004 the number of registered lobbyists in the nation's capital more than doubled, from 16,342 to 34,785. Lobbyists are in such high demand that starting salaries for well-connected former White House aides and congressional staffers willing to switch sides are $300,000 per year![46]

The primary method that lobbyists use to persuade members of Congress is to provide them with information and expertise about their concerns. Representatives of interest groups are very knowledgeable regarding the issues that affect their groups' interests. They are often able to conduct or sponsor research that helps substantiate the case for the goals they are trying to achieve. For example, lobbyists for the National Pork Producers Council might want to get specific provisions included in an agriculture bill that they think will help their business. They would be the ones in the best position to provide the information and data that could demonstrate to Agriculture Committee members the consequences that the hog farmers would have to face if the proposal was not included in the legislation. If they are successful in getting their provisions included in bills, then lobbyists use the same technique of providing knowledge and expertise to legislators when the bill moves on for a full vote. They need to convince not just the committee members, but a majority of the entire legislature, that their bill should be passed. Again, providing the reasons to support such a decision will be significant.

Providing substantive information makes lobbyists a very important part of the legislative process. Lobbyists provide much of the information that legislators use to make their decisions. You might ask a question: Isn't the information that lobbyists present biased? Won't the National Pork Producers Council (NPPC) emphasize only the facts that help its case and ignore evidence that might hurt it? The answers are that of course the information will be biased and that the information provided will place the NPPC's position in the best possible light, but it will not be the only group represented by lobbyists during the legislative process. Competing groups with different points of view will also be making their case. The net result of this process is that legislators will potentially be exposed to multiple perspectives as they make decisions regarding what should, and what should not, be included in any particular federal law or program. This process contributes to the democratic ideal of informed, deliberative decision making.

In addition to providing information and expertise, lobbyists attempt to engage in face-to-face communication with decision makers. One of the most effective ways to convince a person to adopt your point of view is to sit down with him or her and make the case in person. The reason that lobbyists try to make appointments with decision makers in their offices is so they can attempt to persuade them directly. It is also the reason that lobbyists entertain decision makers by hosting various social functions. They do not necessarily think they are guaranteeing a particular decision by taking a legislator out to dinner, but because the lobbyists are picking up the bill, they do have the expectation that they will at least have their case heard.

Working Inside Government

Over time, interest groups and the government officials they come into contact with can develop close ties based on their common goals. Political scientists refer to these relationships as **iron triangles** or **policy subgovernments** because they are formed by close-knit coalitions of three actors: executive branch agencies, congressional committees, and interest groups. By working inside government, interest groups seek to help craft public policy rather than just influence the votes of legislators. The point of access is still public officials. These relationships work through mutual cooperation because each participant has something to offer the other two. Executive agencies provide funding and support to interest groups and get money and power from Congress. Members of Congress provide authorization and money to executive agencies while receiving political support and campaign contributions from interest groups. Interest groups are provided with strong government programs that support their goals, and in turn they support the reelection efforts of members of Congress who help them as well as support the agencies that administer the programs. These coalitions can be difficult for outsiders to penetrate, for iron triangles have every incentive to continue their mutually beneficial relationships. Figure 7.6 describes an example of an agriculture iron triangle.

Although iron triangles once dominated most policy areas, political scientists now believe that in many areas of policy, relationships between interest groups and government officials are less well formed. Rather than iron triangles, **issue networks** characterize decision making in these policy areas.[47] Telecommunications, welfare, and the environment are examples of policy areas characterized in this way. Rather than long-standing relationships, issue networks are based on expertise. The groups of experts in these areas are more diverse, and the relationships between them are more fluid. This diversity is in part the result of the growth in the number and resources of interest groups, the rise of think tanks (home to many policy experts), and increases in the size of legislative staffs. In addition, where iron triangles are characterized by consensus, issue networks are noted for conflict. Friends in one policy battle can be enemies in another. The idea of issue networks indicates that policy making is more open than in areas where iron triangles dominate policy. In the area of environmental policy,

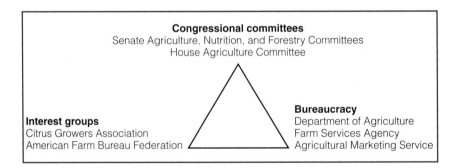

Figure 7.6 An Example of an Iron Triangle: Agriculture. Iron triangles are formed by close-knit coalitions of three actors: executive branch agencies, congressional committees, and interest groups.

for example, rival issue networks have formed with competition between environmentalists and business interests.

Litigation

When interest groups use **litigation** to try to achieve their goals, the courts are their point of access. Interest groups can participate in lawsuits in three ways. They can bring cases themselves, sponsor lawsuits initiated by others, or write *amicus curiae* (friend of the court) briefs in support of other lawsuits. Litigation can be an effective strategy, but only if the goals of the group include actions that the courts have the authority to address. In general, litigation is most likely if the group is attempting to stop an action or activity from occurring. Courts have the authority to order actions to cease if they are deemed in violation of a law or in violation of the Constitution. Courts do not, however, have the authority to institute new laws or programs, which are actions only legislatures can undertake.

Litigation as an interest-group strategy has been used very effectively by civil rights organizations, especially the NAACP (National Association for the Advancement of Colored People). Fifty years ago, the NAACP was trying to stop discriminatory laws—school segregation is one example—which it deemed to be in violation of the Constitution. Without voting rights in a large part of the nation and with little support in Congress, the NAACP took its cause to the courts. In adopting this strategy, the NAACP knew that the courts did not move quickly, so it expected that its goal would be achieved only over a period of time and via a series of incremental decisions. Ultimately, it was able to achieve the goal of ending legal segregation by convincing the Supreme Court that such practices were in violation of the Fourteenth Amendment to the Constitution (see Chapter 4). Conservative groups also use the courts to change public policy. Groups seeking to defend property rights and to allow prayer in schools have been especially active in recent years.

When a group successfully makes a legal claim based on the Constitution, it is likely that this success will be lasting. It is very difficult to change the Constitution, and once the Supreme Court makes a constitutional ruling, the Court is unlikely to alter that interpretation in the foreseeable future. On the other hand, if the basis for the litigation is a congressional statute, the long-term success may not be as assured. If there is opposition to the ruling, it is far easier (through lobbying) to get Congress to alter a law than it is to enact a constitutional amendment.

Shaping Public Opinion

When interest groups try to **shape public opinion,** their point of access is the general public. By influencing the way people think about issues, they then expect that the political system will respond to public opinion. In the current political environment, the most effective way to influence public opinion is

Learn about the strategies that interest groups use.

to make use of the mass media to send a message to the American public. In recent years, pharmaceutical and insurance industry groups have used this method to try to generate support for their points of view in debates regarding health-care policy. Other interests, such as the oil and chemical industries, have used media campaigns to build better public images. One example is the program run by the American Chemical Council. Its slogan is "Good Chemistry Makes It Possible," and its "Responsible Care" program seek to build the image of the industry. The council has chosen these strategies not to generate support for its claims but to diffuse opposition when it is seeking to achieve a goal through other means. Issue ads have grown in recent years. A study by the Annenberg Public Policy Center found that interest groups spent over $404 million during 2003–2004 to influence the public's view on issues in the Washington, D.C., media market alone.[48]

Attempting to shape public opinion through the media is generally an expensive proposition, and many interest groups simply cannot afford broad-based media campaigns designed to influence public opinion. Some groups, however, have successfully generated public support for their goals without having particularly large amounts of resources. A prime example is Mothers Against Drunk Driving (MADD), which has been very successful over the years in achieving its goal of reducing the incidence of drunk driving.

MADD has used traditional lobbying techniques in the legislative process, but it has also convinced the advertising industry that its cause is in the national interest. Consequently, MADD has had public service announcements

MoveOn.org works to build grass-roots support for political ideas and candidates through the Internet. Shown here are MoveOn.org founders Wes Boyd and Joan Blades outside their Berkeley, California, home.

aired with its overall message of "don't drink and drive." MADD has also convinced the entertainment industry to incorporate this message into television programs, thereby sending the message to an even larger audience. Appealing to the public is an especially useful technique for MADD because, in addition to wanting to change public policy, it also wants to convince members of the public to change their individual behavior.

Grass-roots Mobilization

Another method of influencing government is for an interest group to show government officials that they have strong public, or **grass-roots, support.** The point of access is still one or more public officials. This method of influence differs from lobbying in that it involves the general public and differs from shaping public opinion because it asks supporters to be actively engaged in influencing government officials. The most common examples of grass-roots mobilization include letter writing, e-mail and phone-in campaigns, as well as marches and protests. AARP is one group that has used this strategy successfully. Because of its large and active membership, it can literally overwhelm the Congress with mail and phone calls. Elected representatives sometimes claim they are not influenced by these well-orchestrated campaigns, but their effectiveness is hard to discount. When hundreds, or even thousands, of messages come in on a single issue from voters, a public official is likely to listen.

The Internet has become a key tool in grass-roots mobilization in recent years. Technology has allowed groups to connect with disparate people throughout the nation at a moment's notice. One example, noted earlier in the chapter introduction, is MoveOn.org. This liberal group is virtual, with its main presence and gathering place at its website. Launched in October 1998 by Wes Boyd and Joan Blades in their Berkeley, California, home as an online petition encouraging Congress to censure President Clinton over the Lewinsky affair and "move on," it quickly grew and took on new liberal causes. By July 2005, it boasted an e-mail list of over three million people.[49] MoveOn.org uses its website and large list to publicize issues of concern to its members, to gather signatures for petitions, and increasingly to raise funds for political advertising on issues of concern and in political campaigns. In 2004 it ran anti-Bush ads in battleground states. The ads were selected by MoveOn.org members. MoveOn.org has become an important force in American politics, and it is not alone in using technology to mobilize the American people and build grass-roots support. A clear example of this came on July 1, 2005. Within hours of Sandra Day O'Connor announcing her retirement, advocacy groups on both the left and the right had mobilized using technology in a variety of ways.[50] The conservative group Progress for America placed a thirty-second commercial on its website and sent out e-mails announcing it to thousands of activists. NARAL Pro-Choice America placed ads on major newspaper websites urging supporters to visit its website and donate to the cause. Groups on the left and right sent mass e-mails and wrote about the retirement and impending replacement on their blogs. Activists on both the left and right received multiple e-mails in the twenty-four hours after the retirement announcement, including calls to actions and requests for donations.

Electoral Politics

Entering the realm of **electoral politics** is the final method that groups use to try to influence the political process. The point of access is elections. The goal is to elect candidates who are supportive of the group's interests. Groups that are successful with this method should have a much easier time lobbying the officials they helped elect. Interest groups have been involved in electoral politics for a long time, although in recent years the specific means of their involvement have become increasingly controversial.

Traditionally, interest groups have become involved in elections in a number of ways, but the most common one is officially endorsing or opposing candidates running for office. For example, labor unions have a long history of involvement in electoral politics. They officially endorse candidates for office, thereby sending the message to their members that these are the candidates they should vote for. Some interest groups provide lists of candidates that they think should be voted out of office. For example, environmental groups have published the names of those they have designated the "dirty dozen," those officials most opposed to environmental concerns. Groups might also encourage their members to become actively involved in assisting the campaigns of candidates they support.

Over the last quarter-century, campaign contributions by interest groups have become more important. To donate money to a candidate, groups need to establish **political action committees,** better known as PACs. PAC contributions are regulated by federal election law. Under federal law, a multi-candidate PAC can contribute up to $5,000 to a candidate running for federal office and $15,000 to national party committees. There is no upper limit on the total amount that a PAC may contribute to candidates in any calendar year.[51] This means that the PAC may contribute to as many people running for office as it chooses, constrained only by the extent of that group's resources. Top campaign donors in 2004 are listed in Table 7.2. Campaign finance rules are detailed in Chapter 8.

In recent years, there has been a great deal of controversy over the ways that interest groups use unregulated contributions—sometimes referred to as "**soft money**"—to become involved in the electoral process. Campaign finance law has changed in recent years to eliminate unlimited contributions to political parties, but there are still no limits on the amount of money an advocacy group may spend on "independent expenditures": funds spent to forward a policy position or spent on behalf of a candidate as long as the group does not formally coordinate its activities with the candidate's campaign and as long as the group's efforts do not actually say "vote for candidate Smith." The Swift Boat Veterans, MoveOn.org, and the

Should spending on elections be limited?

"The New Soft Money," Jeffrey H. Birnbaum.

Rank	Contributor	Total Contributions	To Democrats	To Republicans	Contributions Tilt
1	Goldman Sachs	$6,551,856	61%	38%	Leans Democratic
2	National Assn. of Realtors	$3,852,527	48%	52%	On the fence
3	Microsoft Corp.	$3,532,505	62%	37%	Leans Democratic
4	Morgan Stanley	$3,397,140	41%	59%	Leans Republican
5	Time Warner	$3,326,217	81%	19%	Strongly Democratic
6	EMILY's List	$3,295,220	100%	0%	Solidly Democratic
7	JP Morgan Chase & Co.	$3,124,304	53%	47%	On the fence
8	Citigroup Inc.	$2,871,362	51%	49%	On the fence
9	Laborers Union	$2,748,355	87%	14%	Strongly Democratic
10	Bank of America	$2,715,325	47%	53%	On the fence
11	National Auto Dealers Assn.	$2,613,050	27%	73%	Strongly Republican
12	UBS Americas	$2,465,414	39%	59%	Leans Republican
13	Intl. Brotherhood of Electrical Workers	$2,443,005	97%	4%	Solidly Democratic
14	SBC Communications	$2,430,972	35%	65%	Leans Republican
15	United Parcel Service	$2,370,317	28%	72%	Strongly Republican
16	Merrill Lynch	$2,369,312	30%	69%	Strongly Republican
17	National Beer Wholesalers Assn.	$2,352,324	24%	75%	Strongly Republican
18	University of California	$2,322,644	91%	9%	Solidly Democratic
19	Assn. of Trial Lawyers of America	$2,238,132	93%	7%	Solidly Democratic
20	General Electric	$2,223,467	47%	53%	On the fence
21	National Assn. of Home Builders	$2,223,237	33%	67%	Strongly Republican
22	Wal-Mart Stores	$2,172,562	19%	81%	Strongly Republican
23	American Medical Assn.	$2,142,310	21%	79%	Strongly Republican
24	Lockheed Martin	$2,139,751	34%	66%	Leans Republican
25	United Auto Workers	$2,118,513	99%	1%	Solidly Democratic

Table 7.2 Top Overall Donors, 2004 Election Cycle   Thirty-two organizations gave over $2 million to federal candidates in 2004, up from ten in 2000. The table lists the twenty-five largest donors. Of the twenty-five, eleven lean toward Republicans, and nine donate significantly more to Democrats. Five groups donate roughly the same amount to Republican and Democratic candidates.

Source: Center for Responsive Politics, http://opensecrets.org/overview/topcontribs.asp?Bkdn= DemRep&Cycle=2004.

other 527 groups noted in the chapter introduction are examples of this growing phenomenon in American electoral politics.

Interest groups increasingly produce and air commercials—on broadcast television, on cable television, and on the Internet—like those described in the opening section of this chapter. In these ads, the group conveys that it either agrees or disagrees with the candidate's position on the issues. The official message to the viewer is to telephone the person running for office and say that you approve or disapprove of his or her position. Although not directly stated, the clear implication of the ads is that you should vote for, or against, the targeted candidate.

Despite changes in campaign finance laws, the number of these political ads has continued to grow, and they have been the source of controversy because they have greatly increased the amount of money spent on political campaigns. The ads have also been criticized because it is not always clear who is paying for them. Such names as Swift Boat Veterans for Truth, America Coming Together, and the Media Fund tell us little about what idea the group represents. Groups obscure their intentions on purpose to gain political advantage.[52] Federal law requires that their name be displayed in the ad, but it does not require that the membership and funding resources of the group be identified in the ad or anywhere else. These "stealth" interest groups have become increasingly prominent in the electoral process. Although it is easy to criticize such actions, it is important to remember that the political pen name has a long history, including James Madison and his coauthors of the *The Federalist Papers*, who wrote under the pseudonym *Publius*.

The Madisonian Dilemma of Interest Groups

As we began this discussion of interest groups, we posed a question: How do we balance the benefits of factions with the problems they create? Clearly, interest groups are well entrenched in the American political system. The ability to express one's viewpoint is a basic civil liberty in the United States. The views expressed in American politics are truly diverse. Interest groups provide a way for the interests of individual citizens to be represented before government. This is truer now than ever before. As we have seen, groups have evolved to support a variety of new causes over the last three decades.

All is not well, however. Two main concerns predominate. First, the system of interest group politics is biased. The views of the wealthy and of corporate America dominate the political landscape.[53] Many of the most influential groups represent the interests of big business, and they are better organized and better financed than most other groups. Second, there may be too many interests today. The complex system of checks and balances was intended to make change difficult.[54] In a system where change is difficult, it is relatively easy for special interests to protect the benefits that government provides for them. It is an irony that a system intended to thwart the power of a majority faction is susceptible to the remarkable growth of minority factions.

Conclusion: Parties and Interests in American Politics

Political parties and interest groups are essential to citizen participation in American democracy. These institutions allow us to influence who wins elected office and to influence the public policies that government officials create. Political parties seek to win elections and control government. Parties recruit candidates, support their electoral efforts, and help organize elections. For the voter—the citizen—parties simplify the electoral landscape. Through electoral competition for voter approval, the people have an opportunity to voice their opinion. Political parties are always searching for individuals to participate in a variety of ways. Interest groups hope to influence public policy. They play an increasingly important role in the American political process. Groups represent a wide range of interests, wider now than ever before. Citizen groups have grown quickly in the last three decades. Even though wealth and big business dominate interest-group politics because of the resources they possess, citizens who band together can and do effect change on the local, state, and national levels. Together, parties and interests are institutions that seek public input and offer opportunities for individual citizens to become involved in the web of American democracy.

Check here for possible post-publication updates to the chapter material.

Key Terms

political party 190
interest group 190
party platform 193
critical realignment 194
critical/realigning
    election 194
Democratic-Republican
    Party 194
Federalist Party 194
Democratic Party 196
Whig Party 196
Republican Party 196
New Deal coalition 198
divided government 198
dealignment 199
split ticket voting 199

minor parties/third
    parties 200
parties in the electorate 201
parties as organizations 201
parties in government 201
party identification 201
straight ticket voting 203
party machines 206
party unity scores 207
factions 209
peak business associations 211
trade associations 211
professional associations 212
labor unions 213
public interest groups 213
intergovernmental lobby 214

material benefits 215
purposive benefits 215
solidary benefits 217
free rider problem 218
access 219
lobbying 219
iron triangles 220
policy subgovernments 220
issue networks 221
litigation 221
shaping public opinion 222
grass-roots support 222
electoral politics 224
elections 224
political action committees 225
soft money 225

Suggested Web Resources

The following sites are related to the study of political parties and interest groups. The following are links to a variety of U.S. political party websites.

The Democratic Party (**http://www.democrats .org**) and the Republican Party (**http://www .rnc.org**) both have well-developed websites. In addition, each party has organizations specifically intended for college students: the College Democrats (**http://www.collegedems.org**) and College Republicans (**http://www.crnconline .org**).

Among the more significant third parties in American politics are the Green Party (**http:// www.greenpartyus.org**), the Reform Party (**http://www.reformparty.org**), and the Libertarian Party (**http://www.lp.org**).

A comprehensive list of American political parties can be found at Politics1.com (**http://www .politics1.com/parties.htm**). In addition to providing a list, the site also provides descriptions of the many American political parties.

Take a look at the interesting Albany, New York, political machine (**http://www.timesunion .com/news/special/century/people**). Two leaders, Dan O'Connell and Erastus Corning, led the city for half a century.

Hundreds of interest groups have websites. The following are links to a variety of websites related to interest groups.

Promoting the general interests of corporate American are such groups as the National Association of Manufacturers (**http://www.nam.org**), the U.S. Chamber of Commerce (**http://www .uschamber.org**), and the Business Roundtable (**http://www.br.org/index.cfm**). Business and trade associations range widely and represent virtually every industry in the United States. Examples include the American Chemistry Council (**http://www.americanchemistry.com**), the National Federation of Independent Business (**http://www.nfib.org/cgi-bin/NFIB.dll/Public/ SiteNavigation/home.jsp**), the National Beer Wholesalers Association (**http://www.nbwa .org**), the American Bankers Association (**http://www .aba.com**), and the Wine Institute (**http://www .wineinstitute.org**). Individual corporations also work hard to influence government. Most are represented on the Web, and some, such as General Electric (**http://www.ge.com/hudson**), use the Web to advocate for their policy views.

Professional associations are important in American politics. Prominent examples include the American Medical Association (**http://www .ama-assn.org**) and the Association of Trial Lawyers of America (**http://www.atlanet.org**). Other examples discussed in the text are the Graphic Artists Guild (**http://www.gag.org**), the American Association of Nurse Anesthetists (**http://www.aana.com**), and the American Political Science Association (**http://www .apsanet.org**).

Major unions include the AFL-CIO (**http://www .aflcio.org**), the National Education Association (**http://www.nea.org**), the United Auto Workers (**http://www.auw.org**), the United Mine Workers (**http://www.umwa.org**), and the American Federation of State, County and Municipal Employees (**http://www.afscme.org**).

Citizen groups in the United States are remarkably diverse. Two, the American Association of Retired Persons (**http://www.aarp.org**) and the National Rifle Association of America (**http://www.mynra .com**), are considered among the most influential interest groups in the United States. Long-established liberal groups include the American Civil Liberties Union (**http://www.aclu.org**), the National Association for the Advancement of Colored People (**http://www.naacp.org**), and the National Organization for Women (**http://www.now.org**). "Good government" groups include Common Cause (**http://www.commoncause.org**) and the League of Women Voters (**http://www.lwv.org**). Conservative groups include the Family Research Council (**http://www.frc.org**), the National Right to Life Committee (**http://nrlc.org**), and the National Taxpayers Union (**http://www.ntu.org**). Another citizen group noted in the text is Mothers Against Drunk Driving (**http://www.madd.org/madd/ home**).

A relatively new set of interest groups are those that represent government: the intergovernmental lobby. Examples include the National League of Cities (**http://www.nlc.org/home**), the U.S. Conference of Mayors (**http://www.usmayors .org**), the National Governor's Association (**http:// www.nga.org**), and the National Conference of State Legislatures (**http://www.ncsl.org**).

If you want access to interest groups that are not listed above, the Internet Public Library (**http:// www.ipl.org/ref/AON**) provides an extensive list of associations.

You can also have access to international political parties and interest groups (http://www.psr.keele.ac.uk/parties.htm).

To examine the role of interest groups and the politics of money, go to OpenSecrets.org (http://www.opensecrets.org).

 A complete study tool kit is available for this chapter and includes the following:
Flashcards
Crossword Puzzle
Critical Thinking Exercises
Interactive Timelines
Chapter Quiz

Elections and Political Participation

■ **Red and Blue America: How Real Is the Divide?**   **227**

■ **Why Elections Matter**   **232**

■ **The Structure of American Elections**   **234**
　　Primary Elections and General Elections   234
　　The Rules of the Election Game   238
　　Financing Federal Election Campaigns   239
　　Candidate-Centered Elections   242

■ **The Race for the White House: The Long Road**   **243**
　　Selecting Presidential Nominees   244
　　Competing in the Primaries and Caucuses   244
　　The National Conventions   247
　　The General Election   247

■ **Running for Congress: The Power
　　of Incumbency**   **250**

■ **Voting**   **252**
　　The Decline of Voter Turnout   253
　　Who Votes?   257
　　How Voters Choose a Candidate   261

■ **The 2004 Election Results**   **265**
　　The Presidency   265
　　The Congress   266

■ **The 2006 Election Results**   **266**

■ **Political Participation Beyond Voting**   **267**

■ **Conclusion: Does It Matter If We Participate?**   **271**

R ed and Blue America: How Real Is the Divide?

In the days and weeks after the 2000 presidential election, two new phrases entered the lexicon of American politics: "red states" and "blue states." By the election of 2004, discussion of the red states and blue states was every-where. The terms have continued to be important in American politics after the 2004 election as well. Where did the concept of red states and blue states come from? Why do they matter?

Protesters gathered in Tallahassee, Florida. On December 9, 2000, supporters of George W. Bush wanted the vote recounts to be stopped. Three days later, the U.S. Supreme Court did just that. The way the outcome of the election ended caused some to question its legitimacy.

The term **"red states"** refers to the states that the Republicans won in the two most recent presidential elections, and **"blue states"** are those states won by the Democrats. The terms are so commonly used that we might believe that these designations have been around a long time, but this is not the case. The television networks have switched colors regularly since the 1960s, when they began using color graphics in their Election Night broadcasts. For example, when Republican President Ronald Reagan won a landslide reelection victory in 1984, television commentators referred to "Lake Reagan": the almost entirely blue map of the United States indicating his victory in forty-nine states. At times, networks have even used colors other than red and blue.[1]

On Election Night 2000, though, all of the networks used red to indicate the states won by then-Texas Governor George W. Bush and blue for states where Vice President Albert Gore was the victor. The election—as we all know now—was remarkably close. Millions of Americans were glued to their televisions waiting for the outcome to become final. Although we would not know the final outcome for over a month, what we saw in the electronic maps of the United States presented by the networks on Election Night was remarkable and undeniable. It was a stark portrait of a divided America: a sea of red states in the South, the Midwest, and the Mountain West surrounded by blue states on the left (the West Coast) and on the upper right (the Northeast and New England). The United States was divided, no doubt about it. There was little change in the state-by-state outcome of the 2004 presidential election. Only three states switched from one party to another—Iowa and New Mexico switched from the Democrats to the Republicans, and New Hampshire switched from the Republicans to the Democrats—but the divide seen in national maps became even clearer.

☐ Won by Bush   ☐ Won by Kerry

Figure 8.1 The 2004 Presidential Election Results, by State. The election map shows states won by George W. Bush in gray (the red states) and states won by John Kerry in blue. The map shows Kerry winning the Northeast, the Midwest and the West Coast President Bush won the remaining states. Is the divide as stark as it seems in this map?

Examine detailed election results.

The switch of New Mexico from blue to red turned the Mountain West entirely red, and the switch of New Hampshire from red to blue turned the Northeast and New England entirely blue (see Figure 8.1).

One story that emerged from the last two elections is that the two major parties share about the same level of electoral support; the nation is closely split politically. In 2000 the two major candidates were divided by less than one-half of one percent in the popular vote, and the electoral college result was just as close. Although President Bush won a clearer victory in 2004, he still won by a razor-thin margin both in the popular vote—50.7 percent voted for President Bush as opposed to 48.3 percent for Senator John Kerry—and in the electoral college, where Bush won 286–251. A similar story is true of House of Representatives voting since 1998.[2]

A second, more powerful story based on the state-level presidential election map emerged as well: that the United States is not one. Rather, we are sharply divided into two nations. This division, we are told, is not only

CHAPTER 8: Elections and Political Participation

evident at the polls. There is a deep cultural divide in America. As one columnist put it, shortly after the 2000 election,

> *This election was Hollywood vs. Nashville, "Sex in the City" vs. "Touched by an Angel," National Public Radio vs. talk radio, "Doonesbury" vs. "B.C.," "Hotel California" vs. "Okie from Muskogee." It was the* New York Times *vs. the* National Review *Online," Dan Rather vs. Rush Limbaugh, Rosie O'Donnell vs. Dr. Laura, Barbara Streisand vs. Dr. James Dobson.*[3]

Those from red states are depicted as churchgoing, intolerant, gun-owning, beer-guzzling conservatives. In contrast, blue state residents are seen as nonreligious, rights-obsessed, passive, wine-sipping, Birkenstock-wearing liberals. No clearer example of this portrayal can be found than the map that emerged on the Internet after the 2004 election depicting the blue states joining Canada as the "United States of Canada" and the remaining red states being depicted as "JesusLand." Conservatives countered that rather than the "United States of Canada," the North and West should be called the "United States of Appeasement." The nation, it was implied, was so divided over the war in Iraq and cultural questions that secession was a possibility.[4] Interest in immigrating to Canada grew as well after the 2004 election, and news reports emerged that at least a few people from blue states were actually leaving.[5]

But is this characterization accurate? Are we really a nation deeply divided? A more sophisticated analysis tells a story that is more complicated, maybe even different. Political commentators and political scientists have questioned how deep the division really is. An essay by the commentator David Brooks titled "One Nation, Slightly Divisible" is an example.[6] He spent time in both blue Montgomery County, Maryland, and red Franklin County, Pennsylvania, and found that the differences were subtler than are often portrayed. Red America was more tolerant than often portrayed, and blue America was not so consistently liberal. As Brooks summarized it, "Although there are some real differences between Red and Blue America, there is not fundamental conflict. There may be cracks, but there is no chasm."[7] Political scientist Morris Fiorina found a similar result after examining survey data on the political attitudes of those living in red and blue states.[8] Yes, differences exist in their attitudes on hot-button cultural issues, such as abortion rights and gay and lesbian rights, but the differences are modest. The similarities are more important than the differences between red and blue America, and on the whole, Americans are centrists, moderates. Surveys done since 2004 have shown that one divide between red and blue America is real: differences of opinion on the war in Iraq and U.S. military expansionism more generally.[9]

A closer look at the 2004 presidential election map also produces a more subtle picture of the American electorate. Figure 8.2 presents three cartograms, maps that take into account population in addition to land mass. In each cartogram, areas won by George W. Bush are in gray and areas won by John Kerry are depicted in blue. The first, Figure 8.2a, presents

"One Nation, Slightly Divisible," David Brooks.

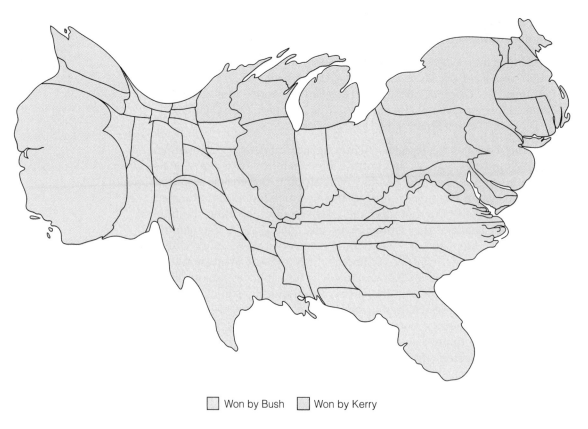

Won by Bush   Won by Kerry

Figure 8.2a Cartogram of the 2004 Presidential Election Results by State, Scaled by Population. This cartogram portrays the election results by state with states resized by population. Bush states are in gray and Kerry states are in blue.

state-level 2004 presidential election results while rescaling the state maps by population. The results shown here make clear the even division of the electorate. The second cartogram, Figure 8.2b, presents a similar map for county-level data. Counties that favored President Bush are in gray, and counties in blue favored Senator Kerry. When the more detailed cartogram is examined, the picture is less clear. There are areas won by each candidate throughout the United States. The division seems to be less about states than about urban and rural areas. The county map shows that what we have is "blue cities" more than blue states. Although there are blue counties that are not urban, they are the exception, not the rule. The final map, Figure 8.2c, depicts county-level data in a more sophisticated way. It shows counties that heavily supported Bush in gray and similar Kerry-supported areas in blue, but counties that were closer are depicted in various shades of dark gray and blue. When looking at the final map, one can see the true complexity of the American electorate. True Republican and true Democratic areas exist,

Won by Bush   Won by Kerry

Figure 8.2b Cartogram of the 2004 Presidential Election Results by County. Examining the election results by county the picture changes. The nation no longer looks like a sea of red with blue on the edges.

but they are much less prominent than we might expect by looking at the simple state map found in Figure 8.1.

The election results tell a similar, more complex story as well. For example, Colorado voted for President Bush in 2000 and 2004, but in 2004 the majorities in both houses of the Colorado legislature switched from Republican to Democratic, and Colorado also elected a Democratic Senator, Ken Salazar. Similarly, New York has voted overwhelmingly for the Democratic presidential candidate in the last four presidential elections, but at the same time has had a Republican governor since 1994. Similar stories can be found in many states.

Why then does American politics feel so divided? There are two clear reasons. First, elected officials are more polarized. Congress in particular is more polarized than in any other time in recent memory.[10] (Polarization in the Senate is discussed in the introduction to Chapter 9.) This polarization has been increased by partisan redistricting after the 2000 census in many states and by the lack of competitiveness in congressional campaigns (this subject is discussed later in this chapter). Morris Fiorina describes the polarization as

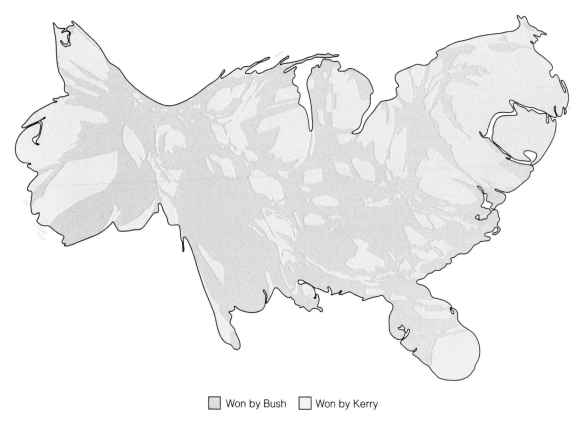

☐ Won by Bush   ☐ Won by Kerry

Figure 8.2c Cartogram of the 2004 Presidential Election Results by County Indicating Size of Victory, Scaled by Population. When election results are measured by size of electoral victory, the nation looks less divided. Counties where Bush won by a large majority are in light gray, those where Kerry won a large victory are in blue.

"the hijacking of American democracy."[11] Second, the presentation of politics in the media clearly adds to the feeling of division and political polarization. Television presents politics as angry and divisive. Talk shows generally have guests with widely divergent viewpoints who express their differences loudly.[12] Blogs and other Internet sites feed the beast of divisiveness further. With political leaders and the media presenting politics in such sharp relief, it is not surprising that we as a nation assume it is true of the rest of us as well.

Why Elections Matter

A democracy depends on the consent of the governed, and **elections** are the key to providing that consent. Elections, then, are central to the web of American democracy for several reasons. Elections are a forum for selecting leaders and for holding those leaders accountable for the decisions they make while in office. They also provide a place to debate public policy. Finally, elections serve to link the people and their leaders, providing legitimacy for the government and its policies. Elections are clearly important in a democracy, but sadly, we will see that they do not always rise to their potential. Low voter turnout and big money—each discussed later in the chapter—serve to limit the impact of elections in the United States.[13]

Elections first and foremost serve as a forum for **selecting leaders** in our representative democracy. Through the selection process, voters communicate with those running their government. Although elections are not the only way that citizens can communicate with leaders—Chapters 5 and 7 discuss the roles of public opinion as well as political parties and interest groups—elections are authoritative; they define clear winners and losers. Once elected, officials must run for reelection to stay in office. Reelection provides a second reason that elections matter; it provides for **democratic accountability.** The ability to turn a leader out of office is a powerful tool for the electorate. It means that elected officials are more attentive and responsive than they otherwise might be. Democratic accountability helps ensure two-way communication between the voter and the official. In practice, the vast majority of officials are returned to office each time they run for reelection, but the possibility of losing is always there.

The leaders we elect create and implement public policy. They can choose to raise taxes or lower them. Leaders can create new programs that benefit us—funding a new park near our home or providing tuition assistance to a wider group of college students—or they can enact laws that we may not like—eliminating subsidized student loans. Elections can **influence public policy;** they can help make clear what policy changes the voters want. This is easiest when voting is on the issues themselves in initiatives and referenda, but instances of direct democracy are relatively infrequent in the United States (see Chapter 1). In some election campaigns, though, the candidates express clear and divergent views. Based on the results, newly elected leaders act to turn their promises into law.

Finally, through elections, citizens provide our public officials with legal authority to govern; they provide **legitimacy** for our elected leaders. We choose our leaders through open and free elections. This fact increases the faith that Americans have in the nation and in the government. Furthermore, because citizens have the chance to participate in choosing their leaders, we are more likely to accept their leadership.

Recent elections—especially the 2000 presidential election—have encouraged Americans to reexamine why elections are important. With the turn of only a few votes, the outcome of the election would have been different. This was surely true of the presidential election, but it was equally true in the Senate as well, where a few thousand votes in Washington state prevented the Republicans from gaining a true majority in 2001. It has been common to hear Americans argue that it does not matter who wins, that there is no difference between politicians or between the political parties. The outcome of the 2000 and 2004 presidential elections, however,

Vice President Gore's concession speech ends the 2000 presidential campaign.

Bush v. Gore (2000).

will change public policy for years to come. It is hard to argue that either a Gore administration or a Kerry administration would have looked like a Bush administration. It is unlikely that either Democratic candidate would have advocated oil exploration in the Arctic National Wildlife Refuge in Alaska or providing funding for faith-based social service agencies.[14] Judicial nominations would have been different, and our response to the 9/11 attacks may well have been different too.[15]

As elections and political participation are examined in this chapter, it is important to keep in mind both the potential and the reality of American elections. The election of 2000 reminded us that democracy is fragile in more ways than one. Democratic citizenship is important. Voting and being knowledgeable about the day's events make a difference in American politics.

The Structure of American Elections

The selection of an elected official in the United States is often a complicated affair. We elect a dizzying array of public officials in a four-year period in many different elections. Although this chapter focuses on presidential and congressional elections, the typical voter is asked to select a governor, both houses of a state legislature and other statewide offices, various county officials, and municipal leaders—such as mayor and city council and school board—as well as vote on occasional ballot issues. Additionally, the rules governing elections vary from state to state. The rules determine who can vote, where voting takes place, how balloting is conducted, and how the votes are counted. As we saw in the 2000 presidential election, these rules can have an impact on who wins. In most states, one must register in advance to vote. Getting a ballot may be difficult for some. College students are a case in point. If you are registered to vote in your hometown, you may have to go home on Election Day or apply for an absentee ballot weeks in advance.

Once a voter examines the ballot, the complexity continues, for there are typically many offices to elect and multiple candidates for each office. It is difficult for the average person to be knowledgeable enough to make an educated decision regarding all these races. Furthermore, as the butterfly ballot used in Palm Beach County, Florida, in 2000, made clear, the ballot itself can be complex and confusing. Yet despite all of this complexity, there are a few basic characteristics that define American elections. Each of these characteristics—like all rules—encourages some outcomes and discourages others.

Read about the problems with the butterfly ballot.

Primary Elections and General Elections

Two types of elections are part of selecting public officials in the United States: primary elections and general elections. In a **primary election,** voters select a political party's nominee for elective office. In a **general election,**

VOTING METHODS: HOW VOTES ARE CAST AND COUNTED IN THE UNITED STATES

The 2000 presidential election forced Americans to examine an aspect of the electoral process that had been taken for granted: the methods used to cast and count the votes. It was, in many ways, the nasty little secret of American politics. At the end of the twentieth century, some areas in the United States, mostly rural counties, were still using voting technology that was developed in the late nineteenth century: 1.3 percent of registered voters used paper ballots in 2000.[1] Among those who were in the business of administering elections, it was generally understood that many of the procedures currently in use regularly miscounted, undercounted, and did not count votes. As long as the election was not close, this did not really make any difference in the outcome, but in a close election, such as the 2000 presidential election where every vote did count in several states, the faulty voting methods became a matter of grave importance.

According to the Federal Election Commission, 17.9 percent of registered voters in 2000 used lever machines, 27.9 percent used the now infamous punch cards, 29.5 percent used some type of optical scan system, and 12.6 percent used direct electronic voting.[2] Lever machines were developed at the end of the nineteenth century and became the most popular method throughout the country through the 1960s. The machines work reasonably well, but they are no longer made and cannot be replaced as they become inoperable. In many locations, this leads to long lines because there are not enough machines for the number of voters.

The method used by the largest proportion of registered voters, punch cards, became popular during the 1960s. They are widely acknowledged as the least reliable method. Their flaws were revealed to the entire nation in 2000 as Florida tried to count, and then recount, votes recorded on punch cards. The process introduced the nation to the many ways in which "chads" could fail to detach from the card, resulting in votes not being counted. Optical scan systems have become more popular in recent years. They are similar to the methods used in many universities to grade multiple-choice exams. Voting for more than one candidate is impossible with this system because the reader will reject any incorrectly filled in ballots. Finally, a small proportion of

(continued)

the population used some type of electronic voting device that has push buttons or touch screens.

In addition to the problems involved in counting votes, citizens across the nation experienced long lines, lost registrations, and confusing ballots. As a response to the problems exposed in the 2000 election, Congress passed the Help America Vote Act of 2002. The law created the United States Electoral Assistance Commission, whose task is to administer funds to replace outdated voting technology and to "establish minimum election administration standards for states and units of local government with responsibility for the administration of Federal elections."

Although it is not accurate to say that the nation's problems of electoral administration have been solved, some progress has been made. For example, only about one-third as many registered voters—13.7 percent—potentially voted with punch-card technology in 2004 as in 1996.[3] The use of more sophisticated technology increased significantly. Almost two-thirds of registered voters had access to either optical scan or electronic voting technology. A Cal Tech–MIT study found that there were over a million fewer "lost votes" in 2004 as compared to 2000.[4] But problems still remain. The Commission on Federal Election Reform, headed by former President Jimmy Carter and former Secretary of State James A. Baker, issued its report in September 2005 and found significant reasons for concern. They urged more uniform registration standards, improved access to voting, and auditable electronic voting to build confidence in American elections.[5]

[1] Kimball Brace, "Overview of Voting Equipment Usage in United States, Direct Recording Electronic (DRE) Voting," United States Election Assistance Commission, May 5, 2004, www.eac.gov/docs/EDSInc_DREoverview.pdf (retrieved November 1, 2005).

[2] Brace, "Overview of Voting Equipment Usage," p. 3.

[3] Brace, "Overview of Voting Equipment Usage," p. 9.

[4] Charles Stewart, "Residual Vote in the 2004 Election" (Cambridge, MA: Cal Tech/MIT Voting Technology Project), http://www.vote.caltech.edu/media/documents/vtp_wp21v2.3.pdf (retrieved November 1, 2005).

[5] Federal Commission on Election Reform, "Building Confidence in U.S. Elections," http://www.american.edu/ia/cfer (retrieved November 1, 2005).

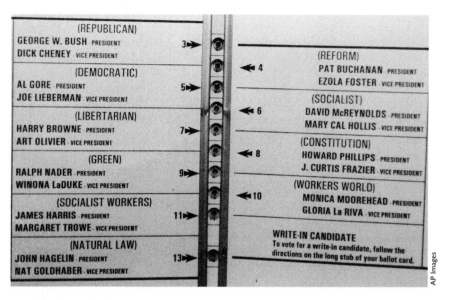

The 2000 presidential ballot—a punch-card ballot—used in Palm Beach County, Florida. Some voters were confused by the layout of the ballot and cast votes for Pat Buchanan instead of for Vice President Al Gore. Fewer voters used punch-card ballots in 2004 than in previous elections.

voters choose between party candidates—and sometimes independents as well—to decide who will hold an elective office. Although voting in primaries is often restricted to party members, all eligible voters may participate in the general election. In practice, voter turnout is much higher for general elections than for primary elections, but primary voters are better informed than are those who vote only in general elections.

The move toward using primaries to select party nominees began in the early twentieth century as a way to take the power to select candidates for office away from party leaders—pejoratively referred to as "bosses"—and to give it to rank-and-file party members. When the party leadership chose candidates, these leaders had the power to reward faithful party workers with the opportunity to run for office and the power to choose the candidate they felt best able to serve the party and most likely to win the election. Party leaders also had the power to control those in office if they wanted to continue holding elective office. Roughly half of the states used primaries from 1900 to 1930. Interest in primaries waned for a time, but since the early 1970s, all states use primaries to decide at least some contested nominations.[16] Removing this power from party leaders is one of the reasons that the influence of parties has diminished in American politics.

Three methods are commonly used to decide contested party nominations in the United States: closed primaries, open primaries, and caucuses. **Closed primaries** allow only registered members of a party to vote for that party's nominees. Most states use closed primaries. In an **open primary,** voters not affiliated with a party may help select a party's nominees by voting in any one primary they choose. Although state laws govern the structure of candidate selection, the U.S. Supreme Court reiterated in an important case in 2000 that political parties can select candidates how they wish, ignoring state laws in the process.[17] In addition, a few states use a **caucus** system for selecting nominees. A caucus is an open meeting of all party members. Those in attendance discuss the candidates and eventually vote for the candidate of their choice. Caucuses require a larger time commitment on the citizens' part. Not surprisingly, turnout for caucuses is generally lower than for primaries.

The Rules of the Election Game

To begin, U.S. public officials are elected to **fixed terms.** The Constitution sets the terms for federal officials. House members serve two-year terms, senators serve six-year terms, and presidents serve four-year terms. Congress has set the date of federal elections since 1845 as the first Tuesday after the first Monday in November of even numbered years. Fixed election dates, as in the United States, can encourage those in power to try to work together to create favorable conditions—such as a growing economy and the passage of new programs—to enhance their chances for reelection. In contrast, most Western democracies have **parliamentary systems** of government that allow the party in power to set the date of the election. This allows the leaders of the government to call for elections when they feel they have the best chance of winning. Fixed election dates also encourage prolonged campaigns. Campaigns in parliamentary systems rarely last longer than four to six weeks, as opposed to the one- to two-year norm in American presidential campaigns.

Unlike the parliamentary systems that exist in most other democratic nations, the selection of the legislature and the executive are **separate and independent elections.** In parliamentary systems, the voters choose a legislature, and that body selects a national leader, generally called the prime minister. This fact links the two institutions in a way that the American electoral system does not. In contrast, our system—wherein Congress and the president are each elected by the people in separate elections—emphasizes the independence of the House, the Senate, and the president. The differing term lengths further accentuate the separation between these institutions.

American elections are generally fought in **winner-take-all single-member districts** and are decided by a **plurality.** This means that in an electoral race, candidates for a specific office are running to fill one seat. The winner will be the candidate receiving the most votes—a plurality—regardless of whether that person garners an absolute majority (50 percent plus one vote). In selecting the U.S. House of Representatives, for example, the 435 seats are divided among the fifty states based on each state's population, and each state legislature divides its state into the appropriate number of equally populated districts. One member of the House is elected in each district; the boundaries of no two districts overlap.

In contrast, many other nations—especially those with a parliamentary system—have a **proportional representation** system. In these systems, party names rather than individual candidate names appear on the ballot, and legislators are elected in multiple-member districts. Each party is then awarded seats roughly in proportion to the percentage of votes a party receives.

Two important implications of the American system are that third parties are discouraged and that racial and ethnic minorities tend to be underrepresented in legislative bodies. Parties with relatively narrow appeal rarely win elections and usually die for lack of success. Two members of the U.S. Senate—Bernard Sanders of Vermont and Joseph Lieberman of Connecticut—won without running on a major party line. Sanders served as an independent member of the U.S. House of Representatives for eight terms before winning his Senate seat in 2006. Lieberman ran as an independent after losing the 2006 Democratic primary. No current members of the House were elected without running as either a Democrat or a Republican. It is worth noting that independents have fared a bit better in gubernatorial elections. Three independent governors were elected in the 1990s: Lowell Weicker of Connecticut, Angus King of Maine, and Jesse Ventura of Minnesota. There are currently no unaffiliated governors.

Historically, it has been difficult for minority candidates to win office except in majority-minority-districts—districts where a majority of the residents are nonwhite. As further discussed in Chapter 9, African Americans—and especially Latinos and Asian Americans—are underrepresented as a percentage of the population in the House of Representatives and Senate. For example, 13.3 percent of Americans are Hispanic, but only 24 House members (5.5 percent) and 2 of 100 senators are Hispanic.

Financing Federal Election Campaigns

In the aftermath of the Watergate political scandal, much of which involved irregularities and abuses tied to campaign funds, Congress revised existing campaign finance laws in the **Federal Election Campaign Act** (1974). The law was designed to (1) reduce the influence of wealthy individuals on elections by eliminating contributions of large sums of money to candidates running for federal office, (2) eliminate the disparities that existed between the financial resources available to the nominees of the two major political parities, and (3) ensure that campaign contributions were not diverted to other, noncampaign-related purposes. To accomplish these goals, the 1974 law established contribution limits, limited public financing for presidential elections, set up procedures that candidates had to follow in accounting for their campaign funds, and established the **Federal Election Commission** (FEC) to enforce the law.

Throughout the 1990s, many argued that the federal campaign finance laws were broken. Money in elections had spiraled out of control, and

Visit the Federal Election Commission website.

interest groups and parties had found major loopholes in the 1974 law. Aside from the requirements that campaigns report their donations and spending, the law had little practical effect. Calls for reform were widespread. In 2002, after years of debate, Congress passed the first major campaign reform law in almost three decades, the **Bipartisan Campaign Finance Reform Act,** also known as the McCain-Feingold Act after its Senate sponsors. The law changed the limits on contributions that individuals and groups can make to candidates and—more important—sought to halt the proliferation of so-called **soft money,** unregulated donations made to political parties that had grown immensely during the 1990s and were used on the behalf of candidates for federal office.

Learn about the Bipartisan Campaign Finance Act at the Campaign Finance Institute's website.

The Elimination of Soft Money

Soft money was exempted from the 1974 campaign finance law if the money was not to be used directly in support of candidates. It was to be used only for "party building" activities, such as voter registration drives and "get out the vote" efforts. In practice, political parties ignored the distinction between hard money—federally regulated donations—and soft money and used soft money to run advertisements directly in support of candidates. Political parties raised millions of dollars in soft money for recent elections. Individual donations over $1 million were not uncommon.[18] Both the Democrats and Republicans ran such ads in support of their presidential candidates in 2000. Although the ads did not note that the candidates were running for president, images of Al Gore and George Bush were prominent.

McCain-Feingold banned these unregulated donations and spending by political parties and congressional campaign committees. As noted below, new limits were placed on donations to political parties and congressional campaign committees. The U.S. Supreme Court upheld the soft money ban in a 2003 decision.[19]

Contribution Limits

The contribution limits established in McCain-Feingold, usually referred to as "hard money," apply to all federal elections. Under these limits, an individual could legally contribute up to $2,100 per candidate per election in the 2006 election cycle—a primary election and a general election are counted separately. New limits were also put into place for other political organizations. Because soft money has been banned, higher contribution limits are allowed to political parties. In 2006 individuals were able to contribute $26,700 per year to a national party committee. Contributions to other political committees, such as **political action committees** (PACs), are limited to $5,000 per year. An individual can contribute no more than $101,400 per election cycle to federally regulated candidates and committees. All of these political contribution limits are pegged to inflation. The limits will increase in future elections. PACs can contribute no more than $5,000 per election to a federal candidate. Unlike individual contributions, PAC contributions are not indexed to inflation.

The New Loophole: 527 Groups

Although one loophole was closed with the passage of McCain-Feingold, another was left in place that allowed groups to collect large donations and spend the funds to influence federal elections and policy debates. These organizations, known as **527 groups,** are named for the section of the Internal Revenue Service code that they are formed under. These groups, which cannot be affiliated with a political party or a candidate for federal elective office, have no limits on the size of contributions that they can raise, nor do they have spending limits. They do have to report their activities to the IRS on a regular basis. As discussed in the introduction to Chapter 7, 527 groups were a major force in the 2004 presidential election. Such groups as MoveOn.org and Swift Boat Veterans for Truth spent millions of dollars in an effort to see their preferred candidate win.

The emergence of 527 groups emphasized the difficulty of truly limiting campaign spending. As Senator John McCain has noted, "Money is like water: it finds cracks in the wall."[20] Efforts to influence elections on the edges of campaign finance laws will continue in the future. The Federal Election Commission has decided that there will be no new regulations on 527s in the 2008 election cycle.[21]

Public Financing for Presidential Candidates

The 1974 law established and the McCain-Feingold act continued a system of partial public financing of presidential elections. (There is no public financing provision for congressional elections, but three states—Arizona, Maine, and New Hampshire—finance legislative and gubernatorial campaigns.) Presidential funding comes through a $3 check-off on tax returns, where taxpayers are asked whether or not they want $3 of their taxes to go to this fund. The money builds up over a four-year period and is used to match individual contributions made to presidential candidates.

To qualify for the funds, a candidate must raise $5,000 in twenty different states in contributions of $250 or less. Once this is accomplished, the first $250 of every individual contribution is matched from the fund. If a candidate accepts the funds, he or she must conform to spending limits in individual states during the primaries. The limits are based on the state's population. In 2004 limits ranged from $746,200 in the least populous states to over $15.5 million in California, with a total during the primary campaign of approximately $45 million.[22] Once the primaries begin, if a candidate drops below 10 percent of the popular vote in two consecutive primaries, he or she loses the matching funds.

In 2000 and in 2004, George W. Bush decided to forgo federal matching funds. In the 2004 election cycle, both former Vermont governor Dr. Howard

Learn about 527 group donations at opensecrets.org.

Visit MoveOn.org.

Participate in a discussion of campaign finance reform.

Dean and Senator John Kerry of Massachusetts, the eventual Democratic nominee, did the same. The two major party nominees together raised over $540 million during the primary campaign. Dr. Dean raised another $51 million.[23] The money raised by Bush and Kerry overwhelmed the spending limits established by the Federal Election Commission for candidates who accepted matching funds. The fact that they were successful makes it likely that most major candidates will forgo federal matching funds in the future, and without changes in the system of federal funding of presidential campaigns, the system may well be rendered meaningless in the future.[24]

The campaign fund pays for the major party conventions, approximately $15 million in 2004. Once the parties have chosen their nominees, each candidate receives the same amount of money to spend in general election efforts (unlike in the primaries, candidates cannot opt out of presidential general election financing). In 2004 both George W. Bush and John Kerry had $74.6 million to spend.[25] Federal spending limits will increase in future elections. Spending limits are tied to inflation.

Third-party presidential candidates can also receive general election funds if their party received 5 percent of the popular vote in the previous general election. Third-party candidates may also receive retroactive funds if they win at least 5 percent of the popular vote in the current election.

Disclosure Provisions

The law also requires all candidates for federal office to keep a thorough record of all campaign contributions and expenditures. They must file periodic reports with the Federal Election Commission. The FEC then makes these records public. It is because of this requirement that the public is able to determine who has contributed to various campaigns for federal office. An additional disclosure provision requires that candidates appear in their own advertisements. Often this is in the form of a voiceover by the candidate: "I am Joe Smith, and I approved this ad."

Examine campaign finance data.

Candidate-Centered Elections

One last point needs to be made about American elections before looking at the particulars of congressional and presidential elections: We have a **candidate-centered** electoral process. This was not always true; at one point, political parties were the dominant forces. Although party is still relevant, one way of thinking about the primacy of candidates over party today is to look at the advertising in an election campaign contested where you live. You may be surprised at how infrequently you see or hear the mention of party. Candidate names dominate advertising to the exclusion of party, even if the party pays for the advertisement.

The dominance of the candidate has grown as the techniques used in political campaigns have changed in the last fifty years. Once grass-roots affairs, campaigns for state and national office are now run by professionals

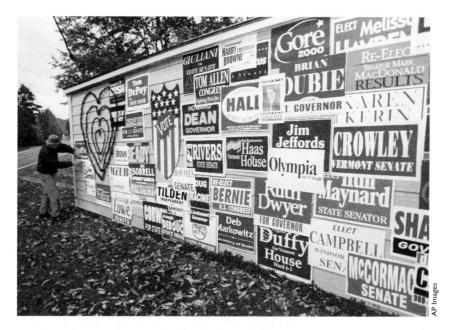

Electoral campaigns in the United States are candidate centered. Note that few if any of the campaign signs here mention the candidate's political party.

and often begin more than a year in advance of Election Day. These professional political consultants conduct polls, develop campaign themes and messages, create and place television and radio advertising, and coordinate the daily events of candidates. This costs a great deal of money that—with the exception of the presidential election—must be raised solely by the candidates themselves from a variety of sources, including interest groups, individuals, and their own pockets. Candidates are political entrepreneurs, raising their own capital and making their own strategic decisions about the product they are selling to the voter on Election Day.

The Race for the White House: The Long Road

Every four years Americans go to the polls to elect a president. The process of running for and winning the presidency is arduous. It begins at least two years before Election Day and formally continues until December of the election year. During this time, any successful candidate will have raised several hundred million dollars, logged hundreds of thousands of miles on airplanes, given hundreds of speeches, and sweated out the results of a few dozen primaries as well as the general election. The road to the White House is a long and twisting one for even the most prepared and well-financed presidential candidate.

Selecting Presidential Nominees

Since the 1830s, party nominations for president have been made by **national party conventions.** These conventions are held in the summer of presidential election years, with the express purpose of choosing the party's presidential candidate. Party delegates come together from each state and cast ballots to select a candidate. Until the 1940s, state party leaders selected most delegates, and until 1968, party rules required that all delegate votes from one state went to one candidate. This allowed state party leaders to negotiate with candidates for support. Often, these negotiations were tense and drawn out over several days. Several ballots were typically required before a nominee was finally chosen. Although the control of party leaders weakened somewhat in the 1950s and 1960s, the system remained substantially in place. For most of our nation's history, the public was largely excluded from the selection process.

The presidential nomination system was transformed in 1972. The key to this transformation was a change in rules by the Democratic Party for the 1972 election and the Republican Party for 1976. The rule changes, especially by the Democrats, encouraged the use of primaries and caucuses to determine whom delegates would support and required that the delegates' votes at the convention were based on the outcome of the primary. Although primaries were held in some states prior to 1972 and about 40 percent of the delegates were selected in this way, the primary outcomes were not always binding on delegates; thus, party leaders were free to ignore the results. Beginning in 1972, most delegates to national conventions—about 80 percent in recent cycles—have been selected by the voting public in primary elections. Delegates were also committed to a particular candidate based on the outcome of the primary. These changes shifted power from political parties—and especially a few party leaders—to the candidates and to the voters.

The type of presidential nominees selected also changed somewhat. The party establishment typically nominated establishment candidates, whereas the electorate now sometimes chooses surprise candidates. Jimmy Carter, the former governor of Georgia, was virtually unknown to the nation in 1974 when he announced he was running for the 1976 Democratic nomination. Yet he was nominated by his party and won the general election over the Republican, President Gerald R. Ford.

The Democrats, concerned that they might nominate a candidate that the party leadership disapproved of, created "superdelegates" in 1984. These delegates, usually elected officials and other party leaders, are unpledged. They are not bound to any candidate. In 2004 superdelegates made up about 20 percent of the delegates at the Democratic National Convention.[26]

Competing in the Primaries and Caucuses

The shift from an elite, party-leader-based system of nominating presidential candidates to a candidate-centered system of state primaries and caucuses means that influencing the mass electorate is key to winning elections.

This in turn has meant that the work of gaining the nomination has changed. It has meant that candidates must raise a great deal of money early in the process to have a real chance at success. A candidate must also create a national organization. Delegate selection begins in early February of the election year with the New Hampshire primary and the Iowa caucuses, but fund-raising and organization building begin at least eighteen months before. Such fund-raising and organization building are important to candidate success in at least two ways. First, without funds a candidate cannot run a modern campaign that requires producing and running television and radio commercials as well as extensive travel. This early money also qualifies candidates for federal matching funds. Once qualified, a candidate is given a match of $1 for every dollar raised up to $250 per donation. Second, without money and organization, the media do not take a candidate seriously. Although the candidate who raises the most money early does not always win—Republicans John Connolly in 1980 and Phil Gramm in 1996 and Democrat Howard Dean in 2004 are examples—candidates with little funding never win.

Candidates spend a great deal of time—many days in the months before delegate selection—in Iowa and New Hampshire trying to make a good impression on the voters of those states and the nation. These two states are small and do not represent the demographics of the nation, but because they select delegates to the national convention first—in late January in 2008—their importance is magnified. It is a chance for candidates to show the nation that they are serious. Candidates who do not do well in either Iowa or New Hampshire often leave the race quickly. For 2008, the Democratic party has moved the Nevada caucuses and the South Carolina primary to late January to increase diversity early in the process.

A fast start has become even more important in recent decades as the presidential nomination process has become **"front loaded."** After Iowa and New Hampshire, the primary season accelerates and the need for early fund-raising and campaign organization is magnified. Since 1992, more states have moved their primaries earlier in the year because states with earlier primaries have greater influence in the nomination process. In 1996 this front loading was clearly evident. Only six weeks after the process began, 75 percent of the Republican delegates had been chosen. The Democrats took only ten weeks[27] (see Figure 8.3). Front loading eased somewhat in 2000, with few primaries held during February, but the structure of the primary season still created difficulties for candidates. Most important, beginning in 2000 New York and California, which once scheduled their primaries late in the process, April and June, respectively, each moved its primary up to early March. Ohio, another populous state, as well as nine other states also had primaries on the same day in early March. This created what amounted to a national primary in which approximately one third of the delegates to both of the major party national conventions were selected on one day.[28]

The Democrats further accelerated their primary process in 2004; within eight weeks of the first delegate selection in Iowa, over 75 percent of delegates had been awarded. Even more importantly, in 2004 seven states ranging in size from North Dakota to Missouri moved their Democratic primaries

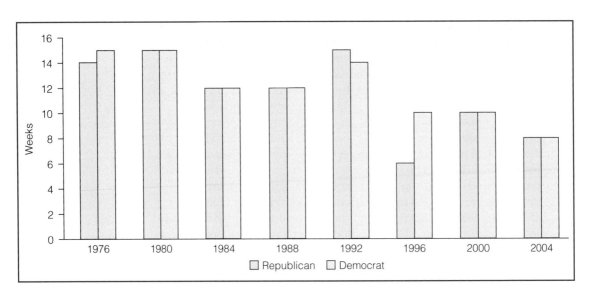

Figure 8.3 Number of Weeks for 75 Percent of Delegates to Be Selected by Party, 1968–2004. The major parties have front-loaded their nomination processes in recent campaigns.

Source: William Mayer, *The Divided Democrats* (Boulder, CO: Westview, 1996). The 2000 and 2004 data are from Jonathon Bernstein, "The Rise and Fall of Howard Dean and Other Notes on the 2004 Democratic Presidential Nomination," *Forum* 2(1), pp. 1–13.

into early February.[29] This put even more pressure for candidates to organize quickly on a national basis and to raise the money required to do so. Although there have been calls for reform, it is unclear that the front loading of presidential nomination campaigns will change for the 2008 election cycle. A number of comprehensive solutions have been proposed, including a national primary, consecutive regional primaries, and a series of primaries with small states going first and moving to larger states in an orderly fashion.[30]

Candidates drop out quickly if they perform poorly in the early primaries. They have difficulty raising money if they do not look like a winner, and they lose federal matching funds if they gain less than 10 percent of the vote in two consecutive primaries. Such was the case in the 2004 Democratic nomination campaign, where a large field of ten Democrats sought to challenge a sitting president whose job approval ratings were hovering below 50 percent. Two candidates, Senator Bob Graham (Fla.) and former Senator Carol Moseley Braun (Ill.), dropped out even before balloting began. Representative and former House Speaker Dick Gephardt left the race after the Iowa caucuses. Senator Joseph Lieberman (Conn.) dropped out shortly thereafter. The two early front-runners—former Vermont Governor Howard Dean and General Wesley Clark—conceded in mid-February. Other candidates, including eventual Democratic vice presidential nominee Senator John Edwards (N.C.), stayed in the race until 2004's version of Super Tuesday, with several large state primaries. But on Super Tuesday, March 2, 2004, Senator John Kerry—the best financed, most organized candidate—had emerged the winner. What is remarkable in the modern campaign is how quickly all of this takes place. What began quietly with fund-raising and organizing more than a year earlier is completed in a hectic flurry of activity over a two-month period.

The National Conventions

As primaries have become central in the nomination campaigns, the national party conventions have become less important, except as political theater. Once the source of exciting and dramatic twists, the outcomes of conventions are now known well in advance, as the delegates simply formalize what was decided in primaries and caucuses months earlier. The convention delegates still have the responsibility to ratify a platform—a statement of policy goals and beliefs—and finalize the rules for the next selection process. The party convention is often a time when the disparate forces inside a party are unified for the upcoming general election campaign.

National party conventions have become, more than anything else, tightly controlled media events. The conventions are seen as the beginning of the fall campaign and an important way of communicating the party's key campaign issues to the whole of the American people. Speeches are timed for prime-time television coverage. The speakers and their topics are carefully chosen so that the party can speak with a clear voice. Each of the major candidates generally gets a "bounce"—an increase in popular support—in public opinion polls in the lead-up to their convention as media coverage focuses on them more exclusively. The post-convention bounces were smaller in 2004 than they had been in the past. Both John Kerry and George W. Bush saw their support in the polls increase modestly after their conventions in July and early September, respectively. Neither bounce was particularly long lasting, though, and the race remained close through Election Day.

Ironically, as the convention has moved from being a decision-making meeting to a made-for-the-media show, television coverage has declined. The major networks once had "gavel-to-gavel" coverage of the conventions and recently had several nights with three hours of coverage each, but only the Public Broadcasting Service and cable outlets CNN, MSNBC, and Fox News have had complete coverage of the two major party conventions in recent campaigns. The three major networks—ABC, CBS, and NBC—sharply limited their coverage and instead broadcast reruns of regular programming.

The General Election

The 2000 presidential election reminded Americans that the election is not simply a national campaign whose goal is to win the **popular vote**— the total votes cast for a candidate nationally. The general election for president comprises fifty-one independent elections (fifty states and the

View Barry Goldwater's presidential nomination acceptance speech.

View George H.W. Bush's presidential nomination acceptance speech.

View video from the 2004 national party conventions.

Democratic presidential nominee John Kerry emphasized his military service in his presidential nomination acceptance speech at the 2004 Democratic National Convention in Boston, Massachusetts, on July 29, 2004.

AP Images

Learn more about the electoral college and participate in discussion on proposals to modify or abolish it.

Look up the results of past presidential elections.

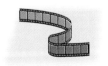

Modern Campaigns: The Election of 1876 and Running for President.

District of Columbia) conducted on the same day. The goal of each candidate is to accumulate a majority of the **electoral vote.** When Americans vote, they are voting for electors who in turn choose the president and vice president as part of the **electoral college.** Each state has the number of electoral votes equal to its total number of U.S. senators plus representatives. For example, Virginia has two U.S. senators and eleven U.S. representatives, for a total of thirteen electoral votes. Residents of the District of Columbia have three electoral votes as the result of the Twenty-Third Amendment. There are a total of 538 electoral college votes. An absolute majority of 270 votes is needed for victory. Figure 8.4 lists the number of electoral votes held by each state.

In forty-eight of fifty states—Maine and Nebraska are the exceptions—it is a winner-take-all system. This means that all of a state's electoral votes are awarded to the candidate with the largest number of popular votes. Even if a candidate wins the general election in Florida by one vote, the candidate gets all twenty-five of Florida's electoral votes. The electors—chosen by party leaders as a reward for service—meet in each of the fifty state capitals in December and formally report the results to Congress, which counts them when the new congressional session begins in early January.

As became abundantly clear with the 2000 election, the outcomes of the popular vote and the electoral vote are not always in accord. On three occasions before 2000—the elections of John Quincy Adams in 1824, Rutherford B. Hayes in 1876, and Benjamin Harrison in 1884—the winner

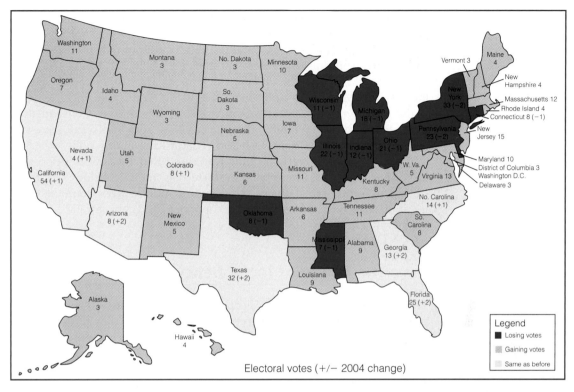

Figure 8.4 Electoral College Votes, 2004 and 2008. As has been the trend in recent decades, electoral college votes moved southward and west after the 2000 census.

Source: http://www.nara.gov/fedreg/elctcoll/index.html.

of the popular vote has lost the election. If no candidate wins an electoral college majority, the House of Representatives selects the president, with each state delegation given one vote. The vice president is selected by majority vote of the Senate.

The presence of the electoral college helps shape the general election campaign in important ways. Unlike the nomination campaign, the general election gives each major candidate the same amount of money to spend. Because the amount of money is fixed, $74.6 million in the 2004 election, all votes are not created equal. First, votes in more populous states—California, Texas, New York, Florida, Pennsylvania, Illinois, and Ohio have the largest populations and more than twenty electoral votes each—are seen as more important than others. Theoretically, a candidate can win an electoral college victory by winning the popular election in the eleven largest states and losing in the remaining thirty-nine. Second, votes in states that are seen as close by the presidential candidates—the so-called battleground states or swing states—are especially valuable. Candidates focus most of their time

View 2004 presidential campaign ad "Act Like Bush."

View 2004 presidential campaign ad "Child's Play."

View 2004 presidential campaign ad "Kerry: International Man of Mystery."

"No Need to Repeal the Electoral College," Norman J. Ornstein.

"Not the People's Choice: How to Democratize American Democracy," Arthur M. Schlesinger, Jr.

and financial resources on these states. Some states consistently support the presidential candidate of one party, others, however, are consistently up for grabs. Swing states in 2004 included electoral-vote-rich Florida, Ohio, and Pennsylvania as well as medium-sized Michigan, Minnesota, and Wisconsin.[31] The major candidates made many trips in the fall of 2004 to these states. Millions of dollars of advertising were spent there as well. Many states vote consistently Democratic or Republican. Consequently, many states, including large states, such as New York and Texas, were virtually ignored by President Bush and Senator Kerry. Early polls indicated that New York was clearly backing Kerry and that Texas was supporting its former governor. The other candidate reasonably concluded in these states and in numerous others that spending money there would be fruitless. Each conceded these states to his opponent and concentrated on states viewed as winnable.

Running for Congress: The Power of Incumbency

Scandal, public perception, and truth.

The process of congressional elections is simpler than that for selecting presidents. These elections are important, but relatively few races are competitive, and for the most part, the **incumbent**—the current officeholder—wins and is sent back to our nation's capital for another term. If there are multiple candidates for a political party's House or Senate nomination, parties use primaries—or primaries in combination with party conventions—to select congressional candidates in all fifty states. Although primaries are not unusual, most sitting members of Congress do not face challenges from within their party, and few lose primaries. Since World War II, fewer than 2 percent of House members seeking reelection have lost primary contests. Only a slightly higher percentage of senators—5 percent—have lost primaries during the same period. Primaries are also not the norm to select a challenger; in most cases, a single potential nominee emerges and is tabbed to run. In some cases, no challenger is named at all. Although no sitting senators ran without a challenge in 2004, thirty-four sitting House members faced no opposition.[32] Twenty-three more faced no major party opposition. In the off-year 2006 election, thirty-four members of the House again ran unopposed and another eighteen ran with no opponent from a major party. No member of the Senate ran unopposed.[33]

The cost of congressional campaigns.

Once nominated, the selected candidates run in the general election, where the winner is the candidate receiving the most votes. As with party candidate selection, general elections are characterized by their lopsided results. In each election year since 1980, over 90 percent of representatives running in the general election won reelection (see Figure 8.5). The percentage of victorious sitting senators has fluctuated during this period, but the story is much the same: Most senators running for reelection win.

Why are incumbents so likely to win reelection? A variety of forces fall into two general categories: the power of incumbency and the advantage

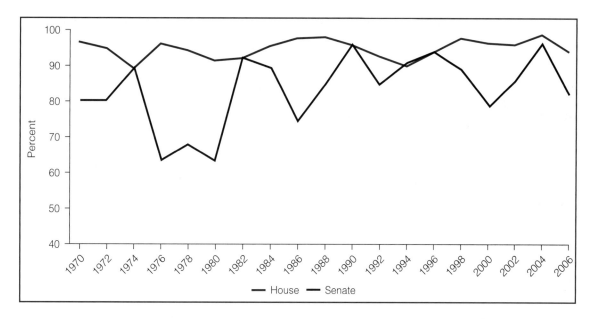

Figure 8.5 Percentage of House and Senate Incumbents Winning Reelection, 1970–2006. Incumbent representatives and senators running for reelection win most of the time. In general, U.S. Congressional elections are not competitive.

Source: Harold W. Stanley and Richard G. Niemi, *Vital Statistics on American Politics 2003–2004* (Washington, DC: CQ Press, 2003). 2004 and 2006 data compiled by authors.

in fund-raising. Incumbency provides a substantial advantage to an officeholder. One of the keys to victory is name recognition: Can voters identify the candidate's name among others on the ballot? Much of what members of Congress do helps create name recognition. As public officials, the local media back home see them as newsworthy. Their press secretary works hard to ensure that the local press knows when their representative or senator has made news. Both chambers now have television studios with satellite feeds to make television interviews easier. Press releases written by congressional staffers are often printed in local papers.

Research fund-raising by congressional candidates in your district.

In addition, members of Congress have the ability to send mail for free. This is known as the **franking privilege.** Ostensibly used to communicate important information to constituents, these messages are often nothing more than self-promotion pieces. Although this free mail cannot be sent out close to election time, it is still important for building name recognition. In addition, constituency work and pork-barrel projects—detailed in Chapter 9—help representatives and senators build goodwill and name recognition.

Raising money is also key to winning an election. Hiring professional consultants, purchasing television and radio time, and conducting polls are expensive and necessary ingredients in a modern campaign. In 2004 the average successful House candidate raised over $1 million, and the average Senate victor spent well over $6 million.[34] Money allows a candidate to build

Type of Candidate	Senate	House
Incumbent	$8,614,011	$1,122,505
Challenger	$962,074	$193,296
Open seat	$2,949,264	$569,738

Table 8.1 Average Campaign Funds Raised by Congressional Incumbents and Challengers, 2004. Incumbents are able to raise much more money than challengers. This gives incumbents a key advantage in congressional elections.

Source: Center for Responsive Politics, http://www.opensecrets.org/overview/incumbs.asp?cycle=2004.

name recognition and to define himself or herself—what kind of person is this candidate and what does he or she stand for—to the voters. In contrast to incumbents, challengers—especially in House races—are typically not well-known and must buy name recognition through television and radio advertising. This is an expensive proposition. And money is often in short supply. In 2004, 160 House challengers reported raising less than $25,000.[35] With this little money, it is impossible to run a modern campaign. Not surprisingly, none of these candidates won. Campaign spending alone cannot guarantee success—in 2004 each of the five incumbents who lost spent over $1 million in their campaign. A challenger has virtually no chance of winning without a good deal of money—in four of five instances where incumbents lost, they were outspent by their opponent, and in the fifth the incumbent outspent his opponent by a narrow margin. (Table 8.1 presents information on money raised by congressional incumbents and challengers in 2004.) In districts with open seats—districts where no incumbent was running—the candidate raising the most funds won in thirty of thirty-two instances.

Thus, relatively few House and Senate campaigns are truly competitive. In 2000 the Center for Responsive Politics analysis categorized 16 percent of House races and 30 percent of Senate races as financially competitive. In contrast, 64 percent of House races and 40 percent of Senate races were defined as "blowouts," races in which one candidate raised more than ten times as much money as another.[36] Although—in principle—elections are intended to be a check on our leaders, that check is a limited one if there is no real alternative candidate running in opposition. This clearly limits us as voters and as citizens.

Voting

Voting is by far the most common form of political participation in the United States. As discussed in Chapter 1, voting is particularly important in a representative democracy where the people choose representatives to make key government decisions. A healthy democracy depends on widespread political participation. Importantly, voting allows broad participation where it would not otherwise be possible. Collectively, voting can influence the decisions that government makes. Voting in a representative political system can be considered the most fundamental right of citizenship because it is "preservative of all rights."[37]

We have already discussed some of the reasons that elections are important to a nation. Voting is important to the individual as well. Over the last two centuries, Americans have struggled for the franchise. In the first presidential election in 1796, only white male property owners had the right to vote. Through concerted efforts on the part of the disenfranchised, constitutional amendments and congressional action now ensure that virtually all citizens can vote (see Chapter 1). Currently, only convicted felons and those deemed mentally incompetent are ineligible to vote in most states.

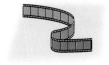

The Internet revolution: Voting online.

The franchise is now a basic right of every American citizen. In the 2004 presidential election, however, just over half of the voting-age population of the United States—55.3 percent—turned out at the polls. This occurred in a nation where four in five Americans believe that voting is either an essential or very important obligation (see Chapter 1). These voting numbers are particularly unflattering compared with those of other nations. As a nation, Americans are often told that they have failed the test of democracy. This section of the chapter will examine voter participation in the United States. One of the great questions in American politics is why voter turnout is so low. After looking at the facts of voter participation in the United States, we will examine alternative answers to this important question.

The Decline of Voter Turnout

Voter turnout, the percentage of the voting-eligible population that goes to the polls on Election Day, was high in the nineteenth century after universal male suffrage became well established. In 1840, 80.1 percent of the eligible electorate participated in selecting John Tyler president. Although the numbers fluctuated somewhat for individual elections, voter turnout was almost identical in 1896—79.3 percent—to what it had been fifty-six years earlier. In all but one election from 1840 through 1900, over 70 percent of the electorate voted, and in 1852—the exception—turnout was 69.6 percent.

The election of 1900 began a decline that continued throughout much of the twentieth century before settling at its current level of roughly 50-percent voter turnout for the last three decades. Since 1900, voter turnout has not approached 70 percent in any national election (see Figure 8.6). The increase in voter turnout in 2004 over 2000 was widely applauded, but voter turnout is still well below that of 1960.[38] Voting in the U.S. is also well below that of most other democratic nations (see Figure 8.7).

Voter Registration

One key difference between the United States and most other nations is the system of **voter registration.** Voter registration was developed a century ago to reduce voter fraud and reduce the power of political party machines. Since then, Americans must take the personal initiative to register to vote,

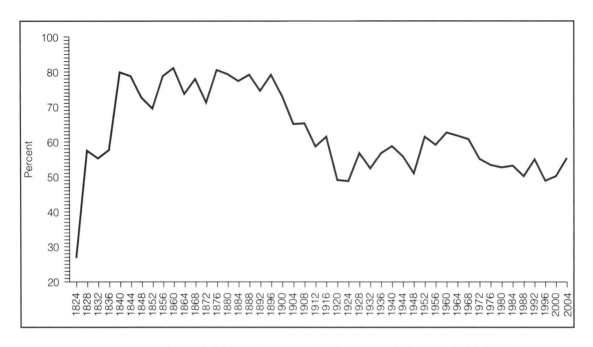

Figure 8.6 Voter Turnout in U.S. Presidential Elections, 1824–2004. Voter turnout in the U.S. peaked around 1900. Even with the recent increase in voter turnout, turnout remains well below past levels of participation.

Source: Department of Commerce, Bureau of the Census, *Historical Statistics of the United States, Colonial Times to 1957* (Washington, DC: Government Printing Office, 1960); *Statistical Abstract of the United States, 2006* (Washington, DC: Government Printing Office, 2006).

Register to vote.

whereas citizens of most other nations are automatically registered to vote by the government. In 2004, 79 percent of the voting-age population in the United States was registered to vote; in most democratic nations, virtually all adults are registered at any one time.[39] If one counts only those people registered to vote, 70 percent of Americans voted in the 2004 presidential election (see Figure 8.7). Voter turnout began to decline in the United States with the advent of registration requirements around 1900.

Each state creates its own rules on how and when voters register. Typically, the voter registration form is simple to fill out, but it can be inconvenient to find the form. The availability of forms and registration deadlines typically are not widely publicized, creating a burden for the potential voter. Most states have similar voter registration requirements in accordance with the U.S. Constitution and federal law. Among them are citizenship, a minimum age of eighteen, and being a resident of the state one is registering in (sometimes for as long as one month before the election). One area in which states vary considerably is in the date of voter registration deadlines. Deadlines are important because many adults think to register only after they have begun to focus on the election. Political scientists have

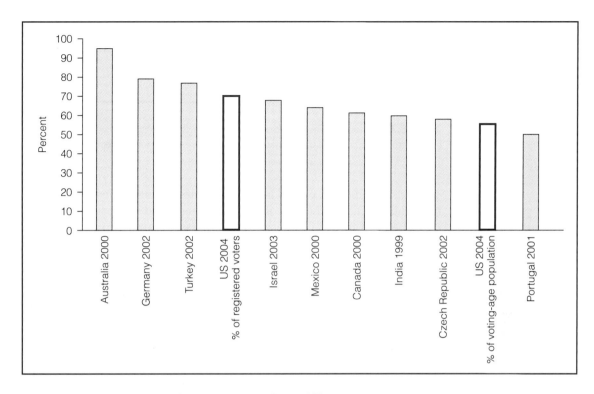

Figure 8.7 Voter Turnout in Selected Recent National Elections. A comparison with other nations shows that voter turnout in the United States trails that of other democracies around the world.

Source: International Institute for Democracy and Electoral Assistance.

found that this often does not occur until a few days before the election. In most states, this is too late to register. Twenty-five of the fifty states require registration to take place a full four weeks in advance of the election.[40] Only six states—Maine, Minnesota, New Hampshire, North Dakota, Wisconsin, and Wyoming—have any form of Election Day registration. Not surprisingly, the states that make it easier for voters to register have significantly higher voter turnout as well (see Table 8.2).

The last decade has seen a renewed effort to register voters in the United States. The most important of these efforts was the passage of the **National Voter Registration Act of 1993** (NVRA), commonly known as the "motor voter" law. The name comes from the requirement that states allow people to register while applying for a driver's license as well as making voter registration available in social services offices and by mail. The passage of this law was controversial. Current officeholders were threatened by the prospect of a host of new voters in the electorate, potentially changing the outcome of future elections. Republicans were particularly worried because those not registered are more likely to be poor, a group that generally

Investigate voter registration requirements

	Voter Turnout
States with same-day registration (N = 6)	70.8%
States requiring advance registration (N = 44 + D.C.)	54.5%

Table 8.2 Turnout by Ease of Voter Registration, 2004. Voter turnout is over fifteen percentage points higher in the six states where voters can register on Election Day.

Source: Compiled by the authors from Federal Election Commission data.

supports Democratic candidates. Some states initially refused to implement the law, citing the cost of administering it and the federal intrusion into an area historically under state control (see Chapter 3).

New voter registration was quite successful in the first two years after the law was passed. Over 18 million Americans were added to the voter rolls between the 1994 and 1996 elections. Millions of new voters continued to be added to voter registration rolls; almost 12 million people were registered in 2003 and 2004.[41] This trend has led to improvements in the percentage of the voting-age population that is registered to vote. In 2004, 79 percent of the voting-age population was registered. In comparison, only 70.6 percent of the voting-age population was registered in 1992 before the NVRA became law. But voter registration efforts have only been partially successful, and there is still a large gap between the number of registered voters and the voting-age population. It is promising, however, that voter turnout has also increased in recent elections as registrations have increased. Furthermore, Republican fears that these new registrants will be Democrats have been unfounded because Republican registration has gained slightly relative to the Democratic Party during the period.[42] Furthermore, whites have been more likely to register under the motor voter law than blacks and other minorities.[43]

Other Reasons for Low Voter Turnout

The impact of the motor voter law shows that registration alone is not the problem. Other forces are at work, as noted by those who study voter turnout. First is the frequency of elections. We are often asked to vote several times a year for a host of offices at all levels of government. It is both confusing and tiring. In contrast, many other democracies vote for national legislators only once every few years. The scheduling of elections is also seen as a problem. Tuesday is a workday. As a larger percentage of Americans work, it is increasingly difficult to find time to get to the polling place. Other nations hold elections on Saturdays or over two days.

Some may believe that it is logical not to vote. Gathering information to make an informed vote is time consuming. Some feel inadequate to the task of learning the facts, but even more important is finding the time to do the work. The most common reason cited in U.S. census surveys of nonvoting is that people are too busy with work or with school.[44] To many, the cost of gathering information is not worth the benefit, given that there is little chance their vote will matter. Of course, the 2000 presidential election emphasized that voting does matter. Finally, others argue that a key problem is that Americans do not feel connected to the community. People have withdrawn from political life and are generally less committed to their communities.[45] In Chapter 5 we found some evidence for a growing distrust in government and a growing belief that government is less responsive than in the past. This disconnectedness may grow. Much of our sense of civic duty comes from our childhood socialization. Current adults are communicating these ideas to the next generation of voters.

Who Votes?

The 55 percent of Americans who turned out to vote in the 2004 presidential election did not look like the American people as a whole. Voters were older, better educated, and wealthier than the voting-age population. White Americans voted more frequently than other races, and women voted at higher rates than men. The voting public in 2004 was typical in most ways of the electorate who have turned out to vote over the last twenty years.[46] (The data in this section come from the November 2004 Current Population Survey done by the U.S. Census Bureau; it is based on reported levels of voting by subjects of the survey. Figure 8.8 presents detailed results from the Current Population Survey.)

Go to the Census Bureau's site and examine voter turnout in past elections.

Age

Age is an important factor in understanding voter turnout. Young Americans vote in remarkably low numbers. Only 41.9 percent of eighteen- to twenty-four-year-olds voted in 2004. (For more on voting and interest in politics by young Americans, see the feature called "Youth Voting in 2004.") There is a steady increase in voting until Americans reach age seventy-five—70.8 percent of sixty-five- to seventy-four-year-olds voted. People seventy-five and older still vote in high numbers, but poor health and immobility erode their turnout numbers.

View news stories on young people voting in the 2004 election.

Education and Income

Americans with a college education are much more likely to vote than those who do not have a high school diploma. Almost three-quarters (74.2 percent) of people with a bachelor's degree or an advanced degree voted in 2004. Fewer than one-third (30.4 percent) of those without a high school diploma voted. Education level is closely tied to an interest in politics and political knowledge. More-educated Americans believe that their voice in politics matters. All of these factors are positively related to voting.[47] Similar to education level, income and voting are strongly linked: A higher income is associated with increased voter participation.

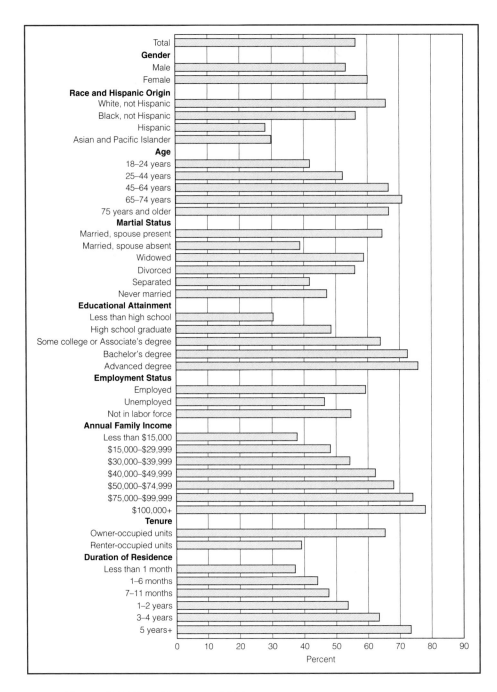

Figure 8.8 Voter Turnout in 2004. Voter turnout varies significantly for different groups. Those who are most likely to vote include those who are older, married, more educated, and have higher incomes.

Source: U.S. Census Bureau, "Voting and Registration in the Election of November 2004," http://www .census.gov/population/www/socdemo/voting/cps2004.html.

CHAPTER 8: Elections and Political Participation

YOUTH VOTING IN 2004

Something unusual happened on college campuses on November 2, 2004: Students waited in long lines to vote in the national election held on that day. In some cases, polls stayed open late to allow all of the students waiting in line to vote. Kenyon College students waited up to 10 hours in freezing rain to vote, and the scene made the national news.[1] Were these scenes typical of young voters across the nation? In a word, yes; voting among the nation's young people was up in 2004. And this is an interesting trend. Since young people were given the right to vote in for the first time in the 1972 presidential election, they have been much less likely to vote than their elders. And there are clear reasons for this. Young people are developing their lives: They are in college, working multiple jobs, and establishing relationships. They are also typically less tied to the community and to politics. They are much less likely to be homeowners or have families. But more is going on as well.

In 2004 voting among the young was up. According to the Current Population Survey done by the U.S. Census Bureau in November 2004, 47.1 percent of eighteen- to twenty-four-year-olds voted and over half of eighteen- to twenty-nine-year-olds voted. As in the past, young people voted in lower numbers than older voters, and voting was up for the electorate as a whole (see Figure 8.6), but the increase in youth voting from 2004 was by far the largest of any age group. Almost 11 percentage points more young people voted in 2004 than in 2000. By contrast, 3.5 percentage points more of the older electorate voted in the most recent presidential election than in 2000.[2] This followed a campaign season where young people were much more engaged in the process and at an earlier point in the election cycle than in the past. For example, a survey of eighteen- to twenty-nine-year-olds found that three-and-one-half times more young people watched the first 2004 presidential debate as compared to 2000.[3]

This increased interest in politics counters a long-term decline in political interest by young people. In 2000 the annual study of college freshmen conducted by UCLA's Higher Education Research Institute found that interest in politics among first-year college students was the lowest recorded in the thirty-four-year history of the survey. The study found only 16.4 percent of students surveyed said they "discussed politics frequently" and only 28.1 percent of respondents thought that "keeping up to date with political affairs" was an "essential" or "very important" objective. The survey has found that interest in politics has rebounded each year since 2000.[4]

(continued)

YOUTH VOTING IN 2004 (Contd.)

Why was voting up in 2004? More than older voters, young voters voted because they cared about the issues. The ongoing conflict in Iraq was one important issue. This was especially true of young, college-educated Americans. For non-college-educated young people, the economy was especially important. Young voters were also motivated by dislike for a candidate as a motivation to go to the polls. They were much likely to cite this than their elders: 83 percent of young people said they voted "because I really disliked one of the candidates," and only 46 percent of older voters agreed with the same statement.

It is unclear if 2004 is a one-time event or if this is part of a positive long-term trend.[5] Because young voters were so issue driven in the last election, we might expect that participation will remain high if the issues that motivated them—Iraq, the economy, and polarizing candidates—continue to be seen as relevant. But if the situation changes between now and 2008, it is unclear that young people will return to the polls.

[1] Guy Gugliotta, "Politics in, Voter Apathy Right Amid Heavy Voter Turnout," *Washington Post,* November 3, 2004.

[2] Mark Hugo Lopez, "The Youth Vote 2004: With a Historical Look at Youth Voting Patterns, 1972–2004," July 2005 (Center for Information Research on Civic Learning and Engagement, Working Paper 35), http://www.civicyouth.org/research/products/working_papers.htm (retrieved November 1, 2005).

[3] Thomas E. Patterson, "Young Voters and the 2004 Election" (Cambridge, MA: The Vanishing Voter Project), http://www.vanishingvoter.org/2004_Releases.shtml (retrieved November 1, 2005).

[4] Linda J. Sax, "Political Engagement Rebounds Among the Nation's College Freshmen," *UCLA's Graduate School of Education & Information Studies' (GSEIS) Forum,* 6(3), http://www.cacampuscompact.org/news/04-06_FreshmanPollInterest.html (retrieved November 1, 2005).

[5] Patterson, "Young Voters," p. 7.

Gender and Race

Gender and race, in comparison, have a limited impact on voter turnout. Over the last twenty years, women have voted in slightly higher numbers than men. Sixty-five percent of women versus 62 percent of men voted in 2004. Similarly, whites vote in higher numbers than blacks. In 2004, 67 percent of whites voted, in comparison to 60 percent of blacks. This gap has shrunk over the last twenty years and is accounted for by the lower education and income levels of blacks, on average. Other racial and ethnic groups also vote in lower numbers.

Life Stability

An alternative way of viewing voters in the United States is to say that those with stable lives are much more likely to vote than those with unstable lives. We have already discussed the impact of age, education, and income. Other breakdowns of voters tell a similar story. Married people living together (64.6 percent) are much more likely to vote than those who are divorced (56.0 percent), separated (41.8 percent), or who have never been married (47.2 percent). Those employed are 14 percentage points more likely to vote than are those who have no job (60.0 versus 46.4 percent). Homeowners vote in much higher numbers than renters (65.3 versus 39.1 percent). And those who have lived in their dwellings five years or longer (73.4 percent) are about twice as likely to vote than those that have lived in their residence for a year or less.

Chapter 5 noted that learning about politics can be a good deal of work that takes time many people cannot afford to give. Much the same picture has been painted here with voting. Those who have stable, comfortable lives participate in democracy through voting, Americans lacking these characteristics tend not to vote.

Examine who votes in U.S. national elections.

How Voters Choose a Candidate

What determines which candidate a voter chooses once in the voting booth? Studies by political analysts have shown that combinations of three key factors are central to understanding voting behavior: the party affiliation of the voter, the candidates' positions on issues, and the candidates' attributes.[48]

Party

Party affiliation is often the key to understanding which candidate a voter chooses in an election. In fact, if all you knew about a voter was his or her party preference in 2004, you would have an 89-percent or higher chance of predicting his or her vote for president: 93 percent of Republicans voted for President George W. Bush, and 89 percent of Democrats voted for Senator John Kerry (see Figure 8.9). Party affiliation is clearly important when voting for president, but it is even more important in choosing a candidate when little information about the candidate's issue positions is available. For example, when someone is running for a local judgeship, judicial ethics limit the ability of a candidate to discuss how he or she would decide issues, so most candidates run a campaign based on experience and background. For average voters, the candidate's party affiliation is the only real distinguishing information they have. Party identification is less important today as the number of independent voters has increased over the last forty years. But in 2004, about three-quarters of the voters were still self-declared as either Democrats or Republicans. Party affiliation remains the most important factor in voter choice.

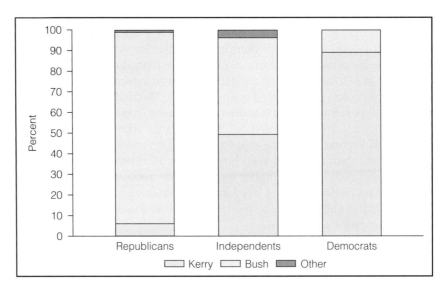

Figure 8.9 Party Identification and Presidential Voting, 2004. More than 90 percent of partisans voted for their party's presidential candidate in 2004.

Source: National Election Pool voter exit poll.

Issues

The issue positions of candidates can be a deciding factor in an election if candidates have clear and opposing views. Many voters do not have a grasp of the detailed positions of candidates on complicated issues, such as Social Security reform. But voters do have a general understanding of the issue positions and ideological leanings of candidates. Often, the sharpest contrasts between candidates are found on **social issues,** such as abortion, gun control, and gay and lesbian rights. These can be compelling for some voters. For some—**single-issue voters**—a candidate's position on just one of these issues may mean a vote for or against a candidate regardless of all else. **Foreign policy** issues typically take a backseat to domestic issues in campaigns. Presidential candidates must spend time articulating their knowledge of international affairs, but voters are more concerned with events closer to home. An exception is when Americans are engaged in war. Such was the case in the 1960s and early 1970s, when the United States was involved in the Vietnam War, and its growing unpopularity led President Lyndon Johnson to drop out of the 1968 presidential race. In 2004, 90 percent of voters who agreed that the war in Iraq was going well for the United States voted for President Bush. In contrast, 82 percent of those who thought the war was going poorly voted for Senator Kerry.[49]

Another kind of issue evaluation often occurs when voters are considering candidates. Voters ask: "Am I better off now than before?" This is called **retrospective voting.** For the most part, voters are making an **economic issue**

Investigate voting in the 2004 election.

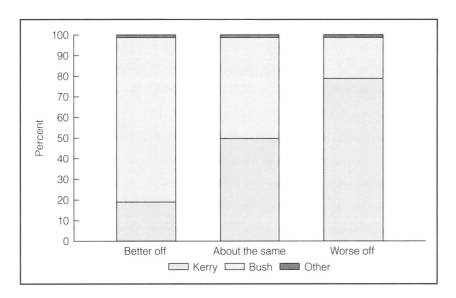

Figure 8.10 Economic Well-Being and Presidential Voting, 2004. A high percentage of voters who felt better off economically in 2004 than in 2000 voted to re-elect President Bush. Those who felt worse off in 2004 than in 2000 voted for Senator Kerry. Those who felt about the same were evenly divided between the two candidates.

Source: National Election Pool voter exit poll.

evaluation when they answer this question. A year before the 1992 election, the incumbent, George H. W. Bush, looked like a shoe-in to win. His approval ratings hovered near 90 percent, and he was the commander in chief during the victorious Gulf War. But after the war, the reality of an economic recession set in with many voters, Bush's ratings sagged, and the Democratic candidate, Bill Clinton, won the election. In the next presidential election, the overall health of the economy helped Clinton cruise to victory despite a string of ethics questions surrounding him and his administration. In the 2004 election, those who believed that they were better off in 2004 than in 2000 voted overwhelmingly for President George W. Bush, and those who saw themselves as worse off in 2004 voted for Senator Kerry, the Democratic nominee (see Figure 8.10).

Candidate Attributes

A voter's evaluation of a candidate as a person may be important in choosing a candidate. This is especially true in elections without compelling issues and for voters who know less about the issues. But even when issue positions are well publicized, candidate attributes can be important. Candidates seen as "presidential" or "senatorial" are more likely to be elected. Candidates who lack these intangible qualities stand less of

Most Important Quality (percentage most important)	Percentage Voting for Bush	Percentage Voting for Kerry
Cares about people (9%)	24%	75%
Religious faith (8%)	91%	8%
Honest/trustworthy (11%)	70%	29%
Strong leader (17%)	87%	12%
Intelligent (7%)	9%	91%
Will bring change (24%)	5%	95%
Clear stand on issues (17%)	79%	20%

Table 8.3 Candidate Characteristics and Presidential Vote, 2004. Voters make clear assessments of the qualities of presidential candidates. These assessments have an impact on the candidate they vote for.

Source: National Election Pool voter exit poll.

a chance of winning. Much of the advertising by candidates is aimed at building an **image of a candidate.** In 1976 Governor Jimmy Carter's perceived honesty was a powerful force in his victory, which came after the Watergate scandal. One attribute that candidates seek to promote is trustworthiness. Voters in 2004 were likely to vote based on the basis of their assessment of candidate characteristics. (See Table 8.3.)

Immutable characteristics can also be important for some voters. Knowledge about the race, ethnicity, religion, or age of a candidate can encourage or discourage some people from voting for a candidate. In 1960 John Kennedy met resistance because he was a Catholic, and some worried that the pope would unduly influence him. In contrast, Senator Joseph Lieberman (D-Conn.)—an Orthodox Jew—was almost universally applauded as the 2000 Democratic vice presidential nominee. Although there may still be some who would not vote for a Jewish candidate, opposition was largely driven underground. Female and black candidates still find resistance among some voters, and in areas of large ethnic communities—Polish Americans in Chicago and Irish Americans in Boston, for example—the right last name can be the difference between winning and losing. In 1996 a sizable minority of people saw Republican presidential nominee Senator Bob Dole's age—he was 73—as a problem.

Summing Up

Although each of these factors—party affiliation, issues, and candidate attributes—has consistently been important in national elections since voter behavior has been studied beginning in the 1950s, no two elections have been alike. In the 1950s, party affiliation was seen as most important, and voters were characterized by their lack of knowledge about the issues. Issue voting was more important in the 1960s. In 1976 and in 1980, character and a desire for change were seen as key elements in the election. In 1996, despite a widespread perception that President Clinton was less than honest, he was returned to office by a large margin, with many Americans supporting him because of the strength of the American economy. In the 2000 election, there was a renewed emphasis on trust among the electorate. George W. Bush prevailed in voter evaluations of most character attributes. Party affiliation was also critically important in voter selection.

The 2004 Election Results

As discussed in the chapter introduction, the election of 2004 showed that the electoral map had changed little since 2000. The 2004 election was close by most standards, but in comparison to the 2000 election it provided a clear victory for Republicans—no need to wait for days and weeks to find out the results. The Democrats were bitterly disappointed in their effort to unseat what they saw as a vulnerable sitting president, but all were relieved that the courts were not involved in deciding the outcome. As is often the case when an incumbent president is running for reelection, the 2004 election was in many ways a referendum on the leadership of President George W. Bush. His victory led increased majorities by the Republicans in both houses of Congress.

The Presidency

The 2004 presidential election was a close but decisive victory for the incumbent, George W. Bush. Bush won 50.7 percent of the popular vote to Kerry's 48.3 percent of the vote. By capturing over 50 percent of the vote, Bush was the first presidential candidate to win a true majority of the popular vote since his father won 53.4 percent of the vote in 1988. It was also the first presidential election since 1988 when a third-party candidate did not win a significant percentage of the vote. In the electoral college, Bush was victorious by a 286 to 252 margin. Aside from the 2000 election, the electoral college majority was the narrowest since 1916.

Review detailed 2004 presidential election results.

John Kerry hoped to capitalize on a soft economy and tap into frustration with the war on terror. He was largely unsuccessful in both areas. Exit polls showed that by a slight margin voters believed that President Bush was more trusted to handle the economy. Kerry, a decorated Vietnam War veteran, needed to show the American people that he could lead them in wartime. He was only partially successful, as Republicans worked hard to undermine his war record and his credibility in this area. One telling statistic was that Kerry lost by a 3 to 2 margin with "security moms," women who worried about safety from terrorism. In recent elections, women had handily favored Democratic presidential candidates. Voter turnout was also a factor in the election. It was up overall, but two groups were especially prominent, young voters and evangelical Christian voters. Kerry was successful in winning a large majority of the much larger youth vote in 2004 (see the feature earlier in the chapter). But this support was not enough to counter the huge Bush majority among evangelical voters. (More details about what groups supported each candidate can be found in Table 8.4.)

As discussed in the introduction to the chapter, the electoral college map was little changed from 2000. Only three states changed hands. President Bush won two states—Iowa and New Mexico—won by Vice President Albert Gore in 2000. Kerry picked up only New Hampshire. The additional increase in the Bush electoral college victory was caused by congressional reapportionment after the 2000 census.

The Congress

Review detailed 2004 congressional election results.

The Republicans solidified control of both houses of Congress in the 2004 election. In the Senate, Republicans had regained a narrow, fifty-one-seat majority in the 2002 elections. In 2004 Democratic senators in five Southern states—Florida, Georgia, Louisiana, North Carolina, and South Carolina—retired, and in each case, the Republican won. The Democrats did pick up two seats previously held by Republicans in Colorado and Illinois, but the Republicans gained four seats overall and established a 55–44 seat advantage over the Democrats. (Senator James Jeffords [Vt.] is an independent who caucuses with the Democrats.) In the most interesting Senate race of the year, then Minority Leader Tom Daschle (D-S.D.) lost in his hotly contested reelection bid to former Congressman John Thune, who was energetically supported by both the White House and the Senate Majority Leader, Bill Frist (R-Tenn.). Daschle was the only incumbent senator to lose in 2004. Remarkably, the race in South Dakota—population 770,883—was the most expensive Senate race in the nation. The two candidates combined to spend about $50 per voter.[50]

Review detailed 2006 congressional election results.

The Republicans also added to their majority in the House in 2004 for the fifth consecutive election, picking up 3 seats. The makeup of the House stood at 232 Republicans, 202 Democrats, and 1 Independent, Bernard Sanders of Vermont. There was little change in the House, with only 7 incumbents losing their seats. Redistricting in Texas was the major source of gains for the Republicans. Three redistricted Democrats lost their seats there.

The 2006 Election Results

In a sharp reversal from the 2004 election, the Democrats did something few thought possible as the 2006 campaign season began: they won majorities in both houses of Congress. Redistricting after the 2000 election created many safe House seats for Republicans and a comfortable 55 to 45 margin in the Senate, so the early analysis argued that the Democrats would be hard pressed to control the House or the Senate after Election Day. Republicans campaigned on the improving economy and their perceived superior ability to fight the War on Terror, but Democrats successfully defined the major issue of the campaign as the war in Iraq and President Bush's leadership. As the war continued with no clear resolution on the horizon and with death tolls for American troops rising, the American people became increasingly disenchanted with the president. His job approval rating dropped below 50 percent in early 2005 and was below 40 percent for much of 2006. His Gallup Poll positive approval rating of 38 percent near Election Day (with a disapproval rating of 56 percent) was the second-lowest midterm approval rating of any president since 1946. Exit polls showed that 36 percent of voters in House races cast ballots to show opposition to President Bush.[51] The president acknowledged the opposition to his Iraq policy when he replaced controversial Secretary of Defense Donald Rumsfeld one day after the election.

A second important issue was a series of scandals involving Republican members of the House. These scandals included influence-selling to lobbyists by then-Majority Leader Tom DeLay (R-Tex.), who resigned in April 2006, and a number of personal transgressions exemplified by Mark Foley (R-Fla.), who resigned in October 2006 after the revelation that he had written sexually suggestive messages to a House page. Fifty-nine percent of voters who said that government scandals were "extremely important" voted for Democratic House candidates.

The Democrats took control of the House for the first time since 1994. They will control at least 230 seats, taking at least 28 seats from Republicans. A minimum of twenty incumbent Republicans lost seats, including four in Pennsylvania alone, while every Democratic incumbent running for re-election was successful. The Democrats also won the majority of open seats—districts with no incumbents. In the Senate, the Democrats captured a narrow 51 to 49 majority. Only 49 Democrats were elected, but the two independent candidates who won, Bernard Sanders of Vermont and three term incumbent Joseph Lieberman of Connecticut—who earlier lost a Democratic primary—will caucus with the Democrats. The Republicans lost six seats, in the states of Missouri, Montana, Ohio, Pennsylvania, Rhode Island, and Virginia. In each instance, the defeated Republican was an incumbent. In addition to the changes in Congress, Democrats took control of six additional governorships and gained majorities in four additional state legislatures.

Political Participation Beyond Voting

Voting is an important form of **political participation** in any democracy, but it is far from the only way that we participate. The ability of Americans to participate in politics beyond voting is part of the richness and potential of our political system. Figure 8.11 shows some of the most significant forms of political participation beyond voting and the percentages of

Social Groups and Presidential Voting, 2000 and 2004.

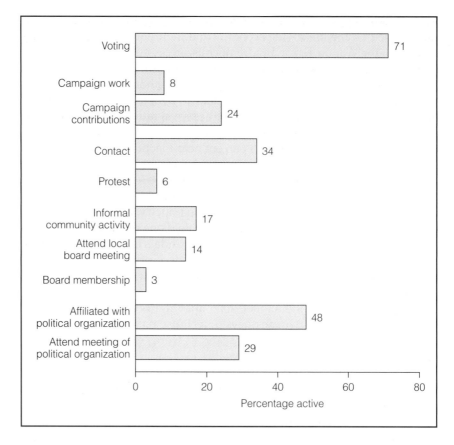

Figure 8.11 Percentage of Americans Engaged in Political Activities. The most common political activity for Americans is voting. Americans are less likely to participate in other more time intensive activities such as attending a meeting or making a campaign contribution.

Source: Sidney Verba, Kay Lehmann Schlozman, and Henry Brady, *Voice and Equality: Civic Volunteerism in American Politics* (Cambridge, MA: Harvard University Press, 1995).

Americans who participate in them. (The data from this table and most of the discussion in this section come from a major study of political participation, *Voice and Equality*, written by political scientists Sidney Verba, Kay Lehmann Schlozman, and Henry Brady in 1995.[52]) The most common forms of political participation, not surprisingly, are those that require the least amount of time commitment: personal contact with a government official, attendance at a political meeting, and campaign contributions. Roughly one-quarter or more of those surveyed said they had been involved in one of these activities. Contacting an official can take many forms—a letter, a phone call, or an e-mail message are possibilities. Members of Congress have literally been overwhelmed with e-mail messages from constituents in recent years.[53] A contact may express a personal concern, such as a sidewalk in need of repair or a town recreation program that is poorly run, or may express a broader national or global concern, such as stating a position on American participation in Bosnia. Twenty-nine percent of Americans attended a political meeting of some sort in the last year before the survey. Much of this attendance is at groups with a particular issue concern—the environment or handguns are examples—or political orientation. These groups are discussed in greater length in Chapter 7. Some Americans—about one-quarter in the survey—are particularly willing to give money to political causes. Often, this "checkbook participation" is at the expense of some other activity.[54]

More intensive activity is less common but important to our political system. Fewer than one in six of us work in campaigns, participate in protests, or serve in leadership positions of political organizations. These forms of political activity are often very time intensive. For example, the 8 percent of Americans who work in campaigns do so for about 7.5 hours a week on average.[55] Those that engage in these more intense activities are more likely to be successful in having an impact on what government does. Although voting is largely anonymous, these more intense activities are personal and allow the participant to more clearly express his or her views.

In contrast to voting, Americans are more likely than citizens of other democracies to participate in politics beyond voting. Figure 8.12 shows comparative data for several types of political participation. Because of our federal system, Americans have many opportunities to participate. There are more elections and more public officials. Weak political parties, discussed in Chapter 7, encourage Americans wishing to influence politics to seek other avenues. The strong national support of individual liberty encourages Americans to pursue their concerns with government officials. In many other democracies, citizens see their governments as unapproachable.

Just as some groups are more likely to vote than others, some types of people are more likely to participate in politics beyond voting. In short, those who participate in politics are more likely to be white males with higher incomes, more education, and more free time. As with voting, the fact that some participate more than others is important and can have a large impact on what issues government concerns itself with.

Participation in civic life extends beyond the narrow bounds of politics as well. Americans are active in the lives of their communities. Charity work, involvement with children at school and in extracurricular activities, and church involvement and attendance are all ways that Americans participate outside of politics. In a 1999 survey, 55.5 percent of adults reported volunteering each year, and 70 percent of American households reported contributing to charities.[56] College students are also clear examples here. Although they vote in low percentages as a group—18- to 24-year-old Americans are less likely to vote than any other age group— students are active in their communities. In 1999, 75.3 percent of college freshmen

"Doing Disservice: The Benefits and Limits of Volunteerism," Drake Bennett.

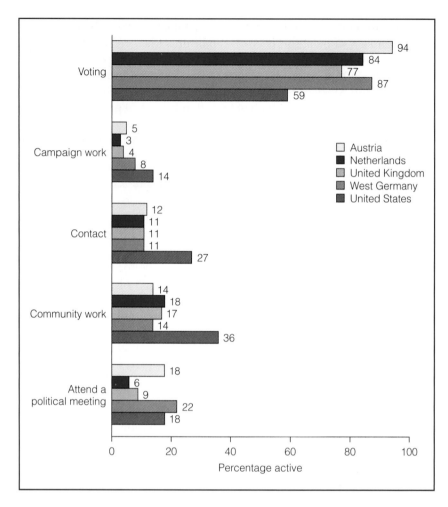

Figure 8.12 A Comparison of Americans' Political Activities with Citizens of Other Nations. American vote at lower rates that citizens of other nations, but they are more likely to participate in other types of political activity than their European counterparts.

Source: Sidney Verba, Kay Lehmann Schlozman, and Henry Brady, *Voice and Equality: Civic Volunteerism in American Politics* (Cambridge, MA: Harvard University Press, 1995).

reported that they had done volunteer work in the past twelve months.[57] Civic volunteerism is high among America's young people.

Despite their common description as lazy and apathetic, the American people are remarkably active in their communities and in their nation, in both politics and especially beyond. Political participation beyond voting has remained relatively constant over the last three decades, with some types of participation—contact with public officials and working on community problems—having grown substantially. Considering all forms of political and nonpolitical participation, 95 percent are connected to civic life in some form. Two-thirds (66 percent) are connected in some way to American politics.[58] Although this does not mean that all is well with American democracy, American apathy as illustrated by low voter participation tells only part of the story.

Conclusion: Does It Matter If We Participate?

The fact that Americans are active in politics beyond voting and in their communities is admirable, but elections, voting, and political participation are at the center of American democracy. Elections are the collective way that we select our leaders and chart the future of our nation. If Americans do not participate in elections, and only half of the citizens do, our democratic system—our nation—is imperiled. Furthermore, we have seen that those who vote are different than nonvoters. Voters tend to be white, older, wealthier, and better educated than those who do not participate. This means that important voices are not heard. In short, those who do not participate give up their influence to those who do. The 2000 election, once again, made this clear to the American public.

Check here for possible post-publication updates to the chapter material.

Key Terms

red states 227
blue states 227
elections 232
selecting leaders 233
democratic accountability 233
influence public policy 233
legitimacy 233
primary election 234
general election 234
closed primaries 237
open primary 238
caucus 238
fixed terms 238
parliamentary systems 238
separate and independent
    elections 238
winner-take-all single-member
    districts 238

plurality 238
proportional representation 239
Federal Election Campaign
    Act 239
Federal Election
    Commission 239
Bipartisan Campaign Finance
    Reform Act 240
soft money 240
political action
    committees 240
527 groups 241
candidate-centered 242
national party
    conventions 244
front loaded 245
popular vote 247
electoral vote 248

electoral college 248
incumbent 250
franking privilege 251
voter turnout 253
voter registration 253
National Voter Registration
    Act of 1993 255
party affiliation 261
social issues 262
single-issue voters 262
foreign policy 262
retrospective voting 262
economic issue 262
image of a candidate 264
immutable characteristics 264
political participation 267

Suggested Web Resources

The following links will take you to websites related to the study of elections and political participation.

To learn more about the 2004 election, try accessing some of the following sites. Detailed presidential results by state can be found can be found on a number of sites, including USelectionatlas.org (http://www.uselectionatlas.org), which also provides detailed results of all presidential elections. Most major news organizations have significant sections of their websites dedicated to the 2004 election. These include CNN (http://clerk.house .gov/members/electionInfo/index.html) and the *Washington Post* (http://www.washingtonpost.com/ wp=dyn/content/politics/elections). Many news sites archive results from past elections. Congressional election results are available at the Clerk of the U.S. House of Representatives (http:// clerk.house.gov/members/electionInfo/ index.html) site.

Information on voter interest during the 2000 and 2004 elections can be found at the Vanishing Voter Project (http://www.vanishingvoter.org) site. This site is the work of Thomas Patterson, professor of public policy at Harvard's Kennedy School of Government.

Campaign commercials and other video including the 2004 party national conventions can be found at C-SPAN.org (http://www.cspan.org).

An excellent online exhibit of past presidential campaign commercials is presented by the American Museum of the Moving Image's "The Livingroom Candidate" (http://livingroomcandidate .movingimage.us/index.php), which provides a selection of commercials from 1952 through 2004.

The National Archives and Records Administration (http://www.archives.gov/federal-register/ electoral-college) provides information about the electoral college and a complete set of electoral college results beginning with the first presidential election in 1789. The site also contains state laws relevant to the electoral college.

You can register to vote (http://www.eac.gov/ register_vote_forms.asp?format=none) by going to the Election Assistance Commission website and following the instructions and links. This site also provides detailed information about state voter registration laws (http://www.eac.gov/ register_vote_deadlines.asp).

Campaign finance data and analysis can be found at the Center for Responsive Government's (http:// www.opensecrets.org) website. This extensive, award-winning site provides data on funds raised and tracks who gave money to candidates and spent money on lobbying. Common Cause (http:// www.commoncause.org) also provides data on campaign finance. Both sites provide information on campaign finance reform efforts. The Federal Election Commission (http://www.cfinst.org/ eguide) is another source of funding data and provides access to the rules of the campaign finance game. The Campaign Finance Institute (http:// www.cfinst.org/eguide) provides an excellent summary of recent changes to federal campaign finance laws.

To find out information about candidates, their voting records, and their views on public policy, go to the Project Vote Smart (http://www.vote-smart.org) website.

The websites of the National Commission on Federal Election Reform (http://www. reformelections.org), co-chaired by former president Jimmy Carter and former Secretary of State James Baker, and the League of Women Voters (http://www.lwv.org//AM/Template.cfm? Section=Home) are excellent resources on election administration reform.

 A complete study tool kit is available for this chapter and includes the following:
Flashcards
Crossword Puzzle
Critical Thinking Exercises
Interactive Timelines
Chapter Quiz

Congress

■ **Partisanship vs. Tradition: The Case of the Filibuster–Nuclear Option Confrontation**   274

■ **Congressional Organization**   277
House and Senate   277
Parties and Party Leadership   279
Committees in Congress   282
The Legislative Process—How a Bill
    Becomes a Law   287
The President in the Legislative Process   290
Divided Government   291

■ **Explaining Congressional Action**   293
The Dominant Goal of Reelection   293
The Incumbency Advantage   295

■ **Who Are Our Representatives?**   298

■ **Conclusion: Lawmaking and Representation**   300

Partisanship vs. Tradition: The Case of the Filibuster–Nuclear Option Confrontation

Alex Wong/Getty Images

Some of the fourteen bipartisan members of the Senate who defused the "nuclear option" in the spring of 2005 at the press conference announcing their agreement.

In the spring of 2005, the national news was full of stories about a passionate debate taking place in the U.S. Senate concerning the use of something called the "nuclear option." Someone simply glancing at the headlines at that time might have concluded that the Senate was debating national security and weapons policies. But such a reader would have been mistaken. The debate was not about weapons of mass destruction; it was about confirming federal judges and possible rule changes in the way that the Senate operates. Although this might not seem like a subject that would result in such highly inflammatory rhetoric, those who were knowledgeable about how Congress operates fully understood the far-reaching implications that invoking the "nuclear option" could have on the operations of the Senate.

The U.S. Senate is often referred to as the world's greatest deliberative body. A large part of the Senate's reputation as a forum for debate and discussion is the unlimited debate rule. There are no time limits on Senate debates; senators discuss an issue until the body agrees that it is done. In contrast, the House of Representatives and most other legislative bodies adhere to strict debate limits to ensure that work gets completed. As a result, the Senate spends more time debating the pros and cons of legislative proposals than do members of the House. Each senator who wishes can have the floor and state his or her position, taking as long as needed. The Senate practice of unlimited debate also means that a senator can refuse to give up the floor and stop speaking, bringing the work of the Senate to a halt. When a senator does this, it is called a *filibuster*. The filibuster rule means that a dedicated minority of senators—in fact, a single senator—can prevent an action from taking place.

The practice of debating legislation for an extended period in Congress goes back to the mid-nineteenth century. In 1917 the Senate adopted the *cloture* rule, which could be invoked to limit debate if two-thirds of the Senate agreed to do so. Because it was extremely difficult to get two-thirds of the senators to agree to stop talking, the Senate changed its rules in 1975 to make ending debate a bit easier, by requiring three-fifths of the Senate, or sixty senators, to end debate.[1] Traditionally, the filibuster has been used to stop legislation from passing, but in 2005 the controversy centered on the use of the filibuster to stop judicial nominations.

One of the responsibilities that the Constitution imposes on the Senate is approving nominations made by presidents for positions in the executive and judicial branches through the power of advice and consent. Executive branch nominees, while sometimes controversial, generally get confirmed, even if the Senate is not controlled by the same political party as the president. No matter how controversial a cabinet appointment might be, if confirmed, his or her term can extend no longer than the president's. In contrast, federal judges, once confirmed, hold their positions until they either retire or die. As a result, the Senate does take its role in the judicial appointment process very seriously.

The usual process for judicial confirmations is for the Senate Judiciary Committee to hold hearings examining the background and credentials of nominees, then pass its recommendations on to the full Senate, which votes to confirm those nominations. Most judicial nominees are confirmed with little attention and controversy even when the Senate is controlled by one party and the presidency is held by the other party. During the 1990s, however, the politics involved in judicial confirmations became increasingly partisan. During much of the Clinton administration, Republicans were the majority party in the Senate; consequently, they controlled the agenda of the Judiciary Committee. They used that advantage to prevent a number of Clinton judicial nominees from ever reaching the floor of the Senate for a vote. When President Bush was elected, the Democrats were the majority party in the Senate, which meant they could do as the Republicans did when Clinton was president and bottle up nominees in committee. This changed after the 2002 election, when Republicans became the majority party. With Republicans in control, controversial Bush nominees made it to the floor of the Senate for a vote, but Democrats engaged in filibusters to prevent confirmation votes on ten occasions. The result was that although thirty-six of Bush's nominees were confirmed by the Senate, there were some controversial nominees that Democrats prevented from being confirmed by using the filibuster.

The Senate Republicans were increasingly frustrated by the Democrats' use of Senate rules to prevent the confirmations. Majority Leader Bill Frist (R-Tenn.) threatened to change the rules of the Senate to "ban filibusters of judicial nominations, but not legislation." Sixty votes are needed to end a filibuster, but only fifty-one votes are needed to change the rules. It would have seemed that with fifty-five Republican senators, the rule would be changed, but it wasn't clear that Frist had the votes needed to change the rules.[2] The proposed change was called the "nuclear option" because it was "so explosive" that Democrats were prepared to bring all Senate business to a halt if the option was exercised.[3] Calling the proposed rules change the "nuclear option" proved to be controversial in itself. Not wanting to be associated with the kind of destruction associated with nuclear weapons, Senate Republicans began to refer to the proposed rule change as the "constitutional option."[4]

As the partisan debate intensified during the spring of 2005 and the nature of the proposal began to receive considerable attention in the press, the American public began to weigh in. A majority of those polled were opposed to changing the rules.[5] Opposition to the rules change was also being expressed by a wide array of interest groups, including groups that traditionally supported Republicans, such as the Gun Owners of America and the National Rifle Association. These groups had benefited from the filibuster in the past and wanted to preserve the rule in case they wanted to make use of it again in the future.[6] Most important, however, members of the Senate from both parties were becoming increasingly disturbed at the prospect of altering a venerated Senate tradition.

In May 2005, fourteen Senators—seven from each party, led by John McCain (R-Ariz.) and Ben Nelson (D-Neb.)—reached a compromise. The group was large enough that if they voted together, they could prevent both a judicial filibuster and the "nuclear option" rule change. They agreed to a vote on three of the controversial nominees but preserved the right of the minority to filibuster "under extraordinary circumstances." As a result, the Senate quickly moved to confirm Priscilla Owens, Janice Brown, and William Pryor as Circuit Courts of Appeal judges, but did not take action on the remaining controversial nominees. The Senators who, together, reached this compromise did so by bypassing the leadership of both parties. Generally seen as "moderates" in their respective parties, the "gang of fourteen" indicated that they reached the agreement in order to, among other things, preserve the traditions of the Senate as an institution. Senator McCain noted that the agreement was in "the finest traditions of the Senate" because it involved "trust, respect and mutual desire to see the institution of the Senate function in ways that protect the rights of the minority."[7] By putting the values of the Senate above partisan considerations, the "moderates" prevented what could have been a significant governmental crisis.

Whether this compromise will hold if there are future controversial nominees, especially for the Supreme Court, will remain to be seen, but the series of events and actions described above illustrates a number of key points about the U.S. Congress in general and the Senate in particular. It highlights the increasingly highly charged partisan nature of debates, especially in decisions that traditionally had been addressed in a bipartisan manner. It demonstrates the importance of rules and procedures in the operations of the legislative branch. Finally, it shows that just because the president enjoys a majority in the Senate, there is no guarantee that senators will simply give the president what he wants—particularly if the traditions and prerogatives of the Senate are at stake.

Watch interviews with members of the "gang of fourteen"

Congressional Organization

As discussed in Chapter 2, the Framers of the Constitution sought to prevent any one institution of the federal government from becoming too powerful, so they created a system of separation of powers and checks and balances. The Framers were particularly suspicious of the legislative branch because it was the part of government most likely to abuse its power and be captured by what James Madison called "factions." Madison feared that a majority faction, seeking to impose its own self-interested views on the nation, could easily capture Congress. As a result, Article I, which describes the powers of Congress, is the most detailed part of the Constitution and imposes a series of checks and balances within Congress itself. In order to understand the operations of the contemporary Congress, it is necessary to learn how Congress is organized, how the legislative process works, and how individual members of Congress go about doing their job.

House and Senate

The first element of congressional organization comes from the **bicameral (two-chamber) legislature,** created by Article I of the Constitution. Congress is composed of two separate chambers: the **House of Representatives** and the **Senate.** The House of Representatives allocates seats to each state based on population. The Senate represents the states equally regardless of size, allocating two senators per state. Originally, only the House was popularly elected, as each state's senators were selected by state legislatures. Since the 17th Amendment was ratified in 1913, senators have been directly elected by the voters in the state they represent.

The Constitution enumerates seventeen specific powers to the Congress. The most significant ones include the power to lay and collect taxes, the power to regulate commerce among the states and with foreign nations, the power to create an armed force, the power to coin money, and the power to declare war. In addition, the Constitution gives Congress the power to "make all laws which shall be necessary and proper to carry into effect its foregoing powers." The necessary and proper clause, or what is sometimes called the "elastic clause," provides Congress with implied powers derived from its enumerated powers (see Chapter 3).

The two chambers of Congress function quite differently. Both the House of Representatives and the Senate are charged with the same basic task of lawmaking, but there are considerable differences in how the two chambers go about legislating. The House has 435 members serving short, two-year terms. Every member of the House is up for election at the same time. Because the House is a large legislative body, it has a more highly structured set of rules and operating procedures. These rules are necessary both to maintain order among members and to ensure that the House can efficiently process the large number of matters before it.

The Senate, on the other hand, is a smaller body of 100 members who serve longer, six-year terms. Senate elections are staggered, with one-third of the Senate up for election every two years. In many ways, the Senate resembles an elite club, a tradition that carries over from the early years of the Republic, when the Senate had only twenty-six members. The members know one another better, and greater deference is paid to individual senators. Although the House has elaborate rules of procedure that limit the power of individual members, the Senate's rules are much less rigid. As the introduction to the chapter indicates, however, the rules can often be a source of controversy because rule changes can influence the decisions that are made and not made. The differences between the House and Senate rules influence how each body operates.

One of the most striking rule differences between the chambers involves the amount of time spent debating legislative proposals (known as bills). Unlike the Senate's unlimited debate or filibuster rule illustrated in the introduction, the House usually restricts the amount of time that members can spend debating a bill before taking a vote. In fact, there is a specific committee in the House, the Rules Committee (described in detail later in the chapter), that establishes the specific conditions for floor debate for every bill considered. The Senate has no comparable committee.

Another difference between the chambers is the one highlighted in the chapter introduction. The Senate lets its members debate measures for as long as they want. Once a senator has been recognized to speak, he or she has "the floor" and can speak indefinitely. Senators can use this privilege as a strategy to derail legislation. If they are opposed to a bill, they can engage in a **filibuster.** They refuse to give up the floor to other senators who want to have a vote on the legislation. Filibusters are used to stop legislation that has majority approval but also has a determined minority that wants to prevent its passage. Filibusters are never used when senators are trying to pass legislation. The mere threat of filibuster gives each senator far more control over the Senate's proceedings than individual members of the House have over the House's proceedings. Filibusters can be ended by a **cloture vote** that needs sixty senators to pass, but it is difficult for sixty senators to agree to anything, much less to agree to stop talking.

The two chambers are structured differently, and they have different constitutional powers. Legislation can proceed only with the approval of both bodies, but technically only the House can begin the consideration of appropriation or spending bills. The Senate is given several important responsibilities in conjunction with the president. The president can nominate judges, ambassadors, and other public ministers, but those nominations are not complete until the Senate provides its "advice and consent" by a simple majority vote. It is for this reason that the fight over judicial nominees described in the introduction took place only in the Senate. Similarly, treaties are negotiated by the president but must be ratified by a two-thirds vote of the Senate to go into effect. In both of these instances, the House has no constitutional role. Finally, the House and Senate share the power of impeachment. Only the House can begin the impeachment process. Once the House votes to impeach the president or a federal judge, the trial takes place in the Senate.

"The Senate Filibuster: A Constitutional Critique," Edward N. Kearny and Robert Heineman.

Watch Congresswoman Barbara Jorden's discussion of impeachment from the Nixon era.

Learn more about the impeachment of President Clinton.

Parties and Party Leadership

Bicameralism divides Congress into two chambers, but a second important organizing factor within Congress is political party. The party affiliation of representatives and senators divides each chamber into the "majority" and "minority." Which party controls the majority is important. The majority party in each chamber names all committee and subcommittee chairs and controls the policy agenda of the institution. Americans were reminded of this fact in May 2001 when—with the Senate divided equally between Republicans and Democrats—Senator James Jeffords (I-Vt.) left the Republican Party, handing control of the Senate to the Democrats. Senator Thomas A. Daschle (D-S.D.) went from minority leader to majority leader. Proposals pushed by the Republicans were presumed dead (school vouchers, for example), and new ones were given life (a medical patient's bill of rights).

The Democratic and Republican members of Congress each have individuals they elect to provide leadership and to speak for the party within each chamber. When the party is in the majority, its leader is called the **majority leader;** when the party is in the minority, its leader is called the **minority leader.** It is possible that a party might be the majority in one chamber and the minority in the other. The leaders are the public face of Congress, often appearing in the media as spokespeople for their party's positions on the issues of the day. **Whips** are party leaders who work to generate unity within the party by encouraging members to vote the party's position on issues. Each party's leadership works to promote the party's platform for governance and to generate unity among party members on important bills.

In the House, political parties decide the leadership of the chamber and determine the membership of committees. The **Speaker of the House** is the presiding member. The Speaker is elected by the membership at the beginning of each two-year session. The election is always by party line, ensuring that a member of the majority party will be Speaker. In addition to the Speaker, the House leadership consists of a majority leader, a minority leader, and party whips, whose job is to instill party unity and discipline among members. The House leadership has considerable power in making committee assignments, selecting committee chairs, and referring bills to specific committees.

See the current House leadership.

The position of Speaker of the House has often carried with it considerable public attention, particularly during the four years the position was held by Representative Newt Gingrich (R-Ga.). Gingrich was the symbol of the House Republican leadership, and he received much more media coverage than the typical Speaker. Gingrich retired from the House in 1999 after the Republicans lost a large number of House seats in the 1998 elections and after Gingrich was the target of an ethics investigation. The current Speaker, Representative Nancy Pelosi (D-Calif.), is likely to be in the media spotlight because she is the first female Speaker of the House and will be leading the first Democratic majority since 1994. Table 9.1 presents the leadership of the 110th Congress.

House of Representatives	Senate
Speaker: Nancy Pelosi (D-Calif.) Majority Leader: Steny Hoyer (D-Md.) Majority Whip: James Clyburn (D.-S.Car.) Minority Leader: John Boehner (R-Ohio) Minority Whip: Roy Blunt (R-Mo.)	Majority Leader: Harry Reid (D-Nev.) Majority Whip: Dick Durbin (D-Ill.) Minority Leader: Mitch McConnell (R-Ky.) Minority Whip: Trent Lott (R-Miss.)
Standing Committees	**Standing Committees**
Agriculture Appropriations Armed Services Budget Education and the Workforce Energy and Commerce Financial Services Government Reform Homeland Security House Administration International Relations Judiciary Resources Rules Science Small Business Standards of Official Conduct Transportation and Infrastructure Veterans Affairs Ways and Means	Agriculture, Nutrition, and Forestry Appropriations Armed Services Banking, Housing, and Urban Affairs Budget Commerce, Science, and Transportation Energy and Natural Resources Environment and Public Works Finance Foreign Relations Health, Education, Labor and Pensions Homeland Security and Government Affairs Judiciary Rules and Administration Small Business Veterans' Affairs **Special, Select, and Other Committees** Select Committee on Intelligence Select Committee on Ethics Indian Affairs Committee Special Committee on Aging

Joint Committees

Joint Economic Committee
Joint Committee on Printing
Joint Committee on Taxation
Joint Committee on the Library

Table 9.1 Committees in the 109th Congress (2005–2006) and the Leadership of the 110th Congress, 2007–2009.

Sources: U.S. House of Representatives, http://www.house.gov; U.S. Senate, http://www.senate.gov (retrieved July 12, 2006). CQPolitics.com http://www.cqpolitics.com/ (retrieved 11/21/06).

Nancy Pelosi (D-Calif.) became the first female Speaker of the House of Representatives in 2007 after the Democrats became the majority party following the 2006 election.

The Constitution states that the vice president shall preside over the Senate. In practice, the vice president does not participate in the day-to-day affairs of the chamber, except to cast a tie-breaking vote. In the absence of the vice president, the Senate is formally presided over by the most senior member of the majority party—the **president pro tempore**—but actual leadership responsibility falls upon the Senate majority leader. There is also a minority leader as well as majority and minority whips. The Senate leaders have less power than their House counterparts due to the structure of the Senate. Senators serve on multiple committees, and personal prerogatives are very important. The Senate rules give considerable discretion to individual members, making it harder for the party leadership to control behavior. Yet the leadership does play an important role in determining the schedule of when legislation will be considered on the floor, although with less control than in the House.

Perhaps the most important responsibility of party leaders is to develop unity and cohesion among party members. They work to convince members to vote with the party's program or, if the president is of the same party, to vote with the president's program. This is not always an easy task, for party leaders do not have much control over members. They cannot remove representatives from office for failing to vote with the party, and they

See the current Senate leadership.

cannot withhold the party's nomination in the next election. They also cannot force members to vote with the party. House leaders can pressure members to vote with the party by threatening to deny preferred committee assignments, but this is an extreme tactic. Most of the time, party leaders try to persuade members that it is in their best interest to vote with the party. At the same time, leaders also recognize that sometimes it may be in a member's interest to vote against the party, especially if reelection is at risk. The role that reelection plays in shaping congressional decision making will be discussed in the second half of this chapter.

Even though the leadership cannot force members to vote with the party, representatives and senators exhibit party unity by voting the party position about 80 percent of the time. Historically, there has been more unity among Republicans than Democrats, probably because for a forty-year period from the 1950s through the early 1990s Republicans were a "permanent" minority in both the House and Senate. As the minority, Republicans perceived the need to "stick together." However, much of the difference between Republicans and Democrats on party unity probably has more to do with the divisions within the Democratic Party, which include a more ideologically diverse coalition. But over the years, the number of "conservative" Democrats (primarily from the South) has dwindled, and those differences have largely disappeared. Indeed, in recent years, party unity has hovered between 80 percent and 90 percent for both parties.[8] This subject is discussed in detail in Chapter 7.

Committees in Congress

Most of the work of Congress does not take place on the floor of the House or Senate, but rather in each chamber's **committees.** The committee system is based on the principle of division of labor. It is not possible for all of the members of Congress to become experts on the wide range of policy issues facing the nation. The committee system means that some members of Congress develop specific expertise in more narrow areas of public policy and share their expertise with the rest of their colleagues. Both the House and the Senate, as well as state legislatures, are organized into committees to complete their work. Table 9.1 lists the specific committees in the 109th Congress. The total number of committees in Congress, including subcommittees, has shrunk considerably since 1985. That year, Congress had 301 committees; by 1997, the total had dropped to 200.[9]

Committee membership and leadership are determined by partisan control of Congress. The majority party leadership names the chairperson of each committee and determines what the partisan makeup of each committee will be. Historically, committee membership has been proportional to party representation in Congress. If the majority party holds 60 percent of the seats in the House, it will control roughly 60 percent of the seats on each committee. In addition to being members of the majority party, chairs are also usually the most senior member of the committee. The minority party on each committee is led by the **ranking member,** usually the member of the minority party who has served for the longest number of years in Congress.

Senators serve on more committees than House members. House members are usually limited to two committee assignments, although members who serve on the Rules Committee (which determines how legislation will be considered on the floor of the House) or the Ways and Means Committee (which deals with matters of taxation) usually serve on only one committee. Senators serve on three or four committees. Members in both chambers are usually placed on committees based on their preferences. Some members want to serve on a committee because of a specific policy interest. Others are concerned with being able to deliver on issues relevant to their district. For example, a House member from rural Iowa, where farm issues are important, would probably want to serve on the Agriculture Committee, whereas a westerner would want to be on the Interior Committee, which has control over federal land policy, a major issue in the West. By serving on committees with jurisdiction over relevant subject matters, members have a greater chance of influencing laws that their constituents care about.

Seniority normally determines committee leadership. From 1910 to 1970, there was a strict seniority system. The most senior member of the committee became chair. This tended to favor members from the South, where a lack of competitive elections (the Republican Party was almost nonexistent in the South from the end of Reconstruction until the 1960s) enabled southern representatives to gain considerable seniority in Congress. Although seniority is still the major factor in determining leadership, it is not automatic. The party leadership may jump over a more senior member to select someone who better fills the party's goals. When Republicans gained control of the House in 1995, then Speaker Newt Gingrich did just this.

Committee Types

There are different types of committees in Congress. They are differentiated based on three factors: whether the committee is permanent or temporary, whether the committee has legislative authority or not, and whether the members of the committee come from one chamber of Congress or both the House and the Senate.[10] **Standing committees** are the most numerous and most important of all committees. They have legislative power, are permanent, and have single-chamber membership. Standing committees have responsibility over specific policy areas. They consider legislation relevant to their jurisdiction and engage in oversight of executive branch departments and agencies that are administering programs in their area of expertise. For example, the House and Senate armed services committees are responsible for legislative decisions that affect the military, and they also oversee

Go to the Senate organizational chart to see the various committees and their respective chairs.

Congressional committees: Discover what committee your representatives serve on.

Go to the House and Senate websites to learn more about congressional committees.

the Department of Defense. The two chambers have similar, but not the same, committee structures, as noted in Table 9.1. In the 109th Congress (2004–2006), the House had twenty standing committees, and the Senate had sixteen.[11]

Most standing committees also have several **subcommittees** that are even more specialized in the substantive policy areas they have responsibility for. For example, the House Armed Services Committee has six standing subcommittees: Tactical Air and Land Forces, Readiness, Terrorism, Unconventional Threats and Capabilities, Military Personnel, Strategic Forces, and Projection Forces.[12]

In addition to standing committees, there are **joint committees, special and select committees,** and **conference committees.** Joint committees are permanent committees without legislative authority, which means they are not directly involved in determining whether a bill becomes a law. They are also dual-chamber committees, which means they have both representatives and senators who serve. There are currently four joint committees. They exist to provide some coordination between the chambers on such issues as the economy, a subject on which it is important for both chambers to be sharing information.

Special and select committees are temporary, they usually do not have legislative authority, and they may or may not have members from both chambers serving on them. Select committees are usually established in order to undertake a specific task not covered by existing committees. When their work is done, they disband. An example of a select committee that no longer exists is the Senate Y2K Committee. It was established to respond to concerns about potential computer problems that might occur when the calendar moved to the year 2000. After that date came and went with no major problems, that committee's job was over, and it no longer exists.

Finally, conference committees are created to work out the differences between legislation passed in different forms by the House and Senate. Conference committees are temporary, have legislative authority, and have members from both the House and the Senate serving on them. Unlike select committees, the other type of temporary committee, conference committees are quite common. They are key components of the legislative process. Bills have to be passed in identical language in both the House and Senate to become law, yet most bills work themselves through each chamber separately and are rarely passed by both houses with identical language. Consequently, virtually every piece of legislation that is passed by Congress goes through a conference committee. These committees consist of members of both chambers and are disbanded when they complete their task.

The Rise of Subcommittees

Subcommittees have become more powerful. Since the 1970s, there has been a decentralization of power in Congress from full committees to subcommittees. In 1974, after the Watergate scandal, newly elected members of Congress demanded reforms in congressional procedure. One of the demands that junior members made was to break the control that committee chairs had over the legislative process. And as committee chairs lost power, it moved to subcommittees. By giving subcommittees more power, less senior members of Congress have more opportunities for leadership within Congress. The expansion of subcommittee power was a direct result of a revolt by younger members unwilling to serve several terms as "apprentices" who were seen but rarely heard. The expansion of subcommittees came at a price, however. By adding another layer to the process by which a bill becomes a law, subcommittees can provide additional stumbling blocks to legislation. Moreover, they only further concerns about iron triangles among subcommittees, executive agencies, and interest groups.

The Work of Committees

Committees have four activities that they undertake. Because most of the work of Congress takes place in standing committees, this is where most of these activities take place. A single standing committee may engage in these activities at different points in time. The first activity is **authorization.** This occurs when a committee works on legislation that establishes or modifies a government program. For example, if a new category of benefits was going to be made available to college students, Congress would have to authorize, or make legitimate, that change. The discussions and decisions about the details of the benefits that should or should not be added to the program would take place in the education committees of the House and Senate. Programs that are authorized by Congress are usually established for a set period of time, such as five or ten years. This feature, known as a sunset provision, ensures after the specified time a program must either be reauthorized or ended.

The second activity is **appropriations.** Spending funds on governmental programs is a yearly process that requires specific legislation. Because this occurs annually and because of the importance of spending decisions, there are specific standing committees in the House and Senate that make decisions only about government spending. The subcommittees of the appropriations committees are organized based on specific areas of spending. The jurisdictions of the subcommittees mirror the Senate standing committees; they include agriculture, homeland security defense, and commerce. When the appropriations committees make their decisions, they can allocate up to the amount of funds authorized, but they are not required to fund programs that are authorized. Consequently, there are any number of programs that are authorized but that do not exist because no funds have been allocated to establish them.

The third activity is **investigation.** In order for Congress to make informed decisions, it has to have a good grasp of the substantive issues that fall under the jurisdiction of the committee. To gain the knowledge needed, congressional committees study and investigate the issues that come before the committee. Much of this work is done by the professional staff members who work for the committee. Most of the investigatory work done by committees could be characterized as basic research, gathering up the facts and evidence needed to make routine decisions. At other times, congressional committees investigate out-of-the-ordinary occurrences that have major policy implications. These investigations often receive a good amount of public and press attention. At times, the issue may be so controversial that Congress may set up a special or select committee to investigate a particular event.

The fourth activity is **oversight** of the executive branch of government. Since the administration of George Washington, Congress has delegated some of its power to the executive branch. Congress regularly enacts laws that create government programs that will be administered by the executive branch, but it maintains authority to oversee the activities of these departments and independent agencies to ensure that they are acting according to Congress's intent. Since the 1940s, committees have authority to conduct oversight to keep a "continuous watchfulness" over the activities of executive agencies within their jurisdictions. Congressional committees regularly conduct oversight hearings into the behavior of the bureaucracy. These hearings might consider how an agency has accomplished a legislative mandated program, or they may focus on future appropriations for the department. Oversight also occurs through informal channels of communication, when members of Congress engage in constituent casework or when legislative staff communicate with agency officials.

Congressional oversight occurs in many forms. There is evidence to suggest that Congress engages in more oversight activities today than it did forty years ago,[13] but it is not altogether apparent how successful oversight is in either monitoring or controlling executive behavior. Part of the problem stems from the sheer size of the executive branch and the relatively small amount of time that individual committees and subcommittees have to devote to matters of oversight. Still, oversight is an important function and one that Congress is not hesitant to engage in regularly.

Committee Hearings

Committees and subcommittees are most visible to the public when they are holding legislative hearings. During hearings, the committee listens to the testimony of those interested in the subject matter. Those testifying can include representatives from interest groups, members of the executive branch, experts in the subject matter of the hearings, and private citizens. Most hearings are rather mundane, of immediate interest only to those closely following the particular issue under consideration. Occasionally, hearings become very dramatic when a major public issue is involved or a very visible congressional decision is taking place, such as a Supreme Court confirmation hearing.

Except under unusual circumstances, such as with national security issues, congressional hearings are open to the public. It is possible for the average citizen to go to Washington when Congress is in session and directly observe congressional hearings. Because this is not practical for most of us, congressional hearings are regularly broadcast on C-SPAN, which provides "gavel-to-gavel" coverage of House proceedings. Senate proceedings are broadcast on C-SPAN2. C-SPAN, a nonprofit organization, is funded by the cable industry, and it also maintains an informative website through which one can get a good understanding of the day-to-day activities of Congress. On rare occasion, the major networks will air congressional hearings, as they did during the Watergate and Iran-Contra investigations during the 1970s and 1980s, but this has become less and less likely with the advent of cable and satellite technologies.

According to Davidson and Oleszek, there are a number of purposes served through the hearing process. These include exploring the need for new legislation, building a public record supporting the legislation, publicizing the committee chair, reviewing executive actions, providing a location for citizens to voice their grievances and frustrations, educating lawmakers and the public on the issues under consideration, and raising the visibility of an issue.[14] Hearings are a concrete place where the democratic process of debate and discussion of issues takes place.

Go to C-SPAN to learn what Congress is doing and to view congressional hearings.

The committee system's greatest strength also contributes to its primary weakness. Committees enable a Congress composed of generalist legislators to ensure that expertise develops for specific subject matters. Because each member serves on only a few committees, he or she gains considerable knowledge over the substantive jurisdiction of the committee. Thus, although a particular member of the House may have little knowledge about the specifics of nuclear power regulation, there are some members who possess that knowledge. This strength can also be a weakness because that subject matter expertise may be self-serving. Committees may serve narrow interests rather than those of the whole body. Iron triangles, discussed in Chapter 8, are an example of this situation.

The Legislative Process— How a Bill Becomes a Law

The legislative process reflects Madison's desire for fragmentation in policy making. It is intentionally difficult to make laws. For a bill to become law, it must clear several hurdles in both chambers. This is done through an intricate set of procedures, rules, and compromise. For Congress to process anywhere from 3,000 to 9,000 bills proposed each year, it is necessary to have the committee system sift through legislation, allowing some bills to go forward and others to die quiet deaths. Figure 9.1 presents a simple schematic description of the process of how a bill becomes

Listen to the Schoolhouse Rock version of this process.

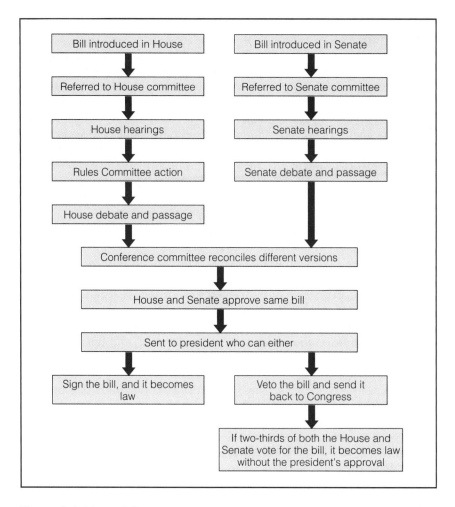

Figure 9.1 How a Bill Becomes a Law

a law. Although not as entertaining as the Schoolhouse Rock version you may remember from grade school, there are several important points from this chart to focus on.

First, any member of Congress can propose a bill, but it is up to the leadership of the House and Senate to determine how to process that bill. The first step is to refer a bill to a committee for its consideration. It is common for complex bills to be referred to more than one committee. When the bill authorizing the establishment of the Department of Homeland Security was introduced, it was referred to more than twelve House standing committees and one select committee.[15] Multiple referrals have become quite common. This further complicates the legislative process, requiring far more coordination between committees and ultimately making it hard for legislation to proceed.

Once the bill reaches a committee, the committee chair might then refer the bill to a subcommittee. It is usually at the subcommittee level that hearings occur. It is also quite possible, indeed likely, that the bill will not get any attention at all. When this happens, the bill is said to "die in committee." After conducting hearings, the subcommittee might "mark up the bill," adding amendments (changes) to it, before sending it back to the full committee. If the subcommittee chooses, it can do nothing with the bill at this point as well, again effectively killing it. The full committee will consider the recommendations of the subcommittee and will vote on the bill before sending it to the House or Senate floor. It can also mark up the bill, making further changes to its text. Once again, if the full committee chooses not to act on the bill, it usually will not be sent to the floor. Each chamber does have procedures, however, to bring legislation to the floor from a committee that refuses to move on it, although doing so is the exception rather than the rule.

The committee stage represents the end for many bills. Thus, committees have considerable discretion—and power—in deciding what legislation is sent to the floor. At each stage, it is possible that a bill will be killed. Even if a bill moves to the next stage, compromises will likely have been to be made to help ensure that the bill continues. By the time a bill passes the full committee, it may look very different from the bill that was first referred.

After approval from the committee, a bill is bound for the floor, but if it is a House bill, it must first clear the **House Rules Committee.** Because of the size of the House of Representatives, it has instituted strict rules of procedure for debate. The Rules Committee membership is controlled by the Speaker of the House, and the power of the Rules Committee gives the Speaker power. The Rules Committee exists to decide if an individual bill will be considered on the House floor and, if so, how it will be considered. For example, the Rules Committee can issue a rule permitting the bill to be debated for two hours, with limited amendments possible (a modified rule). Or the committee could issue a rule to consider the bill without any amendments (a closed rule). In rare circumstances, any amendment a member wishes to make is allowed (an open rule).

In the Senate, which does not have the same set of elaborate procedures as the House, the leadership of both parties work together to schedule bills for debate on the floor. Because the Senate operates on the principle that there are no rules, the leadership cannot control the process to the same degree possible in the House.

Once a bill is on the floor, the full chamber will debate, discuss, and vote on the measure, although much of this debate is for the record. The real, substantive decisions have been made at the committee and subcommittee

Go to Indiana University's Center on Congress to view a learning module on the legislative process. This module presents both the "textbook" and the "real world" view of how a bill becomes a law.

"What I Wish Political Scientists Would Teach About Congress," Lee Hamilton

level. During floor debates, the leadership, especially the whips, make sure that the party members know what the leadership is recommending in terms of a vote. Sometimes, figurative "arm twisting" is employed in situations where the vote is close in order to get the majority of votes needed to move the bill forward. It is during floor debate in the Senate that senators can engage in a filibuster if they want to prevent passage of a measure they oppose.

If a bill passes, it is then in limbo until it is considered by the other chamber. It is usually the case that the same bill is introduced into the House and Senate at about the same time. Because each chamber has its own process of committee consideration and the possibility for amendments, few bills pass both chambers in identical language. At this point a conference committee is established to iron out the differences between the bills. The amended legislation is then sent back to the House and Senate for final passage. Only after both chambers pass the final version of the bill is it ready for the president's signature or veto.

The President in the Legislative Process

For Congress to exercise its powers and to make law, the Constitution requires that identical legislation must be approved by a majority in each chamber and then be sent to the president for his signature. If the president signs the bill, it becomes law. If he rejects or **vetoes** the legislation, it will become law only if a two-thirds majority of both the Senate and House vote to override the president's veto. The Constitution requires that both chambers of Congress concur on legislation before it can become law. Requiring the House and Senate to agree with each other provides a check within Congress that the Framers thought valuable in limiting the potential threat of factions.

The president's role in the legislative process is formally limited to approval or rejection of bills. Yet this understates the full presidential role in lawmaking. When subcommittees and committees consider bills, they do not do so in a vacuum. The administration is an important player. The White House can make it known that it supports a bill or, perhaps even more important, that it opposes a bill in a specific form. Thus, when executive branch officials testify on a bill, they almost always can use the leverage of the presidency to make the point that in its current form the administration opposes this bill—implying that if it passes, the president is likely to veto it. Although an interest group can try to organize opposition to a bill, it cannot make the threat (whether real or imagined) of exercising the presidential veto.

Each year the president seeks to have Congress pass his agenda—those policies and programs central to his preferred policy agenda. The president and his administration will frequently be a source for bills that are introduced in Congress. The president cannot introduce bills, but he can have bills drafted, leaving the formal introduction to members of his own party. For those bills most critical to his agenda, the president can be an active player throughout the entire legislative process. He can intervene when necessary to try to keep his bills moving through the process. This does not mean that the president can personally shepherd preferred legislation through Congress. But it does mean that he can use his influence to keep media attention on a bill, making it harder for Congress to kill a bill without at least voting on it.

Divided Government

The president's role in the legislative process is significantly shaped by the presence or absence of **divided government,** which occurs when one party controls Congress and the other controls the presidency. Divided party control injects increased partisanship and conflict into the legislative process, as each party tries to advance its own partisan agenda. Divided government has been a regular feature of American politics since 1968 (see Table 9.2). During the presidencies of Richard Nixon, Gerald Ford, Ronald Reagan, and George H. W. Bush, the Republicans controlled the White House, but the Democrats controlled Congress. Only Ronald Reagan had the benefit of a Republican-led Senate from 1981 to 1986. Partisan control shifted during the Clinton years, with Republicans gaining control of both chambers of Congress. Control of Congress shifted once more in 2007 when the Democrats became the majority in both houses.

There have been only three short periods of **unified government**—the same party controlling both the Congress and presidency—since 1968. Democrats controlled both the White House and the presidency during the Carter years (1977–1980) and during the first two years of the Clinton presidency (1993–1994). The election of 2000 brought another shift in the partisan makeup of the government, as the Republicans regained control of the White House, resulting in unified Republican control of the presidency and Congress for the first time since the presidency of Herbert Hoover (1929–1932). The 107th Congress (2000–2002) began with unified government by the slimmest of margins. There were 222 Republicans and 210 Democrats (plus 2 independents). A shift of 6 seats could have changed the majority in the House. After the 2000 election, there were 50 Republicans and 50 Democrats in the Senate. The razor-thin majority for the Republicans existed because of the tie-breaking vote of Vice President Cheney. Unified government lasted for only 5 months. In May 2001, Vermont Senator James Jeffords left the Republican Party. Because he caucused with the Democrats, they had a small, 51–49 majority. The Democratic majority was also short-lived. With the gain in Republican seats in the Senate in 2002, Republicans became the majority party in both the House and the Senate. As of November 30, 2006, the 110th Congress (2007–2008) will have 231 Democrats and 201 Republicans in the House; 3 seats are still undecided. There are 49 Democrats, 49 Republicans and 2 Independents in the Senate. Both of the Independents caucus with the Democrats.[16]

Years	Congress	Divided or Unified Government	President	Control of House of Representatives	Control of Senate
1969–1970	91st	Divided	Nixon (Rep.)	Democratic	Democratic
1971–1972	92nd	Divided	Nixon (Rep.)	Democratic	Democratic
1973–1974	93rd	Divided	Nixon/Ford (Rep.)	Democratic	Democratic
1975–1976	94th	Divided	Ford (Rep.)	Democratic	Democratic
1977–1978	95th	Unified	Carter (Dem.)	Democratic	Democratic
1979–1980	96th	Unified	Carter (Dem.)	Democratic	Democratic
1981–1982	97th	Divided	Reagan (Rep.)	Democratic	Republican
1983–1984	98th	Divided	Reagan (Rep.)	Democratic	Republican
1985–1986	99th	Divided	Reagan (Rep.)	Democratic	Republican
1987–1988	100th	Divided	Reagan (Rep.)	Democratic	Democratic
1989–1990	101st	Divided	George H. W. Bush (Rep.)	Republican	Democratic
1991–1992	102nd	Divided	George H. W. Bush (Rep.)	Republican	Democratic
1993–1994	103rd	Unified	Clinton (Dem.)	Democratic	Democratic
1995–1996	104th	Divided	Clinton (Dem.)	Republican	Republican
1997–1998	105th	Divided	Clinton (Dem.)	Republican	Republican
1999–2000	106th	Divided	Clinton (Dem.)	Republican	Republican
2001–2002	107th	Divided	George W. Bush (Rep.)	Republican	Democratic
2003–2004	108th	Unified	George W. Bush (Rep.)	Republican	Republican
2005–2006	109th	Unified	George W. Bush (Rep.)	Republican	Republican
2007–2008	110th	Divided	George W. Bush (Rep.)	Democratic	Democratic

Table 9.2 Control of the Government, 1969–2008.

Source: Facts on File World News Digest, November 4, 2004, p. 857A1.

One of the consequences of divided government is the bitter partisanship and division that have recently characterized the institution. In the Clinton years, partisan bickering and fighting increased to the point that several members chose to retire from the office because the political environment was so venomous that the job lost its appeal. Indeed, civility among members in Congress has diminished dramatically in recent years. Democrats and Republicans have become so polarized that many of them refuse to socialize with members of the other party. There is "open disrespect" for members of the other party. Members have laughed aloud at procedural motions made by members from the other party; there have even been shoving matches on the floor of the House. Although verbal and physical outbursts have occurred throughout the history of Congress, today's Congress is simply more combative, and the parties are less willing to seek amiable working relations with each other than at any other time since 1950.[17] This was most evident during the House impeachment hearings against President Clinton in December 1998. The 110th Congress will once again usher in a period of divided government. In the immediate aftermath of the 2006 election, both parties indicated that they wanted a new period of bipartisan cooperation. Only time will tell whether or not this comes to pass.

Explaining Congressional Action

Although it is important to understand how Congress functions, it is even more critical to explain why Congress acts as it does. Understanding why members of Congress act as they do helps explain a great deal about the institution. What factors determine how members of Congress make their decisions? In a classic work on Congress, political scientist Richard Fenno wrote that "of all the goals espoused by members of the House, three are basic. They are: reelection, influence within the House, and good public policy." These goals are not mutually exclusive: "All congressmen probably hold all three goals. But each congressmen has his own mix of priorities and intensities—a mix which may change over time."[18]

The Dominant Goal of Reelection

Reelection is perhaps the most fundamental goal of members of Congress because reelection is the means to achieving all other legislative goals. If a legislator is not reelected, he or she will ultimately have no ability to pursue other goals, such as power, prestige, or good public policy. The importance of reelection as a means to other ends may seem self-evident because it is reelection that allows legislators to pursue policy and power. However, scholars have also considered the importance of reelection as an end in itself. In a study of the House of Representatives, David Mayhew articulated what today has become the classic argument of the "electoral connection." Mayhew made a "simple assumption about human motivation," and he then speculated about "the consequences of behavior based on that motivation."[19] If we think of legislators as "single-minded seekers of reelection" who structure all of their activities and decisions to maximize the goal of reelection, we can explain three types of activities that legislators engage in: self-advertisement, generating particularized benefits, and position taking. Each of these activities will help a legislator meet his or her primary goal of reelection.

"George W. Bush and Congress: The Electoral Connection," Michael Nelson

First, members **advertise themselves to voters.** Most voters do not know a great deal about candidates in elections. Legislators capitalize on this through the belief that if the voters recognize the incumbent, they will be more likely to vote for him or her. To ensure that they are recognized, legislators "advertise" themselves by making frequent trips home to the district, sending newsletters to voters, and making appearances in the local press whenever possible.

Members spend a lot of time in their districts. Congress is sometimes called the "Tuesday to Thursday Club" because little official business is conducted in Congress on Mondays and Fridays. Members of Congress use these days to return home to their district for the weekend. Rather than an extended holiday, the reality is that members spend most of their weekend engaged in political activities with constituents. They attend local events, such as local sporting championships, parades, awards ceremonies, and other civic events, often spending very little time of their weekend out of the public eye. Maintaining visibility in the district is one of the ways members of Congress advertise themselves and project an image of a representative who is engaged in the affairs of the community. Members also hold official town hall or listening meetings in their districts. These are another opportunity for citizen involvement.

Members of Congress also advertise themselves to their constituents by taking advantage of the **franking privilege** that provides them with free use of the U.S. mail. This enables them to send newsletters to every address in the district at least once or twice per year. The franking privilege provides members with a tangible advantage over their challengers come reelection time, as they can send a mailing to every household in the district without paying for the postage.

The second way that members of Congress enhance their electability is by creating **particularized benefits** for their district. They work hard to enact laws that will bring benefits into the district, a practice known as **pork barrel.** Legislators try to bring federal money into the district and then take credit for these benefits when the next campaign comes around. For example, a member of Congress works to get a new Veterans' Affairs hospital built in her district. This brings all sorts of benefits to the district: It provides jobs to build the hospital; it provides jobs to run the hospital; it provides a service to constituents in the district.

Legislators also use their offices to "service the district." One form of constituency service is **casework.** This involves helping constituents through the red tape of the federal bureaucracy by such activities as speeding up the arrival of a late Social Security check or expediting the issuance of a grazing permit on public land. Congress gives each member a generous budget to staff offices both in Washington and at home. Many of these staff positions are dedicated solely to helping representatives and senators do casework. Casework and pork-barrel legislation enable a member of Congress to engage in taking credit come reelection time. He or she can say to constituents, "Look at what I have done for you in the past two years. I have brought federal dollars to our district, and I have provided you with assistance in dealing with the federal bureaucracy."

Finally, legislators engage in **position taking:** They take stands on issues to please issue-attentive voters. They also make a calculation of what position to take based on their perception of what the voters want to hear. They go on record supporting or opposing certain issues for no reason other than to help generate support for reelection. By taking a position on the issue, the legislator isn't necessarily acting according to what he or she thinks is the best decision; rather, the legislator provides what issue-attentive voters want to hear. The decision is based on what will help the member become reelected rather than on what might be the best course of action.

R. Douglas Arnold has argued that while reelection is the dominant goal of members of Congress, they can pursue other goals as long as their principal goal is not threatened. When reelection is not at risk, members are free to pursue such goals as accumulating power or developing public policy. Implicit in Arnold's argument is the recognition that reelection is only a means to an end. To pursue goals other than reelection, members of Congress will try to shield themselves from potentially negative electoral consequences. This can be achieved through a variety of strategies. They can manipulate the rules so that direct votes are avoided on damaging issues by combining many bills into omnibus packages. Legislators will take a controversial issue and put it into a larger bill, which includes hundreds of issues. This way the legislator can say, "I voted for the omnibus bill because it has an awful lot that is needed." But he or she never voted on just the controversial issue: "Yes, I know that provision was in the bill too, but there was nothing I could do—the whole bill was too important to oppose just because of that issue."

The Incumbency Advantage

Even if reelection is not the only goal of legislators, it clearly is an important one. The strategies identified by Mayhew and others have been extremely successful. They have given legislators what we call an **incumbency advantage** when a current member of the House or the Senate runs for reelection. Challengers have to pay standard postage rates to use the mail to communicate with voters; they cannot engage in casework; they can't bring home the bacon; they usually do not have name recognition with the voters. And perhaps most important, they rarely have the campaign funds raised by incumbents. Chapter 8 examines the huge financial advantage that incumbents have over challengers in raising campaign funds to run an effective campaign. Ultimately, this makes it very difficult to unseat incumbents.

By the late 1980s, House incumbents had achieved reelection rates of close to 98 percent. As Table 9.3 demonstrates, very few incumbents lose their bids for reelection. In 1994 these advantages came to haunt congressional Democrats who had maintained continual control of the House of

Participate in the debate over congressional term limits.

CONGRESSIONAL VOTING WHEN REELECTION IS NOT AT RISK

If a member of Congress perceives a vote as critical to his or her reelection, the choice is quite easy. What, then, decides how individual members vote on bills when reelection does not seem threatened? There are several possibilities:

- **Deference to Committees and Party.** What did the subcommittee or committee decide? How did they vote? Members will often defer to the committee, to their party leaders, or perhaps to the president. If I do not know much about a specific bill, I will look to see how my colleagues are voting. What are my party leaders saying about this bill?
- **Bargaining for Votes.** If an issue is not important to the legislator, he or she may be willing to vote for it because the issue is important to someone who can in turn help the legislator at another time. Legislators engage in horse trading: "I'll vote for your project if you vote for my project." This is also known as *logrolling*.
- **Turning to Lobbyists.** Representatives turn to interest groups who have detailed plans on specific issues. They also turn to campaign contributors. Campaign contributors can influence a legislator's decisions. Campaign contributions may not buy a legislator's vote, but they will buy an insurance policy that the member will consider the contributor's perspective before voting. For example, if the Chemical Manufacturers Association has given a member large contributions over the past five elections, the member is probably going to consider how his or her vote will be perceived by this important campaign supporter.
- **Issue-Aware Voters.** The views expressed by constituents on an issue may also be relevant. Legislators are concerned with how their decisions will play with constituents. They will likely consider how important an issue is in the district. Have many constituents written or called about the issue? Even if reelection is not at stake, will the vote please core constituencies?

Ultimately, legislators are influenced by a combination of these factors, and the particular mix can change on any issue. Although members of Congress will sometimes vote based on their own best judgment of whether the bill is good or not, they also take a wide range of other factors into consideration.

Representatives for forty years, as an anti-incumbency mood in the country turned Democrats out of Congress. In the November 1994 election, thirty-four incumbent Democrats lost their seats, resulting in the first Republican congressional majority in forty years. Not a single Republican incumbent was defeated. Apparently, the voters associated the incumbency problem—that Congress was not responsive to the nation's problems—with the

	Senate			House		
	D	R	Total	D	R	Total
1980	9	0	9	27	3	30
1982	1	1	2	1	22	23
1984	1	2	3	13	3	16
1986	0	7	7	1	5	6
1988	1	3	4	2	4	6
1990	0	1	1	6	9	15
1992	2	2	4	16	8	24
1994	2	0	2	34	0	34
1996	0	1	1	3	17	20
1998	1	2	3	1	5	6
2000	1	5	6	2	4	6
2002	2	1	3	6	2	8
2004	1	0	1	5	2	7
2006	0	6	6	0	19	19*

Table 9.3 Seats Lost by Incumbents, 1980–2004

Sources: National Journal, November 11, 2000, pp. 3557–3562; Federal Election Commission, http://www.fec.gov/pubrec/fe2002/senate.htm#AR (2002); OpenSecrets.org; and CQPolitics.com.

*As of November 21, 2006, seven races were still undecided.

Democrats. A series of controversies and scandals involving prominent Democratic incumbents did not help matters. Two years later, however, only three incumbent Democrats lost their seats, while seventeen incumbent Republicans were defeated. Since 1996, incumbents in both parties have fared quite well. Only six incumbents (two Democrats and four Republicans) lost their bids for reelection in 2000.[20] Reelection is somewhat less certain in the Senate, but the incumbency advantage is still very present. No more than six incumbent senators have lost their bid for reelection in any election since 1986. In 2004 only one incumbent senator was defeated. In that same election, four incumbent members of the House were defeated in the general election, and another three were defeated in redistricted seats where they were running against other incumbents. There were new members of Congress, however, as thirty-three members either retired, resigned, or ran and lost in an election for a different office.[21] 2006 was a bad year for Republican incumbents; six lost their seats in the Senate and at least nineteen lost in the House of Representatives.

The incumbency advantage remains one of the greatest challenges to participatory democracy. It is very difficult for a challenger to unseat an incumbent member of the House of Representatives. Congress has structured itself and its members make decisions to maximize the likelihood of reelection. In the late 1980s and early 1990s, frustration over the inability to unseat incumbents led to the growth of the term limits movement, which sought to limit the number of terms a member could serve in the House or the Senate. Several states eventually passed term limit laws for their state officials and their members of Congress, but the U.S. Supreme Court invalidated term limits for federal officials in 1995.[22]

Who Are Our Representatives?

Historically, Congress has largely been an exclusive club for wealthy white men. Relatively few women or minorities have served in either the House or the Senate. Today's Congress is considerably more representative of the population as a whole, although a small elite—which is still largely white and male—is elected to Congress. The demographic makeup of Congress raises important questions about its representativeness as an institution.

Keith Ellison (D-Minn.), elected in 2006, is the first Muslim to be elected to either chamber of Congress.

To the extent that its membership is markedly different from the population as a whole, segments of the populace may not feel that their interests are genuinely represented in Congress.

The vast majority of members of Congress are men. The 109th Congress (2005–2006) was the most diverse in American history; women held eighty-two seats in the House and Senate combined. There were sixty-eight women representatives (19 percent) and fourteen women senators (14 percent). Women have made considerable gains in the past decade. In the 101st Congress (1989–1990), there were twenty-five women representatives and two female senators. Still, when you consider that 51 percent of the population is female, Congress still reflects the traditional male dominance present through most of American history. Women achieved a major success in 2002 when Representative Nancy Pelosi (D-Calif.) was chosen by her fellow Democrats to serve as the minority leader. She became the first woman in history to be chosen to lead a party in the U.S. Congress.

In relation to the population of the nation as a whole, African Americans and Hispanics have done quite well in securing representation in Congress. Just forty years ago, there were only three African Americans and two Hispanics in the House, with virtually no minority senators. In 2006, however, there were forty-one African American (9 percent) and twenty-six Hispanic (6 percent) representatives. African Americans and Hispanics constitute almost one-quarter of the population (23.8 percent), but they control only 16 percent of the seats in the House. Historically, minorities have not had nearly as much success in the Senate, but the 2004 election resulted in the election of one African American and one Hispanic senator. Even though the Senate largely remains the bastion of white males, it is important to recognize the gains that minorities have made in Congress as a whole. Congress today is considerably more diverse along racial and gender lines than at any other time in U.S. history.[23] But as was true at the founding, the Senate remains the more elite body. This is reflected today in a less diverse membership in the Senate compared to the House.

We can learn considerably more about who represents us in Congress by looking at the backgrounds of individual members. One common misconception about Congress is that the majority of legislators are lawyers. Although the law remains the most common occupation of representatives, in the 109th House, only 160 were lawyers, and more than a third of the members (163) listed their occupation as banking or business. The primary occupation of 163 members was politics or public service. The 109th, Congress included medical doctors, scientists, and even clergy. Lawyers still dominated the Senate (fifty-eight senators), but thirty senators listed business/banking and thirty-two listed public service/politics as their primary occupation.[24] The occupational background of members of the House and Senate is much more diverse than it was a quarter-century ago, although it is hardly reflective of the American people as a whole.

How do members of Congress compare with the general population?

Check the update for details on the members of the 110th Congress (2007–2008).

Conclusion: Lawmaking and Representation

Check here for possible post-publication updates to the chapter material.

This chapter has examined the way Congress is organized, the process by which Congress acts to make laws, and congressional behavior. Congress is a very complex institution, fraught with challenges for governance and democracy. Congress reflects the American system of fragmented policy making and checks and balances. Congress's primary task—lawmaking—is both complicated and difficult to achieve. Thousands of bills are introduced each session, yet only a few hundred become law. It is an institution that is influenced by the president, by average citizens, and by moneyed interest groups.

Congress is also the institution closest to the people in that, unlike the presidency or courts, any citizen is free to communicate with a member of Congress, to raise an issue, or to ask for help with the bureaucracy. When citizens participate in the legislative process, they are not always successful, but as the introduction to the Chapter 1 illustrates, dedicated groups of ordinary citizens can exert a significant influence on congressional decisions. Mary Fetchet and Voices of September 11 illustrate that it is possible for citizens to become involved in the legislative process and to effect change.

Key Terms

bicameral (two-chamber) legislature 277
House of Representatives 277
Senate 277
filibuster 278
cloture vote 278
majority leader 279
minority leader 279
whips 279
Speaker of the House 279
president pro tempore 281
committees 282

ranking member 283
standing committees 283
subcommittees 284
joint committees 284
special/select committees 284
conference committees 284
authorization 285
appropriations 285
investigation 285
oversight 286
House Rules Committee 289
vetoes 290

divided government 291
unified government 291
advertise themselves to voters 294
franking privilege 294
particularized benefits 294
pork barrel 294
casework 294
position taking 295
incumbency advantage 295

Suggested Web Resources

The following websites provide additional resources related to the Congress.

The House (http://www.house.gov) and Senate (http://www.senate.gov) have their own websites where you can find information about members and committees. One caucus mentioned in the text is the Congressional Caucus for Women's Issues (http://www.house.gov/pelosi/womcauc.htm).

The best resource for learning about current legislation is found on Thomas (**http://thomas.loc.gov**), a site maintained by the Library of Congress (**http://www.loc.gov**). An alternative source of information about Congress can be found at Congress.org (**http://www.congress.org/congressorg/home**), which not only includes information about elected officials and current legislation but also provides a form to allow you to send e-mail directly to your representative or senator.

Roll Call (**http://www.rollcall.com**) is the unofficial newspaper of Capitol Hill; it provides detailed information about Congress. CQ.com (**http://www.cq.com**) is the public website of Congressional Quarterly, the publisher of the *Congressional Quarterly Weekly Report,* what is probably the most authoritative resource available for studying Congress. Your university library probably subscribes to the *Weekly Report* in either its print or online version.

If you have cable television or digital satellite service, you probably have access to C-SPAN and C-SPAN II, which provide "gavel-to-gavel" coverage of the House and Senate. C-SPAN's website (**http://www.c-span.org**) provides information about its television coverage and a wide range of other features. C-SPAN also provides access to congressional hearings at Capitol-Hearings.Org (**http://www.capitolhearings.org**).

Regarding the role of money in congressional elections, the Center for Responsive Politics operates Opensecrets.org (**http://www.opensecrets.org**), a website that provides detailed information on both congressional and presidential election fund-raising using data from the Federal Election Commission.

Former Representative Lee Hamilton directs the Center on Congress at Indiana University (**http://congress.indiana.edu**), which includes a number of excellent e-learning modules (**http://congress.indiana.edu/learn_about/index.php**), including "How a Member Decides to Vote" and "The Dynamic Legislative Process."

 A complete study tool kit is available for this chapter and includes the following:
Flashcards
Crossword Puzzle
Critical Thinking Exercises
Interactive Timelines
Chapter Quiz

10 The Presidency and the Executive Branch

■ **George W. Bush and Social Security Reform:
Can the President Lead?** 303

■ **Public Expectations of the Presidency** 305
  Creating the Presidency 306
  Constitutional Powers of the Presidency 310
  Can the President Meet Expectations? 315

■ **Presidential Leadership: The Power of Persuasion** 317
  Leadership as Persuasion 317
  Term Cycles and Presidential Leadership 321

■ **The President and the Executive Branch** 323
  The Executive Office of the President 323
  The Cabinet 326

■ **The Federal Bureaucracy** 328
  Functions of the Bureaucracy 328
  Controlling the Bureaucracy 331

■ **Conclusion: Can the President Lead?** 333

George W. Bush and Social Security Reform: Can the President Lead?

George W. Bush engaged in many public meetings to build support for his Social Security reform proposals during the spring of 2005.

After winning the 2004 election, President George W. Bush was confident that his victory over Massachusetts Senator John Kerry marked a mandate for his domestic agenda. It was widely expected that domestic policy issues, such as Social Security reform, which had been put on the back burner after 9/11, would rise to the surface of the agenda for the Republican-controlled Congress. As expected, Bush announced a major push for reform to Social Security in his 2005 State of the Union Address.[1] The president argued that the Social Security program was "careening toward insolvency"[2] and would go bankrupt by 2042 if something wasn't done now.

The president's solution was to embrace privatization of Social Security—a proposal long favored by conservatives. Bush proposed to create personal accounts for younger workers, in which they would be able to invest a portion of their payroll taxes in a conservative mix of stocks and bonds, theoretically having a higher rate of return on their investment. Bush claimed that establishing these personal accounts would not only save the system but would also give individuals—especially the working poor—a "sense of ownership." The result would be the fostering of an "ownership society" that would encourage investment and greater knowledge in the country's many publicly owned companies and the corresponding investment opportunities.[3] Under the president's plan, Social Security would not be altered at all for those born before 1950.[4] Those born after 1950 would have the option of investing in personal accounts. A young American earning an average of $35,000 annually over the entirety of his or her career would be projected to have over $250,000 invested upon retirement under the President's plan. But the president's plan generated little enthusiasm among the American people, and even less from Congress.

After his State of the Union, the president began a coast-to-coast tour of major cities, holding "town meetings" to build support for his plan. These events were largely controlled—by limiting attendance to his supporters—in order to generate an appearance of support for the television cameras that would be present. In addition, the president asked wealthy Republican donors from his 2004 campaign to contribute funds toward the $50 million he thought would be necessary to run television commercials supporting the initiative. The president was facing an uphill battle. Although 55 percent of Americans polled in January 2005 thought that Social Security had "major problems," only 17 percent thought the system was in "crisis."[5] At the same time that the president mobilized to build support, so did the opponents of Social Security reform. The American Association of Retired Persons (AARP) began running ads opposing the president's plan, arguing that the program's problems were overstated and the "crisis" manufactured.

The debate that was waged in the winter and spring of 2005 was over both the magnitude of the problem and the proposed solution. Critics of the Bush administration in and out of Congress claimed that the president was exaggerating the problem in order to successfully institute his "privatization" agenda.[6] The president argued that he was willing to consider any plan to save Social Security, not just privatization, but something had to be done. The system was just thirteen years away from the point where the government would pay out more in Social Security benefits than it collected in payroll taxes. The result would be budget shortfalls that would continue to grow larger year after year, until the Social Security system went bankrupt in 2042.[7] Critics of the president's plan countered by saying that even if nothing at all were done to Social Security, the system would still be able to pay out 73 percent of promised benefits in 2042, when the trust fund was projected to be depleted.[8] Many critics were convinced that the president's plan wasn't designed to save Social Security, but rather to dismantle it.

Over the course of three months, the president was never able to build public support for his proposal, in spite of traveling to hundreds of cities. By March 2005, a *New York Times* poll found that only 30 percent of Americans supported the way the president was handling Social Security.[9] With such tepid support, few members of Congress were willing to risk the wrath of the AARP—a group that represents over 36 million Americans age fifty or older and that is one of the nation's largest and most influential interest groups—by promoting a proposal that had little support. By May 2005, Republican House Whip Roy Blunt sent an e-mail to the Republican caucus listing major legislation to be considered after the Memorial Day break. Social Security was nowhere to be seen.[10] Indeed, the proposal was all but dead.

Why was the president unable to lead on Social Security reform? He had campaigned on the issue during the 2004 election. Indeed, Social Security played a prominent role during the campaign. But once the proposal was made public, the president was never able to generate enthusiasm for it. There are several factors that might explain the difficulties the president faced. First, the Madisonian system of separation of powers is supposed to make it difficult for policy to be enacted, even when there is strong support. It's even harder when support for an issue is only lukewarm. It is quite probable that the president misjudged the support he would have. Although Bush defeated Kerry by more than one million votes nationwide, 49 percent of the electorate opposed his reelection. Such a close outcome does not produce an environment conducive to major policy shifts (see Chapter 12). Second, the timing of Bush's plan didn't help him; he misjudged the willingness of the nation to accept change. He asked Americans to embrace putting their Social Security retirement savings into the stock market at a time when the market had experienced five years of losses and declines for the private accounts of many Americans. Finally, while the president anticipated opposition to his plan, he may have underestimated the power of the AARP, which was willing to fight against what it saw as an attempt to dismantle Social Security.

George W. Bush was elected by the American people in November 2004. But winning an election and achieving policy objectives are two different things. Social Security reform points out the hazards that a president faces in trying to govern. The very tactics (e.g., town meetings and scripted events) that help win elections do not guarantee victory on policy initiatives. As we will see in this chapter, the American people have high expectations for their president—but they do not always share the president's views on issues. But if the president cannot succeed in achieving the very policy goals he made a centerpiece of his reelection campaign, if he cannot gain support from his own party in Congress, can the president lead?

Public Expectations of the Presidency

George W. Bush's experience with Social Security reform points to an important paradox of the presidency. The American people have high expectations for presidents to lead, even though the Constitution is not structured to make it easy for presidents to exercise such leadership. Over the past sixty years, public expectations of presidential leadership have grown well beyond the expectations that Americans had during the nation's first 150 years. When a president attempts to lead and fails—as was the case with Social Security—the failure to accomplish stated goals makes the president look weak.

The presidency is an elite institution that is removed from the daily lives of the American people, yet it is probably the one part of the government over which people feel the most ownership. Much of this is due to the constant media attention given to the president. Thanks to the media, we know (or can easily find out) what the president does on a daily basis. He dominates the evening news broadcasts and is rarely out of the public eye. This contributes to the high expectations we have for the presidency. In a democratic society, it makes sense that the public has expectations for the president. The president's ability to meet those expectations represents one of the few criteria that citizens can use to evaluate presidential performance at the next election. But are the public's expectations reasonable or attainable?

Do Americans trust the president?

The American people expect the president to be the guardian of the Constitution, the preserver of American values, and the embodiment of American patriotism. The president is the one public official elected by the nation, and he is a symbol of all that is good about the nation. Thus, we expect the president to be a role model, someone to look up to. When presidents fail to live up to our image of what they should be, we are profoundly disappointed. President Bill Clinton learned this the hard way. Most Americans disapproved of the sexual affair he found himself tangled in, not because we could not accept his fallibility, but rather because he let the American people down by lying and because he disgraced the office.

Americans expect the president to be a world leader, steering the nation through the troubled waters of foreign policy, protecting us from our foes, and providing leadership for the world community. We also expect the president to keep watch over the nation's formidable arsenal of nuclear weapons, ensuring that we never need to use them.

The public has substantial expectations for the president to provide leadership for the national government. He must have a political vision and provide an agenda for Congress. It is not enough for the president to deliver a State of the Union Address; he must actively lead Congress, even when the Congress is controlled by the opposition party. We expect the president to be accountable to the voters who provided him with his office and to carry through on his promises.

Of the public's many presidential expectations, none is so great as our expectation that he keep the economy strong, with employment high and inflation low. We place primary responsibility for the nation's economic health on the president. If the economy is prosperous, he can take the credit. If the economy enters a period of recession, he will be blamed.

To more fully understand the role that public expectations play in shaping the modern presidency, we must first examine the origins of the presidency in the Constitutional Convention, the evolution of the office over the past 200 years, and the constitutional powers of the office.

Creating the Presidency

Read *Federalist* No. 70.

Chapter 2 noted that the American Revolution was largely a result of Americans' lack of satisfaction with the king and their beliefs that executive power (that held by kings and governors) was extremely dangerous. The new governments established during the Revolution tried to compensate for the threat of executive power in the states by minimizing the roles of governors. Revolutionary governors were stripped of power and became little more than symbolic figureheads. The Articles of Confederation, which created the first national government, did not even have an executive. The Articles created only a Congress. Thus, it is no wonder that when the Constitution was proposed, the strong executive proposed by it surprised many people. Not only would the government created by the Constitution have an executive; it would have one with considerable power as well.

The Framers of the Constitution were not united on their understandings of how the presidency should be constituted. Some delegates favored a **weak presidency model** to reflect common fears of executive power. The primary function of the executive would be to implement the will of Congress.[11] The executive would be selected by and largely be subservient to Congress. Benjamin Franklin supported a plural executive in which three individuals would share the executive power. About one-quarter of the delegates agreed with him and supported a plural executive as a way to minimize the threat of a single executive from gaining too much power and becoming a tyrant. Even James Madison initially shared this view of the presidency at the outset of the Convention.

The Constitutional Convention also included delegates who thought that a much stronger executive would be needed if the Constitution was to succeed. Advocates of the **strong presidency model** argued that the Constitution required an independent executive empowered with important functions in the Constitution.[12] James Wilson of Pennsylvania sought a single executive, selected by some means other than the legislature, with powers specifically stated in the Constitution. Alexander Hamilton also argued for the strong presidency model, although Hamilton was willing to go even further. Hamilton argued for an elected monarch because "there can be no good government without a good Executive. The English model was the only good one on this subject."[13] Given the American experience with kings, however, most delegates did not take Hamilton seriously.

Read Article II of the Constitution.

Ultimately, the Constitutional Convention opted for a middle ground. The convention created a single chief executive endowed with considerable power balanced by congressional concurrence. For example, the president can nominate justices of the Supreme Court, but they must be confirmed by the Senate. Likewise, he may negotiate treaties with other nations, yet they go into effect only if ratified by two-thirds of the Senate. The Framers created the structure for a strong presidency, but it would take more than a century for the institution to take full advantage of the powers that the Framers provided.

The Evolution of the Presidency

The Constitution did not define the powers of the presidency in great detail. This was a concern for many Anti-Federalists, who feared that the president could easily become an elected monarch. Yet most Americans were less concerned about this because they knew that George Washington, the hero of the Revolution, would be the first president. The people had such trust in Washington that they were willing to take the risk that he might try to abuse the potential powers of the office.

As the first president, George Washington set important precedents for the office, many of which are still in place today. Washington's stature as the "father of the country" gave the office prestige. Almost everything he did was viewed as establishing a tradition that future occupants of the office would follow. For example, when Washington negotiated an Indian treaty in 1789, he went to the Senate to get its advice on how to proceed with the treaty negotiations. When the Senate was unwilling to commit itself to any position on the treaty, Washington became frustrated and left the Senate. Although he received the Senate's consent to the treaty a few days later, he never again sought senatorial advice when negotiating treaties.[14] No president since Washington has ever returned to the Senate for "advice" during treaty negotiations, and the Senate's role has been limited to one of "consent" in approving or rejecting treaties negotiated by the president. Another precedent Washington set is the two-term limit for presidents. Until Franklin Roosevelt was elected to a third and then fourth term in the 1940s, no president served more than eight years in office. After Roosevelt's death, the Constitution was amended limiting presidents to two terms, which permanently formalized Washington's original precedent.

Go to the *Encyclopedia of the American Presidency* to learn about presidential history.

With the exception of Thomas Jefferson, Andrew Jackson, and Abraham Lincoln, most presidents in the nineteenth century had a limited view of their role in American politics. The president was not to be the central actor in American politics; he was not to provide the major agenda-setting focus for government. That task would fall upon the Congress. The president's job was to keep the United States out of "entangling alliances" abroad (yet more of the legacy of Washington) and to provide a check on the Congress, which was the leading force in national legislation. Presidents saw it as their responsibility to faithfully execute policies decided by Congress.

The Two Roosevelts: Defining the Modern Presidency

The presidency of Theodore (Teddy) Roosevelt marked the beginning of what many consider the modern presidency. Teddy Roosevelt, who was a Rough Rider in the Spanish-American War and an outdoor adventurer, brought energy to the presidency by taking on the great "trusts" that developed during the Industrial Revolution in the late 1800s. Trusts were combinations of corporations that exhibited monopolistic tendencies, crushing competition and controlling prices in whole industries. Roosevelt used his authority as president to have the Department of Justice break up the trusts through the use of the Sherman Antitrust Act of 1890. Teddy Roosevelt also actively pursed his own agenda with Congress, pushing to preserve and protect America's great natural resources. He had Congress pass the Antiquities Act, giving him unilateral power to establish national monuments.

Teddy Roosevelt was also one of the first presidents to go directly to the public to promote his agenda. Roosevelt used what he called the "bully pulpit" to generate public support for his proposals and to use that support to pressure Congress to support him. Such strategies today are commonplace in presidential politics, but at the turn of the twentieth century, they were unheard of. No president had ever attempted to use public

Second cousins Theodore Roosevelt and Franklin Delano Roosevelt used their persuasive skills to reshape the American presidency.

opinion to achieve his political goals as Roosevelt did. Unlike most of his predecessors, who did not perceive it as their responsibility to lead the nation, Roosevelt was unwilling to play "second fiddle" to Congress. In an era that had been characterized by congressional dominance of American national politics, Teddy Roosevelt put the presidency at center stage.

Theodore Roosevelt reinvigorated the presidency, but it was his distant cousin who would reshape the office—and all of American national politics—during the 1930s and 1940s. Franklin Delano Roosevelt (FDR) was elected president in 1932, in the midst of the greatest economic depression that America has ever witnessed. FDR was elected on a platform offering Americans a New Deal, a new approach to dealing with the Great Depression set off by the stock market crash of 1929 (see Chapter 12). Roosevelt's New Deal would change the face of American politics forever. The new federal programs that he created vastly expanded the scope of federal power and brought the presidency to the center of American politics.

FDR used his persuasive skills to convince the American public and the Congress of a new, active approach to government. According to Roosevelt, the federal government had the means and should use them to help people overcome problems. Moreover, government should not be limited by historical understandings of dual federalism (see Chapter 3). The federal government should take an active role in ensuring that the democratic process treats people fairly. It should place controls on economic activity to prevent things like the Depression from happening; it should take steps to provide for those with the least in society. In the 1930s, the American people put great trust in FDR and in the ideology of active government. Within thirty years, the notion of a federal government exercising limited

Listen to one of FDR's Fireside Chats.

powers would be gone, and the federal government would legislate in all areas of American life, from public education to welfare to environmental protection.

The acceptance of active government had a profound impact on the presidency. The American people did not simply accept big government on its face; they were willing to accept it only insofar as there was accountability for government action. The people placed that responsibility on the president. As political scientist Theodore Lowi writes, "having given presidents maximum power to govern and all the help they have ever asked for, the public has rationally focused its expectations on them, counting on them to deliver on all the promises they explicitly made and all those explicit and implicit in the policies and programs they vowed faithfully to execute."[15]

Constitutional Powers of the Presidency

The public's expectations for the presidency suggest an office with formidable powers. But is the presidency very powerful or relatively weak? If we look at the array of powers provided to the president in the Constitution, we find that virtually no other world leaders have as many formal limitations on their powers as the Constitution places on the president. As political scientist Richard Neustadt once stated, the Constitution structures the political system in such a way as to guarantee that the president is little more than a clerk.[16] The presidency is not designed for unilateral action. For the president to be a leader and to fulfill the expectations placed on him, he must marshal all of his skills and resources to overcome the limitations.

Enforcement Powers

Article II requires the president to "take care that the laws be faithfully executed." The **take care clause** places responsibility on the president to implement and enforce the laws as passed by Congress. If Congress appropriates funds for a specific program, the president is expected to use that money as intended. President Nixon created considerable controversy when he claimed the right to impound (not spend) funds. Nixon impounded more than $18 billion of funds with the goal of eliminating programs he opposed.[17] Although presidents as early as Thomas Jefferson had impounded funds for reasons that made the spending unnecessary, no one had ever used impoundment in the way Nixon did. Congress responded by passing the **Budget Control and Impoundment Act of 1974,** restricting the president's ability to impound funds.

Although the president must faithfully execute the law, he has some discretion in how he accomplishes this task. Congress does not always specify all the steps that will be required to put a law into effect. Since the president is responsible for the execution of thousands of laws by almost

2.65 million federal employees, he must have some way to provide direction to subordinates in how to implement and enforce laws. The Constitution is silent about this, but the Supreme Court has upheld the president's power to issue **executive orders.** These are directives that the president can issue to employees throughout the executive branch, setting policy and procedures for a specific department or for all the departments. Executive orders can have far-reaching effects, and critics complain that presidents use them to bypass the legislative process. For example, when he became president, Ronald Reagan used executive orders to impose a ban on the use of federal funds to support family planning and abortion abroad. Bill Clinton revoked that ban in his first full day on the job in 1993. Eight years later, George W. Bush restored the Reagan ban.

Executive Privilege and Executive Immunity

Article II begins with the statement "the executive power shall be vested in a president of the United States of America" but does not define executive power. Presidents use the executive power clause as a way to claim vast discretionary privileges when dealing with Congress or the federal courts and to justify claims of executive privilege and executive immunity. **Executive privilege** is the claim that presidents have the prerogative not to provide information to Congress or the courts about activities internal to the operation of the executive branch if doing so would jeopardize national security or limit the president's ability to discharge his duties as the chief executive. The courts show deference to presidential claims of privilege in matters of national security, but they have not been convinced by presidential arguments to use privilege to withhold other information. President Nixon used claims of executive privilege during the Watergate crisis when he refused to turn over copies of the Watergate tapes of conversations held in the Oval Office. The Supreme Court ruled in the landmark case of *United States v. Nixon*[18] against the president's claim of privilege and ordered Nixon to turn over the Watergate tapes to a grand jury.

Listen to the Watergate tapes on the Internet.

Executive immunity is the claim that presidents are not subject to lawsuits that either interfere with carrying out their job or that charge them with a crime or seek civil damages. The Supreme Court has agreed with the first part of this claim.[19] Presidents cannot be stopped from carrying out their official duties by a lawsuit, even if the action damages an individual or organization. Most recently, Bill Clinton was sued for civil damages in a private matter. In this case, Clinton was accused of harassing an Arkansas state employee while serving as governor. Clinton argued that the lawsuit should wait until his term in office ended. It would interfere with his ability to carry out his job. The Supreme Court disagreed, however, ruling that executive immunity did not extend to lawsuits for private actions. The lawsuit could proceed.[20] No sitting president has ever been charged with a crime, leaving that portion of the executive immunity claim untested.

Commander in Chief

The Constitution makes the president the **commander in chief** of the armed forces, meaning that he controls the day-to-day deployment of the military. This gives him considerable discretion in military matters. Yet the Framers of the Constitution did not want to vest the ultimate military power in the president; consequently, the Constitution also provides that only Congress shall have the power to declare war. Presidents often use their power as commander in chief to place American troops into hostile situations leading to undeclared wars. Congress has not declared a war since World War II. Since then, American presidents have brought the United States into three major wars (Korea, Vietnam, and Persian Gulf), plus numerous minor conflicts. By one count, American armed forces have been used abroad at least ninety times since 1941.[21] In the three major undeclared wars alone, more than 15 million American troops were involved and 81,000 died in combat.[22]

Read the War Powers Resolution.

It was not until revelations of presidential abuse of power during Vietnam that Congress sought to rein in presidential war powers. Acting over a presidential veto, Congress passed the **War Powers Resolution** in 1973.[23] The resolution attempted to limit the president's ability to place American armed forces in hostile or potentially hostile situations without congressional approval. The president could introduce troops into hostilities only pursuant to a declaration of war or specific statutory authorization, or in a "national emergency" created by an attack on the United States, its territories or possessions, or its armed forces.[24] In every possible instance, the president is to consult with congressional leaders before commencing hostilities, but if he is unable to do so, he is required to submit a report to Congress within forty-eight hours after introducing troops. The War Powers Resolution then gives the president sixty days (with an additional thirty days if needed) to complete military activities.

The War Powers Resolution can be viewed as an attempt to prevent a president from embroiling the United States into another decade-long conflict like Vietnam. If the president is to use American forces abroad, he must get the job done quickly. But presidents did not accept the resolution. Every president since Richard Nixon has claimed that the War Powers Resolution is unconstitutional and that it is not binding. For example, in 1990, when Saddam Hussein of Iraq invaded Kuwait, President Bush (41) sent well over a half-million troops to the Persian Gulf, an action that led to the 1991 Gulf War against Iraq. Although the president eventually gained authorization from Congress for the military action, he argued that he did not need Congress's consent because his executive power as commander in chief gave him the discretion to prosecute the war. President Clinton made similar arguments in 1999 when he launched an air assault against the Serbs in Yugoslavia in retaliation for their war of ethnic cleansing against the Albanian Kosovars, even after Congress refused to lend its support for the Kosovars. The War Powers Resolution still remains controversial, yet because Congress has been unwilling to invoke it, it has had little impact on presidents—except to prevent them from engaging American troops in long, drawn-out conflicts. President George W. Bush however, had little trouble getting Congress to authorize the 2003 Iraq war. Indeed, military action was authorized a full six months before the war began.

Legislative Powers

The president plays an important role at the beginning and end of the legislative process. The president has the power to suggest a legislative agenda to Congress. The Constitution requires the president "from time to time give to the Congress information on the State of the Union." In presenting what has become an annual State of the Union address, the president acts with constitutional authority in recommending "measures he shall judge necessary and expedient." Although Congress does not have to accept his proposals, the Constitution provides for the president to present a legislative agenda to Congress. Since passing budget reform legislation in 1974, Congress has also mandated that the president submit an annual budget proposal to Congress each year in mid-January. Over the last century, Congress has become very dependent on the president to provide it with a broad agenda. The priorities the president outlines in his State of the Union address and in the bills he sends to Congress play a large role in shaping Congress's agenda. Congress is not limited to considering only his agenda, but given the media attention that usually accompanies the president's proposals, it can rarely ignore the president's program.

The president also has a critical power at the end of the legislative process: He can accept or reject legislation approved by Congress. The Constitution provides the president with a qualified **veto power** over legislation passed by Congress, which enables him to prevent legislation from becoming law unless two-thirds of both houses of Congress override his veto. When both houses of Congress approve a bill, the president has ten days to sign it into law or to veto it. If he vetoes the bill, it is returned to Congress. After that, the bill can become law only if a two-thirds majority of each chamber votes to override the veto. If the president neither signs nor vetoes the bill, it will become law automatically at the end of the ten-day period. If Congress adjourns its session during the ten days after approving a bill, the president can use the **pocket veto,** whereby the bill will automatically be vetoed unless he signs it within ten days.

Presidents have varied greatly in their use of the veto. The veto is an important presidential tool in the legislative process. Although he can suggest legislation, the president cannot force Congress to pass specific bills. The veto is the only way he can stop legislation he dislikes from becoming law. The veto is a formidable power because Congress rarely has the votes needed to override. Thus, the threat of a veto is a real threat to Congress,

Presidential Vetoes, 1789–2005.

and it will likely try to negotiate with presidents over controversial legislation. As George W. Bush, a president who did not veto a single piece of legislation in his first term, has noted, "the best tool I have beside persuasion is to veto."[25] Bargaining to avoid a veto is a regular part of the legislative process. Yet the actual use of a veto is often viewed as a sign of presidential weakness. If a president has to veto legislation, it means that the president has been unsuccessful in convincing Congress to pass legislation he supports. Presidents are more likely to veto legislation when Congress is controlled by the opposition party than when their party controls Congress.

Appointment Power

"From Abe Fortas to Zoe Baird: Why Some Presidential Nominations Fail in the Senate," Glen S. Krutz, Richard Fleisher, and Jon R. Bond.

The Constitution places responsibility for the appointment of judges, ambassadors, and top executive branch officials into the hands of the president and the Senate. The president has the sole power of nomination, but he must secure support of a majority of the Senate to confirm the nominations through its power of "advice and consent." In recent years, most presidential appointments to cabinet-level posts have been confirmed, with a few notable exceptions. In 1989 the Senate refused to confirm President Bush's nomination of former Senator John Tower as secretary of defense in light of allegations of alcoholism and potential conflicts of interest that Tower had from consulting contracts with weapons builders. President Clinton also ran into trouble with several of his nominations, including his choice of Zoe Baird as attorney general in 1993.

When the Senate refused to bring John Bolton, President George W. Bush's nominee for U.N. Ambassador, to the floor for a vote, the president used the power of a "recess appointment" to circumvent the Senate during the August 2005 recess. Recess appointments allow presidents to appoint officials until the end of the current session of Congress. Bush has made 105 recess appointments since taking office, including Charles Pickering as a judge on the Fifth Circuit Court of Appeals, Anthony J. Principi as chairman of the Defense Base Closure and Realignment Commission, and Otto J. Reich as Assistant Secretary of State for Western Hemisphere Affairs. President Clinton used recess appointments 140 times in his eight years in office.[26] Congress dislikes the use of recess appointments but can do little to stop it.

Among the most important nominations that presidents make are justices of the Supreme Court. Because justices have life tenure, a presidential nominee to the court can have an impact upon American politics long after a president has retired. Judicial selection is discussed in greater detail in Chapter 11.

Power over the Executive Branch

Finally, the president has considerable control over those individuals he appoints to positions in the executive branch. The Constitution provides that the president can "require the opinion in writing, of the principal officer, in each of the executive departments, upon any subject relating to the Duties of their respective Offices."[27] The president can direct the activities of executive branch officials, and he can remove them at will. The Supreme Court has held that even though political appointees must be confirmed by the Senate to take their positions, the president has the sole power of removal.[28]

Can the President Meet Expectations?

The constitutional powers given to the president do not suggest a disabled institution. Indeed, the Framers envisioned a president who would play an important role in American politics and serve as a critical check on the Congress. But when we compare the public's expectations for the president with the powers provided to the office, we very quickly see the gap that exists. Brief examinations of the functional roles we expect the president to carry out reveal the limitations of the office.

Chief Legislator

The American people expect the president to provide vision and leadership for the national government. Presidential candidates make many promises about the agenda they intend to achieve if elected. The public expects the president to be the nation's **chief legislator** and to use his legislative powers to achieve his agenda. Of course, we already know that the president's legislative powers are limited to proposing legislation for Congress to consider and vetoing legislation with which he disagrees. The president can present an agenda before Congress, but Congress does not have to accept that agenda. Bill Clinton tried to lead Congress, but the Republican lawmakers who found themselves in the majority for the first time in forty years were not particularly interested in Clinton's agenda after 1995.

George W. Bush had a different experience in 2001. With Republican control of Congress, a major tax cut was passed (see Chapter 12) within his first five months in office. When Senator James Jeffords (R-Vt.) became an independent, resulting in Democratic control of the Senate, Bush found it more difficult to pass legislation. Only one additional major piece of domestic legislation passed—the No Child Left Behind Act—during this period. Bush did enjoy bipartisan support after the terrorist attacks of 9/11, and he easily passed the USA Patriot Act in October 2001. Once Republicans regained the Senate in 2003, Bush succeeded in passing a second tax cut, but he had few other domestic legislative successes, and the second half of his first term was dominated by the ongoing war in Iraq. Bush's second term started with a major initiative on Social Security reform, but as the introduction to the chapter indicates, he was unable to get that agenda enacted into law.

Chief Executive

The public also expects the president to provide leadership over the executive branch. He is supposed to ensure that the laws are faithfully executed. As the only member of the executive branch of government even mentioned by the Constitution, we would expect the president to have considerably more control as chief administrator than he does as chief legislator. But what powers does the president have over the executive branch? The Constitution gives the president authority to appoint (and remove) inferior officers. Yet that power is not unilateral. Although the president can nominate, he must receive the "advice and consent" of the Senate to complete the appointment. If the president does not have senatorial support, his nominations go nowhere.

Once they are appointed, the president can request information from his inferiors; he can order them to carry out specific tasks. He has the sole power of removal. Yet presidents often find that they do not have nearly as much control over their appointees as they would like. Although presidential appointees are responsible to the president, they often serve multiple masters. Cabinet members may want to help the president achieve the administration's policy objectives, but they also have to think about satisfying the demands of the congressional committees, which provide them with statutory authority. They also need to satisfy the demands of the permanent civil servants who work under them, and they have to satisfy the demands of the organized interests that seek to influence the department's decisions.

Chief Diplomat and Commander in Chief

Perhaps the president's greatest abilities to meet expectations lie in the area of foreign affairs. In addition to nominating ambassadors, the president has the sole authority to accept ambassadors from foreign nations. He determines if the United States has diplomatic relations with other countries. Thus, Richard Nixon was able to open relations with China in 1972 after twenty-two years of the United States refusing to recognize the legitimacy of the communist government installed there in 1949. The president has the sole ability to negotiate treaties with foreign countries, although he must gain the support of two-thirds of the Senate for those treaties to be ratified. As the president rarely has a two-thirds majority from his own party in the Senate, he must curry support from both parties to have his treaties ratified. Here we find another limitation on presidential power. Because just over one-third of the Senate can stop a treaty, presidents often avoid treaties in favor of **executive agreements.** Although these are not explicitly mentioned in the Constitution, presidents have used them since early in the nineteenth century, and today presidents sign many more executive agreements than treaties.

The president's greatest foreign power comes from his role as commander in chief of the armed forces. Presidents have used their power as commander in chief to deploy troops to defend American interests abroad. Even though Congress may have the formal authority to declare war, presidents have largely been able to maintain control over foreign policy.

Chief Manager of Economic Prosperity

Finally, we must ask about the ability that the president has to meet the public's expectations of him regarding the economy. How can the president ensure economic growth and prosperity? The president has no formal power over the economy beyond encouraging raising or lowering taxes, encouraging or discouraging spending. He has no ability to command the key investment decisions that shape economic growth; he cannot prevent inflation or control the unemployment rate. Nor does he have any authority beyond appointment powers over the one governmental entity that does have some impact on economic prosperity: the Federal Reserve Board. We discuss this issue in greater length in Chapter 12.

Presidential Leadership: The Power of Persuasion

The Constitution may stack the deck against unilateral presidential action, but it is still possible for a president to be an effective leader. For a president to have a chance at meeting the expectations placed on the office, he must become adept at the power of persuasion. Because the president can rarely command, he must learn how to convince other policy makers— members of Congress, interest groups, executive branch officials and bureaucrats, and the media—that what the president wants is what they should want too. The president must be a leader.

Leadership as Persuasion

Presidency scholar Richard Neustadt suggests that presidential leadership is very much dependent on the personal skills of the individual incumbent. Because American government is not structured to encourage presidents to act alone, the president must marshal all of his resources to convince other Washington policy makers (Neustadt calls them Washingtonians) that what he wants is what they want. To get what he wants, the president must bargain and compromise with others in government. To be an effective leader, the president must act strategically, calculating his every action to maximize his goals.[29] Neustadt argues that there are three factors the president must consider when trying to persuade others of his preferred course of action. The president must (1) effectively use the bargaining advantages of the office, (2) work to develop a professional reputation as a leader who gets what he wants, and (3) cultivate public support for his program.

George W. Bush gestures during a news conference in May 2003 about the Iraq War.

AP Images

Bargaining Advantages

The institution of the presidency gives the American president considerable advantages when bargaining with other policy makers. The president is a powerful figure who inspires considerable awe and easily intimidates. A president needs to use these advantages strategically to give him leverage in his negotiations with other policy makers. A simple presidential phone call to a member of Congress wavering in his or her support of the president's position on a bill can be very effective. Most members of Congress do not have regular interaction with the president, and his personal intervention can yield considerable results. The president who thinks strategically will recognize the potential benefits of an invitation to the Oval Office for a personal meeting or even an invitation to a bill-signing ceremony as a reward for providing critical support for the president's program.

The president must also know that the bargaining advantages of the office are most effective when they are used sparingly. If a member of Congress receives one call from the president, it may have considerable psychological impact in bargaining: "The president must really need my vote." But if the president's intervention becomes commonplace, the bargaining advantages will quickly disappear. He must assess how important a specific issue is and carefully decide when to use the advantages of his office. The president can never focus on just one issue. If he puts everything on the line for an issue today, it can weaken his ability to get what he wants tomorrow, next month, or next year.

Professional Reputation

The president's professional reputation among policy makers is also critical to his success as a leader. Washington policy makers have expectations regarding the president's skills and tenacity as a leader. Their perceptions of the president's leadership abilities and his will to get what he wants strongly shape how Washingtonians react to him. Is the president viewed as a leader who will not settle for defeat? Does he have a reputation as a shrewd negotiator who rarely loses, or is he viewed as a "waffler" who always changes his mind? Does he stand by his promises? Can he be trusted to keep his word? These are all critical questions that shape the president's reputation. Thus, it is in the president's best interest to project an image of himself to Washingtonians as a skilled and tenacious leader. He must constantly evaluate the potential actions he wants to take to determine how they will affect his reputation.

Both Bill Clinton and George W. Bush struggled with their professional reputations. Early in his first term, Clinton seemed to be indecisive, taking long periods of time to make various appointments. By the 1994 elections, Clinton's reputation seemed to be at a low; not only was he unable to pass his major health-care proposals, but his party lost control of Congress for the first time in forty years. One year later, however, the president seemed to gain some ground, as he took a hard stance against the Republicans' spending bills and was willing to let the Republicans shut down the government. Bill Clinton seemed like a new president. The Clinton roller coaster continued when he did great harm to his professional reputation during the Lewinsky affair of 1998. When he wagged his finger, saying, "I did not have sexual relations with that woman," and then seven months later admitted that he lied, he seriously damaged his reputation in Washington. His problem with the Washingtonians was not the extramarital affair. Rather, it was that he told his closest advisors and cabinet members in January that he did nothing wrong, and then they put their reputations on the line for Clinton. The cabinet went on the talk-show circuit and argued for the president's innocence, only to find out seven months later that they had been deceived. Clinton lost the trust and confidence of even his closest allies.

George W. Bush came to office amid major questions over the legitimacy of his presidency, after the 2000 presidential election was decided in the Supreme Court. Bush also faced questions over his fitness for the job, in terms of his intelligence and competence. The allegations, which stemmed

"The Contemporary Presidency: George W. Bush and the Myth of Heroic Presidential Leadership," Jon Roper.

from perceptions raised during the 2000 campaign that Bush was just a "C" student at Yale and lacked the skills needed to be president, were probably unfair. Bush refused to ever acknowledge the legitimacy question, and the question largely went away after the 9/11 attacks, when the president demonstrated strong leadership. His professional reputation changed virtually overnight. Bush cultivated his reputation as a war president throughout his first term. In his second term, Bush suffered his first major legislative failure, in his inability to get Social Security reform passed, but it did not affect his reputation as much as the bungled government response to Hurricane Katrina in August 2005. Poor choices made in the first days after the hurricane struck New Orleans and the Gulf Coast seemed to indicate poor judgment and challenged the image that Bush had carefully cultivated as the president who would keep America safe. It is too early to tell whether the damage to Bush's reputation will be lasting.

Public Prestige and the Rise of Going Public

Measuring public prestige: George W. Bush's approval ratings.

Finally, the president's public prestige outside of Washington is an important factor in how effective he can be at persuasion. Washingtonians are concerned with how the public views the president outside of Washington and how their own constituents will view them if they do what the president wants. If the president has strong public support and is seen as having much prestige, Congress will be more likely to go along with him. As a result, it is essential that the president cultivate his prestige with the nation. The more public support the president can generate for his policies, the more leverage he gains in convincing other Washington policy makers to go along with him. Ronald Reagan, a Hollywood actor who became president, was particularly good at this. Known as the "great communicator," Reagan generated considerable personal popular support. Even when the American public did not support his policies, they supported Reagan as president.

In the past twenty-five years, presidents have used a new technique to try to generate public support: **going public.** Given the vast amount of media attention the president receives, he can appeal directly to the voters to support his policies. In doing so, the president can go over the heads of members of Congress. He can encourage voters to call their representatives and senators to urge them to support him.

"Crisis Leadership: The Symbolic Transformation of the Bush Presidency," Gary L. Gregg II.

Many politicians are discovering the appeal of going public. But going public short-circuits bargaining by making it harder to achieve compromise on important issues. If the president can generate enough public support through going public, he can use the strategy very effectively. But there is also a risk. For example, in 1988 George H. W. Bush focused his campaign for office on a promise of "read my lips: no new taxes." This simple declarative statement was very valuable as campaign rhetoric, but it seriously limited Bush's range of options when dealing with difficult fiscal constraints in the aftermath of the deficits of the 1980s. By going public, the president placed all of his cards on the table. He made it very difficult to bargain.

President George W. Bush greets voters in Ohio during the 2004 presidential campaign. The president's victory in Ohio ensured his reelection.

To make matters worse, when Bush eventually broke his promise in 1990, he instantly created an issue that his opponents could use against him.

Perhaps the most vivid example in recent years is George W. Bush's landing on the deck of the aircraft carrier *U.S.S. Abraham Lincoln* in a Lockheed S-3 Viking jet. He then delivered a speech before a banner announcing "Mission Accomplished," indicating the end of military hostilities in Iraq.[30] Going public isn't just making an appeal to the public; it is the use of public events as a form of political theater and spectacle. Ironically, Bush's shining moment—which he intended to use in the 2004 presidential campaign—backfired, for the insurgency against the American occupation in Iraq began shortly after Bush's mission accomplished speech and continues to the present day.

Going public shows little signs of abating, yet recent research by George Edwards suggests that although presidents use the cultivation of public support as a key strategy in service of accomplishing their goals, presidents are rarely able to move public opinion in support of their key initiatives.[31] Edwards analyzed hundred of public opinion polls and found that presidents with even the strongest of communication skills rarely succeed in moving the public, and they may be better off using the more private method of bargaining.

Term Cycles and Presidential Leadership

The individual strategies for leadership suggested by Richard Neustadt have considerable value, but other presidential scholars have suggested that different strategies can lead to effective presidential leadership. Paul Light's *The President's Agenda* suggests that the opportunities present for presidential leadership differ depending on where the president is within a four-year **term cycle.** Light argues that the election of a president begins a four-year term cycle with identifiable characteristics. When he is first elected, the public and the Congress are likely to give the president greater leeway in proposing an agenda. Congressional support of the president's program will be at its highest in the president's first several months, when the president is given a "honeymoon." During the first months of a new presidency, Congress (and the public) are most willing to support major, nonincremental reform proposals from a president. But like every marriage, the honeymoon between the president and Congress eventually ends. Reality sets in, and the president will find that Congress becomes considerably less supportive of his agenda throughout the rest of his term. After starting at a high level of cooperation, the president will find that cooperation quickly diminishes and conflict increases throughout his term. This suggests that a president who wants to make good on his campaign promises and wants to implement major policy initiatives has a very brief window of opportunity.

Paul Light's term cycle theory has a second part. As congressional support for the president declines, the president's skills and overall effectiveness continually increase throughout his term. When most presidents begin their term, they are at the least effective point in their presidency. Herein lies the problem. A president's skills are at their lowest when Congress is most supportive of the president's program. That is, the opportunity for leadership is highest when the president is least likely to possess the persuasive skills he needs. He is least effective when he needs to be most effective. Thus, the challenge for the president is to overcome the natural tendencies of the term cycle. A president who can come out of the starting blocks of the four-year presidential marathon running will have a much better chance at achieving his goals than one who starts slowly. Yet this is easier said than done, as it is no easy task to transition from campaigning to governing. Bill Clinton learned this the hard way with his health-care legislation. Health-care reform was a major part of Clinton's 1992 campaign, but it took his administration more than ten months to turn a campaign promise into a legislative proposal. By the time Clinton provided Congress with a bill to consider, the first year of his presidency was already finished.

Light's term cycle theory is most applicable during the president's first term. A "honeymoon" is considerably less likely in a second term. There is little novelty to a second term. Although the president's skills are stronger than they were at the beginning of the first term, it is unlikely that congressional support will remain high during the second term. Indeed, many of the president's rivals are already thinking about the next election. The introduction to this chapter illustrates the challenges of a second term. George W. Bush started his second term with an ambitious plan for Social Security reform, but he was unable to generate support for his plan.

The President and the Executive Branch

To this point, we have largely focused on the individual skills needed for presidential leadership. Necessarily, we focus a great deal of attention on the individual in the office. There is a common assumption that the character and leadership style of the individual matter the most. This may lead us to conclude that what it takes to succeed in the presidency is simply the right type of individual.[32] For example, perhaps if George W. Bush was a different individual, he would not have gotten bogged down into a long war in Iraq, or a different Bill Clinton would have succeeded in his health-care reforms or not succumbed to having an affair with an intern. Although it is valid to say that the individual matters, we may overestimate and overemphasize the personal qualities of the presidency. Thus, we may fail to see the structures and institutions that surround the president and affect the president's ability to lead, specifically the Executive Office of the President, the cabinet, and the federal bureaucracy.

The Executive Office of the President

The realities of the modern presidency have made it a necessity for the president to have help to carry out his responsibilities and manage the government. That help has come in the form of the Executive Office of the President. As late as 1933, President Franklin Roosevelt had little more than a dozen full-time employees to assist him with his presidential tasks. Four years later, after one of the most intense periods of presidential activity in American history, Roosevelt had a group of experts conduct a study on how to best manage the presidency and the executive branch. Roosevelt's Committee on Administrative Management issued its report with a simple opening sentence: "The president needs help."[33]

Two years later, Congress passed legislation that fundamentally reorganized the presidency. Help came in the form of the Executive Reorganization Act of 1939, which created the Executive Office of the President (EOP). The EOP was designed to provide the president with personal political assistance as well as objective expert management and policy advice. The former came through the creation of the White House Office (or what is commonly called the White House staff). The latter was provided by the creation of several offices and councils within the White House. Expanded over time, these include the Office of Management and Budget, the National Security Council, the Council of Economic Advisors, and several other minor offices.

Explore the White House website.

The White House Office

The president operated with very little personal staff for the first 120 years of the Republic. As John Burke reports, Congress did not even appropriate funds for a White House staff until 1857, when it provided President Buchanan with one clerk. As late as the presidency of Woodrow Wilson, the president had only seven personal aides.[34] It was not until the passage of the Reorganization Act of 1939 that the **White House Office** was created and the president's staff began to see considerable growth. By the election of Dwight David Eisenhower in 1953, the White House staff had grown to more than 250. By the time Eisenhower's former Vice President Richard Nixon was president in the early 1970s, the White House staff had mushroomed to more than 500. Although President Carter tried to scale the staff back down toward 400, by the time Ronald Reagan was elected in 1980, the White House staff had crept back toward 500, roughly the size it has remained to the present day.[35]

"White House Structure and Decision-Making: Elaborating the Standard Model," Charles E. Walcott and Karen M. Hult.

What impact does a staff of 500 have on the president's ability to lead? The answer to this question is complex, as the modern White House Office can be viewed as both an advantage and a disadvantage for presidential leadership. Because staffers do not require Senate confirmation, the president is free to appoint and fire staff members at will. He can also demand absolute loyalty from his staff, who do not face the problems of cabinet members, with their divided loyalties between the president and their department constituencies. The president is free to shift individual staff members from project to project, using them to best achieve his goals. The White House Office can be thought of as offering the president several hundred extra sets of eyes, ears, and arms to carry out the president's agenda. The White House staff can help manage the president's relations with Congress and with his own executive branch.

The White House staff can also pose serious problems for presidential leadership for many of the same reasons that it can help. Because the job security of White House staff members is entirely dependent on their favor with the president, many staffers are constantly trying to improve their status within the White House. White House staff are always trying to curry favor with the president to ensure their future, and this can have unanticipated consequences. White House staff may not be the best types of advisors for the president. Quite simply, they do not always provide the president with the type of advice that is needed. Out of a desire to please the president, White House staff may be more inclined to tell the president what he wants to hear than what he needs to hear. A classic example includes staffers painting a less than honest portrait of the war in Vietnam for President Johnson. Lyndon Johnson wanted to hear that we were winning the war, so his staffers told him we were winning the war. By their not being completely honest with the president, he was not well served.

A second problem that White House staffs have as policy advisors to the president is that they can be isolated from the rest of the political world. The White House staff can exist in the bubble of the White House. They are at the center of American politics but can be very isolated from the political realities outside of Washington. Because they have only one constituency to serve (the president), they may not be exposed to as many perspectives on issues as cabinet members are.

Office of Management and Budget

Congress created the Bureau of the Budget in 1921 to provide the president with the ability to formulate an executive budget proposal that Congress could consider as a whole. Transferred from the Department of the Treasury in 1939, the bureau began as part of the Executive Office of the President. It was reorganized as the **Office of Management and Budget** (OMB) in 1970. Originally established to provide assistance in formulating the president's budget, which is submitted to Congress for its consideration each year, the mission of the Bureau of the Budget was broadened when it was subsumed into the EOP to include managerial control over the agencies and departments of the executive branch.[36]

Primarily staffed by career civil servants, who provide it with institutional memory and professionalism, the OMB has increasingly become an important part of White House policy making. Since the Nixon presidency, the OMB has been given responsibility for three important tasks: (1) providing assistance to the president in formulating the budget, (2) serving as a clearinghouse for all legislation proposed by executive branch departments to make sure that departmental proposals are consistent with the president's policy goals, and (3) monitoring how executive branch programs are implemented to ensure they are administered economically and efficiently.[37]

Council of Economic Advisors

Another important aspect of the Executive Office of the President is the **Council of Economic Advisors** (CEA). Created in 1946, the CEA consists of professional economists who offer the president professional advice on economic policy. The three-member council provides the president with economic forecasts and suggests ways that the president can meet his economic policy goals through regular memoranda and an annual report on the economy.

The Council of Economic Advisors' importance within a presidency varies with the willingness of the president to heed its advice. Although designed to provide impartial expert advice to the president, EOP units have continually become more and more political. Presidents expect political as well as policy advice from their advisors. It has become increasingly difficult to tell the president what he needs to hear rather than what he wants to hear.

National Security Council

The **National Security Council** (NSC) was created in 1947 with the intention of providing coordination of national security policy to "ensure that the president would take into account professional military advice."[38] The NSC formally consists of the president, vice president, secretary of state, secretary of defense, director of central intelligence, chairman of the joint chiefs of staff, and national security advisor. Over time, the national security advisor and the NSC staff have grown in importance, providing the president with an independent foreign policy staff of more than fifty full-time employees and an additional hundred or so employees on temporary assignment from the armed forces that both coordinate and formulate national security policy. The increased importance of the NSC was made clear in 2005 by the nomination of President's Bush's national security advisor Condoleeza Rice to replace Colin Powell as secretary of state.

The National Security Council provides one of the best examples of the potential problem of staff-driven policy making. During the Reagan administration, the National Security Council was used to implement a secret foreign policy in which the United States would provide military assistance to the counterrevolutionary forces (the Contras) fighting the Sandinista-led socialist government in Nicaragua.[39] But the Congress and the American people never shared the president's support for the Nicaraguan counterrevolution. When Congress passed a law forbidding the United States from providing military assistance to the Contras, the president's NSC staff took matters into their own hands, secretly raising funds (from private donors) for the Contras. NSC staffer Lieutenant Colonel Oliver North masterminded what became known as the **Iran-Contra affair.** The administration secretly entered into an agreement with Iran to exchange arms for hostages. Arms would be sold to Iran in exchange for Americans held hostage in the Middle East, and the profits from the arms deal would be diverted to the Contras in Nicaragua. This violated U.S. law dealing with military assistance to the Contras as well as official U.S. policy not to negotiate with terrorists.

The Cabinet

For the first century and a half of the nation's existence, the primary source of help for the president came from the **cabinet.** The cabinet consists of the secretaries of the executive departments and other individuals whom the president invites to participate, such as the vice president and national security advisor. President Washington, who found it useful, created the cabinet.[40] It originally consisted of the three department secretaries (war, treasury, and state) and the attorney general; today, there are fifteen cabinet-level departments (see Table 10.1). The cabinet was the primary source of advice for the president throughout the nineteenth century, but it declined in importance throughout the twentieth century.

Early presidents used the cabinet as an informal decision-making body, where the president could discuss policy issues and come to a collective decision on a course of action. Given their small personal staffs, presidents could take advantage of the prestige and knowledge of individual cabinet members to provide them with important policy advice and political support. Yet as early as the presidency of Andrew Jackson, some presidents sought other sources of advice outside of the executive branch. Jackson had a group of friends and journalists whom he referred to as his "kitchen

Cabinet Office	Current Officeholder
State	Condoleezza Rice
Treasury	Henry Paulson
Defense	Donald Rumsfeld
Interior	Dirk Kempthorne
Attorney General (Justice Department)	Alberto Gonzales
Agriculture	Mike Johanns
Commerce	Carlos Gutierrez
Labor	Elaine Chao
Health and Human Services	Michael O. Leavitt
Housing and Urban Development	Alphonso Jackson
Transportation	Norman Mineta
Energy	Samuel W. Bodman
Education	Margaret Spellings
Veterans Affairs	Jim Nicholson
Homeland Security	Michael Chertoff
Other Positions in the Cabinet	
Vice President	Dick Cheney
White House Chief of Staff	Joshua B. Bolten
Environmental Protection Agency Administrator	Stephen Johnson
Office of Management and Budget	Rob Portman
United States Trade Representative	Susan Schwab
Office of National Drug Control Policy	John Walters

Table 10.1 The President's Cabinet, 2006

Sources: U.S. White House, http://www.whitehouse.gov/government/cabinet.html; Office of the Director of National Intelligence, http://www.dni.gov.

cabinet." Other informal advisors included Grover Cleveland's "fishing cabinet" and FDR's "brain trust."[41]

The cabinet has seen a gradual decline in importance over the past century for many reasons. First, as the size of the executive branch grew, the cabinet increased with it. The cabinet simply became too large to be an effective advisory and policy body for many presidents. Cabinet members are selected for many reasons and often have little in common with one another. Moreover, many presidents found that it did not make sense to consult the entire cabinet on specific matters that were relevant to only a handful of cabinet members. Most modern presidents prefer to meet with "ad-hoc or functionally-based groups" for policy advice.[42] Second, many of the advisory functions originally carried out by the cabinet were replaced by the White House staff, which has seen continual growth since the presidency of FDR. Presidents simply did not need to seek out cabinet members in the same way they did when they lacked substantial personal staffs. Finally, presidents have found that the cabinet is simply not a good source of advice due to the conflicting interests of members. Cabinet members do not offer undivided loyalty to the president because they are concerned with their own constituencies. As Thomas Cronin and Michael Genovese report, Ronald Reagan's aides did not trust cabinet members to put the president's interest ahead of their own departmental interest. Cabinet members "had generally become advocates of their own constituencies."[43]

The Federal Bureaucracy

Learn about the Web resources of the executive branch.

The institutional presidency surrounding the president represents only a small fraction of the overall executive branch, which spans fifteen departments plus numerous agencies and regulatory commissions. The bureaucracy is responsible for more than 1,400 federal government programs with a $1.7-trillion budget. With more than two and a half million civilian employees, the federal **bureaucracy** represents the bulk of all federal employees and can be a major challenge for the president to control. While the executive departments are responsible to the president, most of the employees in the bureaucracy are **civil servants,** permanent government employees who cannot be removed by the president without cause. Unlike the political staff in the Executive Office of the President, career civil servants are not dependent on the president's favor for their jobs, nor are they necessarily supportive of the president's program for governance. Yet they have substantial powers.

Functions of the Bureaucracy

The bureaucracy has several functions. Its responsibilities are both quasi-legislative and quasi-judicial. First, it implements laws passed by Congress. Most legislation is usually written in general terms, leaving it to the bureaucracy to establish the rules by which legislative goals are applied to specific circumstances. Administrative **rule making** is accomplished by following uniform procedures spelled out in the Administrative Procedure Act,[44] requiring an agency to develop a proposed rule with ample opportunities for public comment and feedback.

The rule-making process is time-consuming and something that most citizens are unaware of. Yet administrative rules have the force of law. Proposed rules are published in the pages of the *Federal Register,* a daily government publication. Although the administrative rule-making process affords opportunities for participation, the system is usually biased toward vested interests, which are more likely to have the resources to track the rule-making processes within each agency. Yet as a quasi-legislative process, administrative rule making can be more open than the actual legislative process in Congress, given the strict process imposed by the Administrative Procedure Act.

Is there waste in the bureaucracy?

Some parts of the bureaucracy do more than establish rules; they enforce the rules they enact. **Regulatory agencies** can be divided into three distinct

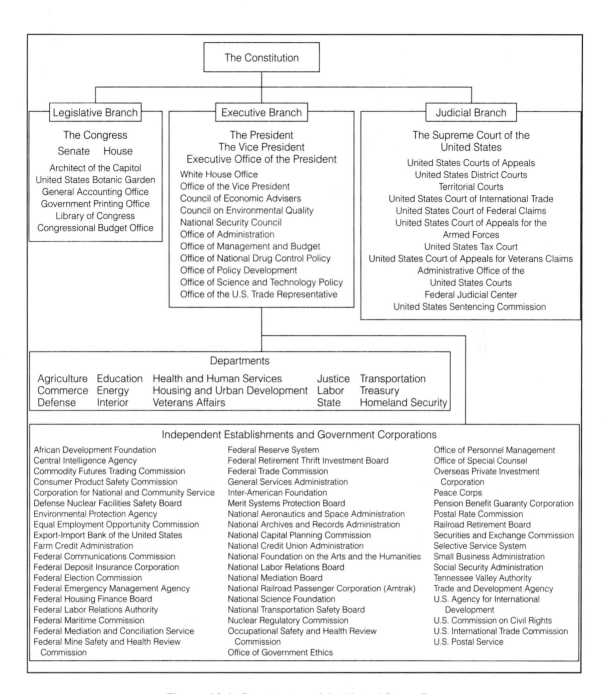

Figure 10.1 Organization of the United States Government

Source: U.S. Government Manual, 2003.

Agency	Year Established	Number of Employees[a]
Consumer Product Safety Commission	1972	466
Environmental Protection Agency	1970	17,943
Equal Employment Opportunity Commission	1965	2,836
Federal Communications Commission	1934	2,017
Federal Deposit Insurance Corporation	1933	6,222
Federal Election Commission	1971	354
Federal Energy Regulatory Commission	1977	1,100
Federal Reserve System	1913	1,693
Federal Trade Commission	1914	1071
Food and Drug Administration	1906	9,000[b]
National Labor Relations Board	1935	2,020
Occupational Safety and Health Administration	1970	2,200
Securities and Exchange Commission	1934	3,085

Table 10.2 Major Regulatory Agencies

Source: Harold W. Stanley and Richard G. Niemi, *Vital Statistics on American Politics 2003–2004*, table 6-13, p. 265.

Note: The Interstate Commerce Commission, established in 1887, was terminated on December 30, 1995. It was succeeded by the Surface Transportation Board.

[a] As of November 1998, except OSHA (February 1999).

[b] Approximate number.

types: agencies within a cabinet department, agencies outside of a department, and independent regulatory commissions. (Table 10.2 lists the major regulatory agencies.) Most are independent regulatory commissions, which means that the president can appoint, but not remove, commissioners. Examples include the Federal Trade Commission, Nuclear Regulatory Commission, and Federal Communications Commission. Agencies that lack the status of independent regulatory commissions are more subject to political control by the administration because the president can remove commissioners. The Occupational Safety and Health Administration (OSHA) is an example of an agency within a department. The Environmental Protection Agency is an example of an agency outside of a cabinet department.

Congress has passed numerous laws designed to regulate the behavior of businesses and groups. Regulatory agencies have both rule-making authority and adjudicatory or quasi-judicial powers, which enable them to investigate and prosecute violations of administrative rules. The adjudicatory process is treated like a court and includes administrative law judges who judge cases. For example, the Environmental Protection Agency has authority to establish emission standards for acceptable amounts of specific pollutants that can be released into the air. Businesses that violate those rules can face civil or criminal penalties.

Controlling the Bureaucracy

The vast majority of federal employees today are civil servants. They are hired through a merit process overseen by the Civil Service Commission. This was not always the case. Throughout most of the nineteenth century, most federal jobs were acquired through **patronage,** or what is sometimes called the **spoils system.** Initiated by President Andrew Jackson, federal jobs were handed out by the president as a reward for past loyalty and work during the campaign. As president, Jackson replaced one-sixth of the federal work force (roughly 11,000 employees) with patronage appointments.[45] By the end of the nineteenth century, the vast majority of federal jobs rotated out with each new administration. It was not until 1883 that Congress took the first steps toward curbing the spoils system by passing the Civil Service Act, which established the beginning of a professional civil service by requiring potential federal employees to take an exam to qualify for a job. It initially covered only about 10 percent of the federal work force, but by the 1930s, it covered more than 80 percent of federal employees.[46]

The creation of a career civil service has resulted in a wealth of policy expertise within each of the executive branch departments and agencies. Many civil servants bring highly technical and scientific knowledge to their jobs, often gained through years of service within a specific agency. This expertise is one of the greatest advantages of the bureaucracy, if not the primary reason for a career civil service. It ensures that the agency will effectively administer the programs it is delegated responsibility for enacting by Congress. But there is no assurance that career civil servants will share the same approaches to public policy as the president.

When Dwight Eisenhower became president in 1953, he was faced with a civil service that had worked under Democratic presidents for twenty years and was committed to the New Deal programs it had authority to administer. Eisenhower was faced with the very real possibility of having a large bureaucracy that was unsympathetic to the new administration's policy approach, yet there was little he could do because he could not replace existing officeholders below the very top levels of each department and agency. His solution was to create a new tier of political appointees (called "schedule c appointments") within each department that would be exempt from civil service requirements. With approximately 1,500 positions spread throughout the bureaucracy, the president could place loyal appointees much deeper into each department.[47] Today, there are almost 5,000 "schedule c" appointees within the government.

Recent presidents have worked hard to control and manage the bureaucracy largely because of their perception that the bureaucracy does not share the same outlook as the administration. Career bureaucrats spend years working in the same policy area. They develop close working relationships with congressional subcommittees and the interest groups that are constituencies of the agency. Chapter 8 describes how these relationships can result in iron triangles and issue networks.

Most bureaucrats become deeply loyal to the programs they administer, which they view as essential to their own personal job security and survival.[48] When a new administration comes to power with the goal of coordinating or directing the activities of the bureaucracy to conform to administration goals, bureaucrats generally resist. Cabinet secretaries and the political appointees below them with authority for specific programs often find themselves in the middle of a war between administration goals and the career staff. It is often a war that the political staff cannot win, as the career bureaucrats have considerable clout. They know that the average political appointee serves only eighteen months in the administration and lacks their specialized knowledge: "Often when the political appointees are seeking a different course of action than the career support staff, a test of wills develops. The career staff will use every tool available to them, including stalling actions and marshalling support from Congress and from interest groups to stop the course of action."[49] They also work to "co-opt" the political staff (sometimes including the cabinet secretary) to convince them to buy into the perspective of the career bureaucracy.

Since Eisenhower, presidents have worked hard to develop strategies to gain control of the bureaucracy, usually with little success. The first step was creating and enlarging the White House Office. By shifting policy-making authority from the departments to the White House, presidents attempted to gain greater control. Although the White House staff has increased in importance, it still lacks the policy expertise of bureaucrats within the departments in administering programs.

President Richard Nixon took a further step by giving the Office of Management and Budget responsibility to review and approve all proposed rules and regulations coming out of the bureaucracy. Nixon also required OMB clearance of all legislative proposals coming from the bureaucracy. Nixon began the process of White House clearance of all political personnel hired within each department. Historically, cabinet secretaries were given free rein in hiring their deputies and bureau chiefs. Nixon required the White House personnel office to clear all political staff within the departments to make sure that appointees were loyal to the administration. In the 1980s, Ronald Reagan raised the stakes, exercising even greater tests of political loyalty. Reagan also used the OMB to control the budgets of the various departments, cutting funding for programs that the administration opposed.[50]

President Clinton took a different approach to controlling the bureaucracy. He operated from the premise that the career staff would be sympathetic to his policies after twelve years of attack by the Reagan and Bush administrations. Clinton tried to gain the support of the career staff by cutting the number of political staff within the agencies. He also worked to eliminate career positions to "reduce the number of points at which his own policies could be thwarted by bureaucratic action." He accomplished the latter goal through his "reinventing government" program and the creation of the National Performance Review. Clinton had Vice President Al Gore lead an effort to reinvent government by making it more efficient, accountable, and effective. The goal would be to streamline government by shifting authority from higher within the bureaucracy to its lower levels, thus enabling departments to act more quickly without multiple levels of review. As an ongoing effort within the Clinton dministration, the National Performance Review eliminated over 291,000 career staff jobs within five years.[51]

Control of the bureaucracy during the presidency of George W. Bush has taken a different focus, largely shaped by 9/11. After the terrorist attacks in 2001, President Bush moved quickly to consolidate several executive branch agencies to enable a more coordinated response to future terrorist attacks and to provide for better domestic security. The Customs Service, Bureau of Citizenship and Immigration Services, Immigration and Customs Enforcement, Coast Guard, Secret Service, and Federal Emergency Management Agency (FEMA) were reorganized under a cabinet-level Department of Homeland Security. Coupled with the USA Patriot Act (see Chapter 4), the executive branch has seen enhanced powers, with greater ability to act outside of public view. The effectiveness of this new approach is still an open question, although the federal government's response to Hurricane Katrina in August 2005 has raised concerns about the government's ability to respond to future terrorist attacks or natural disasters.

Conclusion: Can the President Lead?

This chapter has shown that the president of the United States faces numerous challenges to his leadership. The institution of the presidency provides the president with several powers to carry out his duties, but the American public has large expectations for the office that seem to expand over time. The president needs to cultivate public support for his policies, he needs to demonstrate to other Washington policy makers that he is a skilled leader who must be reckoned with, and he must have the personal skills to strategically advance his interests. The president has been given considerable help to assist with these tasks, but he must be careful that his advisors, assistants, and various councils work to advance his agenda and do not make policy on their own without presidential authorization. And he must manage the bureaucracy so that it promotes his agenda and not that of unelected bureaucrats.

Check here for possible post-publication updates to the chapter material.

The president is far removed from the daily lives of the American people. It is much easier to make contact with and attempt to influence members of Congress than it is the president. But in many ways, the American people feel much closer to the president than they do to Congress. Thanks to constant media attention, Americans feel a sense of ownership over the president, which in itself contributes to the rising expectations of presidential performance.

Key Terms

weak presidency model 307
strong presidency model 307
take care clause 309
Budget Control and
   Impoundment Act
   of 1974 310
executive orders 311
executive privilege 311
executive immunity 311
commander in chief 312
War Powers Resolution 312

veto power 313
pocket veto 313
chief legislator 315
executive agreements 316
going public 320
term cycle 322
White House Office 324
Office of Management
   and Budget 325
Council of Economic
   Advisors 325

National Security Council 325
Iran-Contra affair 326
cabinet 326
bureaucracy 328
civil servants 328
rule making 328
regulatory agencies 328
patronage 330
spoils system 330

Annotated Web Links

The following are links to some resources relating to the presidency and the executive branch. You can find other resources by using Web directories, such as Yahoo or Google.

The White House (**http://www.whitehouse.gov**) runs the official website of the presidency. This site includes both current news about the president and a repository of press releases, speeches, proclamations, and major initiatives of the Bush presidency.

If you are interested in doing research on the Clinton presidency, the National Archives has taken responsibility of maintaining the White House website as it existed from 1994 through January 20, 2001. The Clinton Presidential Materials Project (**http://search2.nara.gov**) includes the ability to search and view the White House website as it existed during the Clinton years. You can see how the site became more sophisticated by viewing each of the different versions. The National Archives also maintains a database (**http://clinton6.nara.gov**) of all the public papers of the Clinton presidency.

The Bush White House website is not nearly as complete as the Clinton White House website was, but there are alternative ways to access most of the same information. The National Archives maintains an online database of "Weekly Compilation of Presidential Documents" (**http://www.access.gpo.gov/nara/nara003.html**) from 1993 through the present.

There are numerous websites chronicling the history of the American presidency. One of the best is *Grolier's Encyclopedia of the American Presidency* (**http://gi.grolier.com/presidents/preshome.html**), which provides resources for all different age levels and includes video and sound clips, historical election results, and more. Microsoft Encarta's website (**http://encarta.msn.com/find/search.asp?search= american%2Bpresidency**) includes a good alternative for encyclopedia-type entries on the presidency.

Virtually every department and agency in the federal government has its own website. There are several Web directories that can point you to specific resources. Probably the best way to start exploring these resources is by using Fed World (http://www.fedworld.gov), which includes links to all executive branch departments and agencies, as well as numerous searchable databases of government websites. Yahoo's U.S. Government directory (http://dir.yahoo.com/Government/U_S_Government) also provides access to thousands of resources for the entire government.

A complete study tool kit is available for this chapter and includes the following:
Flashcards
Crossword Puzzle
Critical Thinking Exercises
Interactive Timelines
Chapter Quiz

■ *Lawrence v. Texas* and the Right to Privacy   337

■ **Courts: Three Institutions in One**   339
    Courts as Institutions of Dispute Resolution   339
    Courts as Legal Institutions   340
    Courts as Political Institutions   342

■ **Court Organization and Structure**   343
    The Modern Federal Judiciary   343

■ **The Modern Supreme Court**   348
    Access to the Court   348
    Who Are the Litigants?   350
    Oral Argument and Decision Making   351

■ **The Politics of Judicial Selection**   352
    Selecting Supreme Court Justices   352
    Selecting Lower Court Judges   358

■ **The Supreme Court and American Politics**   360
    The Development of Judicial Power   360
    Debates over the Appropriate Role
      for the Court   366
    The Court and Public Policy   367

■ **Conclusion: The Least Dangerous Branch?**   368

Lawrence v. Texas and the Right to Privacy

On September 17, 1998, a Texas man named Roger Nance called police and reported that an armed gunman was "going crazy" in his Houston apartment building. Shortly after the phone call, Harris County sheriff's deputies arrived at 794 Normandy Street to investigate the weapons disturbance report. Several deputies entered the building and climbed to the eighth story, where they found an unlocked apartment door and entered. Once inside the room, they didn't find an armed gunman, but instead witnessed a sight none of them would have expected.[1] The tenant, a fifty-five-year-old medical technician named John Geddes Lawrence who worked as a shift supervisor at a local hospital, was inside his apartment engaging in a sexual act with thirty-one-year-old Tyrone Garner.[2] Caught off guard by the incident at first, deputies arrested both men for engaging in "deviate sexual intercourse," a Class C misdemeanor under Texas law.

Tyrone Garner, left, and John Lawrence, center, arrive at the courthouse with one of their attorneys to face charges of homosexual conduct under Texas' sodomy law, Friday, Nov. 20, 1998, in Houston.

The facts in this case were remarkably similar to those of an earlier case from Georgia. In 1982 police entered the home of Michael Hardwick to serve a summons for public drunkenness, and they found him engaged in oral sex with another man. The police arrested Hardwick for violating Georgia's sodomy law—which criminalized both oral and anal sex. Hardwick's case ultimately led to the U.S. Supreme Court's 1986 decision in *Bowers v. Hardwick,* where the court ruled that the Constitution's guarantee of a right to privacy did not extend to the right of homosexuals to engage in private consensual sexual conduct with members of the same sex. Writing for the Court, Justice Byron White argued that proscriptions against homosexual sodomy had "ancient roots" going well beyond the criminal statutes against sodomy that had existed in most states throughout the nation's history. The *Bowers* decision was a setback to advocates of privacy rights for homosexuals, who believed that the Court's privacy jurisprudence in such cases as *Griswold v. Connecticut* and *Roe v. Wade*, which established privacy rights in the fields of birth control and abortion, should extend to the private consensual sexual conduct of adult homosexuals.

The Supreme Court's decision in *Bowers* specifically targeted state proscription of homosexual sodomy, even though the Georgia statute made no such distinction between homosexual or heterosexual acts of sodomy. *Bowers* remained a controversial decision, not only because of what Justice Harry Blackmun called "the court's almost obsessive focus on homosexual activity"[3] but because of the nation's increasing sensitivity to gay rights in recent years as a result of a much more vocal gay rights community. As a result, since 1986, several states have repealed their criminal sodomy statutes, and several state courts have invalidated sodomy laws. Indeed, the very law that Hardwick was convicted under was struck down by the Georgia Supreme Court in 1998.[4]

Texas, however, was one of a few states that maintained a proscription specifically against homosexual sodomy, the law that Lawrence and Garner were convicted under. Its law was enacted in 1973 to ban "unproductive" sexual conduct *only* between people of the same sex.[5] After their arrest, Lawrence and Garner were taken by deputies to a jail, where they were held overnight, charged, and then convicted by a justice of the peace. The defendants exercised their rights to a trial "de novo" (enabling them to retry their case before a court). They challenged their conviction, claiming that their rights to equal protection and privacy under the U.S. and Texas constitutions had been violated. The court upheld the initial conviction and fined them $200. With the assistance of Lamba Legal, an interest group committed to advancing the civil rights of gays and lesbians, Lawrence and Garner appealed to the Texas 14th District Court of Appeals.

The Court of Appeals initially ruled that the conviction violated Texas's Equal Rights Amendment but later reversed that decision upon re-argument by the full court.[6] Lawrence and Garner petitioned the Texas Court of Criminal Appeals—the state's Supreme Court for criminal cases—which declined to hear the case. They then sought review by the U.S. Supreme Court, arguing that the Texas statute which criminalized sodomy between same-sex partners, but not between heterosexual partners, violated their Fourteenth Amendment guarantee of equal protection by discriminating on the basis of sexual orientation and sex without legitimate government justification. On July 16, 2002, the Supreme Court granted a writ of certiorari—reaching down to the 14th District Court of Appeals and bringing the case to the Supreme Court for final resolution. Numerous interest groups on both sides of the issue presented *amicus curiae* ("friend of the Court") briefs urging the Supreme Court to either grant or deny certiorari in the case.[7]

On June 26, 2003, the Court delivered a 6–3 opinion written by Justice Anthony M. Kennedy in which the equal protection argument was thrown out. Instead, the Court decided that the Texas sodomy law violated Lawrence and Garner's vital interests in liberty and privacy protected by the due

"Of 'this' and 'that' in *Lawrence v. Texas*," Mary Ann Case.

process clause of the Fourteenth Amendment. The Texas law was declared unconstitutional, and the Court overturned its precedent from *Bowers*. The decision, known as *Lawrence v. Texas*, was a landmark for gay and lesbian rights groups across the nation, and it gave new life to the Court's privacy jurisprudence (see Chapter 4).[8]

Read *Lawrence v. Texas*.

Lawrence is significant to our study of the judicial system for several reasons. First, the case illustrates the important role that courts play in American politics as policy makers. The Court's decision in *Lawrence* didn't simply resolve a legal dispute between Lawrence and Texas; it also interpreted the U.S. Constitution, invalidated several state laws, and established a binding precedent for future courts. *Lawrence* is also important because it is one of the few instances where the Supreme Court explicitly overruled one of its own precedents in a very short time—only seventeen years had passed since *Bowers*. Finally, *Lawrence* raised many new questions as to how far the right to privacy protected by the decision would extend. Will *Lawrence v. Texas* be the stepping-stone to a privacy interest protecting gay marriage?

Courts: Three Institutions in One

Article III of the Constitution begins with this simple sentence: "The judicial power of the United States shall be vested in one Supreme Court and in such inferior courts that Congress may from time to time ordain and establish." The Constitution describes the types of cases the Supreme Court can hear and the terms of office of Supreme Court justices, but nowhere does it define "judicial power." This chapter will examine the democratic— and undemocratic—aspects of courts. The focus will be primarily on federal courts, particularly the U.S. Supreme Court, where the ultimate power of judicial review rests. Before we can examine the role that the Supreme Court plays in American politics, we first need to understand some basics about the institutions of courts. To understand what courts do, we need to think of them as three institutions in one. Courts are institutions of dispute resolution, they are legal institutions, and they are political institutions. Put another way, courts resolve disputes in society, but they also make law, and their decisions can have considerable consequences for politics and policy making.

Courts as Institutions of Dispute Resolution

First and foremost, courts are institutions of dispute resolution. When you cannot resolve a dispute on your own, you may seek the assistance of a court to provide an authoritative resolution to the disagreement. This is best described in the area of **civil cases,** which involve disagreements between two individuals or between an individual and a corporation or organization. Civil cases have at least one **plaintiff** (who claims to have been injured in some way) and a **defendant** (the person or organization that the plaintiff claims is responsible). Courts provide a forum to resolve the dispute. **Criminal cases** also involve the resolution of disputes, although in these cases the dispute involves an alleged violation of a law (defined later). In a criminal case, there is no plaintiff, but there is usually a **complainant** (a person who reports a possible crime to the police or prosecutors' office).[9]

When courts resolve disputes in criminal or civil cases, they often reward the victor and punish or sanction the loser. If a defendant is found responsible in a civil case, he or she is normally ordered to pay a monetary settlement to correct the problem. The defendant may have to compensate the plaintiff for the loss. In extreme circumstances, the defendant may also have to pay punitive damages as punishment for his or her actions. If a defendant is found guilty in a criminal case, he or she may face more severe sanctions, ranging from a fine, to probation, to time spent in jail or prison, or even the ultimate sanction of death for the most heinous crimes.

By rewarding the victors and punishing the losers, courts serve an important purpose—**behavior modification.** Courts try to encourage some behavior and discourage other behavior in advance. By imposing harsh sanctions on the losers, courts serve a broader societal goal of deterrence. If people know the consequences of their behavior (such as committing murder or robbing a bank), then they are less likely to engage in such discouraged behavior.

Courts as Legal Institutions

American courts are not free to decide cases based on the personal predispositions of the judges because courts are constrained by the law. Courts interpret, apply, and even make law. But what is law?

Definition of Law

Law is not easy to define. Great scholars from before Plato and Socrates through St. Thomas Aquinas to Thomas Hobbes and into the present have debated its meaning. From this debate, a basic definition emerges: **Law** is a body of rules enacted by public officials in a legitimate manner and backed by the force of the state. Laws are rules of conduct that govern the relationships between members of society. Although most organizations (churches, athletic clubs, businesses, etc.) have rules, only those rules enacted by public officials are considered law. Moreover, for laws to be legitimate— or deserving obedience—they must be enacted according to some agreed-upon principles. For example, we accept that Congress can make law because we know that the Constitution gives Congress that authority, as long as it follows certain procedures described in the Constitution. The final point that distinguishes laws from other organizational rules is that only the force of the state backs law. Government alone can legitimately take away life, liberty, or property.

Sources of Law

According to this definition, laws are rules made by public officials in a legitimate manner. There are five different ways that laws are created in the United States: constitutional lawmaking, statutory lawmaking, treaties, administrative actions, and common law development. The most basic source of law in the United States is the U.S. Constitution. As we discussed in Chapter 2, the Constitution provides the framework for government by defining its powers and marking its limits. Ultimately, the Constitution tells us how laws can be made in a legitimate manner. It spells out the authority of Congress to enact laws under the Constitution. Each state also has its own constitution, which is the ultimate source of state law unless it conflicts with the U.S. Constitution. The Constitution can be changed only by amendment.

Statutes are laws passed by legislatures. Statutes differ from constitutions in how they can be changed. The U.S. Constitution is hard to change, but a law passed by a legislature can be changed by enacting another law to modify or repeal it. Cities and counties are authorized under state constitutions to enact statutes, often called ordinances, that are applicable in the local jurisdiction.

Treaties are another form of law that is enacted by government. Treaties are legally binding agreements between the United States and other nations. Only the federal government can enter into treaties. Treaties are negotiated by the president and go into effect only if ratified by two-thirds of the Senate. Treaties have the same force of law as statutes passed by Congress.

When legislatures delegate authority to executive branch agencies or departments, they often give the agency the authority to enact **administrative rules** or **regulations** that have the force of law. To create administrative law, an agency must be given explicit authority from a legislative body to carry out a specific task or program. Legislatures delegate their own authority to agencies because the legislature often lacks the specific expertise over an issue that an agency is better suited to deal with. The president can also issue **executive orders** to employees of the executive branch, setting policy and procedure for a department or the entire executive branch (see Chapter 10). Unless Congress passes a law to overrule them, executive orders are legally binding.

Courts also make law through their decisions. Judicial decisions establish **precedent,** meaning that future courts considering similar cases need to review the results of earlier decisions. When the U.S. Supreme Court decides a case interpreting the meaning of a clause of the Constitution, the decision is said to make **constitutional law** and is binding on all other courts and on the rest of the government, as we saw in *Lawrence v. Texas.* When a court interprets the meaning of statutes, we say it is engaging in **statutory interpretation.** Both types of decisions are equally binding, although it is much easier for Congress to overturn statutory decisions.

Laws made by judicial decision make up part of what is known as the **common law.** Common law consists of all the traditions, principles, and legal practices that have been handed down from one generation to another.[10] American use of common law principles derives from the English legal traditions that were by-products of the English colonial experience. Common law can be considered a combination of both written and unwritten laws that American courts follow. It is out of common law tradition that the practice establishing judicial precedents (known by the doctrine of **stare decisis,** or "let the decision stand") emerged. Many common law practices that were originally unwritten rules have now been written into the text of judicial precedents. Common law is more flexible than statutory law, although it has the same force.

Courts as Political Institutions

The third way to think of courts is as political institutions. When a court hands down a decision that changes the meaning of a law, it is acting as both a legal institution and a political institution. Chapter 1 notes that politics can be defined as "who gets what, when, and how" or "the authoritative allocation of values." When courts interpret laws—when they contract or expand upon rights under the Constitution—they are engaged in politics. The political nature of courts is most clearly seen when a court exercises **judicial review** and invalidates a law. Judicial review is defined as the power of a court to declare a governmental action (usually of the legislature or executive branch) unconstitutional and thus null and void. When courts exercise judicial review, they are declaring that the "democratic process" (represented by Congress and the president) has exceeded its power under the Constitution. By invalidating a law, courts are changing how values are allocated in society. They are altering who gets what, when, and how. By overruling the precedent in *Bowers v. Hardwick*, the Court's decision in *Lawrence* did just this in the field of homosexual privacy rights.

The political nature of courts is not limited to exercising judicial review. When a federal district court orders that a school district use forced busing of students to achieve desegregation of public schools, it is making a political decision. When a court agrees to a plea bargain agreement from a criminal defendant that reduces the sentence to less than what the defendant would have received had he or she been convicted by a jury, the court is making a political decision. The court is, in effect, establishing its own sanctions for crimes, rather than using those established by the democratic process.

Judges like to downplay the political nature of the judicial process, but it is impossible to separate the political role of courts from their other functions. The Framers of the Constitution created the courts to be a coequal, independent branch of government. In the Madisonian system of checks and balances, courts have a responsibility to provide a check on the legislative and executive branches of government. They also have an important job in ensuring that the other branches do not violate the rights of the people under the Constitution (see Chapter 4).

Court Organization and Structure

The Framers of the Constitution could not decide whether it was necessary to have a federal judicial system other than a Supreme Court. Some delegates thought that state courts could hear federal cases, with a final appeal to the Supreme Court. Other delegates feared that state courts might be biased against the new national government. Ultimately, the Constitutional Convention chose not to decide and left to Congress the decision of whether to create additional courts inferior to the Supreme Court.

One of the first acts passed by the new Congress was the **Judiciary Act of 1789,** which established a three-tier system of federal courts. The Judiciary Act created two types of trial courts. District courts hear criminal and civil cases. As originally created, they heard admiralty cases, minor federal criminal cases, and other cases where the United States was a plaintiff. Each district court was within one of three circuit courts, which were both trial and appellate courts. The circuit courts heard diversity cases involving citizens of two states, major federal crimes, and larger cases in which the United States was a plaintiff. Circuit courts also heard appeals from decisions of the district courts.[11] Congress established one district court judgeship for each district, but it chose not to create any circuit judgeships. Circuit courts were staffed by two Supreme Court justices and one district court judge. By the mid-nineteenth century, they were reduced to one Supreme Court justice and two district court judges. The circuit courts were never popular institutions. Supreme Court justices universally detested having to "ride circuit," spending large parts of the year traveling to remote circuit courts to serve as trial judges. Litigants were sometimes mistrustful of the circuit courts because when a case was appealed to the Supreme Court, it had already been heard by one or two Supreme Court justices. Although the justices sought on numerous occasions to eliminate circuit riding, the practice was not abolished until 1912.

The Modern Federal Judiciary

The modern federal court system dates to 1891, when Congress passed the Evarts Act, which created the U.S. Courts of Appeals, appellate courts that would eventually replace the circuit courts. By 1912, the modern three-tiered structure of the federal courts was in place (see Figure 11.1).

U.S. District Courts

With the elimination of the circuit courts, all federal trial jurisdiction was subsumed into the **U.S. District Courts.** The original thirteen district courts have grown to ninety-four districts with 649 judges. Although no judicial district can cross a state border, many states have between two and four district courts. Congress establishes the number of judges in each district. District courts are courts of general jurisdiction, and their judges

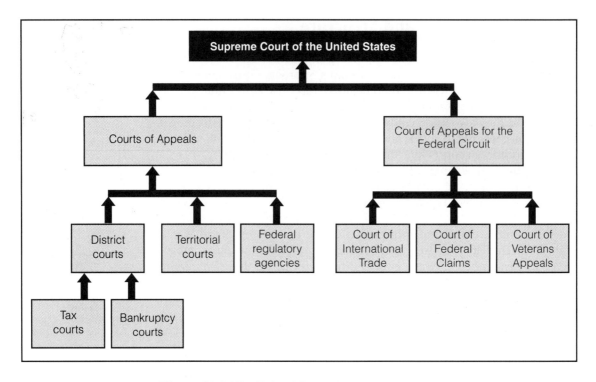

Figure 11.1 The Federal Court System

hear a wide variety of cases, including federal criminal trials, civil diversity actions, violations of federal civil rights law, Social Security claims disputes, bankruptcy cases, and tax disputes. The primary task of the district court is to determine the facts of the case and the appropriate outcome. The district court is assisted in its work by **U.S. Magistrate Judges,** who are "quasi-judicial officers." Magistrate judges are appointed by the district court for an eight-year term and carry out specific tasks for the judges, including arraignments, pretrial motions, consideration of minor matters, and conducting civil trials with the consent of the parties. As adjuncts of the district court, the district judges can always review decisions of magistrate judges.

U.S. Circuit Courts of Appeals

Each district court is included in one of twelve regional **U.S. Circuit Courts of Appeals.** The courts of appeals review decisions from the district courts and federal administrative agencies within the circuit. The courts of appeals correct legal errors made by the district courts interpreting federal laws. They do not make additional factual findings. Courts of appeals decide cases in panels of three judges. When they hear **appeals** from district court cases, the parties submit **briefs,** or written arguments explaining why

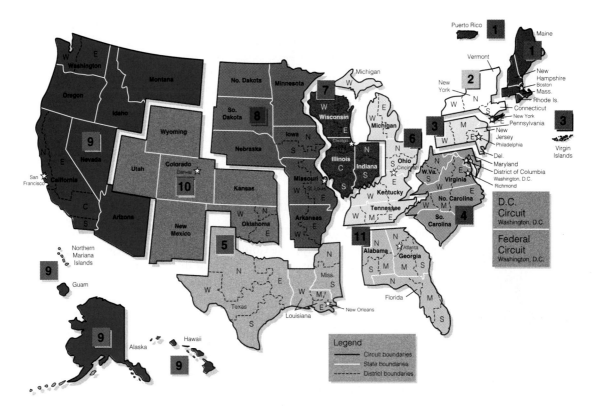

Figure 11.2 Map of the U.S. Courts of Appeals

the district court decision should be upheld or overturned. In many cases, the judges of the courts of appeals hold **oral argument,** in which they let the attorneys for each party make their case before the court. The judges decide almost one-half of their cases without hearing oral argument, basing their decisions solely on the written record. Most cases are decided within ten months after the appeal is filed. Courts of appeals' decisions are written and are binding—they establish **precedent**—on all other district courts within the circuit unless overturned by the Supreme Court. Thus, in addition to its error-correction function, the courts of appeals also make law.

When the courts of appeals were originally established, there were nine circuits, with three judges in each circuit. As the caseload of the federal courts has grown, the courts of appeals have been forced to adapt to meet the demand. Today, the nation is divided into eleven numbered circuits plus a circuit for cases coming from the District of Columbia (see Figure 11.2). The days of circuits with only three judges are also long past. There are now 168 federal court of appeals judges, with seven judges in the first circuit, which covers the New England states, and twenty-eight judges in the vast ninth circuit, including the Pacific states, Alaska, and Hawaii. Even though the size of the courts has grown, the judges still work in panels of three.

In addition to the twelve regional circuits, Congress has also created a court of appeals with national jurisdiction. The **U.S. Court of Appeals for the Federal Circuit** hears cases from several specialized trial courts. The federal circuit hears appeals from the U.S. Court of Federal Claims (which Congress created to decide claims against the federal government as well as cases involving patents and intellectual property issues), the Court of International Trade (dealing with disputes over foreign trade), and the Court of Veterans Appeals (which decides claims brought by veterans regarding their benefits). The federal circuit judges work in Washington, D.C., and they hear cases from all fifty states.

The U.S. Supreme Court

Take a virtual tour of the U.S. Supreme Court building.

The **Supreme Court** of the United States forms the pinnacle of the federal judicial system. The Supreme Court consists of nine justices (one chief justice and eight associate justices) who hear appeals from the U.S. Circuit Courts of Appeals and the fifty state supreme courts in cases dealing with interpretation of parts of the U.S. Constitution and matters of federal law. Unlike the courts of appeals, which work in panels of three judges, all nine justices of the Supreme Court decide cases together (see Table 11.1). The Supreme Court has its greatest power when it exercises judicial review to strike down a federal or state law as unconstitutional.

The U.S. Supreme Court building sits across the street from the Capitol in Washington, D.C. The Supreme Court did not have a home of its own until this building was completed in 1935. For much of its early history, the Court worked out of the old Senate Chamber in the basement of the Capitol.

Justice	Party	Home State	Year Appointed	Age at Appointment	Law School	Undergraduate Education	Previous Judicial Experience
John Paul Stevens	Republican	Illinois	1976	55	Northwestern	Chicago	Seventh Circuit U.S. Court of Appeals
Antonin Scalia	Republican	Illinois	1986	50	Harvard	Georgetown	D.C. Circuit, U.S. Court of Appeals
Anthony Kennedy	Republican	California	1988	51	Harvard	Stanford	Ninth Circuit, U.S. Court of Appeals
David H. Souter	Republican	New Hampshire	1990	50	Harvard	Harvard	New Hampshire Supreme Court, First Circuit U.S. Court of Appeals
Clarence Thomas	Republican	Georgia	1991	43	Yale	Holy Cross	D.C. Circuit, U.S. Court of Appeals
Ruth Bader Ginsburg	Democrat	New York	1993	60	Columbia	Cornell	D.C. Circuit, U.S. Court of Appeals
Stephen B. Breyer	Democrat	Massachusetts	1994	55	Harvard	Harvard	First Circuit, U.S. Court of Appeals
John G. Roberts, Chief Justice	Republican	Indiana	2005	50	Harvard	Harvard	D.C. Circuit, U.S. Court of Appeals
Samuel A. Alito, Jr.	Republican	New Jersey	2006	55	Yale	Princeton	Third Circuit, U.S. Court of Appeals

Table 11.1 The Supreme Court, Its Members, and Their Backgrounds

Sources: Supreme Court Compendium, table 4-4, pp. 207–221; table 4-9, pp. 256–263; *Vital Statistics on American Politics 1999–2000*, table 7-2, pp. 286–273; Wikipedia, http://www.wikipedia.org.

The Modern Supreme Court

When John Marshall assumed the bench as chief justice of the United States in 1801, the Supreme Court had very little work to do. During its first decade, it heard relatively few cases and was unsure of its role in American politics. Today's Supreme Court makes use of many of the traditions and practices begun by Marshall and later justices, but it is a very different institution, operating under very different conditions.

Access to the Court

Only a very small percentage of cases ever make it as far as the Supreme Court. For most litigants, the decision of the court of appeals or the state supreme court is final. For a case to reach the U.S. Supreme Court, it must raise either a constitutional question (challenging a specific clause of the Constitution) or a matter of federal law (a federal question).

The mere presence of a constitutional issue or a federal statutory question does not ensure that the Supreme Court will decide the case. Since 1925, the Court has had considerable discretion in choosing the cases it will decide. Today, the Court controls more than 99 percent of its docket. It has also become increasingly selective in choosing which cases to decide, and since 1990 the Court has cut its annual decisions by more than one-third. At the same time, the number of cases where litigants seek an appeal has grown (see Figure 11.3). When litigants lose at the court of appeals or in a state supreme court, they can petition the Supreme Court to hear the case. Litigants submit written arguments to the Court requesting that it grant a **writ of certiorari.** If the Court decides to grant the writ, it is in effect reaching down to the lower court and bringing the case to the Supreme Court for final resolution. In recent years, the Court has decided fewer than 90 cases, roughly 1 percent of the almost 9,000 cases brought before it annually.[12] When deciding which cases to hear, the justices, with the assistance of their law clerks, review each petition and vote whether or not to grant the petition. For a certiorari petition to be granted, the Court uses the **rule of four.** At least four justices must agree to hear the case. The Court does not require a majority to decide in favor of hearing the case because that might presuppose the case's outcome. The rule of four ensures that if a substantial minority believes that a dispute is important, the Court will decide it.

The Supreme Court issues its decisions on certiorari petitions throughout its term, although it disposes of many petitions in October, at the conclusion of the summer recess. When the Court refuses to grant certiorari, no reasons are given. Sometimes newspapers and broadcast media will report that "today the Supreme Court let a lower court decision stand" on a particular issue. The assumption in the media is that the Supreme Court agreed with the lower court decision and thus decided not to hear the case. Yet this interpretation is hard to sustain because the Court gives no reasons for its certiorari decisions. Indeed, in cases that the Court decides, it often

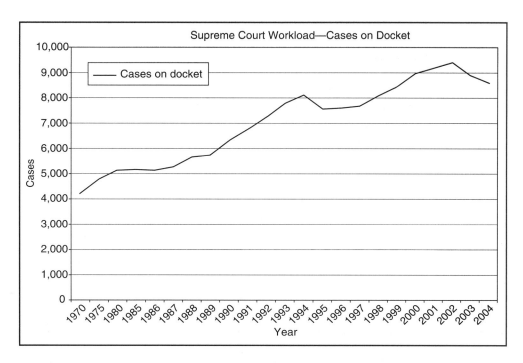

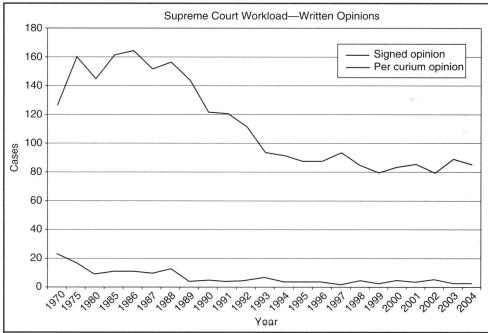

Figure 11.3 Caseload of the U.S. Supreme Court, 1970–2004

Sources: Stanley and Niemi, *Vital Statistics on American Politics 1999–2000,* table 7-7, p. 280; 1998–2004 data from Administrative Office of U.S. Courts, *Judicial Business of the United States Court 2005,* table A-1.

sustains decisions of lower courts after it grants certiorari. If the Court simply wanted to affirm the lower court decision, it could have just refused to grant certiorari.

Why is certiorari granted by the Court in one case and refused in another? We can identify some patterns as to when a certiorari petition is likely to be granted. The characteristics of a case often contribute to its "cert-worthiness." These include cases where the lower court departed substantially from established precedent, conflicting precedents between two or more circuits, the presence of important civil liberties or federalism questions, cases where the U.S. government was a party, and—most important—when the federal government asks the Court to hear the case. The presence of these characteristics does not guarantee that the Court will grant certiorari, but it does increase the odds substantially.

Who Are the Litigants?

The litigants who petition the Supreme Court for certiorari each year are a very diverse group. The vast majority are individuals—mostly criminal defendants seeking final appeals of their convictions. Federal, state, and local governments constitute the largest group of respondents, or litigants brought to the court by petitioners seeking certiorari.[13] The federal government is a petitioner in a very small number of cases, although it is the most frequent litigant at the Court. Political scientist Lawrence Baum reports that in the 1998 term, the federal government was a party in "about one-third of the cases brought to the Court for consideration and in 39 of the 90 cases actually decided by the Court after oral argument."[14] The federal government, represented by the **Office of the Solicitor General,** demonstrates remarkable restraint in filing petitions for certiorari, but it is successful in getting the cases it does petition for granted almost 75 percent of the time. The solicitor general's office will usually seek certiorari only in cases it thinks are extremely important, and once or twice a term, the government will even "confess error" and declare to the Court that a lower court decision favoring the federal government was wrong. The justices generally view the solicitor general with considerable credibility.

Interest groups play a large role in Supreme Court litigation, both by sponsoring cases that eventually arrive at the Court and by seeking to influence the outcome of cases before the Court through the submission of *amicus curiae* ("friend of the court") briefs. Most interest groups themselves cannot be parties in specific cases because they lack standing as litigants, yet they can sponsor cases brought by third parties. By providing legal services to individuals and bearing the substantial costs of litigation, interest groups can shepherd a case through the legal process, hoping eventually to receive a favorable policy ruling from the Supreme Court on an issue important to the group. The **American Civil Liberties Union,** an organization dedicated to the protection of civil liberties, has sponsored numerous cases throughout the years when individual civil liberties have been abridged.

Interest groups also play an important role in trying to influence the Court in deciding which cases to grant certiorari through the submission of *amicus curiae* briefs. With consent of the parties or permission of the Court, interest groups (or individuals) may submit a written brief to supplement a party's arguments. *Amicus* briefs can be submitted on whether the Court should grant certiorari or, if the case has already been granted certiorari, on the merits of the case. Occasionally, the Court may grant permission to an *amicus curiae* party to present arguments in cases, although this is unusual. Interest-group participation through sponsorship or submission of *amicus* briefs is an important way that citizens, acting through their chosen associations, can have an impact on the Court.

Oral Argument and Decision Making

Once the Supreme Court grants certiorari in a case, the clerk of the court assigns the case for oral argument, enabling the parties to argue the merits of their case before the justices in open court. Oral argument usually occurs about three months after the Court grants certiorari, and it is the only public part of the Court's work. The Court permits each party one-half hour to argue the merits of its case before the justices. Oral argument permits the parties to highlight the most important aspects of their case, and it allows the justices to ask questions of the attorneys.

The Supreme Court holds oral argument on Monday, Tuesday, and Wednesday for two weeks each month from October until April. The Court meets in a formal conference, which is closed to the public, on Wednesday afternoons and all day on Friday during argument weeks. Conferences of the Court discuss and decide the cases argued that week and discuss recently submitted certiorari petitions. The justices discuss each case in order of seniority. The chief justice always discusses the case first, and then each associate justice speaks in order of his or her seniority. If the outcome is not apparent from discussion, the chief justice will call for a vote. If the chief justice is in the majority, he will assign one of the justices to write the **majority opinion** of the Court. For important cases, the chief justice will often assign the opinion to himself, although the chief justice is also concerned with ensuring that the Court's workload is distributed reasonably among the justices. If the chief justice is on the losing side of the case, the most senior associate justice in the majority will assign the opinion. The other justices may choose to write a **concurring** or **dissenting** opinion. A concurring opinion is one in which the justice agrees with the outcome of the case but disagrees with the reasoning used by the majority opinion. A dissenting opinion is one in which the justice disagrees with the outcome of the decision. Dissenting opinions do not establish precedents, but justices in future cases often use them as justification for modifying an earlier decision. The number of concurring and dissenting opinions has increased considerably in the past several decades.

Listen to oral argument before the U.S. Supreme Court.

Examine the workload of the Supreme Court.

View the Supreme Court's annual calendar.

Learn how to find a Supreme Court opinion.

The bulk of the Supreme Court's work in a case occurs after oral argument, when the justices are researching and writing their opinions. When writing opinions, individual justices will circulate their drafts with other members of the Court. The goal is to write an opinion that at least four other justices will sign. In closely decided cases, one or two votes could change the outcome of the case, turning an opinion of the Court into a dissenting opinion. To prevent that from happening, justices negotiate with their colleagues. The opinion writer may agree to make a change to his or her opinion to gain the support of another justice, perhaps adopting the language of a proposed concurrence. This process continues until every justice signs one of the circulated opinions, at which point the final decision is prepared and released to the public in an open court session. Since 1989, the Court's decisions have been released both to the media and over the Internet, where they can be read within one hour of their release.

The Politics of Judicial Selection

The selection of federal judges has important consequences for democratic participation because of the special protections given to judges. When the Framers created the Constitution, they wanted to ensure that the justices of the Supreme Court would be insulated from the political pressures of ordinary politics. As a result, federal judges are guaranteed **judicial independence.** The Constitution guarantees that judges exercising "the judicial power of the United States" serve during "good behavior." They can be removed only through the process of impeachment or through attrition by retirement or death. In addition, when Congress sets the salary of federal judges, it can only increase—and never lower—the compensation paid to judges. This prevents members of Congress from "punishing" federal judges by lowering their salaries for unpopular decisions. Collectively, the guarantees of what amounts to life tenure—no Supreme Court justice has ever successfully been removed from office through impeachment—and a guaranteed salary protect federal judges from the potential of undue political pressure. Because federal judges do not face reelection, they are free to decide cases without the worry of pleasing voters with their decisions. The guarantee of life tenure means that the process of judicial selection is extremely important. The Constitution makes the process of selecting federal judges seem fairly straightforward: The president makes the appointment, and the Senate votes whether or not to confirm the judge. If a majority of the Senate votes to confirm, the appointment is complete. The informal political process, however, is considerably more complicated.

Selecting Supreme Court Justices

Most presidents take the responsibility of naming Supreme Court justices quite seriously because of the lasting impact their nominations can have long after the president has left office. Although every president takes a different approach to judicial selection, the president does not select Supreme Court justices in a vacuum. Many factors come into play.

When a vacancy becomes available on the Court, the president usually turns to his top political advisors and the attorney general to identify a replacement. The White House usually maintains a "short list" of potential nominees based on suggestions submitted to the president by friends, senators, party leaders, friends of potential nominees, sitting justices, and others. There is never a shortage of individuals willing to give the president advice on selecting justices. The president's advisors try to narrow the list of possible candidates to a select few for the president to consider after the FBI completes extensive background checks. Sometimes the process to select a nominee can take months—for example, when President Clinton nominated Ruth Bader Ginsberg in 1993—and other times it can be completed fairly quickly. When Thurgood Marshall announced his retirement in 1991, President Bush (41) named Clarence Thomas as his successor in just a few days, suggesting that the administration had anticipated Marshall's retirement and had completed the selection process ahead of time. When Sandra Day O'Connor announced her retirement in July 2005, President Bush (43) named Judge John Roberts in under three weeks. When Chief Justice William Rehnquist died from cancer on September 3, 2005, Bush promptly withdrew Roberts's nomination for associate justice and renominated him as his choice for chief justice less than forty-eight hours after Rehnquist's death. President Bush waited until John Roberts was confirmed as chief justice in October 2005 to name Harriet Miers to the O'Connor seat, although she withdrew her nomination to the Court in less than a month due to controversy over her qualifications.

Watch a story about the conservative controversy over the Miers nomination.

On October 31, 2005, President George W. Bush nominated Samuel A. Alito, Jr., to the O'Connor seat. Alito differed from Harriet Miers in several ways. While Miers never served as a judge, Alito had fifteen years of judicial experience on the Third Circuit Court of Appeals. When President Bush selected Alito, he commented that Alito "has more prior judicial experience than any other Supreme Court nominee in 70 years."[15] Alito had written hundreds of judicial opinions and is widely recognized as a highly qualified jurist. He also had extensive experience as government lawyer. He served as an assistant U.S. attorney, as a deputy assistant to the attorney general, and as U.S. Attorney for New Jersey. It was his judicial record that most clearly distinguished Samuel Alito from Harriet Miers. Although there was no way to verify Mier's conservative credentials, Alito had a proven record as a conservative; he was opposed to abortion and supportive of corporate economic interests. The very reason that pleased conservatives about the selection of Samuel Alito—his conservative record—created opposition from liberals. His confirmation hearings, while contentious, did not generate the support of Democratic senators for a filibuster. Alito was confirmed on January 31, 2006, by a vote of 58–42, the narrowest margin for a Supreme Court nominee since Clarence Thomas was confirmed by a 52–48 vote in 1991.

Presidential Criteria for Selecting a Nominee

Take on the role of the president and see if you can get a Supreme Court nominee confirmed.

Because the Constitution places complete responsibility for selecting a nominee in the hands of the president, there are no formal criteria for selection. Presidents are free to make their selections using whatever criteria they choose, although the individuals that presidents have nominated do suggest several factors that come into play. An obvious criterion that the president uses is political party. Very few presidents select justices from political parties other than their own, although there have been exceptions. Franklin Roosevelt named Republican Harlan Stone to the Court to promote national unity.

Ideology is another important criterion. In selecting a justice, the president can affect the ideological direction the Court takes in future cases. The perceived ideology of a justice can be an important factor in selection. President Reagan used opposition to abortion as a "litmus test" for his nominees both to the Supreme Court and to the lower federal bench. Although the president can try to predict the likely ideological disposition of justices from their past experiences, there is nothing to guarantee that a justice will turn out the way the president hoped. Several Supreme Court justices have been "disappointments" to the presidents who nominated them. Justice David Souter, appointed by President Bush in 1989, is much more moderate than Bush expected. President Eisenhower was disappointed with the decisions of two of his nominees—Earl Warren and William Brennan—although it is not likely that ideology was the controlling factor in either nomination.[16] Ideology was an important reason for Judge John Roberts's 2005 nomination, first as associate justice and then as chief justice. Roberts's solid conservative credentials, coupled with impeccable academic training and work experience as well as a lack of overly controversial decisions made as a judge, made him an ideal candidate for President George W. Bush, who wanted to please his conservative base. Bush's selection of his White House Counsel and personal lawyer Harriet Miers probably was partially driven by ideology as well. Miers's limited public record made her a stealth nominee of sorts, making it difficult to determine her position on controversial issues. Ironically, it was Bush's conservative base that was unhappy with the Miers decision, for social conservatives wanted someone named to the position with a clear record on social conservative issues. Her limited public record made them uncomfortable and uncertain about whether she would rule the way conservatives wanted on such key issues as abortion. It was just as likely that Bush selected Miers based on how he thought she would rule on executive power cases as it was that he selected her based on her likely rulings on social issues. She withdrew her nomination out of a desire not to jeopardize the president's claim to executive privilege, although controversy over her qualifications for the job played a large role as well.[17]

Political reward is the criterion that best explains Eisenhower's nomination of California Governor Earl Warren in 1953. Warren's decision to shift the California delegation, which was pledged to him as a favorite son candidate,

Judge John Roberts responds to questions from the Senate Judiciary Committee during the second day of confirmation hearings for his confirmation as chief justice of the United States Supreme Court in September 2005.

at the 1952 Republican national convention to Eisenhower enabled Eisenhower to win the nomination on the first ballot. Warren's selection as chief justice was a way for Eisenhower both to reward Warren for his actions and to eliminate a potential political rival by isolating him on the Supreme Court.

Geographical and ethnic representation is another factor presidents can use to select justices. Geographical representation on the Court was important to presidents for the first 100 years of the Court's existence. Presidents wanted to ensure that most parts of the nation were represented. As Lawrence Baum reports, because justices had to ride circuit and spend considerable time outside of Washington, "it made sense to choose justices from circuits they would represent."[18] After the practice of circuit riding was abolished, geographical representation became less important, although some presidents have used it to shore up political support. When Richard Nixon named Lewis Powell to the Supreme Court, he was able to satisfy two goals: putting a staunch conservative on the Court and nominating a southerner to strengthen his political support in the region.[19]

Over the last century, representation on the Court for religious and ethic groups and for race and gender has been important. Louis Brandeis was the first Jew to serve on the Court when he was appointed in 1916, and his nomination began the informal practice of having a Jewish seat on the Court. From 1918 until 1969, there was always at least one Jew on the Court.

Likewise, for a long while, there was a Catholic seat. The presence of a Jewish or Catholic seat points to the long-time domination of the Court by Americans of Protestant background. Although both of Bill Clinton's nominees were Jewish, the desire to provide religious diversity seems to have diminished, although the Court's current membership is more diverse than at any other time.[20] George W. Bush's selection of Harriet Miers was the first where membership in an evangelical Christian church was apparently a factor in the selection process, although probably not the key factor.

Today, representation for race and gender is perceived as much more important than religion. George Bush felt considerable pressure to nominate another African American to fill the seat held by Thurgood Marshall since 1965. Ironically, his selection of Clarence Thomas as the second African American on the Court generated controversy within the African American community because the conservative Thomas was ideologically out of the mainstream of most blacks. Ronald Reagan's 1981 appointment of Sandra Day O'Connor as the first woman to serve on the Court was largely viewed as an attempt to build support for Reagan with women. Clinton's nomination of Ruth Bader Ginsberg reflected his desire to seek "greater representation for women in government."[21] Presidents today are under pressure to appoint women, African Americans, and other minorities to the Court, including Hispanics.

The Confirmation Process

Most of the popular media attention given to the selection process for Supreme Court justices surrounds the confirmation hearings and debates in the Senate. Once a nominee is selected, the Senate Judiciary Committee begins a lengthy investigation of the nominee's background and past writings. The Judiciary Committee then conducts what may range from several days to several weeks of public hearings on the nomination, at which point supporters and opponents of the nominee can make arguments before the committee. It is also expected that the nominee will testify on his or her own behalf. Once the hearings conclude, the Judiciary Committee votes on whether to recommend confirmation. Regardless of the vote's outcome, the matter moves to the Senate floor, where the full Senate debates and votes on the confirmation.

Of sixty-three nominations to the U.S. Supreme Court since 1900, the Senate has rejected four nominees, and another three withdrew their name from consideration in light of almost certain rejection. In 1930 Judge John Parker of South Carolina was rejected after opposition arose from both labor groups and civil rights groups. Two Nixon nominees (Clement Haynsworth and G. Harrold Carswell) were rejected in 1969 and 1970 by the Senate as being "mediocre . . . obscure, and unsatisfactory."[22] In 1987 Judge Robert Bork was rejected after widespread opposition arose from liberal interest groups. The three withdrawn nominations were Associate Justice Abe Fortas, Judge Douglas Ginsburg, and Harriet Miers. Fortas was forced to withdraw his nomination as chief justice in light of conflict of interest allegations raised against his role in a private foundation. Ginsburg withdrew his nomination after allegations that he had smoked marijuana with his law students at Harvard Law School in the 1970s. Harriet Miers withdrew her nomination in October 2005 after she failed to gain support from key senators.

When President Reagan named Judge Robert Bork to fill the seat of retiring Justice Lewis Powell, a firestorm of opposition erupted from interest groups concerned about Bork's conservative philosophy. Bork's position on abortion, civil rights, and criminal justice issues set off an extensive interest-group campaign to defeat the nomination, which was viewed as a "swing seat" on the Court and would have major impact on the shaping of the law.[23] Bork's supporters and opponents waged a public relations war over the confirmation, resulting in one of the ugliest confirmation battles in modern times. Bork's ultimate rejection by the Senate created a new term in American politics: **"borking"** a nomination, which is the attempt to defeat the confirmation of a high-ranking official on ideological grounds.

The nomination of Clarence Thomas in 1991 led to another example of confirmation warfare, first over Thomas's conservative views and later over allegations that he had sexually harassed a female employee when he was the chairman of the Equal Employment Opportunity Commission in the 1980s. The Judiciary Committee held a weekend of nationally televised hearings to examine the harassment charges levied by University of Oklahoma law professor Anita Hill. Ultimately, the Senate voted to confirm Thomas, but by the narrowest margin in the twentieth century.[24] The Thomas confirmation illustrates the heightened conflict between the president and the Senate over nominees and the intense media scrutiny and frenzy that are so much a part of the process, particularly when a vacancy could swing the ideological majority on the Court.

The controversy over Supreme Court confirmations varies with the perceived importance of the nomination. The Bork and Thomas nominations were important to many people because of the likely impact these nominees would have on the Court. Supporters of abortion and other liberal causes were concerned that an increasingly conservative Supreme Court could jeopardize Supreme Court precedents established during the 1960s and 1970s. By the time Bill Clinton named Ruth Bader Ginsberg and Stephen Breyer, the Supreme Court had already made an ideological shift to the right. Neither Ginsberg nor Breyer was as liberal as Bork and Thomas were conservative. Consequently, Clinton's nominees were unlikely to have the same impact. As a result, they were relatively uncontroversial. The fact that Clinton had a Democratic majority in the Senate and nominated moderate judges to the Court did not hurt either.

The retirement of Sandra Day O'Connor and then the death of Chief Justice William Rehnquist gave President George W. Bush the first Supreme Court vacancies to fill in over eleven years. It was widely expected that Bush's choices would be controversial and spark a political battle like the ones that had occurred during the Bork and Thomas confirmations. John Roberts, the initial choice to fill O'Connor's seat, was somewhat to the right of O'Connor, but the record of his writings and his short term on the bench made it hard to fully characterize his ideology. This lack of clarity, along with his impeccable academic and work credentials, helps explain why Roberts's nomination failed to generate the political opposition that was expected in the weeks leading up to his confirmation hearings. The inability of Democrats and liberal interest groups to generate sufficient opposition to Roberts's nomination probably played a large part in the president's decision to elevate Roberts to the position of chief justice when William H. Rehnquist died on September 3, 2005. During Roberts's confirmation hearings, Senate Democrats tried to attack the nominee's ideological positions but were mostly frustrated by his unwillingness to directly answer questions that he would likely decide as a justice. In the end, the Roberts nomination sailed through the Judiciary Committee, and the full Senate confirmed him by a vote of 78–22.

A few days after Roberts was confirmed as chief justice, President Bush named his personal lawyer and White House Counsel Harriet Miers to fill Justice O'Connor's seat. The Miers nomination was a surprise, in that Bush selected someone with no previous judicial experience and little public record to serve as a guide to her likely position on issues before the Court. Miers spent most of her career in private law practice before coming to the Bush White House in 2001, and other than a short stint on the Texas Lottery Commission and two years on the Dallas, Texas, City Council, she had no political experience. It was also a surprise that Bush named a close personal friend in the wake of charges of cronyism that plagued the Bush White House in 2005 after the fiasco with the Federal Emergency Management Agency in the aftermath of Hurricane Katrina. Miers's nomination ran into unexpected opposition from conservative interest groups and from conservative Republican senators, who were upset with the president for not naming someone with a clear conservative record and more solid credentials. Members of the Judiciary Committee were also concerned with her unwillingness to provide meaningful answers to the committee's questionnaire used to aid the confirmation process and the White House's refusal to turn over records from her tenure as White House Counsel. In light of the controversy over her nomination, Miers withdrew her name from consideration on October 27, 2005.

Selecting Lower Court Judges

In addition to Supreme Court justices, the president is also responsible for appointing judges to the U.S. district courts and to the U.S. courts of appeals. A president is presented with few opportunities to name Supreme Court justices, but he appoints lower federal judges throughout his tenure in office. The formal process for these appointments is the same as for selecting Supreme Court justices (the president nominates, and the Senate provides advice and consent through confirmation), but there are substantial differences in the practice of appointing lower court judges.

The president usually delegates responsibility for selecting lower court nominees to officials in the Justice Department, although presidents Reagan, Bush, and Clinton have had White House involvement in the process. Reagan and Bush were particularly interested in shaping a conservative judiciary through their judicial nominees. President Clinton created a Judicial Selection Group to oversee judicial nominations. Headed by the White House counsel, the group included Justice Department officials and members of the White House staff.[25] Even with tighter White House control of the selection process, there are still several pressures that influence the president's selection.

The most important factor in determining the selection of lower court judges is **senatorial courtesy.** It is a long-standing tradition that senators of the president's party are given considerable leverage in the process of selecting judges from their state. Senators will submit lists of potential judicial candidates to the White House, sometimes a list with only one name on it. Although the president does not have to accept a senator's recommendation, the senator can hold up the confirmation process in the Senate if he does not. Senators not from the president's party do not have the same influence as those who are. Yet the president may still consider the individuals sought by an opposition party senator out of a desire to build goodwill with the senator, which the president can use on other legislative matters.

Both senators and presidents view lower court judgeships as opportunities for political reward. Most of the individuals who become federal judges have been involved in partisan politics and personally know the senators who sponsor them. Individuals will actively campaign for a judgeship to a much greater degree than will candidates for the Supreme Court. Historically, the confirmation of lower court judges received very little public attention. The vast majority of nominees were confirmed after a brief hearing by the Judiciary Committee and a vote by the full Senate.

During the Clinton years, however, the process of selecting lower court judges ran into a stumbling block. Clinton's poor relations with the Republican-controlled Senate resulted in a slowing down in the process of selecting judges. The Senate Judiciary Committee refused to move many Clinton nominations from committee to the Senate floor. The tables were turned during George W. Bush's presidency. Bush was determined to make an imprint on the federal appellate judiciary by naming staunch conservatives to the courts of appeals. He established a judicial selection committee to screen potential nominees, who must have impeccable conservative credentials to be considered.[26] The result was that in 2001 and 2002, Senate Democrats used their majority in the Senate to slow down consideration of the most controversial of Bush nominees. Once the Republicans regained a majority in 2003, Democrats continued to block ten nominees, whom they considered to be extremists, by threatening to use the filibuster, as described in the introduction to Chapter 9.

Although the Democrats allowed most Bush nominees to go forward (thirty-six were confirmed), the political battle came to a head in 2005, when Bush renominated seven of the ten judges who had been blocked during the president's first term. In January 2005, Senate Majority Leader Bill Frist (R-Tenn.) said that he would move to prevent Democratic-led filibusters by changing the rules of the Senate to require only a simple majority (from the current three-fifths majority) to end debate. The proposed rule change was called the "nuclear option" option because of the potentially catastrophic results the change would have for both sides in future confirmations. The fight over the nuclear option continued until May 2005, when a compromise was struck by a group of fourteen senators—led by John McCain (R-Ariz.) and Ben Nelson (D-Neb.)—preserving the right of the minority to filibuster, but promising not to use it except for the most extreme cases. As a result, the Senate quickly moved to confirm judges Priscilla Owens, Janice Brown, and William Pryor.

The Supreme Court and American Politics

Even though it only hears between 1 and 2 percent of the total number of cases filed in federal and state courts each year, the cases decided by the Supreme Court are quite important because they establish authoritative interpretations of the U.S. Constitution and federal law. Much of the Supreme Court's work involves the power of judicial review, which gives the Court the ability to invalidate federal and state laws that it determines are in conflict with the U.S. Constitution. This is a considerable power—the specific use of which has remained controversial since the Supreme Court first exercised it in *Marbury v. Madison*—because the Constitution is silent about whether the Supreme Court possesses judicial review.

The Development of Judicial Power

Read *Federalist* No. 78.

The first source we have to help determine what the Framers of the Constitution intended for the Supreme Court is *The Federalist Papers*. Alexander Hamilton's *Federalist* **No. 78** provides the most comprehensive argument for judicial review and the Constitution. Hamilton argued that the judiciary should be the least feared branch of government because it is "least dangerous to the political rights of the Constitution. The judiciary does not have power over either the sword or the purse." The judiciary cannot enforce its decisions. It relies on the executive and legislative branches to carry them out. Moreover, Hamilton argued that the judiciary "can be said to have neither force nor will but merely judgment."

Hamilton argued that an independent judiciary with judicial review is essential to a limited Constitution. Only courts can ensure that the limitations of the Constitution are enforced. Hamilton argued that no one could trust the legislature or the executive to place limits on its own powers. But the members of the judiciary can be trusted because they have neither force nor will. They cannot abuse their powers. The courts must rely on the other branches to enforce their decisions. Hamilton assumed that courts would exercise judicial review, but this power was not self-evident to the early Supreme Court. Indeed, the Supreme Court did not first exercise judicial review of a federal law until 1803, when it decided the case of *Marbury v. Madison.*[27]

In *Marbury v. Madison,* the Supreme Court invalidated part of the Judiciary Act of 1789. When the Supreme Court struck down its own power to grant writs of mandamus, the Court claimed that it possessed the power of judicial review—the ability to declare a law unconstitutional and thus null and void. *Marbury* was important because the decision was self-implementing. For the Court to exercise judicial review, it would normally require the executive branch to carry the decision into effect. Yet by nullifying a law that gave power only to the Supreme Court, *Marbury* avoided the possibility of having the president refuse to comply with the Court's order. The brilliance of the decision is that John Marshall exercised judicial review in a case that did not require enforcement by the other branches. In declaring that the Court had the power of judicial review, Marshall took away a small amount of judicial power (that of mandamus) to gain a much larger judicial power (judicial review).

"Marbury v. Madison, Rightly Understood," Peter Schotten.

Chief Justice Marshall was declaring to the nation that the Supreme Court would be a player in American politics. The Court would assume its position as the third independent and equal branch of government. Ultimately, the decision has been given legitimacy by Americans over time. We accept that the Supreme Court has the power of judicial review. Marshall played a large role in legitimizing judicial review because for the remainder of his long tenure on the Court, he never again invalidated a federal law. He never put the Supreme Court in a position where the Congress or the president would be likely to ignore a decision. Instead, he let the idea of judicial review percolate with the American people, slowly gaining legitimacy.

Read Chief Justice Marshall's opinion in *Marbury v. Madison.*

Marshall was more than willing, however, to exercise judicial review over state laws. This was never as controversial, given the Constitution's declaration in Article VI that it was the "Supreme Law of the Land." Throughout the first half of the nineteenth century, the Court regularly examined state laws that conflicted with provisions of the Constitution. Probably the two most important decisions the Court handed down were *McCulloch v. Maryland* (1819) and *Gibbons v. Ogden* (1824), dealing with interpretations of the commerce clause and the necessary and proper clause.[28] (Both cases are covered in Chapter 3.) The Marshall Court consistently interpreted the U.S. Constitution to advance national power over state power.

Read *McCulloch v. Maryland.*

The Supreme Court did not use judicial review to invalidate another federal law until 1857, when it decided *Dred Scott v. Sanford.*[29] In this case, the Court struck down the Missouri Compromise of 1820, which played a critical role in maintaining the fragile balance between free and slave states. Ironically, the Court thought its decision would put an end to the sectional conflict between the states; in reality, it was a catalyst for civil war. The *Scott* decision was disastrous for the Court's attempts to solidify its legitimacy.

Read *Gibbons v. Ogden.*

In the decades after the Civil War, the Supreme Court began a fifty-year period of intense interest in the regulation of economic activity by the federal and state governments. By the end of the nineteenth century, the Court routinely used judicial review to invalidate state efforts to regulate the economy. The majority of justices on the Court interpreted the Constitution as embodying a philosophy of laissez-faire capitalism—the view that government should have a minimal role in regulating markets. Between 1898 and 1937, the Court invalidated more than 200 state and federal laws.

The Court had entered the first great activist period in its history. Although many of its decisions were controversial, the Court did not face a challenge to its legitimacy until the 1930s, when during the Great Depression, it found itself faced with interpreting the New Deal legislation of President Franklin Roosevelt.

The Supreme Court's activist use of judicial review to invalidate the New Deal resulted in a firestorm of controversy for the Court. President Roosevelt viewed the Court as an institution hopelessly out of touch with society's needs, and he proposed a "court-packing" plan to increase the size of the Court. This would enable Roosevelt to appoint several additional justices, tipping the Court's majority in favor of New Deal legislation. The court-packing plan enjoyed neither public nor congressional support, and the justices of the Supreme Court saw it for the threat it was. In early 1937, the Supreme Court saw a switch in its majority and began to uphold New Deal legislation. The decisions in the cases of *NLRB v. Jones and Laughlin Steel* and *West Coast Hotel v. Parrish*[30] were made before Roosevelt's court-packing plan, but they were publicly released after the plan had been announced. As a result, the Court was said to have made a "switch in time that saved nine." Within five years, the Court completely removed itself from invalidating any economic regulations.

The period after the New Deal saw the Supreme Court struggle to find a new role for itself. After fifty years of being a champion for conservative economic policies, the Court had completely changed its approach to economic regulations. As more and more Roosevelt justices were appointed (eight were appointed between 1937 and 1945), the Court's majority took on a philosophy that was considerably more deferential to majoritarian democracy, and it was less willing to strike down laws passed by Congress. For a brief period at mid-century, the Court seemed determined to practice restraint in exercising judicial review.

By the early 1950s, the Supreme Court found itself facing several important cases involving civil rights and liberties. After the appointment of Earl Warren as chief justice in 1953, the Court began the second great period of judicial activism, this time involving civil rights and liberties cases. The **Warren Court** decided numerous cases that would expand the rights of the individual. Landmark decisions on equal protection, freedom of speech, establishment and free exercise of religion, voting rights, and the rights of the accused consistently expanded the individual's rights in relationship to the government. The Supreme Court also began to extend

MARBURY V. MADISON *AND THE BIRTH OF JUDICIAL REVIEW*

Marbury v. Madison is probably the most important decision the Supreme Court ever rendered. *Marbury* can be understood only within the context of the partisan struggle between the Federalists and Democratic-Republicans in the 1800 election. Thomas Jefferson won the presidency in 1800, and his party gained control of both chambers of Congress. The Federalists were desperate to retain some grip on government and used the lame-duck session of Congress after the election of 1800 to seize political control of the judiciary.

First, when the chief justice resigned, President John Adams nominated his secretary of state, the ardent Federalist John Marshall, to the post. The outgoing Senate quickly confirmed the nomination, but Marshall continued to function as secretary of state until Jefferson's inauguration. Second, Congress

Stock Montage/Getty Images

Known as the Great Chief Justice, John Marshall was the third chief justice of the United States, serving from 1801 to 1835. Marshall wrote the opinions of the Court in such cases as *Marbury v. Madison, McCulloch v. Maryland,* and *Gibbons v. Ogden.*

passed the Judiciary Act of 1801, which created six circuit courts and several district courts. In addition, the act reduced the size of the Supreme Court to five justices effective upon the next resignation on the court. This would deny Jefferson an appointment to the Court. Finally, Congress passed the Organic Act of 1801, creating forty-two justice of the peace positions for the new District of Columbia.

In the closing months of his administration, Adams nominated Federalists to fill all the new positions. The Federalist justices of the peace were confirmed in the last days before Jefferson's inauguration. For the new judges to take the bench, Secretary of State Marshall had to attest that they were properly appointed by signing "commissions"

(continued)

for each one. Marshall had the commissions drawn up, the president signed them, and Marshall affixed the Great Seal of the United States on them. But in the chaotic last days of the Adams administration, he failed to deliver seventeen of the forty-two commissions.

Upon Jefferson's inauguration, the new secretary of state, James Madison, discovered the undelivered commissions. Jefferson ordered Madison not to deliver them. If the commissions were not delivered, the Federalist judges could not take their positions on the bench.

William Marbury was one of the justice of the peace appointees who did not receive his commission. He filed a suit in the Supreme Court requesting that the Court order Madison to deliver the commission. The Judiciary Act of 1789 provided the Court with the ability to issue "writs of mandamus" to order governmental officials to carry out their legal responsibilities.

Marbury v. Madison was decided two years later. The case posed a serious dilemma for Chief Justice Marshall. If he ordered Madison to deliver the commission, Jefferson would most likely ignore the order. This would weaken the court and damage its legitimacy. Marshall wanted to find a way to transform the Court into a major player in American politics. If the Court's order were ignored, this would not achieve that goal. Given that the Court had no enforcement powers, it was a likely outcome. The dilemma was made even more difficult given Marshall's other option. If he refused to order Madison to deliver the commission to Marbury, it would be an even clearer victory for Jefferson and a defeat for the Court. Thus, on first look, *Marbury* appears to present a no-win situation to Marshall. It seems that Marshall will lose no matter how he rules.

Marshall wrote an opinion that skirted both no-win scenarios. He transformed the case into an opportunity to firmly assert a strong role for the Court in American politics. How did he do this? First, Marshall began asserting in no uncertain terms that Marbury had been wronged, as he had been properly appointed to the position. Marshall chastised Jefferson for not delivering the commissions, but this was only a slap on the wrist. Marshall then asked, "Could the Court order Madison and Jefferson to comply?" No. Marshall refused to issue the writ of mandamus to Madison because the Court lacked authority to do so. Marshall argued that the Court didn't have this power. The law that gave the Court the power to

(continued)

MARBURY V. MADISON *AND THE BIRTH OF JUDICIAL REVIEW (Contd.)*

issue writs of mandamus was unconstitutional because Congress had given the Court a power that was not specified in the Constitution. Marshall argued that the Court had to strike down the law; otherwise, the Constitution would cease to be a limited form of government. Either the Constitution limits what Congress can do, or Congress can disregard the Constitution. If the Constitution does not define Congress's powers, it is a contradiction and is not a permanent fundamental law.

When faced with upholding an unconstitutional law or disregarding the law, Marshall argued that he would disregard—or nullify—the law. In doing so, he exercised the power of judicial review. Marshall argued that it was uniquely the responsibility of the Supreme Court to exercise judicial review because only the Court could keep the other branches within the limits of the Constitution. In his most famous words, "it is emphatically the province and duty of the judicial department to say what the law is."

individual rights in areas such as personal privacy, which are not found in the text of the Constitution.

By the early 1970s, after the Court had liberalized the law of criminal procedure and had invalidated the abortion laws of more than forty states, conservative politicians began to criticize the Court for being too liberal and ignoring the strict interpretation of the Constitution in its decisions. President Richard Nixon sought to name justices who would slow down the Court's expansion of individual rights. Nixon had mixed success in his appointments, but by the 1980s, the Supreme Court would begin a major shift to the right. After presidents Reagan and Bush were able to name a majority of the justices to the Court, it began to whittle away at the liberal decisions of the Warren and Burger courts in the areas of criminal procedure and equal protection. By the 1990s, the Court began to limit the Congress's power to regulate aspects of the economy, invalidating federal laws under the commerce clause for the first time since the 1940s.[31] At the same time, the Court has not abandoned the field of civil liberties. It has expanded its free speech decisions to include speech on the Internet and has continued to uphold most of the religious freedom doctrines.

The most recent controversy over the Court's legitimacy came at the end of the presidential election of 2000. On December 12, 2000, the Supreme Court handed down the decision in *Bush v. Gore,* ordering an end to the recount of the vote ordered by the Florida Supreme Court ruling in a 5 to 4 *per*

The Role of Personality, Stare Decisis, and Liberty in Constitutional Construction," Robert S. Peck.

curium decision, stating that the Florida recount violated the equal protection clause.[32] The Court's decision was sharply divided, and legal scholars viewed the reasoning within it as flawed. Acting along what appeared to be clearly ideological lines, the Court secured the electoral college victory for George W. Bush. In doing so, it created controversy over its own legitimacy. The threat to the Court's legitimacy played out in the politics of the first nine months of George W. Bush's presidency, but largely disappeared after the nation's attention turned to the war on terrorism after September 11, 2001.

Debates over the Appropriate Role for the Court

"The Supreme Court and US Presidential Election of 2000: Wounds, Self-Inflicted or Otherwise?" James L. Gibson, Gregory A. Caldeira, and Lester Kenyatta Spence.

This brief overview of the development of judicial power since *Marbury v. Madison* illustrates an important debate about the role of the Court in American politics. How actively should justices of the Supreme Court exercise judicial review? To what degree should they be willing to strike down actions of a popular majority? In *Roe v. Wade*, the Court invalidated the laws of more than forty states when it established a woman's right to abortion.[33] We may disagree with the Court's decision, but *Roe v. Wade* illustrates the antidemocratic character of judicial review. In the past twenty-five years, a debate has waged between advocates of **judicial activism** and **judicial restraint.** Judicial activists argue that Supreme Court justices must be willing to make decisions that are contrary to the majority's will because the democratic process does not always result in decisions that protect individual rights and liberties. *Lawrence v. Texas* nicely illustrates this, for many Americans are opposed to expanding the rights of gays and lesbians. The Supreme Court has a special role to ensure individual rights. Proponents of judicial restraint recognize that although judicial review is sometimes necessary, the Supreme Court should be very restrained in exercising it. Judicial restraint and deference to majority rule are necessary because Supreme Court justices are not elected and are accountable to the people only through impeachment.

Is Judicial Activism Democratic?

At first glance, unelected judges striking down actions of popular majorities seems inherently undemocratic. It is if democracy is defined simply as majority rule, but if democracy is defined as majority rule plus protection of individual rights, it may not be. If we recognize that we do not really have a democratic government—we have a representative government—the limitations that judicial activism (and judicial review) place on the majority are not that extraordinary. The Constitution places many limitations on the majority. Judicial review is simply another check on the power of majorities.

Many argue that it is necessary for the Court to practice judicial activism to guarantee individual liberties, particularly when faced with a legislative majority that is hostile to particular freedoms. They state that the Supreme Court may be the only protector of our liberties. How else do we stop a legislative majority from trampling the rights of minorities? But it is a mistake to think that the Court will always be protective of individual rights. The Court's history is replete with examples illustrating this, including such notorious cases as *Dred Scott v. Sanford, Plessey v. Ferguson,* and *U.S. v. Korematsu.*[34]

The debate over the proper use of judicial review continues to the present. Today, the Supreme Court is dominated by political conservatives seeking to undo many of the activist decisions of the Warren and Burger courts of the 1950s, 1960s, and 1970s. Yet the same justices who profess a desire to return to judicial restraint do not hesitate in engaging in a form of judicial activism designed to limit the federal government's powers to regulate the economy and to restore earlier notions of dual federalism (see Chapter 3). These justices speak of practicing judicial restraint, but they are no less activist than the justices of the Warren and Burger courts they criticize.

The Court and Public Policy

By its very nature, the Supreme Court makes public policy. When the Court interprets the Constitution and statutes, it makes law that has consequences for all American citizens. Yet the Court does not make public policy in a vacuum. For its decisions to be implemented by the president, Congress, and states, it is critical that the Court be viewed as a legitimate institution. John Marshall realized this when he was faced with the dilemma of *Marbury v. Madison.* One hundred fifty years later, the justices of the Supreme Court realized this when they handed down the landmark decision in *Brown v. Board of Education,* ruling that segregation of public schools in the American South is an unconstitutional violation of the Fourteenth Amendment equal protection clause. In the *Brown* case, the Court encountered substantial resistance to its decision from not only the South, but also from the president and Congress. Indeed, it took well over a decade before desegregation would occur on a widespread basis throughout the South. And even then, Congress's passage of the Civil Rights Act of 1964, empowering the Department of Justice to force desegregation, was critical (see Chapter 4).

Most Supreme Court decisions, however, are not like *Marbury* or *Brown* and are complied with by the other branches. Occasionally, a controversial Supreme Court decision will result in attempts to overrule it by a constitutional amendment, although even then the decision will be enforced in the interim. When the Court struck down a Texas conviction for flag burning in 1989,[35] ruling that Texas had violated the protestor's right to freedom of speech, a huge controversy arose in Congress. Since the decision was handed down, several constitutional amendments have been proposed to overturn the Court's decision by prohibiting flag burning. Although none of these amendments has received the necessary two-thirds majority in each chamber of Congress to be sent to the states for ratification, the effort indicates that the other branches will not always simply accept the Supreme Court's decision without a fight. Yet Congress can more easily overturn statutory interpretations, and it often does.

The political branches may not always be happy with Supreme Court decisions, but other groups in society often view the Supreme Court as a last resort to achieve policy outcomes that cannot be accomplished through the political process. Interest groups often look for favorable rulings from the Supreme Court to accomplish important policy goals. Perhaps one of the greatest examples of interest-group politics designed to influence constitutional law was the NAACP Legal Defense Fund's attack on segregation from the 1930s until the Court's final decision in *Brown* in 1954. Environmental groups have used litigation in trying to force strict executive branch enforcement of the nation's clean air and water laws. Conservative and liberal civil liberties groups have asked the Court to broaden protection of civil rights and liberties. Interest-group litigation can be viewed as one of the ways that American citizens can seek constitutional or legal change through their associational memberships. We saw this in *Lawrence v. Texas*, when advocates for gay and lesbian rights sponsored Lawrence and Garner's fight against Texas's homosexual sodomy law.

Conclusion: The Least Dangerous Branch?

Check here for possible post-publication updates to the chapter material.

Federal courts play an important role in the separation of powers as a check on the majoritarian branches of government. Courts can also be used by interest groups to try to achieve what the democratic process cannot achieve or to overturn decisions of the majority that limit minority rights. Yet the Supreme Court's use of judicial review remains controversial as a means of making public policy because of the counter-majoritarian nature of a majority of nine unelected judges overruling the decisions of a popular majority. Hamilton's argument that the Supreme Court is the least dangerous branch is debatable today, some 210 years after he wrote *Federalist No. 78*. We cannot discount the role that the Supreme Court and the federal courts have played as a check on the majority at key moments throughout the history of the American Republic.

Key Terms

civil cases 339
plaintiff 339
defendant 340
criminal cases 340
complainant 340
behavior modification 340
law 340
statutes 341
treaties 341
administrative rules/
    regulations 341
executive orders 341

precedent 341
constitutional law 341
statutory interpretation 341
common law 341
stare decisis 342
judicial review 342
Judiciary Act of 1789 343
U.S. District Courts 343
U.S. Magistrate
    Judges 344
U.S. Circuit Courts of
    Appeals 344

appeals 344
briefs 344
oral argument 345
precedent 345
U.S. Court of Appeals for the
    Federal Circuit 346
Supreme Court 346
writ of certiorari 348
rule of four 348
Office of the Solicitor
    General 350
amicus curiae 350

American Civil Liberties
    Union 350
majority opinion 351
concurring opinion 351
dissenting opinion 351

judicial independence 352
borking 357
senatorial courtesy 359
Marbury v. Madison 360
Federalist No. 78 360

Warren Court 362
Bush v. Gore 365
judicial activism 366
judicial restraint 366

Suggested Web Resources

The following links will take you to sites relating to the Supreme Court and the judicial branch. You can find other resources by using Web directories, such as Yahoo or Google.

The U.S. Supreme Court website (http://www.supremecourtus.gov) includes access to the current workload of the Court and to all of the Court's decisions since 2000. The site also includes information about the Court's schedule (docket), as well as information for the tourist interested in visiting the Court.

Although the Supreme Court created its website only in 2000, it had been using the Internet since 1989 (even before the creation of the World Wide Web) to distribute full-text versions of its decisions. The Cornell Law School's Legal Information Institute (http://www.law.cornell.edu) has maintained an excellent archive of Supreme Court decisions (http://supct.law.cornell.edu/supct) since 1989, plus access to a historical database of most of the Court's major decisions dating back to 1789.

Perhaps one of the best websites on the Supreme Court is the Oyez! U.S. Supreme Court Multimedia Database (http://oyez.nwu.edu), which includes access to the actual oral arguments presented before the Court in most of the major cases of the past half-decade. You will need access to

RealPlayer to listen to them, but it is certainly worthwhile to hear the cases as they were argued before the Court. For example, you could listen to the arguments in *Lawrence v. Texas* (http://www.oyez.org/oyez/resource/case/1542/) and then read the actual decision. Oyez! also includes a virtual tour (http://oyez.nwu.edu/tour/index.html) of the Supreme Court building as well as biographical sketches (http://oyez.nwu.edu/justices/justices.cgi) of each of the 109 justices who have served since 1789.

For a more comprehensive set of legal resources, Findlaw.com (http://www.findlaw.com) offers full access to not only all Supreme Court decisions but also those of all federal courts and many state courts as well.

The Administrative Office of U.S. Courts (http://www.uscourts.gov) maintains the official website of the third branch, which provides access to the websites of all the federal courts in addition to a variety of education resources about the judicial system. The Federal Judicial Center (http://www.fjc.gov) is the official research arm of the federal courts, and its website is a valuable resource for anyone studying them. It also includes a wealth of information on the history of the federal court system.

A complete study tool kit is available for this chapter and includes the following:
Flashcards
Crossword Puzzle
Critical Thinking Exercises
Interactive Timelines
Chapter Quiz

12 Politics, Economics, and Public Policy

■ **There and Back Again: Deficits to Surpluses to Deficits** 371

■ **Politics and Policy** 374
The Public Policy Process 374

■ **The Context for Economic Policy Making** 379
Public Expectations for Economic Prosperity
and Their Consequences for Economic Policy 381

■ **Fiscal Policy** 383
The Budget Process 385
Monetary Policy 387

■ **The Politics of Rich and Poor** 390
Income Distribution 390
Wealth and the Widening Gap
Between Rich and Poor 391
Wealth and Income: Why They Matter 393

■ **Conclusion: Policy, Participation, and the Web of Democracy** 396

There and Back Again: Deficits to Surpluses to Deficits

After a bleak period in American history, President Ronald Reagan came to office in 1981 determined to effect a "revolution" in American politics. During the previous decade, the nation's military had been demoralized by its losses in the

President Ronald Reagan holds a dollar bill in his hand during his February 5, 1981, televised address to the nation announcing his economic recovery plan.

Vietnam War; the economy had been hit by high unemployment, skyrocketing inflation, and an energy crisis; and the presidency itself had been tarnished by Watergate. Reagan wanted to set a new course for American public policy. He wanted to strengthen America's defense, he wanted to find a way to end the economic doldrums of the previous six years, and he wanted to shift the focus of governmental authority from the federal government to the states. He embarked on such a course during his first year in office, offering a three-part program.

Reagan asked Congress for large increases in the defense budget to put our military back on course and to provide security in the ongoing Cold War against the Soviet Union. The cost of defense increases would be offset by the savings that Reagan hoped to gain from equally deep cuts in many of the nation's social programs. Reagan proposed reducing the federal budget. He also wanted to turn much of the fiscal responsibility for social programs over to the states. Finally, his economic program included a large tax cut that heavily favored high-income Americans. Reagan was influenced by the theory known as **supply-side economics.** By giving wealthy Americans large tax breaks, they would be encouraged to use their higher after-tax incomes to invest in the economy. Large-scale investment capital would enable businesses to grow, and their success would "trickle down" through the economy to all Americans.

In practice, Reagan's revolution did not work out exactly as he had hoped. Defense spending rose significantly in the early 1980s—increasing by more than 64 percent ($110 billion) from 1981 to 1987—but the offsetting savings from cuts in social programs did not cover the additional costs.[1] Congress was simply unwilling to make the cuts in social programs that Reagan wanted. When the loss in federal revenue that resulted from

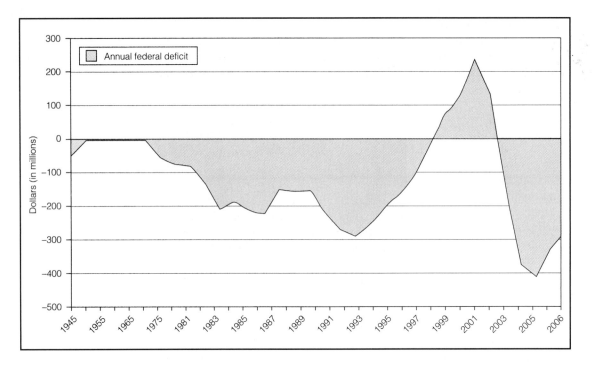

Figure 12.1 Annual Federal Deficit Since 1945

Source: Statistical Abstract of the United States 2004–2005, No. 461, at 308 (retrieved from http://www.census.gov/prod/2004pubs/04statab/fedgov.pdf on June 9, 2005); 2006 data from New York Times; July 12, 2006.

Reagan's tax cut was added to the picture, the result was the beginning of huge federal deficits—where the federal government spends more than it takes in each year.

The federal budget had run a small annual deficit each year since the end of the Johnson administration (see Figure 12.1), but the Reagan-era deficits were much larger in comparison. The nation had a $47-billion deficit in 1945; by 1950, the deficit had shrunk to $3 billion. Beginning in the 1970s, however, annual deficits began rising again. In 1981, Reagan's first year in office, the deficit was roughly $75 billion. By 1990, it had risen to $220 billion. The increased annual deficits led to a rise in the total national debt—the combined totals of all annual deficits. Since 1980, the national debt has grown from $909 billion to $7.8 trillion in 2005.[2]

Much of the national public policy debate in the past twenty years has concerned solving the ongoing problem of the federal deficit, which places severe limits on the federal government's ability to fund new programs in addition to ever-increasing debt financing. The problem of the deficit preoccupied national politics until 1999, when the unprecedented economic expansion of the 1990s resulted in an influx of federal revenues that not

Learn more about the politics of deficits and surpluses.

only eliminated the deficit but created a budget surplus. Met with this booming economy, the federal government took in more than it spent for the next four consecutive fiscal years, resulting in a record-breaking surplus of $236.2 billion in the year 2000.[3] Economists projected surpluses for years to come.

The new age of budget surpluses was not to last, however. The events of the first years of the new millennium resulted in a resurgence of even larger budget deficits than existed in the 1980s and 1990s, reaching an all-time high of $412 billion in 2004.[4] It is not yet clear what will happen to the deficit in years to come. In July 2005, the Bush administration announced that the combination of increased federal revenues, a stronger economy, and the expiration of a temporary tax break for corporations resulted in a significant drop in the deficit in 2005 to an estimated $325 million.[5] Continued increases in federal tax revenues, mostly in the form of corporate taxes, have brought the deficit down to an estimated $296 billion for 2006.[6]

There is no single reason for the resurgence of deficits, but much can be explained by three factors: the passage of two major tax cuts in 2001 and 2003, the economic recession of 2001 and the economic impact of the terrorist attacks of 9/11, and the mounting costs of the war on terrorism and the war in Iraq. During his first term in office, President George W. Bush passed two major tax cuts through Congress. The first was the Economic Growth and Tax Reconciliation Act of 2001, a ten-year, $1.3-trillion tax cut.[7] In 2003 Congress passed the Jobs and Growth Tax Relief Reconciliation Act, which accelerated many of the changes to the tax code implemented by the 2001 act and lowered taxes on income from dividends and capital gains. The Bush tax cuts reflected the "supply side" economic theory that President Reagan had relied upon in the early 1980s. Both acts heavily benefited high-income taxpayers. Those with more than one $1 million in income saw an average tax cut of $59,000, while most Americans saw very modest or no tax relief at all from the new tax law.[8] The loss of federal revenue from these acts has largely been funded with increased federal borrowing. The Congressional Budget Office calculated the impact of the tax cuts to be a $340-billion addition to the 2003 federal deficit.[9]

A second reason for the increased annual federal deficit is the economic recession that began in early 2001. An economic slowdown began following the investment collapse in the technology and "dot-com" industries in the year 2000. Partly responsible for this collapse were higher energy prices and six interest-rate increases between 1999 and 2000. Higher energy costs cut into corporate and family budgets, and the increased interest rates made borrowing less attractive. In turn, the slowdown led to a manufacturing and production recession as companies tried to eliminate stockpiles of unsold goods. The nation's economic troubles were only compounded by the terrorist strikes on New York and Washington in 2001. The 9/11 attacks resulted in cutbacks in travel and hurt consumer confidence. Together, the economic recession and 9/11 resulted in lower federal tax revenues, forcing more spending to be financed through deficits.

Finally, the war on terrorism launched after the 9/11 attacks and the ongoing American military involvement in Afghanistan and Iraq have both played a substantial role in the resurgence of the deficit. Currently, the U.S. government is spending an estimated $1.63 billion per day to fund these conflicts. Military spending and funding are at an all-time high, as the wars have cost the government nearly $277 billion since 2001. In addition, the U.S. government has increased its own operating size by creating anti-terrorism agencies, such as the Department of Homeland Security. Such agencies have created yet another strain on federal spending. For fiscal year 2005, a supplemental war appropriation of nearly $80 billion was requested to fund the fighting in both Iraq and Afghanistan.[10]

Politics and Policy

The choices that the president and Congress need to make in deciding how to eliminate the federal deficit are indicative of the problems involved in economic policy making. The previous chapters have discussed the institutions, political processes, and structure of American politics. In this chapter, *The Web of Democracy* examines how these institutions and agents interact to craft economic policy—that is, what government does to affect the growth and development of the American economy. **Public policy** can be understood as "what government does." Public policy consists of the decisions that government makes and the programs that it enacts. It is the result of the political process.

Policy can be a law that Congress passes, a rule made by an administrative agency, or a decision that a court hands down. Policy can affect all of us or only a few of us. We know that Congress has power to make laws, that the president executes them, and that the judiciary interprets them. But policy decisions do not occur in a vacuum. When the government passes laws, it enacts policies, which are approaches to dealing with an issue in a deliberate and organized way. Policy may be made haphazardly, but it usually develops over a period of time in an incremental fashion, with the government making a series of small changes. Wholesale, nonincremental change is possible, but it is unusual given the nature of the policy process itself.

The Public Policy Process

Public policy making can be understood as a constantly occurring multi-step process. Policy making begins with **agenda setting,** in which problems needing governmental action are identified and prioritized. Not all public issues become part of the government agenda. There are always more potential problems to solve than there are societal resources to solve them. The government's agenda is always changing as new problems are identified and given priority. Some issues remain on the government's agenda for long periods of time, whereas others are on the agenda for a short time and then fade away.

Issues are placed on the policy agenda through a number of avenues. A crisis or major event may bring an issue to the government's attention. For example, in 1989, when the *Exxon Valdez* oil tanker ran aground off the shore of Alaska and spilled millions of gallons of crude oil into Prince William Sound, concern for the environment made a quick rise to the top of the nation's agenda. A crisis with a more lasting impact on the public agenda was the 9/11 terrorist strikes. These events immediately put terrorism on the top of the nation's agenda, where it has largely remained since 2001. Other issues come to the agenda through a "gradual accumulation of knowledge and perspectives among specialists in a given policy arena."[11] New scientific knowledge may push an issue onto the agenda. Over the last several years, scientific development in the area of cloning and genetics has caused government to begin to grapple with the ethical implications of genetic manipulation. When the subject had been purely theoretical, it was not on government's agenda, but once technology made the possibility of human cloning possible, the need for action became more pressing.

"Setting an Agenda for Local Action: The Limits of Expert Opinion and Community Voice," Diana Silver, Beth Weitzman, and Charles Brecher.

Citizens and interest groups can affect the government's agenda by making demands for governmental action. Interest groups continually push elected officials to deal with specific issues—gun control, abortion rights, or the high cost of gasoline. Sometimes, pressure for government action is the result of a court decision. For example, in 2005 the long saga of the Teri Schiavo right-to-die case came to a close amid unusual legislative activity. The Florida courts sided with Schiavo's husband in fulfilling her wishes to be taken off artificial hydration and nutrition, and these rulings resulted in a brief but intensive campaign to get Congress to pass emergency legislation to restore her feeding tube. In an extraordinary session, pressured by Christian conservatives, Congress passed legislation entitling Schiavo's parents to a federal court hearing. Interest groups sometimes pressure the president to follow through with campaign promises. A classic example was in the 1960 election, when John F. Kennedy promised that by signing an executive order he could end racial discrimination in federal housing through "the stroke of a pen." After winning the election narrowly, Kennedy hesitated in carrying out his promise because he was concerned with losing his party's support in the South. When the first year of his presidency ended and Kennedy had not fulfilled his promise, civil rights advocates began mailing him pens by the thousands. Eventually, in response to these actions, the president signed the executive order.

Pressure politics can also be used to try to keep issues off the agenda, as is the case with the National Rifle Association. The NRA has fought hard

Randall Terry, head of the conservative group Society for Truth and Justice, throws his arms in the air during a news conference on October 16, 2003, outside a hospice where Terri Schiavo was a patient in Pinellas Park, Florida. Schiavo had been in a persistent vegetative state following a heart attack in 1990. Her feeding tube was removed the previous day.

to defeat federal gun control legislation. It prefers a federal policy eliminating gun control. The NRA continually pressures elected officials either to vote against gun control proposals or not to allow them to be considered in the first place. The tobacco industry was successful for decades in keeping antitobacco legislation from seeing the light of day. Part of the debate of agenda setting is also focused on defining what is and what is not an appropriate problem for government to solve.

Once an issue makes it on the agenda, the process of **policy formulation** and selection among various policy alternatives begins. Agenda setting begins the policy process by making the claim that government must "do something" about an issue. Policy formulation begins to sort out what government should do and how it should achieve its goals. Policy making would be simplified if it occurred as a form of rational decision making in which policy makers "define their goals rather clearly and then set the level of achievement of those goals that would satisfy them." Policy makers would then consider all of the alternatives to achieve goals, systematically compare the choices, and then "choose the alternatives that would achieve their goals at the least cost."[12]

Ample political science research demonstrates that the reality of policy making is far from a pure cost-benefit determination. In most areas, policy formulation can best be described by the term **incrementalism.** Charles Lindblom has argued that policy makers "muddle through" the policy process by using current practices and policies as a baseline and then make only "small incremental, marginal adjustments in that current behavior." By taking small steps, government is able to effect changes in a particular policy area over time without having to wipe the slate clean and consider every possible solution to a problem.[13]

As an alternative to incremental policy making, John Kingdon argues that policy formulation can be understood as "solutions looking for problems." Policy making consists of three sets of processes that occur independently and occasionally converge to form policy: "People recognize problems, they generate proposals for public policy change, and they engage in such political activities as election campaigns and pressure group lobbying." At the same time that problems are coming to the attention of government, there are policy specialists working in loosely formed issue networks (see Chapter 7)—bureaucrats within the executive branch, congressional staffers, academic researchers, and interest groups—who generate policy proposals: "They each have their pet ideas or axes to grind; they float their ideas up and the ideas bubble around in these policy communities." Some ideas are ignored, whereas others are further developed.[14] But the key point is that solutions are always being developed, even if a problem is not on the policy agenda.

Kingdon argues that when problems are being identified and solutions developed, the "political stream" is always changing: "The political stream is composed of things like swings of national mood, vagaries of public opinion, election results, changes of administration, shifts in partisan or ideological distributions in Congress, and interest group pressure campaigns."[15] Ultimately, policy formulation comes about through the convergence of these three processes: A problem is identified and makes it to the agenda, a viable solution is available to solve that problem, and the political climate seems right for action, enabling government to act (see Figure 12.2): "Advocates develop their proposals and then wait for problems to come along to which they can attach their solutions, or for a development in the political stream like a change of administration that makes their proposals more likely to be adopted."[16] Policy windows open for short periods of time, when conditions are right for a specific problem and solution to take a high position on the agenda.

A good example of policy windows opening and closing is in relation to the growing problem of obesity in America. As the problem of obesity moved up the policy agenda, government moved to change foods available in schools, the Department of Agriculture revised its "food pyramid," and lawsuits were filed blaming such restaurants as McDonald's of causing obesity through their marketing of fatty and high-calorie meals. With the popularity of "low-carb" diets, such as Atkins and South Beach, a policy window appeared to open, making government more likely to pursue reforms aimed at fighting obesity. This window may have been short-lived, however, as restaurants and food manufacturers have tried to convince us that there is no role for government regulation in this area. These industries argued

Explore the policy process with the Medical Marijuana Debate simulation.

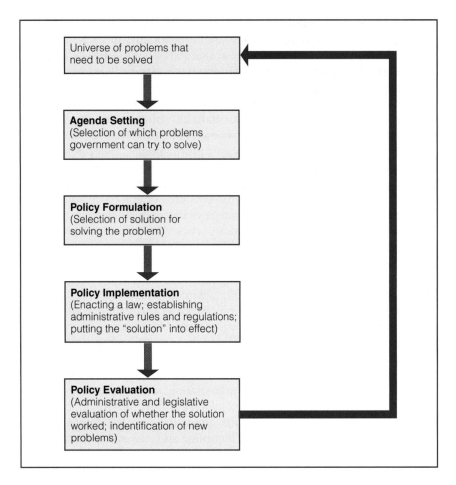

Figure 12.2 The Policy Process

that lawsuits should be banned and that food is a matter of personal choice best left to the market. The food industry has spent millions to persuade Americans that obesity is just hype and not an epidemic.[17]

The policy process is completed with **policy implementation** and **policy evaluation.** Once a law is passed to enact a specific public policy, it must be implemented. Specific agencies are identified and given authority to carry out a policy. Once the policy goes into effect, both formal and informal kinds of assessment and evaluation begin. Did the policy achieve its stated goal? Is it effective? What were the unintended consequences of the policy? The answers to these questions can lead back to the beginning of the policy process if problems are identified that merit placing the issue back on the government's agenda. Here again, citizens and interest groups can affect the policy process by voicing their support or opposition to specific policies. For example, even after Congress enabled satellite television subscribers to receive local channels in major markets, the two primary providers of digital broadcast satellite (DirecTV and DishNetwork) have encouraged their subscribers to write to Congress to eliminate those remaining restrictions on receiving distant broadcast networks.

All aspects of the policy process—agenda setting, policy formulation, implementation, and evaluation—are occurring simultaneously within different policy areas. The agenda is constantly shifting, and new policies are formulated while others are implemented. At the same time that foreign policy decisions are implemented, other policies are formulated in such areas as transportation and nuclear energy, and new issues make their way to the government's agenda. For the rest of this chapter, we turn to a detailed discussion of one policy area: how government attempts to regulate and direct the course of the American economy.

The Context for Economic Policy Making

Regulating the nation's economy is arguably the most important function of the federal government today, even though that task was not anticipated by the Constitution. The Framers of the Constitution were preoccupied with political power. They went into great detail describing the institutions of government. They were more interested in the procedures of governmental decision making than they were in the outcomes of those decisions. This is nowhere more evident than in the area of economic policy.

The Framers were fairly silent when it came to explaining the relationship between the government and economics, even though it was economic conflict that brought about the Constitution in the first place. The Framers were well aware of the economic problems of the 1780s, and they were determined to protect the rights of property owners when designing the Constitution. They gave the government the ability to deal with economic problems—the commerce clause, the power to coin money, and limits on state ability to enter into foreign trade agreements—but they did not attempt to prescribe an economic system in the Constitution, nor did they specify the government's role in maintaining the economy. Nonetheless, the Constitution created an environment favorable to a capitalist economic system by protecting property rights and emphasizing individual liberty.

Capitalism is an economic system based on the principles of a profit motive and private ownership of the means of production. In a capitalist economy, individuals own businesses and try to produce goods and services that can be sold to others in a competitive marketplace. Consumers seek to buy goods and services at the lowest prices, whereas sellers want the highest price the market will bear for their goods. Principles of supply and demand shape economic decisions. When demand for a product is high and supply is low, prices will be high. When the demand drops and supply increases, prices will drop in turn. We often refer to this type of economy as a free market or free enterprise system because private individuals make most of the decisions governing economic transactions.

Americans are committed to free market capitalism. It is deeply rooted in the core American values discussed in Chapter 1. Capitalism flourishes in a society that values individualism, property rights, and liberty. The purest form of capitalism, identified by Adam Smith in *The Wealth of Nations* (1776), envisions an economic system free of any government intervention. In the past two centuries, however, most Americans have come to expect the government to play at least some role in regulating the free market. Without regulation, capitalism is prone to fluctuations between periods of economic prosperity and economic downturn caused by changes in employment and inflation.

During good times, when few people are unemployed, consumers spend more and businesses make greater profits, enabling them to invest profits back into the business. If the economy grows too quickly, there are often fears about rising **inflation,** which results when prices increase faster than wages, decreasing consumer spending power. If inflation increases, the economy will begin to slow, which in turn can cause unemployment to rise. This situation can cause the cycle of "high employment, increased spending, and greater profits" to reverse itself. During periods of increased inflation, people become more cautious and spend less, causing profits to diminish and companies to lay off workers. Instead of growing, the economy shrinks. If the economy shrinks for three consecutive quarters, we enter a **recession,** which is a period of diminished economic output.

When recessions hit, unemployment levels rise, creating greater economic pressures or demands on the political system. Recessions are a normal part of the business cycle, although they are not always labeled as severe. When they are, an even worse economic scenario occurs: a **depression.** In a depression, economic output diminishes to such a degree that the economy begins to collapse. A depression is characterized by high unemployment and low confidence in the economy and in financial institutions at the same time that prices fall and inventories rise.

The United States last experienced a depression in the 1930s. The **Great Depression** was a worldwide phenomenon caused by both the economic imbalances created by World War I and the collapse of the American financial markets after the stock market crash of 1929. Within four years, unemployment was as high as 40 percent in some places. More than 5,000 banks failed, resulting in millions of Americans losing their life savings. The magnitude of the economic crisis caused the federal government to fundamentally change its approach to economic policy making. The government had regularly intervened to deal with economic problems throughout the post–Civil War era, particularly to deal with economic panics created by shortages in the money supply and the political battles over the valuation of gold and silver in the late nineteenth century. But the Great Depression and New Deal period mark the true beginning of widespread government intervention into the economy. Before this time, Americans accepted the

Learn more about the Great Depression.

Known simply as "Migrant Mother," Dorothea Lange's photo of California migrant worker Florence Owen and her three children came to symbolize the Great Depression for many Americans.

© CORBIS

limited role of the national government. This change brought about the beginnings of public expectations that the government needed to take actions to maintain economic prosperity on a regular basis.

Public Expectations for Economic Prosperity and Their Consequences for Economic Policy

When Franklin Roosevelt was elected president, his primary goal was to find a way to end the Great Depression. His New Deal included a set of public policy proposals that offered radical steps to try to improve the economic situation of the country. The plan was based on an expansion of the scope of federal government powers. His first goal was to find ways to put Americans to work. His second goal was to take steps to prevent an economic calamity of the scale of the Great Depression from ever happening again. Chapter 10 describes how Roosevelt fundamentally changed the dominant ideology of governance. FDR was guided by the principle that if government had the means to help solve economic problems, it was incumbent on it to do so. Americans placed their trust in President Roosevelt and ultimately accepted the notion of "big government" that went with his policies. But they did so at a price.

In abandoning the ideology of a limited role of government in economic matters in favor of a view that called for a much larger government role in the economy and in all areas of life, the American people have placed high expectations on the government's ability to maintain economic prosperity. If the economy prospers, the public allows public officials to take credit for the "good times," but if the economy falters, the public is quick to blame officeholders come reelection time. Of the last five American presidents, two lost their bids for reelection largely due to economic downturns. Jimmy Carter was unseated in 1980 after the nation experienced double-digit inflation and a recurring energy crisis throughout his term. George Bush paid the price for the 1991–1992 economic recession by losing to Bill Clinton, a candidate who designed his entire campaign on the idea "It's the economy, stupid." Despite lingering economic troubles, President George W. Bush was able to narrowly win reelection largely due to the American people's focus on the war on terrorism. These expectations are centered on the American president, but the concern for maintaining economic prosperity is spread throughout the government and makes economic policy a chief governmental concern.

The public's expectations that the government should maintain economic prosperity create challenges for elected officials because they have relatively few tools available to shape the economy. The primary method that the president and Congress have to influence the economy is **fiscal policy,** which is the use of government spending and taxation. The government can also use **monetary policy** to control the money supply and interest rates. But for the most part, the president and Congress are locked out of those decisions because the **Federal Reserve Board** has exclusive control over monetary policy. Although there is nothing preventing government from limiting business's ability to make such investment decisions, it runs counter to the capitalist economy ideology that Americans have chosen as their model for economic decision making through the implicit and explicit policy choices made over the past two hundred years.

Not only do elected officials have few tools available, but they are faced with the reality that the most significant decisions affecting the economy—those involving large-scale investment capital—are largely outside of government control. In a capitalist economy, private actors control the means of production. The owners and directors of major corporations—and those who provide major sources of investment capital to business—make decisions that have a significant impact on the economy. Corporate leaders can decide to build new production facilities, or they can outsource their operations to Third World countries. Key investment decisions can mean the difference between increased research and development or greater profit taking; they can make the difference between increased employment and corporate downsizing. Ultimately, these private actors make decisions that shape productivity, employment levels, and overall growth. Yet, as private actors, they are not accountable to the American public. If General Motors decides to close down domestic production facilities in favor of factories in Mexico, where labor costs are a fraction of what they are in Michigan, the corporation does not pay a political price for the impact that those decisions have on such places as Flint, Michigan. If a local or regional economy enters a recession due to corporate decisions, the corporate CEO does not pay a price, but the region's political leaders along with its citizens do. Local governments have long recognized this power. Many communities have established economic development commissions, which are charged specifically with encouraging businesses to relocate to their regions, offering low-interest loans and tax breaks, among other incentives, to bring corporations in the area and keep them there.

Recognizing the power of corporations, political leaders at all levels work hard to encourage corporate leaders to make the "right" decisions. The president and Congress regularly consider the likely response of **Wall Street**—the New York financial markets and heart of the American economy—to government policy proposals. The last thing Washington policy makers want is to adopt a policy proposal that investors perceive as hostile to their interests and causes them to lose confidence in the economy. When investors are confident about the economy, they are more willing to invest. If Wall Street loses confidence, economic growth can be short-circuited almost overnight. This does not mean that government will never act in a way that business dislikes; rather, government will rarely act without considering the economic ramifications of its decisions.

Fiscal Policy

Fiscal policy is the attempt to influence the business cycle through manipulation of federal revenue and spending. It is largely based on the economic theories of John Maynard Keynes, which marked a revolution in economic philosophy. In the classic economic theory espoused by Adam Smith and later economic liberals, the market is understood to be self-correcting and able to work out economic problems. Government's role in the economy is "to ensure the integrity of the market while not distorting the natural operations of market forces."[18] As long as government protects the people's right to property, including maintaining respect for the obligations of economic contracts and preventing monopolies, the market will function efficiently. Economic problems will be solved through the normal course of the business cycle.

Keynes departed from traditional economic theory by urging a more activist role for the government in the economy. Government had "an obligation to secure the reliable performance of the economy as a whole."[19] The Great Depression suggested to Keynes that the rampant unemployment of the period would not be fixed by Smith's "invisible hand of the market." The problem was that during bad economic times, people were more likely to save money than spend it, making it harder to increase the demand that sparks economic growth. The less people spend, the less profits there are for businesses, and businesses are then forced to lay off even more people. Keynes argued that the solution to the problem was increased government spending. The economy needed a jump start, and only the government could provide it. Increased government spending—even deficit spending—would provide the demand that the economy needed to grow.[20]

Keynesian theory was not limited to periods of economic downturns. Government could use spending to increase demand anytime it appeared that market forces were "insufficient to create enough demand to keep unemployment at acceptable levels." Although Keynes preferred government spending as a means to influence the economy, he also recognized that tax cuts could achieve the same result. Decreasing taxes would put more money in the hands of consumers, who would then spend more, resulting in greater demand. The two primary tools of Keynesian fiscal policy are government spending and taxation. Adjusting government spending and taxing makes it possible for the president and Congress to affect economic conditions.

Government choices in fiscal policy must also take into account the potential costs that spending can have on inflation. When unemployment falls, inflation rises because the "scarcity of labor drives up wage rates" as employers compete to hire workers, thus inflating the price of goods. So in its attempts to increase demand through spending, government has the potential of inadvertently creating inflation, which can then short-circuit the government's goals. In this way, fiscal policy can be a Catch-22. Efforts to create demand can generate inflation. Attempts to control inflation can result in higher unemployment.[21] Faced with such a trade-off, fiscal policy must be formulated to find a balance between unemployment and inflation.

Alternative economic theories became popular in the late 1970s and 1980s. when Keynesian economics seemed incapable of solving the unanticipated problem of **stagflation.** The economy had entered a period of both high unemployment and high inflation. The inverse relationship of unemployment and inflation no longer seemed to work. This caused some economists to urge a departure from the "demand-side" policies of Keynesian fiscal policy to what was called "supply-side" economics. To such supply-siders as economist Arthur Laffer, the primary problem to be dealt with was inflation, not unemployment. In supply-side theory, government should encourage savings rather than spending. The more money people saved, the more investment capital there would be to support economic growth. As we saw in the introduction to this chapter, this was one of President Reagan's primary goals in effecting his "revolution" of 1981. The theory was that if those at the top were given large tax cuts, they would have more money to invest in the economy.

Supply-side economics did not work out as its proponents hoped. The Reagan tax cuts did result in higher after-tax income for wealthy Americans, but they did not result in additional savings. Personal savings declined during the 1980s. Rather than investing their additional money, those at the top did exactly what Keynesian theory suggested: They spent it on luxury items. The result, described in the last section of this chapter, was a growing disparity between rich and poor.

Learn about federal income tax policy.

Explore debates over tax policy.

As the introduction to this chapter points out, political leaders regularly differ over the best way to implement fiscal policy, and approaches to fiscal policy usually break down along partisan lines. Democrats tend to support accomplishing fiscal policy goals through government spending, whereas Republicans favor the supply-side approach of achieving fiscal results through tax cuts. Here too there can be disagreements. Should taxes be **progressive,** in which people are taxed based on their ability to pay, or should they be **regressive** or **flat,** where everyone pays the same tax rate regardless of income? Democrats tend to favor progressive taxes, and Republicans seek regressive taxes, but the stereotypes do not always work, for not all Democrats and all Republicans think the same way.

The Budget Process

Coordination of fiscal policy is shared between the president and Congress through the legislative process. Fiscal policy is developed through the annual budgetary process, which determines the levels for government spending and taxes, and the appropriations levels for specific programs. Each year, Congress must develop a budget for the next fiscal year (October–September) by setting overall revenue and expenditure levels. It must also pass a series of appropriations bills to provide every government agency with the opportunity to spend during the year. Perhaps no other issue has generated as much political controversy as has control of the federal budget.

Try to balance the federal budget with the Budget Simulation.

The current budgetary process began in 1921, with passage of the Budget and Accounting Act. This law created the Bureau of the Budget (later renamed the **Office of Management and Budget**) within the executive branch and gave the president greater control over submission of a unified budget for the executive branch to Congress. Congress also reformed its committee structure so that each chamber's appropriations committees had sole control over all spending bills. The appropriations committees developed standing subcommittees to deal with specific funding requests and to work with the relevant standing committees. Many of the battles for funding are played out at the subcommittee level, as various interest groups try to influence a subcommittee's decision-making process.

The presidency's role in budgetary politics has increased over time with the expansion of federal programs during the New Deal period and then again throughout the 1960s. As the federal budget became more complex, Congress found itself more and more dependent on the Office of Management and Budget (OMB) for expert information on the budget. When Richard Nixon came to office, beginning the modern period of divided government, the Democratic Congress found itself at a disadvantage to the presidency in budget matters.[22] In the wake of the Watergate scandal, Congress passed the **Budget and Impoundment Control Act of 1974,** which gave Congress more control over the budget process, allowing Congress to establish firm time lines for action on the budget and to establish budgetary priorities. The act created standing budget committees in each chamber, with responsibility to establish overall tax and spending limits. It also required the House and Senate to pass "concurrent budget resolutions" in order to "establish targets for total budget authority, budget outlays, and revenues for the upcoming year." The initial concurrent resolution is not binding and does not require the signature of the president. It is intended to provide an initial baseline for approval of the final budget resolution, which does require presidential approval. The act also created a "reconciliation process to conform revenue, spending, and debt legislation to the levels specified in the final budget resolution."[23] Finally, the budget act established a **Congressional Budget Office** (CBO) to provide Congress with independent expert advice on economic forecasts and budget scenarios, similar to the advice that the OMB provides the president.

Although the nation's elected officials want to make fiscal policy in a way that will ensure economic prosperity, they also must respond to the numerous interest groups and constituencies that want to see specific programs enacted. The federal budget does more than simply influence economic growth; it funds programs sought by citizens, and it establishes priorities across the full spectrum of domestic and foreign policy. Given finite resources, policies designed to promote one issue (for example, maintaining lost cost for heating energy) will affect the funds available for programs in other areas. Thus, fiscal policy is not a closed process. Citizens can pressure the government to solve specific problems, and interest groups can lobby for desired policies. These activities all take place within the annual budget and appropriations process. The priorities and pressures, in addition to prevailing economic conditions, shape the formulation and development of fiscal policy.

Fiscal policy making does not occur in a bubble, isolated from the substantive issues that various groups want to see funded. Although a tax cut may be framed explicitly in terms of its impact on the economy, budgetary politics cuts across all substantive policy issues. A good example of the pressures that citizens and interest groups can put on government was seen during the budget battles of 1995. When Republicans gained control of Congress for the first time in forty years, they began to promote their own agenda, which was quite different from that of President Clinton. Republicans owed their new majority in no small part to the efforts of the New Right, the Christian conservatives who wanted to put their own mark on American politics. They placed considerable pressure on Republican lawmakers to enact their agenda, including cuts in social programs, such as family planning, and cuts in support for the National Endowment of the Arts, the Corporation for Public Broadcasting, and legal services for the poor, among others—all programs favored by liberals.

The New Right was explicit in its demands of Congress, as Gary Bauer, then of the Family Research Council, made clear: "We want the people who are in office because of our votes to take us seriously and quit acting as they sometimes do, as if we're the black sheep of the family."[24] Christian conservatives pushed hard for their agenda, and many Republican lawmakers responded. The House Appropriations Committee considered proposals to slash housing programs, environmental regulations, summer jobs programs, and many of President Clinton's most cherished projects, including the National Service Initiative, the Goals 2000 education reform program, and grants to hire more police across the nation. This ultimately led to a showdown between the Republicans and President Clinton, who opted to shut down the government rather than accept what he considered "draconian" cuts.[25]

In the Bush years, the New Right has maintained pressure on President Bush to enact socially conservative legislation. Bush pleased Christian conservatives with his refusal to allow federal monies to be used for stem-cell research, beyond the existing thirty or so stem-cell "lines" already in existence. Bush has found resistance to his plan from the House of Representatives, which voted 238–194 to lift the president's ban on exploring new stem-cell research lines.[26] The issue remained on the agenda in 2006. The Senate approved the legislation in July 2006, and President Bush vetoed the bill. This was the first use of the veto in the six years of the Bush presidency.[27]

Monetary Policy

Although fiscal policy is made on an ongoing basis through the dynamics of the legislative process, in recent decades it has taken a backseat to monetary policy as the primary way to influence economic policy. Government spending and tax policy can affect the economy, but they can take anywhere from six months to five years to have their full impact. Monetary policy, however, can be changed overnight and have an immediate impact. Monetary policy is the attempt to influence demand in the economy through manipulating the amount of money in circulation. By increasing the money supply, more funds will be available to spend; constricting the money supply will shrink the economy. Monetary policy can be used to fight runaway inflation, to jump-start a sluggish economy, or to slow down the economy to prevent inflation. It can affect the "volume of money, credit and their price—interest rates. In this way it influences employment, output, and the general level of prices."[28] This in turn affects individual citizens when they seek to borrow money for school loans, car loans, and mortgages. Unlike fiscal policy, which is in the hands of the president and Congress, monetary policy is under the control of the nation's central bank: the Federal Reserve Board and the regional federal reserve banks.[29]

Congress created the Federal Reserve System in 1913 to regulate the nation's banking system. It includes a board of governors and twelve regional federal reserve banks. About one-third of the nation's private banks are members of the system. These banks hold more than 70 percent of the

Learn more about the Federal Reserve System.

nation's banking reserves and 40 percent of all deposits.[30] The twelve regional federal reserve banks serve as the backbone of the system, providing currency to the nation's banks, collecting and clearing checks between private banks, and maintaining the system of reserve funds that enables banks to function.

The regional federal reserve banks maintain the day-to-day operations of the nation's banking system, but the heart of the Federal Reserve Board (the Fed) is its board of governors and, most specifically, its chairman. The president, with the advice and consent of the Senate, appoints the chairman and vice chair for four-year terms staggered in between presidential elections. The remaining five governors are appointed for fourteen-year terms. Once appointed, the Fed's governors function as independent policy makers, free from presidential or congressional control. This independence enables the Fed to make the decisions it thinks are in the nation's best economic interest, without being subject to partisan control. Moreover, the president cannot remove the Fed's governors simply because of decisions with which the president disagrees.

All seven governors are equal voting members of the board, and the Fed's chairman is at the helm. Indeed, the power of the chairman has grown considerably under the stewardship of the last two men to hold the position: Paul Volker and Alan Greenspan. Greenspan served as chairman from 1986, when President Reagan appointed him, until his retirement in 2006. Presidents Bush (41), Clinton, and Bush (43) have subsequently reappointed him as chair. Chairman Greenspan has elevated the importance of the Federal Reserve Board to the degree that he is probably the most important economic policy maker in the nation, if not the entire world.

The Fed directs monetary policy through several mechanisms, the three most important of which are setting reserve levels, open market operations, and discount rates. All three can affect interest rates, encourage or discourage economic growth, and push the economy in one direction or another. By setting reserve rates, the Fed establishes what percentage of a bank's assets the bank must hold in reserve. When the Fed lowers the reserve rate, banks have more money available to lend; likewise, when it raises the reserve rate, banks have less money and are likely to raise the interest rates they charge.

Open market operations involve the buying and selling of government securities to and from member banks to affect interest rates. By selling government securities to the highest bidders, the Fed depletes reserves, making less funds available to lend. When the Fed buys securities at the lowest price, it adds to the nation's reserve.

Finally, the Fed can manipulate the federal funds rate and the discount rate to affect interest rates. The discount rate is the interest rate that banks are charged to borrow directly from the regional Fed banks. By increasing the discount rate, the Fed makes credit more expensive; by lowering it, credit becomes cheaper. The Fed can also change the **federal funds rate,** which is the interest rate that federal depository institutions charge banks for overnight loans. Because banks respond quickly to changes in the federal funds rate, changes in the rate have been a highly effective means of making minor corrections to keep the economy on course.

In the past decade, changes to the federal funds rate have been the preferred monetary policy tool in the Greenspan-led Federal Reserve. For example, in January 2001 the Fed lowered the federal funds rate by a half-percentage point twice within twenty-eight days to send a strong signal of its desire to avert a recession in the face of the most significant economic slowdown in five years. Likewise, the Fed began to raise interest rates starting in 2004 to curb inflationary fears.

Compromises, deal making, and pressure-group politics of the legislative process characterize fiscal policy making, but monetary policy is crafted under very different circumstances. The Federal Reserve Board can make its own decisions largely free from the influences of partisan politics. The Fed's decisions can stimulate or slow the economy. They can result in great profits or great losses for investors. Given public expectations, the Fed can make or break a presidency. If the Fed chairman thinks there is too much of a threat of inflation, he can manipulate monetary policy in such a way that could send the economy spiraling into recession. The actions of Greenspan's predecessor, Paul Volker, did exactly that in 1980, when his Fed fought to bring an end to double-digit inflation. In the industrialized world, no other nation gives as much unchecked authority to its central bank as the United States vests in the Federal Reserve Board.

The Fed is not without its critics. Given its attention to investment capital, the Fed is often viewed as representing the interests of Wall Street and big business at the expense of the American worker. The Fed has been viewed as excessively concerned with preventing inflation, even if the result is increased unemployment levels to achieve that goal. Economists argue that a tight labor market can create inflationary pressures on the economy. As more people are employed, corporations have a harder time finding employees and must pay higher wages than when there is a glut of available workers. Thus, when unemployment reached its lowest levels in decades in the late 1990s (with just 4 percent of Americans out of work), the Fed became particularly concerned with the potential of inflation rearing its ugly head. To combat this, the Fed raised interest rates six times between June 1999 and September 2000. The Fed then began to lower interest rates over a three-year period to try to stimulate the economy. With inflationary fears present again in 2004 and 2005, the Fed has raised interest rates fifteen times since 2004. From the perspective of the American worker, however, the Fed's actions suggest a bias toward the interests of big business and its investors. Scarcity in the labor market is not necessarily bad, particularly if you are a worker and can demand higher wages. But the Fed tends to represent the interests of those at the top of the socioeconomic spectrum. Higher wages might be good for the worker, but they are not for corporate investors. Of course, the counterargument is that if business expenses increase, they will ultimately be passed on to the consumer.

The Politics of Rich and Poor

Economic policy affects all Americans, but unfortunately, not everyone benefits from economic prosperity in the same way. Likewise, there is also an unequal impact from economic downturns. Any examination of economic policy would be incomplete if it did not consider the question of who wins and who loses in the American economy. The United States is the wealthiest nation in the world, blessed with abundant natural resources and an economy unmatched by any other nation. The United States is also a representative democracy based on the principle that all are equal before the law. Yet when it comes to an individual's ability to succeed economically, Americans recognize and accept huge differences among people. Most people do not expect, or even hope for, equality of results in the socioeconomic world. People should have the opportunity to succeed or fail based on their own efforts. As a result, Americans allow, and maybe even encourage, social and economic inequality among individuals.

Income Distribution

The median **income** in the United States has risen by more than 30 percent in real dollars since 1967. In 2005 the U.S. Census Bureau reported that the median income for U.S. households in 2004 was $44,389. Median income was unchanged from 2002–2004 in real terms. Yet the official poverty rate had also increased from 11.8 percent in 2000 to 12.7 percent in 2004.[31] In 2004, 37 million people were living in poverty, an increase of 1.1 million since 2003. These statistics are indeed an indication that the economic boom of the 1990s had an impact on the lives of Americans. Although the median income had risen a full $5,000 during the previous decade, it meant that a full 50 percent of American households earn less than $44,000 per year. Table 12.1 provides a graphic representation of the large disparities in income distribution that continue to exist among Americans.

As of 2004, the bottom 40 percent of American households controlled only 12.1 percent of the nation's total income. The bottom 20 percent controlled a mere 3.4 percent of the income. When compared with the top 40 percent of the population, there is a huge difference; the top 40 percent controlled 73.3 percent of all income, and the top 20 percent controlled 50.1 percent. Income in America is distributed very unevenly, with a large gap between the top and bottom of the scale. If we separate the top 5 percent of households out of the top quintile, we will see even more of the divide: The top 5 percent controlled almost 22 percent of the nation's income.

There has always been a wide distribution of income in the United States, but the distribution has widened substantially since 1980. From 1947 to 1979, all households saw real increases in income, and it was the bottom 20 percent that saw the largest increases. Since 1980, however, that trend has changed considerably. Almost all of the real gains in income have gone to the top 20 percent, and the bulk of that to the top 5 percent of

Year	Lowest	Second	Middle	Fourth	Highest	Top 5%
2004	3.4	8.7	14.7	23.2	50.1	21.8
2000	4.3	9.8	15.5	22.8	47.4	20.8
1995	3.7	9.1	15.2	23.3	48.7	21.0
1990	3.9	9.6	15.9	24.0	46.6	18.6
1985	4.0	9.7	16.3	24.6	45.3	17.0
1980	4.3	10.3	16.9	24.9	43.7	15.8
1975	4.4	10.5	17.1	24.8	43.2	15.9
1970	4.1	10.8	17.4	24.5	43.3	16.6

Table 12.1 Household Shares of Aggregate Income by Income Quintile, 1970–2004

Source: U.S. Census Bureau, *Current Population Reports,* March 1968–2004, "Historical Income Tables—Households," table H-2, "Share of Aggregate Income Received by Each Income Quintile and Top Five Percent, 1967–2004," http://www.census.gov/hhes/income/histinc/h02ar.html.

the population. The bottom 20 percent has seen a drop in real income (adjusted for inflation) of 5 percent. If you examine Table 12.1 again, you will see that the bottom 20 percent has not seen any of the increase in income percentage. It earns 3.4 percent of the nation's income, almost a full percentage point less than it did in 1980. The top 20 percent, however, has seen its percentage income go from 43.7 to 50.1 percent. The economic boom of the 1990s was very much skewed toward the top.

When the ratio between pay taken by corporate chief executive officers (CEOs) is compared with their workers' salaries, it becomes clear where the income has gone. In 1980 the ratio between CEO compensation and worker wages was 42 to 1, meaning that on average CEOs earned $42 for every $1 earned by their employees. A decade later, in 1990, the ratio had more than doubled, to 85 to 1. During the 1990s, however, CEO pay exploded, and by 2003 the CEO to worker ratio reached 301 to 1.[32]

Wealth and the Widening Gap Between Rich and Poor

Income distribution shows us what Americans earn. We can learn even more by examining **wealth,** or the total amount of assets that people own. Wealth is the total value of tangible assets (including equity in a home, car, and other consumer durables) plus financial assets (stocks, bonds, savings accounts) minus debts. If we know how much wealth an individual or household has, we have a much clearer picture of its overall economic standing than we gain simply by examining earnings.

These photos point to the wide gap between rich and poor in America's neighborhoods. Although many Americans are enjoying the benefits of middle-class suburbia, others still toil in the poverty of the inner city.

	Bottom 50%	Next 40%	90–95%	95–99%	Top 1%
1989	3	29.9	13	24.1	30.1
1992	3.3	29.6	12.5	24.4	30.2
1995	3.6	28.6	11.9	21.3	34.6
1998	3	28.4	11.4	23.3	33.9
2001	2.8	27.4	12.1	25	32.7
2004	2.5	27.9	12	24.1	33.4

Table 12.2 The Distribution of Wealth in the United States, 1989–2004

Source: Arthur B. Kennickel, "Current and Undercurrents: Changes in the Distribution of Wealth, 1989–2004," Table 5, p. 11; Federal Reserve Board, Washington, D.C., January 30, 2006. Accessed from http://www.federalreserve.gov/Pubs/oss/oss2/papers/concentration.2004.3pdf.

The estimated total net worth of all Americans today is approximately $26.1 trillion, which is up more than 55 percent from 1983 ($17.8 trillion).[33] Yet that wealth is highly concentrated in a small percentage of the American population. The bottom 40 percent of the population controls 12.1 percent of the nation's income, but that same portion of the population literally controls none of the nation's wealth. The bottom 50 percent of the population controls a mere 2.5 percent of the wealth. More than 97 percent of the nation's wealth is concentrated in the top 50 percent of the population. But here too, wealth is not evenly distributed, as the top 10 percent of the population controls 69.5 percent of all wealth.

As was true for income, wealth is not equally distributed within the top 10 percent. Table 12.2 shows that the top 1 percent of the population controls 33.4 percent of the nation's wealth. The next 4 percent of the population controls almost a quarter of the wealth (24.1 percent). Thus, the top 5 percent of the population controls 57.5 percent of the wealth. Perhaps the most important point to learn from the historical trend in Table 12.2 is that almost all of the increase in wealth has gone to the wealthiest 1 percent of the population, although the top 5 percent has done very well in the 1980s and 1990s. The remainder of the top 10 percent held its own, but the remaining 90 percent of the population saw its share of the nation's wealth shrink. Since the Reagan years and through the Clinton years, we have seen a continual growth in the gap between rich and poor.

Wealth and Income: Why They Matter

We have seen how income and wealth are distributed in America. Statistics paint a picture of a society with a large gap between rich and poor. Those at the top of the socioeconomic ladder have seen huge gains over the

THE SUPER-RICH: LEADING THE PACK

The top 1 percent of Americans, sometimes called the **super-rich,** have seen their fortunes balloon during the 1980s and 1990s. During the twentieth century, the top 1 percent had the largest share of the nation's wealth (44 percent) in 1929, the same year the stock market crashed and the Great Depression began. From the 1930s through the 1970s, however, the top 1 percent saw its share of wealth drop from a high of 36.4 percent in 1939 to a low of 19.9 percent in 1976. From 1979 until 1998, the wealth of the top 1 percent almost doubled, from 20.5 to 38.1 percent. It dipped 5 percentage points to 33.4 percent in 2001, but this was probably a short-term result of the 2001 recession and the "bursting" of the "dot-com" bubble in 2000. There are several factors that can explain the remarkable success of the top 1 percent of the population, including favorable corporate pay structures, a strong economy in the 1990s, and tax policies favorable to the wealthiest Americans.

The top 1 percent can be broken into an even smaller and more elite group—the top 0.1 percent or top 145,000 taxpayers. It is in this group of Americans where wealth is truly astounding. According to the *New York Times,* members of this group have seen their share of income double since the 1970s, reaching 10 percent of all incomes in the year 2000. They have estimated average incomes of $1.5 million or higher in the year 2005. And even the top 0.1 percent pales in comparison to the income of the top 0.01 percent (14,000 taxpayers), who average $5.5 million or more in income.

Source: "The Richest Are Leaving Even the Rich Far Behind," *New York Times,* June 5, 2005, p. A17.

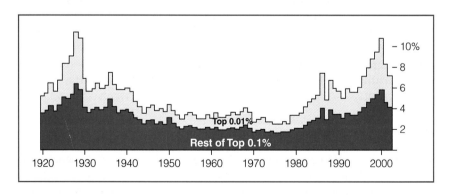

Figure 12.3 Percentage of income earned by top 0.1% of taxpayers

past two decades, and the bottom 60 percent of the population has fallen behind. Although median incomes for all Americans have risen in the past decade, the real economic rewards remain tilted toward the top. What remains to be examined are the consequences of the disparities between rich and poor for American politics.

In a capitalist economy, we would fully expect that some people will be rich and others will be poor; some will succeed and others will fail. Yet at the same time, in a democracy we expect formal equality before the law. Rich and poor alike can cast one vote in an election; the laws of the nation apply to all equally. Wealth provides many advantages that those with the median income simply do not have. For example, nothing prevents any American from contributing to a candidate's campaign fund, but the reality is that those at the top of the socioeconomic spectrum have far more disposable income available for such activities than the average American. Given the increased access to policy makers that campaign contributions bring (see Chapter 8), this is not insignificant.

Ask yourself this question: How likely is it that you would make a $2,100 contribution (the maximum permitted by law for the 2006 election cycle) to a candidate for federal office or a $5,000 contribution to an interest group if your annual family income was $50,000? With roughly $35,000 in after-tax income to spend during the year on housing, food, utilities, and all other living expenses, it is probably not very likely that you would have either the resources or the desire to make such a contribution. Yet in the 2004 election alone, candidates raised more than $2.5 billion. When PACs, party committees, and 527 groups are included, over $3.9 billion was spent on the election. In the 2002 congressional elections, less than one-tenth of one percent of the American people gave 83 percent of the $728 million raised by candidates.[34] One study of contributors to congressional candidates in the 1996 election found that only 19 percent of all "large donors"—those giving more than $200—had a family income of less than $100,000. Only 5 percent of large donors had incomes under $50,000. Yet 35 percent of large donors had incomes of $100,000 to $250,000, another 26 percent had incomes between $250,000 and $500,000, and a full 20 percent of large donors reported incomes over $500,000.[35] The wealthiest Americans are far more likely to make large contributions to candidates than those making the median income, or even those earning twice the median income ($85,000). They simply have more resources to support their favorite candidates and favorite causes.

There is nothing illegal, immoral, or unjust about wealthy Americans participating in the political process through campaign and interest-group contributions. The problem stems from the uneven playing field that wealth creates. Money does not buy candidates, but it does buy access. It buys an insurance policy of sorts that an elected official will at least consider the interests of his or her contributors when voting on an issue. Wealthy Americans have a disproportionate level of access to policy makers in comparison to those earning the median income. And ultimately, the wealthy tend to see their policy preferences achieved far more often as well. Wealth has a louder voice in American politics.

Explore how social welfare policy affects people differently.

In economic policy, the wealthy tend to win in the formulation of both fiscal and monetary policy. The federal tax code is filled with loopholes that provide benefits—through added deductions—to wealthy Americans. Three of the last four presidents have made a tax cut for upper-income Americans a centerpiece of their agendas. President George W. Bush's tax cut provides $1.3 trillion in tax relief to individuals. The Bush tax cut lowers the rate at which the top 1 percent of Americans pay from 39.6 percent to 35 percent by 2006. High-income taxpayers also benefit from the easing of the estate tax, or "death tax," as the amount of money that can be passed to one's heirs tax free rises dramatically over the next decade from $675,000 in 2001 to $3.5 million in 2009. The top estate tax rate drops from 50 percent in 2001 to 45 percent in 2007.[36] An analysis of the 2001 and 2003 tax cuts shows that individuals making between $100,000 and $200,000 are likely to pay taxes at a higher rate than Americans making more than $10 million in income.[37] The Bush tax cut does not just provide relief to the wealthiest Americans; it lowers tax rates across the board. But we still must confront the question of whether there is a relationship between Bush's tax cut and the fact that he collected more than $100 million in campaign contributions in the 2000 elections and $275 million in the 2004 election, which is more than any candidate has ever raised in the history of American presidential campaigns. Is Bush's tax policy a reward to those who contributed large sums of money to his campaign?

In many ways, the formulation of monetary policy is even more explicitly tilted toward the interests of wealth. The Federal Reserve Board's concern with keeping inflation in check benefits the interests of investment capital far more than it does people with median incomes. Not only does the Fed seem unconcerned about raising wages for the American worker; it tends to be biased against seeing it happen.[38]

Conclusion: Policy, Participation, and the Web of Democracy

Check here for possible post-publication updates to the chapter material.

Economic policy is only one of the many areas in which the federal government makes policy. But given its impact on the lives of all Americans, it is one of the most critical. Responsibility for economic policy making is divided between the Federal Reserve Board's tight control over monetary policy and the many points of influence among the president, Congress, bureaucracy, interest groups, and citizens that shape fiscal policy. Economic policy making cannot be understood outside the context of the capitalist economic system and the rewards and benefits that capitalism gives to those at the top of the socioeconomic ladder. Capitalism is deeply imbedded in American political culture, but the rich-poor gap has grown so large that it has had an impact on the development of public policy. The wealth gap has created an "access gap" whereby those with financial resources have far greater access to policy makers and are much better situated to win in American politics than are Americans without such resources.

In the last twenty-five years, American elections have become increasingly reliant on big money through both direct contributions and soft money (see Chapter 8). In the 2000 presidential primaries, frustration over the role of money in politics began to emerge through the popular support that Senator John McCain received in his bid for the Republican nomination. McCain's single-minded focus on the need for campaign finance reform resonated with both Republican and Democratic voters. McCain's popular appeal suggests that Americans are growing tired of the undue influence that money has in American politics. Governor Howard Dean's fund-raising success in the 2004 Democratic primaries illustrates the possibility for change. Dean was able to raise more than 60 percent of the $51 million his campaign spent from donations of less than $200. Only 11 percent of his contributors gave $2,000 or more. Compare this with 49 percent for George W. Bush and 36 percent for John Kerry.[39] Given the reliance that members of Congress have on campaign funds to maintain their strong incumbency advantage, campaign finance reform is a difficult task. Members of Congress, however, are increasingly supportive of the idea, including some who had previously opposed it.

Write a letter to your representative about a policy issue you care about.

The Web of Democracy began by urging you to become active participants in the American political process. This chapter ends by examining one of the greatest challenges facing American democracy. Yet our goal is not to turn you away from participating in politics. It is possible to disregard the wealth gap and still be successful in American politics. When Senator Russell Feingold (D-Wis.)—Senator McCain's co-sponsor in support of campaign finance reform—ran for reelection in 1998, he voluntarily adhered to the campaign finance rules that he has advocated. Many thought it would doom his reelection bid. Although it was a close election, Feingold did win, and this demonstrates that it is possible to combat the influence of money in politics and still be reelected. In fact, Feingold won again in 2004 while refusing to accept political action committee money. It is also the case that money does not guarantee success—witness multimillionaire Steve Forbes's two failed attempts to win the Republican nomination for the presidency. Despite our concern with the damaging influence of money on the political process, we believe that only through an awareness of the issues and challenges that face American politics will it be possible to work for change.

Key Terms

supply-side economics 371	capitalism 379	Federal Reserve
public policy 374	inflation 380	Board 382
agenda setting 374	recession 380	Wall Street 383
policy formulation 376	depression 380	stagflation 384
incrementalism 376	Great Depression 380	progressive tax 385
policy implementation 378	fiscal policy 382	regressive tax 385
policy evaluation 378	monetary policy 382	flat tax 385

Office of Management and
    Budget 385
Budget and Impoundment
    Control Act of 1974 385

Congressional Budget
    Office 386
federal funds rate 388
income 390

wealth 391
super-rich 394

Suggested Web Resources

The following are links to some resources relating to economic policy making. You can find other resources by using Web directories, such as Yahoo or Google.

The Federal Reserve Board (**http://www .federalreserve.gov**) maintains a website that provides up-to-date access to the activities of the Federal Reserve Board. The site also provides educational materials about monetary policy, the nation's banking system, and detailed economic statistics.

There are numerous interest groups and think tanks that are engaged in the study of economic policy, such as the Center for Economic and Policy Research (**http://www.cepr.net**) and the Levy Economics Institute (**http://www.cepr.net**) of Bard College.

Many of the major Washington think tanks are engaged in economic policy research. The Brookings Institution Economic Studies Program (**http:// www.brookings.org/es/es_hp.htm**) and the American Enterprise Institute for Public Policy Research (**http://www.aei.org**) are two good examples.

The federal government publishes the *Statistical Abstract of the United States* (**http://www.census .gov/statab/www**) annually. This is an excellent resource for policy research of any issue. You can also access the *State and Metropolitan Area Data Book* (**http://www.census.gov/statab/www/ smadb.html**) in its entirety on the U.S. Census Bureau's website.

There are numerous websites dedicated to exploration of issues surrounding fiscal policy. One example is the Center on Budget and Policy Priorities (**http://www.cbpp.org**). The National Center for Policy Analysis (**http://www.ncpa.org/pi/taxes**) presents arguments against government regulation and for "pro-growth" approaches to taxation. The Cato Institute (**http://www.cato.org/fiscal/ index.html**) is an organization that promotes a libertarian approach to tax policy. A competing point of view is offered by the Progressive Policy Institute (**http://www.ppionline.org/ppi_ka.cfm? knlgAreaID=125**), an organization affiliated with the Democratic Leadership Council.

There are numerous resources available on the Great Depression of the 1930s and its impact on American history. The Library of Congress has a photo album titled *America from the Great Depression to the Second World War* (**http://memory.loc.gov/ ammem/fsowhome.html**), which provides a pictorial history of the Depression. *The Internet Modern History Sourcebook—The Depression* (**http://www .fordham.edu/halsall/mod/modsbook41.html**) includes links to other Internet sources on the Depression.

Finally, on page 394, this book includes a famous photo by Dorothea Lange. Titled "Migrant Mother" (**http://xroads.virginia.edu/~UG97/fsa/ lang.html**), this photo captures the essence of the impact of the Great Depression on American life. You can learn more about this photo by reading this account (**http://www.migrantgrandson.com**) written by the grandson of the woman memorialized by Lange's photo.

A complete study tool kit is available for this chapter and includes the following:
Flashcards
Crossword Puzzle
Critical Thinking Exercises
Interactive Timelines
Chapter Quiz

American Foreign Policy

■ **Wal-Mart, China, and the Impact of
Globalization on American Foreign Policy**   400

■ **American Foreign Policy**   403

■ **Constitutional Powers in Foreign Policy**   403
Struggle over the War Power   403
Treaties and Executive Agreements   405
Diplomatic Powers   405

■ **The Players in American Foreign Policy**   406
Foreign Policy in the Executive Branch   406
Foreign Policy and Congress   410

■ **A Brief History of American Foreign Policy**   411
The Beginning of Interventionism   411
The Two World Wars   412
The Creation of the United Nations   413
The Cold War   414
Deterrence and the Arms Race   415
The End of the Cold War   416

■ **Current Problems in American Foreign Policy**   418
The War on Terrorism   418
Al-Qaeda and Osama bin Laden   418
The Afghanistan War and the Escape of
bin Laden   420
Strategies in the War on Terror   420

■ **The War in Iraq and Its Consequences**   421
Buildup to War   422
"Mission Accomplished" and the Rise
of the Insurgency   423

■ **Global Warming and Foreign Policy**   427
What Is Global Warming?   427
International Efforts to Curb
Greenhouse Emissions   429

■ **Conclusion: Foreign Policy and
the Web of Democracy**   430

Wal-Mart, China, and the Impact of Globalization on American Foreign Policy

A family of shoppers walks through a parking lot towards a Wal-Mart store. Wal-Mart is known for its low prices. Many of its products are manufactured in China.

Watch a story about Wal-Mart.

When most Americans think of Wal-Mart, they probably do not think about American foreign policy. Wal-Mart is the store where most Americans go to do their shopping—a vast amount of their shopping— for clothes, toys, electronics, and groceries. Americans shop at Wal-Mart because it has built a reputation as having the lowest prices. Shopping for groceries at Wal-Mart can save as much as $30 per week over grocery shopping at a traditional grocery chain. As a result of the savings offered to customers, Wal-Mart has become the nation's largest employer, and also the largest corporation in the world, with more than $260 billion in annual sales and close to $10 billion in annual profits.

The primary way that Wal-Mart is able to keep its prices lower than those of virtually all of its competitors is through the corporation's vast size and its approach to manufacturers and vendors. With more than 3,000 stores, Wal-Mart is able to dictate the price it is willing to pay to the thousands of manufacturers and vendors that want their goods on Wal-Mart's shelves. At the corporation's headquarters in Bentonville, Arkansas, thousands of corporations learn that if they want to sell to Wal-Mart, they need to cut their prices—something that Wal-Mart is ruthless about. Many vendors realize that if they are to succeed, they need to find cheaper sources of labor to meet Wal-Mart's demands. The result is that many Wal-Mart vendors look outside of the United States for their manufacturing facilities. In the past decade, this has almost exclusively meant relocating manufacturing to China and other low-wage countries—a practice entirely supported and encouraged by Wal-Mart itself. By 2004, the *Washington Post* reported that "more than 80 percent of the 6,000 factories in Wal-Mart's worldwide database of suppliers are in China," with Wal-Mart spending more than $15 billion on Chinese-made goods, "accounting for nearly one-eighth of all Chinese exports to the United States."[1] Wal-Mart is not the only corporation to embrace China, but it is the largest, and its position as the world's largest corporation sets the tone for many of its competitors.

For most of the past fifty years, China was closed off to the West. A "sleeping giant," China had more than a billion people locked in a mostly preindustrial society, controlled by a brutal communist regime. In the 1990s, however, the giant awoke, as China realized that if it were to succeed economically, it would have to embrace capitalism. And embrace capitalism it did. The Chinese took advantage of their massive labor pool and low wages to begin a manufacturing boom unlike any ever seen before. Perhaps the best example is the city of Shenzen, located on the Chinese border near Hong Kong. Twenty years ago, Shenzen was mostly rice fields; today, it is a vibrant manufacturing city of more than seven million people.[2] Shenzen has become one of the hubs of the new China: a city filled with manufacturing facilities for many of the world's largest corporations.

Learn more about China and globalization.

China's embrace of capitalism was encouraged not only by corporations like Wal-Mart, but by the U.S. government as well. President Bill Clinton strongly supported China's entrance into the World Trade Organization (WTO). The president was not alone; the Business Roundtable—an organization of the chief executive officers of major American corporations—strongly supported the legislation needed to enable China's entrance into the WTO. Big business saw China as a great opportunity to reach over 1.2 billion new potential customers.

The opening of China to big business is an important example of **globalization**—the changes in societies and the world economy that come from dramatically increased international trade. For a corporation such as Wal-Mart, globalization provides a cheap source of goods, enabling Wal-Mart to keep prices down for its customers. But China is more than a source of goods; it also represents the world's largest untapped consumer market and, consequently, the opportunity for even more profits. Many large corporations share the excitement of potentially selling their goods in China. Thus far, China has welcomed corporations wanting to produce goods for export, but it has made it very difficult for corporations to sell within China. The communist government has imposed many trade restrictions and has tried to protect its own industries from foreign imports. China has also undervalued its currency, giving its exports a huge advantage in the global market.

Globalization and the opening of China to corporations like Wal-Mart have many consequences not only for American domestic politics but for foreign policy as well. Domestically, the reliance on foreign-made goods has contributed to the decline of American manufacturing. Every time an American corporation moves its production facilities to China, the result is that American factories are shut down and American workers are out of well-paying jobs. Often, these workers are forced to take new positions at considerably lower wages.

Not only is there a loss of American manufacturing jobs, but the success of Chinese manufacturing has a direct impact on the American trade deficit as well. American foreign policy is affected by the rising trade deficit between American imports and exports. American big business had thought that the opening of China would result in new markets for

American goods, but the reality of the past five years has been something different. Although some inroads have been made into Chinese markets, most of the flow of trade has been from China to the United States. The year 2004 saw a $162-billion trade deficit between the United States and China, with a $200-billion deficit projected for 2005.[3]

The meaning of this trade deficit can be illustrated by looking at the port of Long Beach, California—one of the major ports of entry for goods traded between China and the United States. In 2003, $36 billion in Chinese goods came into the United States through Long Beach, while only $3 billion in goods left Long Beach for China. The relationship has become one that resembles the mercantilist economic system between the American colonies and England in the eighteenth century. The United States produces raw materials, which are sent to China, where they are made into finished products and then sent back to the United States, where they are sold. As the director of communications at the Long Beach port reported to PBS's *Frontline*, "We export cotton, we import clothing, we export hides, we bring in shoes. We export scrap metal. We bring back machinery. We're exporting waste paper, we bring back cardboard boxes with products inside them."[4]

Some of the trade deficit may be the result of the protectionist policies that the Chinese government has placed on imports coming into China. This has put pressure on the U.S. government to impose restrictions on Chinese imports and to try to require the Chinese to "play fair" if they are going to be a part of the international marketplace. The United States has put pressure on China to more accurately value its currency, by moving away from a fixed-rate valuation of the yuan. The House of Representatives went so far as to pass a nonbinding resolution by a 411–1 vote to ask China to change its currency valuation.[5] In November 2005, the United States entered into a new trade agreement with China that placed some limits on Chinese textile exports to the United States for the next three years. The European Union entered into a similar agreement earlier in the year.[6] This agreement might have a small effect on the U.S.-China trade deficit, but Wal-Mart's purchase of garments will probably be unaffected, for the corporation has already shifted to buying much of its textiles from Bangladesh, where labor costs are one-third of what they are in China.

Thomas Friedman of *The New York Times* has argued in his best-selling book *The World Is Flat* that globalization is here to stay and that it is incumbent on the United States to come to terms with the consequences of a "flat world"—a world in which instantaneous communication technologies have made a global marketplace a reality. It is an environment that encourages the shifting of manufacturing facilities to lower-cost nations, such as China. Thus, it is unlikely that high-paying manufacturing jobs will come back to the United States. As a result, Americans will have to develop skills to effectively compete with China, Bangladesh, and other nations around the world. In addition, the architects of American foreign policy will have to work just as hard to develop an international economic environment open to competition, based on a level playing field.

American Foreign Policy

The globalization of international trade is probably not what most people think of when they hear the words "foreign policy." But given the economic stimulus underlying globalization, it is unlikely that the United States will ever again be able to retreat behind its borders, isolated from the rest of the world. And although the central images of foreign policy—matters of diplomacy, intelligence gathering, and war and peace—are still important, much of foreign policy is dedicated to solving conflicts over economic issues. In this chapter, we end *The Web of Democracy* with a brief examination of the major issues in formulating foreign policy. If public policy is defined as the decisions that government makes and the programs it enacts, **foreign policy** can be understood as the decisions that government makes in dealing with foreign nations and also as the goals the government wants to achieve in the world. To explore foreign policy, it is important to understand the institutional mechanisms by which foreign policy is made, the origins and development of American foreign policy, and some key issues in contemporary foreign policy.

Constitutional Powers in Foreign Policy

If there is one area of American politics where the separation of powers is unbalanced, it is in foreign policy. Although Congress and the president are partners in making domestic policy, the foreign policy environment is structured in a way that strongly favors the president, providing him with the greatest ability to act unilaterally. Yet even here we will see that the Constitution creates an environment that is ripe for a struggle for control between the branches.

The Constitution's allocation of powers to the Congress and the president is seen in several areas related to foreign policy: the power to declare and make war, the power to make treaties and agreements with other nations, and the power to enter into diplomatic relations with other nations.

Struggle over the War Power

Perhaps the most important power in foreign policy is the war power. Article II of the Constitution designates the president as **commander in chief** of the armed services, which gives him the ability to control the use of American troops. But Article I, section 8, gives Congress the "power to declare war." The Framers of the Constitution struggled over the war power. Their experience with executive power under the English king was such that whoever controlled the army and navy had the greatest power, and standing armies were dangerous to the rights of the people. By placing the war power in the Congress, the Framers were trying to ensure that there would be deliberation over the decision to go to war, not to leave it solely in the hands of the president. Yet the Framers also recognized that the constitutional language should also not be too narrow. Congress is given the power to "declare" war, not to "make war." There was concern that if the nation was attacked, the latter language would preclude the president from responding to an attack; thus, the language was changed to "declare" to provide more flexibility.[7]

The existence of a commander-in-chief clause and a congressional power to declare war has created tension in American politics, because American presidents, from Abraham Lincoln to the present, have interpreted the commander-in-chief clause in such a way as to expand their power considerably. Presidents have used their power as commander in chief to deploy troops into potentially hostile situations and have led the nation into more than 125 "undeclared wars," ranging from small incursions in Latin America and the Middle East to large-scale police actions, such as the three-year war in Korea and the ten-year war in Vietnam. Presidents have used the commander-in-chief power so many times that the American people, as well as Congress and the courts, have largely accepted the president's power. Table 13.1 describes some of the major American military actions that have occurred without a declaration of war.

Congress has declared war only five times in the nation's history—the War of 1812, the Mexican-American War (1848), the Spanish-American

Quasi-Naval War with France, 1798	Cuba, 1962
Tripoli, 1801–1805	Vietnam War, 1964–1973
Mexico, 1806	Cambodia, 1970
Spanish Florida, 1814	Grenada, 1983
Algiers, 1815	Lebanon, 1983
Nicaragua, 1853, 1854, 1857, 1867, 1894, 1896, 1898	Libya, 1986
Panama, 1860, 1865, 1873, 1885, 1902, 1903–1914	Panama, 1989
Colombia, 1868	Gulf War, 1991
Hawaiian Islands, 1874, 1889	Somalia, 1992
Haiti, 1888, 1891	Bosnia/Serbia, 1993–1997
China, 1898–1899, 1900	Afghanistan, 2001
Korean War, 1950–1953	Iraq No-Fly Zone, 1993–2003
Guatemala, 1954	War in Iraq, 2003–present

Table 13.1 Selected U.S. Military Actions Without a Declaration of War

Source: Susan Collier, "Instances of Use of United States Forces Abroad, 1789–1993," Naval Historical Center (retrieved from http://www.history.navy.mil/wars/foabroad.htm).

War (1898), World War I, and World War II—and has provided authorization short of a declaration of war in just a handful of recent conflicts, including the 1991 Gulf War and the 2003 Iraq War.

Treaties and Executive Agreements

Article II of the Constitution provides the president with the power to make treaties with other nations, with the advice and consent of two-thirds of the Senate. **Treaties** are formal agreements with other nations, and these agreements have the force of law. Unlike other laws, treaties do not require the consent of both chambers of Congress to be enacted, as the House of Representatives has no authority to approve or reject treaties. Enforcement and interpretation of treaties are largely an executive function.

Although the constitutional authority to make treaties is shared by the president and Congress, the negotiation of treaties is largely an executive function, even though the Constitution declares that treaties are made with the "advice and consent" of the Senate. When President George Washington sought the advice of the Senate when negotiating an Indian treaty, he became extremely annoyed when the senators refused to commit to any position that day. The president left the Senate and never again returned for its advice.[8] Since then, no other president has formally sought advice when negotiating treaties. In the past one hundred years, however, presidents have come to realize that although they do not need to formally consult the Senate when negotiating treaties, they have better success getting treaties ratified when they solicit the informal assistance of key senators during the negotiation stage.

Unlike treaties, **executive agreements** do not require Senate approval. The president has the power to enter into agreements with other heads of state. Such agreements are not binding on future presidents, and Congress is under no requirement to fund programs arising from them. Executive agreements were first used by President Franklin Roosevelt during World War II,[9] and they have become the preferred tool for presidents to use. For example, during the 1990s, 249 treaties were enacted, but presidents made 2,857 executive agreements.[10] The U.S. Supreme Court has ruled that executive agreements have the same legal force as a treaty.[11] The downside of using them is that they do not necessarily have the political support that a treaty does.

Diplomatic Powers

The president has several other critical foreign powers at his disposal, including the ability to appoint ambassadors to foreign nations and the power to receive ambassadors from other nations. The power to name ambassadors and other government ministers or counsels is provided in Article II, requiring the Senate's advice and consent. The president's choice for an ambassador can have significant impact on American foreign policy. For example, when President George W. Bush used a recess appointment to name John Bolton as ambassador to the United Nations (see Chapter 10), he selected an individual who had a reputation as being hostile to the United Nations, and thus his choice suggested disdain for the organization on the part of the administration. Although Bolton's appointment may be viewed critically by supporters of the United Nations, it is generally true that ambassadors are less important and less autonomous today than they once were.

The power to receive ambassadors is important because it vests in the president the ability to establish diplomatic relations with other nations. When President Richard Nixon decided to receive the ambassador from the People's Republic of China in 1972, he was formally acknowledging China's place in the world of nations. Since the Chinese Revolution in 1949, the United States had recognized Taiwan, also known as the Republic of China, as the legitimate Chinese government in exile. Nixon's decision ultimately resulted in Communist China being recognized in the United Nations and enabled it to take its seat on the Security Council. Likewise, the decision not to accept an ambassador is equally important. The United States has not had diplomatic relations with Cuba since that nation's 1959 revolution.

Presidential power over **diplomacy** is critical to foreign policy because it is through diplomatic relations that the United States is able to develop and maintain relationships with other nations. Diplomacy occurs at multiple levels. While presidents engage in frequent dialogues with the leaders of other nations, lower-level diplomats within the State Department are engaged in constant discussion with their foreign counterparts. Presidential skills in foreign policy are in many ways similar to the negotiations and bargaining the president must do with Congress (see Chapter 10). However, the additional layers of protocol when interacting with foreign leaders, as well as overcoming cultural and language differences that are usually not a part of domestic policy making, make foreign policy negotiations more complicated. Diplomacy occurs not only in a one-on-one relationship, but through the many international organizations, such as the United Nations, the Organization of American States, and the World Trade Organization, which bring representatives of many nations together.

The Players in American Foreign Policy

Foreign Policy in the Executive Branch

The president does not control foreign policy on his own. The executive branch has a large foreign policy apparatus in both cabinet-level departments and in other key agencies. Table 13.2 provides a listing of the key positions and their current officeholders.

Position	Current Officeholder
President	George W. Bush
Vice President	Dick Cheney
Secretary of State	Condoleezza Rice
Secretary of Defense	Donald Rumsfeld
Director of National Intelligence	John D. Negroponte
National Security Advisor	Stephen J. Hadley
United Nations Ambassador	John Bolton
U.S. Trade Representative	Susan C. Schwab
U.S. House Armed Services Committee	Rep. Duncan Hunter
U.S. House Committee on International Relations	Rep. Henry J. Hyde
U.S. House Permanent Select Committee on Intelligence	Rep. Peter Hoekstra
U.S. Senate Armed Services Committee	Sen. John Warner
U.S. Senate Select Committee on Intelligence	Sen. Pat Roberts
U.S. Senate Committee on Foreign Relations	Sen. Richard G. Lugar

Table 13.2 The Players in American Foreign Policy, 2005

Department of State

The Department of State is the one cabinet department whose sole purpose is to coordinate and maintain the United States' diplomatic relations. It is the oldest executive department, created in 1789. The State Department maintains diplomatic relations with more than 190 nations and with many organizations, including the United Nations and the Organization of American States. The State Department maintains the system of embassies and consulates that the United States has across the globe. More than 60,000 federal employees from 30 government agencies are housed in embassies and consulates.[12]

The State Department is headed by the secretary of state, who historically has been the president's primary foreign policy advisor. The secretary of state is responsible for advising the president on the ends and means of foreign policy, collecting and sharing information about events abroad, providing services to American citizens traveling abroad, and regulating foreign travel to the United States. Most presidents rely heavily on their secretary of state, but such is not always the case. Former Secretary of State Colin Powell found himself on the outside of key foreign policy decisions in the events leading up to the 2003 Iraq War. President George W. Bush relied much more heavily on Vice President Dick Cheney, Secretary of Defense Donald Rumsfeld, and National Security Advisor Condoleezza Rice. Since Dr. Rice took over for General Powell as secretary of state in early 2005, the secretary has again become a central advisor and the State Department has again risen in stature.

The U.S. ambassador to the United Nations also plays a key role in voicing the United States' position on issues through the United Nations. The United Nations ambassador is responsible for coordinating the day-to-day work of representing the United States at the United Nations, including the many U.N. committees and councils that the United States must participate in, such as the Security Council. On important issues—for instance, when the United States was trying to build support for a possible war in Iraq—the secretary of state also plays a key role in representing the United States. At least once per year, the president addresses the U.N. General Assembly.

Department of Defense

The Department of Defense is the largest single department in the U.S. government, with more than 2.3 million men and women in the armed services, almost three-quarters of a million civilian employees, and a budget of $450 billion in 2004.[13] The Defense Department is responsible for carrying out defense policy and is the front line in ensuring national security. Headed by the secretary of defense, the department has become an increasingly important part of the nation's foreign policy apparatus, as American troops are stationed across the globe.

The secretary of defense is assisted by a large and complex bureaucracy made up of both civilians and military officers responsible for ensuring that the president's orders as commander in chief are carried out effectively. This is not always easy, as there are long-standing rivalries between the armed services, internal battles for funding and prioritization, and tensions between civilians and military personnel for control of policy. The president is advised by the secretary of defense and by the joint chiefs of staff: the heads of the army, navy, air force, and the Marine Corps. The chairman of the joint chiefs of staff is appointed by the president and is a key military advisor.

Department of Homeland Security

Created by a presidential executive order after the terrorist attacks of September 11, 2001, the Office of Homeland Security was elevated to cabinet status by Congress in March 2003. The Department of Homeland Security brought together more than 180,000 federal employees from twenty-two federal agencies and departments (see Chapter 10). Homeland Security is responsibility for advising the president on all aspects of domestic security. The Defense Department is the nation's front line for national defense from external threats, but Homeland Security serves the same role for internal threats. It plays a critical role in coordinating federal, state, and local governments in responding to potential terrorist strikes.

The Department of Homeland Security is supposed to serve as an information clearinghouse between agencies, coordinating communications within the government and working to enhance the nation's homeland defenses. In its first two years in existence, it has been subject to many criticisms, including challenges from previously independent agencies that came under its control, as well as conflicts over budget and mission.[14] The department's color-coded national alert system did not help matters in building support from the public, which found the system to be confusing and the constantly shifting states of alertness in the years following 9/11 to be frustrating.

One of the department's most public faces, the Transportation Security Agency (TSA), also had a rough start with the public. Multiple security checks while boarding airplanes, intrusive searches of airline passengers who had already gone through a complete security clearance, and images of eighty-year-old women being practically strip-searched as they boarded an aircraft have not given the agency a positive public image.[15]

The National Security Council

Described in Chapter 10, the National Security Council plays a critical role in advising the president on all matters of domestic, foreign, and military policy. The National Security Council brings together all of the key players in foreign policy and can be an important policy wielder in its own right. It was created by the National Security Act of 1947 to provide coordination of national security policy. Over time, the National Security Council has grown to having a staff of more than fifty full-time personnel. The National Security Council provides the president with an independent foreign policy staff, separate from the executive departments. Yet the development of an independent foreign-policy-making apparatus inside the White House can have its problems, as we saw in Chapter 10 with the National Security Council's role in the Iran-Contra scandal.

The National Security Council is headed by the national security advisor, also known as the assistant to the president for national security affairs. The national security advisor is one of the few individuals with daily access to the president. The appointment of Henry Kissinger as national security advisor by President Richard Nixon transformed the importance of the position, putting the national security advisor on the same footing as the secretary of state and the secretary of defense. President George W. Bush's appointment of Dr. Condoleezza Rice as national security advisor was initially intended for her to provide more of a coordination role, but after 9/11 she became a key actor in the Bush foreign policy team.[16]

"The Contemporary Presidency: Condoleezza Rice as NSC Advisor: A Case Study of the Honest Broker Role," John P. Burke.

Director of National Intelligence

Beginning in World War II, it became critical for the nation to have an effective and comprehensive program of international intelligence gathering. For most of the past fifty years, chief responsibility for that task has fallen on the Central Intelligence Agency (CIA). The CIA provides the president with up-to-the-minute intelligence on the political, military, and economic activities of other governments. The CIA collects intelligence by monitoring foreign news sources and through covert operations involving intelligence agents (spies) on the ground in foreign nations. There are numerous other intelligence gathering agencies, such as the National Security Agency, the Federal Bureau of Investigation (limited to domestic policy), the Defense Intelligence Agency, and intelligence gathering units in the individual armed forces, as well as the departments of treasury, energy, state, and homeland security. In 2004 Congress enacted intelligence reform legislation that consolidated intelligence gathering responsibility under a new **director of national intelligence** in response to criticisms of intelligence failures leading to 9/11. It is too early to know what impact the consolidation of intelligence gathering under one entity will have on foreign policy making and on the interagency rivalries that have been such a major part of contemporary intelligence gathering.

U.S. Trade Representative

The Office of the U.S. Trade Representative is part of the Executive Office of the President (see Chapter 10) and is separate from the State Department. It plays an equally important yet more specialized role in foreign policy. The **U.S. trade representative** is treated as a cabinet-level position, although it is technically not within the cabinet. The trade representative is responsible for negotiating the United States' position on matters of international trade. Former U.S. Trade Representative Rob Portman negotiated the recent trade agreement with China regarding textile exports that was discussed in the chapter introduction.

Foreign Policy and Congress

The Congress is also a player in foreign policy, although the president and executive branch tend to be more visible. Congress has the power to declare war, and Congress funds and regulates the armed forces. The Senate has responsibility to confirm ambassadors, and it has the power to ratify treaties. On some trade agreements, such as the 1993 North American Free Trade Agreement between the United States, Canada, and Mexico, both chambers of Congress were needed to approve the agreement, which was not treated as a treaty. Congressional committees on intelligence, foreign relations, armed services, and homeland security play a large role in overseeing U.S. foreign policy—and hold power in their ability to withhold funding for specific projects that affect foreign policy.

Since the Vietnam War, Congress has tried to play a larger role in matters of war and peace. The War Powers Resolution of 1973, discussed in Chapter 10, attempted to place limits on the president's ability to unilaterally commit the nation to war. Congress required the president to consult with Congress before committing troops, but most presidents have viewed the resolution as unconstitutional and have agreed to consult with Congress only after the fact. After 9/11, Congress gave the president broad power to use force against those responsible for the terrorist attacks on New York and Washington. For the two largest military actions since Vietnam—the 1991 Gulf War and the 2003 War in Iraq—presidents George H. W. Bush and George W. Bush both sought and received authorization short of a declaration of war before the initiation of hostilities.

Read the War Powers Resolution.

A Brief History of American Foreign Policy

For much of its history, the United States approached its relations with other nations through a policy known as **isolationism.** Beginning with President George Washington, the United States considered itself as a unique experiment in democracy, different from the rest of the world, and because of its separation from Europe by three thousand miles of ocean, it made sense for the United States to adopt a policy of isolating itself from the concerns of other nations. This policy approach was pragmatic as well as ideological. The United States was a new, relatively poor nation with no sizable navy, and it was largely unable to defend itself against the European powers. By staying outside of the affairs of Europe, Americans hoped to avoid what George Washington referred to as "entangling alliances."

The Beginning of Interventionism

In 1820 President James Monroe articulated what has become known as the **Monroe Doctrine.** In his address to Congress, the president warned the European powers not to intervene in the politics and affairs of the nations of North, Central, and South America. In return, the United States would stay out of European politics. The Monroe Doctrine set the path for U.S. domination of politics in Latin America. This policy provided the United States with a buffer from Europe. With the United States promising to stay out of European affairs, Europe would stay out of affairs in the Western Hemisphere.

Read the Monroe Doctrine.

The Monroe Doctrine reinforced isolationism, but it also led to American **interventionism** within the Western Hemisphere. Interventionism can be defined as a nation's active participation into the affairs of another nation's political, economic, or military affairs. The United States saw Central and South America as its own sphere of influence, and over the course of the nineteenth century the United States became more and more involved in the affairs of Latin American governments. This was particularly true in the decades after the Civil War, when the U.S. economy began to industrialize, and economic advancement resulted in more trade between American corporations and Latin American nations. Moreover, European nations were never really willing to abandon their colonial interests in Latin America, causing ongoing conflict between the United States and Great Britain, France, and Spain.

Spanish control over the Caribbean island of Cuba, a mere ninety miles from the southernmost tip of Florida, came to a head in the Spanish-American War (1898), which began over controversy about the mysterious sinking of the *U.S.S. Maine,* an American naval ship moored in Havana. When Spain lost the war, it turned control over Cuba and Puerto Rico to the United States. At the same time, Spain also ceded to the United States several of its colonial holdings in the Pacific, including Guam and the Philippines. Almost overnight, the United States had become a colonial power, and with the acquisition of these colonies came the opportunity to further develop American economic interests in Asia.

American economic interest in Asia had begun some forty years earlier, when President Millard Fillmore used "gunboat diplomacy" with Japan in 1853. The United States had tried to open trade relations with Japan in the years prior, but the Japanese emperor refused to open Japan to American markets. Fillmore deployed naval ships to Tokyo, and the Japanese soon agreed to a treaty allowing for American trade.[17] American interests in the Pacific were not limited to Japan. Hawaii had long been viewed as important to the United States because it was halfway between the United States and Asia. In 1893 the United States sponsored a coup against the Hawaiian monarchy after the Hawaiians were unwilling to agree to a treaty favorable to the United States. Within a few days after the coup, Hawaii signed a treaty of annexation with the United States.[18]

The Two World Wars

Although the United States continued to build an economic empire in Latin America and the Pacific, the nation still clung to the theory of isolationism when it came to Europe. When the Great War (World War I) broke out in 1914, President Woodrow Wilson declared a policy of **neutrality**— the United States would not take sides in the conflict. Ultimately, however, the United States was forced into the war after German submarines sunk U.S. ships on their way to Britain. After the war ended, President Wilson tried to build the **League of Nations** as a way to establish a new international order based on the idea of **collective security,** in which war would "be renounced as an instrument of statecraft" and world leaders would "pledge to defend each other in the case of outside aggression."[19] The League of Nations would be a permanent international organization where diplomatic relations between nations could be carried out and nations could solve problems short of war. In addition, to be part of the league, nations had to pledge to support disarmament, decolonization, freedom of the seas, open markets, and the end of secret diplomacy. Wilson's plan for a League of Nations was well received by other nations, but not by Americans. After the war ended, most Americans wanted to return to isolationism, and the Senate refused to ratify the League of Nations, leaving the United States out of the new organization.

American isolationism with Europe continued through the 1920s and into the 1930s. Once the Great Depression hit in late 1929, and the world was overcome by a global depression in 1930, the conditions were ripe for the rise of Nazism in Germany. Adolph Hitler gained power at roughly the same time as Franklin Roosevelt began his presidency in the United States. World War II began when Germany invaded Poland in 1939. During the Battle of Britain in 1940, the United States maintained its official policy of neutrality, but President Roosevelt entered into an agreement with Britain whereby the United States would provide military aid to Britain in return for use of British islands in the Caribbean as a port for American naval ships. All through 1940 and 1941 the United States began building up its military for a likely war. After the Japanese surprise bombing attack on Pearl Harbor in Hawaii in December 1941, the United States officially entered the war, allying itself with Great Britain and the Soviet Union to fight Nazi Germany, Mussolini's Fascist regime in Italy, and the Japanese Empire.

Listen to FDR's request to Congress for a declaration of war in 1941.

The Creation of the United Nations

One of the positive results of World War II was the creation of the **United Nations.** Unlike the League of Nations, which Wilson tried to create after World War I, the United Nations was begun during World War II as an attempt to build a permanent world body, yet one significantly different from the League of Nations. The United Nations charter dedicated the organization to "save succeeding generations from the scourge of war," to "reaffirm faith in human rights," to "establish conditions under which justice and respect for the obligations arising from treaties and other sources of international law can be maintained," and to "promote social progress and better standards of life."[20]

Explore the United Nations website.

The United Nations was based on the principle of sovereign equality—each member nation would have equal rights. Yet the largest and most powerful nations would have considerable control within the organization.[21] The Security Council would be the primary organizational means of dealing with international conflict. It would consist of five permanent members—the United States, Great Britain, France, the Soviet Union, and China—and ten additional members whose membership would rotate. The permanent members of the Security Council would have veto power over any action of the council.

The Cold War

The U.S. alliance with the Soviet Union was a fragile one, and once the war ended with the defeat of Japan, the alliance quickly disintegrated as the Soviet Union quickly moved to gain control over most of Eastern Europe. Unlike after World War I, Americans were not able to retreat back under the banner of isolationism—the United States was the only major power left largely unscathed by the war. Very quickly, the world became divided into two blocs: East versus West, communism versus democracy. By 1949, when the Soviet Union gained the technology to create an atomic bomb, the **Cold War** began with the prospect that conflict between the United States and the Soviet Union could lead to a nuclear winter—and world-wide destruction.

Explore the history of the Truman Doctrine at the Truman Library.

President Harry S Truman was faced with the prospect of another war with much greater consequences, just two years after the defeat of Germany and Japan. The Soviets were determined to extend their sphere of domination across Europe, and the president was faced with the reality that all of Western Europe had been devastated by six years of war. In 1947 President Truman announced what became known as the **Truman Doctrine,** an effort to stop the spread of communism in Europe. First, the United States offered $400 million in aid to Greece and Turkey to prevent them from being taken over by the Soviets. Second, the president began a massive infusion of aid, coordinated by General George Marshall, into the nations of Western Europe so that they could rebuild after the war. Over a five-year period, more than $17 billion in aid was given to sixteen nations to rebuild their economies under what became known as the **Marshall Plan.**[22] Rebuilding Western Europe would serve two purposes. First, it would provide stability, while further preventing the spread of Soviet communism. Second, the Marshall Plan would provide strong markets for American economic interests. Together, the Truman Doctrine and the Marshall Plan would mark the beginning of what has become known as the doctrine of **containment:** Although the United States would do nothing to remove communism from areas already under Soviet influence, it would take clear and decisive action to prevent the spread of communism elsewhere in the world.

Initially, containment would be implemented through economic and military aid, as with Greece and Turkey in 1947. By 1950, however, the containment policy would face its first test, after the North Korean invasion of South Korea. With U.S. support, the United Nations Security Council voted to use force to repel the North Koreans from South Korea. The Soviet Union had been boycotting the Security Council at the time and were thus unable to use their veto power as a permanent member of the Security Council to stop the U.N. authorization for the "police action." Ultimately, the Korean War would go on for three years, and while the Soviets largely remained out of it, American and U.N. forces would fight North Korea (assisted by the Chinese Army) for much of that time.

In the 1960s, the United States would become involved in an even longer war in Southeast Asia, in the former French colony of Vietnam. Unlike the Korean War, which was backed by the United Nations, Vietnam involved a civil war between the Communist North and the prodemocratic South. The United States began to support the South Vietnam government after the defeat of the French by North Vietnam's Ho Chi Minh. What began as a small force of 16,000 American military "advisors" under President John F. Kennedy escalated to more than 500,000 American troops under presidents Lyndon Johnson and Richard Nixon. Ultimately, more than 57,000 Americans died and over 300,000 troops were injured in ten years of conflict. Vietnam became a "quagmire" because there appeared to be no exit and no clear indication of what we were fighting for. Once a peace agreement allowed American troops to leave Vietnam in 1973, the North Vietnamese quickly took control of the entire Vietnamese peninsula, and in 1975 Saigon was occupied as the last Americans left.

Deterrence and the Arms Race

Korea and Vietnam were examples of the types of wars that would become common during the Cold War—wars where the goal of the United States was to stop the spread of communism, or contain it. Once the Soviet Union, and then later China, acquired nuclear weapons, the risk was too great for the major powers to fight each other directly. If the United States and the Soviets became embroiled in an armed conflict, the chance of a nuclear war with the potential of eliminating human life as we know it was very high. As a result, in the 1950s and 1960s, foreign policy became dominated by a kind of nuclear chess game, where each side tried to strengthen its cause by building bigger and more powerful nuclear weapons. The goal of these weapons was to serve as a deterrent to war. If a nuclear war occurred, there would be no winner; thus, it was important to make the other side believe that a nuclear confrontation could never be allowed to occur. Underlying the theory of deterrence was the principle of **mutually assured destruction**—if the United States and Soviets engaged in a military conflict, both sides were assured that although they might destroy their other side, they would be destroyed as well.[23]

The Cuban Missile Crisis of October 1962 helped reinforce this standoff, as the Soviet decision to place medium-range and long-range ballistic missiles in Cuba prompted a U.S. naval blockade of all Soviet ships going to Cuba. The Cuban Missile Crisis pushed the Cold War to the brink, as the world came closer than at any other time to a full-scale nuclear exchange.

The early 1970s saw a cooling-off period between the United States and the Soviet Union, for both sides realized that the threat of nuclear war was becoming too great and that the cost of the arms race was too high. As both sides began to stockpile more and more weapons, it became more likely that eventually they would be used. This period is described as one of **détente**—a French word meaning "relaxing of tension." The United

Watch President John Kennedy's speech on the Cuban Missile Crisis.

National Archive/Getty Images

The United States conducted many atomic tests in the South Pacific from the mid-1940s through the early 1960s. This mushroom cloud is from a detonation on July 25, 1946, at Bikini Atoll.

States and the Soviet Union began a series of arms reduction talks, culminating in the Strategic Arms Limitation Treaty (SALT I) of 1972. This treaty placed limits on the development of antiballistic missile defense systems and limited the number of new offensive weapons that each nation could develop. From 1973 to 1979, the United States and the Soviets negotiated SALT II, which intended to further limit the manufacture of strategic weapons. Although this treaty was never ratified by the U.S. Senate, both sides honored it.

The End of the Cold War

Détente ended abruptly in December 1979, when the Soviet Union invaded the Central Asian nation of Afghanistan to support a pro-communist government there. Afghanistan would become the Soviet Union's Vietnam, and the Soviet-Afghan war would last until 1989. The world response to the Soviet invasion was harsh. U.S. President Jimmy Carter responded by deciding to boycott American participation in the 1980 Summer Olympic Games, scheduled to be held in Moscow. Four years later, the Soviets would counter by boycotting the 1984 Los Angeles Summer Olympics.

The election of Ronald Reagan to the presidency in 1980 further escalated the tensions between the United States and the Soviet Union due to

Reagan's desire to both strengthen American armed forces and to develop new weapons systems, including what became known as "Star Wars," the Strategic Defense Initiative. Star Wars would be a multi-billion-dollar space missile defense system. As Reagan upped the ante in the arms race, it put increasing pressure on the Soviets to spend more and more as well. The U.S. economy could absorb the increased costs, but the Soviet economy could not. Beginning in 1985, President Reagan began meeting with Soviet Premier Mikhail Gorbachev on a new arms-reduction pact. In 1987 the United States and the Soviet Union agreed to the Intermediate Range Nuclear Force Treaty, which required the immediate dismantling of several thousand missiles.

Watch President Ronald Reagan's speech calling for a "Star Wars" missile defense system.

The arms-reduction treaty came too late, however, for Gorbachev, who had begun a reform movement known as *perestroika* in 1987 that was designed to reform the Soviet economy and make it more robust. He accompanied this by a policy known as *glasnost* that provided for a new openness in decision making, making the nation's governance more transparent and open to debate. Gorbachev hoped *glasnost* would build support for his economic reforms. These policy changes within the Soviet Union had a major impact, but not necessarily what Gorbachev intended. Beginning in 1989, the Soviet Union began to relinquish the tight control it held over Eastern Europe as pro-democracy movements in Poland, Germany, Romania, and Czechoslovakia grew in strength. In 1989 the Berlin Wall fell, and East and West Germany moved to unify. The new freedoms of free speech unleashed long-repressed frustrations with Soviet rule. When Gorbachev tried to restructure the Constitution to provide greater autonomy for the individual states, it caused pro-communist opponents of Gorbachev to attempt a *coup d'état*. The Russian people, under the leadership of Boris Yeltsin, stopped the coup attempt, but instead of restoring Gorbachev to power, Yeltsin moved to establish an independent Russian state. On December 26, 1991, the Soviet Union was officially dissolved.

The Post–Cold War Era

The end of the Soviet Union marked a new period in world history. After fifty years of Cold War, the Soviet Union had broken into several independent states. The United States was effectively the only "superpower" left. The long-standing goal of containing communism was instantaneously brought to an end. China remained a communist state, but it had never had the expansionist goals of the Soviet Union, and the remaining communist states—Vietnam, Cuba, and North Korea—were largely isolated and disengaged from the rest of the world. As we saw in the chapter introduction, however, even China would take a new path in the 1990s, opening itself up to capitalist markets.

Beginning in the 1990s, foreign policy would go through the growing pains of adapting to a multipolar—as opposed to a bipolar—world. Instead of two superpowers, the world now has several important nations, including the United States, the newly unified European Union, China, and the newly democratic Russia. And although the arms race that had dominated the previous thirty years ended, new problems emerged. Instead of the vast majority of the world's nuclear weapons being under the control of two nations, there were nuclear weapons spread across several former Soviet republics. Other nations, such as China, France, and India, also possessed nuclear weapons. Perhaps most important, with the end of the cold war, regional conflicts that might have been subsumed by the rivalries of years past began to take greater importance in the world. Ethnic conflicts in the former Yugoslavia, genocide in Africa, and the ongoing Arab-Israeli conflict in the Middle East, and with it the rise of extremist Islamic terrorism, would grow to dominate world politics. It is to some of these issues that we now turn.

Current Problems in American Foreign Policy

The War on Terrorism

Watch President George W. Bush speaking at the ruins of the World Trade Center in September 2001.

American politics changed dramatically on September 11, 2001, after the terrorist strikes on the World Trade Towers and the Pentagon. For the first time since Pearl Harbor, the United States had been attacked on its home soil. The impact of 9/11 was widespread, affecting many areas of American life and fundamentally shifting American foreign policy. In the days after 9/11, President George W. Bush began what he called the **war on terror.** The initial target was Osama bin Laden; his terrorist organization, al-Qaeda; and the Taliban regime of Afghanistan. Al-Qaeda had been identified as the group responsible for the attacks in New York and Washington. The Taliban had been allowing al-Qaeda to operate freely in Afghanistan. They were given fair warning that any country or organization harboring or supporting al-Qaeda would be treated as an enemy of the United States. Within one month, U.S. troops were fighting in Afghanistan with three goals: to topple the Taliban regime that had supported al-Qaeda, to capture Osama bin Laden, and to eliminate al-Qaeda as a viable organization. The first of these goals was accomplished quickly, as the Taliban government was overturned. The other two goals proved more elusive.

Al-Qaeda and Osama bin Laden

Al-Qaeda is an Islamic fundamentalist group led by Osama bin Laden, with roots in the Afghani uprising against Soviet occupation in the mid-1980s. Osama bin Laden, a wealthy Saudi, was the main financier for an organization that recruited Muslims from mosques around the world. These fighters, known as the *mujahideen*, were crucial in defeating the Soviet forces in Afghanistan.[24] During the Soviet war bin Laden used his riches to help bring in more than 9,000 Arab fighters. While in Afghanistan, "bin Ladin came under the influence of the Islamic Jihad, the militant Egyptian group responsible for the assassination of president Anwar el-Sadat in 1981."[25] After the Soviet withdrawal of troops from Afghanistan, bin Laden returned to Saudi Arabia, where he was viewed by radical Muslims as a hero of sorts. By 1991, however, he was expelled from the country for "anti-government activities." After his expulsion from Saudi Arabia, bin Laden established the al-Qaeda headquarters in Khartoum, Sudan. Osama bin Laden despised the Saudi government's decision to host the U.S. military during the first Gulf War in 1991, and he viewed the United States as trying to continue its world dominance at the cost of Muslims throughout the world. He used his family wealth as the starting point to build a global network aimed at destroying the United States. From Sudan, bin Laden issued his first *fatwa*—an Islamic religious ruling—declaring a holy war on Americans, whom he viewed as "occupying the land of the two holy places."[26]

Bin Laden used al-Qaeda as the focal point for his holy war, or jihad, against the United States: "Rather than carrying out the attacks itself, bin Ladin's group provides financial and other assistance that allows smaller independent organizations to operate."[27] By organizing itself into small decentralized "cells" spread throughout the Middle East, Europe, the United States, and the Philippines and Indonesia, al-Qaeda has proven remarkably effective at achieving its goals, and even harder to fight.

Al-Qaeda leader Osama bin Laden, the prime suspect behind the Sept. 11, 2001, terrorist attacks in the United States, speaks in 1998 at a meeting at an undisclosed location in Afghanistan. The United States has tried unsuccessfully to capture bin Laden since 2001.

AP Images

Eventually, after being forced to leave the Sudan, bin Laden relocated his terrorist training camps in the rugged terrain of Afghanistan, where he was welcomed by the fundamentalist Islamic Taliban regime that came to power in the years after the Soviet occupation. Al-Qaeda claimed responsibility for the 1998 bombings of the U.S. embassies in Kenya and Tanzania, and for the 2000 bombing of the *U.S.S. Cole* in Bahrain. Al-Qaeda was implicated in (but never definitively blamed for) several other terrorist attacks, including the 1993 bombings of the World Trade Center in New York and the 1995 bombing of U.S. military barracks in Saudi Arabia. Then it masterminded the attacks of 9/11.

The Afghanistan War and the Escape of bin Laden

The American war in Afghanistan was relatively brief. On September 18, 2001, the United Nations Security Council issued a resolution ordering the Taliban to turn over Osama bin Laden and to close all terrorist training camps. By early October, American and British special forces infiltrated Afghanistan to make contact with the Northern Alliance, a group that had been fighting a civil war against the Taliban for several years. On October 7, 2001, a bombing campaign began. Within a month, the Taliban had been forced to flee Kabul, the Afghani capital. Taliban and al-Qaeda fighters began retreating to their few strongholds, namely the city of Kandahar and also the cave complex of Tora Bora, on the Pakistan border. By early December 2001, the war was over.

The Taliban was removed from power, and the al-Qaeda terrorist camps were eliminated, but the United States failed in one of the major goals of the campaign: capturing Osama bin Laden and his chief lieutenants. They escaped from the caves of Tora Bora, most likely to the White Mountains of Pakistan. In the years since 2001, the United States has never been able to find bin Laden, although he has periodically issued video statements proving that he is still alive. Some al-Qaeda operatives have been captured in the years since 2001, but the group's decentralized organization has proved to its advantage, for the organization has been impossible to destroy, although it has most certainly been weakened.

Strategies in the War on Terror

Upon declaring a global war on terror, President Bush refocused his foreign and domestic policy decisions toward eradicating all global terrorist organizations. The administration has based its counterterrorist strategies on the following several steps: denying safe havens where terrorists can train and equip members, restricting funding of terrorist organizations, degrading terrorist networks by capturing or killing intermediate leaders, detaining suspected terrorists, interrogating captured terrorists in order to gain insight on possible terrorist activities, and expanding and improving the efficiency of intelligence capabilities in foreign and domestic situations.[28]

These goals have been met with some success: Many countries have refused to be safe havens for terrorist activities, several terrorist leaders have been captured or killed, and intelligence has been made more efficient with the restructuring of the CIA and FBI. These successes have been made in spite of several obstacles, including support within Saudi Arabia and other places in the Middle East for terrorists and legal opposition within the United States to its methods of detaining suspected terrorists.

"Can Democracy Stop Terrorism?" F. Gregory Gause III.

The War in Iraq and Its Consequences

After defeating the Taliban in Afghanistan, President George W. Bush began to further refocus the war on terror by working to prevent other nations from carrying out future acts of terrorism against the United States.[29] The president identified an "axis of evil," a group of rogue nations that he considered a major threat to world security. Among these nations were Iraq, Iran, and North Korea.

"Understanding the Bush Doctrine," Robert Jervis.

The statue of Iraqi president Saddam Hussein in Baghdad is symbolically pulled down by an American armored vehicle with the assistance of about a hundred Iraqis after the fall of Baghdad in April 2003.

© Olivier Coret/In Visu/Corbis

The nations of the axis of evil were reportedly linked through common terrorist activities. Of these three, Iraq was viewed as the most serious threat, and discussions began within the White House for an invasion of Iraq to bring to a close the conflict that began during the George H. W. Bush administration. George W. Bush believed that Iraq posed an immediate threat to world security. This threat was founded on the principle that Iraq owned and would continue to create and possess weapons of mass destruction (WMD) that could be used against the United States.

Buildup to War

Throughout 2002, the Bush administration made it clear that removing Saddam Hussein from power was a major goal, but the administration argued that war could be avoided if the Iraqis made major changes in policy. But as the year progressed, it became clear that the administration expected to invade Iraq in the near future. The major justifications for invasion were the Iraqi production of WMD, Saddam Hussein's links to terrorist organizations, major human rights violations in Iraq, and Iraq's failure to abide by numerous U.N. Security Council resolutions passed in the decade since the 1991 Gulf War. The most prominent of these goals and objectives were the weapons of mass destruction and Iraq's purported links to al-Qaeda. It was believed at the highest levels of the U.S. government that Saddam Hussein had, or was currently developing, nuclear missile capabilities and that he was also linked to Osama bin Laden and the terrorist attacks on 9/11. A 2002 report presented to the president by the CIA detailed that Iraq did in fact have WMD capability. This report was relied on heavily as key decisions were made regarding the invasion. The content and validity of this report would later be hotly contested as the war played itself out, but it was generally accepted as valid at the time it was released. The purported link between al-Qaeda and Saddam Hussein was capitalized on heavily by the administration in the run-up to the war.[30] Links between 9/11 and Saddam Hussein drew skepticism as new evidence weakened the idea that there was an actual pact between Saddam and al-Qaeda. Eventually, the 9/11 Commission would find no credible link between the two.[31]

In the fall of 2002, the president sought and received congressional support to enable him to enforce the U.N. resolutions on Iraq and to use force if necessary.[32] At the same time, the president gathered what he termed a "coalition of the willing." This forty-nine-nation coalition included such countries as the United Kingdom, South Korea, Australia, Denmark, and Poland. However, the coalition and its plan for invasion were met with heavy opposition by U.N. Security Council members France, Germany, and China. This U.N. opposition would call into question the legality of the invasion of Iraq under international law. The Bush administration would justify its intentions through Resolution 1441 of the U.N. Security Council. This resolution concluded that Iraq would face "serious consequences" if it did not come into compliance with past weapons resolutions. However, this resolution did not authorize the use of force against Iraq.[33]

The United States and other coalition members decided to forgo the authority of the United Nations and ultimately gave Saddam and his government a forty-eight-hour period to leave the country. Saddam refused this request, and the war began on March 20, 2003, about ninety minutes after the lapse of the forty-eight-hour deadline.

The invasion of Iraq was swift, with the Iraqi government collapsing in only three weeks. The oil infrastructure, which sustained only limited damage, was rapidly secured. Securing the oil fields was seen as fundamental because, during the first Gulf War, desperate Iraqi soldiers set oil fields ablaze to distract coalition forces. As the invasion moved northward toward Baghdad, it avoided major cities except when necessary to secure river crossings at the Tigris and Euphrates rivers. Coalition forces encountered some resistance in the vicinity of Karbala, but they were able to quickly push toward Baghdad, which fell in early April 2003. With the fall of Baghdad, the regime of Saddam Hussein was over. Saddam himself had vanished, his whereabouts unknown. The symbolic moment that signified the end of the former regime was the toppling of a Saddam Hussein statue in central Baghdad by a U.S. tank. Overall, the official military operations in Iraq were quick, lasting a mere twenty-eight days. The invasion incurred only minimal losses while trying to avoid large numbers of civilian deaths and even higher numbers of fatalities among the Iraqi military forces. The invasion, at least militarily, was seen as an overwhelming success because it did not require a huge force as the 1991 Gulf War did.

"Mission Accomplished" and the Rise of the Insurgency

On May 3, 2003, President George W. Bush declared that major combat operations in the Iraq war were over, with only 107 American fatalities. However, the conclusion of major combat did not necessarily mean that peace had returned to Iraq. Very shortly after the president declared "mission accomplished," the U.S. occupation forces in Iraq began to come under attack by Sunni insurgents from within Iraq. Under Saddam Hussein, the Sunni Arab minority was able to control the larger population of Shia Arabs and Kurds. Once Saddam was removed from power, the Sunnis found themselves without power, and this helped fuel the insurgency. Using guerilla warfare tactics, roadside bombs, and suicide bombings, Iraqi insurgents opposed to the U.S. invasion and occupation made the rebuilding of Iraq increasingly difficult, and their efforts resulted in far more deaths than the "official" war did.[34] The insurgency has continued for more than two years, with little signs of it abating. As of November 4, 2006, the list of American fatalities in Iraq had grown to 2853, with another 21,572 troops wounded. News reports of American deaths continue on an almost daily basis.

The war in Iraq was part of the Bush foreign policy of eliminating terrorist regimes and providing a model for democracy in the Middle East (see

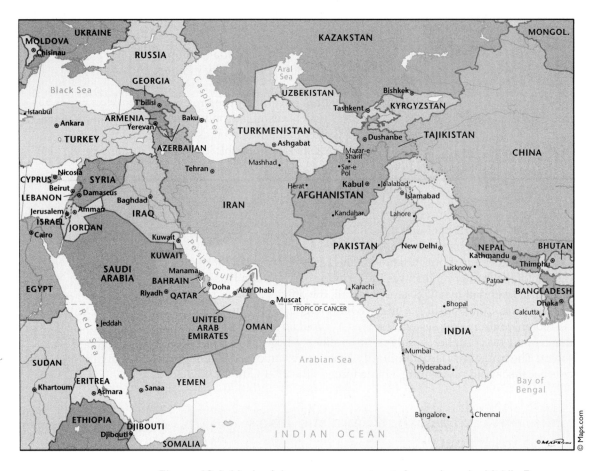

Figure 13.1 Much of the war on terrorism is focused on the Middle East. U.S. troops are currently deployed in Iraq and Afghanistan, with additional bases in Saudi Arabia, Kuwait, and Qatar. Iran and Syria remain sources of tension in American foreign policy.

Figure 13.1). The administration's policy goals have proven difficult to accomplish. The president has encountered opposition to his policies at home. Domestic opposition to the war grew when it became apparent that the rationale used by the administration to justify the war—Iraq's stockpile of weapons of mass destruction—proved to be unfounded. As soon as the war ended, the U.S. military began an extensive search for WMD, and to its surprise, not a single WMD was found. The lack of WMD was used by the opponents of the war to suggest that the president had either lied to the nation about the rationale for the war, had exaggerated the nature of the threat, or, at a minimum, had received very bad intelligence. When coupled with the ongoing insurgency, the mounting American casualties, the high price of the war (estimated as much as $251 billion as of October 2005),[35] and reports of abuse of Iraqi prisoners by American captors at Abu Ghraib prison in

THE RWANDAN GENOCIDE AND THE WORLD'S FAILURE TO ACT

Much of foreign policy deals with economic issues, such as foreign trade or access to markets, but protection of human rights is one of the more difficult issues that foreign policy makers are faced with. Perhaps one of the worst human rights violations since the Holocaust occurred in the spring of 1994 in the African nation of Rwanda. Even though almost one million Rwandans died, most Americans were unfamiliar with what occurred here until the 2004 film *Hotel Rwanda* was released. Rwanda had been in a long civil war between the Tutsi minority and the ruling Hutu majority. Shortly after a peace negotiation was signed to allow for a U.N. peacekeeping mission in the Rwandan capital of Kigali, the president of Rwanda was killed when his plane was shot down. At this point, the fragile peace broke down. Armed Hutu militia began an organized campaign to kill all Tutsi and moderate Hutus. Using machetes and machine guns, the Hutus turned Rwanda into a bloody battleground, murdering thousands of Tutsi. Lacking a mandate to protect civilians, the United Nations peacekeeping force abandoned Kigali.

© Gideon Mendel/Corbis

The skulls of victims from the 1994 Rwanda genocide are a gruesome reminder of the horror of the events that took almost one million lives while most of the world sat by and did nothing to prevent it.

(continued)

THE RWANDAN GENOCIDE AND THE WORLD'S FAILURE TO ACT (Contd.)

In the next three months, anywhere from 800,000 to one million Tutsi and moderate Hutus were murdered in the Rwandan **genocide.** By some estimates, almost 500,000 Tutsi were killed in the first month alone.[1] Given the magnitude of the Rwandan genocide, the world's reaction and response—or lack of response—were particularly telling.

When the genocide began in Rwanda, the United States and the United Nations did nothing to stop it. Even though there were media reports of the genocide coming out of Rwanda, President Clinton chose not to act. Instead, Clinton urged Rwanda's government to negotiate with the Tutsis, "the group the Hutu-led government had targeted for killing."[2] The United Nations also ignored calls for help, describing the events in Rwanda as an internal affair. It was only after the genocide ended that the president acted, sending a small contingent of 200 troops to Kigali to help oversee the relief efforts coordinated by the United Nations.

Why did the world of nations not react to the crisis in Rwanda? Perhaps part of the reason was that political leaders are generally reluctant to intervene in foreign crises unless they perceive the intervention to be in their own political interest.[3] For President Clinton, Rwanda was probably viewed through the lens of the U.S. experience in Somalia the year before. In the closing weeks of George H. W. Bush's presidency, U.S. troops were sent to provide peacekeeping support in the East African nation of Somalia and to prevent relief aid from being stolen by warring clans. When eighteen U.S. troops were killed in a gunfight, American support for the peacekeeping effort soured. In March 1994, U.S. troops withdrew from Somalia. When the Rwanda genocide began, just a month after U.S. troops left Somalia, there was little desire to return to East Africa.

It was only after the genocide ended that the world admitted its failure to act. U.N. Secretary General Kofi Anan said in 1998 that "the world failed Rwanda at that time of evil. The international community and the United Nations could not muster the political will to confront it." That same year, President Clinton visited Rwanda and admitted that "We did not act quickly enough after the killing began. . . . We did not call these crimes by their rightful name: genocide."[4]

[1] Sarah Glazer, "Should the US and UN Take Action in Sudan?" *CQ Researcher*, August 27, 2004, pp. 687–707.

[2] Glazer, "Should the US and UN Take Action?" p. 688.

[3] Glazer, "Should the US and UN Take Action?" p. 689.

[4] Glazer, "Should the US and UN Take Action?" p. 688.

Baghdad, many Americans began to question both the underlying rationale for the war and how the United States could emerge from Iraq without creating a Vietnam-like "quagmire" where troops would be in hostilities with no end in sight. As a result, George W. Bush began a slow but steady drop in approval ratings beginning in mid-2003.

Two-and-a-half years after the original invasion, American troops were still in Iraq, and the insurgency continued, now identified by the name "al-Qaeda in Mesopotamia" or "al-Qaeda in Iraq." Yet post-Saddam Iraq has made positive steps toward achieving the goal of a democracy. A constitution was drafted and ratified by Iraqi voters in October 2005. Elections were held under the new constitution in December 2005. What the future will hold for Iraq, however, is uncertain. Iraq remains under a mostly American occupation, and it is unclear how long U.S. troops will remain there. And although pressure exists within the United States to begin a slow withdrawal from Iraq, President Bush has suggested that troops could be needed as late as 2009.

Read an update on the reconstruction of Iraq and the status of the insurgency.

Global Warming and Foreign Policy

Not all issues in foreign policy involve matters of terrorism or war and peace. In recent decades, environmental issues have also made their way onto the foreign policy agenda of many nations. This chapter concludes with a brief discussion of one of those issues—global warming. Global warming is a difficult foreign policy issue because of domestic controversies over the seriousness of the problem and shifts in government policy from administration to administration.

What Is Global Warming?

Global warming is the common name for global climate change caused by human interference with the environment through increased emissions of hydrocarbons, or greenhouse gases, that cause the Earth's atmosphere to warm. Most of these emissions stem from the burning of fossil fuels—oil, natural gas, and coal—in automobiles, homes, and factories. When burned, fossil fuels release carbon dioxide (CO_2) into the atmosphere. Increased levels of CO_2 serve the same effect as a greenhouse: They trap the radiant heat and reflect it back to the Earth's surface, warming the temperature of the planet. Scientists measured gases trapped in icebergs dating back 20,000 years and were able to determine that "carbon dioxide levels had held relatively steady until the beginning of industrialization in about 1800, when they began to rise."[36] In addition to the increase of atmospheric carbon dioxide, scientists have measured a one-degree increase in average global temperatures since 1900, and although that might seem like a small increase, it has had a large effect.

Evening rush-hour traffic crawls along Highway 91, a major commuter route between Riverside and Orange counties, in Southern California. Automobiles are among the major sources of greenhouse gas emissions responsible for global warming. In California, they are also a primary cause of the smog that pollutes the air.

Continued global temperature increases can have several serious effects, including melting of the polar ice caps, which causes an increase in ocean levels and could be disastrous for tropical island nations—or low-lying nations, such as the Netherlands. Increased water temperature can cause more frequent violent storms, as witness the string of Category 4 and 5 hurricanes that have hit the United States in recent years. It is difficult to tell if global warming is responsible for increased hurricane activity or if ocean temperatures are going through normal fluctuations, but increased temperatures can change the ecosystems as far north as Alaska and deep into the tropics. If temperatures rise, it is possible that the range of disease-carrying mosquitoes could spread to larger parts of the Earth's surface.[37]

The theory of global warming caused by greenhouse gas emissions was first suggested by the Swedish scientist Svante Arrhenius in 1896. It took most of the twentieth century for scientists to substantiate his theory. Beginning in the 1960s, scientists began to use satellites to provide support for global warming. In 1995 the United Nations Intergovernmental Panel on Climate Change—a group of 2,500 scientists from across the globe—declared that "the evidence of global warming was undeniable" and that "the balance of evidence suggests that there is a discernible human influence on global climate."[38]

Even though most scientists concur with the argument that global warming is a real problem, some scientists remain unconvinced, arguing that we do not know that changes in the Earth's temperature reflect anything other than normal fluctuations in the planet's life cycle. These critics argue that the Earth's temperature has warmed and cooled several times in its history and that there isn't enough proof to be sure that increased levels of CO_2 in the atmosphere are at fault. Although there is debate over global warming, the majority of the world's scientists believe that global warming is happening and that the problem is one demanding a concerted effort by the international community.

International Efforts to Curb Greenhouse Emissions

International efforts to deal with global warming began in earnest in 1988, when the United Nations created the Intergovernmental Panel on Climate Change to provide advice to world leaders. Many political leaders were initially reluctant to take steps to deal with this problem—largely out of concern for the economic costs that would come from retooling industry to reduce emissions from factories. President George H. W. Bush was willing to acknowledge that global warming could be a problem, but he was unwilling to act without further evidence proving global warming. Bush faced serious criticism from his European counterparts, who accused the United States of ignoring the problem to protect American industry.[39] Bush did agree to sign the 1992 United Nations Framework Convention on Climate Change, which required most industrialized nations to reduce their emissions to 1990 levels by the year 2000. The treaty was ratified by the U.S. Senate in September 1992.

When President Clinton came into office, environmental protection was one of his top priorities. The president's initial approach to meeting the 2000 emission reductions was to create a series of incentives for American industries to voluntarily reduce their emissions. For example, the Environmental Protection Agency created a "Green Lights" program to encourage business to install energy-efficient lighting, which would reduce electricity needed for lighting and save as much as 800,000 tons of greenhouse gases.[40] By 1995, however, President Clinton shifted away from voluntary reduction programs to more stringent requirements as it became clear that voluntary programs would not achieve the goal of 1990-level emissions by 2000.

In 1997 the members of the U.N. Framework group met in Kyoto, Japan, to sign amendments to the 1992 treaty. The Kyoto Protocol, as it was called, was an attempt to both strengthen the original 1992 treaty and to establish emissions reductions in the years after 2000 for an additional 5.2% beyond 1990 emission levels. President Clinton sent Vice President Al Gore to Kyoto to sign the new treaty. But President Clinton never sent the treaty to the Senate for ratification because he knew that it would never receive the required two-thirds majority. There was—and remains—intense opposition from American corporate interests against the Kyoto Protocol and any mandatory reductions in greenhouse emissions. Critics of Kyoto "say that achieving the treaty's emissions targets would require a massive shift to non-fossil fuels, imposing unacceptable costs on the U.S. economy."[41] Indeed, in 1998 the U.S. Senate passed a resolution by a 98–0 vote decreeing that the "United States should not be a signatory to any treaty that did not include binding targets and timetables for both developing and already developed nations."[42] Much of the opposition stemmed from the Kyoto Protocol's division of reductions between developed and developing nations. Since the United States is both the world's largest consumer of fossil fuels and the largest source of CO_2 emissions—by 2002, emissions reached 1.592 million metric tons—the Kyoto Protocol placed higher requirements on the United States than on other nations. Yet Clinton pledged to meet Kyoto requirements regardless of whether the United States ratified the treaty.

When George W. Bush became president, the United States' position on the Kyoto Protocol, and on global warming itself, changed course dramatically. Unlike Clinton, Bush is skeptical about the global warming argument. President Bush's background in the oil industry put him squarely on the side of global-warming critics. He has also been supported by oil and gas interests in his presidential election campaigns.

In 2001 President Bush officially withdrew the United States from the Kyoto Protocol.[43] In its place Bush proposed his "Clear Skies Initiative" in 2002 as an alternative way to reduce air pollution through a series of incentives for industry by placing caps or limits on specific pollutants. Companies can buy "emission credits" that will allow them to go over the limits from another company that is below the limits. If enacted into law, Clear Skies will reduce emissions 18 percent by 2012.[44] As of 2006, Congress has not moved to pass the Bush initiative, and its future remains uncertain.

The president's repudiation of Kyoto has placed the United States among a very small minority of nations unwilling to follow the Kyoto Protocol. The European Union, Canada, Britain, and Russia all have ratified the treaty. Of the twenty nations that are the highest producers of CO_2 emissions, only the United States and Australia have failed to ratify the agreement. Although China, the second highest emitter of CO_2, is exempt from the initial round of emission reductions, it has begun taking steps to reduce emissions as well. The European Union is considerably ahead of the United States in embracing renewable and clean energy solutions. It is likely that other nations will put pressure on the United States to participate more fully in international efforts to curb global warming. Debate continues in the United States over the seriousness of global warming, but the issue is one that is likely to remain a foreign policy issue for years to come.

Conclusion: Foreign Policy and the Web of Democracy

Check here for possible post-publication updates to the chapter material.

In this chapter we have provided an overview of several of the major issues in American foreign policy. Foreign policy issues involve the interaction of political leaders with their counterparts from other nations; thus, these issues may seem far removed from the daily lives of ordinary Americans. Yet the decisions made in American foreign policy affect citizens, and citizens can have an impact on them. Citizens make decisions that affect foreign policy every time they demand low prices by shopping in a Wal-Mart. By shopping at Wal-Mart, they contribute toward the loss of American manufacturing jobs and increase the nation's trade deficit. Could people make a difference by telling Wal-Mart—perhaps by refusing to shop there—that they are willing to pay more for items if it will save American jobs? Likewise, public opinion can play a role in foreign policy issues, such as African genocide. If the American people make it clear that they want the government to do something to prevent genocide, it is likely that politicians will act.

What do the American people think about foreign policy issues?

Although it is most certainly true that many foreign policy decisions seem to be far from the daily lives of people, these decisions are really no different than any other government policy. The more citizen input that political leaders receive on an issue, the more they are likely to follow that input. Thus, we end *The Web of Democracy* with a call for citizen participation. For some of you, your political participation may end with the completion of the semester in which you take your introductory course in American politics. For the majority of you, however, we hope that *The Web of Democracy* will provide you with the knowledge and tools to become active citizens. We encourage you to bookmark many of the Web resources we have provided on *The Web of Democracy's* website. Use the many resources of the World Wide Web as a citizen's toolbox to learn about politics, to investigate issues, and to make up your own mind about the issues of the day. Then use your knowledge to play a part in politics. Vote. Find a cause that you care about, and pursue it.

Key Terms

globalization 401
foreign policy 403
commander in chief 403
treaties 405
executive agreements 405
diplomacy 406
director of national
   intelligence 410
U.S. trade representative 410

isolationism 411
Monroe Doctrine 411
interventionism 411
neutrality 412
League of Nations 412
collective security 412
United Nations 413
Cold War 414
Truman Doctrine 414

Marshall Plan 414
containment 414
mutually assured
   destruction 415
détente 415
war on terror 418
genocide 426
global warming 427

Suggested Web Resources

The following links will take you to sites relating to American foreign policy. You can find other resources by using Web directories, such as Yahoo and Google.

The White House (http://www.whitehouse.gov) includes many resources on American foreign policy and links to the president's national security strategy (http://www.whitehouse.gov/nsc/nss.html), as well as links to the National Security Council (http://www.whitehouse.gov/nsc), the U.S. trade representative (http://www.ustr.gov), and major speeches of the president on the war

on terror (http://www.whitehouse.gov/news/releases/2005/08/20050824.html). The White House Cabinet page (http://www.whitehouse.gov/government/cabinet.html) includes links to the departments of state, defense, and homeland security. The Office of the Director of National Intelligence (http://www.dni.gov) includes links to all of the intelligence agencies, including the Central Intelligence Agency and the National Security Agency.

There are many web resources on Wal-Mart and globalization. We would start with the PBS *Frontline* story "Is Wal-Mart Good for America?" (http://www.pbs.org/wgbh/pages/frontline/shows/walmart). This site includes transcripts of the PBS special and in-depth interviews. There are several websites critical of Wal-Mart, including Wal-Mart Watch (http://www.walmartwatch .com). Wal-Mart has its own website (http://www .walmartfacts.com), which counters some of the criticism.

PBS *Frontline* has a detailed website on the Rwandan genocide (http://www.pbs.org/wgbh/pages/frontline/shows/evil).

There are numerous sites on global warming, including the Environmental Protection Agency (http://yosemite.epa.gov/oar/globalwarming .nsf/content/index.html), the National Resources Defense Council (http://www.nrdc.org/globalWarming/default.asp), the National Oceanic and Atmospheric Administration (http://www .ncdc.noaa.gov/oa/climate/globalwarming.html), and the United Nations Framework Convention on Climate Change (http://unfccc.int/2860.php). An organization called Cooler Heads maintains a website critical of global warming (http://www .globalwarming.org).

 A complete study tool kit is available for this chapter and includes the following:
Flashcards
Crossword Puzzle
Critical Thinking Exercises
Interactive Timelines
Chapter Quiz

Notes

Chapter 1

1 http://www.voicesofsept11.org/mission_statement.php (retrieved July 14, 2005).

2 Michele Norris, "Mary Fetchet Discusses Her Opinion of Today's Testimony by Condoleezza Rice Before the 9-11 Commission," *All Things Considered*, National Public Radio, April 8, 2004 (transcript retrieved through LexisNexis, July 12, 2005).

3 The commission's final report can be found at http://www .gpoaccess.gov/911.

4 Dana Milbank, "Two Mothers Helped Move Mountain on Post-9/11 Bill," *Washington Post*, December 9, 2004, final edition (retrieved through LexisNexis, July 12, 2005).

5 Abraham Lincoln, Gettysburg Address, lcweb.loc.gov/ exhibits/gadd/4403.html.

6 It is important to realize that the Greeks did not consider all residents of a city-state (their basic political community) citizens. The Greek economy was based on a system of slave labor, and slaves were not citizens, nor were women and non-Greeks. It is not until the late nineteenth and twentieth centuries that the idea developed that all residents of a political community constituted its citizenry.

7 J. G. A. Pocock, *The Machiavellian Moment: Florentine Political Thought and the Atlantic Republican Tradition* (Princeton, NJ: Princeton University Press, 1975).

8 Justice Matthews, *Yick Wo v. Hopkins*, 118 U.S. 356 (1886).

9 Richard McCormick, *The Second American Party System: Party Formation in the Jacksonian Era* (Chapel Hill: University of North Carolina Press, 1966).

10 Lee Epstein and Thomas G. Walker, *Constitutional Law for a Changing America: Rights, Liberties, and Justice*, 2nd ed. (Washington, DC: CQ Press, 1995), pp. 775–789.

11 *Elk v. Wilkins*, 112 U.S. 94 (1884).

12 *New York Public Library American History Desk Reference* (New York: Stonesong/Macmillan, 1997).

13 James Madison, *Federalist* No. 10, www.law.ou.edu/hist/ federalist.

14 The Initiative and Referendum Institute, http://www .iandrinstitute.org; *Ballotwatch*, September 2004, http:// www.iandrinstitute.org/BW%202004-0%20(List).pdf (retrieved July 21, 2005).

15 Robert A. Putnam, *Bowling Alone: The Collapse and Revival of American Community* (New York: Simon & Schuster, 2000), p. 19.

16 Putnam, *Bowling Alone*, p. 46.

17 *The Public Perspective* (February/March 1997), p. 14 (from the 1996 Survey of American Political Culture).

18 Janet Kornblum, "So Proudly We Hail Our Freedom," *USA Today*, June 29, 2005, final edition, p. 4D.

19 Harold Dwight Lasswell, *Politics: Who Gets What, When, How* (New York: McGraw-Hill, 1936).

20 David Easton, *The Political System: An Inquiry into the State of Political Science*, 2nd ed. (New York: Knopf, 1971).

21 Robert A. Putnam, "Bowling Alone: America's Declining Social Capital," *Journal of Democracy*, 6.1 (1995), pp. 65–78.

Chapter 2

1 E. James Ferguson, *The American Revolution: A General History, 1763–1790* (Homewood, IL: Dorsey, 1974), pp. 90–93; The History Place, "Boston Tea Party, An Eyewitness Account by a Participant," www.historyplace .com/unitedstates/revolution/teaparty.htm.

2 Ferguson, *The American Revolution*, pp. 204–206; The History Place, "A New Nation," www.historyplace .com/unitedstates/revolution/rev-nation.htm.

3 Eric Black, *The Constitution: The Myth That Binds Us* (Boulder, CO: Westview, 1988).

4 Walter Murphy et al., *American Constitutional Interpretation*, 2nd ed. (Westbury, NY: Foundation, 1995), pp. 45–47.

5 Black, *The Constitution*, p. x.

6 Black, *The Constitution*, p. xi.

7 James Madison, *Federalist* No. 51.

8 Donald S. Lutz, "The Relative Influence of European Writers on Late Eighteenth-Century American Political Thought," *American Political Science Review*, 78 (March 1984), p. 190.

9 James Madison, *Federalist* No. 39.

10 Gordon S. Wood, *The Radicalism of the American Revolution* (New York: Vintage, 1993), p. 109.

11 Wood, *Radicalism*, p. 105.

[12] Gordon S. Wood, *The Creation of the American Republic, 1776–1787* (New York: Norton, 1972), p. 53.

[13] Wood, *Radicalism*, p. 229.

[14] Wood, *Radicalism*, p. 240.

[15] The use of gendered language is intentional in this context as women, albeit an important component of colonial society and an influence in the politics of the day behind the scenes, were not empowered to participate in the official public life of the colonies, nor were they able to participate in the political life of the new state once independence was declared. It was not until after the Civil War that women, in significant numbers, began to become a formal component of the American citizenry. The vast majority of African Americans were slaves, and they, too, did not share in the formal political practices of the country until after the Civil War.

[16] Bernard Bailyn, *The Origins of American Politics* (New York: Vintage, 1967), p. 63.

[17] Bailyn, *The Origins of American Politics*, p. 88.

[18] Ferguson, *The American Revolution*, pp. 9–11.

[19] Ferguson, *The American Revolution*, pp. 67–78.

[20] Ferguson, *The American Revolution*, pp. 85–90.

[21] An official secretary recorded the proceedings, and James Madison kept extensive notes of the debates, proposals, and actions. It is primarily through these documents that we know what did occur behind the closed doors in Philadelphia. Max Farrand, *The Framing of the Constitution of the United States* (New Haven, CT: Yale University Press, 1913). These documents can be found on the World Wide Web at memory.loc.gov/ammem/amlaw/lwfr.html.

[22] Herbert J. Storing and Murray Dry, *What the Anti-Federalists Were For* (Chicago: University of Chicago Press, 1981).

[23] It is worth noting that Rhode Island, the state where democratic political practices were most firmly adhered to and that did not send delegates to the Constitutional Convention, did not ratify the Constitution and formally join the new nation until 1790.

Chapter 3

[1] Medical Marijuana ProCon.org, "Voting/Polling on Medical Marijuana 2000 to Present," http://www.medicalmarijuanaprocon.org/pop/votes2000.htm (accessed July 18, 2005).

[2] Joan Biskupic, "Patients Who Use Marijuana Fear Worst If Forced to Stop," *USA Today*, June 7, 2005.

[3] Dan Hurley, "Medical Marijuana on Trial," *New York Times*, March 29, 2005; Biskupic, "Patients Who Use Marijuana Fear Worst If Forced to Stop. "

[4] The facts are largely derived from the 9th Circuit Court of Appeals decision, *Raich v. Ashcroft*, 352 F.3d 1222 (9th Cir. 2003).

[5] Andrew Taylor, "House OKs Medical Pot Prosecutions," *Washington Post*, June 28, 2006; Elana Schor, "New Lobbying Group Presses for Medical Marijuana Use," *The Hill*, June 21, 2006.

[6] *Federalist* No. 51.

[7] Hamilton and others wanted the president to appoint governors and give Congress the power to veto state laws.

[8] *United States v. Curtiss-Wright Corporation*, 99 U.S. 304 (1936).

[9] Sue Davis and J. W. Peltason, *Corwin & Peltason's Understanding the Constitution*, 16th ed. (New York: Harcourt, 2004), pp. 149–150.

[10] Ken I. Kersch, "Full Faith and Credit for Same Sex Marriages?" *Political Science Quarterly*, 112 (Spring 1997), pp. 117–136.

[11] Kevan Peterson, "Same-Sex Unions—A Constitutional Race," http://www.stateline.org/live/ViewPage.action?siteNodeId=136&languageId=1&contentId=20695 (accessed September 1, 2005).

[12] *Saenz v. Roe*, 526 U.S. 489 (1999).

[13] *McCulloch v. Maryland*, 17 U.S. 316, 424 (1819).

[14] *Gibbons v. Ogden*, 22 U.S. 1 (1824).

[15] *Dred Scott v. Sanford*, 60 U.S. 393 (1856).

[16] *Lochner v. New York*, 198 U.S. 45 (1905).

[17] Morton Grodzins, "The Federal System," in *Goals for Americans: The Report of the President's Commission on National Goals* (New York: Prentice Hall, 1960), pp. 265–282.

[18] Calvin Jillson, *American Government* (Fort Worth, TX: Harcourt Brace, 1999), p. 79.

[19] These figures are in constant 1992 dollars.

[20] Timothy Conlan, *From New Federalism to Devolution: Twenty-Five Years of Intergovernmental Reform* (Washington, DC: Brookings Institution Press, 1998), p. 5.

[21] Conlan, *From New Federalism to Devolution*, p. 6.

[22] Conlan, *From New Federalism to Devolution*, p. 65.

[23] U.S. Department of Commerce, *Statistical Abstract of the United States* (Washington, DC: U.S. Government Printing Office, 1994), pp. 317–318.

[24] Conlan, *From New Federalism to Devolution*, pp. 212–229.

[25] John Kincaid, "Political Coercion and Administrative Cooperation in U.S. Intergovernmental Relations" (paper presented at the biennial conference of the European Union Studies Association, Austin, Texas, March 31–April 2, 2005), http://aei.pitt.edu/archive/00003351 (accessed September 10, 2005).

26 Louis Uchitelle, "Minimum Wages, City by City," *New York Times*, November 19, 1999.

27 This program was modified in 1987 and repealed in 1995.

28 The law is formally known as the National Voter Registration Act of 1993.

29 Timothy Conlan and David R. Beam, "Federal Mandates: The Record of Reform and Future Prospects," *Intergovernmental Relations* (Fall 1992), p. 9.

30 Paul Light, *Shrinking Government: Federal Headcounts and the Illusion of Smallness* (Washington, DC: Brookings Institution Press, 1999).

31 National Council of State Legislatures, "Mandate Monitor," http://www.ncsl.org/standcomm/scbudg/manmon.htm (accessed September 10, 2005).

32 Ronald E. Weber and Paul Brace, "States and Localities Transformed," in *American State and Local Politics: Directions for the 21st Century* (New York: Chatham, 1999), p. 7.

33 Conlan, *From New Federalism to Devolution*, pp. 269–272.

34 The law is formally known as the Personal Responsibility and Work Opportunity Reconciliation Act of 1996.

35 *Printz v. United States* and *Mack v. United States*, 521 U.S. 898 (1997).

36 *New York v. United States*, 505 U.S. 144 (1992).

37 *United States v. Lopez*, 514 U.S. 549 (1995).

38 *United States v. Morrison*, 529 U.S. 598 (2000).

39 *Alden v. Maine*, 527 U.S. 706 (1999); *Seminole Tribe of Florida v. Florida*, 517 U.S. 44 (1996); and *Florida Prepaid Postsecondary Education Expense Board v. College Savings Bank*, 527 U.S. 627 (1999).

40 *Kimel v. Florida Board of Regents*, 528 U.S. 62 (2000); *City of Boerne, Texas v. Flores*, 521 U.S. 507 (1997).

Chapter 4

1 Material for this section is based on Edward J. Cleary, *Beyond the Burning Cross: The First Amendment and the Landmark R.A.V. Case* (New York: Random House, 1994), and *R.A.V. v. St. Paul*, 505 U.S. 377 (1992).

2 *Chicago, Burlington and Quincy Railroad Company v. Chicago*, 166 U.S. 226 (1897).

3 *Gitlow v. New York*, 268 U.S. 652 (1925).

4 Otis H. Stephens, Jr., and John M. Scheb II, *American Constitutional Law*, 2nd ed. (Belmont, CA: West/Wadsworth, 1999), pp. 348–351.

5 *Schenck v. United States*, 249 U.S. 47 (1919).

6 *Schenck v. United States*, 249 U.S. 47 (1919).

7 *Brandenburg v. Ohio*, 395 U.S. 444 (1969).

8 *Texas v. Johnson*, 491 U.S. 397 (1989).

9 *Near v. Minnesota*, 283 U.S. 697 (1931).

10 *Chaplinsky v. New Hampshire*, 315 U.S. 568 (1942).

11 *New York Times v. Sullivan*, 376 U.S. 254 (1964).

12 *Miller v. California*, 413 U.S. 15 (1973).

13 *Reno v. American Civil Liberties Union*, 521 U.S. 844 (1997).

14 Linda Greenhouse, "Court, 5–4, Blocks a Law Regulating Internet Access," *New York Times*, June 30, 2004, p. 1 (retrieved via LexisNexis, September 10, 2005).

15 *Engel v. Vitale*, 370 U.S. 421 (1962); *Abington School District v. Schempp*, 374 U.S. 203 (1963).

16 *Lee v. Weisman*, 505 U.S. 577 (1992).

17 *Santa Fe Independent School District v. Doe*, 530 U.S. 290 (2000).

18 Stephens and Scheb, *American Constitutional Law*, p. 538.

19 *ABC World News Tonight*, September 22, 2000.

20 The PEW Forum on Religion and Public Life, "School Vouchers," http://pewforum.org/school-vouchers (retrieved September 10, 2005); Linda Greenhouse, "The Supreme Court: School Tuition; Supreme Court, 5–4, Upholds Voucher System That Pays Religious Schools Tuition," *New York Times*, June 28, 2002, p. 1 (retrieved via LexisNexis, September 10, 2005).

21 *Goldman v. Weinberger*, 475 U.S. 503 (1986).

22 *Employment Division v. Smith*, 494 U.S. 872 (1990).

23 *Church of the Lukumi Babalu Aye, Inc. v. City of Hialeah*, 508 U.S. 520 (1993).

24 Thomas McIntyre Cooley, *A Treatise on the Law of Torts or the Wrongs Which Arise Independent of Contract* (Littleton, CO: F. B. Rothman, 1993).

25 Samuel Warren and Louis Brandeis, "The Right to Privacy," *Harvard Law Review* 4 (1890), pp. 193–220.

26 *Pierce v. Society of Sisters*, 268 U.S. 510 (1925); *Skinner v. Oklahoma*, 316 U.S. 535 (1942); *Loving v. Virginia*, 388 U.S. 11 (1967).

27 *Griswold v. Connecticut*, 381 U.S. 479 (1965), 485.

28 *Eisenstadt v. Baird*, 405 U.S. 438 (1972).

29 *Roe v. Wade*, 410 U.S. 113 (1973).

30 *Planned Parenthood of Southeastern Pennsylvania v. Casey*, 505 U.S. 833 (1992), 846.

31 *Webster v. Reproductive Health Services*, 492 U.S. 490 (1989); *Planned Parenthood v. Casey* (1992).

32 *Stenberg v. Carhart*, 530 U.S. 914 (2000).

33 *Lawrence v. Texas*, 539 U.S. 558 (2003).

34 *Cruzan by Cruzan v. Director, Missouri Department of Health*, 497 U.S. 261 (1990); *Washington v. Glucksberg*, 521 U.S. 702 (1997).

35 Don Colburn, "Fewer Turn to Assisted Suicide," *Oregonian*, March 11, 2005.

36 *Gonzalez v. Oregon*, 546 U.S. ____(2006).

37 *Michigan State Highway Patrol v. Sitz*, 496 U.S. 444 (1990).

38 *Arizona v. Hicks*, 480 U.S. 321 (1987).

39 *United States v. Leon*, 468 U.S. 897 (1984).

40 *Hudson v. Michigan*, 547 U.S.____(2006).

41 *Miranda v. Arizona*, 384 U.S. 436 (1966).

42 *Dickerson v. United States*, 530 U.S. 428 (2000).

43 *Gideon v. Wainwright*, 372 U.S. 335 (1963); *Argersinger v. Hamlin*, 407 U.S. 25 (1972).

44 *Duncan v. Louisiana*, 391 U.S. 145 (1968).

45 *Georgia v. McCollum*, 505 U.S. 42 (1992); *J.E.B. v. Alabama ex rel T.B.*, 511 U.S. 127 (1994).

46 *Furman v. Georgia*, 408 U.S. 238 (1972).

47 *Gregg v. Georgia*, 428 U.S. 153 (1976).

48 Alex Kotlowitz, "In the Face of Death," *New York Times Magazine*, July 6, 2003; "Public Opinion About the Death Penalty," Death Penalty Information Center, September 12, 2005, http://www.deathpenaltyinfo.org/article. php?did=209&scid=23.

49 *Wiggins v. Smith*, 539 U.S. 1231 (2003).

50 *Kansas v. March*, 548 U.S.____(2006).

51 Bernard Bailyn, et al., *The Great Republic: A History of the American People*, vol. 1 (Lexington, MA: Heath, 1977), p. 749.

52 *Plessy v. Ferguson*, 163 U.S. 537 (1896).

53 *Brown v. Board of Education I*, 347 U.S. 483 (1954).

54 Harvard Sitkoff, *The Struggle for Black Equality 1954–1980* (New York: Hill & Wang, 1981), p. 166.

55 Susan M. Hartmann, *From Margin to Mainstream: American Women and Politics Since 1960* (New York: Knopf, 1989), pp. 54–55.

56 T. R. Reid, "Same-Sex Marriage Measures Succeed: Bans in Several States Supported by Wide Margins," Washington Post.com, posted Wednesday, November 3, 2004, http://www.washingtonpost.com/wp-dyn/articles/A20471-2004Nov3.html (retrieved September 17, 2005).

57 Linda Greenhouse, "The Supreme Court: Affirmative Action; Justices Back Affirmative Action by 5 to 4, but Wider Vote Bans a Racial Point System," *New York Times*, June 24, 2003, p. 1 (retrieved via LexisNexis, September 10, 2005).

Chapter 5

1 David W. Moore, "Clinton Leaves Office with Mixed Public Reaction," Gallup News Service, January 12, 2001, gallup.com/poll/releases/pr010112.asp.

2 For dates of events, see, generally, "Clinton Accused: A *Washington Post* Special Report," and "Time Line," www.washingtonpost.com/wp-srv/politics/special/clinton/timeline.htm.

3 John F. Harris and Dan Balz, "Clinton Forcefully Denies Affair, or Urging Lies," *Washington Post*, January 27, 1998, p. A1.

4 David Marannis, "First Lady Launches Counterattack," *Washington Post*, January 28, 1998, p. A1.

5 Peter Baker and Juliet Eilperin, "Clinton Impeached," *Washington Post*, December 20, 1998, p. A1.

6 Moore, "Clinton Leaves Office."

7 Molly Sonner and Clyde Wilcox, "Forgiving and Forgetting: Public Support for Bill Clinton During the Lewinsky Scandal," *PS: Politics and Political Science*, 33 (September 1999), pp. 554–558.

8 Richard Morin and Claudia Deane, "Public Gives Clinton Blame, Record Support," *Washington Post*, February 15, 1999, p. A1.

9 John Zaller, "Monica Lewinsky's Contribution to Political Science," *PS: Political Science and Politics*, 32 (June 1998), pp. 182–189.

10 Peter Baker et al., "The Train That Wouldn't Stop," *Washington Post*, February 14, 1999, p. A1.

11 Steven A. Peterson, *Political Behavior: Patterns in Everyday Life* (Newbury Park, CA: Sage, 1990).

12 Donald R. Kinder and David O. Sears, "Public Opinion and Political Action," in Gardner Lindzey and Elliot Aronson, eds., *The Handbook of Social Psychology* (New York: Random House, 1985).

13 Anthony D. Lutkus, Andrew R. Weiss, Jay R. Campbell, John Mazzeo, and Steven Lazer, National Assessment of Educational Progress 1998 Civics Report Card for the Nation (website). U.S. Department of Education, 1999 (cited 2000). Available from nces.ed.gov/nationsreportcard/civics/new.results.asp.

14 David O. Sears and Carolyn L. Funk, "Evidence of the Long-Term Persistence of Adults' Political Predispositions," *Journal of Politics*, 61.1 (1999), pp. 1–28.

15 Kinder and Sears, "Public Opinion and Political Action"; Sears and Funk, "Evidence of the Long-Term Persistence."

16 Stanley Feldman and John Zaller, "The Political Culture of Ambivalence: Ideological Responses to the Welfare State," *American Journal of Political Science*, 36 (1992), pp. 268–307.

17 Quoted in Byron G. Massialas, *Education and the Political System* (New York: Addison Wesley, 1969), p. 2.

18 Doris A. Graber, *Mass Media and American Politics*, 5th ed. (Washington, DC: CQ Press, 1996), p. 193.

[19] Lance W. Bennett, *News: The Politics of Illusion,* 5th ed. (White Plains, NY: Longman, 2002).

[20] Robert D. Putnam. "Tuning In, Tuning Out: The Strange Disappearance of Social Capital in America," *PS: Political Science and Politics,* 28 (December 1995), pp. 664–683.

[21] Stephen Earl Bennett, "Comparing Americans' Political Information in 1988 and 1992," *Journal of Politics,* 57 (1995), p. 524.

[22] Michael X. Delli Carpini and Scott Keeter, *What Americans Know About Politics and Why It Matters* (New Haven, CT: Yale University Press, 1996), p. 271.

[23] Benjamin Page and Robert Shapiro, *The Rational Public* (Chicago: University of Chicago Press, 1992), p. 383.

[24] Delli Carpini and Keeter, *What Americans Know About Politics,* pp. 133–134.

[25] Lawrence R. Jacobs and Robert Y. Shapiro, "Lyndon Johnson, Vietnam, and Public Opinion: Rethinking Realists' Theory of Leadership," *Presidential Studies Quarterly,* 29 (1999); Lawrence R. Jacobs and Robert Y. Shapiro, "Issues, Candidate Image, and Priming: The Use of Private Polls in Kennedy's 1960 Presidential Campaign," *American Political Science Review,* 88 (1994); Lawrence R. Jacobs and Robert Y. Shapiro, "The Rise of Presidential Polling: The Nixon White House in Historical Perspective," *Public Opinion Quarterly,* 59 (1995).

[26] Frank Bruni, "Tax Fight: Where George Bush Leads, Who Will Follow?" *New York Times,* February 25, 2001, sec. 4, p. 16.

[27] Barbara A. Bardes and Robert W. Oldendick, *Public Opinion: Measuring the American Mind,* 2nd ed. (Belmont, CA: Wadsworth, 2003), pp. 32–33.

[28] Presidential Radio Address, August 27, 2005, www.whitehouse.gov/news/releases/2005/08/20050827.html.

[29] Herbert Asher, *Polling and the Public: What Every Citizen Should Know,* 4th ed. (Washington, DC: CQ Press, 1998), pp. 10–11.

[30] Asher, *Polling and the Public,* p. 10.

[31] Historical *New York Times*/CBS poll results can be found at http://www.nytimes.com/library/national/index-polls.html.

[32] Page and Shapiro, *The Rational Public.*

Chapter 6

[1] CBS News, "Dan Rather: Witness to History," November 23, 2004, http://www.cbsnews.com/stories/2004/11/23/entertainment/main657372.shtml (retrieved August 27, 2005).

[2] Bill Carter, "Post-Mortem of a Flawed Broadcast," *New York Times,* January 11, 2005, Section C, p. 1 (retrieved via LexisNexis, August 28, 2005).

[3] Al Tompkins, "Mapes: Decision to Air National Guard Story Was Made by CBS Superiors, Including Heyward," *Poynter Online,* January 10, 2005, http://www.poynter.org/content/content_view.asp?id=76700 (retrieved August 31, 2005).

[4] William Safire, "Those Discredited Memos," *New York Times,* September 13, 2004, Section A, Editorial Desk, p. 23.

[5] Corey Pein, "Blog-Gate," *Columbia Journalism Review,* January/February 2005, http://www.cjr.org/issues/2005/1/pein-blog.asp (retrieved August 31, 2005).

[6] Mallory Jensen, "Emerging Alternatives: A Brief History of Weblogs," *Columbia Journalism Review,* September/October 2003, http://www.cjr.org/issues/2003/5/blog-jensen.asp (retrieved August 21, 2005).

[7] Howard Kurtz, "In the Blogosphere, Lightning Strikes Thrice," *Washington Post,* February 13, 2005, p. D1 (retrieved via LexisNexis, August 28, 2005).

[8] "Two-Thirds of Americans Online," *Cyber Atlas,* internet.com, May 10, 2000, cyberatlas.internet.com/big_picture/demographics/article/0,1323,5901_358791,00.html.

[9] Richard Davis and Diana Owen, *The New Media and American Politics* (New York: Oxford University Press, 1998), pp. 1–27.

[10] Heather Hayes, "On the Virtual Campaign Trail: How the Web Is Changing the Nature of Running for Office," Civic.com, November 1, 1999, www.civic.com/civic/articles/1999/CIVIC_110199_32.asp.

[11] David Schultz, "Celebrity Politics in a Postmodern Era: The Case of Jesse Ventura," *Public Integrity,* 3.4 (2001), pp. 92–116.

[12] Pew Research Center for the People and the Press, " Cable and Internet Loom Large in Fragmented Political News Universe," January 11, 2004, http://people-press.org/reports/display.php3?ReportID=200 (retrieved September 9, 2005).

[13] Davis and Owen, *The New Media and American Politics,* p. 7.

[14] Davis and Owen, *The New Media and American Politics,* p. 27.

[15] Doris A. Graber, *Mass Media and American Politics,* 5th ed. (Washington, DC: CQ Press, 1997), pp. 13–18.

[16] Pew Research Center for the People and the Press, "News Audiences Increasingly Politicized: Online News Audience Larger, More Diverse," June 8, 2004, http://people-press.org/reports/pdf/215.pdf (retrieved September 19, 2005).

[17] Thomas E. Patterson, *Out of Order* (New York: Random House, 1994); W. Lance Bennett, *The Governing Crisis:*

Media, Money, and Marketing in American Elections, 2nd ed. (New York: St. Martin's, 1996).

[18] Matthew Robert Kerbel, *Remote and Controlled: Media Politics in a Cynical Age* (Boulder, CO: Westview, 1999), pp. 28–30; also Calvin R. Exoo, *The Politics of the Mass Media* (Minneapolis, MN: West, 1994), pp. 117–123.

[19] Kerbel, *Remote and Controlled,* pp. 41–45.

[20] Ben H. Bagdikian, *The Media Monopoly,* 5th ed. (Boston: Beacon, 1997), p. xiii.

[21] Ben H. Bagdikian, *The New Media Monopoly* (Boston: Beacon, 2004), p. 27.

[22] Bagdikian, *The Media Monopoly,* p. ix.

[23] John W. Wright, ed., *The New York Times Almanac: The Almanac of Record* (New York: Penguin, 2005), p. 382.

[24] W. Lance Bennett, *News: The Politics of Illusion,* 5th ed. (New York: Addison Wesley Longman, 2003), p. 29.

[25] Bennett, *News,* pp. 190–217.

[26] Exoo, *The Politics of the Mass Media,* pp. 50–51.

[27] David Schultz, "The Cultural Contradictions of the American Media," in David Schultz, ed., *It's Show Time! Media, Politics, and Popular Culture* (New York: Peter Lang, 2000), pp. 19–21.

[28] Graber, *Mass Media,* pp. 106–108.

[29] Patterson, *Out of Order,* pp. 78–84.

[30] Patterson, *Out of Order,* pp. 20–21.

[31] Graber, *Mass Media,* pp. 170–176.

[32] Schultz, "The Cultural Contradictions," pp. 22–25.

[33] Tracey L. Gladstone-Sovell, "Criminals and Buffoons: The Portrayal of Elected Officials on Entertainment Television," in David Schultz, ed., *It's Show Time!* pp. 117–132.

Chapter 7

[1] Jim VandeHei and John F. Harris, "Kerry: 'America Can Do Better,'" *Washington Post,* July 30, 2004.

[2] Michael Dobbs, "Swift Boat Accounts Incomplete," *Washington Post,* August 22, 2004.

[3] OpenSecrets.org.

[4] Gail Russell Chaddock, "Money Lessons from a Year on the Campaign," *Christian Science Monitor,* November 8, 2004.

[5] The Center for Public Integrity, http://www.publicintegrity.org/527/report.aspx?aid=435 (retrieved July 10, 2005).

[6] Chaddock, "Money Lessons."

[7] Ellyn Ferguson, "Ex-Bush Supporter Endorses Kerry," *Statesman Journal* (Salem, OR), August 21, 2004.

[8] Peter Baker, "Parties Gear Up for High Court Battle," *Washington Post,* June 27, 2005.

[9] Mark J. Rozell and Clyde Wilcox, *Interest Groups in American Campaigns: The New Face of Electioneering* (Washington, DC: CQ Press, 1999), pp. 29–31.

[10] From George Washington's Farewell Address, in Jared Sparks, ed., *The Writings of George Washington* (Boston: F. Andrews, 1840), p. 224.

[11] Morris Fiorina, *Divided Government,* 2nd ed. (Needham Heights, MA: Allyn & Bacon, 1996).

[12] For example, Joel H. Silbey, *The American Political Nation, 1838–1983* (Stanford, CA: Stanford University Press, 1991). For a general discussion, see L. Sandy Maisel, *Parties and Elections in America: The Electoral Process,* 3rd ed. (Lanham, MD: Rowman & Littlefield, 1999).

[13] *2004 Official Presidential General Election Results,* http://www.fec.gov/pubrec/fe2004/2004presgen.shtml (retrieved June 20, 2005).

[14] James Dao, "Angry Democrats, Fearing Nader Cost Them Presidential Race, Threaten to Retaliate," *New York Times,* November 8, 2000, p. B3.

[15] See, generally, Steven J. Rosenstone, Roy L. Behr, and Edward H. Lazarus, *Third Parties in America: Citizen Response to Major Party Failure* (Princeton, NJ: Princeton University Press, 1984).

[16] See, for example, Walter Dean Burnham, "American Parties in the 1970s: Beyond Party," in Louis Sandy Maisel and Paul M. Sacks, eds., *The Future of Parties* (Beverly Hills, CA: Sage, 1975); James L. Sundquist, *Dynamics of the Party System* (Washington, DC: Brookings Institution Press, 1973); David Broder, *The Party's Over* (New York: Harper & Row, 1971).

[17] See, for example, Paul S. Herrnson, "The Revitalization of National Party Organizations," in L. Sandy Maisel, ed., *The Parties Respond* (Boulder, CO: Westview, 1998); and Xandra Kayden and Eddie Mahe, Jr., *The Party Goes On* (New York: Basic, 1985).

[18] Martin P. Wattenberg, *The Rise of Candidate-Centered Politics* (Cambridge, MA: Harvard University Press, 1991).

[19] Paul Allen Beck, *Party Politics in America,* 8th ed. (New York: Longman, 1997).

[20] The Center for Responsive Politics, http://OpenSecrets.org (retrieved July 5, 2005).

[21] John Bibby, "State and Local Politics in a Candidate-Centered Age," in Ronald E. Weber and Paul Brace, eds., *American State and Local Politics* (New York: Chatham, 1999), pp. 194–210.

[22] Daniel M. Shea, *Transforming Democracy: Legislative Campaign Committees and Political Parties* (Albany, NY: State University of New York Press, 1995).

23 Bibby, "State and Local Politics."

24 Thomas E. Patterson, *Out of Order* (New York: Vintage, 1994).

25 Gerald Pomper and Susan Lederman, *Elections in America* (New York: Longman, 1980).

26 See, for example, Richard Fleisher and Jon R. Bond, " Assessing Presidential Support in the House II: Lessons from George Bush," *American Journal of Political Science* 37 (1992), pp. 525–541; and Cary R. Covington, J. Mark Wrighton, and Rhonda Kinney, "A 'Presidency-Augmented' Model of Presidential Success on House Roll Call Votes," *American Journal of Political Science* 39 (1995), pp. 1001–1024.

27 "Party Unity History," *CQ Weekly*, January 9, 2006, p. 98.

28 Theodore Lowi, *The End of Liberalism*, 2nd ed. (New York: Norton, 1979).

29 The classic statement is David Truman, *The Governmental Process* (New York: Knopf, 1951).

30 Jeffrey Birnbaum, *The Lobbyists: How Influence Peddlers Work Their Way in Washington* (New York: Times Books, 1993).

31 Alexis de Tocqueville, *Democracy in America*, ed. J. P. Mayer, trans. George Lawrence (New York: Anchor, 1969), p. 513.

32 Frank R. Baumgartner and Beth L. Leech, "Interest Niches and Policy Bandwagons: Patterns of Interest Group Involvement in National Politics," *Journal of Politics*, 63 (2001), pp. 1191–1213.

33 Baumgartner and Leech, "Interest Niches and Policy Bandwagons."

34 Jeffrey H. Birnbaum, "The Road to Riches Is Called K Street," *Washington Post*, June 22, 2005.

35 "Report to NAM Members: 108th Congress Achievements," 2005, http://www.nam.org/s_nam/sec .asp?CID=26&DID=24 (retrieved June 21, 2005).

36 Michael Massing, "Strong Stuff," *New York Times Magazine*, March 22, 1998, p. 39.

37 Massing, "Strong Stuff," p. 40.

38 Birnbaum, "The Road to Riches."

39 *Statistical Abstract of the United States, 2004–2005*, table 639.

40 Troy Smith, "When States Lobby: Welfare Reform (1993–1997)" (paper presented at the 1998 annual meetings of the American Political Science Association).

41 Robert Salisbury, "An Exchange Theory of Politics," *Midwest Journal of Political Science*, 13 (February 1969), pp. 1–32.

42 Jeffrey Berry, *The Interest Group Society*, 3rd ed. (New York: Longman, 1997), p. 72.

43 Mancur Olson, *The Logic of Collective Action* (Cambridge, MA: Harvard University Press, 1965).

44 E. E. Schattschneider, *The Semi-Sovereign People: A Realist's View of Democracy in America* (New York: Holt, Rinehart and Winston, 1960), p. 35.

45 Sidney Verba, Kay Lehman Schlozman, and Henry E. Brady, *Voice and Equality: Civic Volunteerism in American Politics* (Cambridge, MA: Harvard University Press, 1995).

46 Birnbaum, "The Road to Riches."

47 Hugh Heclo, "Issue Networks and the Executive Establishment," in Anthony King, ed., *The New American Political System* (Washington, DC: American Enterprise Institute, 1978); and Berry, *The Interest Group Society*.

48 Erika Falk, Erin Grizard, and Gordon McDonald, *Legislative Issue Advertising in the 108th Congress*, Report No. 47 (Washington, DC: Annenberg Public Policy Center, 2005), http://www.annenbergpublicpolicycenter .org/issueads05 (retrieved on June 20, 2005).

49 http://moveon.org (retrieved July 13, 2005).

50 Mark Memmott, "O'Connor Action Triggers Major Political Campaign," *USA Today*, July 1, 2005, http://www .usatoday.com/news/washington/2005-07-01-scotus-battle_x.htm (retrieved July 13, 2005).

51 Trevor Potter, "Chapter 2: The Current State of Campaign Finance Law," *The New Campaign Finance Sourcebook* (Washington, DC: Brookings Institution, 2005), pp. 5–6, http://www.brookings.edu/gs/cf/newsourcebk.htm (retrieved June 20, 2005).

52 Falk, Grizard, and McDonald, *Legislative Issue Advertising in the 108th Congress*.

53 G. William Domhoff, *Who Rules America Now?* (Englewood Cliffs, NJ: Prentice Hall, 1983).

54 Lowi, *The End of Liberalism*.

Chapter 8

1 Kevin Drum (*The Washington Monthly's* Political Animal), "Red States and Blue States . . . Explained!," http:// www.washingtonmonthly.com/archives/individual/ 2004_11/005157.php (retrieved November 1, 2005).

2 Morris Fiorina, *Culture War? The Myth of a Polarized* America (New York: Pearson-Longman, 2005), p. 7 (with Samuel J. Abrams and Jeremy C. Pope).

3 Terry Mattingly, "The Map Spoke Volumes About Our Country's Divisions," *Knoxville News-Sentinel*, December 30, 2000, B2 (as cited in Fiorina, *Culture War?*).

4 Joseph Curl, "Blue States Buzz over Secession," *Washington Times*, November 9, 2004.

[5] Tom Zeller, Jr., "Looking North?" *New York Times,* November 7, 2004, p. 4-2; Susan Bourette, "Feeling Blue in the Blue States? Canada Rolls Out Welcome Mat," *Christian Science Monitor,* December 7, 2004, p. 1.

[6] David Brooks, "One Nation, Slightly Divisible," *Atlantic Monthly,* December 2001.

[7] Brooks, "One Nation," p. 65.

[8] Fiorina, *Culture War?*

[9] Pew Research Center for the People and the Press, "Beyond Red and Blue," May 2005, http://people-press.org/reports/display.php3?ReportID=242 (retrieved November 1, 2005).

[10] Roin Toner, "Good-Will Reserves Run Low for Social Security Talks," *New York Times,* December 19, 2004, p. A41.

[11] Fiorina, *Culture War?* p. 99.

[12] "A Polarized Nation," *Washington Post,* November 14, 2004, p. B6.

[13] Stephen J. Wayne, *Is This Any Way to Run a Democratic Election?* (Boston: Houghton Mifflin, 2001), pp. 3–5.

[14] Adam Clymer, "Suddenly Bush's Smooth Ride Turns Bumpy," *New York Times,* April 1, 2001, sec. 4, p. 1.

[15] David Remnick, "The Wilderness Campaign: Al Gore Lives on a Street in Nashville," *New Yorker,* September 13, 2004.

[16] Wayne, *Is This Any Way?* pp. 137–138.

[17] *California Democratic Party v. Jones,* 530 U.S. 567 (2000).

[18] The Center for Responsive Politics, "Soft Money," http://www.opensecrets.org/softmoney/index.asp (retrieved November 1, 2005).

[19] *McConnell v. Federal Election Commission,* 540 U.S. 93 (2003).

[20] Quoted in Nancy Gibbs and Karen Tumulty, "A New Day Dawning," *Time,* April 9, 2001, p. 50.

[21] Thomas B. Edsall, "FEC Adopts Hands-Off Stance on '527' Spending," June 1, 2006.

[22] The Federal Election Commission, "Presidential Spending Limits 2004," http://www.fec.gov/pages/brochures/pubfund_limits_2004.shtml (retrieved November 1, 2005).

[23] The Center for Responsive Politics, "2004 Presidential Election," http://www.opensecrets.org/presidential/index.asp (retrieved November 1, 2005).

[24] Thomas B. Edsall, "Top FEC Officials Urge Higher Spending Limit," February 10, 2005.

[25] The Federal Election Commission, "FEC Press Office Backgrounders for Reporters: Presidential Election Campaign Fund," http://www.fec.gov/press/bkgnd/fund.html (retrieved November 1, 2005).

[26] CNN, "America Votes 2004: The Primaries, the Delegate Selection Process," http://www.cnn.com/ELECTION/2004/primaries/pages/misc/more.html (retrieved November 1, 2005).

[27] William Mayer, *The Divided Democrats* (Boulder, CO: Westview, 1996); 2000 and 2004 data found in Jonathon Bernstein, "The Rise and Fall of Howard Dean and Other Notes on the 2004 Democratic Presidential Nomination," *The Forum* 2(1), pp. 1–13.

[28] William G. Mayer and Andrew E. Busch, *The Front-Loading Problem in Presidential Nominations* (Washington, DC: Brookings Institution Press, 2004), chapter 2.

[29] Bernstein, "The Rise and Fall of Howard Dean," pp. 4–7.

[30] Mayer and Busch, *The Front-Loading Problem,* chapter 5.

[31] David S. Broder, Dan Balz, and Charles Babington, "Bush, Kerry in Reach of Electoral Win," *Washington Post,* October 31, 2004, p. A1.

[32] Compiled by the authors from "The 2004 Elections," *New York Times,* November 4, 2004, pp. P12–P13.

[33] Compiled by the authors from CNN's website, http://www.cnn.com/ELECTION/2002/pages/house/index.html and http://www.cnn.com/ELECTION/2002/pages/senate/index.html (retrieved November 1, 2005). Data for 2006 from author analysis of election returns.

[34] Campaign Finance Institute, "House Winners Average $1 Million for the First Time; Senate Winners Up 47%," http://www.cfinst.org/pr/110504a.html (retrieved November 1, 2005).

[35] Author analysis of data found on the Center for Responsive Politics website, http://opensecrets.org/overview/bigspenders.asp?Display=A&Memb=H&Sort=D (retrieved November 1, 2005).

[36] The Center for Responsive Politics, "The Competitive Edge," http://www.opensecrets.org/pubs/whospay00/competitive.asp (retrieved November 1, 2005).

[37] Justice Matthews, *Yick Wo v. Hopkins,* 118 U.S. 356 (1886).

[38] Martin Wattenberg, "Elections: Turnout in the 2004 Presidential Election," *Presidential Studies Quarterly* 35 (March 2005), pp. 138–146.

[39] The United States Election Project, using data from the Federal Election Commission and state election commissions, http://elections.gmu.edu/Voter_Turnout_2004.htm (retrieved November 1, 2005).

[40] The United States Electoral Assistance Commission, "State Voter Registration Deadlines," http://www.eac.gov/register_vote_deadlines.asp (retrieved November 1, 2005).

[41] The United States Election Assistance Commission, "The Impact of the National Voter Registration Act, 2003–2004: A Report to the 109th Congress," June 30, 2005, http://www.eac.gov/election_resources.asp?format=none (retrieved November 1, 2005).

42 James L. Tyson, "Motor Voter Law Yields Results, Some Reproach," *Christian Science Monitor*, October 11, 1996.

43 Raymond E. Wolfinger and Jonathan Hoffman, "Registering and Voting with Motor Voter," *PS: Political Science & Politics*, 34 (March 2001), pp. 85–92.

44 Lynne M. Casper and Loretta E. Bass, *Current Population Reports: Voting and Registration in the Election of November 1996* (P20–504) (Washington, DC: U.S. Department of Commerce, 1998), p. 4.

45 Robert D. Putnam, "Bowling Alone: America's Declining Social Capital," *Journal of Democracy* (January 1995); Ruy A. Teixeria, *The Disappearing American Voter* (Washington, DC: Brookings Institution Press, 1992), p. 57.

46 Data are from the Current Population Survey, U.S. Census Bureau, "Voting and Registration in the Election of November 2004," http://www.census.gov/population/www/socdemo/voting/cps2004.html (retrieved November 1, 2005).

47 M. Margaret Conway, *Political Participation in the United States*, 3rd ed. (Washington, DC: CQ Press, 1999).

48 Data in this section are from exit polling done by the National Election Pool (a consortium of ABC News, the Associated Press, CBS News, Fox News, and NBC News), reported in Marjorie Connelly, "Election 2004: How Americans Voted: A Political Portrait," *New York Times*, November 7, 2004, p. WK4.

49 CNN, "Election 2004" http://www.cnn.com/ELECTION/2004/pages/results/states/US/P/00/epolls.0.html (retrieved November 1, 2005).

50 The Center for Responsive Politics, http://www.opensecrets.org/overview/topraise.asp?cycle=2004 (retrieved November 1, 2005).

51 Robin Toner, "A Loud Message for Bush," *New York Times*, November 8, 2006.

52 Sidney Verba, Kay Lehman Schlozman, and Henry Brady, *Voice and Equality: Civic Volunteerism in American Politics* (Cambridge, MA: Harvard University Press, 1995).

53 Craig Gustafson, "55,000 Dear Senators," *Minneapolis Star Tribune*, March 23, 2001, p. 16A.

54 Verba et al., *Voice and Equality*, p. 67.

55 Verba et al., *Voice and Equality*, p. 53.

56 "Executive Summary: Giving and Volunteering in the United States," 1999 ed., www.independentsector.org/GandV/default.htm.

57 L. J. Sax, A. W. Astin, W. S. Korn, and K. Mahoney, *The American Freshman: National Norms for Fall 1999* (Los Angeles, CA: Higher Education Research Institute, UCLA, 1999).

58 Verba et al., *Voice and Equality*, p. 83.

Chapter 9

1 http://www.senate.gov/artandhistory/history/common/briefing/Filibuster_Cloture.htm.

2 Charles Babington, "Senate Work May Come to Halt If GOP Bars Judicial Filibusters," *Washington Post*, March 16, 2005, p. A4 (retrieved via LexisNexis August 5, 2005).

3 Sheryl Gay Stolberg, "As Vote on Filibuster Nears, G.O.P. Senators Face Mounting Pressure," *New York Times*, April 20, 2005, p. 19 (retrieved via LexisNexis August 5, 2005).

4 Mark Leibovich, "In the Senate, the Escalation of Rhetoric," *Washington Post*, May 17, 2005, final edition (retrieved via LexisNexis August 5, 2005).

5 Richard Morin and Dan Balz, "Filibuster Rule Change Opposed; 66% in Poll Reject Senate GOP Plan to Ease Confirmation of Bush's Judicial Nominees," *Washington Post*, April 26, 2005, p. A1 (retrieved via LexisNexis August 5, 2005).

6 Dana Milbank, "Republicans Enlist History in Fight Against Filibusters," *Washington Post*, April 10, 2005, p. A4 (retrieved via LexisNexis August 5, 2005).

7 Charles Babington and Shailagh Murray, "A Last-Minute Deal on Judicial Nominees; Senators Agree On Votes for 3; 2 Could Still Face Filibusters," *Washington Post*, May 24, 2005, p. A1 (retrieved via LexisNexis August 5, 2005).

8 See Norman J. Ornstein, Thomas E. Mann, and Michael J. Malbin, *Vital Statistics on Congress 1999–2000*, "Party Unity Scores in Congressional Voting" (Washington, DC: American Enterprise Institute Press, 1999), table 8-4, pp. 202–203.

9 Ornstein et al., *Vital Statistics*, table 4-2, p. 117.

10 Christopher J. Deering and Steven S. Smith, *Committees in Congress*, 3rd ed. (Washington, DC: CQ Press, 1997), pp. 11–18.

11 U.S. House of Representatives and U.S. Senate websites, www.house.gov and www.senate.gov.

12 U.S. House of Representatives, Committee on Armed Services website, http://armedservices.house.gov/about/subcommittees.html (retrieved October 17, 2005).

13 Joel D. Aberbach, *Keeping a Watchful Eye: The Politics of Congressional Oversight* (Washington, DC: Brookings Institution Press, 1990), p. 419.

14 Roger H. Davidson and Walter J. Oleszek, *Congress and Its Members*, 9th ed. (Washington, DC: CQ Press, 2004), p. 215.

15 Congressional Information Service, Bill Tracking Report, "Tracking H.R. 5005 Homeland Security Act of 2002" (retrieved via LexisNexis, October 27, 2005).

16 Mildred L. Amer, "Membership of the 109th Congress," *CRS Report for Congress*, Report #RS22007, May 31, 2005.

[17] Elizabeth Drew, *The Corruption of American Politics: What Went Wrong and Why?* (New York: Birch Lane, 1999), pp. 37–39.

[18] Richard F. Fenno, Jr., *Congressmen in Committees* (Boston: Little Brown, 1973), p. 1.

[19] David Mayhew, *Congress: The Electoral Connection* (New Haven, CT: Yale University Press, 1974).

[20] Eliza Newlin Carney, David Baumann, and Bill Ghent, "A House Divided," *National Journal*, November 11, 2000, pp. 3555–3559.

[21] http://www.opensecrets.org/overview/casualties .asp?cycle=2004 (retrieved October 11, 2005).

[22] *U.S. Term Limits, Inc. v. Thorton*, 514 U.S. 779 (1995).

[23] Amer, "Membership."

[24] Amer, "Membership."

Chapter 10

[1] Michael A. Fletcher, "Bush Promotes Plan for Social Security," *Washington Post*, January 12, 2005, p. A4.

[2] Fletcher, "Bush Promotes Plan," p. A4.

[3] White House Official Website, Special Page on the President's Plan for Social Security (retrieved from http://www.whitehouse.gov September 22, 2005).

[4] President's Plan for Social Security Reform.

[5] Wikipedia.org, http://en.wikipedia.org/wiki/Social_ Security_reform (retrieved October 1, 2005).

[6] Fletcher, "Bush Promotes Plan," p. A4.

[7] President's Plan for Social Security Reform.

[8] Fletcher, "Bush Promotes Plan," p. A4.

[9] Robin Toner and Glen Justice, "For Social Security, 2 Crucial Weeks Near," *New York Times*, March 16, 2005.

[10] Patrick O'Connor, "Social Security in Limbo," *The Hill: The Newspaper for and About Congress*, June 1, 2005.

[11] Norman C. Thomas, Joseph A. Pika, and Richard A. Watson, *The Politics of the Presidency*, rev. 3rd ed. (Washington, DC: CQ Press, 1992), p. 14.

[12] Thomas et al., *The Politics*, p. 15.

[13] Max Farrand, ed., *The Records of the Federal Convention of 1787*, vol. 1 (New Haven, CT: Yale University Press, 1966), p. 289.

[14] Louis Fisher, *Constitutional Conflicts Between the Congress and the President*, 3rd ed. (Lawrence: University Press of Kansas, 1991), pp. 218–219.

[15] Theodore Lowi, *The Personal President* (Ithaca, NY: Cornell University Press, 1984), p. 20.

[16] Richard Neustadt, *Presidential Power and the Modern Presidents: The Politics of Leadership from Roosevelt to Reagan* (New York: Free Press, 1990), p. 7.

[17] Robert E. DiClerico, *The American President*, 5th ed. (New York: Prentice Hall, 1999), pp. 88–89.

[18] *United States v. Nixon*, 418 U.S. 683 (1974).

[19] *Mississippi v. Johnson*, 71 U.S. 475 (1866); *Nixon v. Fitzgerald*, 457 U.S. 731 (1982).

[20] *Clinton v. Jones*, 520 U.S. 681 (1997).

[21] Harold W. Stanley and Richard G. Niemi, *Vital Statistics on American Politics 1999–2000* (Washington, DC: CQ Press, 2000), Table 9-5, p. 334.

[22] Stanley and Niemi, *Vital Statistics*, Table 9-6, p. 335.

[23] The War Powers Resolution, HJ Res 542; Pub.L. 93-148 (1973); 87 Stat. 555; 50 U.S.C. §§1541–1548. Passed over presidential veto, November 7, 1973.

[24] War Powers Resolution, §2(c).

[25] Andrew Rudalevige, "The Executive Branch and the Legislative Process," in *The Executive Branch*, Joel Aberbach and Mark A. Peterson, eds. (New York: Oxford University Press, 2005), p. 441.

[26] Elisabeth Bumiller and Sheryl Gay Stolberg, "President Sends Bolton to U.N.; Bypasses Senate," *New York Times*, August 2, 2005.

[27] U.S. Constitution, Article II, § 2.

[28] *Meyers v. United States*, 272 U.S. 52 (1926).

[29] Neustadt, *Presidential Power*, chapters 2–5.

[30] David E. Sanger, "Aftereffects: The President; Bush Declares 'One Victory in a War on Terror,'" *New York Times*, May 2, 2003, p. A1.

[31] George C. Edwards III, *On Deaf Ears: The Limits of the Bully Pulpit* (New Haven, CT: Yale University Press, 2003).

[32] James David Barber offers a psychological theory of the presidency that argues just that point; James David Barber, *Presidential Character: Predicting Performance in the White House*, 4th ed. (New York: Prentice Hall, 1992).

[33] Lowi, *The Personal President*, p. 1.

[34] John P. Burke, "The Institutional Presidency," in Michael Nelson, ed., *The Presidency and the Political System*, 6th ed. (Washington, DC: CQ Press, 2000), p. 417.

[35] Burke, "The Institutional Presidency," p. 420.

[36] James P. Pfiffner, *The Modern Presidency* (New York: St. Martin's, 1994), p. 103.

[37] DiClerico, *The American President*, p. 220.

[38] Pfiffner, *The Modern Presidency*, p. 105.

[39] Bill Moyers, *The Secret Government: The Constitution in Crisis* (New York: Seven Locks, 1988), p. 20.

[40] Ronald C. Moe, "The President's Cabinet," in James P. Pfiffner and Roger H. Davidson, eds., *Understanding the Presidency* (New York: Longman, 1997), p. 137.

[41] Moe, "The President's Cabinet," pp. 140, 142.

42 Thomas E. Cronin and Michael A. Genovese, *The Paradoxes of the American Presidency* (New York: Oxford University Press, 1988), p. 284.

43 Cronin and Genovese, *Paradoxes*, p. 283.

44 *Administrative Procedures Act of 1946*, 5 U.S.C. 551–559, 701–706.

45 Shirley Anne Warsaw, *The Keys to Power: Managing the Presidency* (New York: Longman, 2000), p. 203.

46 Warsaw, *Keys to Power*, pp. 204–206.

47 Warsaw, *Keys to Power*, pp. 206–207.

48 Cronin and Genovese, *Paradoxes*, p. 311.

49 Warsaw, *Keys to Power*, p. 208.

50 Richard Nathan, *The Administrative Presidency* (New York: John Wiley, 1983).

51 Warsaw, *Keys to Power*, pp. 225–226.

Chapter 11

1 Keith Boykin, "Life After *Lawrence*," Keithboykin.com, August 11, 2003 (retrieved from http://www.keithboykin.com/arch/000805.html on July 13, 2005).

2 "John Geddes Lawrence, a Brief Biography" (retrieved from http://en.wikipedia.org/wiki/John_Geddes_Lawrence on July 13, 2005).

3 *Bowers v. Hardwick*, J. Blackmun, dissenting, 478 US 186, at 199.

4 *Powell v. State*, 270 Ga 327 (1998).

5 http://www.outsmartmagazine.com (retrieved July 13, 2005).

6 Texas Court of Criminal Appeals, *John Geddes Lawrence and Tyron Garner v. The State of Texas: Petition for Discretionary Review of Appellants John Geddes Lawrence and Tyron Garner*, April 13, 2001 (retrieved from http://www.lambdalegal.org/cgi-bin/iowa/cases/brief.html?record=824 on September 10, 2005).

7 The Supreme Court's official docket lists *amicus* briefs filed in the case. See http://www.supremecourtus.gov/docket/02-102.htm.

8 *Lawrence and Garner v. Texas*, 539 U.S. 558 (2003).

9 Lawrence Baum, *American Courts: Process and Policy*, 4th ed. (Boston: Houghton Mifflin, 1998), p. 7.

10 Robert A. Carp and Ronald Stidham, *Judicial Process in America*, 4th ed. (Washington, DC: CQ Press, 1998), p. 7.

11 Russell R. Walker and Cynthia Harrison, *Creating the Federal Judicial System*, 2nd ed. (Washington, DC: Federal Judicial Center, 1992), p. 4.

12 Administrative Office of U.S. Courts, *Judicial Business of the United States Courts 2004*, Table A-1 (retrieved from http://www.uscourts.gov/judbus2004/contents.html on September 5, 2005).

13 Baum, *American Courts*, p. 84.

14 Lawrence Baum, *The Supreme Court*, 7th ed. (Washington, DC: CQ Press, 2001), p. 99.

15 Elisabeth Bumiller and Carl Hulse, "Court in Transition: The Overview; Bush Picks U.S. Appeals Judge To Take O'Connor's Seat," *New York Times*, November 1, 2005.

16 Ed Cray, *Chief Justice: A Biography of Earl Warren* (New York: Simon & Schuster, 1997), p. 336.

17 David Stout and Timothy Williams, "Miers Failed to Win Support of Key Senators," *New York Times*, October 27, 2005.

18 Lawrence Baum, *The Supreme Court*, 7th ed. (Washington, DC: Congressional Quarterly, 1998), p. 41.

19 Baum, *Supreme Court*, 6th ed., pp. 46–47.

20 Baum, *Supreme Court*, 6th ed., p. 48.

21 Baum, *Supreme Court*, 6th ed., p. 48.

22 Henry J. Abraham, *Justices, Presidents, and Senators* (Lanham, MD: Rowman & Littlefield, 1999), p. 262.

23 Abraham, *Justices*, pp. 297–299.

24 Abraham, *Justices*, pp. 312–313.

25 Baum, *Supreme Court*, 6th ed., p. 107.

26 Neil A. Lewis, "President Moves Quickly on Judgeships," *New York Times*, March 11, 2001.

27 *Marbury v. Madison*, 5 U.S. 137 (1803).

28 *McCulloch v. Maryland*, 17 U.S. 316 (1819); *Gibbons v. Ogden*, 22 U.S. 1 (1824).

29 *Dred Scott v. Sanford*, 60 U.S. 393 (1857).

30 *West Coast Hotel v. Parrish*, 300 U.S. 379 (1937); *NLRB v. Jones & Laughlin Steel Company*, 301 U.S. 1 (1937).

31 *U.S. v. Lopez*, 514 U.S. 549 (1995); *U.S. v. Morrison*, 120 S.Ct. 1740 (2000).

32 *Bush v. Gore*, 531 U.S. 98 (2000).

33 *Roe v. Wade*, 410 U.S. 113 (1973).

34 *Scott v. Sandford*, 60 U.S. 393 (1856); *Plessy v. Ferguson*, 163 U.S. 537 (1896); *Korematsu v. United States*, 323 U.S. 214 (1944)

35 *Texas v. Johnson*, 491 U.S. 397 (1989).

Chapter 12

1 William A. Niskanen, "More Defense Spending for Smaller Forces: What Hath DoD Wrought?" Cato Institute, Policy Analysis No. 110 (July 29, 1988), www.cato.org/pubs.

2 Bureau of the Public Debt, U.S. Treasury Department (retrieved from http://www.publicdebt.treas.gov/opd/opdpenny.htm on June 13, 2005).

[3] CNN.com, "President Clinton Announces Another Budget Surplus" (retrieved from http://archives.cnn.com/2000/ALLPOLITICS/stories/09/27/clinton.surplus on June 14, 2005).

[4] *Statistical Abstract of the United States 1999* (Washington, DC: U.S. Government Printing Office, 2000), Table 542, p. 348.

[5] Edmund L. Andrews, "Sharp Increase in Tax Revenue Will Pare U.S. Deficit," *New York Times,* July 13, 2005, p. A1.

[6] Edmund L. Andrews, "White House Forecasts Drop in Deficit," *New York Times,* July 12, 2006.

[7] *Economic Growth and Tax Relief Reconciliation Act of 2001* (retrieved from http://en.wikipedia.org on June 16, 2005).

[8] Tax Policy Center (William G. Gale, Peter Orszag, and Isaac Shapiro), "Distributional Effects of the 2001 and 2003 Tax Cuts and Their Financing" (retrieved from http://www.taxpolicycenter.org/publications/template.cfm?PubID=8888 on July 5, 2005).

[9] *Jobs and Growth Tax Relief Reconciliation Act of 2003* (retrieved from http://en.wikipedia.org on June 16, 2005).

[10] Jonathan Weisman, "Record '05 Deficit Forecast: War Costs to Raise Total to $427 Billion," *Washington Post,* January 26, 2005.

[11] John W. Kingdon, *Agenda, Alternatives, and Public Policies* (New York: HarperCollins, 1984), p. 18.

[12] Kingdon, *Agenda,* p. 82.

[13] Kingdon, *Agenda,* pp. 83–84; see Charles E. Lindblom, "The Science of Muddling Through," *Public Administration Review,* 14 (Spring 1959), pp. 79–88.

[14] Kingdon, *Agenda,* pp. 92–93

[15] Kingdon, *Agenda,* p. 93.

[16] Kingdon, *Agenda,* pp. 93–94.

[17] Melanie Warner, "The Food Industry Stikes Back Again," *New York Times,* July 7, 2005.

[18] Gosling, *Politics and the American Economy* (New York: Longman, 1998), p. 9.

[19] Gosling, *Politics and the American Economy,* p. 9.

[20] Gosling, *Politics and the American Economy,* pp. 9–10.

[21] Gosling, *Politics and the American Economy,* p. 11.

[22] Gosling, *Politics and the American Economy,* p. 83.

[23] James A. Thurber, "If the Game Is Too Hard, Change the Rules: Congressional Budget Reform in the 1990s," in James A. Thurber and Roger Davidson, eds., *Remaking Congress: Change and Stability in the 1990s* (Washington, DC: CQ Press, 1995), p. 131.

[24] Steven V. Roberts, "Church Meets State," *U.S. News &World Report,* April 24, 1995, p. 26.

[25] *CQ Almanac 1995,* 11–3; *CQ Weekly Report* (November 18, 1995), p. 3506.

[26] Richard Alonso Zaldivar, "House Defies the President on Stem Cells," *Los Angeles Times,* May 25, 2005.

[27] David Stout, "In First Veto, Bush Blocks Stem Cell Bill," *New York Times,* July 19, 2006.

[28] Federal Reserve Board, *The Federal Reserve Board, Purposes and Functions,* p. 17, www.federalreserve.gov/pf/pdf/frspf2.pdf.

[29] Gosling, *Politics and the American Economy,* pp. 5–6.

[30] Jeffrey E. Cohen, *Politics and Economic Policy in the United States* (Boston: Houghton Mifflin, 1997), p. 224.

[31] U.S. Census Bureau, "Income, Poverty, and Health Insurance Coverage in the United States 2004," August 30, 2005 (retrieved from http://www.census.gov/hhes/www/income/income03.html on September 7, 2005).

[32] Dan Ackman, "Outsourcing CEOS to Get Big Pay Hikes," Forbes.com (retrieved from http://www.forbes.com/work/management/2004/08/31/cx_da_0831topnews.html on July 6, 2005).

[33] Steve Forbes, "Fact and Comment" (retrieved from http://www.forbes.com/forbes/2005/0523/027.html on July 5, 2005).

[34] Center for Responsive Politics, "Big Time Donors Small in Number" (retrieved from http://www.crp.org/pressreleases/DonorDemographics02.asp on July 6, 2005).

[35] John Green, Paul Herrnson, Lynda Powell, and Clyde Wilcox, *Individual Congressional Campaign Contributors: Wealthy, Conservative, and Reform Minded* (Chicago: Joyce Foundation of Chicago, 1998) (retrieved from http://www.opensecrets.org/pubs/donors/donors.htm).

[36] David Cay Johnston, "The Tax Bill Up Close: Some Facts, Some Tips," *New York Times,* June 3, 2001.

[37] David Cay Johnson, "The Richest Are Leaving the Rich Behind," *New York Times,* June 5, 2005 (retrieved from http://www.nytimes.com/2005/06/05/national/class/HYPER-FINAL.html?ex=1120795200&en=74362ebd51517133&ei=5070 on June 5, 2005).

[38] "The Federal Reserve: Is the Fed Too Aggressive in Fighting Inflation?" *CQ Researcher* (September 1, 2000), pp. 677–678.

[39] Center for Responsive Politics, "2004 Donor Demographics" (retrieved from http://www.crp.org/presidential/donordems.asp on July 6, 2005).

Chapter 13

[1] Peter S. Goodman and Phillip P. Pan, "Chinese Workers Pay for Wal-Mart's Low Prices," *Washington Post,* February 8, 2004.

[2] Bill Moyers, "Is Wal-Mart Good for America?" *PBS Frontline,* November 16, 2004 (transcript available at

http://www.pbs.org/wgbh/pages/frontline/shows/walmart/etc/script.html).

3 Associated Press, "China's Trade Surplus Grew to $12 Billion in October," *New York Times*, November 10, 2005.

4 Ned Barker, "U.S. Trade with China: Expectations vs. Reality," in *PBS Frontline*, "Is Wal-Mart Good for America?" November 16, 2004 (retrieved from (http://www.pbs.org/wgbh/pages/frontline/shows/walmart/china/trade.html on November 9, 2005).

5 Gene B. Sperlin, "U.S. and China Are on a Collision Course," *International Herald Tribune*, November 4, 2003.

6 James Kanter and Keith Bradsher, "A Return to Quotas," *New York Times*, November 9, 2005.

7 See Louis Fisher, *Presidential War Power*, 2nd ed. (Lawrence, KS: University Press of Kansas, 2004).

8 Louis Fisher, *Constitutional Conflicts Between Congress and the President*, 3rd ed. (Lawrence, KS: University Press of Kansas, 1991), pp. 218–219.

9 Steven W. Hook and John Spanier, *American Foreign Policy Since World War II*, 16th ed. (Washington, DC: CQ Press, 2003), p. 160.

10 James M. McCormick, *American Foreign Policy and Process*, 4th ed. (Belmont, CA: Wadsworth, 2004), p. 262.

11 *United States v. Belmont*, 301 U.S. 324 (1937); *United States v. Pink*, 315 U.S. 203 (1942).

12 Steven W. Hook, *U.S. Foreign Policy: The Paradox of World Power* (Washington, DC: CQ Press, 2004), p. 161.

13 Hook, *U.S. Foreign Policy*, p. 170.

14 Hook, *U.S. Foreign Policy*, p. 176.

15 "80-Year-Old Woman Strip-Searched," *United Press International*, July 2, 2002 (retrieved from http://www.upi.com/inc/view.php?StoryID=02072002-043959-6030r on November 19, 2005).

16 McCormick, *American Foreign Policy*, pp. 364–365.

17 Hook, *U.S. Foreign Policy*, p. 29.

18 Hook, *U.S. Foreign Policy*, p. 29.

19 Hook, *U.S. Foreign Policy*, p. 32.

20 United Nations Charter (retrieved from http://www.un.org/aboutun/charter).

21 Hook, *U.S. Foreign Policy*, p. 263.

22 McCormick, *American Foreign Policy*, p. 52.

23 McCormick, *American Foreign Policy*, p. 89.

24 Laura Hayes, "Al-Qaeda: Osama bin Ladin's Network of Terror," *Infoplease* (retrieved from http://www.infoplease.com/spot/terror-qaeda.html).

25 Charles S. Clark, "Bin Laden's War on America," in "War on Terror," *CQ Researcher*, October 12, 2001.

26 Clark, "Bin Laden's War on America."

27 Clark, "Bin Laden's War on America."

28 "War on Terrorism" (retrieved from at http://en.wikipedia.org/wiki/War_on_terrorism).

29 David Masci, "Confronting Iraq," *CQ Researcher*, October 4, 2002, pp. 793–816.

30 Susan Taylor Martin, "Bush Dismisses Facts By Linking 9/11, Iraq," *St. Petersburg Times*, June 30, 2005, p. A6.

31 "Putin: Russia Warned US of Iraq Terror," *CNN.com International*, June 18, 2004 (retrieved from http://edition.ccn.com/2004/WORLD/meast/06/18/saddam.terror).

32 "In Their Own Words: Iraq's Imminent Threat," *Center for American Progress*, January 29, 2004 (retrieved from http://www.americanprogress.org/site/pp.asp?c=bi-JRJ8OVF&b=24970).

33 Transcript, "Speech to U.N. Security Council, November 8: 'U.S. Wants Peaceful Disarmament of Iraq, Negroponte Says'" (retrieved from http://manila.usembassy.gov/wwwhira3.html).

34 "Operation Iraqi Freedom" (retrieved from http://www.globalsecurity.org/military/ops/iraqi_freedom.htm).

35 Amy Belasco, "The Cost of Iraq, Afghanistan, and Enhanced Base Security Since 9/11," *CRS Report for Congress*, October 7, 2005.

36 Mary H. Cooper, "Global Warming Update," *CQ Researcher*, November 1, 1996, p. 972.

37 Cooper, "Update," p. 962.

38 Cooper, "Update," p. 962.

39 Cooper, "Update," p. 972.

40 Cooper, "Update," p. 975.

41 Mary H. Cooper, "Bush and the Environment," *CQ Researcher*, October 25, 2002, p. 874.

42 United States Senate, *S. RES. 98*, 105th Congress, 1st Sess., July 25, 1997 (retrieved from http:thomas.loc.gov on October 20, 2005).

43 Robert Longley, *Alternatives to Global Warming: US Policy*, U.S. Government Information/Resources (retrieved from http://usgovinfo.about.com/od/technologyandresearch/a/warmingpolicy.htm on October 20, 2005).

44 Cooper, "Bush and the Environment," p. 874.

Glossary

527 groups Named for the section of the Internal Revenue Service code that they are formed under, these groups, which cannot be affiliated with a political party or a candidate for political office, can spend unlimited funds on political campaigns. They have multiplied and become controversial in recent elections.

1936 Literary Digest poll A straw poll that incorrectly predicted that Alf Landon would win the election over FDR. It is a famous example of an unscientific poll.

Actual malice The standard that applies when a public official or public figure files a libel claim. Such a person must be able to be show that the person making the statement either knew that it was false when it was stated or acted with "reckless disregard of whether it was false or not."

Actual representation The idea that the only person who can legitimately speak for a group of citizens is someone they actually choose.

Administrative rules/regulations Decisions by executive departments or agencies that have the force of law. In order for an agency to enact administrative law, Congress must specifically provide it with authority to do so.

Advertising to voters By making frequent trips home to the district, sending newsletters to voters, and making appearances in the local press, members of Congress promote themselves to their constituents.

Affirmative action A term used to encompass a variety of governmental programs and corporate initiatives that make a concerted, proactive effort to ensure equal opportunity in practice as well as in theory.

Agenda setting A process in American politics through which the media raise the issues that are deemed important to the public and also frame the manner in which we discuss those issues.

Agents of socialization Institutions and events that help define our political beliefs. Important examples include family, school, generational effects, the media, community groups, and peers.

Alexander Hamilton One of the authors of the *Federalist Papers,* which were designed to convince people that the Constitution ought to be ratified.

American Civil Liberties Union An organization dedicated to the protection of civil liberties.

American political culture The set of beliefs, values, and traditions that most Americans share.

Amicus curiae A "friend of the court"; a brief (a document containing a legal argument supporting a desired outcome in a particular case) filed by a third party, or amicus curiae, who is not directly involved in the litigation but who has an interest in the outcome of the case.

Anti-Federalists A political group that opposed the adoption of the Constitution because of the document's nationalist tendencies and because it did not include a bill of rights.

Appeals When a case from a lower court (usually a trial court) is reviewed by an appellate court to correct errors made by the lower court.

Appropriations Legislative committee activity that determines the funds that will be spent on governmental programs. Allocating funds is a yearly process that requires specific legislation.

Aristocracy One of Aristotle's six forms of government, in which a select minority of the population governs for the public good.

Aristocratic republic Where a minority of the citizenry is given the power to choose representatives for the government.

Aristotle Greek philosopher who examined the forms of government known to him at the time he was writing. He argued that it was possible to characterize governments by looking at (1) who governs and (2) whose interests are being served by the decisions made by those in power.

Articles of Confederation The nation's first national constitution, established following the American Revolution. The articles provided for a government in which each state retained its own sovereign power and the central government had few powers.

Authorization Legislative committee activity that focuses on legislation that establishes or modifies a government program.

Ballot initiative An electoral procedure through which citizens directly decide the outcome of a policy issue.

Baron de Montesquieu French philosopher who embodied the conventional wisdom on the correct construction of a republic upon which our government is based. He argued that to maintain a republic it was vital to maintain strict *separation of powers* between the basic branches of government.

Behavior modification By rewarding the victors and punishing the losers, courts try to encourage some behavior and discourage other behavior. By imposing harsh sanctions on the losers, courts serve a broader societal goal of deterrence.

Bicameral legislature A legislature made up of two chambers, or parts. The United States has a bicameral legislature, composed of the House of Representatives and the Senate.

Bill of Rights The first ten amendments to the U.S. Constitution. They list the freedoms—such as the freedoms of speech, press, and religion—that a person enjoys and that cannot be infringed on by the government.

Bill of attainder A legislative act that singles out an individual or group for punishment without a trial.

Bipartisan Campaign Finance Reform Act of 2002 The first major change since 1974, it changed the limits on contributions that individuals can donate to political parties and, more important, sought to halt the proliferation of soft money.

Black codes Laws that existed primarily in the southern states that constrained the activities of African Americans. They included prohibitions on gun ownership and assembling after dark.

Block grants Federal programs that provide funds to state and local governments for general functional areas, such as criminal justice or mental-health programs. These grants provide more flexibility for state and local government than categorical grants.

Blue states The states that the Democratic Party won in the 2000 and 2004 elections. These states are often characterized as being liberal.

Borking The attempt to defeat the confirmation of a high-ranking official on ideological grounds. Named for the battle over the failed Supreme Court nomination of Robert Bork.

Boston Tea Party Act of civil disobedience undertaken by the American colonists. It involved the open defiance of British law.

Briefs Written arguments explaining why a court decision should be upheld or overturned.

Broadcast media Media that transmit information in "real time" using electronic technology.

Brown v. Board of Education The Supreme Court case decided in 1954 whereby the Court changed its interpretation of the Fourteenth Amendment. It rejected the "separate but equal" standard and required that the states treat all their citizens the same, regardless of race.

Budget and Impoundment Control Act of 1974 An Act of Congress that restricts the president's ability to impound funds. Passed after President Nixon refused to spend funds appropriated by Congress.

Bureaucracy A large organization that is structured hierarchically to carry out specific functions.

Cabinet A presidential council consisting of the secretaries of executive departments and other individuals the president invites to participate. The cabinet is supposed to provide the president with advice on how to do his job, but its importance has declined over time.

Candidate image The intangible qualities that are part of a candidate's persona and advertising such as: honesty, trustworthiness, and looking presidential.

Candidate-centered elections Individual candidates are the center of the electoral process. They individually choose to run, raise their own funds, and plan their own strategies. Political parties play a support role to candidates.

Capitalism An economic system based on the principles of profit motive and private ownership as the means of production.

Casework The term used when members of Congress help their constituents deal with the red tape of the federal bureaucracy.

Categorical grants A federal grant targeted for a specific purpose, as defined by a federal law.

Caucus An open meeting of party members designed to select candidates and propose policies.

Censorship Governmental prohibition of specific forms of expression.

Checks and balances A major principle of American government, in which each branch of government is given the means to check (restrain or balance) the actions of the other two.

Chief legislator The expectation the public has for the president to provide leadership for Congress and to use his legislative powers to achieve his agenda.

Civic education The study, throughout the elementary and secondary school years, of important events and figures in our nation's political history—intended to educate the nation's youth on what it means to be a citizen.

Civic obligation The sense that we should learn about and participate in politics because it is the right thing to do.

Civic virtue The idea that the ruling element of society must put the good of the whole above individual or class interests when making public decisions.

Civil cases Legal cases that involve noncriminal disagreements between two individuals or between an individual and a corporation or organization.

Civil liberties Personal freedoms that are protected for all individuals.

Civil rights The guarantees that each citizen has in the United States that his or her privileges of citizenship are the same as for all other citizens.

Civil Rights Act of 1964 Law that addressed the problems of *de facto* racial discrimination, which was practiced by individuals and businesses rather than governmental entities.

Civil rights movement The movement in the 1950s and 1960s, by African Americans and concerned whites, to end racial segregation.

Civil servants Permanent government employees who cannot be removed by the president without cause.

Closed primary A primary election in which only party members can vote to choose that party's candidates.

Cloture vote A vote of sixty senators to end a filibuster.

Cluster sampling A technique for creating a sample to poll that begins with the pollster selecting increasingly smaller clusters—regions, a county, a residential block, for example—before randomly selecting a household to contact.

Coercive federalism A derogatory term used to describe the increasingly restrictive rules placed on federal grants-in-aid beginning in the 1960s.

Coercive or Intolerable Acts Retaliatory acts by the British government after the Boston Tea Party. Most of the acts were directed toward Massachusetts.

Cold War Political, economic, and military rivalry between the United States and the Soviet Union that began after World War II. It intensified when the Soviet Union gained access to nuclear weapons, but remained short of actual warfare.

Collective security The idea that war is renounced as a means of statecraft, and participating nations pledge to defend each other in the case of outside aggression.

Commander in chief A constitutional power granted by Article II that makes the president the supreme commander of the military forces of the United States and of the state National Guard units when they are called into federal service.

Commerce clause The clause in Article I, Section 8, of the Constitution that gives Congress the power to regulate interstate commerce (commerce involving more than one state). It is a major source of congressional power.

Commercial speech Advertising statements that describe products. Commercial speech receives less protection under the first amendment than ordinary speech.

Committees Where most of the work of Congress is done. Membership and leadership are determined by partisan control of Congress: the majority party leadership names the chairperson for each committee and determines the partisan makeup of each committee.

Common law Judge-made law that originated in England from decisions shaped according to prevailing customs. Decisions were applied to similar situations and thus gradually became common to the nation.

Complainant A person who reports a possible crime to the police or prosecutor's office.

Concentration of ownership The situation that currently exists where increasingly fewer media outlets are owned by a small number of extremely large corporations.

Concurrent powers Powers held jointly by the national and state governments.

Concurring opinion A separate opinion, prepared by a judge who supports the decision of the majority of the court but who wants to make or clarify a particular point or to voice disapproval of the grounds on which the decision was made.

Conditions of aid Accompany categorical grants and instruct state and local governments how to run programs.

Confederation A league of independent states that are united for the purpose of achieving a common goal or goals.

Conference committees Committees composed of members of both chambers who are appointed to reconcile differences when bills pass the two chambers of Congress in different forms.

Congressional Budget Office Office within Congress created to give Congress independent advice on economic forecasts and budget scenarios.

Conservatives Those espousing a political ideology characterized by a desire to limit the role of government; they believe that private solutions are often the best way to work out societal ills.

Constitutional Convention This meeting of delegates from the states was held in Philadelphia in 1787 for the purpose of amending the Articles of Confederation. Instead, the delegates wrote a new constitution (the U.S. Constitution) to replace the Articles.

Constitutional law Decisions of the U.S. Supreme Court are said to make constitutional law, and are binding on all other courts and on the rest of the government.

Constitutionalism A term used to describe the belief that there is a fundamental law, the Constitution, and that all other laws, to be valid, must conform to the Constitution.

Containment The American foreign policy started by President Truman to stop the spread of communism by containing communist nations within their current territorial limits.

Content bias/political bias The idea that reporters and news organizations are promoting a specific political perspective or agenda in the content of their stories.

Content neutral A limitation on freedom of expression that exists for reasons other than restricting expression and where no particular message is being singled out for restriction.

Convergence A bringing together of media sources.

Cooperative federalism The theory that the states and the national government should cooperate in solving problems.

Corporate foundation A source of structural bias. With few exceptions, media outlets are for-profit entities.

Council of Economic Advisors A three-member council of professional economists created in 1946 to advise the president on economic matters.

Creative expression The various means that people have at their disposal to display their creative impulse in the arts, literature, and music.

Criminal case A case in which an individual, the defendant, is charged with violating a law and, if found guilty, faces deprivation of life, liberty or property as a sanction.

Criminal syndicalism laws Laws that made it a crime to advocate the violent overthrow of the American government.

Critical election An election in which the change of party control, a critical realignment, occurs.

Critical realignment A dramatic change in the party control of American politics. This change takes place in a critical election.

Crosscutting requirements A method of control that allows the national government to impose federal rules on the states as a condition of accepting federal money.

Crossover sanctions A method of federal government control that requires a state or local government to meet specific guidelines to receive federal dollars.

***De facto* Segregation** Racial segregation that occurs not as a result of deliberate intentions but because of past social and economic conditions and residential patterns.

***De jure* Segregation** Racial segregation that is legally mandated, i.e., racial segregation that occurs because of laws or decisions by government agencies.

Dealignment When political parties become too weak to organize the electoral system; critical realignment then is no longer possible.

Declaration of Independence The document declaring that the thirteen colonies were separating from Great Britain. It set forth principles and political ideals that would later be incorporated into the state constitutions, the U.S. Constitution, and the Bill of Rights.

Declaration of Rights Put forth by the first Continental Congress, it asserted that the colonists' political rights and freedoms as British citizens were being violated by the British government.

Defendant In a civil case, the person or organization the plaintiff claims is responsible for the complaint. In a criminal case, the person accused of committing a crime.

Definition of news A source of structural bias. News is defined based on the following criteria: 1. strong impact; 2. violence, conflict, disaster, scandal; 3. familiarity; 4. proximity; 5. timeliness and novelty.

Deliberative Type of principle involved in democratic decision-making, which holds that decisions should be based on a full examination and discussion of the issue at stake—also implies that a variety of perspectives are discussed and debated prior to making a final determination of what should be done.

Democracy A system of government in which the people have ultimate political authority. The word is derived from the Greek *demos* (people) and *Kratia* (rule).

Democratic accountability The ability that voters have to turn officials out of office. This ability helps to insure two-way communication between the voters and officials, since the official must run for re-election to stay in office.

Democratic Party Formed by Andrew Jackson after the 1824 election from the remnants of the disintegrating Democratic-Republican Party; it remains one of the two major American political parties today.

Democratic republic Where the entire citizenry has the power to choose representatives for the government.

Democratic-Republican Party Founded by Thomas Jefferson and James Madison, this party, also known as the Jeffersonian Republican Party, formed in opposition to George Washington's administration's economic policies. The party had the support of agrarian interests in the South and the West.

Depression A period of severe economic recession when output diminishes to such a degree that the economy begins to collapse. It is characterized by high unemployment and low confidence in the economy.

Détente A French word meaning "relaxing of tension," détente refers to the effort by the United States and the Soviet Union to de-escalate the Cold War. Détente began with the Strategic Arms Limitation Treaty of 1972, and ended with the Soviet invasion of Afghanistan in 1979.

Devolution revolution A movement that began in the 1990s to transfer to the states some of the responsibilities assumed by the national government since the 1930s.

Digital divide A term used to describe the difference between those who have access to information technology and those who—because of their economic circumstances—do not.

Diplomacy The conduct by government officials of negotiations and other relations between nations.

Direct democracy/participatory democracy A system of government in which political decisions are made by the people themselves rather than by elected representatives.

Discrimination To make distinctions and to treat people differently based on those distinctions.

Dissenting opinion A separate opinion in which a judge dissents from or disagrees with the conclusion reached by the majority on the court and expounds his or her own views about the case.

Divided government A situation where no one major political party controls the presidency and the other two houses of Congress. This has been common over the last three decades.

Dred Scott v. Sanford An 1856 decision of the Supreme Court that held that slavery was protected by the Constitution and that slaves were the property of their owners regardless of where they traveled with their owner. Its effects served as a catalyst to the dissolution of the Union.

Dual federalism A system of government in which the states and the national government each remain supreme within their own spheres. The doctrine looks on nation and states as coequal sovereign powers.

Due process Procedures used to guarantee the rights of those accused of committing a crime. These guarantees are critically important in the criminal justice system because they are based on the presumption of legal innocence.

Due process clause The constitutional guarantee, set out in the fifth and fourteenth amendments, that the government cannot deprive a person of life, liberty, or property without due process of law.

Elastic clause Article I, Section 8, Clause 18, of the Constitution, it grants Congress the power to do whatever is necessary to execute its specifically delegated powers. Also known as the necessary and proper clause.

Elections The method for selecting leaders in a representative democracy. Elections also serve as a method for holding leaders accountable and for influencing public policy.

Electoral College The formal method of selecting the president and vice president in the United States. When Americans vote they are voting for electors who in turn meet in state capitols to decide who the president and vice president will be.

Electoral politics A method that interest groups use to influence public policy. Techniques include endorsing candidates, providing workers for campaigns, and—especially—donating money to candidates through political action committees (PACs).

Electoral vote The vote taken by the electoral college to decide who the president and vice president will be. Each state has electoral votes equal to the total number of U.S. senators plus representatives.

Electorate Those who are empowered to vote.

Empirical judgment A determination of what actually is the case that is based on substantive and credible evidence.

Enlightenment The period of intellectual history that covers the seventeenth and eighteenth centuries. During this period, ideas about politics and government changed markedly from previous eras.

Entertainment Values A source of structural bias. The idea that television news producers are more interested in entertaining their audiences rather than focusing on traditional hard news items.

Enumerated Powers Powers specifically granted to the national government by the Constitution. Most are spelled out in Article I, Section 8 of the Constitution.

Equal protection clause Section 1 of the Fourteenth Amendment, which states that no state shall "deny to any person within its jurisdiction the equal protection of the laws."

Equal Rights Amendment First introduced into Congress in 1923, this Amendment stated that "Equality of Rights under the law shall not be denied or abridged by the United States or by any state on account of sex."

Equality of conditions The idea that certain levels of material services and goods should be provided to citizens so that they can function as citizens regardless of their economic circumstances. Public education is an example of this concept.

Equality of opportunity An application of equality to the economic realm. It is the view that everyone should be able to advance his or her own material circumstances based on his or her own abilities and willingness to work hard.

Equality of results The idea that certain levels of material services and goods should be provided to citizens so that they can function as citizens regardless of their economic circumstances. Public education is an example of this concept.

Establishment clause The section of the First Amendment that prohibits Congress from passing laws "respecting an establishment of religion." Issues concerning the establishment clause often center on prayer in public schools, the teaching of fundamentalist theories of creation, and government aid to parochial schools.

Ex post facto **law** A criminal law that punishes individuals for committing an act that was legal when the act was committed but that has since become a crime.

Exclusionary rule The legal rule that does not allow evidence gathered by unconstitutional means to be used in a trial.

Executive Agreements Agreements with other nations that are made by the president instead of through the treaty process. Executive agreements have been used for more than 100 years, and avoid having to gain Senatorial ratification to go into effect.

Executive immunity The claim that the president is not subject to lawsuits that interfere with the duties of the president, that charge the president with a crime, or that seek civil damages from the president.

Executive orders A rule or regulation issued by the president that has the effect of law. Executive orders can implement and give administrative effect to provisions in the Constitution, to treaties, and to statutes.

Executive privilege The claim that presidents have the prerogative not to provide information to Congress or the courts about activities internal to the operation of the executive branch if doing so would jeopardize national security or limit the president's ability to discharge his duties as chief executive.

Exit polls Polls used to predict the outcome of elections before the polls are closed and the votes are counted; done by interviewing voters as they leave the polling place.

Faction(s) The term used by James Madison in *Federalist* No. 10 to describe groups of people in the electorate with a common interest that is contrary to the public good.

Federal Election Campaign Act of 1974 The first major effort at campaign finance reform. The act was designed to reduce the influence of wealthy individuals on elections, eliminate the disparities in available financial resources that existed among candidates, and to ensure that campaign contributions were not diverted to non-campaign related purposes. In large part, this act remains the basis of current federal campaign finance law.

Federal Election Commission Established by the Federal Election Campaign Act (1974) to enforce the terms of the law.

Federal funds rate The interest rate that federal depository institutions charge banks for overnight loans.

Federal Reserve Board An independent executive agency that has exclusive control over monetary policy. Enacted to enforce the Federal Reserve System so the government can regulate the nation's banking system.

Federal Trade Commission An example of the expanding reach of the federal government, the FTC, created in 1914, is charged with enforcing antitrust laws and other laws against unfair business practices.

Federalism A system of government that divides power and sovereignty over a territory between two or more separate governments, typically a national government and regional governments.

Federalist Papers A series of arguments by Alexander Hamilton, James Madison and John Jay that provided an explanation of how the proposed Constitution would work and were intended to convince the public that the Constitution ought to be ratified.

Federalist Party An political party led by Alexander Hamilton and John Adams that supported the adoption of the Constitution. Support came from commercial interests, the cities, and generally from the North.

Fifteenth Amendment Stated that voting rights were not to be denied to an individual due to race or "previous condition of servitude." This remedy was short lived because the states of the former Confederacy restricted the voting rights of former male slaves and their descendants with procedures such as grandfather clauses, poll taxes, white-only primaries, and literacy tests.

Filibuster The Senate rule that allows for unlimited debate on an item. It is used to halt or delay action on a particular bill.

Fireside chats Radio broadcasts by Franklin D. Roosevelt during the Depression.

First Continental Congress The first gathering of delegates from twelve of the thirteen colonies, held in 1774.

Fiscal policy The primary method that the president and Congress have to influence the economy—via government spending and taxation.

Fixed term The length of time a federal official holds office is set by the Constitution. For example, U.S. senators serve six-year terms. In many nations, elected officials do not have fixed terms.

Flat tax An approach to taxation in which everyone is taxed at the same rate.

Food and Drug Act of 1906 An early and important regulatory scheme created by Congress, it prohibited interstate commerce of mislabeled and impure food, drink, and drugs. Inspired by Upton Sinclair's *The Jungle.*

Foreign policy The decisions that government makes in dealing with foreign nations and the goals the government wants to achieve in the world.

Fourteenth Amendment Stated that states had to provide equal protection of the laws and due process of the laws to all citizens (while at the same time formally excluding women and non-taxed Indians from voting). Ratified in the aftermath of the Civil War (1868), it provided for additional limitations on the powers of states. It was not fully adhered to until the *Brown v. Board of Education* decision and the Civil Rights Act of 1964.

Franchise The right to vote.

Franking privilege The ability of members of Congress to send mail to constituents without paying postage. It is part of the electoral advantage that incumbents have over challengers.

Franklin Delano Roosevelt President from 1933 to 1945, Roosevelt led Congress to pass a series of "New Deal" measures intended to stabilize the economy during the Great Depression, which expanded the scope of federal power. He was also the only U.S. president to be elected four times.

Free exercise clause The provision of the First Amendment stating that the government cannot pass laws "prohibiting the free exercise" of religion.

Free media News coverage of political campaigns. Candidates do not pay for this air time.

Free rider problem A question that interest groups face: how to prevent free riders, people who do no work but get the benefits of the work that interest groups do? Groups use a variety of techniques to encourage membership and activism.

Freedom of expression The ability of a person, or group of people, to publicize their views and creative undertakings through a range of communicative technologies and methods.

Front loaded nomination process The acceleration of the presidential nomination selection process by the two major political parties. Holding more primaries and caucuses earlier in the process requires candidates to be better organized and obtain funding earlier.

Full faith and credit clause One way interstate relations are governed in the Constitution. Basically, this clause means that legal documents such as mortgages, marriages, wills, and deeds recorded in one state must be accepted by the other states as valid.

Fundamental law The law that all other laws have to conform to.

General election An election where voters chose between party candidates to decide who will hold elective office. Federal elections are held in even-numbered years on the first Tuesday after the first Monday in November.

General revenue sharing A program that began in 1972; it gave state and local governments billions of dollars and the freedom to spend it as they wished, with only minor strings attached.

Generational effects Long-lasting effects of events of a particular time period on the political opinions or preferences of those who came of political age at that time.

Genocide The deliberate and systematic extermination of a national, racial, political, or cultural group.

Gibbons v. Ogden Decided by the Supreme Court in 1824. In an opinion written by John Marshall, the Court interpreted the commerce clause for the first time. By interpreting "commerce among the several states" broadly, it empowered the national government.

Global warming The theory that global climate change is caused by human interference with the environment through increased emissions of hydrocarbons or greenhouse gases, causing the Earth's atmosphere to warm.

Globalization The changes in society and the world economy that come from dramatically increased international trade.

Going public A new phenomenon in presidential politics where the president will appeal directly to the voters to support his policies instead of bargaining with Congress behind closed-doors.

Grants-in-aid Money given by the national government to state and local governments.

Grassroots support Broad public support for an interest group's issues, which might involve letterwriting, email and phone-in campaigns, as well as marches and protests.

Great Compromise The compromise between the New Jersey and the Virginia plans that resulted in representation in the House of Representatives being based on population and that gave each state equal representation in the Senate.

Great Depression A period of deep economic distress in American history that began with the stock market crash of 1929 and quickly spread to create high unemployment, bank failures, and increased homelessness. The federal government response, the New Deal, led to a larger, more active national government.

Great Society A series of federal government programs created in the 1960s by Lyndon Johnson. It expanded the scope of the national government.

Horse race coverage The way the media frames elections, emphasizing who is ahead and who is behind in the campaign.

House of Representatives The lower house of Congress. It has 435 members serving 2-year terms. Representation is based on population, so that larger states have more seats and the smallest states have a single seat.

House Rules Committee Exists to decide how, and if, individual bills will be considered on the House floor.

Human nature The essential nature of human beings. This concept was important to Enlightenment philosophers when they addressed the question of why government was necessary.

Immutable characteristics Characteristics that a political candidate cannot change, for example: race, ethnicity, religion, or age. Some voters see these characteristics as important in deciding whom to vote for.

Implied powers The powers of the federal government that are implied by the expressed powers in the Constitution, particularly in Article I, Section 8. These powers derive from the "necessary and proper" clause.

Income The amount of money that is earned by an individual or household during a year.

Incorporation doctrine The principle the Supreme Court uses to apply the Bill of Rights to the states; it relies on the due process clause of the Fourteenth Amendment.

Incrementalism The theory of policy formulation in which policy makers "muddle through" the policy process using current practices as a baseline and then only make small adjustments in current behavior.

Incumbency advantage The ability of a candidate who is already in office to be reelected to the same office because of certain perks that they have as an elected official.

Incumbent The person currently holding an elective office.

Independent judicial branch The "least democratic branch of government." This branch of government has the power to judge and is not subject to political pressure.

Indirect democracy/representative democracy Political and policy decisions are made by representatives chosen by the citizenry rather than being made directly by the citizens.

Individual rights The idea that social and political life is based on rights that are inherent in every person.

Individualist conservatives Those who espouse a political ideology committed to the idea of individual freedom and the nineteenth-century idea of rugged individualism.

Inflation Economic phenomenon that results when prices increase faster than wages, decreasing consumers' spending power.

Influencing public policy Voters have the opportunity to influence public policy by making clear to their elected leaders what policy changes they want.

Inherent power The powers of the national government that, although not expressly granted by the Constitution, are necessary to ensure the nation's integrity and survival as a political unit. Inherent powers include the power to make treaties and the power to wage war or make peace.

Interest group An organization that seeks to promote its interests by trying to influence public policy.

Intergovernmental lobby A special interest lobby formed by government officials—governors, mayors, highway commissioners, and others—for the purpose of other government officials.

Internet The Internet is a global network of publicly accessible computer networks. Email and the World Wide Web are examples of services that rely on the Internet to share information electronically.

Interstate Commerce Act of 1888 The first major regulatory scheme created by Congress, it established the Interstate Commerce Commission, which regulated the rates charged for moving railroad freight across state lines.

Interventionism A nation's active intrusion into another nation's political, economic, or military affairs.

Investigation Committee activity that seeks to gain the knowledge needed to make informed decisions about the issues that come before the committee.

Iran-Contra Affair When Congress forbade the United States from providing assistance to counterrevolutionary forces (Contras) fighting in Nicaragua, Lt. Col. Oliver North orchestrated a secret agreement with Iran to exchange arms for hostages and divert the profit from the arms sales to the Contras.

Iron triangles A three-way alliance among legislators, bureaucrats, and interest groups to make or preserve policies that benefit their respective interests.

Isolationism The policy of isolating one's country from the affairs of other nations by declining to enter into alliances, foreign economic commitments, or international agreements. Doctrine first established by President George Washington.

Issue networks In some issue areas, the environment for example, groups of diverse experts are influential in making public policy. These experts may include legislators or legislative staff members, interest-group leaders, bureaucrats, the media, scholars, and others. Policy making is more open in areas characterized by issue networks as opposed to those with iron triangles.

Jacksonian democracy This political movement of the 1820s sought to expand the right to vote to all males. It argued that economic status should not be a prerequisite to voting rights. However, at the time the argument only included white males.

James Madison Often called the "father of the Constitution," Madison was instrumental in drafting the Constitution. He also wrote many of the *Federalist Papers*.

Jim Crow The familiar term for *de jure* segregation. These laws, passed in the post–Civil War era in the southern states, required that separate public facilities had to be established for whites and blacks.

John Locke English political philosopher who heavily influenced the writing of the Declaration of Independence.

John Marshall Considered the nation's greatest Supreme Court justice, he presided over the Court from 1801–1833. He wrote opinions in major decisions such as the *McCulloch v. Maryland* (1819) and *Gibbons v. Ogden* (1824) cases. He favored nation-centered federalism.

Joint committees Consisting of members from both the House and Senate.

Judicial activism A doctrine holding that the Supreme Court should take an active role in using its powers to check the activities of Congress, state legislatures, and administrative agencies when those government bodies exceed their authority.

Judicial independence The special protection given to Supreme Court justices and other federal judges to insulate them from the political pressures of ordinary politics. Article III of the Constitution provides these justices and judges with a guaranteed salary that cannot be diminished while in office, and the ability to serve during "good behavior," meaning that they cannot be removed from office other than by impeachment.

Judicial restraint A doctrine holding that the Supreme Court should defer to the decisions made by the elected representatives of the people in the legislative and executive branches.

Judicial review The power of a court to declare a law unconstitutional and thus null and void.

Judiciary Act of 1789 One of the first acts passed by the new Congress, it established a three-tier system of federal courts.

Kennedy-Nixon debates In 1960, the first televised debate between presidential candidates. It has come to be seen as one of the key events that heralded the increasing importance of the role of the media in elections.

Labor unions Groups that bring together workers who share an occupation or work in the same industry. They seek to negotiate better pay and working conditions for their members as well as influence government to benefit their members and workers generally.

Law A body of rules enacted by public officials in a legitimate manner and backed by the force of the state.

Layer cake federalism Term used by political scientists before the New Deal to describe the relationships between the levels of government—national, state, and local—in which each had clearly defined powers and responsibilities.

League of Nations An international organization promoted by President Woodrow Wilson to promote world peace and cooperation after World War I. The League of Nations was created by the Treaty of Versailles, but the United States Senate never ratified U.S. membership.

Legal equality The idea that each citizen is equal under the law and that the rules apply the same to all persons regardless of their wealth, race, gender, and/or status in the community.

Legitimacy A reason for holding elections. By electing officials in open and free elections, the faith of the people in their leaders and their government is increased.

Libel A published report of a falsehood that tends to injure a person's reputation or character.

Liberals A political ideology characterized by the advocacy of an active government in solving society's problems.

Life, liberty, property The three rights that Locke argued naturally belonged to all individuals. These were later incorporated into the Declaration of Independence as "life, liberty, and the pursuit of happiness."

Litigation A technique used by interest groups of bringing a lawsuit, sponsoring a lawsuit, or writing an *amicus curiae* brief in support of a lawsuit, to try to achieve their goals through the court system.

Lobbying A method that interest groups use to influence government officials by persuasion, especially by providing officials with information and expertise about their concerns.

Local government These governments make up about 97 percent of the nation's governments and offer individual citizens remarkable potential for access and influence, but have no status under the Constitution.

Local media Media outlets with a regional rather than a national audience.

Majority leader The leader elected by the majority party in the House or Senate.

Majority opinion A court opinion reflecting the views of the majority of the judges on a court.

Majority rule The basic decision-making rule used in democracies.

Mandates A requirement or an order that a state or local government implement a national government program.

Marble cake federalism Term used to describe the relationships between the levels of government after the New Deal in which the lines between national, state, and local governments are skewed.

Marbury v. Madison An 1803 case where the Supreme Court first exercised judicial review. The decision of this case invalidated part of the Judiciary Act of 1789 and claimed the Court's ability to declare a law unconstitutional.

Margin of error The positive or negative range for inaccuracy in the results of a poll. The margin of error is based on the size of the survey sample.

Marshall Plan Part of the Truman Doctrine, the Marshall Plan was an American policy designed to rebuild western Europe after World War II by injecting $17 billion of reconstruction aid.

Mass media Communication channels, such as newspapers as well as radio and television broadcasts, where large numbers of people can be sent the same message at the same time.

Material benefits Financial incentives and information that are offered to people to become members of interest groups.

McCulloch v. Maryland Decided by the Supreme Court in 1819, this dispute was over the constitutionality of the Bank of the United States. In finding the Bank constitutional, it increased the power of the national government by providing an expansive reading of implied powers and the supremacy clause.

Medical marijuana The legalization of marijuana for medical use. Marijuana is said to provide relief from nausea, vomiting, seizures, chronic pain, and the lack of appetite caused by a number of diseases and their treatment. Its use remains controversial and has been the subject of a power struggle between the states and the national government.

Minor parties Also known as third parties, these political parties do not often win elections, but they can be influential by bringing up new policy ideas.

Minority leader The leader elected by the minority party in the House or in the Senate.

Miranda **rule** The Supreme Court rule that requires law enforcement officials to notify those being accused of crimes of their rights before being questioned.

Mob rule Exists when the majority of people engage in rash, irrational behavior. This action often involves violence and usually does not conform to the rule of law.

Moderate A political ideology characterized by holding no consistent belief in either conservative or liberal ideas.

Monarchy A form of government in which a single ruler (king, queen, emperor, etc.) governs in the best interests of the society at large.

Monetary policy The use of changes in the amount of money in circulation to alter credit markets, employment, and the rate of inflation.

Money supply The amount of money in circulation within an economy.

Monroe Doctrine Foreign policy doctrine established by President James Monroe in an 1820 address to Congress. The Monroe Doctrine put European powers on notice not to intervene in the politics and affairs of the Western Hemisphere. In return, the United States would stay out of European politics.

Moralist conservatives Reflecting a political ideology rooted in a fundamentalist or evangelical religious perspective, they have a passionate commitment to a clear and true set of moral rights and wrongs, which come from the word of God.

Moralist liberals People who reflect a political ideology that is rooted in the goal of achieving a more just and equitable society that often comes from deeply held religious or spiritual convictions. Often described as idealists.

Mutually assured destruction Part of the theory of deterrence of nuclear war, mutually assured destruction asserts that if the United States and Soviet Union engage in a military conflict, both sides are assured that although they might destroy the other side, they would be destroyed as well.

NAACP National Association for the Advancement of Colored People. Founded in 1910, it is an interest group dedicated to the eradication of racial segregation and discrimination.

National media Media outlets that are available to people throughout the nation.

National party convention Major meetings of political parties held every four years to create a platform and select a presidential nominee. Once presidential nominees were chosen by party leaders, but today they formalize what was decided in the primaries and caucuses.

National Security Council A council established in 1947 that was created to provide the president with coordination of national security policy.

National Voter Registration Act of 1993 Commonly known as the "motor voter" law, it requires that states allow people to register to vote while applying for a driver's license as well as making voter registration available in social service offices and by mail.

Nation-centered federalism The idea that the national government should be stronger, more dominant in relation to the state governments.

Necessary and proper clause Article I, Section 8, Clause 18, of the Constitution, which gives Congress the power to make all laws "necessary and proper" for the federal government to carry out its responsibilities. Also known as the elastic clause.

Negative image ads Political ads where the candidate will suggest that his or her opponent does not have the integrity needed to hold the office.

Negative issue ads Political ads where a candidate criticizes his or her opponent's positions on specific public policy issues.

Neutrality The policy or status of a nation that does not participate in a war between other nations.

New Deal A program ushered in by the Roosevelt Administration in 1933 to bring the United States out of the Great Depression. The New Deal included many government spending and public-assistance programs, in addition to thousands of regulations governing economic activity.

New Deal coalition The broad and diverse group of supporters—blue-collar workers, southerners, northern liberals, intellectuals, Catholics, Jews, African Americans, and the poor—of the Democratic Party during FDR's presidential terms and afterward.

New Deal liberals People who reflect the ideology of the traditional base of support for the Democratic Party in the United States. Their highest political values are equality, social progress, and the efficacy of the existing political system.

New federalism A plan, first proposed by Richard Nixon and later advocated by Ronald Reagan, to both limit the national government's power to regulate and to restore power to state governments. Essentially, the new federalism was designed to give the states greater ability to decide for themselves how government revenues should be spent.

New Jersey Plan Proposed in 1787, this plan would have kept the balance of power between the states as it was under the Articles of Confederation.

New media Non-news forums used to communicate with the public about politics. New media includes talk radio, television talk shows, television news magazines, electronic town hall discussions, MTV, print and electronic tabloids, and the Internet.

News media Organizations that have as their primary purpose informing the public about current political and policy issues.

Nineteenth Amendment Ratified in 1920, it gave women the right to vote.

Normative question A question involving values, principles, and the rationales used to justify why certain actions are desirable.

Objectivity A standard in the media which emerged in the nineteenth century as newspapers began to lose their partisan character. It is the idea that the media are supposed to be neutral in their political reporting.

Obscenity A category of creative expression that is not protected by the First Amendment. Material is legally obscene if it appeals "to the prurient interest in sex," portrays "sexual conduct in a patently offensive way," and, taken as a whole, has no "serious literary, artistic, political, or scientific value."

Office of Management and Budget An agency in the Executive Office of the President that assists the president in preparing and supervising the administration of the federal budget.

Office of the Solicitor General The office in the U.S. Department of Justice that represents the government in all cases before the U.S. Supreme Court.

Oligarchy A government where a select minority of the population govern in their own self-interest rather than for the public good.

Open primary A primary election in which voters who are not affiliated with a particular party, as well as party members, may participate in selecting a party's nominee.

Oral arguments Verbal arguments presented in person by attorneys to an appellate court. Each attorney presents reasons to the court why the court should rule in his or her client's favor.

Oversampling A process that is used in polling to insure that a poll will survey enough members of a small group—such as blacks or Hispanics—to allow for independent analysis.

Oversight Committee activity that follows up on enacted laws to ensure that they are being enforced and administered in the way in which they were intended.

Parliamentary system A method of selecting a government where the voters choose a legislature and that body selects a national leader. Parliamentary election campaigns tend to be shorter than in the United States, and the elections generally do not have fixed dates.

Partial preemption A policy where the federal government creates a minimum requirement and allows state and local governments to exceed it if they wish, thereby not pushing them out of a policy area altogether. The minimum wage is an example.

Particularized benefits A way to enhance a Congressperson's electability by enacting laws that will bring benefits, including federal money, into his or her district; also known as "pork barrel" legislation.

Parties as organizations One of three perspectives through which we view political parties. Parties are fragmented networks of local, state, and national organizations that work to elect candidates to office.

Parties in government One of three perspectives through which we view political parties: a group of elected and appointed officials that are affiliated with a party organize government and try make their policy ideas law.

Parties in the electorate One of three perspectives through which we view political parties. Parties are labels that voters use to help them make decisions when voting.

Partisan press Newspapers that existed during the late eighteenth century as offshoots of political parties. They were used to convey and promote specific political agendas.

Party affiliation The political party that an individual supports. Although not all people have a clear party affiliation, for those that do it is the most important factor in understanding voter choice.

Party identification An emotional or psychological link to a particular political party that is often carried over from generation to generation in a family and is often converted to a vote.

Party machines Powerful local party organizations, especially prevalent between 1875 and 1950, that control government employment and government contracts.

Party platform A document drawn up by a party platform committee at each national convention, it outlines the policies, positions, and principles of the party; it is then submitted to the entire convention for approval.

Party unity scores The percentage of votes on legislation where a majority of one party votes against a majority of the other party. High scores are indicators of party unity.

Patronage A system of rewarding the party faithful and workers with government jobs or contracts. Also referred to as the spoils system.

Peak business associations An example of business interest groups, they promote the general interests of corporate America. Examples are the U.S. Chamber of Congress and the National Association of Manufacturers.

Plaintiff The party in a civil case who claims to have been injured in some way.

Plea bargain An agreement between the prosecutor and the defendant that determines the outcome of a criminal case. Often used in place of a jury trial.

Plessy v. Ferguson This 1896 case upheld a Louisiana law that required railroad companies to provide separate cars for blacks and whites. It established what came to be called the "separate but equal" interpretation of the equal protection clause of the Fourteenth Amendment.

Plurality A method of declaring a winner of an election where the candidate who receives the most votes wins, regardless of whether that candidate wins a majority (over 50 percent of the votes) or not. Most elections in the United States are decided by a plurality vote.

Pocket veto A special type of veto power used by the chief executive. Bills that are not signed by the president after the legislature has adjourned die after a specified period of time and must be reintroduced if Congress wishes to reconsider them.

Police powers The power of the states to create laws for the protection of the health, morals, safety, and welfare of the people.

Policy evaluation The act of assessing public policies through formal and informal means after the policy has gone into effect.

Policy formulation The part of agenda setting that begins to sort out what government should do and how it should achieve its goals by selecting among alternative solutions to policy problems.

Policy implementation The process of putting a policy into place after a new law is passed.

Policy subgovernments See iron triangle.

Political action committees Better known as PACs, they are organizations set up under federal law. Representing a corporation, labor union, or special interest group, PACs raise and give campaign donations on behalf of these organizations or groups. PACs are limited in the amount of money they can donate to any individual candidate and to federal candidates as a whole.

Political agenda The issues that politicians will address; often determined by the media.

Political equality The idea that all citizens should have the right to vote, serve on juries, and participate in the civic life of the nation.

Political expression Putting forth views about public issues.

Political ideology A well-developed set of views that guide an individual's thinking on politics.

Political participation Various practices that are necessary for a healthy democracy which require citizens to pay attention to, and be involved in, public affairs. Examples include voting, contacting an elected official, and working on a political campaign.

Political party An organization that seeks to elect candidates to office under its label and, once elected, run the government.

Political socialization A learning process through which individuals learn about and form their attitudes and beliefs about government politics.

Polity A system of government in which the majority governs for the public good. Aristotle believed this form of government was rare and unstable because the majority of citizens were usually incapable of making disinterested decisions.

Poll timing The concept that it is critical to know when a poll was conducted to accurately interpret the results. Events can change public opinion quickly.

Popular vote The total number of votes cast by the American people in the presidential election.

Pork barrel An informal term for legislation that directly benefits a member's district. (See particularized benefits.)

Position taking Taking stands on issues to please issue-attentive voters.

Positive image ads Political ads where the candidate presents a picture of himself or herself that appeals to voters' ideas about what constitutes a good leader.

Positive issue ads Political ads that promote a candidate's stand on specific public policy issues.

Pragmatic liberals Voters who reflect a political ideology that shares some values with both New Deal and moralistic liberals but is tempered by a strong belief in capitalism and a willingness to compromise to meet their goals.

Precedent A rule of law where future courts considering similar cases need to review the results of prior cases. Judges often rely on precedents in deciding cases.

preemption A doctrine rooted in the supremacy clause of the constitution that provides that national laws or regulations governing a certain area take precedence over conflicting state laws or regulations governing that same area.

President Under the executive branch of government, this single executive has the authority to administer the federal government.

President pro tempore The member of the majority party who has been in the Senate for the longest time and who formally presides over the Senate.

Primary election A preliminary election held for the purpose of choosing a party's candidate for the general election.

Print media Communication channels that consist of printed materials, such as newspapers and magazines.

Prior restraint Restraining an action before the activity has actually occurred. The formal term for censorship.

Privileges and immunities clause An important provision affecting interstate relations. It means that no state can discriminate against someone from a different state and that no state can normally afford special privileges to its own citizens.

Probability sampling A well-established set of mathematical principles that allows scientific polling to be done. It is based on some form of random selection.

Professional associations These groups bring together individuals with the same occupations, most commonly occupations requiring technical training or expertise, to advocate for their professional interests before government.

Progressive tax rates Tax system where people are taxed based on their ability to pay.

Proportional representation A system of selecting a legislature where legislators are elected in multiple-member districts and each political party is then awarded seats roughly in proportion to the percentage of votes a party receives.

Public accommodations Services provided to the general public by private entities such as restaurants, hotels, movie theaters, and other retail establishments.

Public figures Public officials, movie stars, and generally all persons who become known to the public because of their positions or activities.

Public interest The idea that the best interests of the collective, overall community, rather than the narrow interests of a self-serving group, should be the basis for political decision-making.

Public interest groups A range of citizen groups that are concerned with issues that benefit the larger community, not just their members. They represent both conservative and liberal interests.

Public official Someone who holds either elected or appointed public office.

Public opinion The collective view of a community on a political issue or idea.

Public policy The decisions that government makes and the programs that it enacts.

Purpose of government What should government be trying to achieve?

Purposive benefits The rewards individuals get by joining an interest group whose goals they believe in.

Push polls An effort by a political group to give a person negative information about an opponent with the intent of changing that view or vote. This is done by phone under the pretense of conducting a public opinion poll.

Racism The belief that there are superior and inferior races of people and that individual members of those races should be treated accordingly.

Ranking member The most senior member of the minority party on each congressional committee.

Rational The capacity of human beings to improve their circumstances through the use of logic and systematic inquiry.

Realigning election See critical election.

Recession A period of diminished economic output that occurs when the economy shrinks for three consecutive quarters.

Red states The states that the Republican Party won in the 2000 and 2004 elections. These states are often characterized as being conservative.

Referendum An electoral device whereby legislative or constitutional measures are referred by the legislature to the voters for approval or disapproval.

Regressive tax rates A tax system in which tax rates decrease as income increases.

Regulatory agencies Agencies that enforce administrative rules enacted in specific areas like environmental protection, nuclear power, or occupational health and safety.

Representation A system in which individuals are chosen by the citizenry to make political decisions rather than having the citizens make those decisions directly.

Republic A form of government based on representation, the principle of a mixed constitution, and the concept of separation of powers. The ultimate political authority rests with the people, who elect individuals to represent them in lawmaking and other decisions.

Republican Party Formed in 1854 by opponents of the expansion of slavery, it first won the presidency in 1860 with the election of Abraham Lincoln. It remains as one the two major American political parties.

Republicanism The political principles and ideals that inspired the founding generation of American politics.

Reserved powers Created by the Tenth Amendment, these powers are left exclusively to the states. The extent of these powers has been controversial.

Retrospective voting A process that a voter goes through in deciding who to vote for when a voter poses the question: "Am I better off now than before?"

Right to a jury trial The constitutional guarantee that determinations of guilt are made by citizens serving on juries.

Right to Privacy A set of constitutional protections afforded to individuals that are not explicitly listed in the Constitution. They are generally understood to include the right to make choices about one's body and lifestyle free of government intrusion.

Roger Taney Replacing John Marshall as Chief Justice in 1835, he was a strong advocate of state-centered federalism and turned the Court in that direction.

Rule making The process undertaken by an administrative agency when formally proposing, evaluating, and adopting a new regulation.

Rule of four A United States Supreme Court procedure requiring four affirmative votes to hear the case before the full Court.

Sampling error In the context of opinion polling, the difference between what the sample results show and what the true results would have been had everybody in the relevant population been interviewed. Sampling error generally decreases as the sample size increases.

Scientific sampling The idea that you can identify the views of an entire population by interviewing a small number of individuals.

Second Continental Congress The 1775 Congress of the colonies that established an army.

Segregation To separate. In racial terms, it means separate treatment of people based on their race.

Selecting leaders The primary reason for holding elections in most democracies.

Self-interest The idea that political decisions are made to benefit the personal interests of the decision maker rather than being made to benefit the public at large (see public interest.)

Senate The upper house of Congress with 100 members. Senators serve six-year terms. One-third of the members are up for re-election every two years. Each state has two senators.

Senatorial courtesy A longstanding tradition in the U.S. Senate that senators of the president's party are given considerable leverage in the process of selecting judges from their state.

Separate and independent elections An election system, in contrast to a parliamentary system, where the legislature and the executive are each voted on by the people in separate elections.

Separate but equal A Supreme Court doctrine holding that the equal protection clause of the fourteenth amendment did not forbid racial segregation as long as the facilities for blacks were equal to those provided for whites. The doctrine was established in *Plessy v. Ferguson* and overturned in *Brown v. Board of Education*.

Separation of powers The principle of dividing governmental powers into separate and independent executive, legislative, and judicial institutions.

Shaping public opinion A method that interest groups use to influence government by trying to modify the views of the general public.

Shays' Rebellion A rebellion of angry farmers in western Massachusetts in 1786, led by former revolutionary war Captain Daniel Shays.

Single-issue voters Voters who are focused on one issue above all else. They will vote on the basis of a candidate's position on a single issue, often a social issue, regardless of all else.

Slander The public uttering of a false statement that harms the good reputation of another.

Social capital Social capital is defined as "connections among individuals" as experienced in social networks and voluntary organizations.

Social contract A voluntary agreement among individuals to create a government and to give that government adequate power to secure the mutual protection and welfare of all individuals.

Social issues Issues such as abortion, gun control, and gay and lesbian rights on which candidates are often sharply divided. These issues are important to many voters.

Soft money Campaign contributions that evade contribution limits by being given to parties and party committees to help fund general party activities. The Bipartisan Campaign Finance Reform Act of 2002 limited donations to federal candidates and national parties, but independent 527 groups are still allowed.

Solidary benefits The sense of community, friendship, and connections that some individuals get from joining an interest group of like-minded people.

Sound bites Brief, memorable comments that easily can be fit into news broadcasts.

Speaker of the House Presiding officer of the House of Representatives. Elected at the beginning of each two-year session, the election is always by party line.

Special/select committees Congressional committees that deal with specific issues that arise outside the jurisdiction of standing committees. They are established temporary committees that exist for designated periods of time.

Split ticket voting When a voter selects candidates from more than one party on an election ballot.

Spoils system The system initiated by President Andrew Jackson where federal jobs were handed out by the president as a reward for past loyalty or work during the presidential campaign.Also known as patronage.

Stagflation An economic phenomenon that occurs when both inflation and unemployment are rising.

Stamp Act (1765) The first direct tax imposed on the colonies because custom revenues were insufficient to raise the amount of money the British government required.

Stamp Act Congress (1765) The first time that a number of states gathered together formally to complain about British rule and brought a petition to the king protesting the Stamp Act that was later repealed by Parliament.

Standing committees Permanent committees in Congress that deal with legislation concerning a particular area, such as agriculture or foreign relations.

Stare decisis From the Latin, "to stand on decided cases"; the judicial policy of following precedents established by past decisions.

State of nature A situation where there is no government. Consequently, in that state human nature is expressed without restraint.

state-centered federalism The belief that the national government should be held to the enumerated powers listed in the Constitution and that the national government is limited by the Tenth Amendment.

Statutes Laws passed by legislatures that can be changed by enacting another law to modify or repeal it.

Statutory interpretation When courts engage in interpreting the meaning of statutes.

Straight ticket voting When a voter selects candidates from only one party on an election ballot.

Strong presidency model The theory argued by members of the Constitutional Convention that the Constitution required an independent executive empowered with important functions in the Constitution.

Structural bias Referring to what occurs as a result of news organizations' systems of selecting some kinds of information as news and rejecting other kinds as not.

Subcommittee A division of a larger committee that deals with a particular part of the committee's policy area. Each of the standing committees in Congress has several subcommittees.

Super rich The top 1 percent of Americans who control the largest share of the nation's wealth.

Supply-side economics An economic theory that supports tax cuts for wealthy Americans and corporations to stimulate the economy. Also known as "trickle-down economics," supply-side economics argues that tax relief for the wealthy provides them with more funds to invest, the benefits of which "trickle down" to the poorest in society.

Supremacy clause Article VI, Clause 2, of the Constitution, which makes the Constitution and federal laws superior to all conflicting state and local laws.

Supreme Court Forms the pinnacle of the federal judicial system and consists of nine justices who hear appeals from the U.S. Circuit Courts of Appeals and the fifty state supreme courts in cases dealing with interpretation of the Constitution and federal law.

Symbolic expression Everything from slogans to insignias through which a person can indicate to others his or her political position.

Take care clause Power given to the president in Article II of the Constitution that gives the president responsibility to implement and enforce the laws as passed by Congress.

Term cycle Theory about opportunities for presidential leadership that suggests that the opportunities present for leadership differ depending on where the president is within a four-year term.

Thomas Hobbes An Enlightenment political thinker who had harsh views of human nature, calling it a state of "war of all against all," where life was "solitary, poor, nasty, brutish, and short."

Thomas Jefferson Jefferson (1743–1826) drafted the Declaration of Independence and later became the third president of the United States.

Three-fifths Compromise A compromise reached during the constitutional convention by which it was agreed that three-fifths of all "other persons" were to be counted both for tax purposes and for representation in the House of Representatives.

Time constraints A component of structural bias. The limited amount of time news programs have to present the day's important events.

Tracking polls Polls conducted over several days and weeks to look for trends or changes in voter attitudes over time.

Trade association An interest group formed by members of a particular industry, such as the oil industry or the trucking industry, to influence government for the benefit of that industry.

Traditional conservatives Reflecting a political ideology committed to preserving the values and institutions that they believe are the real source of the nation's greatness and well-being, traditional conservatives are concerned with the decline in standards and civility in contemporary culture.

Treaties Legally binding agreements between nations—in the United States, proposed by the president and ratified by two-thirds of the U.S. Senate.

Truman doctrine Also known as containment, the doctrine established by President Harry S Truman in 1947 to stop the spread of communism by containing communist nations to their current territorial limits.

Twenty-Sixth Amendment Ratified in 1971 during the Vietnam War, it lowered the voting age from twenty-one to eighteen.

Tyranny The arbitrary or unrestrained exercise of power by an oppressive individual or government.

U.S. Circuit Courts of Appeals Federal appellate courts that review decisions from both the district courts and federal administrative agencies within the circuit and correct any legal errors made by the district courts in interpreting federal laws. Organized into twelve geographic circuits.

U.S. Court of Appeals for the Federal Circuit Specialized federal appellate court that hears cases from the U.S. Court of Federal Claims and the Court of International Trade.

U.S. District Courts Trial courts that hear both criminal and civil cases under the U.S. Constitution and federal law.

U.S. magistrate judges Judges who are appointed by the U.S. District Courts for eight-year terms and carry out specific tasks for district court judges. Magistrate judges hear minor criminal matters and can try civil cases with the consent of the parties.

Unfunded mandates A requirement or an order that a state or local government implement a national government program that comes without the money to pay for it.

Unified government Where the same political party controls both the Congress and the presidency.

Unitary system A centralized governmental system in which one national government has the authority make decisions for the entire territory. Local or regional governments exercise only those powers given to them by the central government.

United Nations An international organization created in 1945 by the Allied Powers in World War II to promote international peace, security, and cooperation among nations.

Veto The power held by the president of the United States to refuse to sign a bill into law.

Veto power A constitutional power that enables the president to reject legislation and return it to the legislature with reasons for the rejection. This prevents the bill from becoming law, unless the veto is overridden by two-thirds of both chambers of Congress.

Virginia Plan A plan proposed by the Virginia delegates to the Constitutional Convention that called for a strong national government with the ability to veto actions taken by the state legislatures and called for representation based on population that would have given the balance of power to the large states.

Virtual representation The idea that representatives do not have to be directly chosen by the citizens being represented, nor do they have to live in the area represented.

Voices of September 11th A nonprofit advocacy group founded by Mary Fetchet in order to assist those affected by the 9/11 terrorist attacks.

Voter registration Developed a century ago to reduce voter fraud and reduce the power of political party machines. Unlike many democracies, Americans must take the initiative to register to vote.

Voter turnout The percentage of the voting-eligible population that goes to the polls on Election Day.

Voting Rights Act of 1965 A law which was directed toward removing the barriers that prevented most African Americans in the country at the time from voting.

Wall Street The location of the New York Stock Exchange and other major financial institutions, Wall Street is a symbol of the nation's financial markets and economic power.

War on Poverty A national program proposed by Johnson in 1964 to combat poverty and discrimination.

War on terror The war on terror is the name given to the United States' effort to combat global terrorism in the wake of the 2001 attacks on the World Trade Center and the Pentagon.

War Powers Resolution A 1974 Act that attempted to limit the president's ability to place American armed forces into hostile or potentially hostile situations without congressional approval.

Warren Court The second period of judicial activism with Earl Warren as Chief Justice of the Supreme Court that ruled on several important civil rights and liberty cases.

Weak presidency model The theory argued by members of the Constitutional Convention that the primary function of the executive would be to implement the will of Congress.

Wealth The value of an individual's tangible assets (equity in one's home, car, and other consumer durables) plus financial assets (stocks, bonds, savings accounts) minus debts. Wealth is a much better indicator of economic power than income.

Weighted results A process of interpreting and presenting poll results so that they correspond to the demographics of the population being studied.

Welfare reform Passed in 1996, it replaced numerous categorical grants with a major block grant to states and gave flexibility to the states to run welfare programs as they saw fit. It is a major example of devolution.

Whig Party It emerged out of a faction of the old Democratic-Republican Party in the 1830s and became the second major party until the 1850s. The Whigs would go on to elect two presidents in the 1840s. They were a diverse and splintered group of northern industrialists and southern planters.

Whip A member of Congress who assists the majority or minority leader in the House or in the Senate in managing the party's legislative preferences.

White House Office The personal office of the president. The White House Office provides the president with a staff of more than 500 individuals who are solely dedicated to advancing the president's agenda.

Winner-take-all single-member districts A method of election in which only one candidate can win election to each office. A term used to describe the Electoral College System, in which the candidate who receives the largest popular vote in a state is credited with all that state's electoral votes—one vote per elector.

Wording of questions A major concern in public opinion polling because the way a question is worded can alter the results of a poll.

Writ of certiorari An order issued by a higher court to a lower court to send up the record of a case for review. It is the principal vehicle for cases decided by the U.S. Supreme Court.

Written constitutions The embodiment of social contract theory. In written constitutions, the details of the governing system are specified and ratified by the public.

Index

A

AARP, 213, 219, 304
Abolitionists, 110
Abortion rights, 103–4, 188
Abu Ghraib, 424
Access
    to court, 348–50
    to politicians, 214, 396
Accused, rights of, 104, 106
ACLU, 210, 350, 396
Actual malice, 98
Adams, President John, 19, 191
Adams, President John Quincy, 248
Adams, Samuel, 27
Adirondack Mountain Club, 213
Adjudicatory powers, 330
Administrative Procedure Act, 328
Administrative rules, 341
Advertising, campaign, 175–76
Advocacy of ideas, 95
Ad watch articles, 176
Affirmative action, 118–19
Afghanistan War, 130, 134, 416, 417, 419, 420
African Americans, 116, 356
    equal rights for, 11, 110
Agenda setting process, 178, 374
Agents of socialization, 128
Aid to Families with Dependent Children
    (Welfare), 75
Alito, Justice Samuel, 82, 353
Al Qaeda, 418–19, 422
Amendment 2, in Colorado, 313–15
American Bar Association, 106
American Center for Law and Justice, 120, 211
Americans with Disabilities Act, 79, 117
Amicus curiae, 217, 338, 350, 351
Annual budget proposal, 313
Anti-Federalists, 46, 64, 307
Antiquities Act, 308
Appointment power, 314
Aristotle, 6
Arms Race, 415–16
Article I, 49, 50, 277
Article II, 51, 311, 403
Article III, 339
Articles of Confederation, 28–42, 64, 306
Asian-American immigrants, 10
Audiences, media, 159–60
"Axis of evil", 421

B

Bagdikian, Ben, 167
Ballot initiative, 13
Ballots, place of parties on, 197
Bank of the United States, 70
Bargaining advantages, of presidency, 318–19
Benefits
    of interest groups, 212–13
    particularized, 293
Bias, question of, 168–73
Bicameral legislation, 37, 49
Bicameral legislature, 277
Bill, how it becomes law, 287–89
Bill of Rights, 16, 17, 44, 45, 47, 50, 53, 85, 90, 96
    incorporation of, 91–92
Bills of attainder, 52
Bin Laden, Osama, 418–19, 420
Bipartisan Campaign Finance Reform Act, 240
Black, Justice Hugo, 95
Black civil rights movement, 11
Black codes, 111
Blair, Tony, 137
Block grants, 77
Blue states, 227–29
Blunt, Roy, 304
Bork, Robert, 357
Boston Tea Party, 27–30, 39
Bowers v. Hardwick, 337
Brady, James, 82
Brady Handgun Violence Prevention Act, 82
Brandeis, Justice Louis, 95, 355
Brennan, Justice William, 95, 354
Breyer, Justice Stephen, 357
Broadcast media, 157, 159
Brown v. Board of Education, 11, 90, 113, 114,
    116, 367
Bryan, William Jennings, 178
Buchanan, President James, 323
Budget, 371–74, 385–87
Budget and Accounting Act, 385
Budget Control and Impoundment Act of 1974,
    310, 385
Bully pulpit, 308
Bureaucracy, federal, 328–33
Bureau of the Budget, 325, 385
Burger Court, 367
Burning cross, 86
Bush, President George H.W., 78, 195, 197, 263,
    320, 429

Bush, President George W., 4, 101, 137, 143–44, 148, 174, 186, 195, 197, 203, 204, 227, 228, 231, 240, 261, 263, 265, 267, 301–3, 315, 319, 320, 321, 322–23, 326, 333, 353, 356, 359, 366, 373, 382, 397, 406, 421, 425, 429, 430
Bush v. Gore, 226, 365
Business associations, 207–9
Business interests, 207
Byrd, Senator Harry, 197

C
Cabinet, 326–28
Cable technology, 159, 163
Calhoun, Senator John C., 72
California, ballot initiative in, 13
Campaign ads, 175–76
Campaign contributions, 240
Campaign finance reform, 186, 397
Campaigns, financing, 239–42
Canada, 60, 410
Candidates, 142–43
    attributes of, 263–64
    how voters choose, 261–65
    recruiting, 189
Capitalism, 18, 379
Career civil service, 331
Carter, President Jimmy, 142, 177, 244, 264, 324, 382, 416
Casework, 294
Categorical grants, 76
Catholics, 356
Caucus system, 238
Censorship, 93
Center for Media and Public Affairs, 174
Cheney, Vice President Dick, 137
Changing the Constitution, 52–53
Checkbook participation, 269
Checks and balances, 46, 47, 48, 49, 206, 342
Chicago, machine politics, 203
Chief diplomat, 316–17
Chief executive, 316
Chief legislator, 315
Child Online Protection Act (COPA), 98–99
Children, political views of, 128–29
China, 400–402, 417
Chinese Exclusion Act, 10
Christian Right, 188, 211
Churches, 132
Circuit Courts of Appeals, 344–46
Circuit courts, 344
Citizen groups, 210–11
Citizen participation, 125–27
Citizenship
    responsibilities of in democracy, 5
    restricted, 36
    restricted understanding of, 9

Civic education, 130
Civic involvement, 181
Civic obligation, 140
Civic virtue, 8, 35
Civil cases, 339
Civil disobedience, 28
Civil liberties, 88, 90–108
Civil rights, 89, 108–16
    current issues, 118
Civil Rights Act, 11, 60, 115–16
Civil rights movement, 11, 21, 115, 178, 217
Civil servants, 328
Civil Service Act, 331
Civil Service Commission, 331
Civil War, impact of, 10, 72–73, 111, 193
Class Action Fairness Act of 2005, 78–79, 188
Clear and present danger test, 94
Cleveland, President Grover, 327
Clinton, President Bill, 78, 81, 123–24, 128, 141, 143, 160, 161, 167, 174, 176, 195, 203–4, 219, 263, 275, 311, 314, 322–23, 332–33, 353, 356–57, 382, 386–87, 429
    and gun control, 319
    support for, 123–25
Clinton, Senator Hillary Rodham, 124, 161
Cloture vote, 278
Cluster sampling, 146
Coercive Acts, 39
Cold War, 414, 416–18
Colonial assemblies, 37
Commander in chief, 316–17, 403–4
Commerce clause, 65, 71
Commercial speech, 93
Committee on Administrative Management, 323
Committees, in Congress, 282–87
Common law, 341
Communications Decency Act of 1996, 98
Communist Party, 94
Community groups, 132
Concerted political activity, 9
Concurrent powers, 67
Concurring opinion, 351
Conditions of aid, 76
Confederation, 64
Confirmation, of judges, 356–58
Congress, U.S., 216, 306, 308, 322
    changing the Constitution, 52–53
    committees in, 282–87
    and devolution revolution, 80–81
    and lawmaking, 287–92
    organization of, 277–92
    party leadership and, 279–82
    running for, 250–52
    women in, 298–99
Congressional Budget Office, 373, 386
Congressional elections, 266

Congressional oversight, 286
Conlan, Timothy, 76
Conservatives, 133
    individualist, 136
    moralist, 136–37
    traditional, 136
Constituency work, 294
Constitution, U.S., 26–56, 30–31, 53–54
    changing, 52–53
    equality and, 110–16
    federalism and, 64–66
    general provisions of, 48–52
    national government in, 65–66
    as source of law, 341
    written, 33
Constitutional amendments, 10, 11, 12, 18
Constitutional Convention, 34, 42–44, 307
Constitutionalism, 30
Constitutional law, 341
Containment, 414
Content bias, 171
Content neutral, 94
Continental Congress
    First, 39, 40
    Second, 39
Contraception, 102–3
Contract with America, 144, 203
Contributions, limits on, 240
Conventions, 242, 244, 247
Convergence, of media sources, 168–70
Cooperative federalism, 75
Core American beliefs, 15–16
Corporate foundation, 171
Corporation, 209
    power of, 383
    rise of large, 73
Council of Economic Advisors, 325
Council of State Governments, 211
Counsel, right to, 105
Court of Appeals, 338, 343, 346
Court packing plan, 74, 362
Courts, 217, 339
    access to, 348–49
    district, 344–46
    organization of, 343–48
    as political institutions, 342
Creative expression, 93
Creditor-dominated state government, 29
Criminal cases, 341
Criminal law, 66
Criminal syndicalism laws, 94
Critical realignment, 191
Cronkite, Walter, 166
Crosscutting requirements, 79
Crossover sanctions, 79
Cruel and unusual punishment, 106

C-SPAN, 287
Cuban Missile Crisis, 415

D
Daily Show, 162
Daley, Richard J., 203
Daschle, Senator Thomas, 266, 279
Dealignment party, 196
Dean, Howard, 163, 242, 397
Death penalty, 106
Death with Dignity Act, 104
Debates, televised, 162–63, 166, 176–78
Debt, unpaid, 41
Decision making, in Supreme Court, 351–52
Declaration of Independence, 9, 31, 33, 36, 40, 108
Declaration of Rights, 39
Defense, Department of, 408
Defense of Marriage Act (DOMA), 68
Deficits, 371–74
Deliberative process, 14
Democracy
    and American politics, 4–5
    current state of American, 20–23
    direct, 13
    framers' understanding of, 36–38
    indirect, 13
    Internet and, 24
    meaning and history of, 5–8
    participatory, 13
    representative, 13
    transformation of, 9–12
Democratic accountability, 233
Democratic Party, 142, 188–89, 193, 198, 282
    emergence of, 191, 193
Democratic-Republicans, 191, 193
Depression, economic, 41, 191, 380
Détente, 415
Deterrence, 415, 415–16
Digital divide, 157
Diplomacy
    presidential power over, 406
Diplomatic relations, 316
Direct democracy, 13
Director of National Intelligence, 410
DirecTV, 159
Disadvantaged groups, 116–18
Disclosure, 242
Discrimination, 112, 378
    reverse, 119
Disney, 167–68
    holdings of, 169
Dispute resolution, 339–41
Dissenting opinion, 351
District courts, 338, 343–44, 358–59
Divided government, 195–96, 291–92
Donaldson, Sam, 167

"Dot.com" industries, 373
Dred Scott v. Sanford, 72, 111, 361, 367
Due process clause, 90, 103

E
Economic Growth and Tax Reconciliation Act of
    2001, 373
Economic issue evaluation, 262–63
Economy
    promotion of nation's, 70
    role of president in keeping strong, 317
Eighteenth Amendment, 53
Eisenhower, President Dwight, 114, 165, 195, 324,
    331, 332, 354
Elastic clause, 50, 65
Election coverage, patterns of, 174–75
Elections
    of 2000, 220, 227, 234, 319, 365
    of 2004, 14, 197, 227, 230, 233, 246, 254, 265–66
    of 2006, 195, 239, 250, 266–67
    candidate-centered, 242–43
    general, 234, 237–38, 247–50
    organizing, 189
    presidential, 243–50, 265–66
    primary, 234, 237–38
    rules of, 238–39
    structure of, 234–43
    why they matter, 232–34
Electoral clause
Electoral college, 51, 248, 366
Electoral politics, 220–22
Electoral process, mediated, 173–78
Electoral vote, 248
Electorate, 38
    parties in, 198–200
Electronic media, 165
Electronic technologies, 157
Elite, of colonial society, 37
Elk v. Wilkins, 10
Empirical judgment, 8, 9
Enforcement powers, of president, 310–11
Enlightenment, political ideas of, 31–32
Entangling alliances, 411
Entertainment, 160
Entertainment influences, 180
Entertainment values, 172
Enumerated powers, 50, 60, 65
Environmental groups, 212
Environmental Protection Agency, 429
Equality, 18–19, 89
    of conditions, 109
    and the Constitution, 98–105, 110–16
    legal, 109
    for disadvantaged groups, 106–07
    understandings of, 109–10

Equal Pay Act of 1963, 116
Equal protection clause, 88
Equal Rights Amendment, 117
Establishment clause, 99–101
European Union, 402
Evarts Act, 343
Excluded groups, 9
Exclusionary rule, 105
Executive agreements, 316, 405
Executive branch
    oversight of, 286
    president and, 323–28
Executive Office of the President, 323
Executive orders, 311, 341
Executive power, 50–51
Executive privilege, 311
Executive Reorganization Act of 1939, 323
Exit polls, 142
Ex post facto laws, 52
Expression, unprotected, 97–99
Exxon Valdez, 375

F
Face-to-face communication, 215
Factions, 47, 206
Fairness and Accuracy in Reporting (FAIR), 171
Family, 128–29
Family Research Council, 211, 386
Family values, maintaining, 179
Farmers, small, 28
Federal Bureau of Investigation (FBI), 353, 410
Federal Communication Commission (FCC), 330
Federal Election Campaign Act, 239
Federal Election Commission (FEC), 239
Federal Emergency Management Agency
    (FEMA), 358
Federalism, 52, 60
    American, 60–63, 69–78
    and American industrialization, 73–74
    coercive, 78–80
    in Constitution, 64–68
    cooperative, 75
    creative, 77
    double security of, 60
    dual, 69–70, 309
    nation-centered, 70–74
    new, 77–78
    recent developments in, 78–82
Federalist Papers, 46, 47, 360
Federalist Party, 191
Federalists, 191
Federal matching funds, 245
Federal Reserve Board, 387, 396
Federal Reserve System, 382, 387
Federal Trade Commission (FTC), 74, 330

Feingold, Senator Russell, 241
Fetchet, Mary, 2, 20
Fifteenth Amendment, 10
Fifth Amendment, 18, 90
Filibuster, 115, 274, 278, 360
Filibuster-Nuclear Option Confrontation, 274, 275–76
Filtering function, 13
Fireside chats, 165
First Amendment, 87–88, 90, 92, 95, 102
Fiscal policy, 382, 383–85
Five Twenty Seven (527) Groups, 185–86, 186–87, 222, 241
Fixed terms, 238
Flag burning, 95–96, 367
Florida, 143, 234, 366
Food and Drug Act of 1906, 74
Ford, President Gerald, 177, 244
Foreign policy, 262, 316, 400–430, 410, 411
Fortas, Justice Abe, 356
Fourteenth Amendment, 8, 10, 82, 88, 90, 92, 111, 114, 217, 338
Fourth Amendment, 104–5
France, 60
Franchise, expansion of, 10
Franking privilege, 251–92
Franklin, Benjamin, 307
Freedom, 89
Freedom of expression, 92–96
Freedom of religion, 89, 99–102
Freedom of speech, 92
Freedom of the press, 96–97
Free enterprise system, 380
Free exercise clause, 99, 101–2
Free rider problem, 213
French and Indian War, 38
Frontloading, 245
Full faith and credit clause, 68
Fundamental law, 33
Fund raising, 241–42, 245, 251, 252

G
Gallup Organization, 146
Gallup Poll, 144
Gender-based crimes, 82
General revenue sharing, 77
Generational effects, 130
Germany, 60
Ghana, 60
Gibbons v. Ogden, 71, 361
Gingrich, Representative Newt, 81, 144, 203, 279, 283
Ginsberg, Justice Ruth Bader, 353, 356, 357
Gitlow v. New York, 90
Glasnost, 417

Globalization, 401
Global warming, 427–28
    and foreign policy, 427–30
Going public, 321
Gorbachev, Soviet premier Mikhail, 417
Gore, Vice President Al, 143, 227, 234, 240, 333
Government, 212–13
    creditor-dominated state, 29
    divided, 291–92
    local, 60, 62–63
    organizing the, 190
    parties in, 203–5
    plan of, 34–36
    purpose of, 33–34
    restrictions on authority of, 52
    state, 66–67
    trust in post 9/11, 22–23
    working inside, 215–16
Government spending, 384
Grants-in-aid, 75
Graphic Artists Guild, 209–12
Grassroots mobilization, 219–20
Great Compromise, 43–44
Great Depression, 74, 130, 195, 362, 380–81, 383
Great Society, 75–77
Greenhouse emissions, 427–29
Greenspan, Alan, 388
Griswold v. Connecticut, 102–3
Grodzins, Morton, 75
Gulf War, 312, 411, 422, 425
Gun control movement, 82

H
Hamilton, Alexander, 44, 57, 64, 307, 360
Handgun Control, Incorporated, 211
Hard money, 201, 240
Harrison, President William Henry, 193
Hastert, Representative Dennis, 137, 139
Hate crime laws, 88
Henry, Patrick, 44
Highway funding contingent, 80
Hill, Anita, 357
Hispanics, 118, 356
Hobbes, Thomas, 32, 33, 340
Holmes, Justice Oliver Wendall, Jr., 94, 95
Homeland Security, Department of, 333, 374, 408–9
Honeymoon, presidential, 322
Hoover, President Herbert, 74, 195
Horse race coverage, 173
House of Representatives, 43, 49, 204, 249, 277–78
House Rules Committee, 289
Houston, Charles Hamilton, 113
Human nature, 32
Hurricane Katrina, 63, 320, 333, 358
Hussein, Saddam, 312, 422

I

Image ads, 175–76
Immutable characteristics, 264
Impeachment, 167, 278
Implied powers, 65
Income distribution, 390–91, 393–96
Incorporation doctrine, 90
Incrementalism, 376
Incumbency
    advantage of, 295–98
    power of, 250–52
Incumbents, 142, 250
Independents, 198
India, 60
Indian Citizenship Act, 11
Indirect democracy, 13
Individualism, 16
Individualist conservatives, 136
Individual rights, 33, 34, 36, 364–66
Inflation, 380
Inherent power, 65
Interest groups, 127, 142, 143, 184–206, 206–22,
    354, 368
    benefits of, 212–13
    Madisonian dilemma of, 222
    political parties and, 187–88, 223
Intergovernmental lobby, 211
Internet, 23, 157, 159, 162, 167
    and democracy, 24
Interstate commerce, 71–73
Interstate Commerce Act of 1888, 73
Interstate relations, 67–69
Interventionism, 411–12
Intolerable Acts, 27, 39
Iran, 421
Iran-Contra affair, 326, 409
Iraq
    insurgency in, 423
Iraq War, 130, 134, 143–44, 229, 312, 315, 408,
    421–23, 424
Irish, 116
Iron triangles, 215
Isolationism, 411
Israel, 60
Issue networks, 216
Issue positions of candidates, 262–63

J

Jackson, President Andrew, 191, 193, 308, 326, 331
Jacksonian Democracy, 10
Jay, John, 44
Jefferson, President Thomas, 5, 9, 19, 33, 36, 40, 191,
    308, 310
Jeffersonian-Republicans, 191
Jeffords, Senator James, 239, 315

Jews, 116, 355
Jim Crow laws, 111
Jobs and Growth Tax Relief Reconciliation
    Act, 373
Johnson, President Lyndon, 75–77, 115, 166,
    324, 372
Jones, Paula, 123
Judges (See also individual justices)
    confirmation of, 356–60
Judicial activism, 362, 366
Judicial independence, 352
Judicial interpretation, 51
Judicial power, 51–52, 360–65
Judicial restraint, 366
Judicial review, 51, 342, 361, 363–64
Judicial selection
    birth of, 363–64
    politics of, 352–60
Judiciary Act of 1789, 343
Judiciary Act of 1801, 363
Jury trial, right to, 105–6
Justice, Department of, 307

K

Keeter, Scott, 141
Kennedy, Justice Anthony, 103, 338
Kennedy, President John F., 115, 143, 166,
    264, 375
Kennedy-Nixon debates, 176–77
Kerry, Senator John, 161, 185, 197, 228, 234,
    250, 261, 263, 305, 397
Keynes, John Maynard, 383
King, Angus, 197, 239
King, Martin Luther, Jr., 115
Kissinger, Henry, 409
Kitchen cabinet, 326
Korean War, 414, 415
Ku Klux Klan, 95
Kyoto Protocol, 429–31

L

Law
    definition of, 340
    sources of, 341
Lawmaking, Congress and, 287–90
Lawrence, Kansas, 170
Lawrence v. Texas, 337–38, 366, 368, 412
Leadership, from president, 317–22, 333
League of Nations, 412
League of Women Voters, 210
Legislation, developing, 287
Legislative powers, 49–50, 313–14
Legitimacy, 233
Leiberman, Senator Joseph, 264
Lewinsky, Monica, 124–25, 141, 219, 319

Libel, 93, 94–95
Liberals, 132
 moralist, 134
 New Deal, 134–35
 pragmatic, 135
Libertarian Party, 197
Life term provision, 51
Light, Paul, 80
Lincoln, President Abraham, 4, 191, 193, 308, 404
Litigation, 217
Lobbying, 214–15
Lobbyist, 207
Locke, John, 18, 32, 33, 34
Lott, Senator Trent, 156

M
Madison, President James, 32, 34, 43–44,
 45–46, 60, 64, 69, 191, 206–7, 304, 307
Magistrate judges, 344
Majority leader, 281
Majority opinion, 351
Majority party, 279
Majority rule, 14
Mandates, 80
Mann, Horace, 129
Marbury v. Madison, 360, 361, 363–65, 366–67
Margin of error, 146
Marshall, Chief Justice, 70–71, 113, 353, 361
Marshall Plan, 414
Mason, George, 64
Massachusetts, western colonial, 28
McCain, Senator John, 161, 241, 360, 397
McCain-Feingold Act, 240
McCarthy, Senator Joseph, 165
McCullough v. Maryland, 70, 71, 361
McKinley, President William, 194
Media, 131–32, 156–80
 audiences of, 159–60
 broadcast, 157
 changing role of, 163–67
 formats of, 156–59
 free, 173–74
 mass, 131, 156–60
 new, 160–61
 paid, 174–76
 and political socialization, 179–80
 trends in ownership of, 167–68
Medical marijuana laws, 82
Mexico, 410
Miers, Harriet, 356–57
Military presence, 41
Minority groups, 147
Minority rights, 109
Minor parties, role of, 197–98
Miranda rule, 104, 105

Miranda v. Arizona, 105
"Mission Accomplished", 425
Missouri Compromise, 111, 361
Mob rule, 7
Moderates, 133
Monetary policy, 382, 385–89
Money, raising, 189
Money supply, 388
Monroe, President James, 193
Monroe Doctrine, 411
Montesquieu, Baron de, 34–35
Moralist conservatives, 136–37
Moralist liberals, 134
Mothers Against Drunk Driving (MADD),
 211, 218
Motor Voter law, 255
MoveOn.Org, 219
Murrow, Edward R., 166
Mutually Assured Destruction, 415

N
NAACP, 11, 113, 114, 210, 217, 368
Nader, Ralph, 197, 211
Name recognition, 251
NARAL Pro-Choice America, 219–20
National Commission on Terrorist Attacks Upon
 the United States (9/11 Commission), 3
National debt, 372–73
National Governors' Association, 211–12
Nationalism, American, 19
National League of Cities, 211
National Organization for Women (NOW), 210
National Performance Review, 333
National Pork Producers, 215
National Rifle Association (NRA), 211, 375–76
National Security Act of 1947, 409
National Security Council (NSC), 325–26, 409,
 409–10
National Taxpayers Union, 211
National Voter Registration Act of 1993, 255–56
National Wildlife Federation, 210
Native people, 10–11, 112
Natural rights, 33
Nature Conservancy, 210
Navigation Acts, 38
Nazi Germany, 413
Near v. Minnesota, 97
Necessary and proper clause, 50, 65
Networks, 247
New Deal, 69, 74, 83, 309, 331, 362, 380–81, 385
New Deal coalition, 195
New Deal liberals, 134–35
New Jersey Plan, 43
New Orleans, 320
New Right, 386

News, history of in America, 164–65
News media, 160
    definition of, 172
News organizations, 143
Newspapers, 160, 168
Nineteenth Amendment, 11, 117
Ninth Amendment, 102
Nixon, President Richard, 77, 78, 97, 166, 195, 310, 312, 316, 324, 326, 332, 355, 356, 365, 385, 409
No Child Left Behind Act of 2002, 79, 315
Normative question, 5
North American Free Trade Agreement (NAFTA), 410
Nuclear Regulatory Commission, 330
Nuclear weapons, 417

O
Objectivity, standard of, 171
Obscenity, 93, 98
Occupational Safety and Health Administration (OSHA), 330
O'Connor, Justice Sandra Day, 82, 103, 187, 219, 353, 356, 357, 358
O'Donnell, Rosie, 162
Office of Management and Budget (OMB), 323, 325, 332, 385
Office of the Solicitor General, 350
Omnibus packages, 295
Opportunity, equality of, 109
Oral arguments, at Supreme Court, 351–52
Organization building, 245
Organization of American States (OAS), 406
Oversampling, 147

P
Pacific Legal Foundation, 211
Page, Benjamin, 141
Paine, Thomas, 39
Paper money, 41
Parliamentary systems, 238
Partial Birth Abortion Law, 103
Partial preemption, 79
Participatory democracy, 13
Partisan press, 164
Partisanship, 291–92
Partisan voting, 200, 204, 205
Party affiliation, 261
Party bosses, 237
Party dealignment, 195–96
Party identification, 198
Party machines, 203
Party platform, 190
Party unity scores, 204
Patriot Act, 107–8, 128, 315, 333
Patronage, 331
Patronage jobs, 203
Peers, 132

Pentagon Papers case, 97
Perestroika, 417
Perot, Ross, 160, 197
Personal freedoms, 16
Physician-assisted suicide, 104
Platform, party, 247
Plea bargain, 106
Pledge of Allegiance, 130
Plessy v. Ferguson, 111, 113, 367
Plural executive, 307
Plurality, 238
Pocket veto, 313
Police powers, 66
Policy agenda, 290
Policy evaluation, 378
Policy formulation, 376
Policy implementation, 378
Policy promises, 203–4
Policy solutions, 190
Policy subgovernments, 215–16
Politainer, 161
Political action committees (PACs), 220, 240
Political advertising, 174, 176
Political agenda, 178
Political bias, 171
Political culture, American, 16
Political expression, 93
Political ideology, 126, 132–37
Political institutions, courts as, 342
Political participation, 14, 267–71
Political parties, 188–206
    decline of, 163
    first, 191–93
    in government, 203–4
    history of, 190–91
    and interest groups, 187–206
    leadership of, 279–81
    membership in, 212
    as organizations, 200–201
    reassessing in America, 205–6
Political party identification, 129
    in the electorate, 198–99
Political practices
    colonial, 37–38
    democratic, 12–15
Political principles
    of America's founding, 33–42
Political socialization, 127–32, 179–80
Political stream, 377
Politics, 32
    American and constitutionalism, 30–31
    American and democracy, 4–5
    electoral, 220–22
    how much Americans know about, 137–41
    negative view of, 20
    young people in, 4

Polity, 7
Poll, who sponsored and conducted, 142–44
Polling, 144–46
    in-person, 148
    mail, 148
    methods, 145
    public opinion, 142–50
    telephone, 148
Poll results, 147
Poll tax, 12
Popular vote, 247
Population, information on views of, 144
Pork-barrel projects, 251, 294
Position taking, 295
Powell, Colin, 136, 326, 407
Power to tax, 67
Pragmatic liberals, 135
Precedent, 341, 345
Preemption, 78
Presidency, 302–16
    bargaining advantages of, 318
    creating, 306–7
    public expectations of, 305–7
President, 50, 143
    constitutional powers of, 310–15
    enforcement powers of, 310–11
    and executive branch, 323–28
    in legislative process, 290–91
    persuasion of, 317–23
Presidential debate, television, 166
Presidential nominees
    selecting, 244
President pro tempore, 281
Primaries, 234, 237–38, 244–47
Print media, 156–57
Prior restraint, 93
Privacy, right to, 102–4, 337–38
Private property, 18
    right to, 73
Privileges and immunities clause, 68
Probability sampling, 145
Pro-choice candidates, 188
Professional associations, 209–10
Professional political consultants, 243
Prohibition, 53
Proportional representation system, 239
Pseudo-polls, 145
Public accommodations, discrimination in, 115
Public figure, 98
Public financing, 241–42
Public interest, 6, 35
Public interest groups, 210
Public official, 98, 215
Public opinion, 123, 126, 141–49
    advertising to influence, 217
Public opinion polls, 141–49

Public policy, 367, 374–79
Public schools, 99
Push polls, 144

Q
Questions, wording of in poll, 147

R
Racism, 112
Radio, 147, 165–66
Rather, Dan, 154, 167, 174
    bloggers and, 154
Ratification, debate on, 44–48
Rational thought, capacity for, 32
R.A.V. v. St. Paul, 86–89
Reagan, President Ronald, 78, 142, 167, 195,
    227, 320, 324, 332, 333, 356, 359, 371,
    388, 416
Recession, 380
Red and blue America, 227
Red states, 227, 227–29
Reelection, goal of, 293
Referendum, 13
Regulatory agencies, 328, 330
Rehnquist, Justice William, 82, 353, 357, 358
Reinventing government, 333
Religion, 99–102
Religious practices, 101–2
Reorganization Act of 1939, 324
Representation, 7, 43
Representative democracy, 13
Representatives, 29
Republic, 6, 7
    nature of, 44
Republicanism, 34–36
Republican Party
    dominance of, 194
    emergence of, 193–94
Reserved powers, 66
Retrospective voting, 262
Reverse discrimination, 119
Revolution, events leading to, 38–40
Revolutionary War, 28
Rice, Condoleeza, 326, 409
Rights, protection of, 47
Roberts, Chief Justice John, 82, 353, 357–58
Rock the Vote, 161
Roe v. Wade, 103, 366
Role model, president as, 306
Roosevelt, President Franklin Delano, 50, 74, 75,
    130, 142, 165, 195, 308, 309, 323, 327, 362,
    381, 405
Roosevelt, President Theodore, 194, 197, 308–10
Rousseau, Jean Jacques, 33
Rule making, 328–30
Rule of four, 348

Russia, 60
Rwanda genocide, 425–26

S
Same-sex unions, 68
Sample size, 140
Sampling error, 146
Sanders, Representative Bernard, 267
Satellite technology, 159, 163
Scalia, Justice Antonin, 82, 88
Schattschneider, E. E., 213
Schedule c appointments, 331
Schenck v. United States, 94
Schiavo, Teri, 375
School prayer, 99–100
Schools, 129–30
School voucher programs, 100–101
Scientific sampling, 145
Search and seizure, 104–5
Secretary of State, 407
Segregation, 113
    de facto, 113
Self-incrimination, 105
Senate, 49, 204, 277–78, 308
Senate Judiciary Committee, 275, 356–57, 359
Senatorial courtesy, 359
Seniority, 282–83
Separate but equal, 111, 114
Separation between church and state, 99
Separation of powers, 35, 42, 48
September 11th attacks on U.S., 2, 81, 130, 131, 148,
        366, 373, 375, 410
    aftermath of, 2
    commission, 126
Sequencing, 148
Service the district, 294
Sexual orientation, 118
Shapiro, Robert, 141
Shays, Daniel, 29
Shays' Rebellion, 27–29, 36, 41
Sheehan, Cindy, 135
Sherman Antitrust Act of 1890, 308
Sierra Club, 210
Sixth Amendment, 105
Slander, 97
Slavery, 10, 44, 110–11
    institution of, 110
Smith, Adam, 380, 383
Soap opera story, 174
Social contract, 33
Socialist Party, 197
Social Security, 176, 198
Sodomy laws, 104, 338
Soft money, 175, 220, 240
Sound bites, 172

Souter, Justice David, 55, 331, 60
Soviet Union, 417
Speaker of the House, 279
Split ticket voting, 196, 200
Spoils system, 331
Stagflation, 384
Stamp Act, 28, 38–39
Stare decisis, 342
Starr, Kenneth, 123–25
"Star Wars" Strategic Defense Initiative (SDI), 417
State, Department of, 407–8
State government, 59
State of nature, 32
State of the Union address, 303, 306, 313
States
    changing of Constitution by, 52
    in Constitution, 66–67
States, constitutions of, 40–42
Statutes, 341
Statutory interpretation, 341
Stewart, Jon, 162
Stock Market Crash of 1929, 309, 380
Straight ticket voting, 200
Stratetic Arms Limitation Treaties (SALT), 416
Strong presidency model, 307
Structural bias, 171–72
Student government, 130
Subcommittees, 284
Suffrage, women's, 117
Supply-side economics, 371, 384
Supreme Court, 52, 69, 276, 307, 314, 319, 346–52,
        348–51
    and federalism, 70
    and First Amendment, 89–92, 94, 98–99
    and politics, 360–67
    and public policy, 367–68
    as reigning national power, 81–82
    supremacy clause, 52, 65
Surplus, 371–74
Survey of American Political Culture, 16, 17
Sweden, 60
Symbolic expressions, 93

T
Taft, President William Howard, 194, 197
Take care clause, 310
Taney, Roger, 71
Tax, power to, 67
Taxation, 373, 385
Taylor, President Zachary, 193
Tea Act, 27, 39
Telecommunications Act, 1998, 168
Telecommunications Reform Act, 251
Television, 131, 157, 159, 165
    debates on, 176–77

elected officials depicted on, 180
rise of, 174–75
Temporary Assistance for Needy Families grant, 81
Tenth Amendment, 66, 69
Term cycles, 321–22
Term limits movement, 298
Texas v. Johnson, 87, 95
Third parties, 197, 242
Thirteenth Amendment, 10, 111
Thomas, Justice Clarence, 353, 356, 357
Three-Fifths Compromise, 44
Thurmond, Senator Strom, 197
Time constraints, 172
Timing, of poll, 148
Title VI, 79
Title VII, 116
Tocqueville, Alexis de, 16, 207
Town hall format, 177
Tracking polls, 142
Trade associations, 207–9
Traditional conservatives, 136
Transportation Security Agency, 409
Treaties, 341, 405
power to negotiate, 308
Trickle-down economics, 371
Twenty-Fourth Amendment, 12
Twenty-Second Amendment, 50
Twenty-Sixth Amendment, 12
Twenty-Third Amendment, 12
Two-party system, 191, 196
Two-term limit, 308

U
Unfunded Mandate Reform Act, 80
Unified government, 291–92
Unions, 132, 188, 210
Unitary system, 60
United Nations (UN), 406, 408, 413
General Assembly, 408
United Nations Framework Convention on Climate Change, 429
United Nations Intergovernmental Panel on Climate Change, 427–29
United States v. Nixon, 311
Universal manhood suffrage, 10
Unprotected expression, 97–98
Upper-class bias, 213
U.S. Conference of Mayors, 211

V
Van Buren, President Martin, 193
Ventura, Jesse, 161, 197, 239
Veto, 48, 290, 313–14
Vice president, 281

Vietnam War, 12, 154, 185, 195, 262, 312, 324, 371, 411, 415
Virginia Plan, 43
Visual demands, 172
Visually literate, 181
Voices of September 11, 2
Volker, Paul, 388, 389
Voter choice, simplifying, 189
Voter registration, 253–56
Voter turnout
decline of, 253–57
demographics of, 257–61
Voting age, 12
Voting methods, 235–36
Voting Rights Act, 10–12, 115–16

W
Wallace, George, 197
Walmart, 400
War on Poverty, 76
War on Terrorism, 356, 374, 382 418, 418, 420, 420–22
War power, 403
War Powers Resolution, 312
Warren, Justice Earl, 90, 354, 362
Warren Court, 362, 367
Wars, undeclared, 404
Washington, President George, 42, 50, 188, 307–8, 326, 405, 411
Watergate crisis, 166, 178, 195, 287, 311
Weak presidency model, 307
Wealth, 391–96, 393–95
Weapons of Mass Destruction (WMD), 422–24
Weighted results, 147
Welfare system, overhaul of, 85
West Wing, The, 180, 323
Whig Party, 193
Whips, 279
White, Justice Byron, 337
White House Office, 197, 323–24, 332
Wilson, President Woodrow, 194, 323, 412
Wire services, 168
Women, 109, 116–17
in Congress, 118, 298–99
right to vote for, 11, 36, 117
Women's suffrage, 11, 117
Wood, Gordon, 35
World leader, president as, 306
World Trade Organization (WTO), 406
World Wars, 412–13
Writ of certiorari, 348

Y
Yellow journalism, 150
Youth voting in 2004, 259–60